RAND McNALLY

Road Atlas

2020

Contents

National Parks

Our editors' picks of America's 60 national parks—big and small, west and east—showcase this country's astonishing beauty, highlight essential visitor information, and offer insightful travel tips.

Pages ii–vii

Mileage Chart

Driving distances between 90 North American cities and national parks.

Page viii

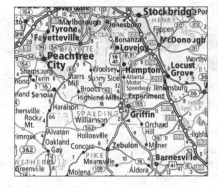

Maps

Maps: **pages 2–128**
Legend: **inside front cover**
Index: **pages 129–136**

Mileage and Driving Times Map

Distances and driving times between hundreds of North American cities and national parks.

Inside back cover

©2019 RM Acquisition, LLC d/b/a Rand McNally. All rights reserved. Rand McNally and the globe logo are registered trademarks of RM Acquisition, LLC. All other trademarks appearing in this publication are trademarks of third parties and are the responsibility of their respective owners.

For licensing information and copyright permissions, contact us at permissions@randmcnally.com.

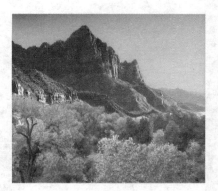

If you have a comment, suggestion, or even a compliment, please contact us at randmcnally.com/contact or write to:
Rand McNally Consumer Affairs
P.O. Box 7600
Chicago, Illinois 60680-9915

Published and printed in U.S.A.

1 2 3 BU 20 19

The Sustainable Forestry Initiative® (SFI) program promotes responsible environmental behavior and sound forest management.

Printed by Quad Graphics

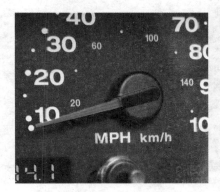

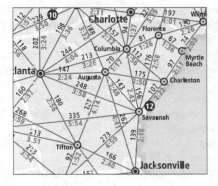

America's 60 national parks not only inspire wonder and awe but also restore our souls. Here are 6 of our favorite parks—big and small, west and east—that showcase this country's astonishing beauty.

DENALI NATIONAL PARK & PRESERVE, AK

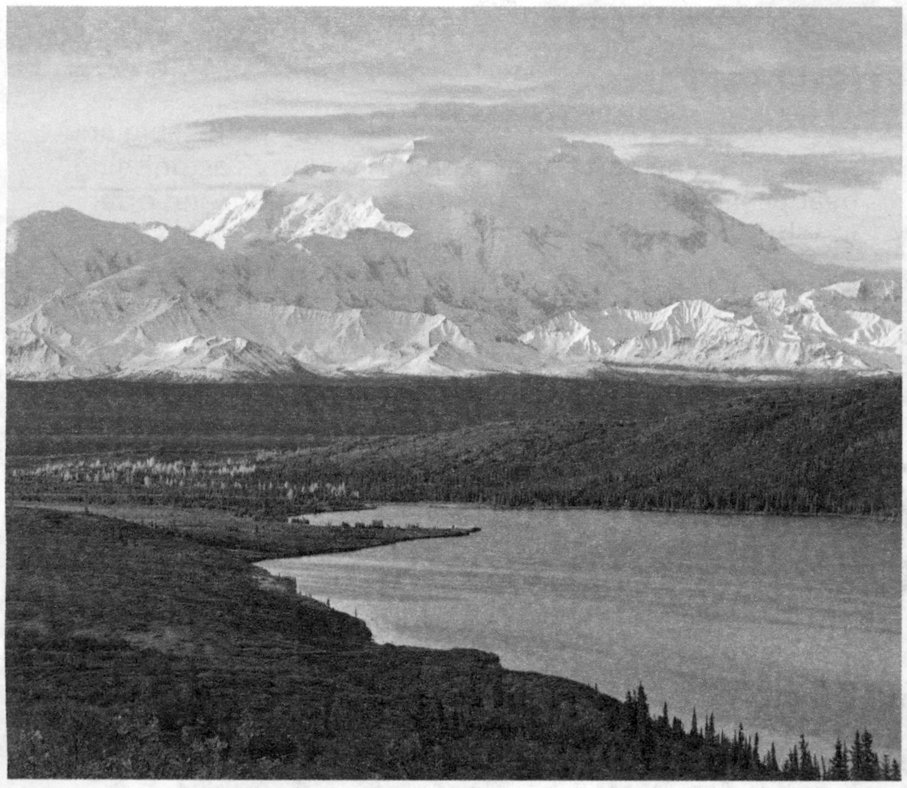

Fall color of Denali and Wonder Lake

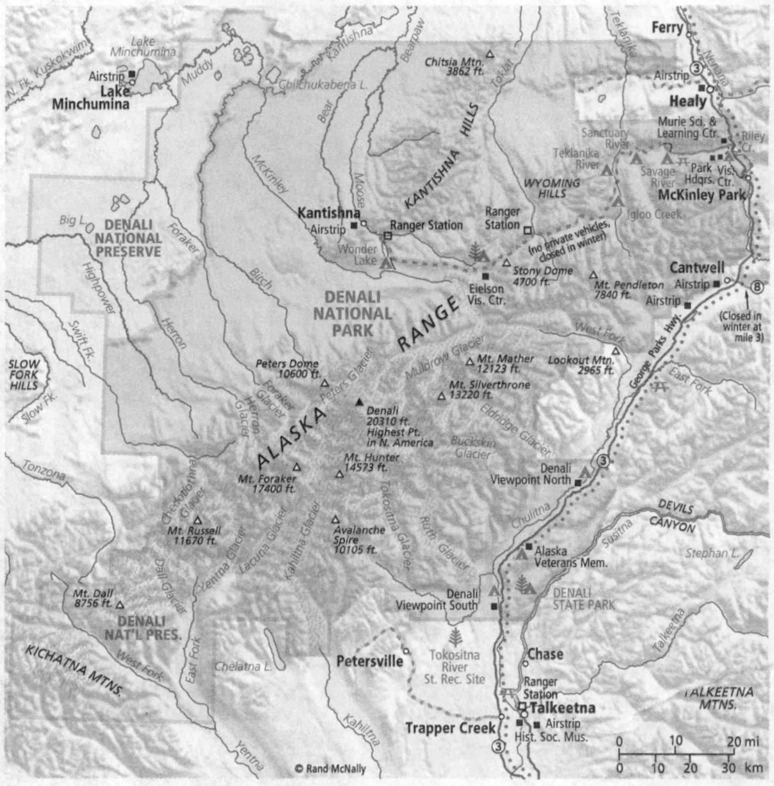

Atlas map **p. 6, E-7**

This vast tract of central Alaskan outback surrounds North America's highest point: the park's 20,310-foot namesake peak, which translates to "the tall one" and "mountain-big" in Native Alaskan languages. No park in the lower 48 is as untouched: The only way to traverse its one road is via shuttle bus, which lets you truly focus on the sweeping tundra and mountain scenery.

GETTING ORIENTED

Denali is west of AK 3 (aka George Parks Highway). Gateway airports include Ted Stevens Anchorage International (243 miles south) and Fairbanks International (120 miles north). **Denali Visitor Center** is just inside the park's one entrance, on the east side. **Eielson Visitor Center** (Mile 66, Park Rd.) is 66 miles west of the entrance. **Walter Harper Talkeetna Ranger Station** (B St., Talkeetna, 907/733-2231) is 152 miles south of the park.

A few in-park wilderness lodges operate on inholdings (private lands), including **Camp Denali** (Mile 92, Park Rd., 907/683-2290, campdenali.com). Reservations (800/622-7275, www.reservedenali.com) are recommended at the park's six campgrounds. Nearby towns with amenities include **Healy** (www.denalichamber.com), 11 miles north of the park entrance, and **Talkeetna** (www.talkeetnachamber.org), 152 miles south. **Park Contact Info:** ***907/683-9532, www.nps.gov/dena.***

PARK HIGHLIGHTS

Natural Attractions. The minds behind Denali National Park made a bold decision when they chose to ban passenger cars from entry, and it has paid off in an authentic wilderness with an intact ecosystem. The prime visiting season runs from early June to mid-September.

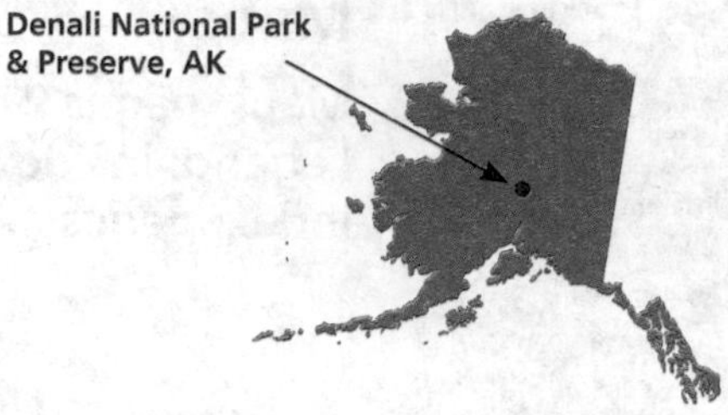

It's hard to ignore **Denali** (formerly known as Mt. McKinley), the park's massive centerpiece. While other peaks are higher, the more than 18,000-foot ascent from Denali's surrounding lowlands is greater than Mt. Everest's rise above the Tibetan Plateau. The park's boundaries encompass numerous other peaks of the Alaska Range, including 17,400-foot **Mt. Foraker**, North America's sixth-highest peak, and the glaciated, 13,220-foot **Mt. Silverthrone** on the park's east side.

Treeless **tundra** atop perpetually frozen permafrost dominates the landscape. Below 3,000 feet, a 6-foot thicket of dense brush can cover the tundra; above 3,000 feet, alpine tundra has less vegetation and is easier to traverse on foot. Fed by glaciers and mountain snow, numerous **braided rivers**—including the Toklat, Savage, and Teklanika—are so named for their multiple, ever-changing channels in wide gravel floodplains that crisscross the tundra.

Brown bear near Mt. Galen

Denali is also a prime **wildlife habitat**. You may see grizzly bears and many hoofed mammals—such as moose, Dall sheep, and caribou—roaming the tundra.

Trails, Drives & Viewpoints. Denali is a hiker's paradise but has few developed trails; many routes follow the braided rivers. **Stony Creek** (Mile 60, Park Rd.) makes a great access point for exploring the tundra or mountains; the first 3 miles are relatively flat. Near the park entrance, the difficult 5-mile round trip to the **Mt. Healy Overlook** culminates in sweeping views of the Alaska Range.

Although Park Road is closed to private vehicles, the two-lane **Denali Highway** (aka AK 8) runs parallel to the Alaska Range for 135 miles from Paxson to Cantwell, 27 miles south of the park entrance. Only 22 miles of the highway are paved; the rest is gravel. The entire highway, however, stretches along jaw-dropping scenery and offers countless opportunities for wildlife watching, hiking, and boating. The main route to the park from either Anchorage or Fairbanks, the **George Parks Highway** also has plenty of spellbinding views.

Programs & Activities. The park concessionaire operates **shuttle buses** (800/622-7275, www.reservedenali.com) that go as far as Kantishna (92 miles one-way, 13 hours round-trip) and offers some bus tours. Reserve shuttles and tours; two-thirds of the seats are sold in advance. Ranger-led **Discovery Hikes**, available daily in summer, are for experienced hikers only; sign up in person at the Denali Visitor Center.

Offering a different perspective, the **Alaska Railroad** (800/544-0552, www.alaskarailroad.com) runs between Anchorage and Fairbanks, stopping near the park entrance daily in summer. You can see Denali from above on a "flightseeing" trip with **Denali Air** (907/683-2261, denaliair.com) that departs from a private airstrip near the park entrance. **Denali Outdoor Center** (907/683-1925, www.denalioutdoorcenter.com) guides rafting trips on the Nenana River, just east of the park.

JOSHUA TREE NATIONAL PARK, CA

Joshua tree landscape

Joshua Tree National Park, CA

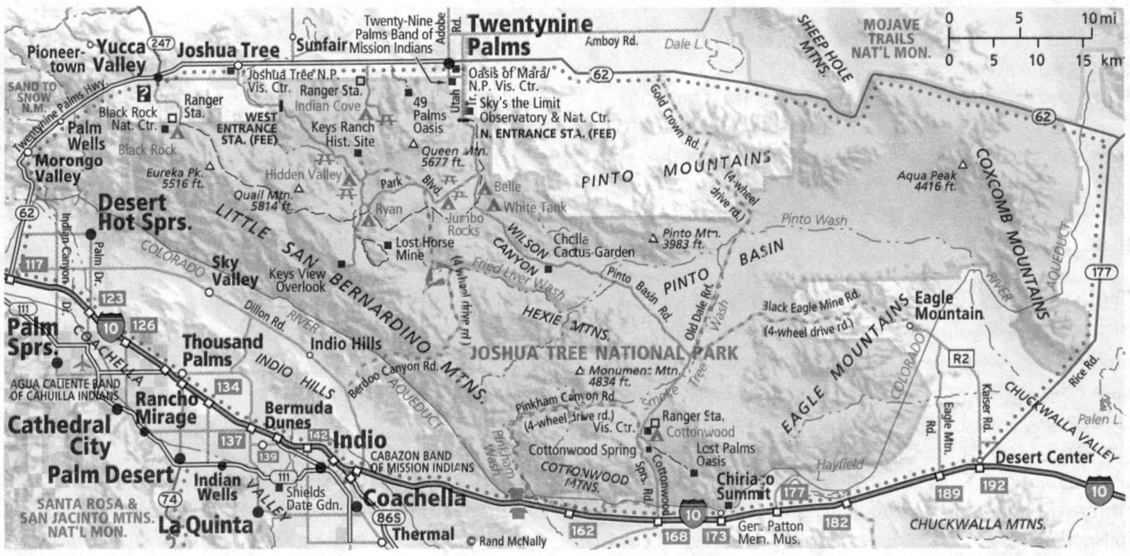

Atlas map **p. 14, SJ-16**

Trees that aren't trees. Boulders that look like skulls. A vast, dry plateau hiding an oasis. Distant snowcapped peaks. Welcome to weird, wild wonderful Joshua Tree, named for the tall, Dr. Seuss–like trees that are actually flowering yucca plants. It's also home to cacti, piñon pines, cottonwoods, bighorn sheep, and many bird species. What's more, spectacularly starry night skies make this park a 24/7 masterpiece.

GETTING ORIENTED

The **Joshua Tree Visitor Center** is 142 miles east of Los Angeles International Airport and 39 miles northeast of smaller Palm Springs International Airport via I-10 and Twentynine Palms Highway (CA 62); 16 miles farther east along CA 62, near the town of **Twentynine Palms** (www.ci.twentynine-palms.ca.us), is the **Oasis of Mara Visitor Center**. The southern **Cottonwood Visitor Center** is 26 miles east of **Indio** (www.discoverindio.com) off I-10.

Make reservations for the popular **Black Rock** (99 sites) and **Indian Cove** (101 sites) campgrounds through Recreation.gov; other campgrounds are first-come, first-served. Lodgings abound in trendy **Palm Springs** (www.visitpalmsprings.com) and along CA 62 in **Yucca Valley** (www.yucca-valley.org), **Joshua Tree** (www.joshuatreechamber.org), and Twentynine Palms. **Park Contact Info:** *760/367-5500, www.nps.gov/jotr.*

PARK HIGHLIGHTS

Natural Attractions. Joshua Tree's striking scenery is due in no small part to the fact that it stretches between parts of two famous deserts: the higher-in-elevation Mojave to the north, and the lower-in-elevation Colorado to the south. Temperatures are high June through September, so try to visit October through May.

Joshua trees are everywhere but are especially striking in the park's northwestern section; bizarre boulder formations dot the northeastern section. The southern section, in and around Cottonwood Visitor Center, occasionally closes due to flash floods. Nevertheless, it's worth exploring some excellent trails through the cottonwoods. This is also a premier birding spot; more than 250 species have been recorded in the park.

Trails, Drives & Viewpoints. The 25-mile drive along scenic **Park Boulevard**, which connects the two northern park entrances and visitor centers, can be done in 40 minutes without stopping. Don't do that, since you'd miss, well, virtually everything, including the curvaceous **Arch Rock** (an easy 0.5-mile loop walk); the pockmarked mounds of **Skull Rock** (a moderate 1.5-mile loop trail); **Barker Dam** (an easy 1.3-mile loop where you might see bighorn sheep); and the sublime **Oasis of Mara**, an 0.5-mile stroll behind the visitor center of the same name.

Sunset is a no-brainer: **Keys View** (Keys View Rd., 20 minutes off Park Blvd.), an overlook at 5,100 feet, gives you a view westward across Coachella Valley—particularly stunning when the sun dips behind the snow-covered San Jacinto Mountains. Bring your camera, tripod, and binoculars: It's worth the trouble, especially to capture iconic Joshua trees in the foreground of those burnished desert sunsets.

Museum. Head down to **Keys Ranch**, built by ranchers and homesteaders Bill and Frances Keys. They raised five children, planted an orchard, built several structures, and lived on-site for 60 years until 1969. Ranch tours, the only way to see this spectacular piece of desert history, require tickets that you purchase at the Oasis of Mara Visitor Center on the morning of the tour.

Programs & Activities. Joshua Tree's ranger-led programs mesh perfectly with what the park is all about. They include the **Joshua Tree Rocks!** geology walk (1 mile, near Skull Rock), an **oasis walk** (easy 0.5-mile stroll from the Oasis of Mara Visitor Center), the **I Speak for the Trees** walk (easy 0.4-mile walk along the Cap Rock Nature Trail), and the more strenuous, steep 3-mile hike to **Mastodon Peak**.

After sunset, you can appreciate the spectacular, star-filled skies that have made Joshua Tree a designated International Dark Sky Park. The **Night Sky Festival**, usually held in early November, features free talks and solar viewing by day and astronomy programs by night. The park's geology makes it a favorite destination for rock climbing; **Joshua Tree Rock Climbing School** (760/366-4745, www.joshuatreerockclimbing.com) offers courses for all levels. Joshua Tree's backcountry roads and trails are also perfect for **mountain biking** and **horseback riding**.

Climbing

ZION NATIONAL PARK, UT

The Narrows

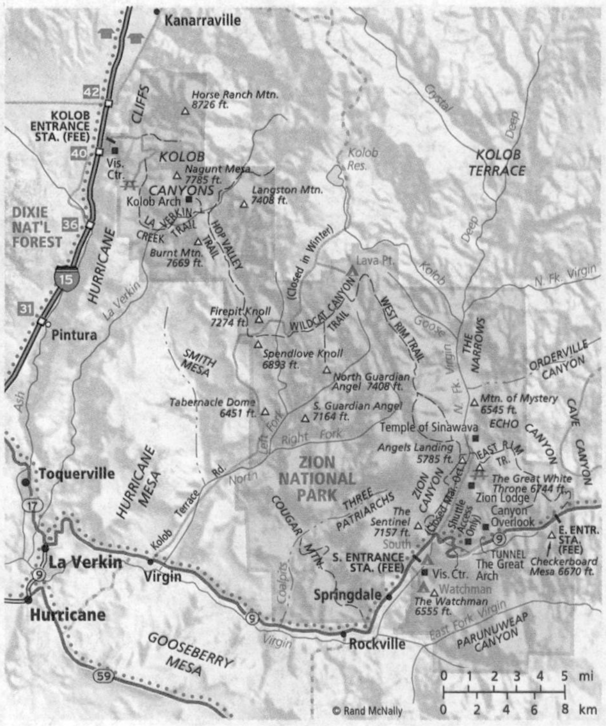

Atlas map **p. 102, M-6**

Zion National Park, UT

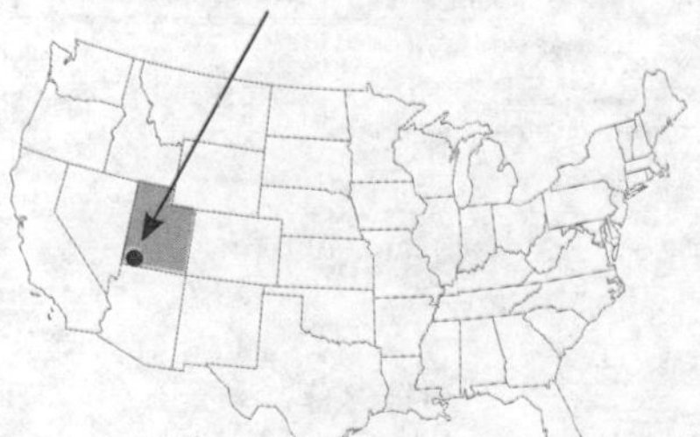

Burnished red Navajo sandstone cliffs rise from the Colorado Plateau, forming a series of majestic outcroppings illuminated by the sun amid a deep-blue Utah sky. Zion Canyon, one of this park's most striking formations, features 2,000-foot-high walls carved over millennia by the snaking Virgin River. On any given day, thousands of people gaze up at the canyon's walls and its intrepid rock climbers.

GETTING ORIENTED

Zion is in southwestern Utah, near the Nevada and Arizona borders. Las Vegas' McCarran International Airport is 160 miles southwest of the South Entrance, mainly via I-15; Salt Lake City International Airport is 313 miles northeast, also via I-15. It's 40 miles on UT 9 and I-15 between the South Entrance and the less-trafficked, northwestern Kolob Canyons Entrance. The even quieter East Entrance, on UT 9, accesses the scenic Zion–Mount Carmel Highway.

In-park lodging is limited to camping (Recreation.gov). Motels and inns line UT 9 in Springdale and Rockville (www.zionpark.com for both). St. George (www.visitstgeorge.com), 41 miles west of the South Entrance, and Kanab (www.visitsouthernutah.com), 40 miles east, are also good bases for exploring Zion as well as Bryce Canyon and the Grand Canyon's North Rim. **Park Contact Info:** ***435/772-3256, www.nps.gov/zion.***

PARK HIGHLIGHTS

Natural Attractions. With more than 4 million visitors annually, Zion is one of America's most popular national parks. (It has even considered introducing an online reservation system to address overcrowding and potential environmental damage.) It's wise to book in-park campsites and rooms at nearby hotels well in advance.

The sheer walls of Zion Canyon and many other mesas, buttes, and rusty red outcroppings are the park's main draws. You can see formations like the Court of the Patriarchs and Weeping Rock as you move in to the canyon, and it's impossible to say whether the canyon itself is more spectacular seen from its floor looking up or from its top looking down.

Zion displays a more desert-style landscape in its southwest corner (accessible by two trailheads off UT 9); the varied landscape of the high-elevation Kolob Canyons area in the northwest, however, is worth a full extra day. Few explore Kolob's hikes and views or the stunning 287-foot span of Kolob Arch, a strenuous 14-mile (round-trip) hike that is one of the park's hidden treasures.

Trails, Drives & Viewpoints. The 7-mile (one-way) Zion Canyon Scenic Drive from the South Entrance visitor center, which ends at the natural amphitheater called the Temple of Sinawava, and the 12-mile (one-way) Zion–Mount Carmel Highway, connecting the park's South Entrance to the East Entrance, are unmissable. Zion Canyon can be visited only via park shuttle bus mid-March through October (and weekends in November), but the spectacular narrowing and rising of the canyon's walls inspires awe as you travel farther in. The winding Zion–Mount Carmel Highway is one of America's most beautiful roads, with striated mesas and canyon views.

The Narrows begin at the north end of Zion Canyon; here, the canyon's walls are sometimes only 20 or 30 feet wide. The easy 2.2-mile round-trip Riverside Walk Trail is where you can examine The Narrows for yourself. For a spectacular bird's-eye view of Zion Canyon, the strenuous, 5.4-mile round-trip Angels Landing Trail from the Grotto trailhead, with its cliff-hugging stone steps and helpful (and necessary) chain handholds, is one of Zion's greatest experiences.

Programs & Activities. Rangers lead a great mix of summer programs, including a moderate 2.5-hour, 3.3-mile round-trip hike on the Watchman Trail that climbs to a great view of Zion Canyon. In mornings and afternoons, rangers conduct Patio Talks on wildlife and geology; evening programs generally feature more personal stories.

Zion Canyon Scenic Drive is open for cycling, as is the pedestrian-and-bike-only Pa'rus Trail (3.5 miles round-trip). Zion Canyon's sheer cliffs and narrow slot canyons draw thousands for climbing every year, and canyoneering (a combination of climbing, rappelling, and scrambling) is becoming increasingly popular. Permits for canyoneering and overnight climbs are required.

Sandstone landscape

ROCKY MOUNTAIN NATIONAL PARK, CO

Studded by peaks soaring majestically above the timberline, this north-central Colorado park is marked by a treeless ecosystem that's home to some of Earth's hardiest living things. The wide swath of high-country alpine tundra is largely dormant for half the year as snow falls, winds howl, and temperatures plunge. In warmer months, low-country forests, verdant meadows, and shimmering lakes and rivers define the landscape of this hiker's paradise.

GETTING ORIENTED

Rocky Mountain is 40 miles northwest of Boulder via US 36 and 35 miles west of Loveland via US 34. Denver International Airport is 78 miles southeast of the Beaver Meadows Visitor Center. The largest of the park's five campgrounds (Recreation.gov) is near the Moraine Park Discovery Center, 2 miles southwest of Beaver Meadows.

Amenities-filled gateway towns include Estes Park (www.visitestespark.com)—3 miles east of Beaver Meadows and 4 miles southeast of the Fall River Visitor Center—and Grand Lake (grandlakechamber.com), 2 miles south of the Kawuneeche Visitor Center. Trail Ridge Road (closed late Oct.–June) runs 48 miles between Estes Park and Grand Lake. Alpine Visitor Center, near Trail Ridge Road's high point (12,183 feet), is 22 miles west of Beaver Meadows. **Park Contact Info:** ***970/586-1206, www.nps.gov/romo.***

Rocky Mountain National Park, CO

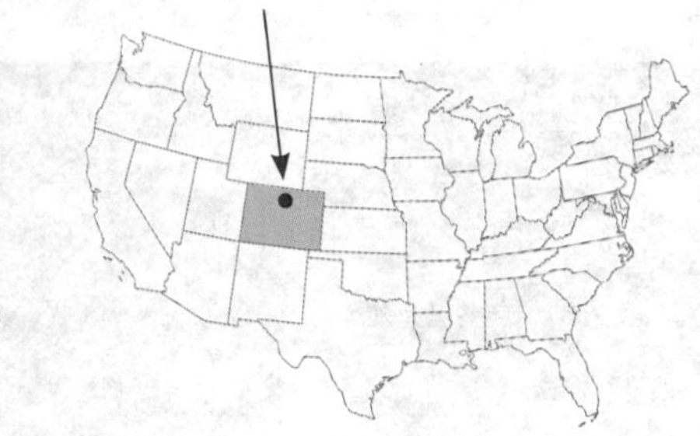

Hiking in the park

PARK HIGHLIGHTS

Natural Attractions. Although the park is home to elk, black bears, and mountain lions, the star attractions are its namesake Rocky Mountains. Their formation began about 70 million years ago, when geologic uplift began pushing ancient rocks about a mile skyward. Of the park's 124 named peaks, 20 have summits higher than 13,000 feet. At 14 259 feet, Longs Peak is the tallest, and a draw for climbers from all over the world.

Subalpine forests and meadows dominate the mountains' lower flanks. Pine beetles, insects the size of a grain of rice that kill trees by feasting inside the bark, have ravaged many of the forests. Above 11,000 feet, woods and meadows give way to alpine tundra, which makes up more than a third of the park's land area. Windswept and devoid of trees, this fragile ecosystem typically sees at least a little snowfall every month of the year.

Trails, Drives & Viewpoints. Rocky Mountain has more than 300 miles of trails. The easy, 0.6-mile loop around Bear Lake is a good scenic introduction to the east side. From the Glacier Gorge trailhead nearby, it's a moderate 0.6 miles to Alberta Falls and a moderate 2.8 miles to Mills Lake.

In the Wild Basin Unit, the Ouzel Falls Trail offers a moderate, 5.4-mile round-trip to a waterfall named for the bird also known as the American dipper. Just north of Grand Lake, the North Inlet Trail is a moderate, 6.8-mile round-trip to Cascade Falls by way of a wide mountain valley; more experienced hikers can continue to a pair of lakes and Flattop Mountain.

Twisting, turning, and gaining more than 3,000 feet along its 48 miles, the seasonally open Trail Ridge Road ranks among the highest and most scenic roads in the United States. Numerous endless-view overlooks merit a stop, including Far View Curve and Rainbow Curve. Old Fall River Road, the park's original automobile route, is a curving one-way, 11-mile drive that connects with Trail Ridge Road; it has been called "a motor nature trail."

Museums & Sites. On Rocky Mountain's west side, Holzwarth Historic Site was homesteaded in 1917 and later became a dude ranch. It's open for guided tours. The area also has a mining legacy: Reachable by a 2.8-mile hike from the Longs Peak Trailhead on the park's east side, Eugenia Mine was abandoned in 1919 but has intriguing ruins. The remains of Lulu City, a mining boomtown that went bust in the 1880s, are 3.7 miles from the Colorado River Trailhead near Grand Lake.

Programs & Activities. In summer, ranger-led activities include guided hikes, talks on ecology and geology, and stargazing programs. Guided snowshoe walks are available in winter. Horseback riding is a staple, and the park has two stables: Glacier Creek (970/586-3244, www.sombrero.com) and Moraine Park (970/586-2327, www.sombrero.com).

Climbers flock to Longs Peak and other mountains. The Colorado Mountain School (341 Moraine Ave., Estes Park, 720/387-8944, coloradomountainschool.com) offers guided mountaineering and climbing expeditions.

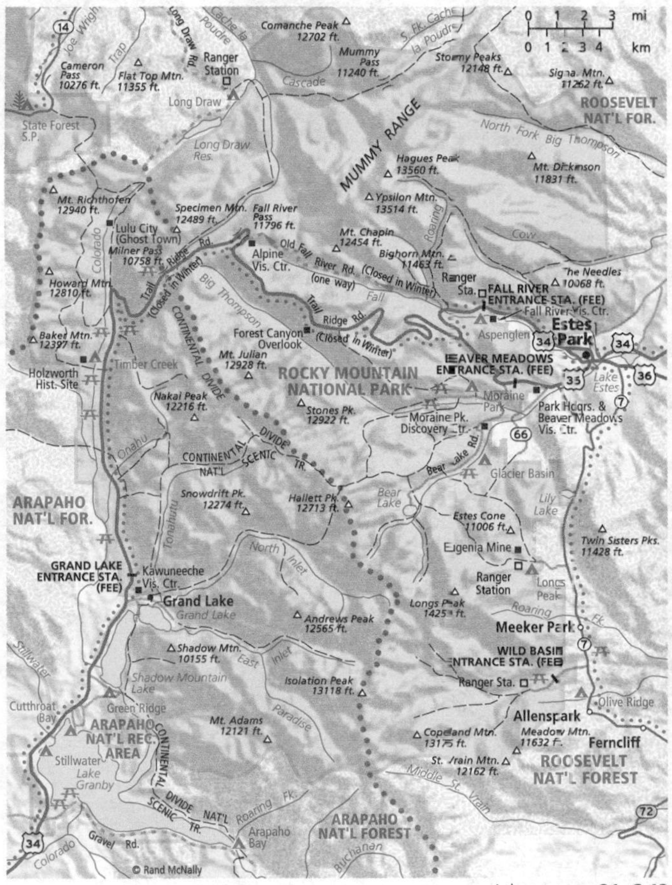

Atlas map **p. 21, C-12**

A Rocky Mountain National Park vista

GATEWAY ARCH NATIONAL PARK, MO

Downtown St. Louis skyline

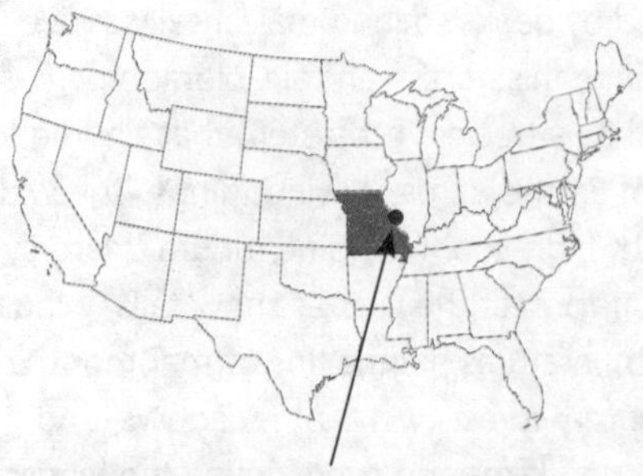

Gateway Arch National Park, MO

America's newest national park is also its smallest. As the saying goes, though, "Big things come in small packages." And this package contains the country's tallest manmade monument, an iconic structure that memorializes a whole lot of history. Rising 630 feet and framing the dome of the Old Courthouse, also part of the park, the Arch was completed in the late 1960s—a Mid-Century metaphor for manifest destiny ideals.

GETTING ORIENTED

Gateway Arch is edged by **St. Louis** (explorestlouis.com) on one side and the Mississippi River (across from East St. Louis in Illinois) on the other. Interstate 44 cuts through the park between downtown and the river. A pedestrian-friendly land bridge connects the Old Courthouse with the Arch and its grounds. North of downtown, I-70 runs to I-44 from the west—including the 15 miles from St. Louis Lambert International Airport—as well as from the east. In the south, I-64, I-44, or I-55 get you to the park.

Numerous downtown hotels and public parking lots are within walking distance. **Metro system** (www.metrostlouis.org) buses—including hop-on-hop-off #99 Downtown Trolley—and trains serve both Missouri and Illinois. **Park Contact Info:** ***314/655-1600 (recorded info), 877/982-1410 (to buy timed-entry tickets), www.nps.gov/jeff.***

PARK HIGHLIGHTS

Viewpoints. Plenty of national parks feature spectacular views as part of a visit. Here, though, the views are arguably *the* reason to visit. One bank of windows atop the 630-foot **Arch** looks across the Mississippi River and into Illinois. Windows on the other side take in the west as far as the eye can see, which, on a clear day, is roughly 30 miles.

To experience the park's recently refurbished glory and classic vistas, purchase timed-entry, **Journey to the Top** tickets for 4-minute tram rides up well in advance through **GatewayArch.com**, the park's concessionaire partner. Although the tram system accommodates up to 6,400 visitors daily, tickets can sell out. Also, arrive at least 30 minutes early to allow time for airport-style security screening. Stay in the observation area as long as you like; trams for the 3-minute ride down depart every 10 minutes or so. Note, though, that there are no restrooms or other facilities at the top; plan accordingly.

If you prefer to stay grounded, you can check out top-side views on live web cams; see the documentary *Monument to the Dream*, covering the Arch's construction and significance; and visit the underground Museum of the Gateway Arch (formerly the Museum of Westward Expansion).

History, Museums & Activities. Some people wonder why this very small, very urban site was made a national park in 2018. To be fair, the National Park Service has always overseen it, and it does commemorate a pioneering history without which there might be fewer vast, wild spaces farther west for the park service to protect.

Established in 1935 by President Franklin Roosevelt as the Jefferson National Expansion Memorial, the site honors not only Thomas Jefferson's vision of westward expansion but also the Louisiana Purchase and the Lewis & Clark Expedition.

It was just northwest of St. Louis, where the Mississippi and Missouri rivers meet, that the Corps of Discovery began its 1804–06 journey across uncharted territory to the Pacific. The onset of World War II and other issues delayed the memorial's development. In 1947–48, a design competition was held, and Eero Saarinen's concrete and stainless-steel Arch won out over 172 other entries, including one by his father, Eliel.

Six refurbished galleries in the **Museum of the Gateway Arch** look back across all this history using very forward-facing technology. Video and other interactive displays cover the Native American and Creole cultures of early St. Louis; Jefferson's vision for westward expansion; the steamboats, railroads, and other industries that helped to propel expansion; and the building of the Arch itself.

Two historic legal cases are highlighted on the daily, 45-minute, ranger-led tours of the **Old Courthouse**: The landmark Dredd Scott Case, involving emancipation and heard here in 1847 and 1850 (before a U.S. Supreme Court decision in 1857), and the 1870 case of Virginia Minor, a suffragette who sued for the right to vote.

For a leisurely park experience, board a replica 19th-century steamboat for a one-hour **riverboat cruise** (GatewayArch.com) with fantastic views of the Arch from Old Muddy. For a more active approach, look into biking, in-line-skating, or walking/running along the paved, 11-mile **St. Louis Riverfront Trail** (www.traillink.com).

Old Courthouse

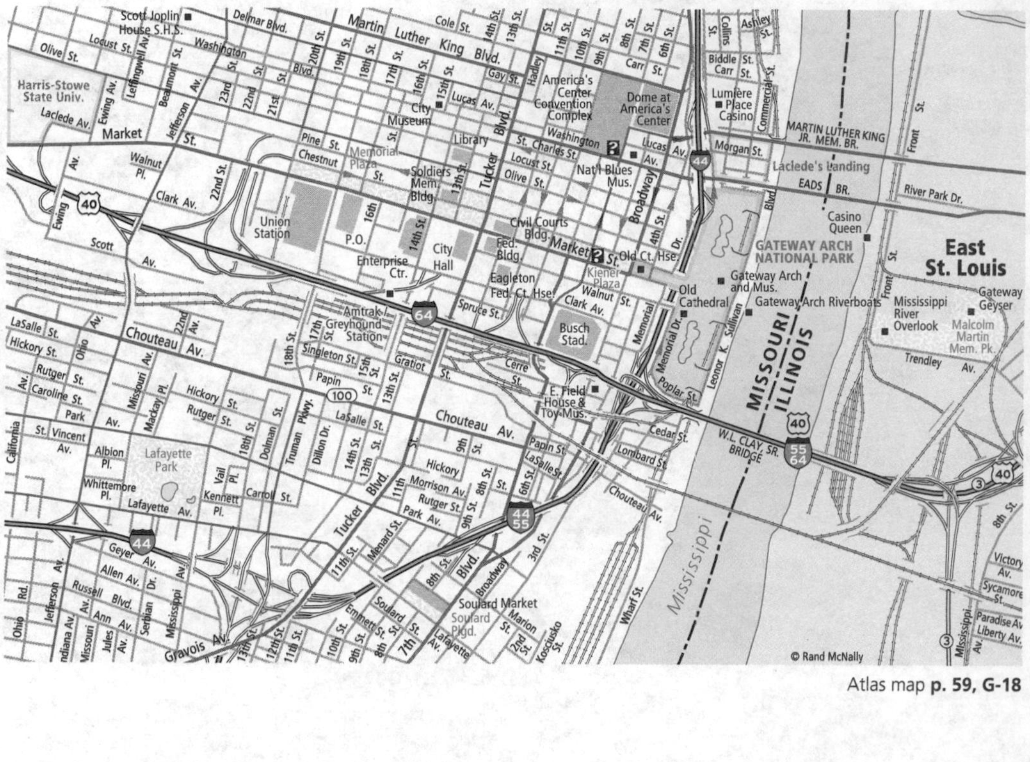

Atlas map **p. 59, G-18**

MAMMOTH CAVE NATIONAL PARK, KY

Cave entrance

On the surface, it looks as if Mammoth Cave National Park has little to offer, but its 586,000 annual visitors are drawn by what's below: more than 400 surveyed miles of passageways and chambers. Even in the 19th century, Mammoth was recognized as one of America's natural wonders, a reputation that would grow with the cave itself. In 1972, spelunkers discovered that it connected to a neighboring network, establishing it as the world's longest cave system.

Mammoth Cave National Park, KY

GETTING ORIENTED

Mammoth Cave is in south-central Kentucky. Louisville International Airport is 85 miles north of the park entrance, and Tennessee's Nashville International is 95 miles south. From Louisville, take I-65 south to Exit 53 in Cave City; from Nashville, take I-65 north to Exit 48 in Park City. Mammoth Cave is 28 miles northeast of Bowling Green via I-65.

In the park's main visitor area, a pedestrian bridge connects the visitor center to the Lodge at Mammoth Cave (171 Hotel Rd., 844/760-2283, mammothcavelodge.com); the main cave entrance is just down the hill. Nearby towns with lodging and other amenities include Cave City (cavecity.com), Park City, and Bowling Green (www.visitbgky.com). The park also has three campgrounds (Recreation.gov). **Park Contact Info:** ***270/758-2180, www.nps.gov/maca.***

PARK HIGHLIGHTS

Cave Tours. You need to take a tour to see the cave. The roster of offerings changes seasonally, with tours lasting from 75 minutes to 6 hours and prices varying accordingly. Sign up in advance if possible since tours sell out quickly, especially in summer. Some tours enter at the Historic Entrance (aka Natural Entrance) by the visitor center; others require a 10-minute bus ride to the New Entrance.

Among the easiest and most popular is the 75-minute Frozen Niagara Tour highlighting stalactites, stalagmites, flowstones, and Frozen Niagara itself, a formation that looks like a freeze-dried waterfall. Going deeper into the cave, the moderate, 2-hour Domes and Dripstones Tour descends nearly 300 steps to dazzling domes, pits, and dripstone formations before returning to sights seen on the Frozen Niagara Tour.

The moderate, 2-hour Historic Tour uses the Historic Entrance and leads to places familiar to visitors in the 1800s, including the Rotunda, Broadway, and Fat Man's Misery. Designed for people who use a walker or wheelchair, the 2-hour Mammoth Cave Accessible Tour visits unique gypsum formations, historical cave writing, and the Snowball Room, where gypsum nodules cover the ceiling.

Specialty cave tours supplement regularly scheduled tours and explore the cave in different ways. The strenuous, 4-mile Violet City Lantern Tour visits the cave Tom Sawyer–style: you carry a flickering lantern. A handful of "wild" tours, including the very strenuous, 5-mile Wild Cave Tour, are for those who can handle tight spaces and don't mind getting dirty. This one finds you donning gloves, knee pads, and a helmet as you walk, kneel, crouch, and crawl your way through the cave.

Trails & Viewpoints. More than 80 miles of trails fan out across the park, with the easiest and most accessible being the 7 miles of routes that surround the visitor center. On these you can see the Green River, walk along ridges that provide lovely views of Doyle Valley, and trek beside huge depressions caused by sinkholes.

The easy, 0.75-mile Heritage Trail passes the Old Guides Cemetery, where you can see the grave of cave explorer Stephen Bishop, a mixed-race slave who, in the mid-19th century, navigated uncharted passages to create detailed cave maps. A popular 9-mile path adjacent to an old railroad bed, the Mammoth Cave Railroad Bike and Hike Trail runs from the visitor center to Park City and accommodates bicyclists, pedestrians, joggers, and dogs on a leash. Hybrid bikes can handle the hard-packed gravel.

Programs & Activities. Outside the cave, rangers host free "surface" talks and presentations that vary by season. In summer, evening presentations are held nightly in the Amphitheater (less often in other seasons), highlighting topics related to Mammoth Cave. There are short Porch Talks about the park's cultural heritage; a 45-minute Heritage Walk explaining Mammoth Cave Estate and the Old Guides Cemetery; and a 45-minute Sloans Pond Crossing Walk. Mammoth Cave is along the Mississippi Flyway, and rangers host two-hour birding excursions.

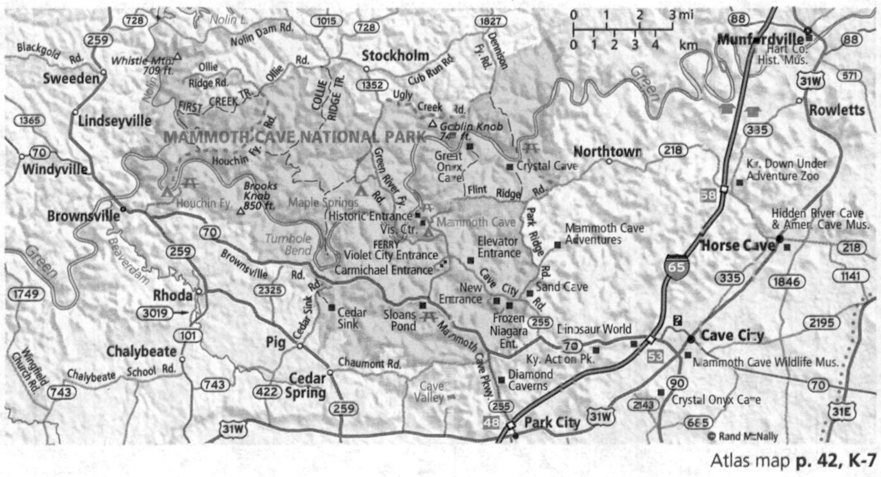

Atlas map **p. 42, K-7**

Cave interior, Frozen Niagara section

Mileage Chart

This handy chart offers more than 2,400 mileages covering 90 North American cities and U.S. national parks. Want more mileages? Visit **randmcnally.com/MC** and type in any two cities or addresses.

	Albuquerque, NM	Amarillo, TX	Atlanta, GA	Baltimore, MD	Billings, MT	Birmingham, AL	Boise, ID	Boston, MA	Branson, MO	Brownsville, TX	Buffalo, NY	Charleston, SC	Charleston, WV	Charlotte, NC	Cheyenne, WY	Chicago, IL	Cincinnati, OH	Cleveland, OH	Columbus, OH	Dallas, TX	Denver, CO	Des Moines, IA	Detroit, MI	El Paso, TX	Fargo, ND	Grand Junction, CO	Hartford, CT	Houston, TX	Indianapolis, IN	Jackson, MS	Jacksonville, FL	Kansas City, MO	Las Vegas, NV	Little Rock, AR
Acadia N.P., ME	2490	2206	1366	671	2507	1448	2935	283	1704	2469	728	1241	1014	1112	2198	1254	1142	911	1034	2035	2242	1570	997	2626	1900	2484	372	2115	1208	1683	1417	1692	2988	1718
Albuquerque, NM		284	1386	1887	998	1241	938	2219	864	990	1782	1703	1543	1626	546	1333	1387	1598	1457	647	446	983	1570	260	1318	380	2118	884	1279	1047	1636	784	572	877
Amarillo, TX	284		1102	1602	965	957	1243	1935	580	788	1498	1419	1259	1342	515	1049	1103	1314	1173	363	424	765	1286	407	1002	607	1834	589	995	762	1352	570	857	593
Anchorage, AK	3672	3641	4338	4321	2660	4284	2707	4495	3788	4430	4155	4532	4111	4389	3128	3617	3914	3965	3975	4097	3227	3450	3905	3940	2935	3288	4513	4339	3804	4302	4689	3572	3424	3959
Atlanta, GA	1386	1102		682	1831	146	2177	1095	652	1145	894	317	502	244	1439	715	461	714	567	780	1404	902	722	1418	1361	1643	996	794	533	380	346	800	1959	515
Baltimore, MD	1887	1602	682		1952	780	2378	400	1079	1801	372	571	361	442	1644	699	513	369	409	1368	1673	1015	524	2003	1346	1916	300	1448	584	1017	744	1068	2420	1050
Big Bend N.P., TX	592	470	1344	1929	1393	1201	1530	2325	973	625	1939	1661	1610	1588	938	1442	1495	1755	1614	561	838	1182	1678	325	1525	949	2226	637	1388	964	1505	988	1043	880
Billings, MT	998	965	1831	1952		1780	620	2236	1241	1758	1786	2132	1742	1990	453	1246	1546	1596	1606	1425	551	946	1535	1257	607	662	2143	1652	1435	1688	2182	1026	971	1407
Birmingham, AL	1241	957	146	780	1780		2126	1177	507	1020	908	463	564	390	1386	660	464	716	569	636	1329	848	724	1274	1307	1573	1078	668	478	237	434	749	1814	370
Boise, ID	938	1243	2177	2378	620	2126		2660	1588	1928	2214	2473	2123	2336	736	1693	1943	2020	2013	1702	830	1360	1960	1205	1227	620	2566	1930	1835	2048	2528	1372	624	1786
Boston, MA	2219	1935	1095	400	2236	1177	2660		1433	2198	453	970	744	841	1927	983	870	638	763	1764	1970	1299	724	2373	1629	2210	101	1844	937	1412	1146	1421	2714	1447
Branson, MO	864	580	652	1079	1241	507	1588	1433		1005	995	968	755	868	851	545	601	808	668	435	806	400	784	985	816	1049	1327	602	493	432	968	209	1437	172
Brownsville, TX	990	788	1145	1801	1758	1020	1928	2198	1005		1853	1459	1525	1388	1303	1474	1409	1669	1528	547	1213	1230	1673	814	1614	1370	2099	354	1379	793	1225	1036	1550	794
Buffalo, NY	1782	1498	894	372	1786	908	2214	453	995	1853		866	435	656	1478	533	434	190	326	1378	1521	849	273	1908	1180	1762	397	1499	500	1125	1037	984	2266	1061
Calgary, AB	1542	1511	2357	2332	541	2305	747	2615	1783	2299	2165	2542	2122	2400	998	1627	1925	1976	1985	1967	1096	1461	1915	1809	956	1154	2524	2209	1814	2239	2703	1567	1284	1958
Charleston, SC	1703	1419	317	571	2132	463	2473	970	968	1459	866		471	207	1740	908	620	721	636	1099	1706	1199	826	1734	1557	1946	871	1105	726	697	235	1103	2276	831
Charleston, WV	1543	1259	502	361	1742	564	2123	744	755	1525	435	471		264	1389	491	196	250	162	1049	1355	788	352	1684	1136	1595	644	1171	312	801	642	752	2099	732
Charlotte, NC	1626	1342	244	442	1990	390	2336	841	868	1388	656	207	264		1600	769	477	514	426	1023	1566	1057	616	1662	1414	1810	742	1038	583	624	379	961	2199	754
Cheyenne, WY	546	515	1439	1644	453	1386	736	1927	851	1303	1478	1740	1389	1600		960	1210	1288	1281	971	100	628	1227	807	787	340	1834	1202	1104	1316	1792	634	829	1055
Chicago, IL	1333	1049	715	699	1246	660	1693	983	545	1474	533	908	491	769	960		289	342	354	926	1002	332	280	1455	641	1242	888	1085	181	738	1068	526	1746	650
Cincinnati, OH	1387	1103	461	513	1546	464	1943	870	601	1409	434	620	196	477	1210	289		248	106	934	1187	580	259	1569	937	1427	767	1055	108	686	796	584	1932	617
Cleveland, OH	1598	1314	714	369	1596	716	2020	638	808	1669	190	721	250	514	1288	342	248		142	1194	1330	659	168	1721	990	1570	562	1315	315	937	892	799	2073	868
Columbus, OH	1457	1173	567	409	1606	569	2013	763	668	1528	326	636	162	426	1281	354	106	142		1039	1261	653	191	1578	1000	1501	661	1174	176	790	812	657	2004	724
Crater Lake N.P., OR	1307	1595	2580	2772	1033	2528	422	3054	1990	2305	2609	2866	2515	2736	1129	2086	2336	2413	2406	1976	1223	1753	2353	1473	1640	972	2959	2212	2227	2375	2931	1775	754	2178
Dallas, TX	647	363	780	1368	1425	636	1702	1764	435	547	1378	1099	1049	1023	971	926	934	1194	1039		880	683	1163	635	1079	1124	1665	228	873	402	992	489	1220	319
Denver, CO	446	424	1404	1673	551	1329	830	1970	806	1213	1521	1706	1355	1566	100	1002	1187	1330	1261	880		670	1270	707	873	243	1876	1035	1083	1226	1756	603	747	965
Des Moines, IA	983	765	902	1015	946	848	1360	1299	400	1230	849	1199	788	1057	628	332	580	659	653	683	670		599	1124	475	909	1206	938	474	828	1253	193	1413	573
Detroit, MI	1570	1286	722	524	1535	724	1960	724	784	1673	273	826	352	616	1227	280	259	168	191	1163	1270	599		1702	930	1508	668	1319	288	945	1002	764	2013	885
El Paso, TX	260	407	1418	2003	1257	1274	1205	2373	985	814	1908	1734	1684	1662	807	1455	1569	1721	1578	635	707	1124	1702		1370	642	2300	744	1398	1038	1619	929	718	954
Fargo, ND	1318	1002	1361	1346	607	1307	1227	1629	816	1614	1180	1557	1136	1414	787	641	937	990	1000	1079	873	475	930	1370		1115	1538	1321	825	1265	1708	600	1579	988
Grand Canyon N.P., AZ	400	684	1786	2294	1072	1641	861	2618	1264	1390	2182	2102	1943	2025	774	1729	1786	1997	1857	1047	676	1344	1969	600	1546	433	2518	1284	1679	1446	2036	1184	275	1277
Grand Junction, CO	380	607	1643	1916	662	1573	620	2210	1049	1370	1762	1946	1595	1810	340	1242	1427	1570	1501	1124	243	909	1508	642	1115		2115	1279	1324	1470	1994	844	506	1207
Grt. Smoky Mts. N.P., TN	1440	1151	189	536	1806	289	2142	940	684	1310	705	333	313	190	1408	585	293	548	406	882	1375	873	561	1522	1230	1614	843	962	399	528	510	771	2010	567
Halifax, NS	2865	2581	1742	1046	2878	1823	3306	660	2079	2844	1103	1616	1390	1488	2569	1624	1517	1286	1409	2410	2612	1940	1335	3042	2271	2854	747	2490	1583	2059	1792	2067	3358	2093
Hartford, CT	2118	1834	996	300	2143	1078	2566	101	1327	2099	397	871	644	742	1834	888	767	562	661	1665	1876	1206	668	2300	1538	2115		1745	834	1313	1047	1318	2619	1348
Houston, TX	884	589	794	1448	1652	668	1930	1844	602	354	1499	1105	1171	1038	1202	1085	1055	1315	1174	228	1035	938	1319	744	1321	1279	1745		1021	439	871	732	1457	439
Indianapolis, IN	1279	995	533	584	1435	478	1835	937	493	1379	500	726	312	583	1104	181	108	315	176	873	1083	474	288	1398	825	1324	834	1021		671	874	482	1828	583
Jackson, MS	1047	762	380	1017	1688	237	2048	1412	432	793	1125	697	801	624	1316	738	686	937	790	402	1226	828	945	1038	1265	1470	1313	439	671		590	664	1620	261
Jacksonville, FL	1636	1352	346	744	2182	434	2528	1146	968	1225	1037	235	642	379	1792	1068	796	892	812	992	1756	1253	1002	1619	1708	1994	1047	871	874	590		1152	2210	832
Kansas City, MO	784	570	800	1068	1026	749	1372	1421	209	1036	984	1103	752	961	634	526	584	799	657	489	603	193	764	929	600	844	1318	732	482	664	1152		1349	381
Key West, FL	2099	1815	809	1251	2646	905	2992	1659	1431	1688	1544	742	1149	886	2256	1534	1275	1399	1325	1455	2222	1726	1515	2082	2178	2466	1560	1334	1348	1053	507	1617	2673	1294
Las Vegas, NV	572	857	1959	2420	971	1814	624	2714	1437	1550	2266	2276	2099	2199	829	1746	1932	2073	2004	1220	747	1413	2013	718	1579	506	2619	1457	1828	1620	2210	1349		1450
Little Rock, AR	877	593	515	1050	1407	370	1786	1447	172	794	1061	831	732	754	1055	650	617	868	724	319	965	573	885	954	988	1207	1348	439	583	261	832	381	1450	
Los Angeles, CA	786	1072	2174	2670	1240	2029	842	2983	1651	1630	2535	2491	2330	2414	1102	2015	2172	2342	2244	1437	1015	1682	2281	796	1848	774	2888	1550	2068	1838	2421	1616	270	1665
Louisville, KY	1300	1016	420	604	1539	366	1877	978	510	1314	540	613	244	470	1144	296	97	347	206	836	1109	586	361	1474	944	1349	877	960	113	586	772	507	1854	520
Memphis, TN	1008	720	379	914	1477	234	1825	1312	274	929	922	696	597	619	1091	531	482	729	587	453	1097	617	742	1089	1054	1340	1213	575	464	209	677	451	1581	137
Mexico City, DF	1392	1332	1718	2372	2301	1592	2330	2768	1548	570	2424	2029	2095	1962	1846	2017	1979	2239	2098	1090	1756	1790	2254	1124	2158	1772	2669	924	1963	1364	1796	1598	1755	1364
Miami, FL	1952	1668	661	1082	2497	746	2844	1482	1284	1538	1385	583	990	728	2107	1381	1127	1240	1164	1307	2069	1567	1354	1934	2025	2308	1385	1186	1198	905	349	1466	2525	1147
Milwaukee, WI	1354	1132	809	792	1173	754	1732	1074	630	1557	630	1002	589	867	1000	90	381	434	445	1010	1042	371	374	1497	569	1282	980	1163	272	830	1163	565	1786	724
Minneapolis, MN	1225	1009	1127	1112	838	1072	1461	1396	643	1475	946	1323	902	1180	865	408	703	756	766	928	913	242	696	1377	235	1152	1304	1171	591	1040	1474	436	1656	815
Mobile, AL	1234	949	328	1003	1874	258	2236	1427	620	821	1166	602	816	571	1504	917	721	973	826	589	1414	998	978	1215	1451	1657	1328	468	733	188	403	850	1808	449
Montpelier, VT	2203	1919	1165	498	2207	1247	2636	179	1417	2268	428	1068	813	928	1899	954	855	611	747	1824	1942	1270	718	2347	1601	2184	198	1914	921	1482	1245	1405	2688	1506
Montréal, QC	2129	1845	1218	548	2099	1299	2523	310	1342	2311	393	1118	822	980	1790	847	824	578	714	1722	1832	1163	560	2261	1496	2072	328	1884	847	1517	1294	1330	2576	1451
Nashville, TN	1219	932	248	703	1586	192	1925	1099	464	1140	712	549	388	407	1192	469	273	525	378	664	1158	656	534	1300	1116	1397	1000	786	287	414	596	555	1792	348
New Orleans, LA	1165	881	468	1124	1868	343	2216	1520	597	700	1248	742	908	712	1488	923	804	1057	910	519	1398	1008	1066	1095	1445	1638	1421	347	818	183	547	844	1739	425
New York, NY	2001	1716	882	192	2041	960	2465	207	1201	1981	395	768	530	641	1733	787	637	460	533	1548	1775	1105	613	2201	1438	2014	108	1632	707	1198	939	1196	2518	1230
Norfolk, VA	1910	1632	558	228	2132	715	2525	569	1158	1716	569	437	403	328	1792	878	605	551	570	1350	1758	1196	704	1986	1529	1997	470	1362	720	948	613	1155	2486	1035
Oklahoma City, OK	542	256	844	1346	1203	699	1497	1678	323	738	1242	1160	1002	1084	720	792	846	1057	917	204	631	545	1029	660	875	870	1577	437	739	603	1160	348	1112	335
Omaha, NE	863	647	992	1153	845	939	1225	1436	402	1192	987	1293	943	1151	492	470	722	797	792	656	534	137	736	1004	420	774	1345	898	613	852	1343	187	1278	574
Orlando, FL	1730	1446	440	889	2275	534	2622	1288	1062	1319	1184	380	792	526	1885	1153	905	1043	954	1086	1851	1339	1144	1712	1807	2095	1189	965	968	683	141	1246	2303	925
Philadelphia, PA	1924	1640	780	98	2011	880	2435	306	1138	1900	388	668	466	539	1703	757	571	428	468	1467	1732	1074	583	2102	1405	1975	207	1547	643	1115	844	1127	2480	1150
Phoenix, AZ	462	746	1844	2349	1210	1700	914	2681	1326	1259	2245	2165	2005	2088	1008	1795	1849	2060	1920	1066	908	1445	2032	424	1780	571	2580	1178	1742	1466	2050	1246	285	1340
Pittsburgh, PA	1641	1357	684	246	1713	748	2137	570	851	1708	216	654	225	446	1405	459	288	131	184	1221	1447	777	285	1774	1107	1686	469	1354	359	971	825	840	2190	905
Portland, ME	2315	2031	1192	496	2333	1274	2761	110	1529	2294	553	1066	840	938	2024	1079	967	736	859	1861	2067	1395	825	2455	1726	2309	197	1940	1034	1509	1243	1518	2813	1543
Portland, OR	1363	1669	2603	2804	891	2551	428	3086	2013	2354	2639	2904	2554	2761	1161	2118	2369	2446	2439	2128	1256	1786	2385	1630	1497	1046	2992	2356	2260	2473	2954	1797	1022	2211
Québec, QC	2283	1999	1372	694	2257	1455	2681	396	1497	2472	552	1264	979	1134	1948	1004	979	735	870	1876	1991	1320	715	2416	1650	2230	427	2123	1001	1676	1440	1484	2734	1606
Raleigh, NC	1761	1474	408	302	2067	555	2444	702	1003	1556	637	278	322	168	1712	816	521	572	486	1191	1678	1107	677	1826	1460	1917	602	1202	628	789	449	1074	2334	889
Rapid City, SD	843	714	1508	1616	323	1456	942	1900	920	1515	1450	1811	1410	1670	298	912	1208	1260	1270	1061	397	626	1200	1110	550	639	1808	1291	1100	1371	1860	704	1039	1093
Regina, SK	1284	1253	1904	1882	472	1850	1092	2090	1321	2046	1721	2066	1674	1937	740	1151	1445	1503	1510	1510	838	1016	1441	1551	513	1080	2080	1753	1337	1805	2220	1104	1443	1525
Reno, NV	1019	1304	2396	2599	956	2262	422	2881	1806	1998	2433	2698	2342	2555	956	1913	2163	2240	2234	1668	1051	1581	2180	1166	1564	799	2786	1904	2056	2067	2748	1591	447	1898
Saint Louis, MO	1037	752	555	829	1278	501	1622	1182	249	1177	746	856	506	714	888	296	348	560	421	630	854	354	533	1157	841	1095	1080	784	243	491	906	250	1600	345
Salt Lake City, UT	599	883	1878	2081	552	1826	339	2365	1288	1589	1915	2180	1829	2037	437	1398	1647	1725	1718	1403	533	1065	1664	866	1160	283	2271	1634	1541	1749	2229	1073	419	1488
San Antonio, TX	712	510	986	1642	1480	861	1651	2039	708	274	1654	1300	1324	1230	1025	1202	1210	1457	1314	276	935	960	1439	554	1343	1092	1940	197	1149	635	1066	766	1272	594
San Diego, CA	810	1097	2138	2695	1301	1994	958	3046	1675	1552	2596	2459	2354	2381	1162	2080	2196	2407	2269	1359	1077	1747	2346	718	1908	835	2930	1472	2089	1759	2343	1597	331	1676
San Francisco, CA	1086	1370	2472	2816	1173	2327	639	3098	1950	2010	2650	2789	2564	2712	1172	2130	2380	2458	2451	1734	1268	1798	2397	1175	1781	968	3004	1929	2273	2133	2723	1808	569	1963
Sault Ste. Marie, ON	1777	1493	1040	852	1273	1014	1893	923	991	1918	514	1156	683	947	1411	471	577	496	521	1370	1428	710	347	1910	665	1692	904	1527	540	1180	1333	951	2196	1089
Savannah, GA	1634	1350	247	605	2078	393	2418	1014	900	1320	909	106	514	251	1687	951	664	764	680	996	1651	1150	870	1632	1609	1890	915	971	770	580	135	1048	2206	763
Seattle, WA	1438	1743	2649	2770	818	2597	503	3054	2059	2428	2604	2950	2560	2808	1225	2063	2363	2414	2424	2193	1320	1764	2353	1705	1424	1121	2960	2431	2253	2537	3000	1844	1128	2275
Shenandoah N.P., VA	1794	1488	556	119	1951	634	2399	519	1016	1655	382	516	260	317	1650	698	474	368	389	1223	1614	1014	523	1863	1345	1855	420	1306	563	872	687	1012	2359	904
Spokane, WA	1320	1505	2369	2491	540	2318	425	2774	1780	2296	2325	2671	2281	2528	993	1785	2084	2135	2144	1964	1091	1484	2075	1587	1147	1002	2682	2192	1973	2229	2720	1564	1138	1948
Tampa, FL	1746	1462	451	942	2291	537	2638	1342	1078	1329	1235	433	840	578	1901	1166	916	1091	1007	1102	1860	1354	1178	1728	1813	2099	1242	980	984	699	198	1252	2319	941
Thunder Bay, ON	1566	1348	1376	1288	1049	1322	1670	1298	983	1830	942	1570	1118	1382	1210	656	949	932	957	1270	1253	583	784	1718	441	1492	1305	1522	840	1361	1728	776	1996	1156
Toronto, ON	1800	1516	963	472	1771	968	2194	548	1014	1919	98	964	535	756	1462	519	493	290	426	1393	1504	834	232	1932	1167	1744	490	1551	518	1186	1135	1001	2247	1120
Tucson, AZ	449	735	1732	2320	1326	1588	1030	2669	1314	1145	2233	2052	1994	1975	995	1784	1836	2048	1908	952	895	1433	2020	312	1769	687	2569	1066	1728	1353	1936	1234	401	1271
Vancouver, BC	1574	1878	2785	2906	953	2733	638	3188	2195	2564	2740	3086	2696	2944	1372	2198	2499	2548	2560	2338	1465	1900	2487	1841	1559	1256	3094	2565	2389	2675	3136	1980	1264	2421
Washington, DC	1885	1600	637	39	1951	744	2375	439	1078	1765	382	530	362	398	1642	697	512	367	407	1332	1671	1014	522	1966	1344	1914	340	1411	582	980	706	1066	2428	1014
Wichita, KS	591	382	955	1260	1064	810	1338	1613	292	896	1176	1272	945	1092	608	724	779	992	851	361	519	391	964	730	685	759	1512	595	674	707	1272	193	1164	446
Winnipeg, MB	1538	1222	1582	1570	723	1532	1345	1729	1033	1834	1403	1779	1360	1638	1006	864	1158	1214	1222	1298	1092	699	1153	1590	222	1334	1760	1541	1049	1484	1932	817	1692	1208
Yellowstone N.P., WY	963	977	1904	2145	175	1852	418	2410	1316	1813	1960	2207	1906	2076	469	1418	1710	1772	1787	1436	563	1094	1710	1229	782	632	2315	1664	1602	1826	2256	1100	769	1519
Yosemite N.P., CA	989	1289	2391	2695	1129	2246	594	2979	1868	1939	2529	2708	2403	2619	1051	2012	2264	2339	2335	1636	1045	1680	2279	1104	1735	802	2888	1858	2155	2052	2642	1649	415	1870

	Los Angeles, CA	Louisville, KY	Memphis, TN	Miami, FL	Milwaukee, WI	Minneapolis, MN	Mobile, AL	Montpelier, VT	Nashville, TN	New Orleans, LA	New York, NY	Norfolk, VA	Oklahoma City, OK	Omaha, NE	Orlando, FL	Philadelphia, PA	Phoenix, AZ	Pittsburgh, PA	Portland, ME	Portland, OR	Raleigh, NC	Rapid City, SD	Reno, NV	Saint Louis, MO	Salt Lake City, UT	San Antonio, TX	San Diego, CA	San Francisco, CA	Savannah, GA	Seattle, WA	Spokane, WA	Tampa, FL	Washington, DC	Wichita, KS
Acadia N.P., ME	3256	1249	1583	1760	1348	1667	1698	293	1370	1791	478	840	1949	1707	1559	577	2952	841	172	3360	972	2171	3154	1453	2636	2310	3317	3371	1285	3325	3045	1613	710	1884
Albuquerque, NM	786	1300	1008	1952	1354	1225	1234	2203	1219	1165	2001	1910	542	863	1730	1924	462	1641	2315	1363	1761	843	1019	1037	599	712	810	1086	1634	1438	1320	1746	1885	591
Amarillo, TX	1072	1016	720	1668	1132	1009	949	1919	932	881	1716	1632	256	647	1446	1640	746	1357	2031	1669	1474	714	1304	752	883	510	1097	1370	1350	1743	1505	1462	1600	382
Anchorage, AK	3412	3919	4093	5004	3545	3165	4486	4318	4093	4485	4428	4506	3894	3391	4782	4380	3681	4082	4443	2448	4436	2995	3026	3825	3006	4152	3532	3084	4585	2276	2387	4798	4319	3736
Atlanta, GA	2174	420	379	661	809	1127	328	1165	248	468	882	558	844	992	440	780	1844	684	1192	2603	408	1508	2396	555	1878	986	2138	2472	247	2649	2369	451	637	955
Baltimore, MD	2670	604	914	1082	792	1112	1003	498	703	1124	192	228	1346	1153	889	98	2349	246	496	2804	302	1616	2599	829	2081	1642	2695	2816	605	2770	2491	942	39	1260
Big Bend N.P., TX	1128	1400	1015	1820	1525	1427	1102	2395	1226	981	2128	1912	650	1102	1598	2028	757	1794	2422	1956	1753	1190	1491	1145	1191	404	1050	1507	1558	2021	1912	1614	1892	807
Billings, MT	1240	1539	1477	2497	1173	838	1874	2207	1586	1868	2041	2132	1203	845	2275	2011	1210	1713	2333	891	2067	323	956	1278	552	1480	1301	1173	2078	818	540	2291	1951	1064
Birmingham, AL	2029	366	234	746	754	1072	258	1247	192	343	960	715	699	939	534	880	1700	748	1274	2551	555	1456	2262	501	1826	861	1994	2327	393	2597	2318	537	744	810
Boise, ID	842	1877	1825	2844	1732	1461	2236	2636	1925	2216	2465	2525	1497	1225	2622	2435	914	2137	2761	428	2444	942	422	1622	339	1651	958	639	2418	503	425	2638	2375	1338
Boston, MA	2983	978	1312	1482	1074	1396	1427	179	1099	1520	207	569	1678	1436	1288	306	2681	570	110	3086	702	1900	2881	1182	2365	2039	3046	3098	1014	3054	2774	1342	439	1613
Branson, MO	1651	510	274	1284	630	643	620	1417	464	597	1201	1158	323	402	1062	1138	1326	851	1529	2013	1003	920	1806	249	1288	708	1675	1950	900	2059	1780	1078	1078	292
Brownsville, TX	1630	1314	929	1538	1557	1475	821	2268	1140	700	1981	1716	738	1192	1319	1900	1259	1708	2294	2354	1556	1515	1998	1177	1589	274	1552	2010	1320	2428	2296	1329	1765	896
Buffalo, NY	2535	540	922	1385	630	946	1166	428	712	1248	395	569	1242	987	1184	388	2245	216	553	2639	637	1450	2433	746	1915	1654	2596	2650	909	2604	2325	1235	382	1176
Calgary, AB	1557	1930	2028	3018	1555	1221	2481	2380	2116	2419	2438	2516	1763	1386	2797	2390	1524	2093	2505	787	2446	865	1276	1820	869	2021	1617	1500	2620	678	424	2833	2330	1606
Charleston, SC	2491	613	696	583	1002	1323	602	1068	549	742	768	437	1160	1293	380	668	2165	654	1066	2904	278	1811	2698	856	2180	1300	2459	2789	106	2950	2671	433	530	1272
Charleston, WV	2330	244	597	990	589	902	816	813	388	908	530	403	1002	943	792	466	2005	225	840	2554	322	1410	2342	506	1829	1324	2354	2564	514	2560	2281	840	362	945
Charlotte, NC	2414	470	619	728	867	1180	571	928	407	712	641	328	1084	1151	526	539	2088	446	938	2761	168	1670	2555	714	2037	1230	2381	2712	251	2808	2528	578	398	1092
Cheyenne, WY	1102	1144	1091	2107	1000	865	1504	1899	1192	1488	1733	1792	720	492	1885	1703	1008	1405	2024	1161	1712	298	956	888	437	1025	1162	1172	1687	1225	993	1901	1642	608
Chicago, IL	2015	296	531	1381	90	408	917	954	469	923	787	878	792	470	1153	757	1795	459	1079	2118	816	912	1913	296	1398	1202	2080	2130	951	2063	1785	1166	697	724
Cincinnati, OH	2172	97	482	1127	381	703	721	855	273	804	637	605	846	722	905	571	1849	288	967	2369	521	1208	2163	348	1647	1210	2196	2380	664	2363	2084	916	512	779
Cleveland, OH	2342	347	729	1240	434	756	973	611	525	1057	460	551	1057	797	1043	428	2060	131	736	2446	572	1260	2240	560	1725	1457	2407	2458	764	2414	2135	1091	367	992
Columbus, OH	2244	206	587	1164	445	766	826	747	378	910	533	570	917	792	954	468	1920	184	859	2439	486	1270	2234	421	1718	1314	2269	2451	680	2424	2144	1007	407	851
Crater Lake N.P., OR	738	2270	2235	3246	2126	1874	2562	3038	2318	2494	2858	2917	1889	1618	3025	2828	1039	2530	3156	250	2837	1351	310	2015	691	2028	858	410	2810	422	493	3041	2768	1731
Dallas, TX	1437	836	453	1307	1010	928	589	1824	664	519	1548	1350	204	656	1086	1467	1066	1221	1861	2128	1191	1061	1668	630	1403	276	1359	1734	996	2193	1964	1102	1332	361
Denver, CO	1015	1109	1097	2069	1042	913	1414	1942	1158	1398	1775	1758	631	534	1851	1732	908	1447	2067	1256	1678	397	1051	854	533	935	1077	1268	1651	1320	1091	1860	1671	519
Des Moines, IA	1682	586	617	1567	371	242	998	1270	656	1008	1105	1196	545	137	1339	1074	1445	777	1395	1786	1107	626	1581	354	1065	960	1747	1798	1150	1764	1484	1354	1014	391
Detroit, MI	2281	361	742	1354	374	696	978	718	534	1066	613	704	1029	736	1144	583	2032	285	825	2385	677	1200	2180	533	1664	1439	2346	2397	870	2353	2075	1178	522	964
El Paso, TX	796	1474	1089	1934	1497	1377	1215	2347	1300	1095	2201	1986	660	1004	1712	2102	424	1774	2455	1630	1826	1110	1166	1157	866	554	718	1175	1632	1705	1587	1728	1966	730
Fargo, ND	1848	944	1054	2025	569	235	1451	1601	1116	1445	1438	1529	875	420	1807	1405	1780	1107	1726	1497	1460	550	1564	841	1160	1343	1908	1781	1609	1424	1147	1813	1344	685
Grand Canyon N.P., AZ	490	1699	1408	2351	1716	1586	1634	2603	1619	1565	2406	2314	942	1208	2130	2324	218	2041	2715	1286	2160	1070	722	1436	522	1112	551	788	2033	1351	1243	2146	2285	990
Grand Junction, CO	774	1349	1340	2308	1282	1152	1657	2184	1397	1638	2014	1997	870	774	2095	1975	571	1686	2309	1046	1917	639	799	1095	283	1092	835	968	1890	1121	1002	2099	1914	759
Grt. Smoky Mts. N.P., TN	2224	286	430	862	682	996	520	1015	220	633	716	485	896	964	624	637	1903	496	1042	2577	326	1479	2371	527	1852	1151	2249	2528	378	2624	2344	640	502	908
Halifax, NS	3627	1624	1958	2145	1724	2037	2073	668	1745	2166	853	1216	2324	2078	1935	952	3328	1216	550	3731	1348	2541	3524	1828	3006	2685	3688	3741	1661	3695	3416	1988	1085	2259
Hartford, CT	2888	877	1213	1385	980	1304	1328	198	1000	1421	108	470	1577	1345	1189	207	2580	469	197	2992	602	1808	2786	1080	2271	1940	2930	3004	915	2960	2682	1242	340	1512
Houston, TX	1550	960	575	1186	1163	1171	468	1914	786	347	1632	1362	437	898	965	1547	1178	1354	1940	2356	1202	1291	1904	784	1634	197	1472	1929	971	2431	2192	980	1411	595
Indianapolis, IN	2068	113	464	1198	272	591	733	921	287	818	707	720	739	613	968	643	1742	359	1034	2260	628	1100	2056	243	1541	1149	2089	2273	770	2253	1973	984	582	674
Jackson, MS	1838	586	209	905	830	1040	188	1482	414	183	1198	948	603	852	683	1115	1466	971	1509	2473	789	1371	2067	491	1749	635	1759	2133	580	2537	2229	699	980	707
Jacksonville, FL	2421	772	677	349	1163	1474	403	1245	596	547	939	613	1160	1343	141	844	2050	825	1243	2954	449	1860	2748	906	2229	1066	2343	2723	135	3000	2720	198	706	1272
Kansas City, MO	1616	507	451	1466	565	436	850	1405	555	844	1196	1155	348	187	1246	1127	1246	840	1518	1797	1074	704	1591	250	1073	766	1597	1808	1048	1844	1564	1252	1066	193
Key West, FL	2884	1238	1159	162	1632	1944	866	1758	1063	1010	1446	1120	1623	1807	387	1357	2514	1332	1756	3417	956	2326	3211	1370	2693	1529	2806	3186	642	3464	3185	402	1213	1735
Las Vegas, NV	270	1854	1581	2525	1786	1656	1808	2688	1792	1739	2518	2486	1112	1278	2303	2480	285	2190	2813	1022	2334	1039	447	1600	419	1272	331	569	2206	1128	1138	2319	2428	1164
Little Rock, AR	1665	520	137	1147	724	815	449	1506	348	425	1230	1035	335	574	925	1150	1340	905	1543	2211	889	1093	1898	345	1488	594	1676	1963	763	2275	1948	941	1014	446
Los Angeles, CA		2085	1794	2735	2055	1925	2014	2957	2006	1894	2787	2707	1326	1546	2515	2713	370	2428	3082	963	2548	1312	470	1821	688	1357	120	380	2422	1134	1215	2525	2670	1377
Louisville, KY	2085		384	1085	390	710	620	962	174	705	740	649	759	699	858	676	1762	388	1074	2310	568	1214	2104	263	1586	1111	2109	2321	658	2357	2077	872	606	701
Memphis, TN	1794	384		1012	622	831	382	1369	212	394	1094	898	466	641	778	1014	1471	768	1408	2245	753	1160	2029	283	1524	727	1819	2095	626	2299	2018	779	879	577
Mexico City, DF	1839	1884	1500	2111	2100	2032	1392	2838	1710	1272	2571	2286	1282	1735	1889	2471	1469	2279	2865	2756	2126	2139	2202	1721	1991	821	1700	2218	1906	2830	2711	1905	2335	1440
Miami, FL	2735	1085	1012		1475	1791	719	1587	913	861	1288	950	1476	1658	229	1180	2362	1173	1585	3260	797	2173	3063	1221	2544	1379	2656	3038	483	3315	3035	255	1044	1587
Milwaukee, WI	2055	390	622	1475		336	1011	1054	564	1015	879	969	875	509	1258	849	1817	551	1176	2062	914	840	1953	379	1437	1285	2118	2170	1045	1990	1712	1260	788	763
Minneapolis, MN	1925	710	831	1791	336		1224	1367	881	1223	1204	1295	788	372	1573	1171	1687	874	1492	1727	1227	575	1818	563	1308	1205	1986	2040	1374	1655	1377	1578	1110	634
Mobile, AL	2014	620	382	719	1011	1224		1497	447	144	1202	887	791	1038	497	1101	1643	1000	1523	2661	737	1557	2255	645	1936	662	1936	2320	502	2727	2478	509	965	894
Montpelier, VT	2957	962	1369	1587	1054	1367	1497		1160	1589	306	668	1662	1408	1387	405	2666	612	220	3061	800	1871	2854	1166	2336	2096	3018	3071	1113	3025	2746	1440	538	1597
Montréal, QC	2845	931	1314	1646	938	1262	1549	133	1105	1640	381	717	1588	1302	1436	454	2591	603	258	2948	850	1766	2743	1092	2228	1998	2912	2960	1162	2916	2638	1490	587	1529
Nashville, TN	2006	174	212	913	564	881	447	1160		532	884	688	677	747	683	802	1682	560	1196	2357	542	1262	2151	310	1633	939	2030	2306	495	2404	2124	700	666	688
New Orleans, LA	1894	705	394	861	1015	1223	144	1589	532		1304	1026	722	1032	641	1222	1523	1090	1616	2642	878	1551	2186	675	1920	541	1816	2252	642	2716	2409	651	1087	880
New York, NY	2787	740	1094	1288	879	1204	1202	306	884	1304		370	1460	1245	1089	97	2463	369	304	2891	502	1708	2685	954	2170	1822	2809	2902	811	2858	2580	1138	228	1391
Norfolk, VA	2707	649	898	950	969	1295	887	668	688	1026	370		1366	1335	755	270	2373	425	666	2962	183	1799	2744	911	2238	1557	2730	2973	481	2949	2671	808	189	1349
Oklahoma City, OK	1326	759	466	1476	875	788	791	1662	677	722	1460	1366		452	1254	1384	1005	1100	1775	1922	1218	857	1563	496	1200	468	1351	1627	1092	1948	1710	1270	1343	158
Omaha, NE	1546	699	641	1658	509	372	1038	1408	747	1032	1245	1335	452		1436	1212	1325	914	1533	1650	1266	525	1445	439	930	920	1613	1662	1239	1663	1383	1445	1151	298
Orlando, FL	2515	858	778	229	1258	1573	497	1387	683	641	1089	755	1254	1436		986	2145	975	1385	3048	597	1956	2841	999	2323	1160	2436	2816	280	3093	2814	84	849	1365
Philadelphia, PA	2713	676	1014	1180	849	1171	1101	405	802	1222	97	270	1384	1212	986		2387	304	402	2861	399	1675	2656	888	2140	1742	2738	2873	703	2828	2550	1040	137	1319
Phoenix, AZ	370	1762	1471	2362	1817	1687	1643	2666	1682	1523	2463	2373	1005	1325	2145	2387		2104	2778	1332	2224	1305	733	1499	653	985	352	749	2091	1414	1381	2153	2348	1053
Pittsburgh, PA	2428	388	768	1173	551	874	1000	612	560	1090	369	425	1100	914	975	304	2104		666	2563	499	1378	2357	604	1842	1495	2452	2574	697	2530	2252	1023	244	1035
Portland, ME	3082	1074	1408	1585	1176	1492	1523	220	1196	1616	304	666	1775	1533	1385	402	2778	666		3186	798	1996	2979	1279	2461	2136	3143	3196	1111	3150	2871	1438	535	1710
Portland, OR	963	2310	2245	3260	2062	1727	2661	3061	2357	2642	2891	2962	1922	1650	3048	2861	1332	2563	3186		2897	1214	578	2050	765	2076	1083	635	2844	172	351	3064	2800	1764
Québec, QC	3003	1086	1470	1792	1096	1417	1703	259	1262	1795	524	863	1742	1457	1582	600	2745	760	275	3107	996	1921	2901	1246	2386	2152	3067	3119	1308	3074	2795	1636	733	1683
Raleigh, NC	2548	568	753	797	914	1227	737	800	542	878	502	183	1218	1266	597	399	2224	499	798	2897		1735	2690	830	2172	1397	2551	2847	322	2885	2605	648	262	1227
Rapid City, SD	1312	1214	1160	2173	840	575	1557	1871	1262	1551	1708	1799	857	525	1956	1675	1305	1378	1996	1214	1735		1167	959	649	1242	1372	1384	1756	1141	862	1960	1615	699
Regina, SK	1712	1454	1594	2570	1078	743	2009	1914	1659	1985	1994	2037	1307	927	2348	1946	1682	1619	2039	1120	2002	532	1428	1360	1024	1774	1773	1645	2117	1046	767	2360	1878	1149
Reno, NV	470	2104	2029	3063	1953	1818	2255	2854	2151	2186	2685	2744	1563	1445	2841	2656	733	2357	2979	578	2690	1167		1844	518	1720	558	217	2644	720	793	2857	2595	1558
Saint Louis, MO	1821	263	283	1221	379	563	645	1166	310	675	954	911	496	439	999	888	1499	604	1279	2050	830	959	1844		1326	906	1845	2061	802	2096	1817	1008	827	442
Salt Lake City, UT	688	1586	1524	2544	1437	1308	1936	2336	1633	1920	2170	2238	1200	930	2323	2140	653	1842	2461	765	2172	649	518	1326		1311	750	735	2125	839	720	2339	2079	1042
San Antonio, TX	1357	1111	727	1379	1285	1205	662	2096	939	541	1822	1557	468	920	1160	1742	985	1495	2136	2076	1397	1242	1720	906	1311		1278	1736	1161	2150	2018	1170	1606	625
San Diego, CA	120	2109	1819	2656	2118	1986	1936	3018	2030	1816	2809	2730	1351	1613	2436	2738	352	2452	3143	1083	2551	1372	558	1845	750	1278		501	2356	1256	1468	2447	2693	1401
San Francisco, CA	380	2321	2095	3038	2170	2040	2320	3071	2306	2252	2902	2973	1627	1662	2816	2873	749	2574	3196	635	2847	1384	217	2061	735	1736	501		2720	807	874	2832	2812	1775
Sault Ste. Marie, ON	2465	649	972	1685	398	538	1268	740	823	1355	921	1037	1236	850	1475	911	2240	614	871	2165	1007	1118	2364	740	1848	1646	2502	2581	1201	2090	1812	1492	851	1150
Savannah, GA	2422	658	626	483	1045	1374	502	1113	495	642	811	481	1092	1239	280	703	2091	697	1111	2844	322	1756	2644	802	2125	1161	2356	2720		2896	2616	333	575	1202
Seattle, WA	1134	2357	2299	3315	1990	1655	2727	3025	2404	2716	2858	2949	1948	1663	3093	2828	1414	2530	3150	172	2885	1141	720	2096	839	2150	1256	807	2896		278	3109	2768	1828
Shenandoah N.P., VA	2582	506	768	1035	798	1111	886	618	558	978	320	181	1233	1155	847	217	2238	245	616	2824	263	1615	2604	768	2107	1496	2586	2842	567	2769	2490	885	82	1207
Spokane, WA	1215	2077	2018	3035	1712	1377	2478	2746	2124	2409	2580	2671	1710	1383	2814	2550	1381	2252	2871	351	2605	862	793	1817	720	2018	1468	874	2616	278		2830	2490	1600
Tampa, FL	2525	872	779	255	1260	1578	509	1440	700	651	1138	808	1270	1445	84	1040	2153	1023	1438	3064	648	1960	2857	1008	2339	1170	2447	2832	333	3109	2830		902	1381
Thunder Bay, ON	2265	957	1153	2041	585	341	1547	1121	1130	1545	1349	1473	1127	720	1822	1339	2028	1049	1246	1938	1443	913	2006	870	1648	1547	2326	2224	1613	1866	1588	1828	1286	974
Toronto, ON	2517	601	983	1483	609	933	1222	465	774	1306	489	669	1259	974	1284	497	2262	316	592	2620	737	1438	2414	763	1899	1669	2583	2632	1007	2588	2310	1333	482	1188
Tucson, AZ	485	1749	1406	2250	1805	1675	1530	2654	1617	1410	2448	2303	990	1313	2029	2383	116	2092	2766	1447	2142	1293	848	1485	776	871	407	864	1949	1529	1496	2040	2283	1040
Vancouver, BC	1275	2493	2437	3451	2125	1790	2894	2982	2540	2851	2993	3084	2083	1799	3229	2963	1550	2665	3286	313	3021	1277	890	2232	973	2286	1398	947	3032	141	413	3245	2903	1973
Washington, DC	2670	606	879	1044	788	1110	965	538	666	1087	228	189	1343	1151	849	137	2348	244	535	2800	262	1615	2595	827	2079	1606	2693	2812	575	2768	2490	902		1258
Wichita, KS	1377	701	577	1587	763	634	894	1597	688	880	1391	1349	158	298	1365	1319	1053	1035	1710	1764	1227	699	1558	442	1042	625	1401	1775	1202	1828	1600	1381	1258	
Winnipeg, MB	1965	1164	1273	2252	791	456	1721	1552	1336	1664	1659	1749	1095	640	2029	1629	2000	1331	1677	1474	1684	745	1684	1062	1277	1562	2025	1912	1829	1401	1121	2047	1568	905
Yellowstone N.P., WY	1037	1611	1624	2569	1345	1016	2014	2381	1658	1950	2213	2314	1182	958	2356	2182	1002	1892	2506	833	2178	497	755	1356	351	1535	1098	972	2151	760	481	2356	2142	1072
Yosemite N.P., CA	308	2159	2009	2957	2051	1922	2239	2950	2212	2162	2802	2811	1533	1547	2735	2754	678	2457	3075	751	2762	1263	214	1899	615	1665	429	189	2639	923	967	2751	2695	1564

Mileages in this chart are based upon the routes usually followed by motorists. Highway systems include interstate, U.S., and state highways.

RAND McNALLY

Road Atlas 2020

Maps

Maps

Map Legend **inside front cover**

United States Overview Map **2–3**

States and Cities **4–116**

Canada Overview Map **117**

Provinces and Cities **118–127**

Mexico Overview Map and Puerto Rico **128**

Indexes

United States Index **129–136**

Canada Index **136**

Mexico Index **136**

Quick Map References

State & Province Maps

United States

Alabama 4–5
Alaska 6
Arizona 7–9
Arkansas 10–11
California 12–19
Colorado 20–22
Connecticut 23
Delaware 24
Florida 24–27
Georgia 28–30
Hawaii 30
Idaho 31
Illinois 32–35
Indiana 35–37
Iowa 38–39
Kansas 40–41
Kentucky 42–43
Louisiana 44
Maine 45
Maryland 46–47
Massachusetts 48–49
Michigan 50–52
Minnesota 53–55
Mississippi 56
Missouri 57–59
Montana 60–61
Nebraska 62–63
Nevada 64–65
New Hampshire 65
New Jersey 66–67
New Mexico 68
New York 69–73
North Carolina 74–76
North Dakota 77
Ohio 78–81
Oklahoma 82–83
Oregon 84–85
Pennsylvania 86–90
Rhode Island 91
South Carolina 92
South Dakota 93
Tennessee 94–96
Texas 96–101
Utah 102–103
Vermont 104
Virginia 105–107
Washington 108–110
Washington, D.C. 111
West Virginia 112
Wisconsin 113–115
Wyoming 116

Canada

Alberta 118–119
British Columbia 118–119
Manitoba 121
New Brunswick 126
Newfoundland and Labrador 127
Nova Scotia 126–127
Ontario 122–123
Prince Edward Island 126–127
Québec 124–125
Saskatchewan 120–121

Selected City Maps

This list contains only 70 of more than 350 detailed city maps in the Road Atlas. To find more city maps, consult the state & province map list above and turn to the pages indicated.

Albany / Schenectady 70
Albuquerque 68
Allentown / Bethlehem 88
Atlanta & Vicinity 30
Austin 98
Bakersfield 14
Baltimore 46
Baton Rouge 44
Birmingham 5
Boston & Vicinity 48
Bridgeport / New Haven 23
Buffalo / Niagara Falls 70
Charlotte & Vicinity 76
Chicago & Vicinity 34–35
Cincinnati 80
Cleveland & Vicinity 81
Columbus 81
Dallas / Fort Worth & Vicinity 97
Dayton 80
Denver & Vicinity 22
Detroit & Vicinity 52
Fresno 15
Grand Rapids 52
Greensboro / Winston-Salem / High Point 76
Hampton Roads: Norfolk / Virginia Beach / Newport News 105
Hartford 23
Honolulu 30
Houston & Vicinity 96
Indianapolis 35
Jacksonville 26
Kansas City & Vicinity 58
Las Vegas 64, 65
Little Rock 11
Los Angeles & Vicinity 18–19
Louisville 42
Memphis & Vicinity 94
Mexico City (Ciudad de México) 128
Miami / Fort Lauderdale & Vicinity 25
Milwaukee & Vicinity 113
Minneapolis / St. Paul & Vicinity 53
Montréal 124, 125
Nashville 94
New Orleans 44
New York & Vicinity 72–73
Oklahoma City & Vicinity 82
Omaha 63
Orlando 27
Oxnard / Ventura 17
Philadelphia & Vicinity 90
Phoenix & Vicinity 7
Pittsburgh & Vicinity 90
Portland & Vicinity 85
Providence 91
Raleigh / Durham / Chapel Hill 76
Richmond / Petersburg 105
Rochester 69
Sacramento 16
St. Louis & Vicinity 57
Salt Lake City & Vicinity 103
San Antonio 101
San Diego & Vicinity 17
San Francisco Bay Area: San Francisco / Oakland / San Jose 13, 16
Seattle / Tacoma & Vicinity 110
Tampa / St. Petersburg & Vicinity 25
Toronto 122
Tucson 9
Tulsa 82
Vancouver 118
Washington & Vicinity 111
Worcester 49

National Park Maps

Acadia National Park 45
Arches National Park 103
Banff / Glacier / Kootenay & Yoho National Parks 119
Black Canyon of the Gunnison National Park 20
Bryce Canyon National Park 103
Canyonlands National Park 103
Capitol Reef National Park 103
Colonial National Historical Park 105
Crater Lake National Park 85
Denali National Park & Preserve 6
Gettysburg National Military Park 87
Grand Canyon National Park 7
Grand Teton National Park 116
Great Sand Dunes National Park 20
Great Smoky Mountains National Park 76
Hot Springs National Park 11
Isle Royale National Park 50
Joshua Tree National Park 14
Mammoth Cave National Park 42
Mesa Verde National Park 20
Mount Rainier National Park 110
Petrified Forest National Park 7
Rocky Mountain National Park 22
Sequoia and Kings Canyon National Parks 14
Waterton-Glacier International Peace Park 60
Yellowstone National Park 116
Yosemite National Park 12
Zion National Park 102

Rand McNally updates this Road Atlas annually, and every effort has been made to provide accurate information. Changes can and do occur, however, and we cannot be legally responsible for any errors, changes, omissions, or any loss, injury, or inconvenience sustained by any person or entity as a result of information or advice contained in this book.

Photo credits: Table of contents: (t to b) ©John Cox / Getty, ©Rand McNally (3); p. ii (t to b), ©Lijuan Guo Photography / Getty, ©Jeffrey D. Walters / Getty; p. iii (t to b) ©Joshua Miller / Getty, ©Kyle Sparks / Getty; p. iv (t to b) ©Matteo Colombo / Getty, ©Joe Rockey; p. v (t to b) ©Eija Huhtikorpi / Getty, ©MargaretW / Getty; p. vi (t to b) ©Joecho-16 / Getty, ©Joe Daniel Price / Getty; p. vii (t to b) ©zrfphoto / Getty, ©Nancy Nehring / Getty; p. 5 ©Blazen Images / Getty; p. 7 ©skiserge 1 / Getty; p. 9 ©Mimi Ditchie Photography / Getty; p. 11 ©Wesley Hitt / Getty; p. 13 ©Mariusz Blach / Getty; p. 15 ©Matteo Colombo / Getty; p. 16 ©ETham Photo / Getty; p. 17 ©Santa Barbara Conference & Visitors Bureau and Film Commission/J. Sinclair; p. 18 ©Rand McNally; p. 19 ©Sitnic Sofia / EyeEm / Getty; p. 21 ©Michael Russell / Getty; p. 22 ©Shutter18 / Getty; p. 25 ©Buena Vista Images / Getty; p. 27 ©Damocean / Getty; p. 29 ©Sean Pavone / Getty; p. 33 ©Ron Thomas / Getty; p. 34 ©City of Chicago/Hedrich Blessing; p. 35 ©The Children's Museum of Indianapolis; p. 37 ©Stevegeer / Getty; p. 39 ©Teddi Yaeger Photography / Getty; p. 41 ©Shoemcfly / Getty; p. 43 ©Kentucky Tourism; p. 47 ©Remsberg Inc. / Design Pics / Getty; p. 49 ©Gregobagel / Getty; p. 51 ©ehrlif / Getty; p. 52 ©Robert J. Eovaldi; p.53 ©Walker Art Center; p. 55 ©Wildnerdpix / Getty; p. 57 ©MO Div. of Tourism; p. 59 ©Eric Bowers Photo / Getty; p. 61 ©Matt Anderson / Getty; p. 63 ©zrf photo / Getty; p. 67 ©Aneese / Getty; p. 71 ©Getty; p. 72 ©Photodisc; p. 73 ©Getty; p. 75 ©NC Div of Tourism Film & Sports Dev.; p. 76 ©tonda / Getty; p. 79 ©Drnadig / Getty; p. 81 ©Holly Hildreth / Getty; p. 83 ©Getty; p. 85 ©zschnepf / Getty; p. 87 ©zrfphoto / Getty; p. 89 ©GPTMC; p. 90 ©f11photo / Getty; p. 95 ©FangXiaNuo / Getty; p. 96 ©Kingsport CVB; p. 97 ©S. Greg Panosian / Getty; p. 99 ©eric foltz / Getty; p. 101 ©ejesposito / Getty; p. 103 ©Getty; p. 105 ©wmay / Getty; p.107 ©Pam Susemiehl / Getty; p. 109 ©Christopher Kimmel / Getty; p. 110 ©Rene Frederick / Getty; p. 113 ©Kenosha Area CVB; p. 115 ©Wisconsin Dept. of Tourism; p. 123 ©Benedek / Getty; p. 125 ©Posnov / Getty.

If you have a comment, suggestion, or even a compliment, please visit us at randmcnally.com/contact or write to:
Rand McNally Consumer Affairs
P.O. Box 7600
Chicago, Illinois 60680-9915

Published and printed in U.S.A.

1 2 3 BU 20 19

United States

Capital: Washington, G-17
Land area: 3,531,905 sq. mi.

Selected National Park Service locations

- Acadia National Park C-20
- Arches National Park G-6
- Badlands National Park E-9
- Big Bend National Park L-8
- Biscayne National Park M-18
- Bryce Canyon National Park. G-5
- Canyonlands National Park G-6
- Capitol Reef National Park. G-5
- Carlsbad Caverns National Park. J-7
- Channel Islands National Park H-1
- Congaree National Park I-17
- Crater Lake National Park D-2
- Cuyahoga Valley National Park F-16
- Death Valley National Park G-3
- Denali National Park. L-4
- Dry Tortugas National Park M-17
- Everglades National Park M-17
- Glacier Bay National Park. M-6
- Glen Canyon Nat'l Recreation Area . . G-5
- Grand Canyon National Park. H-4
- Grand Teton National Park E-6
- Great Sand Dunes Nat'l Park & Pres. . . H-7
- Great Smoky Mountains Nat'l Park. . H-15
- Guadalupe Mountains Nat'l Park J-7

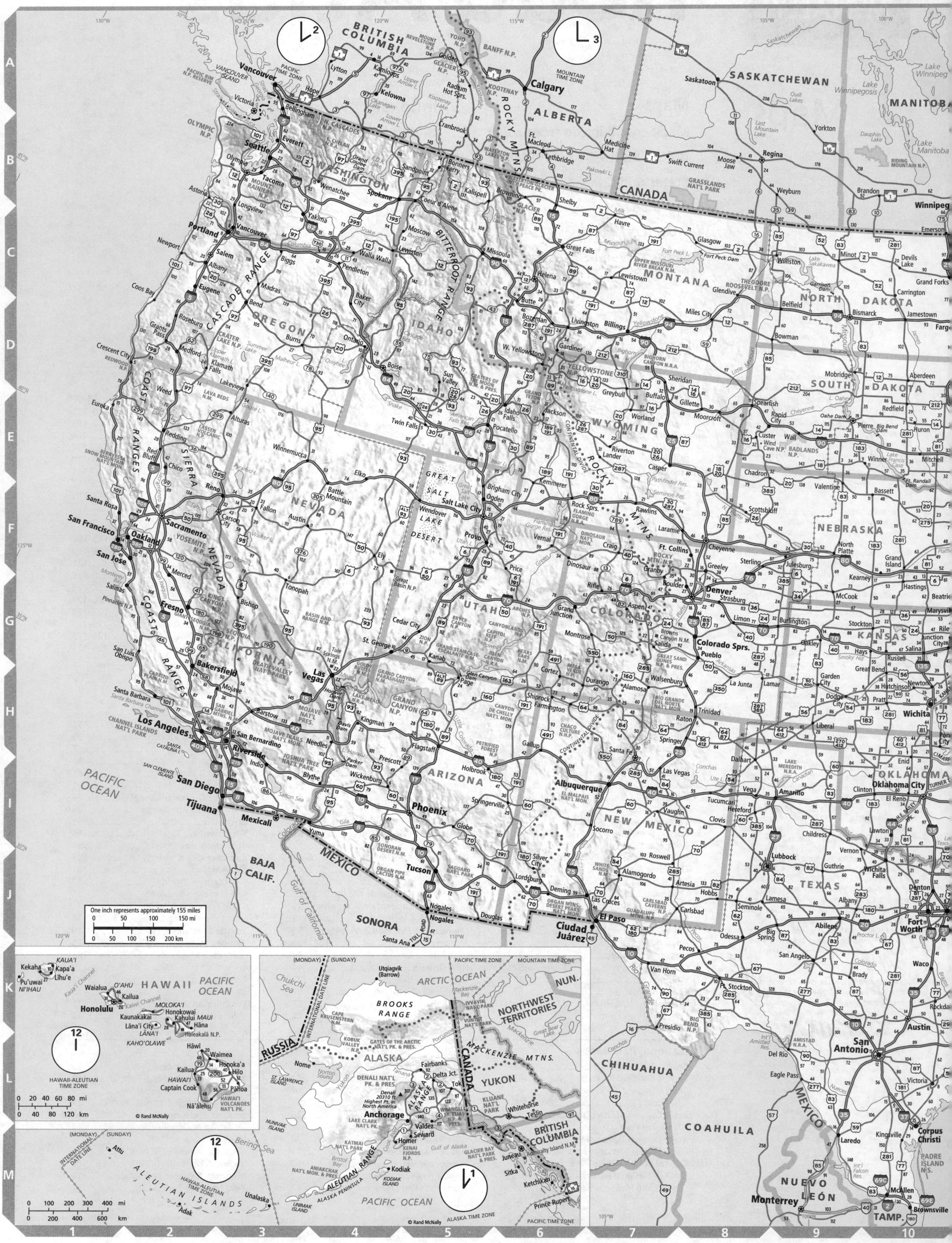

Population: 308,745,538
Largest city: New York, 8,175,133, E-18

Selected National Park Service locations

- Haleakalā National Park L-2
- Hawai'i Volcanoes National Park. L-2
- Hot Springs National Park I-12
- Isle Royale National Park C-13
- Kings Canyon National Park G-2
- Lake Mead Nat'l Recreation Area H-4
- Lassen Volcanic National Park E-2
- Mammoth Cave National Park H-14
- Mesa Verde National Park H-6
- Mount Rainier National Park B-3
- North Cascades National Park B-4
- Olympic National Park B-3
- Petrified Forest National Park I-5
- Redwood National Park D-1
- Rocky Mountain National Park F-7
- Sequoia National Park G-2
- Shenandoah National Park G-17
- Theodore Roosevelt National Park . . . D-8
- Voyageurs National Park C-12
- Waterton-Glacier Int'l Peace Park B-5
- Wind Cave National Park E-8
- Yellowstone National Park D-6
- Yosemite National Park F-2
- Zion National Park G-5

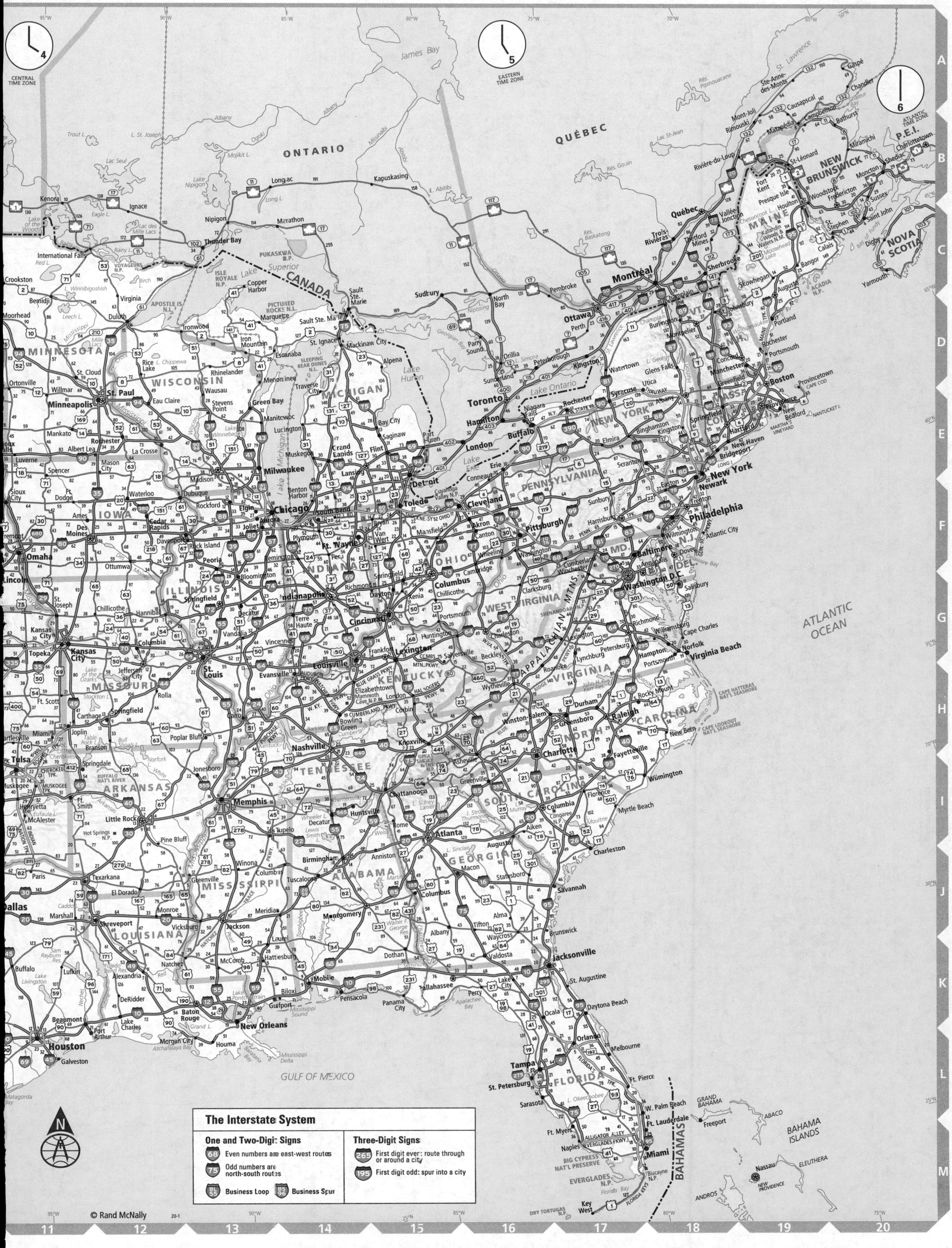

Alabama

Nickname: The Heart of Dixie
Capital: Montgomery, J-8
Land area: 50,645 sq. mi. (rank: 28th)
Population: 4,779,736 (rank: 23rd)
Largest city: Birmingham, 212,237, F-7

Index of places Pg. 129

Travel planning & on-the-road resources

Tourism Information
Alabama Tourism Dept.: (800) 252-2262, (334) 242-4169; tourism.alabama.gov

Road Conditions & Construction
(888) 588-2848; algotraffic.com, www.dot.state.al.us

Toll Road Information
No tolls on state or federal highways

Determining distances along roads

Highway distances (segments of one mile or less not shown):
Cumulative miles (red): the distance between red arrows
Intermediate miles (black): the distance between intersections & places

Interchanges and exit numbers
For most states, the mileage between interchanges may be determined by subtracting one number from the other.

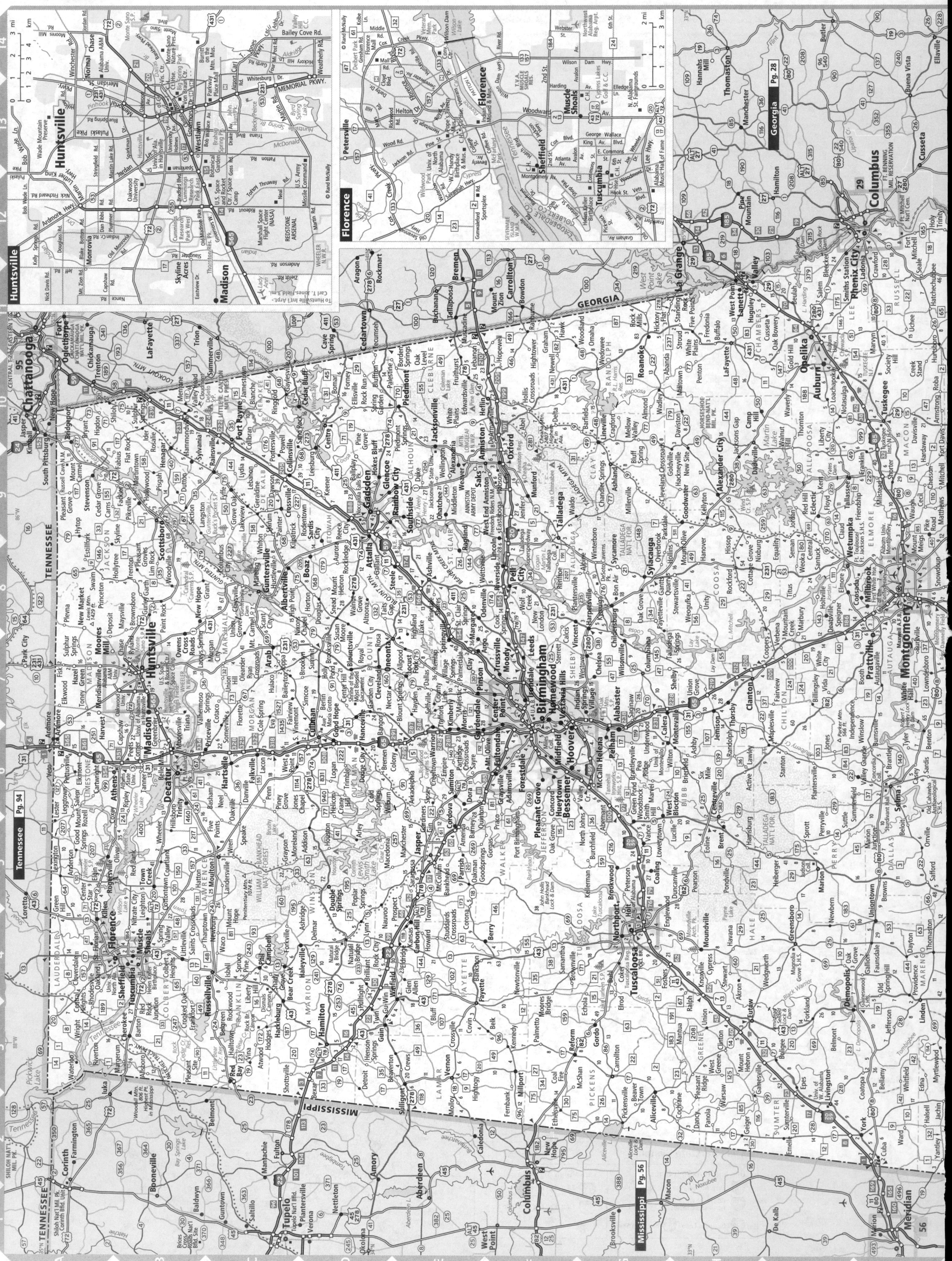

Mileages between cities	Andalusia	Anniston	Auburn	Birmingham	Chattanooga, TN	Columbus GA	Dothan	Florence	Gadsden	Grove Hill	Huntsville	Meridian, MS	Mobile	Montgomery	Selma	Tuscaloosa
Atlanta, GA	252	90	108	146	117	106	206	263	119	294	181	289	328	160	210	201
Birmingham	181	64	109		146	141	196	118	61	155	102	146	258	90	87	58
Chattanooga, TN	322	119	221	146		219	319	166	89	300	102	291	399	232	228	203
Dothan	74	207	118	196	319	99		311	252	169	294	253	196	103	148	210
Huntsville	279	104	210	102	102	243	294	64	72	254		244	356	189	188	155
Mobile	123	280	222	258	399	256	196	376	313	82	356	133		168	159	203
Montgomery	91	110	54	90	232	87	103	205	148	134	189	153	168		50	104
Tuscaloosa	194	118	159	58	203	192	210	123	118	121	155	93	203	104	75	

Total mileages through Alabama

- 10: 66 miles
- 20: 215 miles
- 59: 241 miles
- 65: 367 miles

More mileages at randmcnally.com/MC

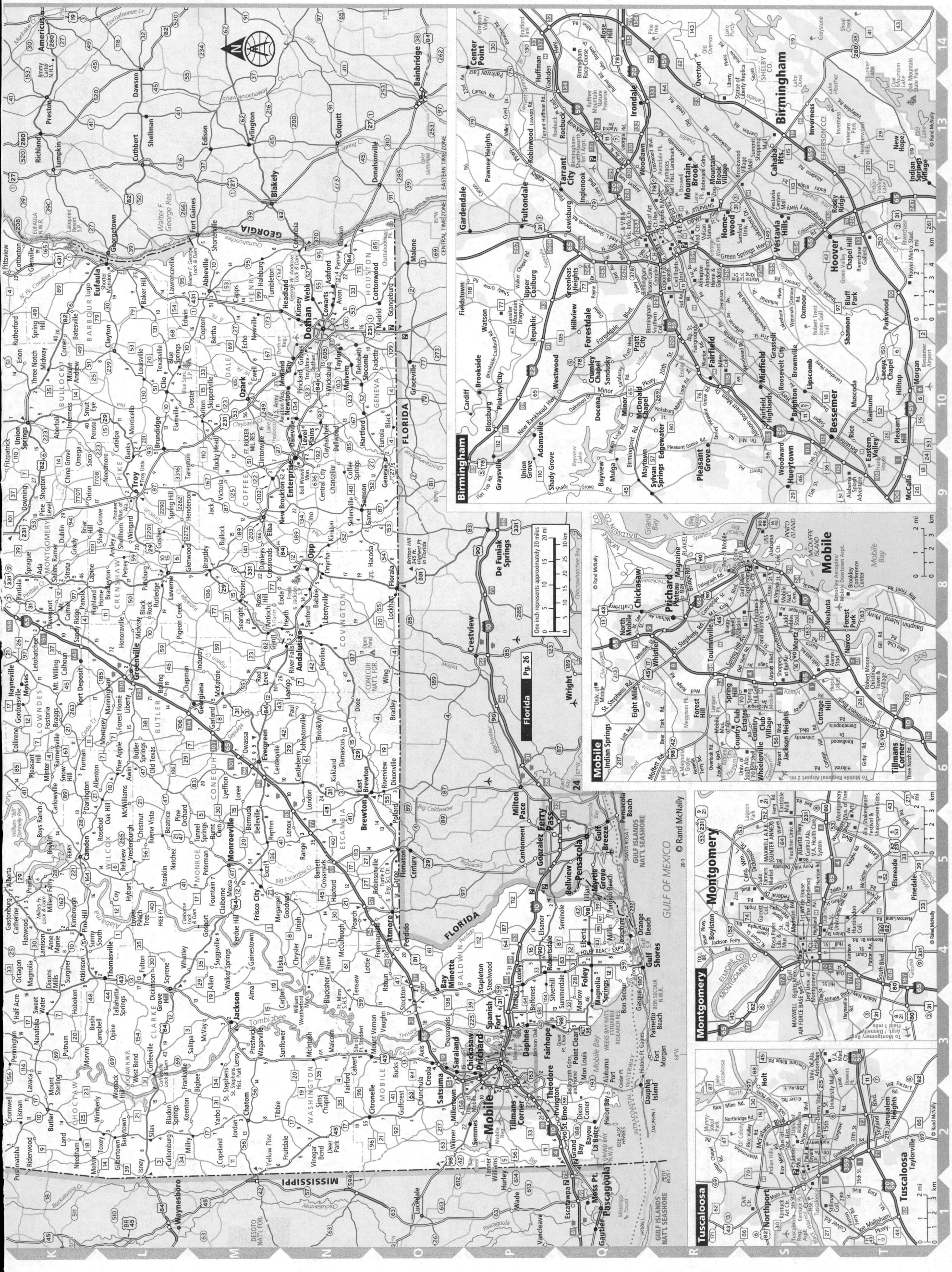

Alaska

Nickname: The Last Frontier
Capital: Juneau, H-12
Land area: 570,641 sq. mi. (rank: 1st)
Population: 710,231 (rank: 47th)
Largest city: Anchorage, 291,826, G-7

Index of places Pg. 129

Mileages between cities

	Anchorage	Denali N.P.	Fairbanks	Haines	Homer	Prince Rupert, BC	Tok	Valdez
Anchorage		236	358	756	221	1557	317	297
Fairbanks	358	122		640	578	1441	202	362
Haines	756	762	640		975	919	438	691
Homer	221	457	578	975		1776	537	277
Kenai	157	393	514	911	83	1713	473	213
Seward	126	362	483	880	168	1682	442	182
Tok	317	324	202	438	537	1240		252
Valdez	297	346	362	691	277	1493	252	

Total mileages through Alaska
① 408 miles ③ 325 miles
② 202 miles

More mileages at randmcnally.com/MC

Travel planning & on-the-road resources

Tourism Information
Alaska Tourism: www.travelalaska.com

Road Conditions & Construction
511, (866) 282-7577
www.511.alaska.gov, www.dot.state.ak.us

Toll Road Information
No tolls on state or federal highways

Determining Distances
(segments of one mile or less not shown)
Cumulative miles (red): the distance between red arrows
Intermediate miles (black): the distance between intersections & places

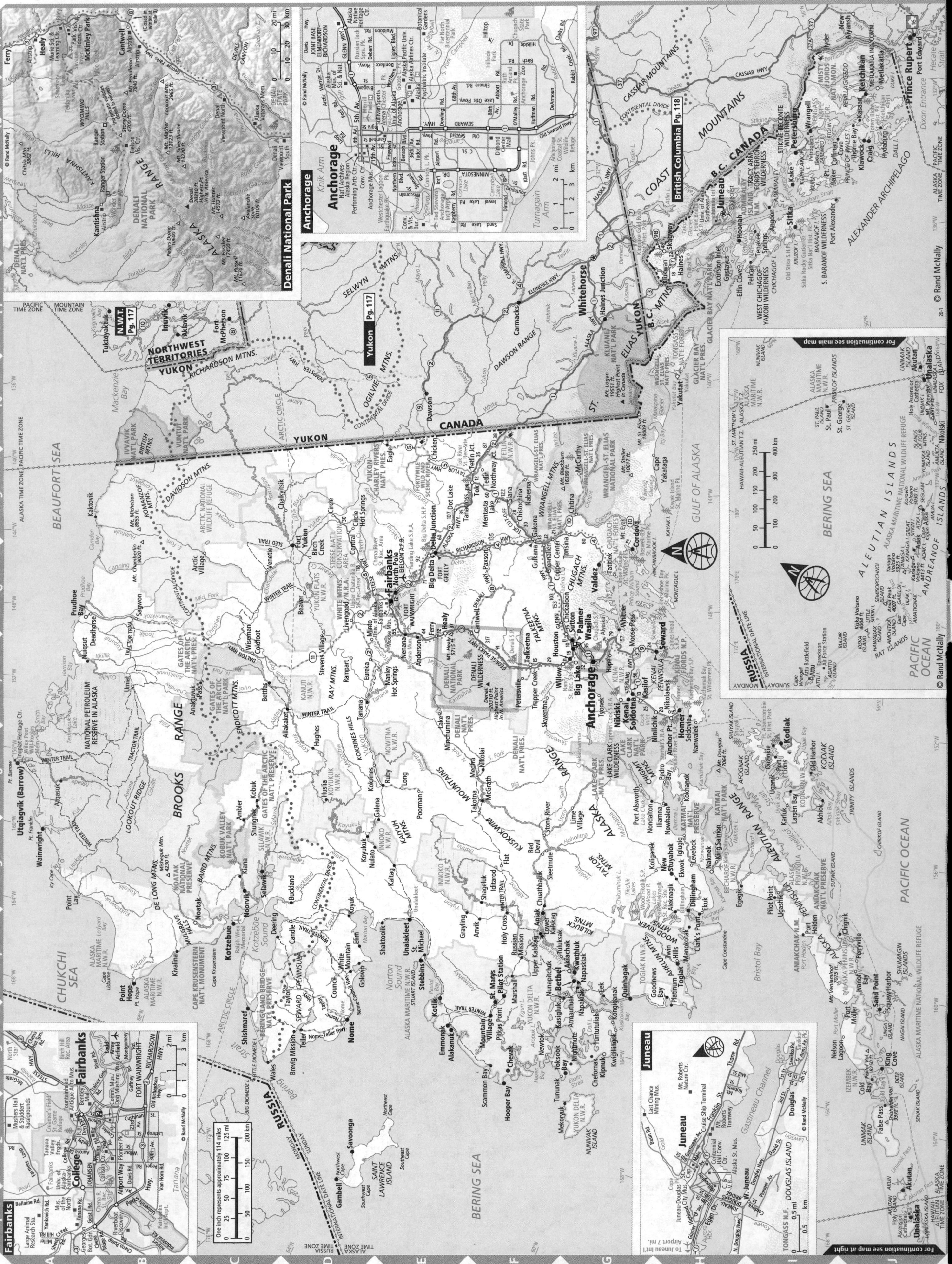

Havasu Falls

Sights to see

- Arizona Historical Society Sanguinetti House Museum, Yuma L-6
- Arizona Museum of Natural History, Mesa J-7
- Arizona Science Center, Phoenix M-3
- Arizona State Capitol, Phoenix M-1
- Heard Museum, Phoenix L-2
- Painted Desert Inn Museum, Petrified Forest N.P. L-10
- Phoenix Art Museum, Phoenix L-2
- Taliesin West, Scottsdale H-7
- Tusayan Ruin and Museum, Grand Canyon N.P. D-9
- Yavapai Point Overlook, Grand Canyon N.P. B-1
- Yuma Territorial Prison State Historic Park, Yuma L-6

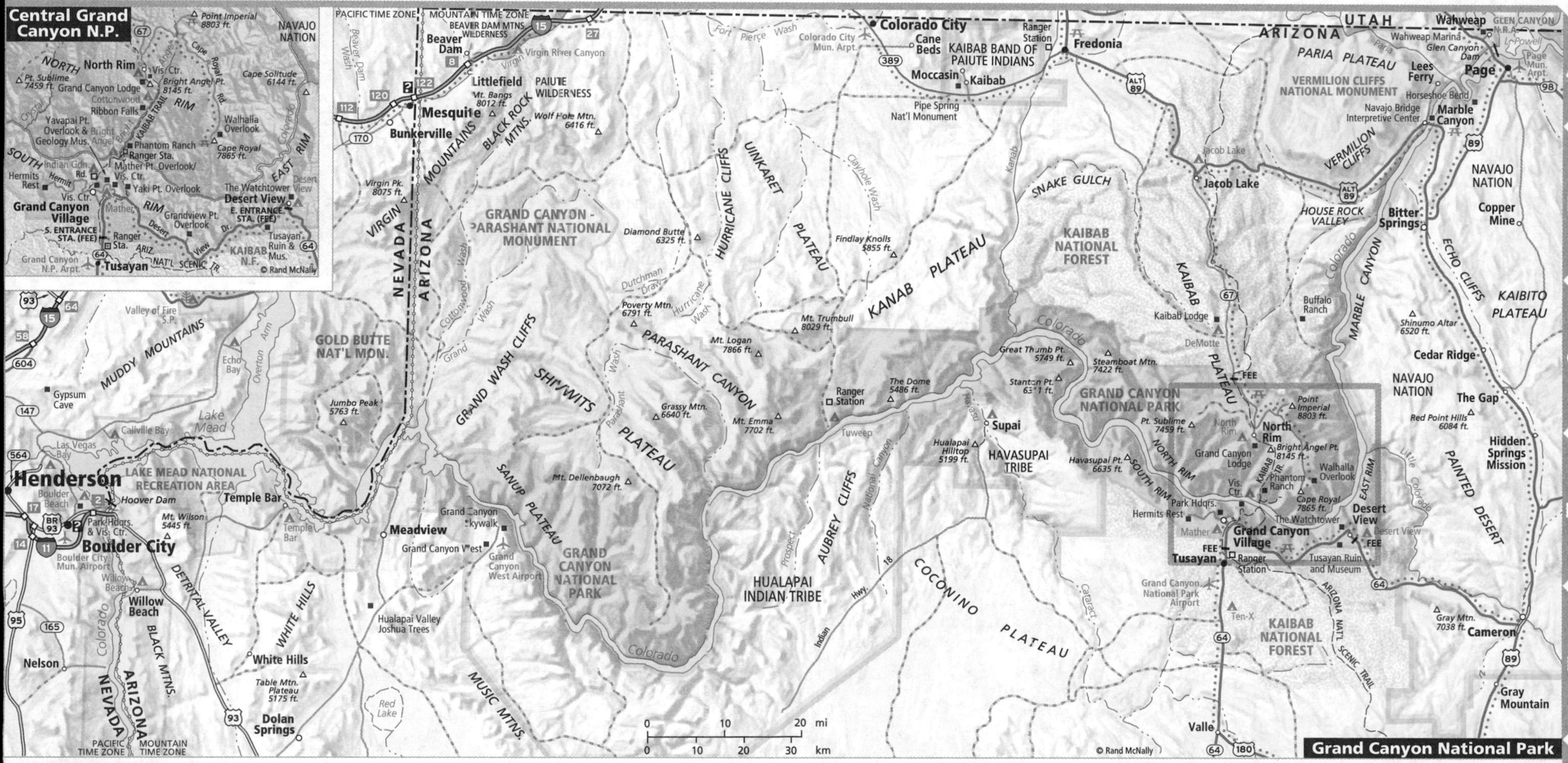

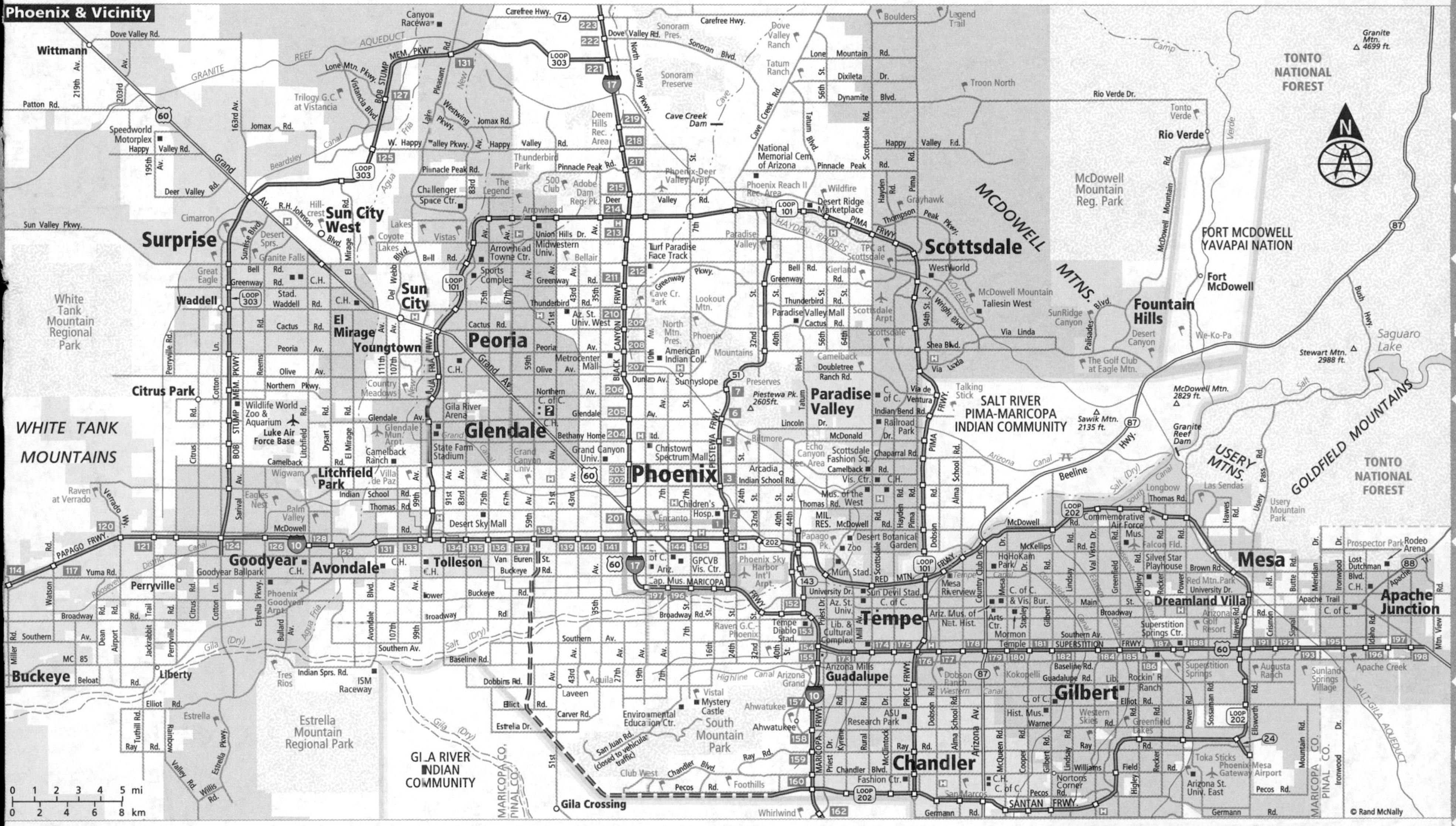

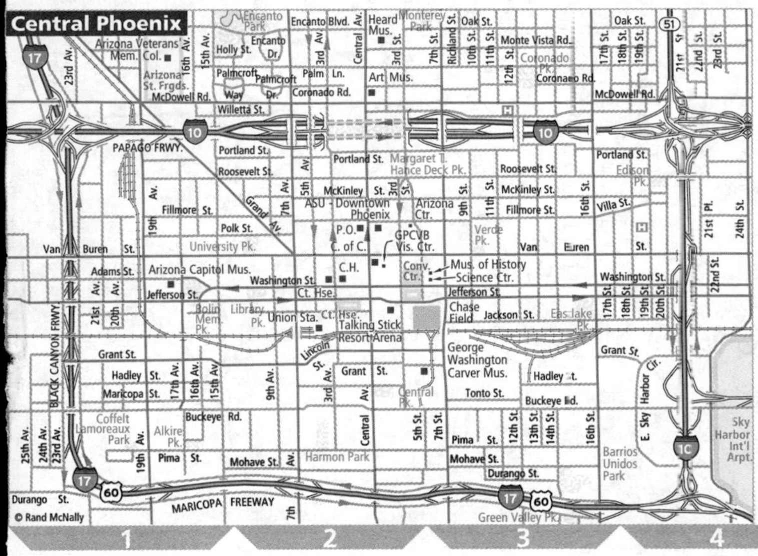

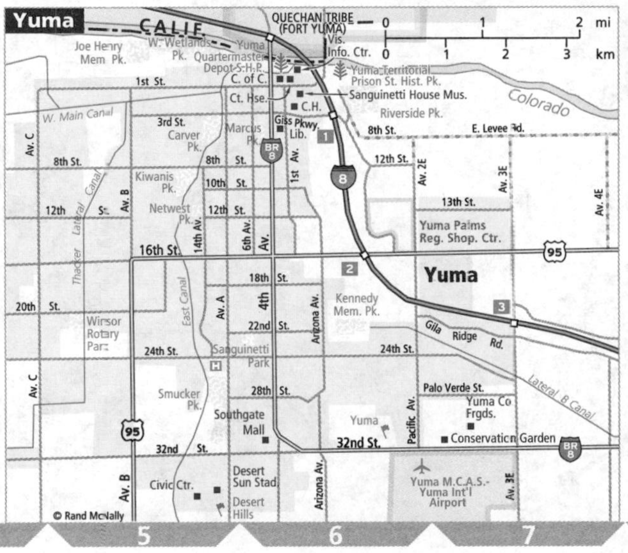

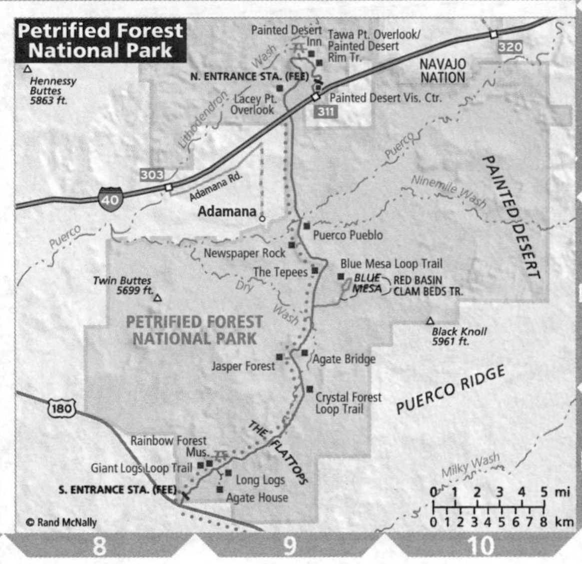

Arizona

Nickname: The Grand Canyon State
Capital: Phoenix, J-7
Land area: 113,594 sq. mi. (rank: 6th)
Population: 6,392,017 (rank: 16th)
Largest city: Phoenix, 1,445,632, J-7

Index of places Pg. 129

Travel planning & on-the-road resources

Tourism Information
Arizona Office of Tourism: (866) 275-5816, (602) 364-3700; www.visitarizona.com, tourism.az.gov

Road Conditions & Construction
511, (888) 411-7623; www.az511.com, www.azdot.gov

Toll Road Information
No toll on state or federal highways

Determining distances along roads

Highway distances (segments of one mile or less not shown):
Cumulative miles (red): the distance between red arrows
Intermediate miles (black): the distance between intersections & places

Interchanges and exit numbers
For most states, the mileage between interchanges may be determined by subtracting one number from the other.

Mileages between cities	Casa Grande	Chinle	Eagar	Flagstaff	Gallup, NM	Grand Canyon	Holbrook	Kingman	Lake Havasu City	Las Vegas, NV	Lordsburg, NM	Nogales	Page	Phoenix	Tucson	Yuma
Flagstaff	191	213	176		185	79	90	146	204	250	374	321	133	139	255	318
Holbrook	220	123	86	90	94	167		237	295	340	264	304	214	230	238	409
Las Vegas, NV	336	463	427	250	435	275	340	104	152		558	467	271	285	401	292
Page	324	204	301	133	255	137	214	281	340	271	499	455		275	390	453
Phoenix	48	353	226	139	324	218	230	182	198	285	268	179	275		116	181
Prescott	148	306	270	93	278	126	184	148	206	251	368	278	227	97	213	214
Tucson	66	361	238	255	333	334	238	297	314	401	156	66	390	116		236
Yuma	172	532	399	318	502	397	409	213	155	292	392	301	453	181	236	

Total mileages through Arizona

8: 178 miles; 17: 146 miles; 10: 392 miles; 40: 359 miles

More mileages at randmcnally.com/MC

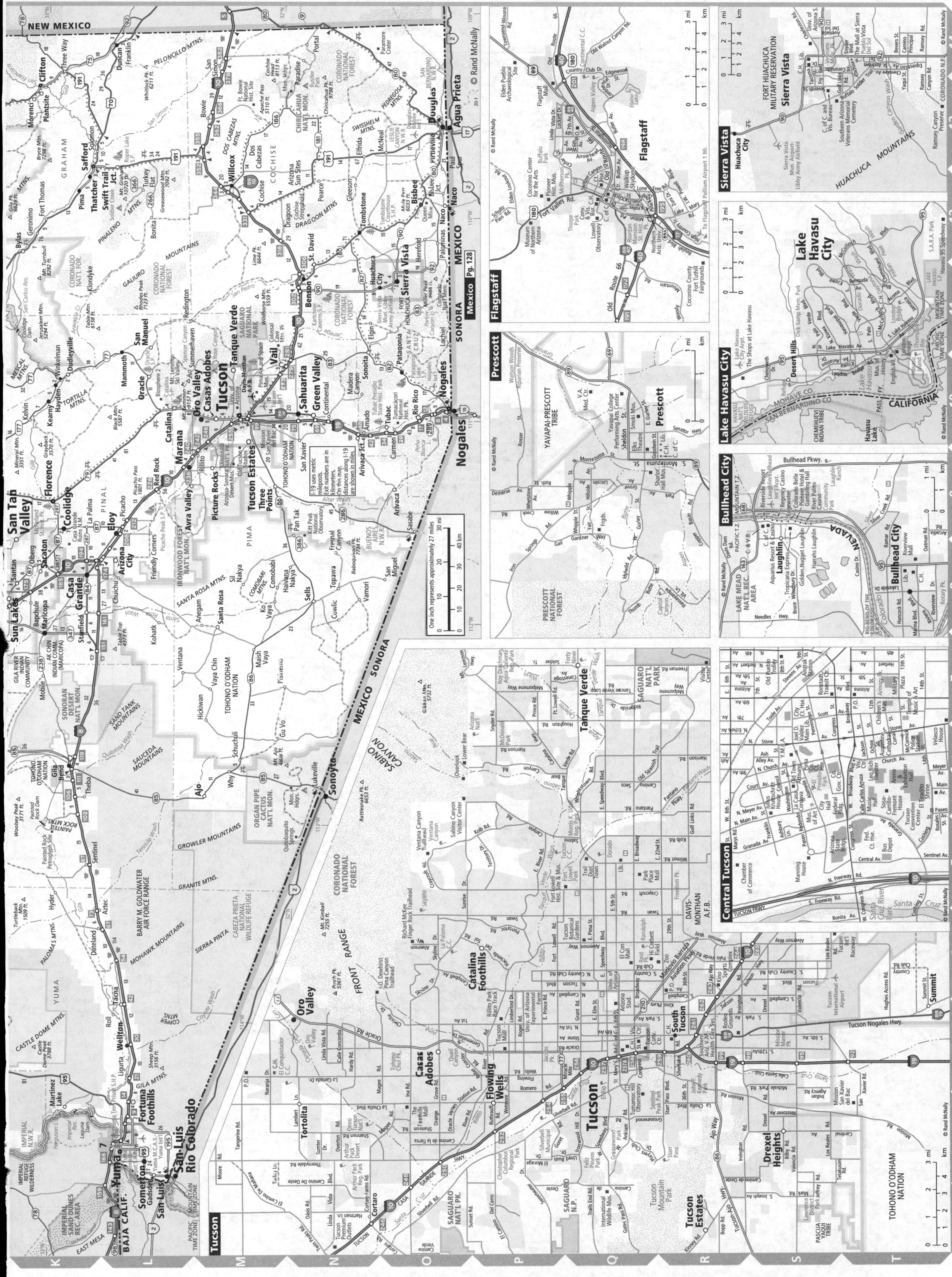

Nickname: The Natural State
Capital: Little Rock, G-7
Land area: 52,035 sq. mi. (rank: 27th)
Population: 2,915,918 (rank: 32nd)
Largest city: Little Rock, 193,524, G-7

Index of places Pg. 129

Travel planning & on-the-road resources

Tourism Information
Arkansas Department of Parks & Tourism; (501) 682-7777; www.arkansas.com

Road Conditions & Construction
(800) 245-1672, (501) 569-2227; www.idrivearkansas.com, www.arkansashighways.com

Toll Road Information
No tolls on state or federal highways

Determining distances along roads

Highway distances (segments of one mile or less not shown):
Cumulative miles (red): the distance between red arrows
Intermediate miles (black): the distance between intersections & places

Interchanges and exit numbers
For most states, the mileage between interchanges may be determined by subtracting one number from the other.

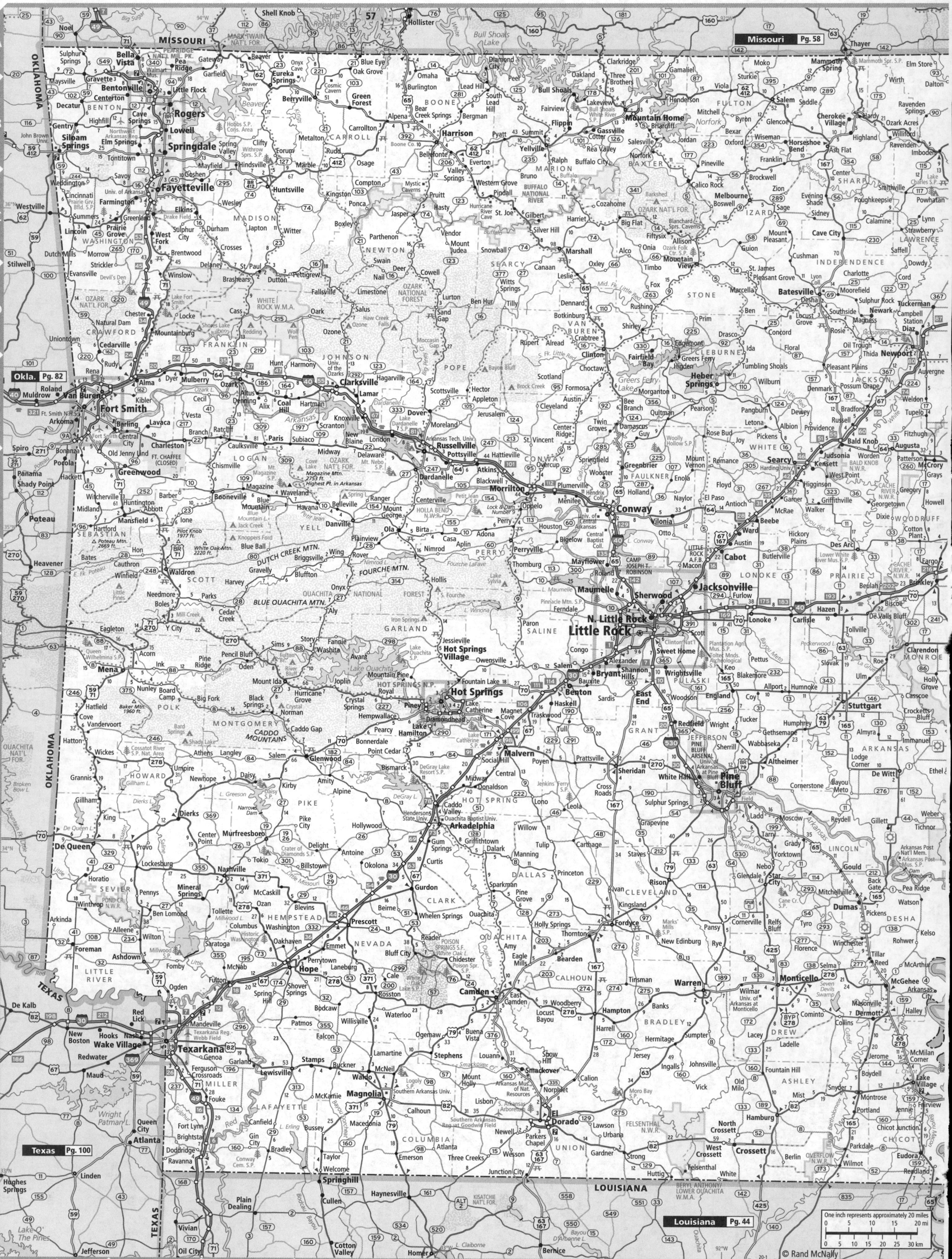

Ozark National Forest

Mileages between cities	Batesville	Branson, MO	DeQueen	El Dorado	Fayetteville	Fort Smith	Greenville, MS	Hot Springs	Jonesboro	Little Rock	Memphis, TN	Mountain Home	Pine Bluff	Rogers	Russellville	Texarkana
El Dorado	209	287	141		304	227	109	121	245	118	250	268	91	325	190	88
Fayetteville	251	98	184	304		58	335	184	250	188	318	123	231	24	115	236
Fort Smith	219	158	130	227	58		304	130	261	158	286	187	199	81	84	182
Jonesboro	68	203	272	245	250	261	219	182		130	70	126	171	253	173	270
Little Rock	94	172	143	118	188	158	147	54	130		137	151	43	208	74	142
Memphis, TN	119	274	278	250	318	286	152	188	70	137		195	152	339	204	276
Mountain Home	78	83	287	268	123	187	298	198	126	151	195		194	126	125	287
Texarkana	234	306	54	88	236	182	198	110	270	142	276	287	152	258	209	

Total mileages through Arkansas

- 30: 143 miles
- 55: 72 miles
- 40: 284 miles
- 65: 309 miles

More mileages at randmcnally.com/MC

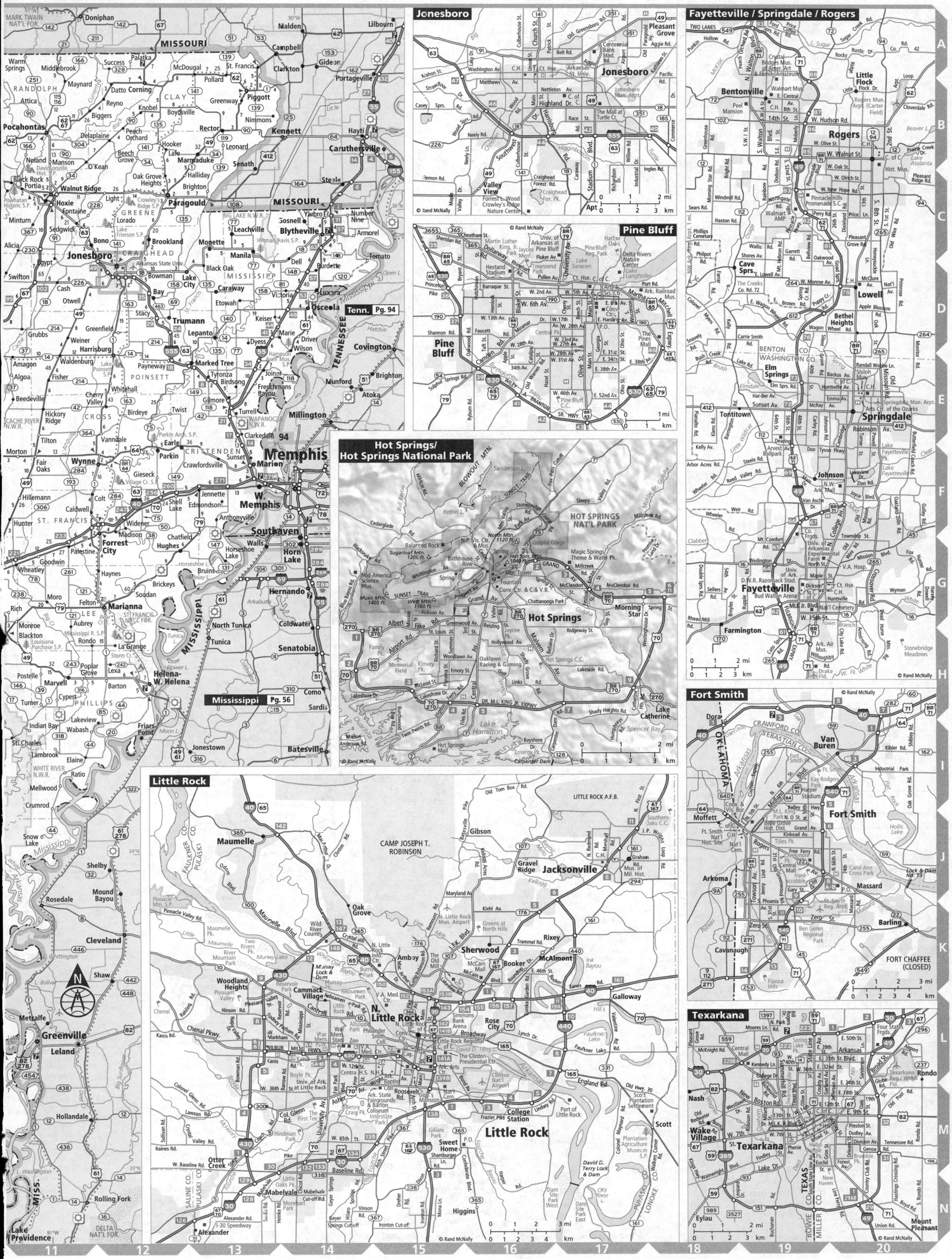

Nickname: The Golden State
Capital: Sacramento, NK-7
Land area: 155,799 sq. mi. (rank: 3rd)
Population: 37,253,956 (rank: 1st)
Largest city: Los Angeles, 3,792,621, SJ-11

Index of places Pg. 129

Travel planning & on-the-road resources

Tourism Information
California Tourism: (877) 225-4367, (916) 444-4429; www.visitcalifornia.com

Toll Bridge Information
Golden Gate Bridge (San Francisco Bay area) (*FasTrak*): (415) 921-5858; www.goldengate.org
Bay Area Toll Authority (all other San Francisco Bay area bridges) (*FasTrak*): (415) 778-6700, (415) 778-6757; mtc.ca.gov

Road Conditions & Construction

www.dot.ca.gov	
Eastern Sierras District 9:	511, (800) 427-7623; www.dot.ca.gov/d9
Inland Empire region:	511, (877) 694-3511; www.ie511.org
Los Angeles metro area:	511, (877) 224-6511; go511.com
Sacramento region:	511, (877) 511-8747; www.sacregion511.org
San Diego area:	511, (855) 467-3511; www.511sd.com
San Francisco Bay area:	511, (888) 500-4626; 511.org
San Luis Obispo area:	511, (866) 928-8923

Mileages between cities	Bishop	Crescent City	Los Angeles	Oroville	Redding	Sacramento	San Francisco	San Jose	Santa Rosa	S. Lake Tahoe	Stockton	Susanville	Ukiah	Vallejo	Yosemite N.P.	Yreka
Alturas	371	280	648	225	144	302	357	385	365	228	349	103	330	329	392	176
Bishop		614	265	326	400	269	295	290	364	176	224	286	418	328	138	454
Eureka	546	81	644	222	146	289	272	315	217	392	325	259	158	262	454	198
Redding	400	208	544	54		161	216	244	198	264	209	112	188	187	332	98
Sacramento	269	372	383	68	161		87	115	95	100	47	217	145	58	160	257
San Francisco	295	355	380	150	216	87		45	55	187	82	303	115	30	189	312
San Jose	290	396	340	178	244	115	45		96	215	74	330	156	64	182	340
S. Lake Tahoe	176	472	445	157	264	100	187	215	195		147	143	248	159	189	311

Mileages © Rand McNally

Total mileages through California

5: 797 miles; 101: 791 miles

80: 199 miles

More mileages at randmcnally.com/MC

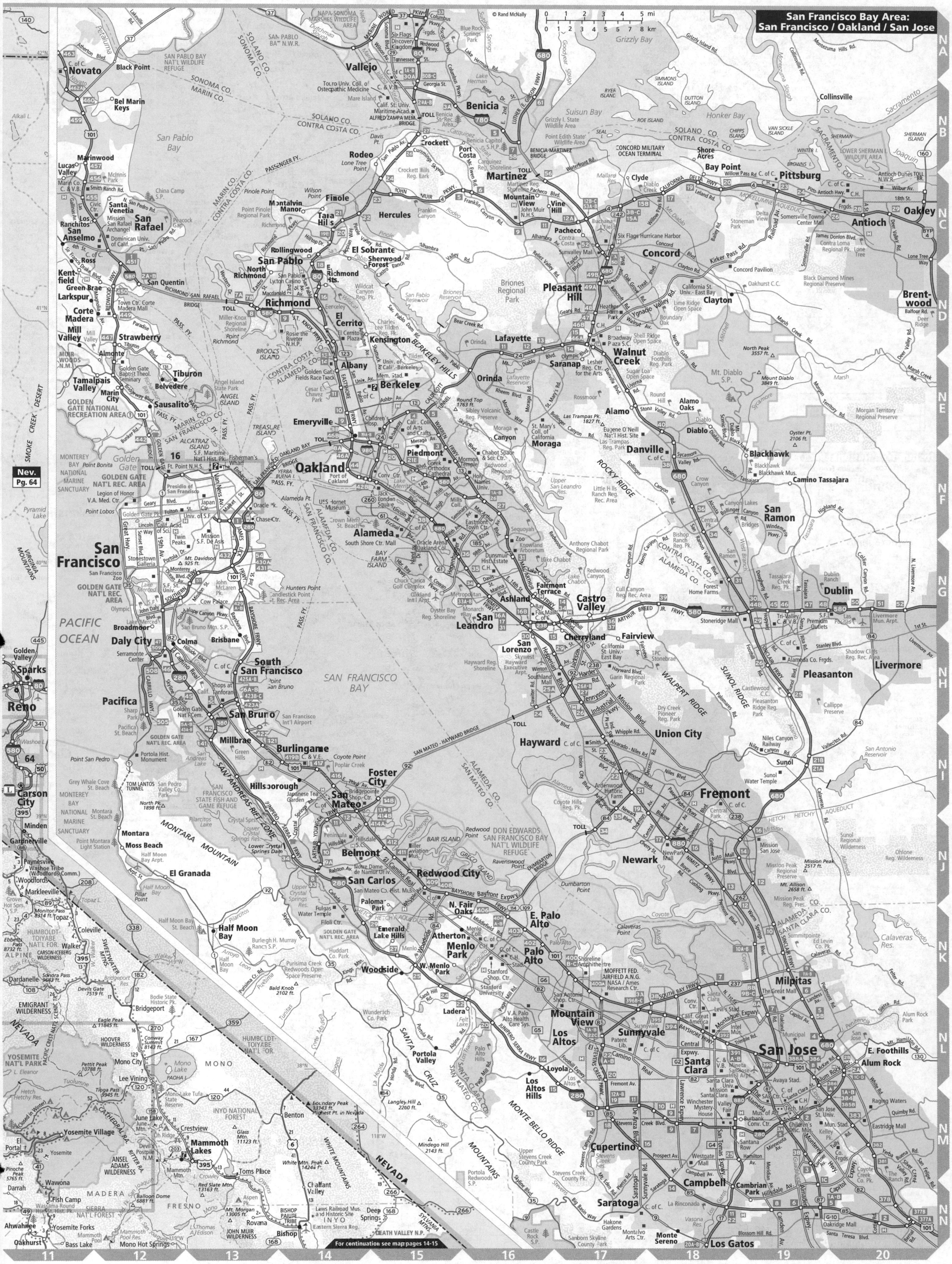

Nickname: The Golden State
Capital: Sacramento, NK-7
Land area: 155,799 sq. mi. (rank: 3rd)
Population: 37,253,956 (rank: 1st)
Largest city: Los Angeles, 3,792,621, SJ-11

Index of places Pg. 129

Travel planning & on-the-road resources

Tourism Information
California Tourism:
(877) 225-4367
(916) 444-4429
visitcalifornia.com

Toll Road Information *(FasTrak)*
91ExpressLanes (Orange Co.): (800) 600-9191; www.91expresslanes.com
I-15 (San Diego Co.): (888) 889-1515; 511sd.com
Metro Express Lanes (Los Angeles Co.):
(877) 812-0022; www.metroexpresslanes.net
South Bay Expwy. (San Diego Co.): (619) 661-7070; www.southbayexpressway.com
The Toll Roads of Orange Co.: (949) 727-4800; www.thetollroads.com

Road Conditions & Construction 511
www.dot.ca.gov
Eastern Sierras District 9: 511, (800) 427-7623; www.dot.ca.gov/d9
Inland Empire region: 511, (877) 694-3511; www.ie511.org
Los Angeles metro area: 511, (877) 224-6511; go511.com
Sacramento region: 511, (877) 511-8747; www.sacregion511.org
San Diego area: 511, (855) 467-3511; www.511sd.com
San Francisco Bay area: 511, (888) 500-4626; 511.org
San Luis Obispo area: 511, (866) 928-8923

Joshua Tree National Park

Mileages between cities	Bakersfield	Barstow	El Centro	Fresno	Las Vegas, NV	Los Angeles	Monterey	Needles	Palm Springs	Riverside	San Bernardino	San Diego	San Francisco	San Luis Obispo	Santa Barbara	Sequoia N.P.
Bakersfield		129	322	109	286	112	222	272	216	166	166	232	284	130	147	122
Fresno	109	239	429		395	218	150	381	323	271	273	339	183	130	254	77
Las Vegas, NV	286	156	312	395		270	507	110	278	234	225	331	569	415	358	410
Los Angeles	112	114	212	218	270		319	256	107	54	60	120	380	189	94	232
Monterey	222	350	530	150	507	319		494	424	372	373	439	112	142	237	226
Palm Springs	216	123	108	323	278	107	424	188		52	54	139	486	296	201	338
San Diego	232	176	113	339	331	120	439	317	139	97	106		501	313	214	352
Santa Barbara	147	203	306	254	358	94	237	345	201	148	150	214	325	94		268

Mileages © Rand McNally

Total mileages through California

- I-5: 797 miles
- I-15: 287 miles
- I-10: 243 miles
- I-40: 155 miles

More mileages at randmcnally.com/MC

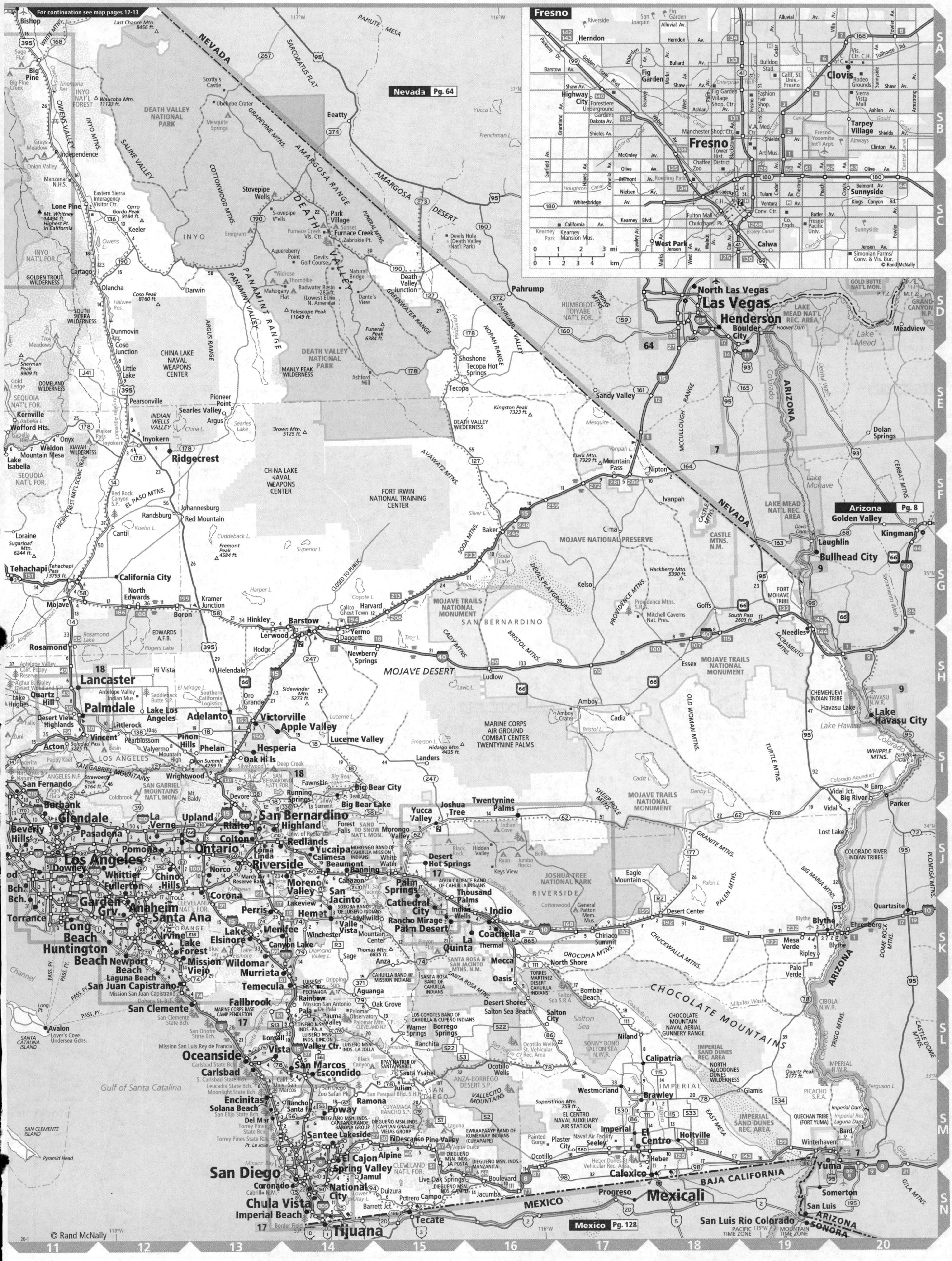

Sights to see

- California State Capitol, Sacramento I-6
- California State Railroad Museum, Sacramento H-6
- Chinatown, San Francisco C-8
- Coit Memorial Tower, San Francisco B-8
- Crocker Art Museum, Sacramento I-5
- Fisherman's Wharf, San Francisco A-7
- Ghirardelli Square, San Francisco B-7
- Golden Gate Bridge, San Francisco A-2
- Monterey Bay Aquarium, Monterey M-1
- Pier 39, San Francisco A-8
- San Francisco Cable Car Museum, San Francisco C-8
- Squaw Valley U.S.A., Olympic Valley F-8

Chinatown, San Francisco

Central San Francisco

PACIFIC OCEAN

GOLDEN GATE NATIONAL RECREATION AREA

San Francisco Bay

© Rand McNally

Sacramento

Roseville · Granite Bay · Elverta · Rio Linda · North Highlands · Foothill Farms · Citrus Heights · Antelope · Orangevale · Fair Oaks · Folsom · Carmichael · Arcade · Gold River · Rancho Cordova · Arden Town · La Riviera · Sacramento · West Sacramento · Broderick · Bryte · Rosemont · Florin · Parkway · Vineyard · Freeport

© Rand McNally

Central Sacramento

West Sacramento

© Rand McNally

Lake Tahoe Region

Truckee · NEVADA · Washoe City · New Washoe City · Incline Village · Tahoe Vista · Kings Beach · Crystal Bay · Carson City · Olympic Valley · Tahoe City · Homewood · Tahoma · Meeks Bay · Glenbrook · Lakeridge · Zephyr Cove · Skyland · Genoa · S. Lake Tahoe · Stateline · Kingsbury · Camp Richardson · Gardnerville · Minden

Lake Tahoe

© Rand McNally

Modesto

Modesto · Empire · Ceres

© Rand McNally

Santa Rosa

Fulton · Santa Rosa · Roseland · Rohnert Park

© Rand McNally

Stockton

Morada · Lincoln Village · Garden Acres · Stockton · French Camp

© Rand McNally

South Monterey Bay Area: Monterey to Salinas

PACIFIC OCEAN

MONTEREY BAY NATIONAL MARINE SANCTUARY

Monterey Bay

Castroville · Prunedale · Gabilan Acres · Bolsa Knolls · Marina · Salinas · Boronda · Spreckels · Pacific Grove · Monterey · Sand City · Seaside · Del Rey Oaks · Del Monte Forest · Pebble Bch. · Carmel Woods · Carmel-by-the-Sea · Carmel Hills · Carmel Pt.

FORT ORD NATIONAL MONUMENT

© Rand McNally

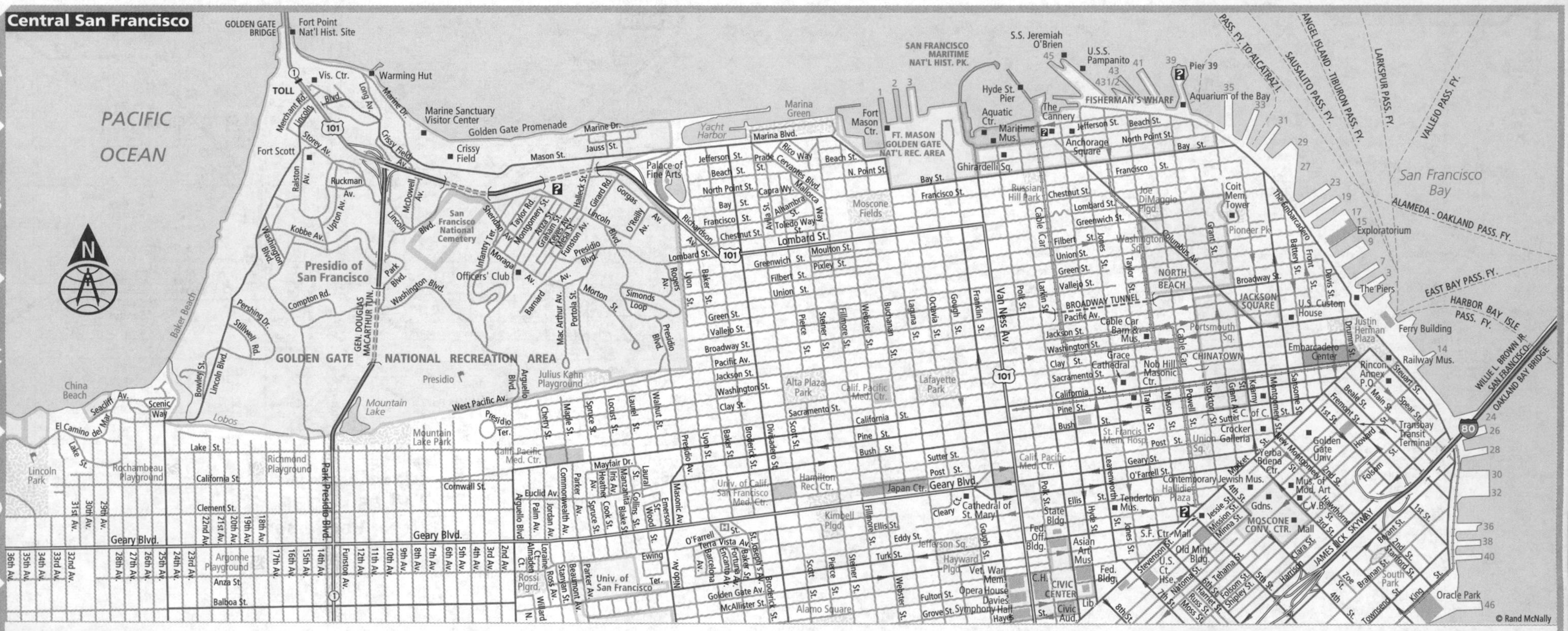

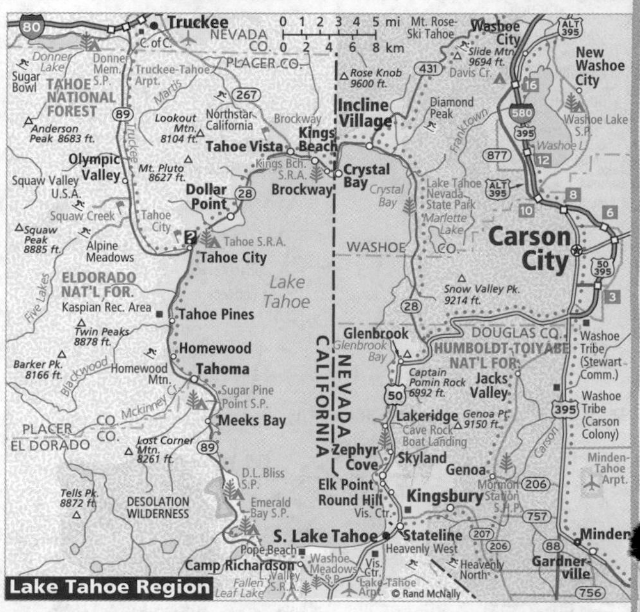

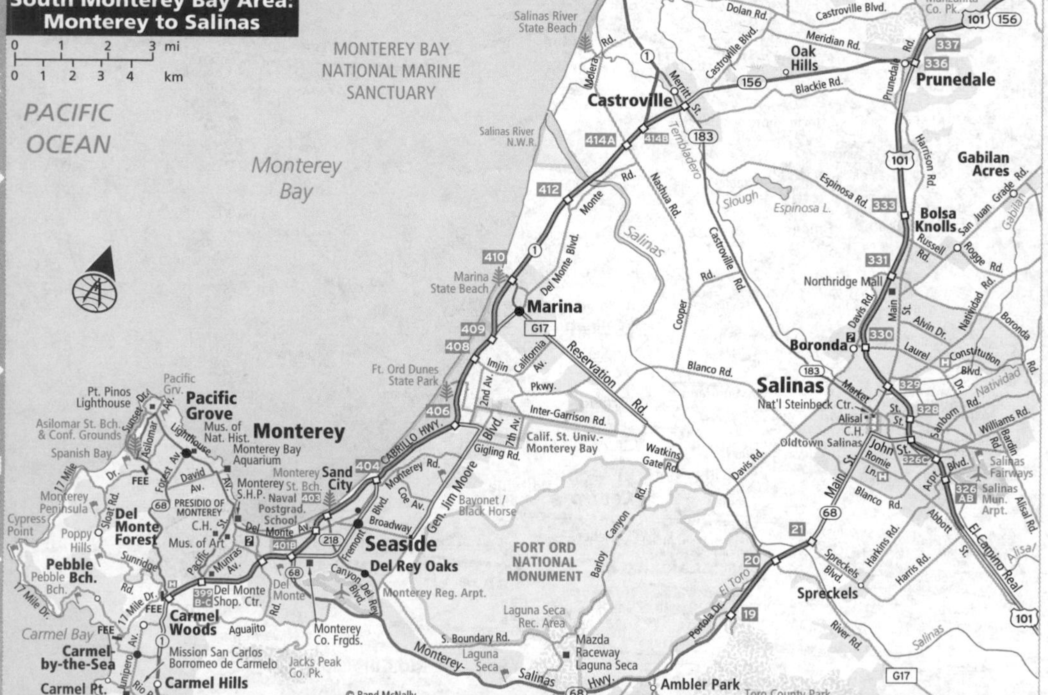

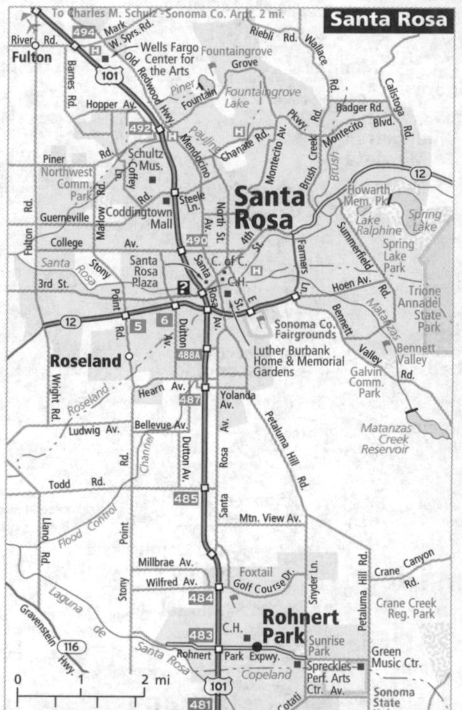

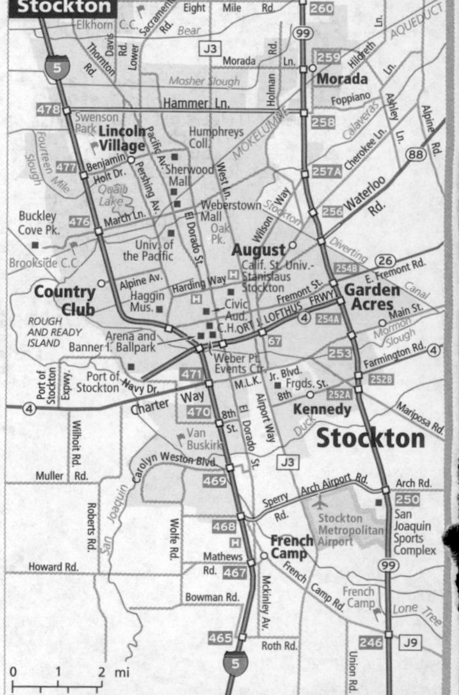

Santa Barbara harbor and coastline

Sights to see

- Balboa Park, San Diego K-10
- Birch Aquarium at Scripps Institute, San Diego G-1
- Cabrillo National Monument, San Diego K-1
- Gaslamp Quarter Historic District, San Diego M-9
- Legoland California, Carlsbad J-8
- The Living Desert Zoo and Gardens, Palm Desert ... G-10
- Museum of Contemporary Art, San Diego L-8
- Palm Springs Art Museum, Palm Springs E-7
- San Diego Air & Space Museum, San Diego K-9
- San Diego Zoo, San Diego J-3
- SeaWorld, San Diego I-1
- Stearns Wharf, Santa Barbara B-5

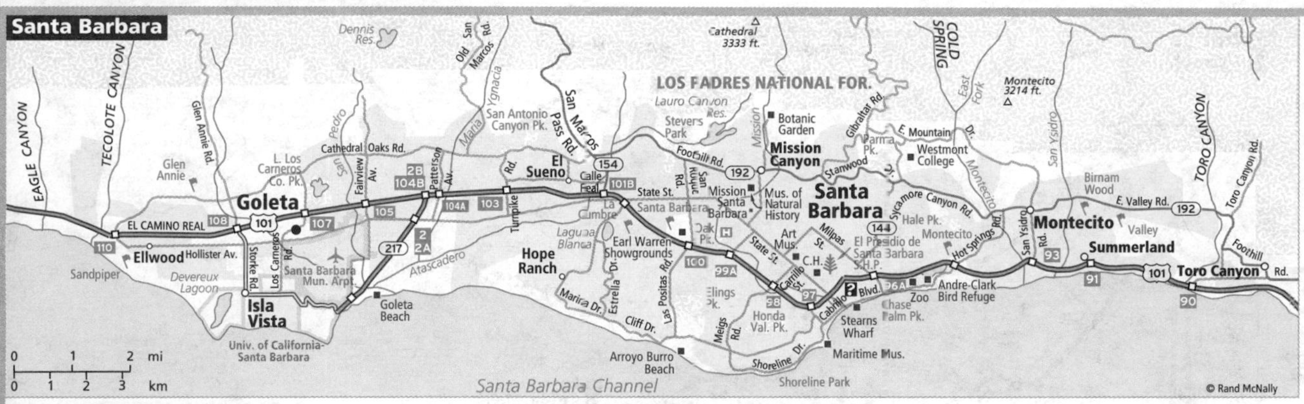

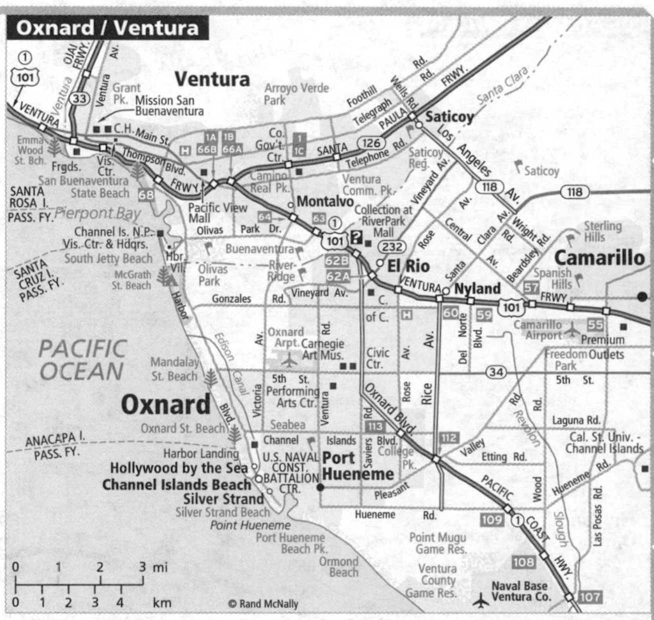

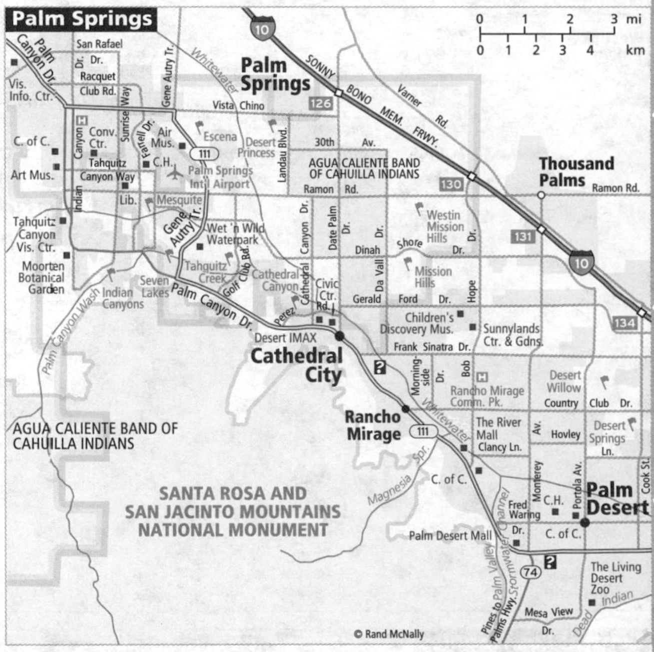

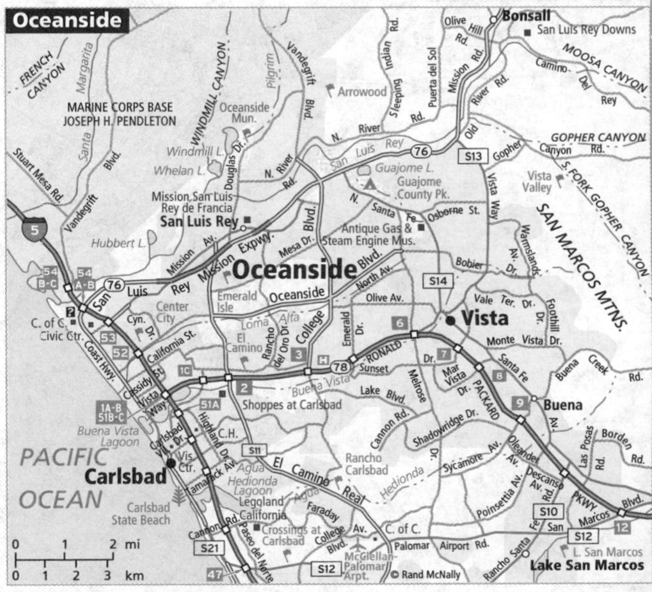

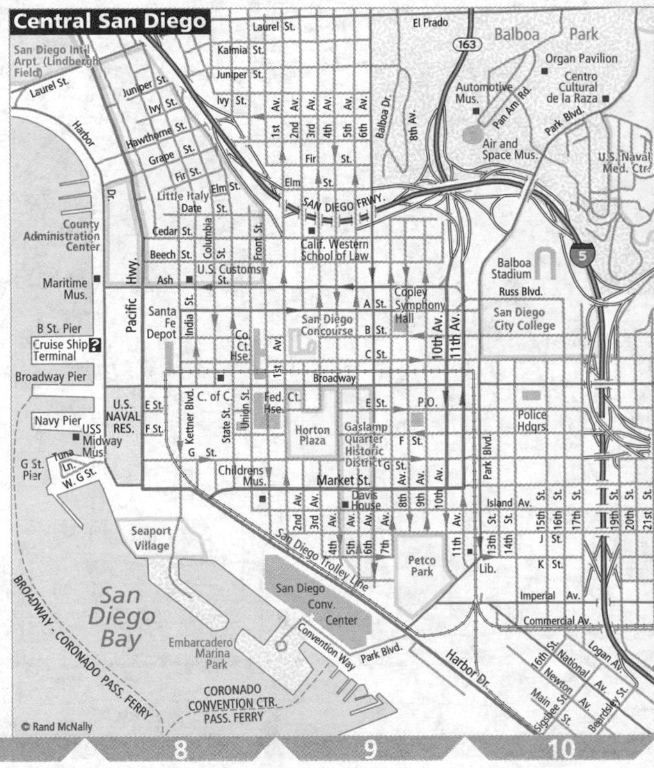

Sights to see

- Aquarium of the Pacific, Long Beach J-8
- Disneyland, Anaheim I-11
- Dodger Stadium................................ E-7
- El Pueblo de Los Angeles K-2
- Getty Center.................................... E-4
- Hollywood Bowl.................................. D-6
- Huntington Library, San Marino D-8
- Japanese American National Museum K-3
- Knott's Berry Farm, Buena Park H-10
- Los Angeles County Art Museum.................... E-5
- Los Angeles Maritime Museum J-7
- Los Angeles Zoo and Botanical Gardens............ D-6

Walt Disney Concert Hall

Santa Monica Pier

Sights to see

- Mission San Juan Capistrano, San Juan Capistrano . . M-14
- Old Pasadena, Pasadena D-8
- Oldest Winery in California, Rancho Cucamonga . . . D-14
- The Queen Mary, Long Beach J-8
- Richard M. Nixon Library & Birthplace, Yorba Linda H-12
- Santa Monica Pier, Santa Monica. F-4
- Universal City D-5
- Venice Boardwalk F-4
- Walt Disney Concert Hall K-1
- Warner Bros. Studio, Burbank D-6
- Will Rogers State Historic Park, Pacific Palisades E-4

Colorado

Nickname: The Centennial State
Capital: Denver, E-13
Land area: 103,642 sq. mi. (rank: 8th)
Population: 5,029,196 (rank: 22nd)
Largest city: Denver, 600,158, E-13

Index of places Pg. 129

Travel planning & on-the-road resources

Tourism Information
Colorado Tourism Office:
(800) 265-6723; www.colorado.com

Road Conditions & Construction
511, (303) 639-1111
www.cotrip.org, www.codot.gov

Toll Road Information
E-470 (Denver metro) *(ExpressToll)*:
(888) 946-3470, (303) 537-3470; www.expresstoll.com
Express Lanes (CO DOT) (Denver metro) *(ExpressToll)*:
www.codot.gov/programs/expresslanes
Northwest Parkway (Denver metro) *(GoPass)*:
(303) 533-1200; www.northwestparkway.org

Determining distances along roads
Highway distances (segments of one mile or less not shown):
Cumulative miles (red): the distance between red arrows
Intermediate miles (black): the distance between intersections & places

Interchanges and exit numbers
For most states, the mileage between interchanges may be determined by subtracting one number from the other.

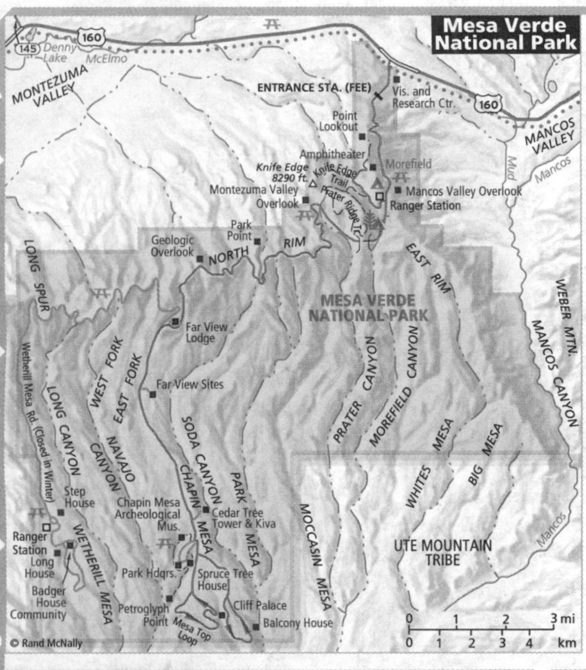

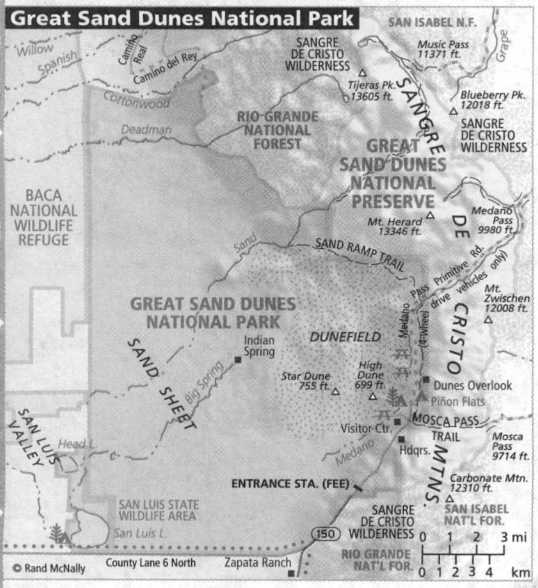

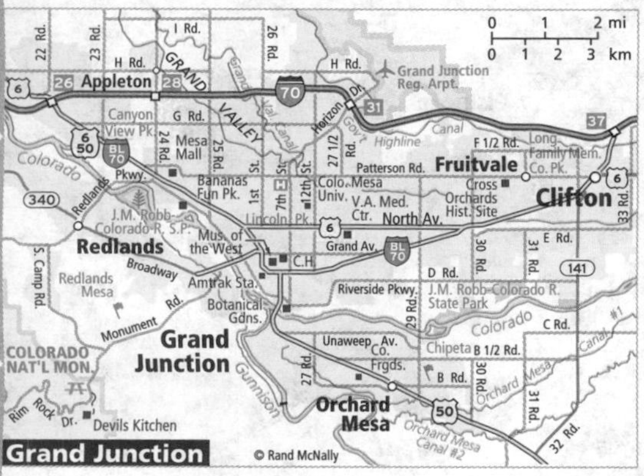

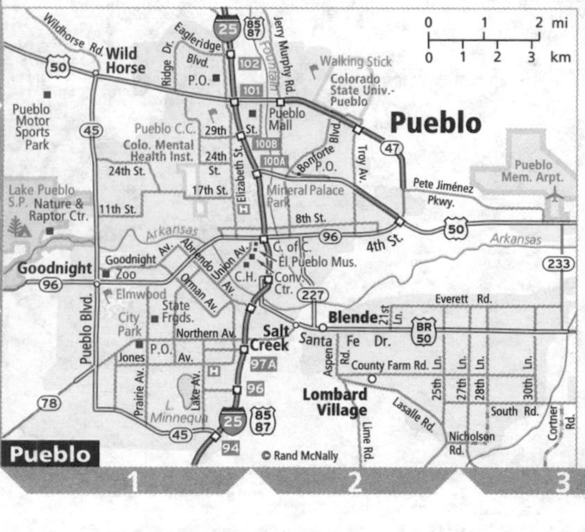

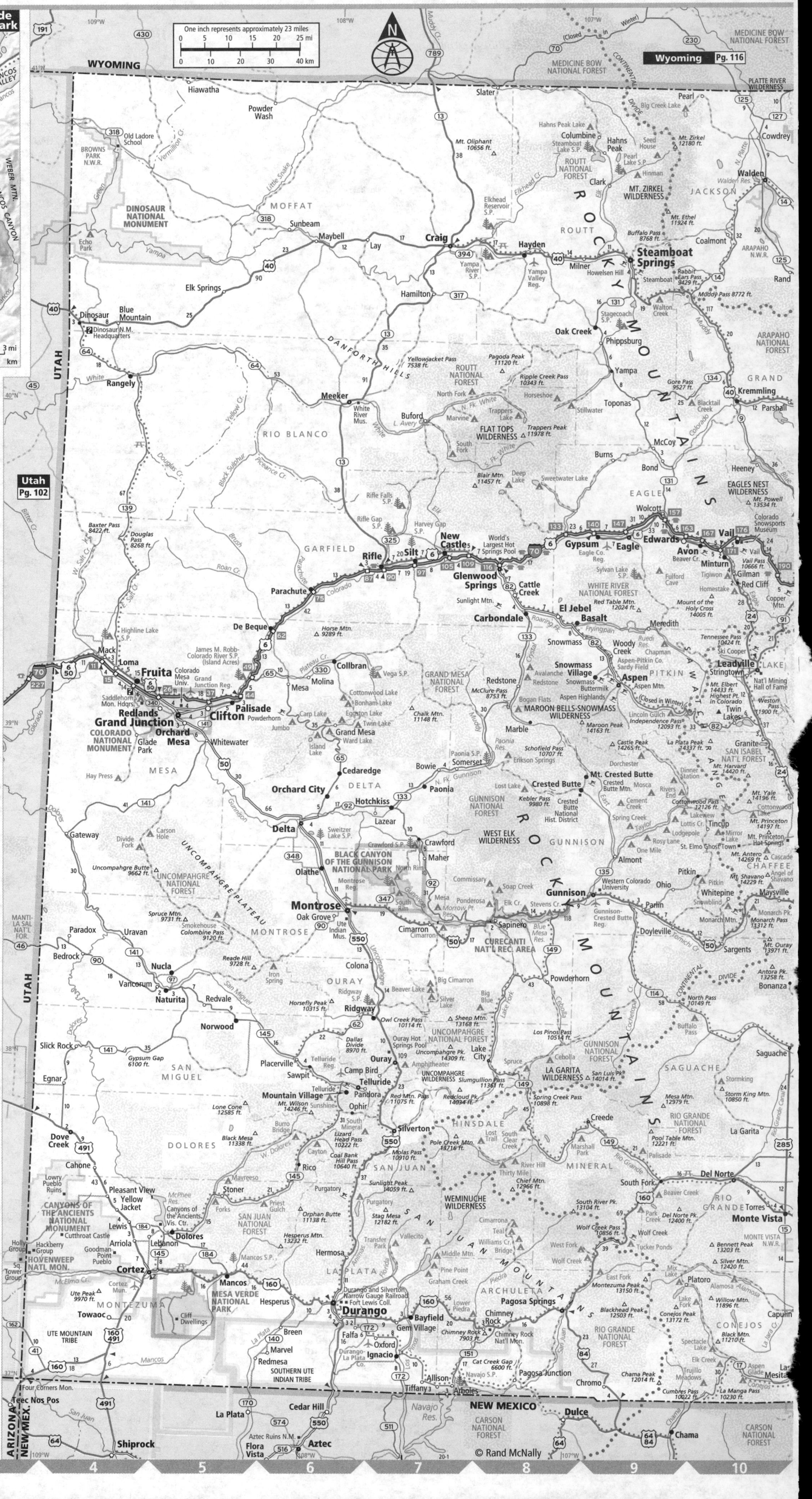

Garden of the Gods

Mileages between cities	Alamosa	Aspen	Burlington	Colorado Springs	Craig	Denver	Durango	Estes Park	Fort Collins	Grand Junction	Gunnison	Lamar	Leadville	Pueblo	Sterling	Trinidad
Burlington	311	363		151	363	166	460	222	220	408	324	108	265	189	142	230
Colorado Springs	163	155	151		264	69	313	133	133	309	166	158	121	42	194	128
Denver	234	197	166	69	197		336	64	63	243	200	208	99	112	125	198
Durango	149	246	460	313	312	336		402	396	168	142	351	253	269	458	258
Fort Collins	296	258	220	133	201	63	396	42		303	260	261	160	175	102	261
Grand Junction	247	128	408	309	151	243	168	258	303		126	448	174	287	364	370
Leadville	135	58	265	121	145	99	253	143	160	174	102	276		154	222	204
Trinidad	109	232	230	128	392	198	258	262	261	370	209	136	204	85	322	

Mileages © Rand McNally

Total mileages through Colorado

25 300 miles, 76 185 miles

70 451 miles, 50 467 miles

More mileages at www.randmcnally.com/MC

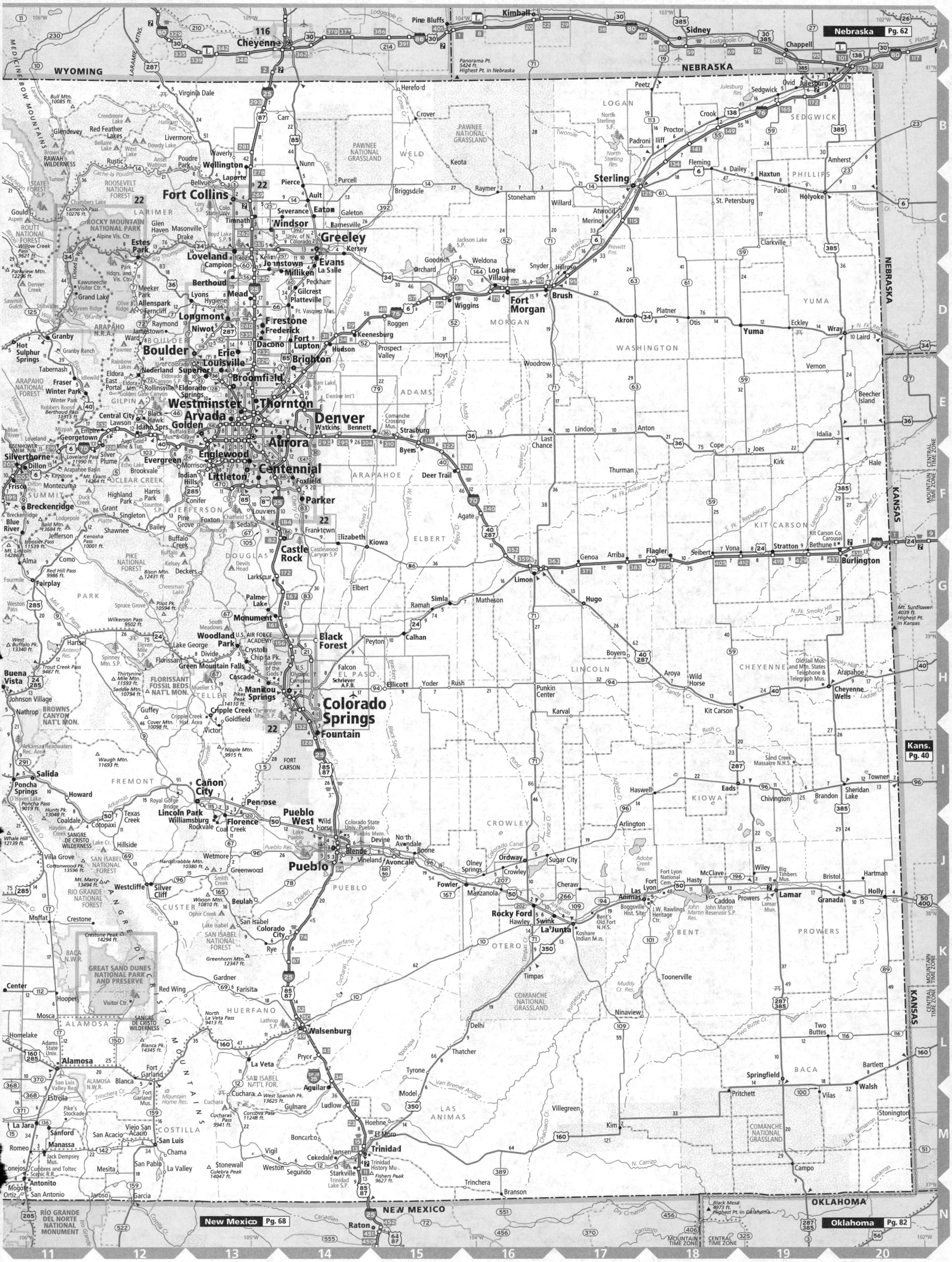

Sights to see

- Black American West Mus. & Heritage Ctr., Denver. . . . B-7
- Cave of the Winds, Colorado Springs L-8
- Colorado History Museum, Denver C-6
- Colorado State Capitol, Denver C-6
- Denver Art Museum, Denver C-6
- Denver Museum of Nature & Science, Denver I-5
- Garden of the Gods, Colorado Springs L-8
- National Center for Atmospheric Research, Boulder . . . F-1
- ProRodeo Hall of Fame, Colorado Springs K-9
- U.S. Air Force Academy, Colorado Springs J-9
- United States Mint, Denver C-6
- World Figure Skating Hall of Fame, Colorado Springs. . M-9

Denver Art Museum

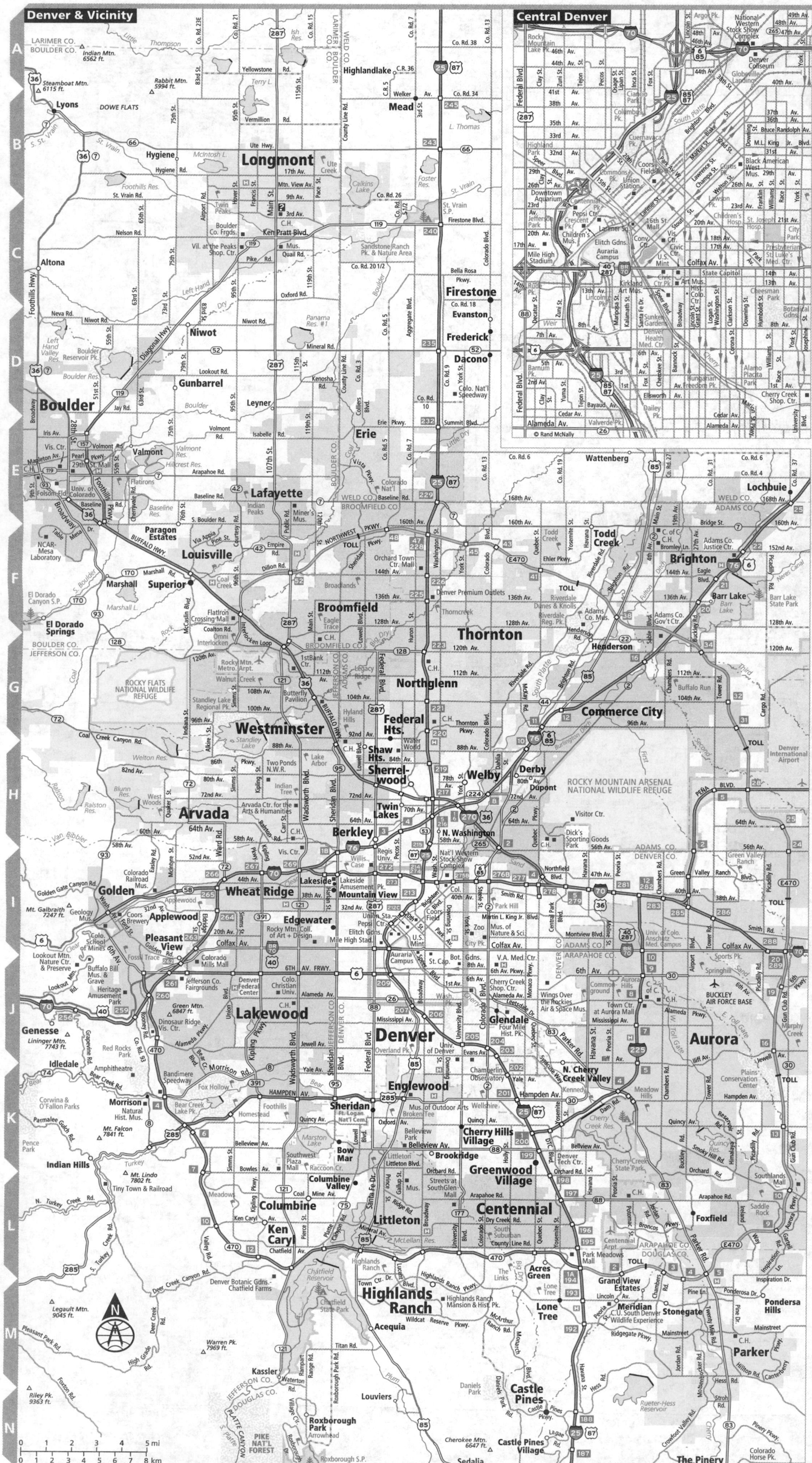

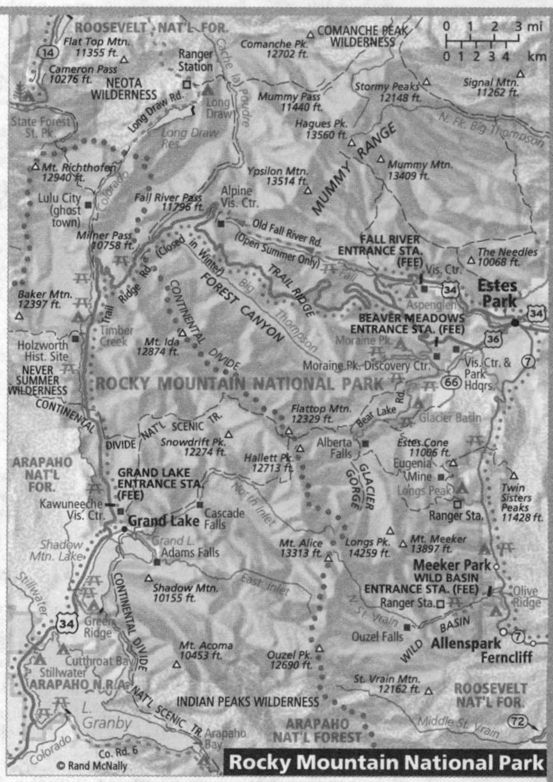

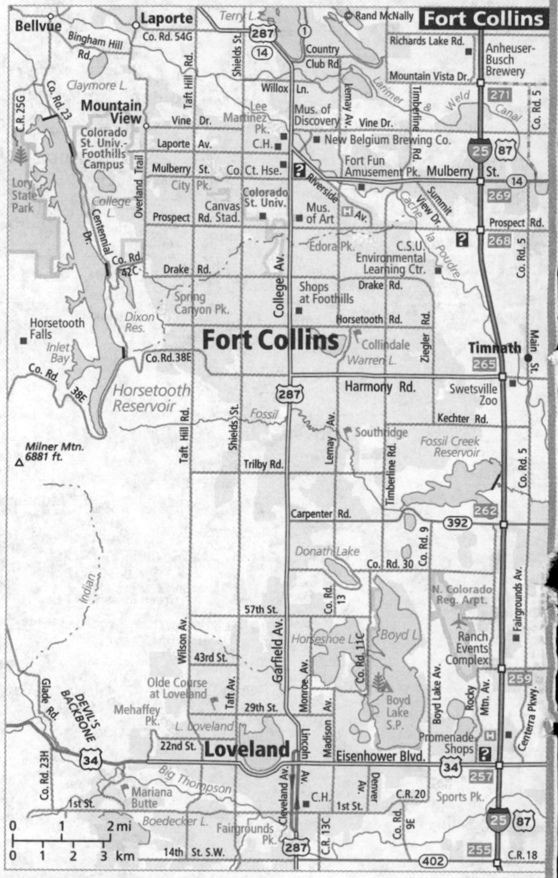

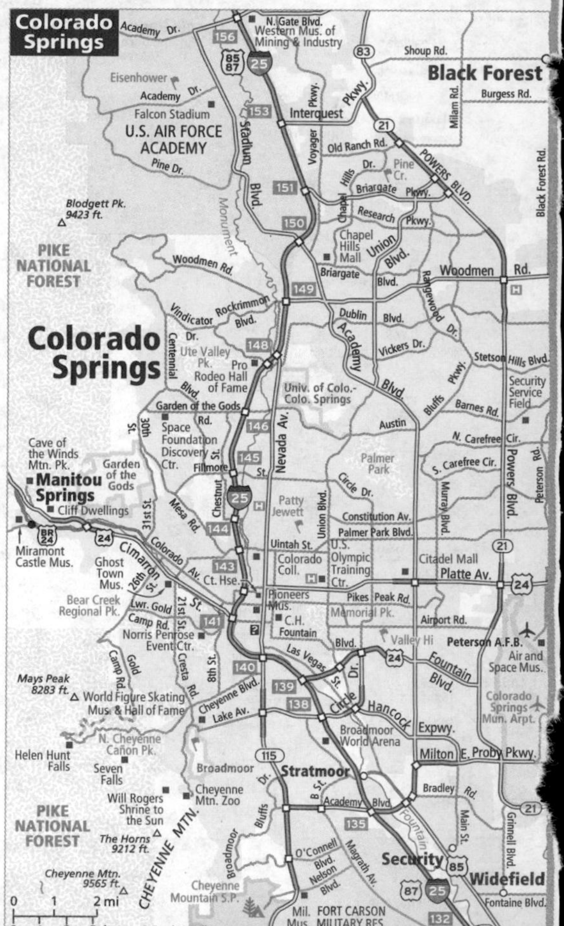

Travel planning & on-the-road resources

Tourism Information
Conn. Office of Tourism:
(888) 288-4748
(860) 500-2300
www.ctvisit.com

Road Conditions & Construction
(860) 594-2650
(860) 594-2000
cttravelsmart.org
www.ct.gov/dot

Toll Road Information
No tolls on state or federal highways

Determining Distances
9 / 4 3 2 (segments of one mile or less not shown)
Cumulative miles (red): the distance between red arrows
Intermediate miles (black): the distance between intersections & places

Total mileages through Connecticut
84: 98 miles
95: 112 miles
91: 58 miles
395: 55 miles

More mileages at randmcnally.com/MC

Mileages between cities	Bridgeport	Hartford	New Haven	New London	New York, NY	Putnam	Torrington	Waterbury
Bridgeport		55	18	64	54	107	50	30
Danbury	29	57	35	81	62	104	47	27
Hartford	55		38	45	108	47	26	30
New Haven	18	38		46	72	89	43	22
New London	64	45	46		118	47	79	63
Putnam	107	47	89	47	162		73	78
Torrington	50	26	43	79	109	73		20
Waterbury	30	30	22	63	89	78	20	

Nickname: The Constitution State
Capital: Hartford, C-9
Land area: 4,842 sq. mi. (rank: 48th)
Population: 3,574,097 (rank: 29th)
Largest city: Bridgeport, 144,229, H-5

Index of places Pg. 129

Nickname: The First State
Capital: Dover, G-2
Land area: 1,949 sq. mi. (rank: 49th)
Population: 897,934 (rank: 45th)
Largest city: Wilmington, 70,851, C-2

Index of places Pg. 129

Mileages between cities	Dover	Georgetown	Lewes	Milford	Philadelphia, PA	Salisbury, MD	Selbyville	Wilmington
Dover		36	40	20	80	56	55	50
Georgetown	36		15	16	114	27	20	85
Lewes	40	15		21	119	43	29	90
Middletown	26	62	66	46	56	84	81	27
Millville, NJ	94	124	128	108	45	147	143	53
Newark	46	80	85	64	43	102	99	14
Selbyville	55	20	29	36	133	24		104
Wilmington	50	85	90	70	29	107	104	

Mileages © Rand McNally

Total mileages through Delaware
95: 23 miles
1: 104 miles
13: 108 miles

More mileages at randmcnally.com/MC

Travel planning & on-the-road resources

Tourism Information
Delaware Tourism Office:
(866) 284-7483; www.visitdelaware.com

Road Conditions & Construction
(800) 652-5600, (302) 760-2080
www.deldot.gov

Toll Road Information *(E-ZPass)*
Delaware Department of Transportation:
(888) 397-2773, (302) 678-7000; www.ezpassde.com
Delaware River & Bay Authority (Del. Mem. Bridge & Lewes/Cape May Ferry):
(302) 571-6300; www.drba.net

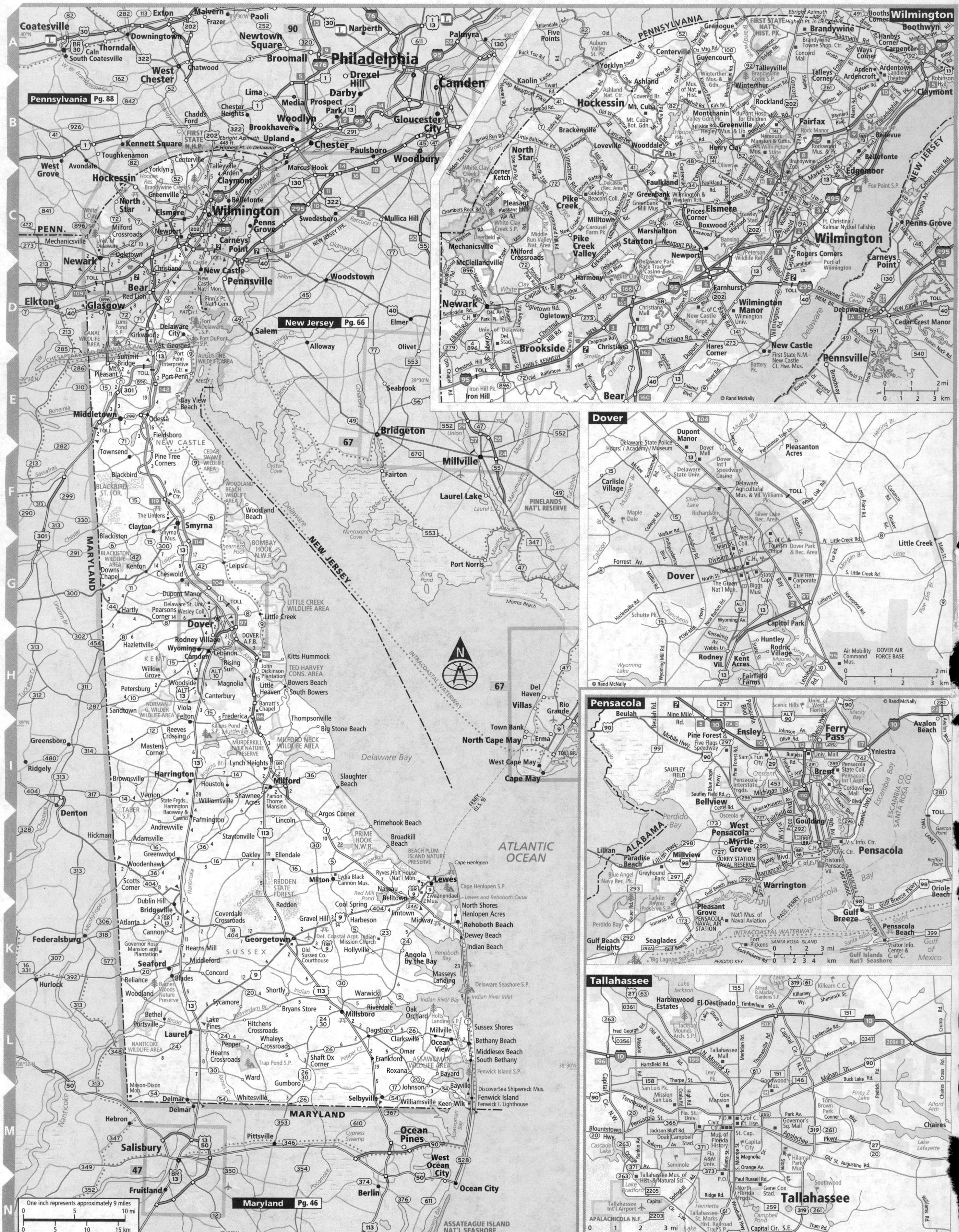

Sights to see

- Art Deco National Historic District, Miami Beach L-9
- Busch Gardens, Tampa B-4
- Hugh Taylor Birch State Park, Fort Lauderdale. H-9
- Marie Selby Botanical Gardens, Sarasota H-3
- Miami Seaquarium, Miami M-9
- Norton Museum of Art, Palm Beach B-10
- Ringling Center for the Cultural Arts, Sarasota G-3
- Salvador Dali Museum, St. Petersburg. D-2
- St. Petersburg Museum of History, St. Petersburg D-2
- Thomas A. Edison & Henry Ford Winter Estates, Fort Myers M-2
- Vizcaya Museum and Gardens, Miami. M-8

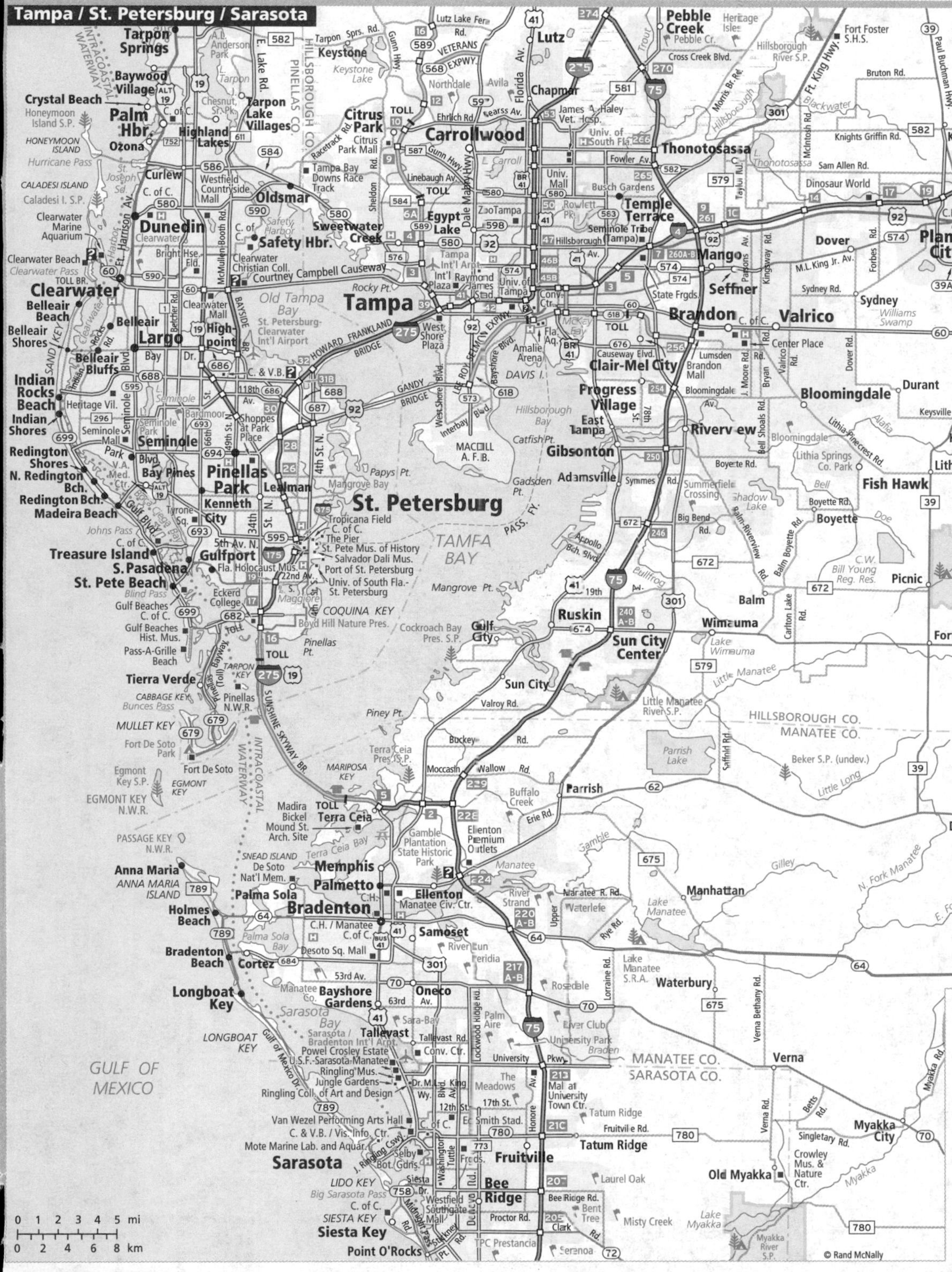

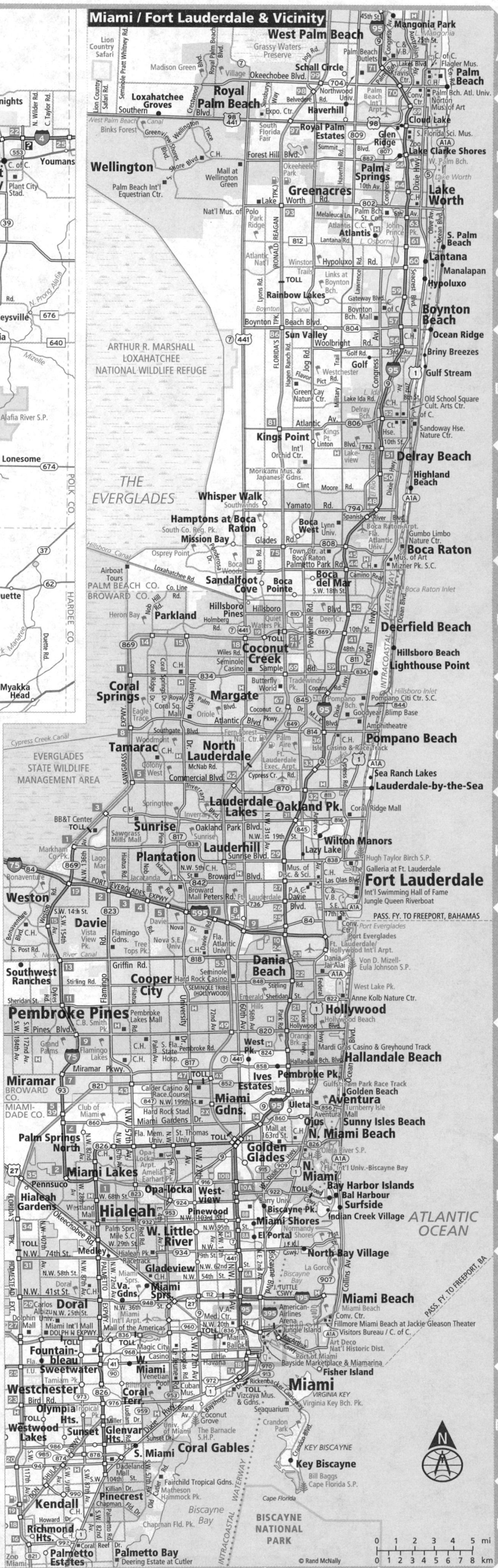

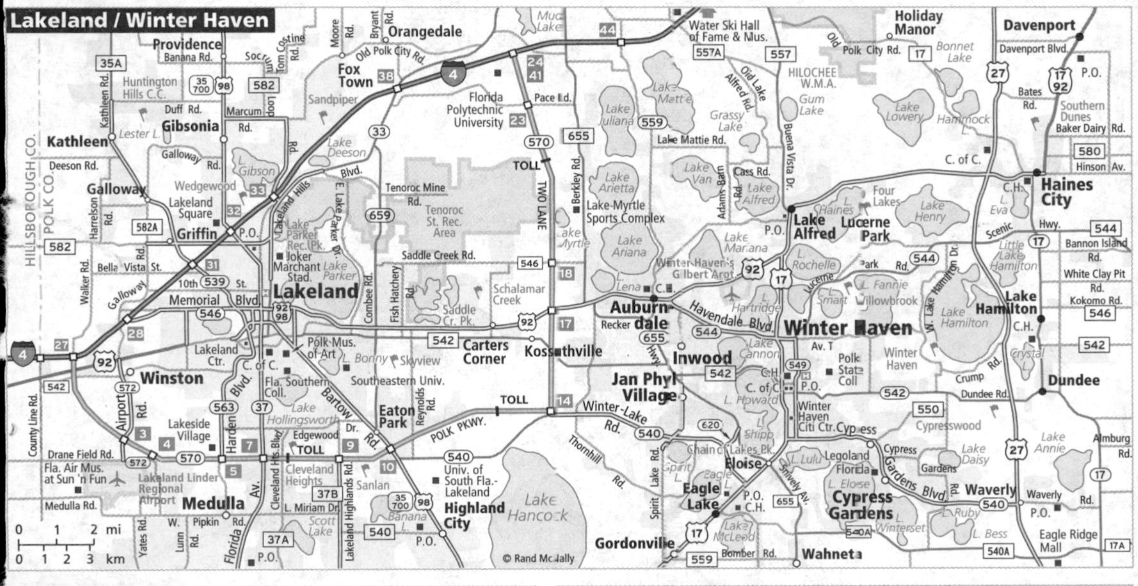

Nickname: The Sunshine State
Capital: Tallahassee, B-2
Land area: 53,625 sq. mi. (rank: 26th)
Population: 18,801,310 (rank: 4th)
Largest city: Jacksonville, 821,784, C-9

Index of places Pg. 129

Travel planning & on-the-road resources

Tourism Information
Visit Florida: (888) 735-2872
(850) 488-5607; www.visitflorida.com

Road Conditions & Construction
511, (866) 511-3352
fl511.com, fdot.gov

Toll Road Information *(all use SunPass unless otherwise noted)*
Florida Express Lanes (FL DOT): floridaexpresslanes.com
Florida's Turnpike Enterprise: (800) 749-7453; floridasturnpike.com
Central Florida Expressway Authority (Greater Orlando) ***(also E-Pass)***: (800) 353-7277, (407) 823-7277; www.cfxway.com
Miami-Dade Expressway Authority: (855) 277-0848, (305) 637-3277; www.mdxway.com
Osceola Co. Expressway Authority ***(E-Pass only)***: (407) 742-0552; www.osceolaxway.com
Tampa Hillsborough Expressway Authority: (813) 272-6740; www.tampa-xway.com

Toll Bridge Info. *(all use SunPass)*
Escambia Co. (Bob Sikes Br.): (850) 916-5421; myescambia.com
Santa Rosa Bay Br. Auth.: (800) 749-7453 www.garconpointbridge.com
Town of Bay Hbr. Islands (Broad Causeway): (305) 866-6241 www.bayharborislands-fl.gov

Coral reef near Key West

Mileages between cities	Daytona Beach	Fort Myers	Fort Pierce	Gainesville	Jacksonville	Key West	Miami	Orlando	Panama City	Pensacola	St. Petersburg	Sarasota	Tallahassee	Tampa	Titusville	West Palm Beach
Fort Myers	225		128	254	312	279	152	171	497	589	117	80	397	130	209	124
Jacksonville	92	312	227	72		507	349	141	264	355	222	253	164	198	136	284
Key West	414	279	284	483	507		162	387	727	821	390	352	627	402	371	231
Miami	256	152	123	336	349	162		229	579	663	262	225	479	255	213	68
Orlando	54	171	110	114	141	387	229		357	451	106	132	257	84	39	159
Pensacola	442	589	549	338	355	821	663	451	102		458	511	193	459	487	594
Tallahassee	253	397	364	148	164	627	479	257	96	193	257	328		273	295	413
Tampa	137	130	151	127	198	402	255	84	373	459	23	60	273		124	202

Total mileages through Florida

- 4: 132 miles
- 75: 471 miles
- 10: 362 miles
- 95: 382 miles

More mileages at randmcnally.com/MC

Nickname: The Peach State
Capital: Atlanta, E-4
Land area: 57,513 sq. mi. (rank: 21st)
Population: 9,687,653 (rank: 9th)
Largest city: Atlanta, 420,003, E-4

Index of places Pg. 130

Travel planning & on-the-road resources

Tourism Information
Explore Georgia: (800) 847-4842; www.exploregeorgia.org

Road Conditions & Construction
511, (877) 694-2511; www.511ga.org

Toll Road Information
State Road & Tollway Authority (Greater Atlanta) *(Peach Pass)*: (855) 724-7277; www.stra.ga.gov

Determining distances along roads

Highway distances (segments of one mile or less not shown):
Cumulative miles (red): the distance between red arrows
Intermediate miles (black): the distance between intersections & places

Interchanges and exit numbers
For most states, the mileage between interchanges may be determined by subtracting one number from the other.

Forsyth Park, Savannah

Mileages between cities	Albany	Athens	Atlanta	Augusta	Bainbridge	Brunswick	Chattanooga, TN	Columbus	Gainesville	Jacksonville, FL	Macon	Rome	Savannah	Toccoa	Valdosta	Vidalia
Atlanta	182	69		148	240	275	117	106	54	346	82	70	247	94	228	172
Augusta	211	98	148		268	193	265	249	140	254	123	217	134	132	217	99
Chattanooga, TN	300	172	117	265	348	397		219	121	465	201	71	364	155	346	289
Columbus	85	171	106	249	128	258	219		161	292	98	144	249	201	173	175
Jacksonville, FL	198	310	346	254	204	66	465	292	396		270	416	135	375	121	164
Macon	106	91	82	123	163	193	201	98	132	270		152	165	143	152	90
Savannah	226	222	247	134	249	77	364	249	297	135	165	317		255	167	90
Valdosta	79	243	228	217	83	120	346	173	278	121	152	298	167	317		118

Mileages © Rand McNally

Total mileages through Georgia

- I-20: 203 miles
- I-85: 180 miles
- I-75: 355 miles
- I-95: 112 miles

More mileages at randmcnally.com/MC

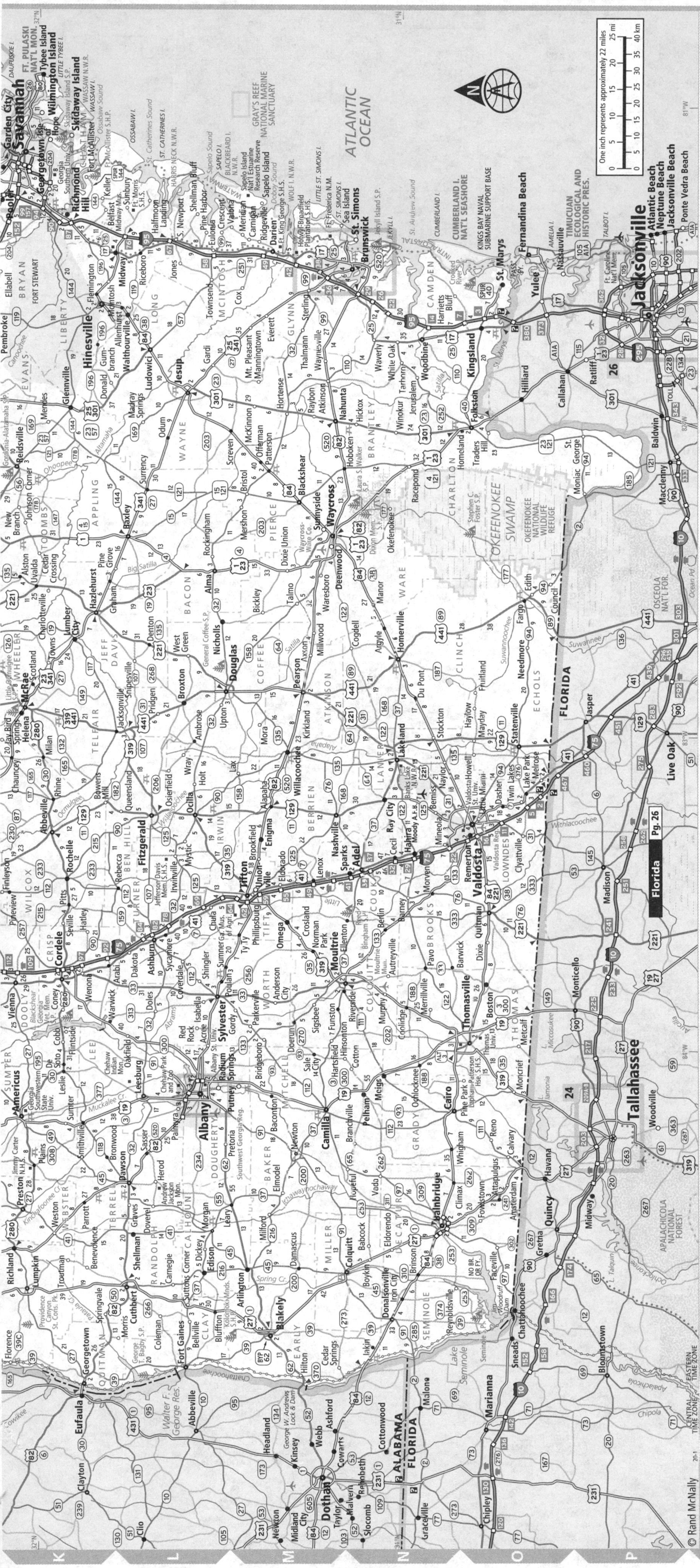

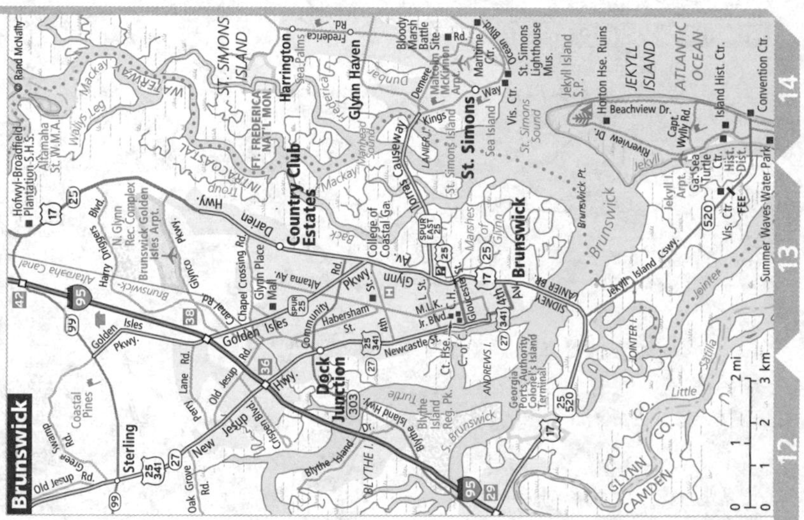

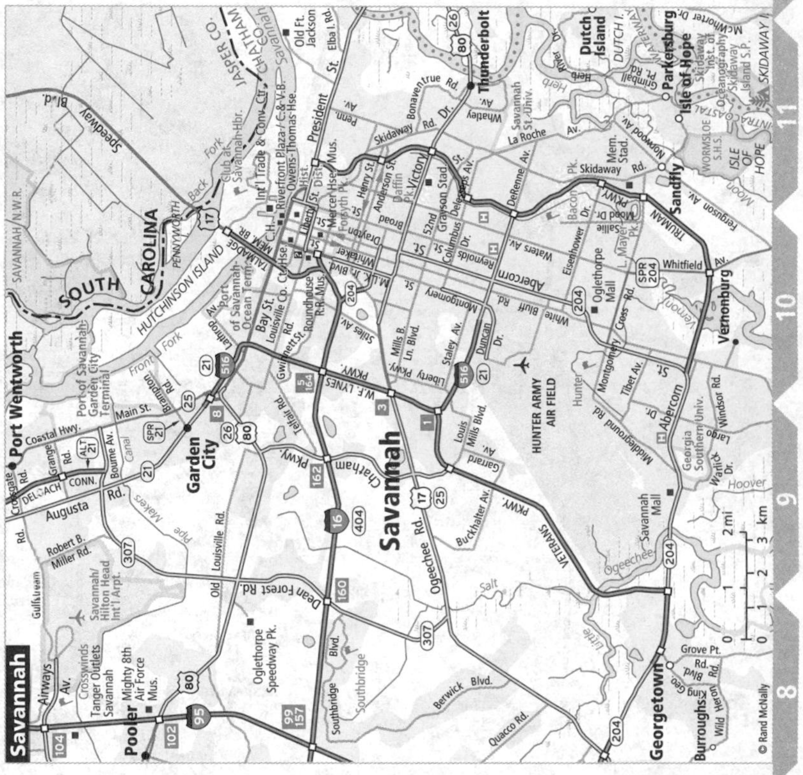

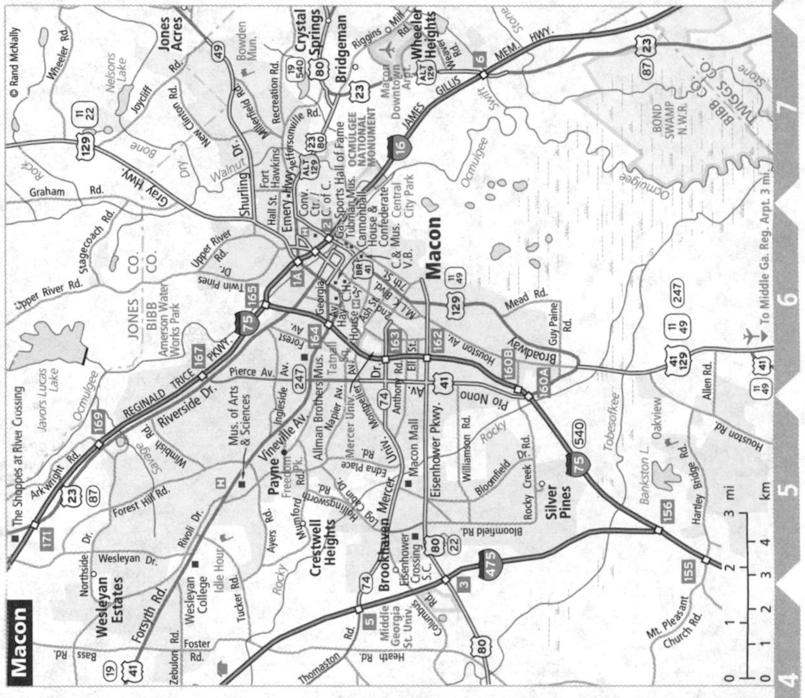

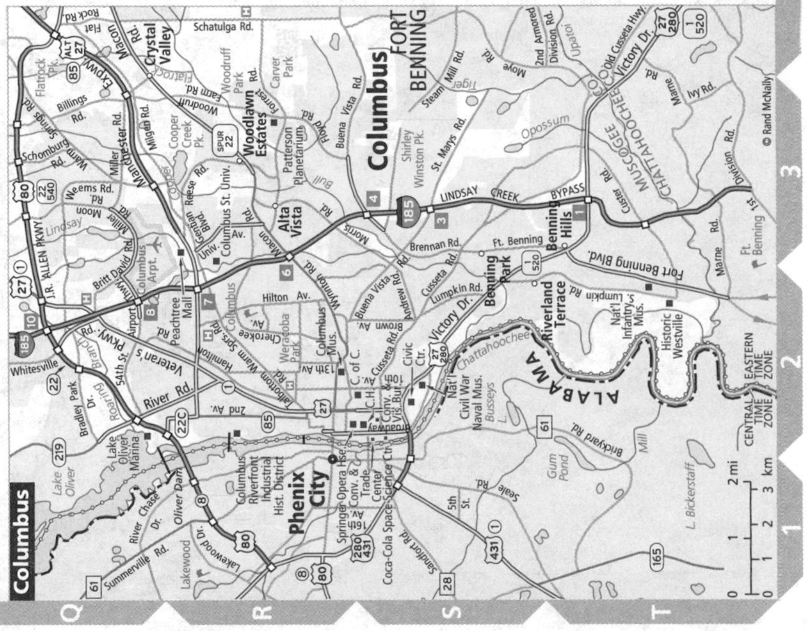

Nickname: The Aloha State
Capital: Honolulu, N-4
Land area: 6,423 sq. mi. (rank: 47th)
Population: 1,360,301 (rank: 40th)
Largest city: Honolulu, 337,256, N-4

Index of places Pg. 130

Mileages between cities *Via plane

	Hilo	Honolulu	Kahului	Kailua	Kailua Kona	Kapa'a	Lahaina	Wahiawā
Hilo		225*	127*	237*	74	337*	149*	236*
Honolulu	225*		108*	11	177*	116*	130*	20
Kahului	127*	108*		22*	93*	214*	22	119*
Kailua Kona	74	177*	93*	188*		283*	116*	188*
Kapa'a	337*	116*	214*	128*	283*		236*	128*
Kaunakakai	177*	68*	55*	79*	144*	174*	77*	79*
Lahaina	149*	130*	22	43*	116*	236*		141*
Wahiawā	236*	20	119*	26	188*	128*	141*	

Total mileages through Hawaii
H1 27 miles
H3 15 miles
H2 8 miles

More mileages at randmcnally.com/MC

Travel planning & on-the-road resources

Tourism Information
Hawaii Visitors & Convention Bureau: (800) 464-2924
www.gohawaii.com

Toll Road Information
No tolls on state or federal highways

Road Conditions & Construction
(808) 587-2220
hidot.hawaii.gov
O'ahu: 511
www.goakamai.org

Determining Distances
(segments of one mile or less not shown)
Cumulative miles (red): the distance between red arrows
Intermediate miles (black): the distance between intersections & places

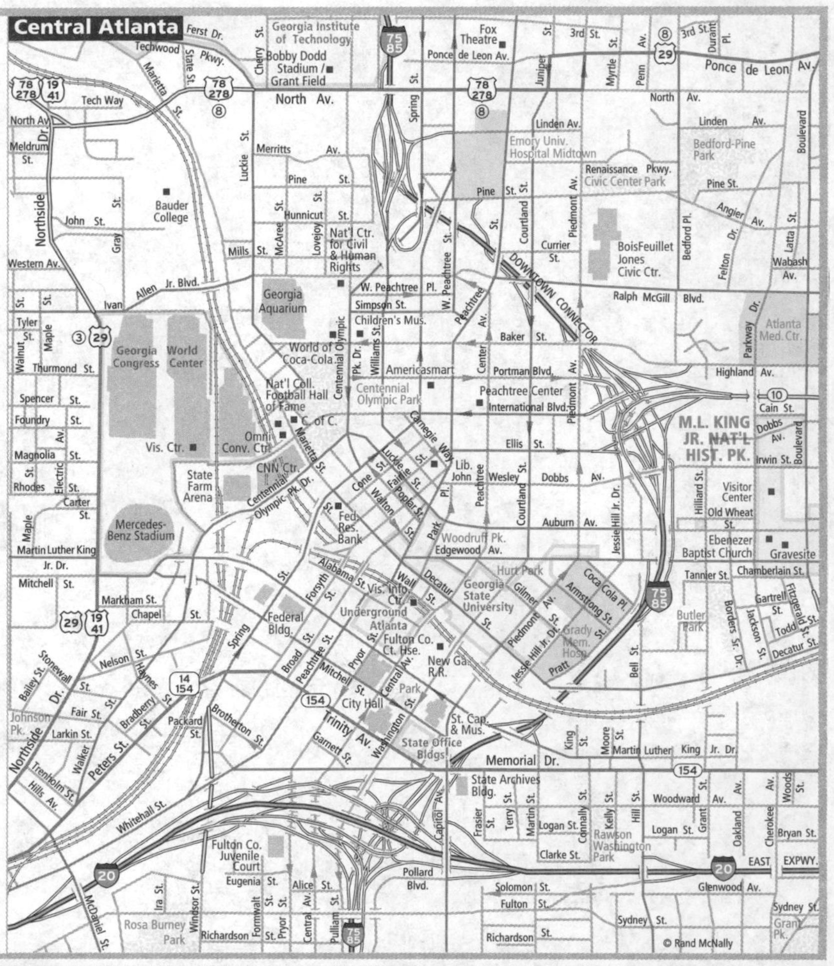

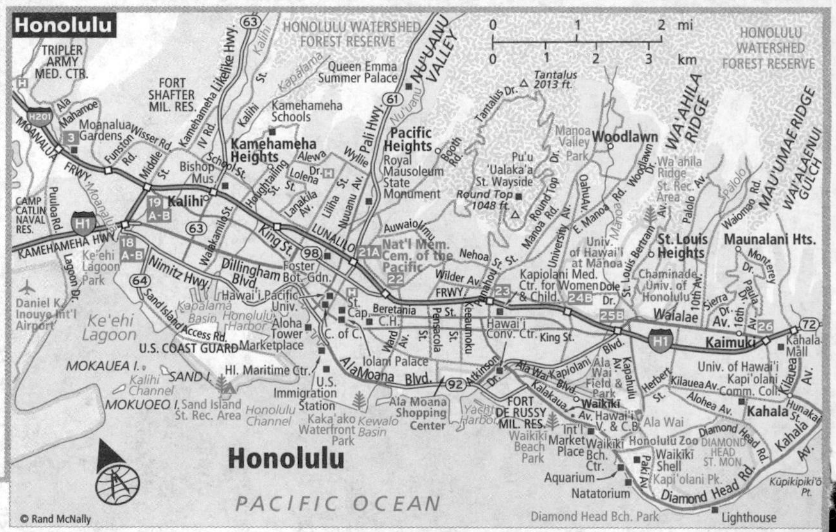

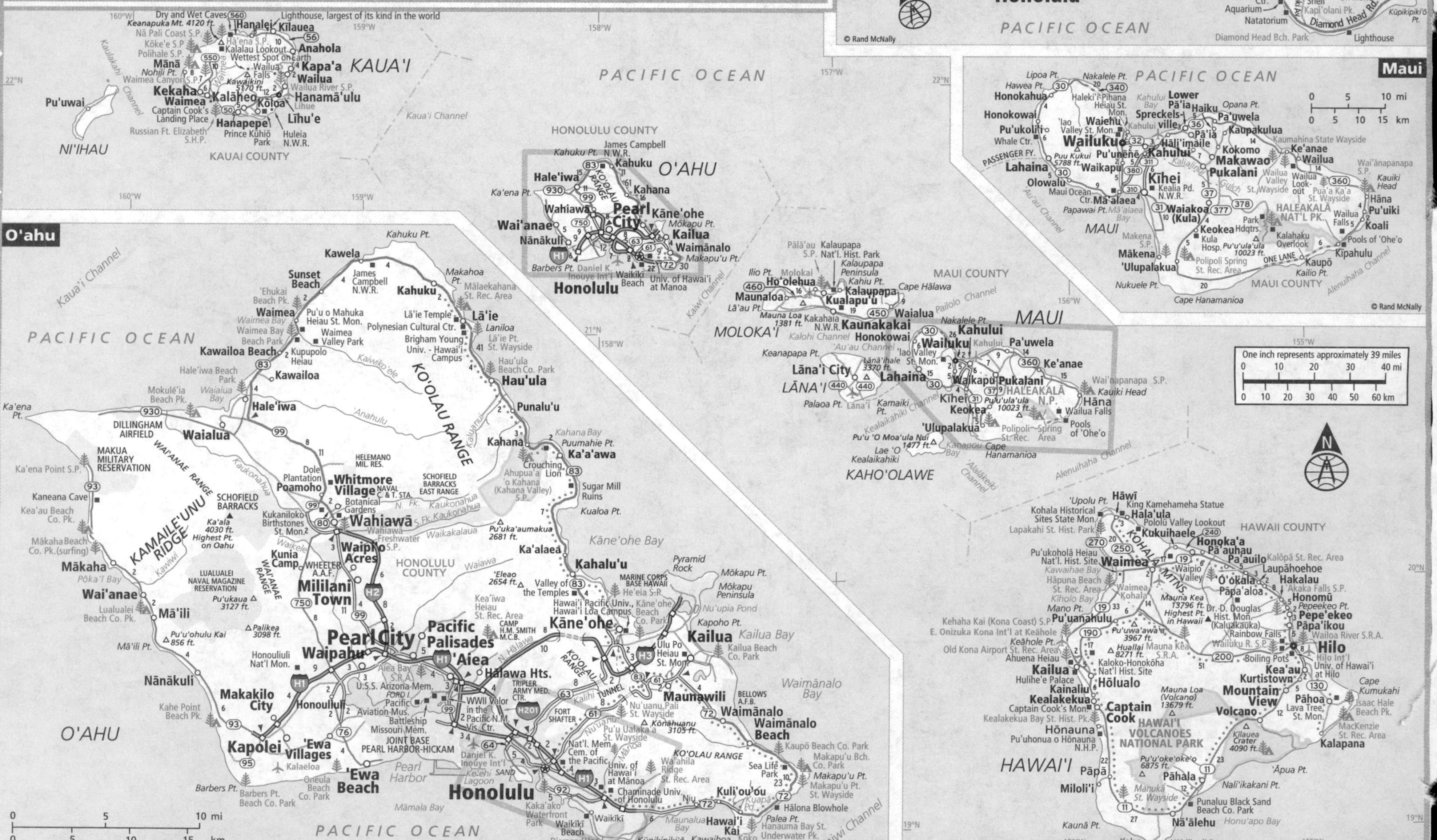

Travel planning & on-the-road resources

Tourism Information
Idaho Tourism:
(800) 847-4843, (208) 334-2470; visitidaho.org

Road Conditions & Construction
511, (888) 432-7623
www.511.idaho.gov, www.itd.idaho.gov

Toll Road Information
No tolls on state or federal highways

Determining Distances
(segments of one mile or less not shown)
Cumulative miles (red): the distance between red arrows
Intermediate miles (black): the distance between intersections & places

Total mileages through Idaho
15: 196 miles
84: 276 miles
86: 63 miles
90: 74 miles

More mileages at randmcnally.com/MC

Mileages between cities

	Boise	Coeur d'Alene	Lewiston	Missoula, MT	Mountain Home	Pocatello	Salmon	Twin Falls
Boise		383	268	367	44	234	247	128
Bonners Ferry	459	76	191	212	504	573	351	589
Coeur d'Alene	383		115	166	428	525	303	513
Idaho Falls	279	478	526	312	237	49	160	159
Lewiston	268	115		214	313	504	332	398
Pocatello	234	525	504	361	191		209	114
Salmon	247	303	332	138	287	209		247
Twin Falls	128	513	398	384	85	114	247	

Mileages © Rand McNally

Idaho

Nickname: The Gem State
Capital: Boise, K-2
Land area: 82,643 sq. mi. (rank: 11th)
Population: 1,567,582 (rank: 39th)
Largest city: Boise, 205,671, K-2

Index of places Pg. 130

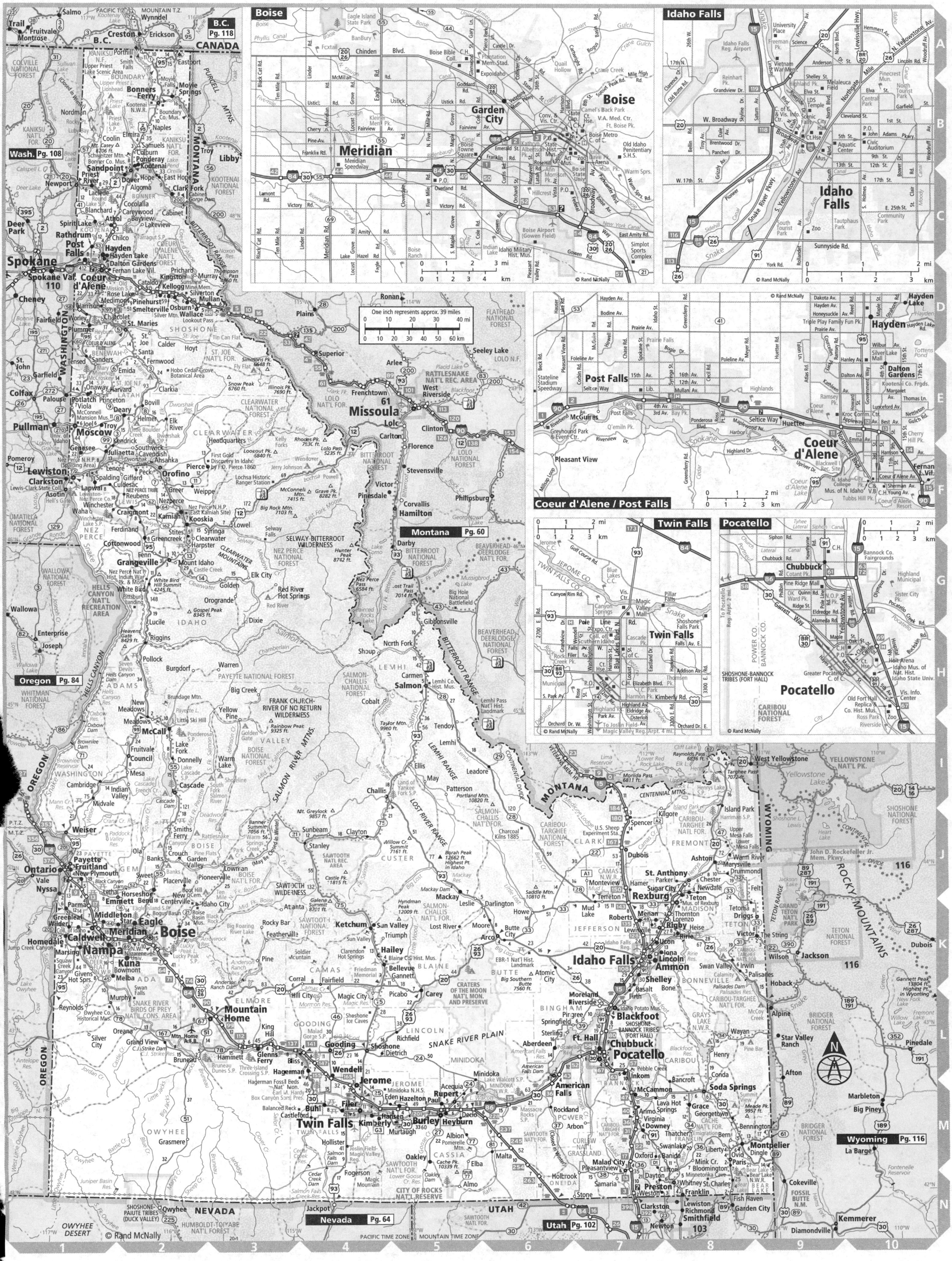

Illinois

Nickname: Land of Lincoln
Capital: Springfield, J-8
Land area: 55,519 sq. mi. (rank: 24th)
Population: 12,830,632 (rank: 5th)
Largest city: Chicago, 2,695,598, C-13

Index of places Pg. 130

Travel planning & on-the-road resources

Tourism Information
Illinois Office of Tourism: (800) 226-6632, (312) 814-4732; www.enjoyillinois.com

Road Conditions & Construction
(800) 452-4368; www.gettingaroundillinois.com, www.dot.il.gov

Toll Road/Bridge Information
Illinois Tollway (*I-Pass*): (800) 824-7277, (630) 241-6800; www.illinoistollway.com
Skyway Concession Co. (Chicago Skyway) (*I-Pass*): (773) 356-5555; www.chicagoskyway.org

Determining distances along roads

Highway distances (segments of one mile or less not shown):
Cumulative miles (red): the distance between red arrows
Intermediate miles (black): the distance between intersections & places

Interchanges and exit numbers
For most states, the mileage between interchanges may be determined by subtracting one number from the other.

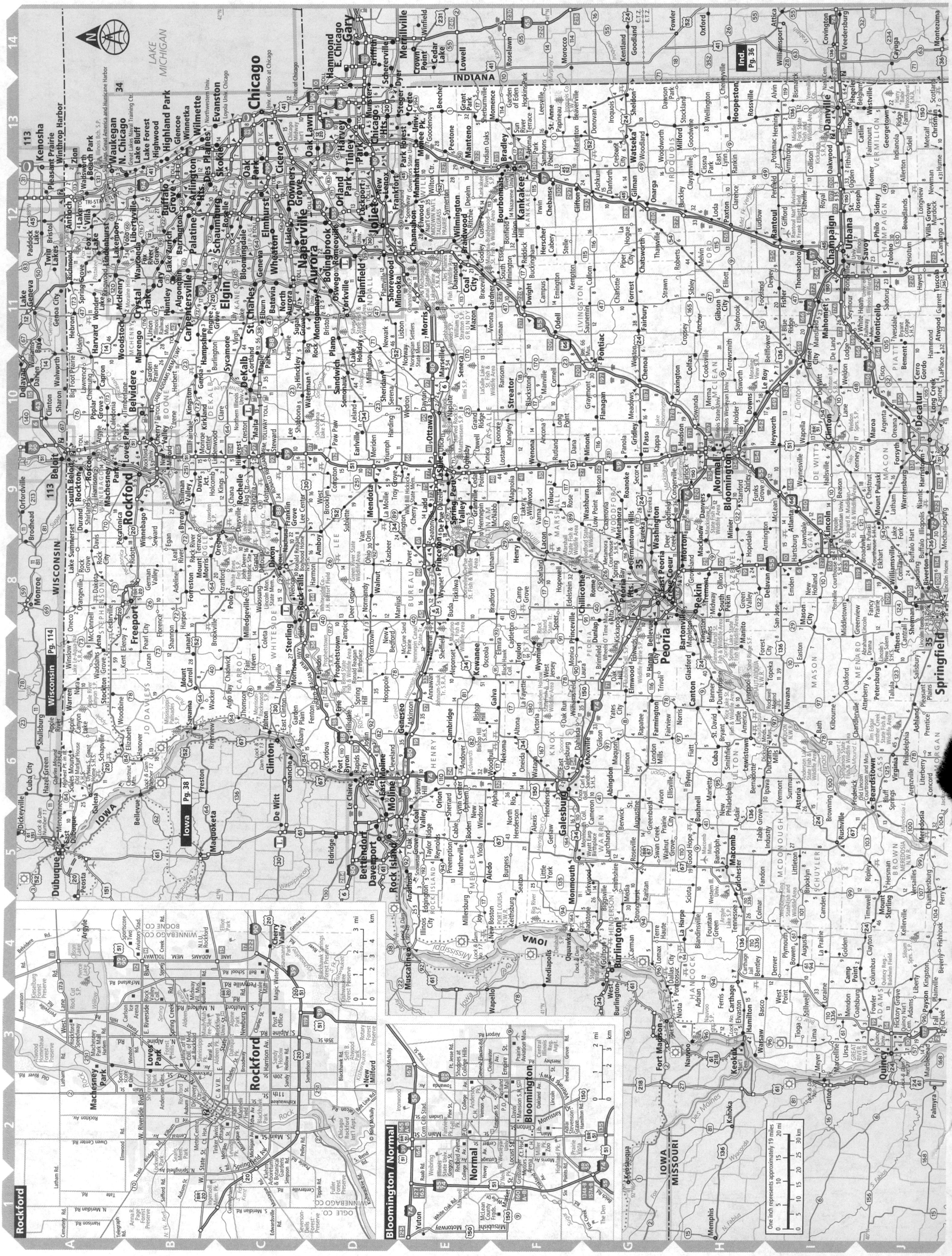

Navy Pier, Chicago

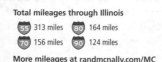

Mileages between cities	Bloomington	Carbondale	Champaign	Chicago	Decatur	Dubuque, IA	Kankakee	Lawrenceville	Moline	Mt. Vernon	Peoria	Quincy	Rockford	St. Louis, MO	Springfield	Waukegan
Carbondale	245		200	330	176	406	272	146	332	57	240	240	379	104	170	374
Champaign	51	200		135	48	256	78	130	182	147	89	194	185	180	85	180
Chicago	132	330	135		179	177	58	247	166	277	154	309	84	296	198	38
Moline	131	332	182	166	171	75	158	307		308	93	148	120	261	164	190
Peoria	38	240	89	154	78	167	108	214	93	215		130	138	168	71	184
Rockford	132	379	185	84	180	93	139	309	120	326	138	268		294	197	73
St. Louis, MO	162	104	180	296	135	335	252	144	261	79	168	139	294		98	326
Springfield	56	170	85	198	38	238	157	153	164	138	71	112	197	98		229

Mileages © Rand McNally

Total mileages through Illinois

- 55: 313 miles
- 80: 164 miles
- 70: 156 miles
- 90: 124 miles

More mileages at randmcnally.com/MC

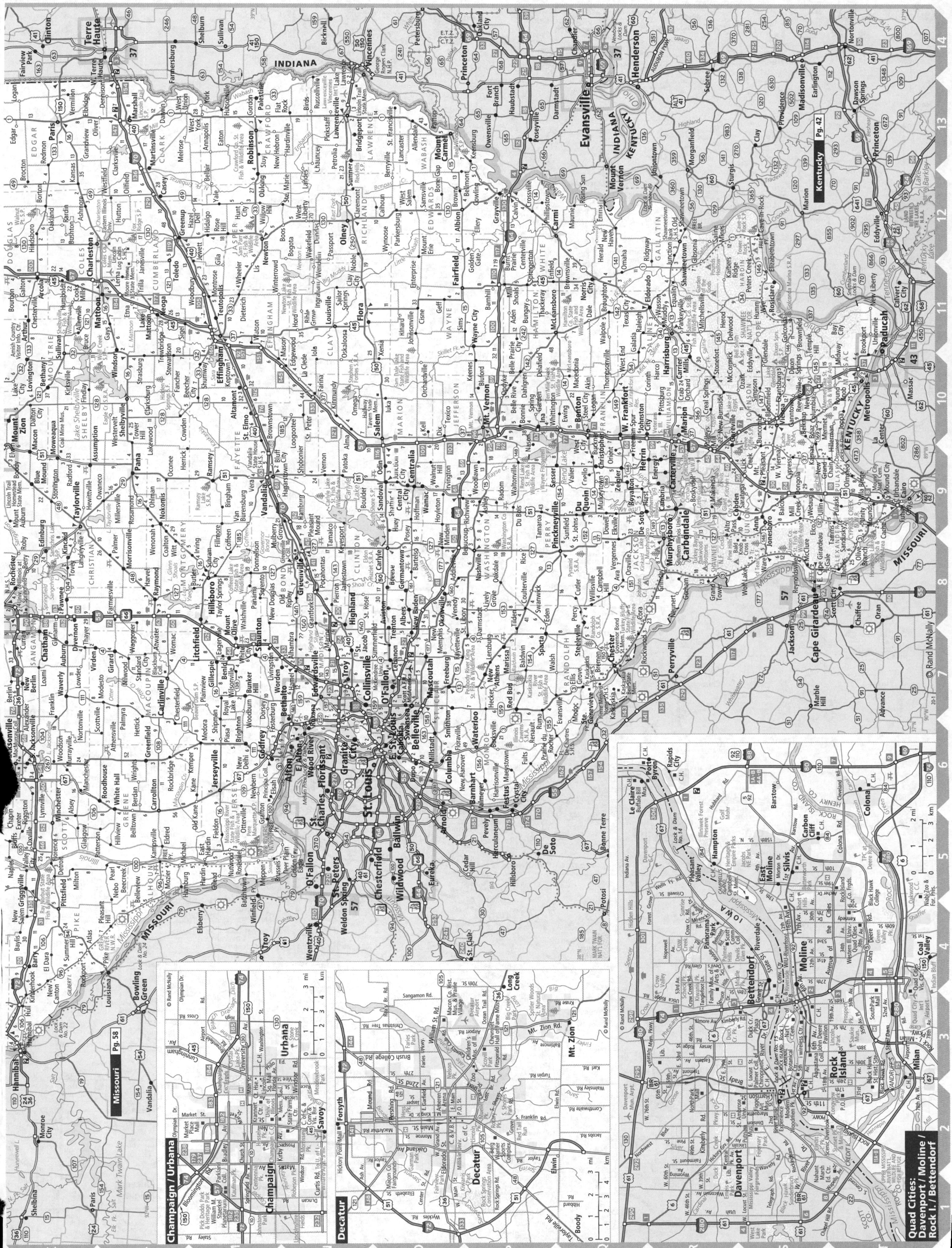

Chicago Cultural Center

Sights to see

- Adler Planetarium G-15
- Art Institute of Chicago E-13
- Chicago Botanic Garden, Glencoe D-8
- Field Museum G-14
- Frank Lloyd Wright Home & Studio, Oak Park H-8
- John G. Shedd Aquarium G-14
- Lincoln Park Zoo H-9
- Millennium Park E-13
- Museum of Science & Industry J-10
- Navy Pier D-14
- Willis Tower E-12
- Wrigley Field G-9

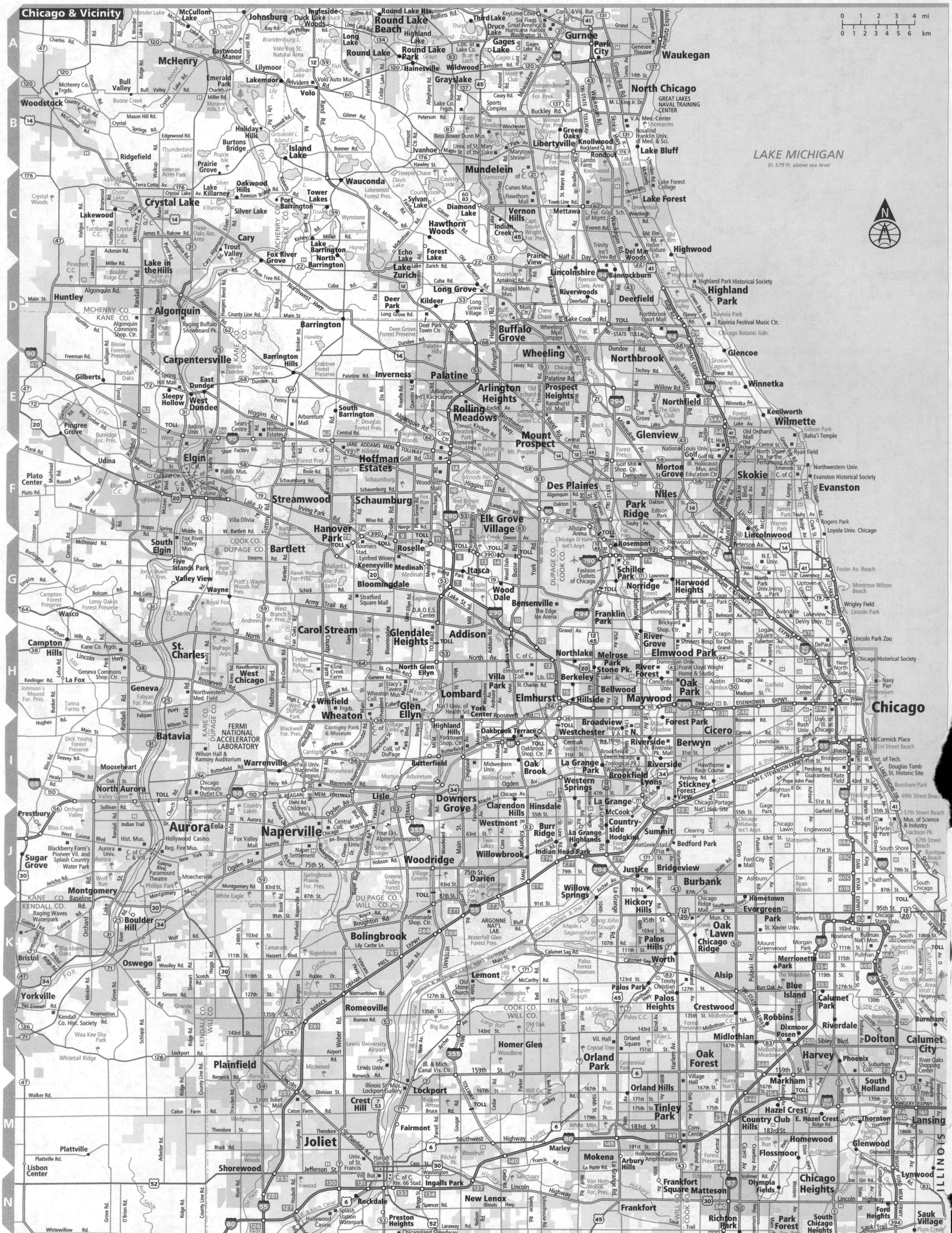

Children's Museum of Indianapolis

Sights to see

- Abraham Lincoln Presidential Library & Museum, Springfield M-16
- Buckingham Fountain, Chicago F-13
- Children's Museum of Indianapolis, Indianapolis D-18
- Fort Wayne Children's Zoo, Fort Wayne L-19
- Illinois State Capitol Complex, Springfield M-16
- Indiana State Capitol, Indianapolis H-19
- Indiana State Museum, Indianapolis H-19
- Indianapolis Motor Speedway and Hall of Fame Museum, Indianapolis D-16
- NCAA Hall of Champions, Indianapolis H-18
- President Benjamin Harrison Home, Indianapolis F-20

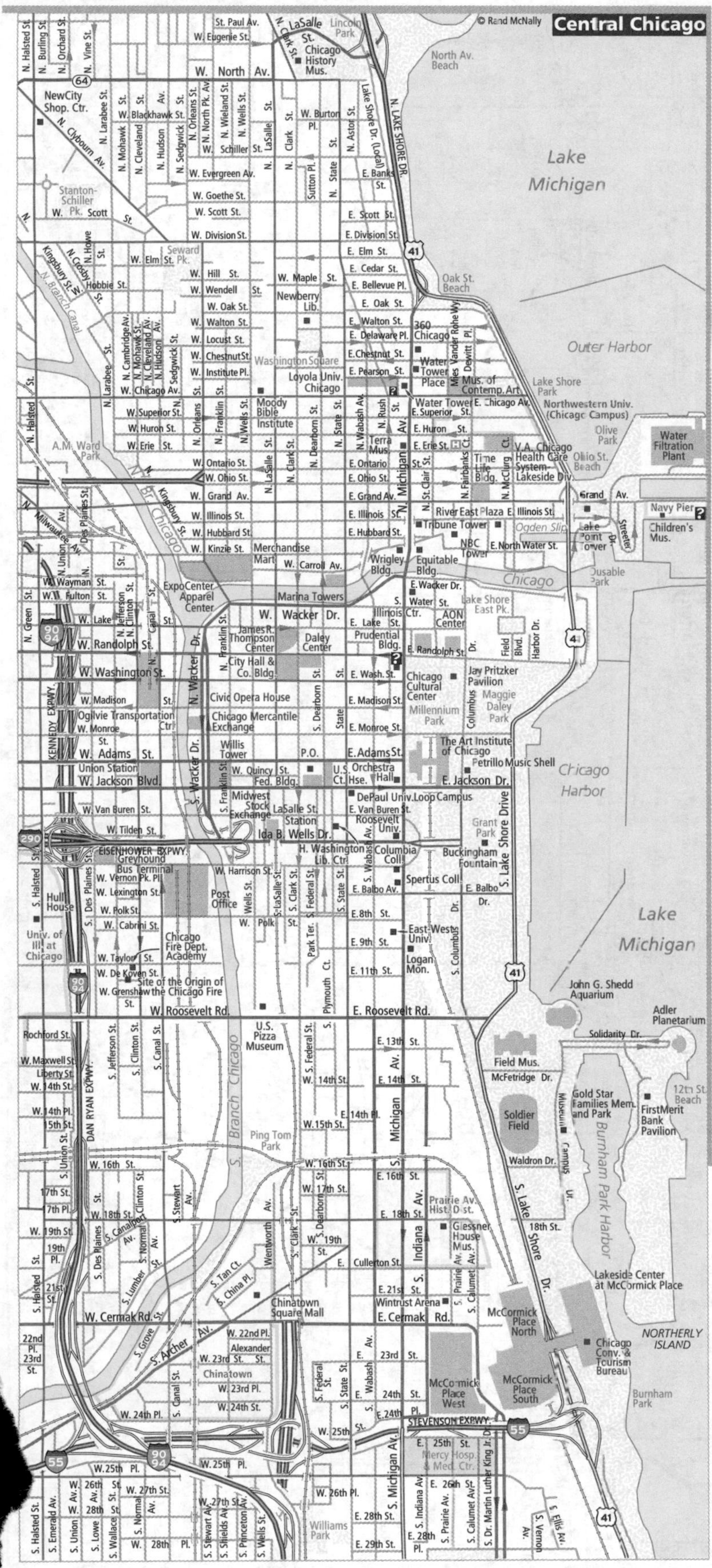

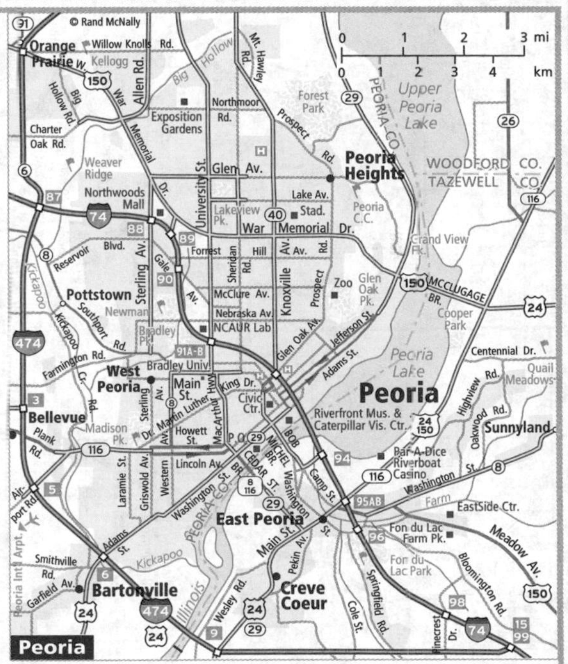

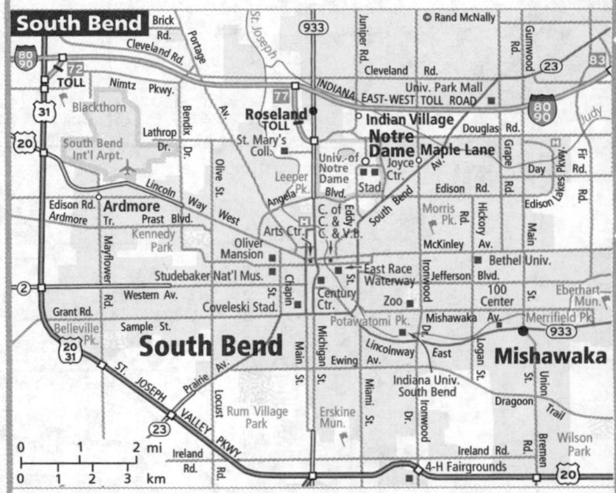

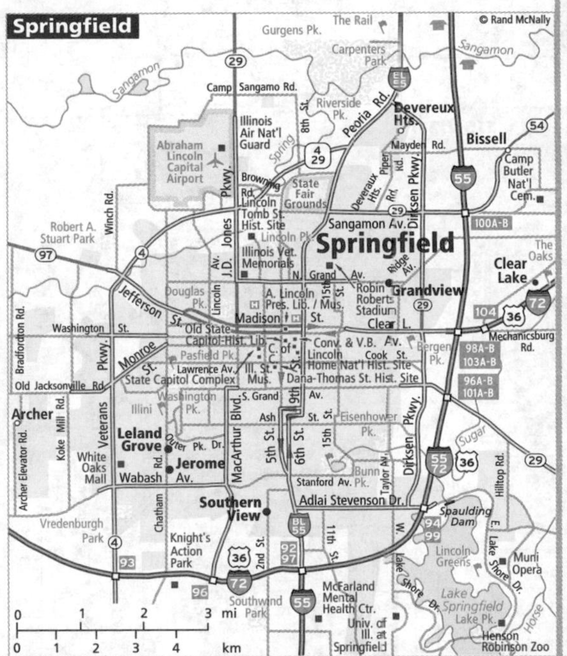

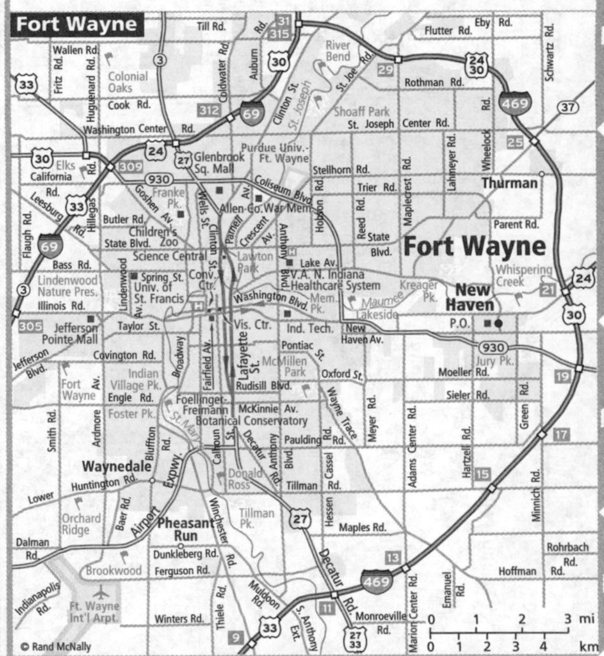

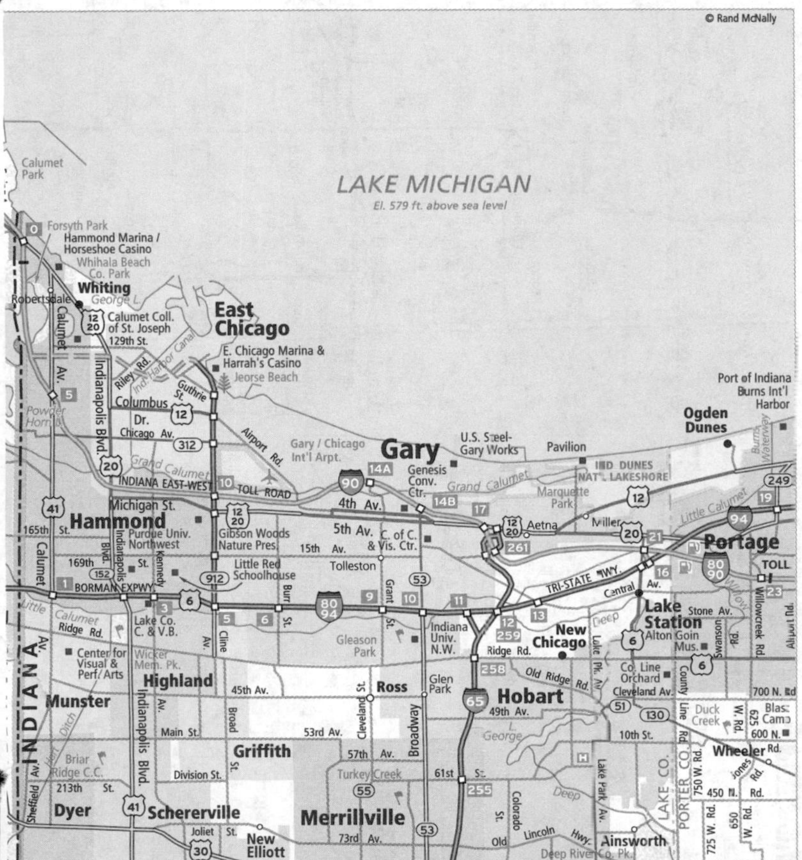

Nickname: The Hoosier State
Capital: Indianapolis, J-9
Land area: 35,826 sq. mi. (rank: 38th)
Population: 6,483,802 (rank: 15th)
Largest city: Indianapolis, 820,445, J-9

Index of places Pg. 130

Travel planning & on-the-road resources

Tourism Information
Indiana Office of Tourism Development: (800) 677-9800; visitindiana.com

Road Conditions & Construction
(800) 261-7623, (855) 463-6848; www.in.gov/indot/2420.htm, indot.carsprogram.org

Toll Road Information
Indiana Toll Road Concession Co. (*E-ZPass*): (574) 675-4010; www.indianatollroad.org
RiverLink (Louisville area toll bridges) (*RiverLink or E-ZPass*): (855) 748-5465; www.riverlink.com

Determining distances along roads

Highway distances (segments of one mile or less not shown):
Cumulative miles (red): the distance between red arrows
Intermediate miles (black): the distance between intersections & places

Interchanges and exit numbers
For most states, the mileage between interchanges may be determined by subtracting one number from the other.

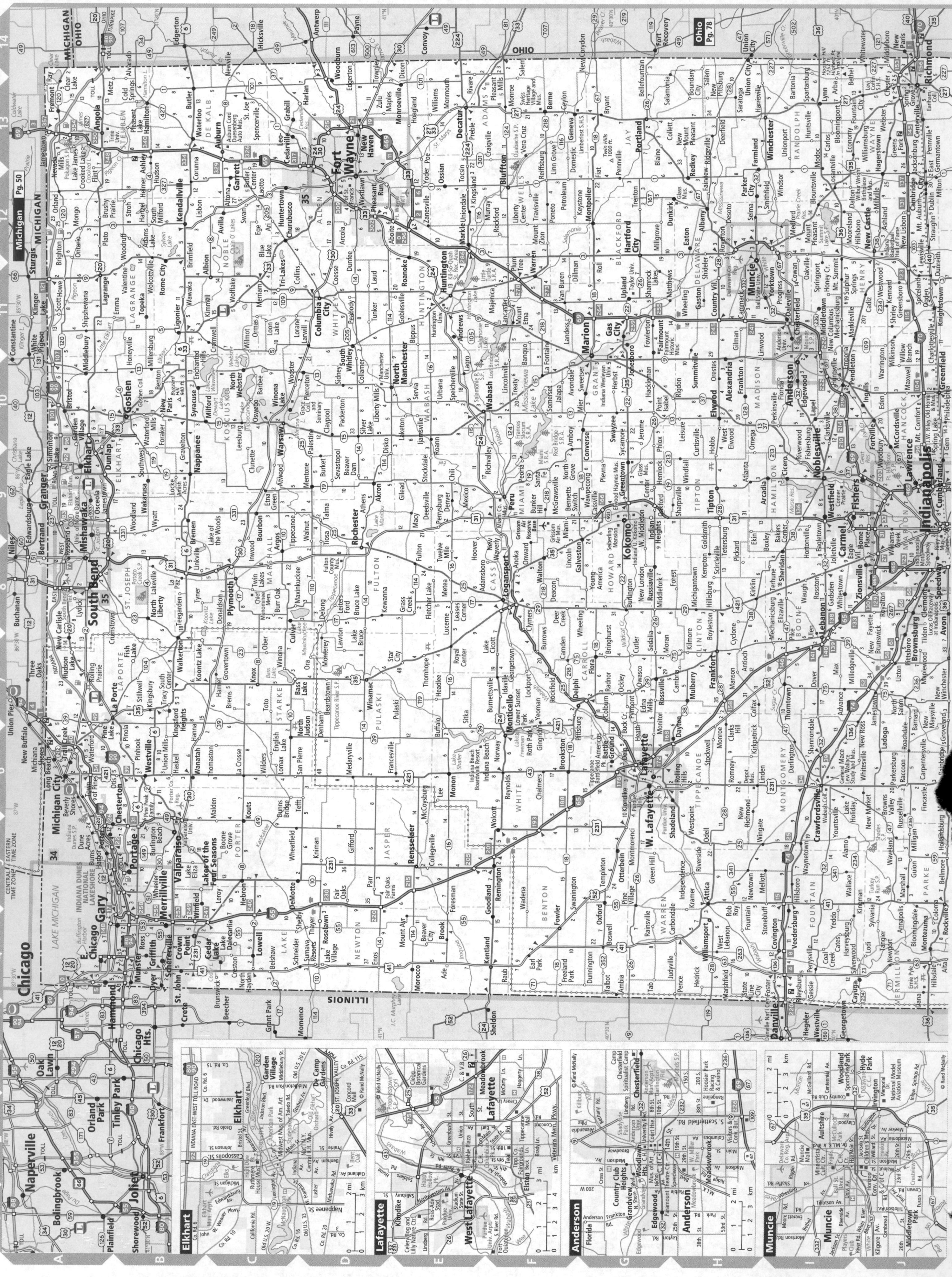

Indiana Dunes National Lakeshore

Mileages between cities	Angola	Bloomington	Chicago, IL	Crawfordsville	Evansville	Fort Wayne	Gary	Greensburg	Indianapolis	Kokomo	Lafayette	Muncie	New Albany	Richmond	South Bend	Terre Haute
Evansville	347	120	289	178		309	273	202	180	234	198	244	112	255	320	109
Fort Wayne	39	178	160	162	309		132	147	129	86	117	72	238	92	89	205
Gary	135	200	30	118	273	132		203	151	127	91	196	266	222	64	164
Indianapolis	166	52	181	49	180	129	151	50		51	63	61	114	73	145	76
New Albany	276	88	296	163	112	238	266	94	114	168	178	172		184	256	146
Richmond	139	123	252	119	255	92	222	62	73	115	134	43	184		202	150
South Bend	77	195	93	135	320	89	64	183	145	87	106	143	256	202		216
Terre Haute	242	58	180	58	109	205	164	123	76	129	89	139	146	150	216	

Total mileages through Indiana

65: 261 miles
74: 172 miles
70: 157 miles
90: 156 miles

More mileages at randmcnally.com/MC

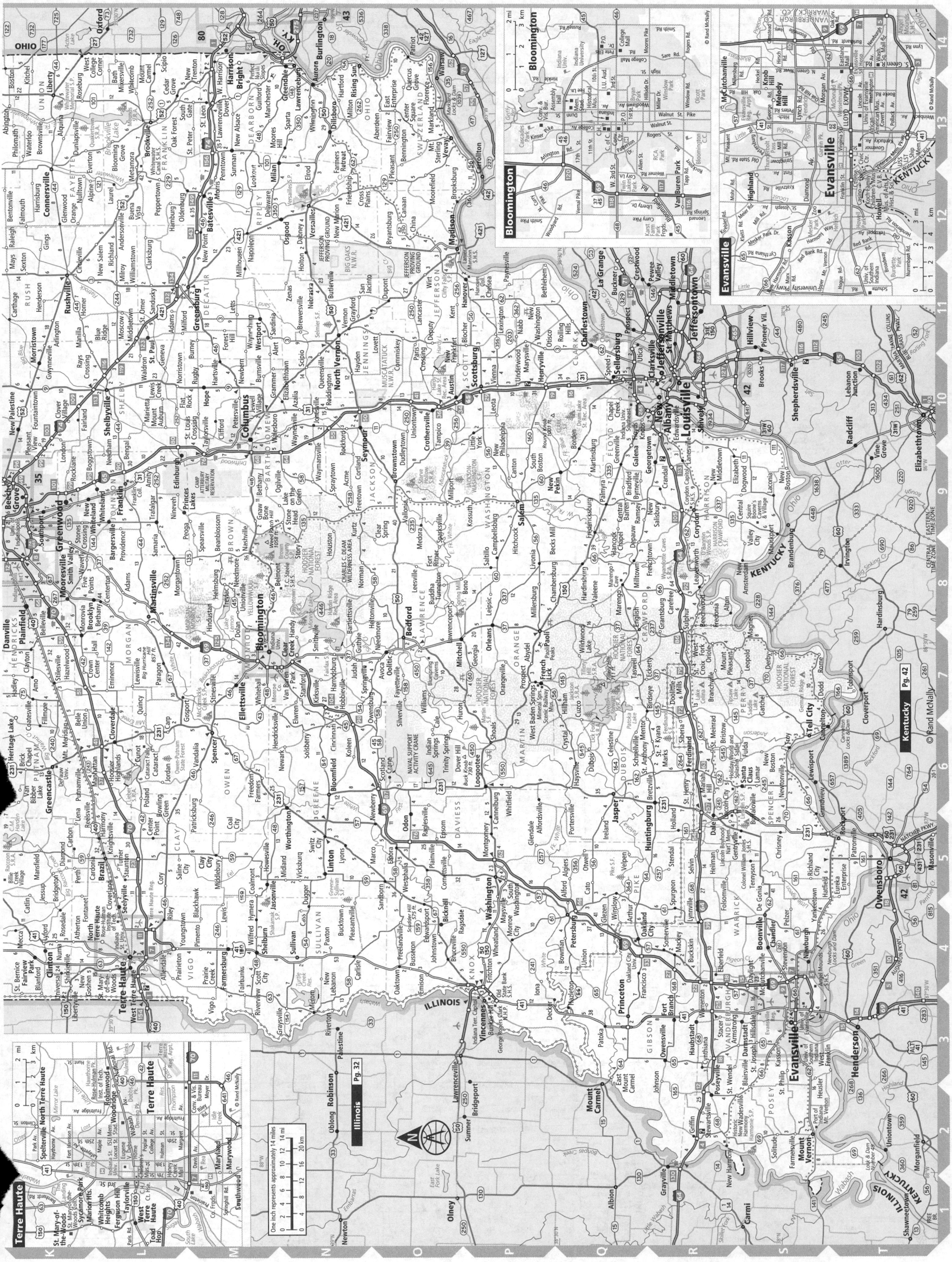

Iowa

Nickname: The Hawkeye State
Capital: Des Moines, I-10
Land area: 55,857 sq. mi. (rank: 23rd)
Population: 3,046,355 (rank: 30th)
Largest city: Des Moines, 203,433, I-10

Index of places Pg. 131

Travel planning & on-the-road resources

Tourism Information
Iowa Tourism Office: (800) 345-4692; www.traveliowa.com

Road Conditions & Construction
511, (800) 288-1047; www.511ia.org, www.iowadot.gov

Toll Road Information
BNSF Railway (Fort Madison Toll Bridge): en.wikipedia.org/wiki/Fort_Madison_Toll_Bridge

Determining distances along roads

Highway distances (segments of one mile or less not shown):
Cumulative miles (red): the distance between red arrows
Intermediate miles (black): the distance between intersections & places

Interchanges and exit numbers
For most states, the mileage between interchanges may be determined by subtracting one number from the other.

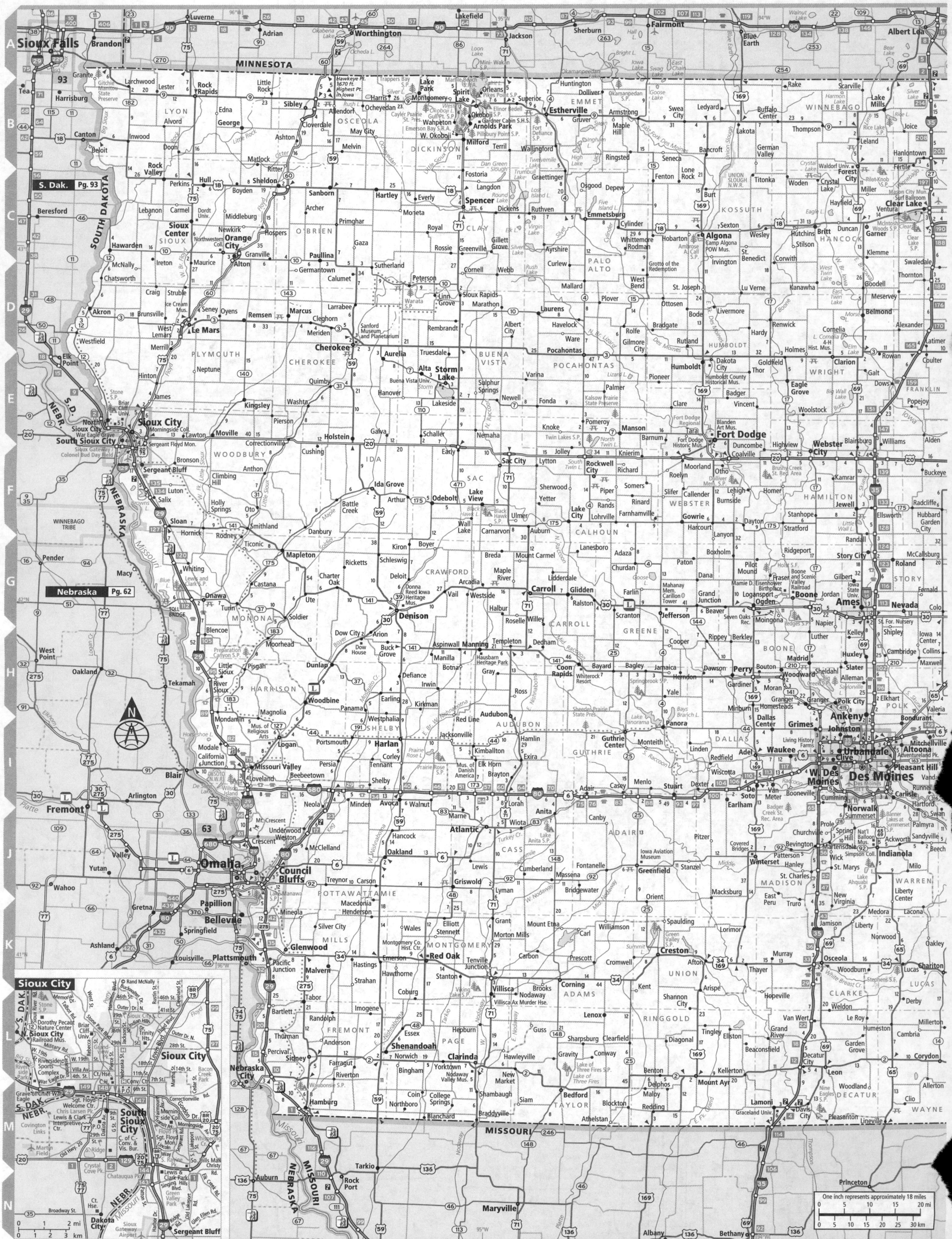

Hogback Covered Bridge, Madison County

Mileages between cities	Ames	Burlington	Cedar Rapids	Council Bluffs	Davenport	Decorah	Des Moines	Dubuque	Iowa City	Mason City	Ottumwa	Sioux City	Sioux Falls, SD	Spirit Lake	Storm Lake	Waterloo
Burlington	209		100	294	77	206	167	150	77	238	78	366	451	355	312	155
Cedar Rapids	108	100		253	82	105	126	70	28	136	110	268	357	252	212	53
Council Bluffs	160	294	253		295	328	127	327	241	246	213	94	180	176	122	253
Davenport	191	77	32	295		167	167	71	57	220	133	366	441	336	294	136
Des Moines	33	167	126	127	167	201		199	114	119	86	198	283	200	154	126
Dubuque	185	150	70	327	71	96	199		84	174	184	305	395	290	249	91
Mason City	91	238	136	246	220	88	119	174	165		203	200	222	118	135	83
Sioux City	175	366	268	94	366	304	198	305	312	200	285		85	109	78	218

Total mileages through Iowa

- 29: 155 miles
- 80: 303 miles
- 35: 218 miles
- 218: 257 miles

More mileages at randmcnally.com/MC

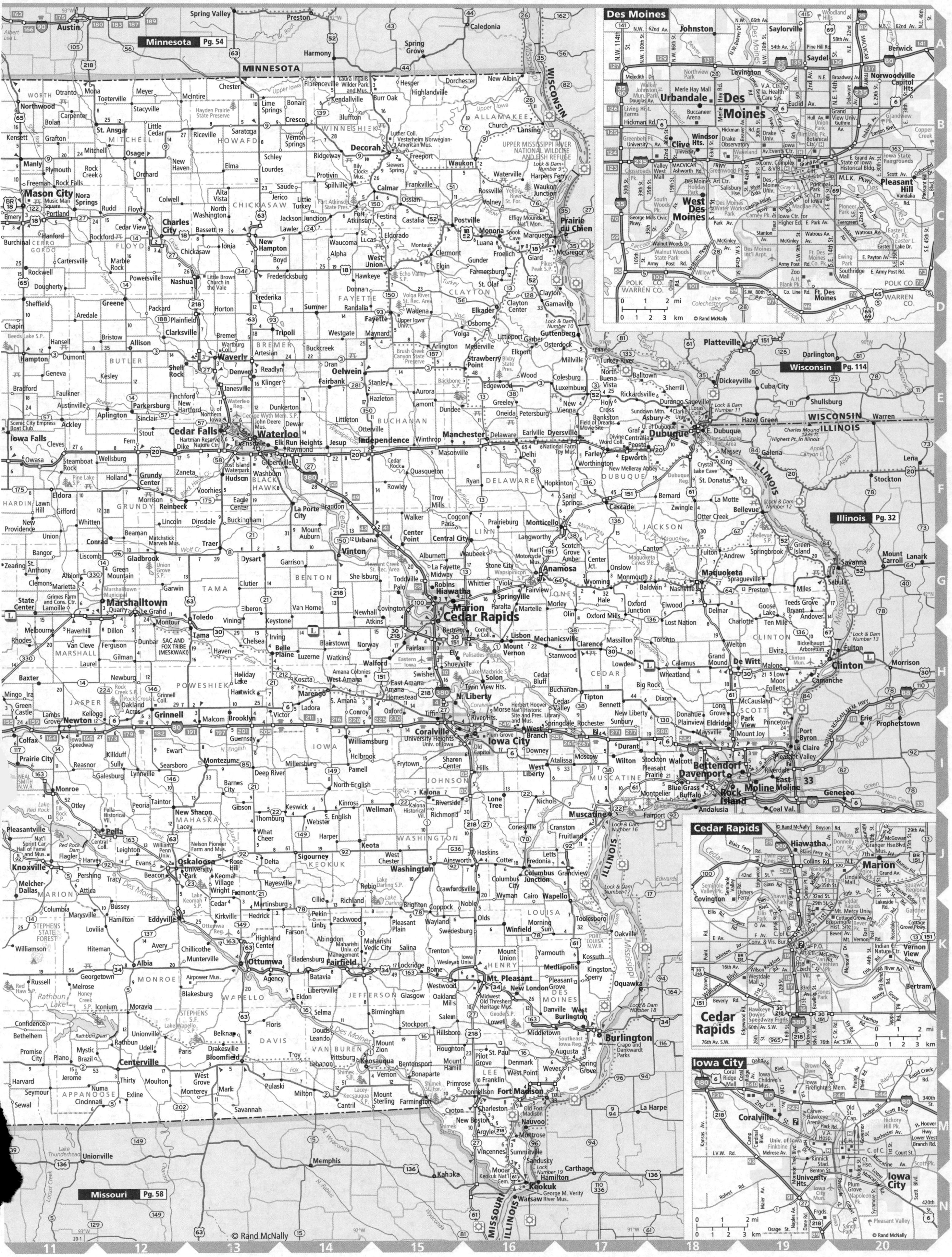

Nickname: The Sunflower State
Capital: Topeka, D-16
Land area: 81,759 sq. mi. (rank: 13th)
Population: 2,853,118 (rank: 33rd)
Largest city: Wichita, 382,368, H-13

Index of places Pg. 131

Travel planning & on-the-road resources

Tourism Information
Kansas Tourism Office: (785) 296-2009; www.travelks.com

Road Conditions & Construction
511, (866) 511-5368; www.kandrive.org, www.ksdot.org

Toll Road Information
Kansas Turnpike Authority *(K-TAG)*: (800) 873-5824, (316) 682-4537; www.ksturnpike.com

Determining distances along roads

Highway distances (segments of one mile or less not shown):
Cumulative miles (red): the distance between red arrows
Intermediate miles (black): the distance between intersections & places

Interchanges and exit numbers
For most states, the mileage between interchanges may be determined by subtracting one number from the other.

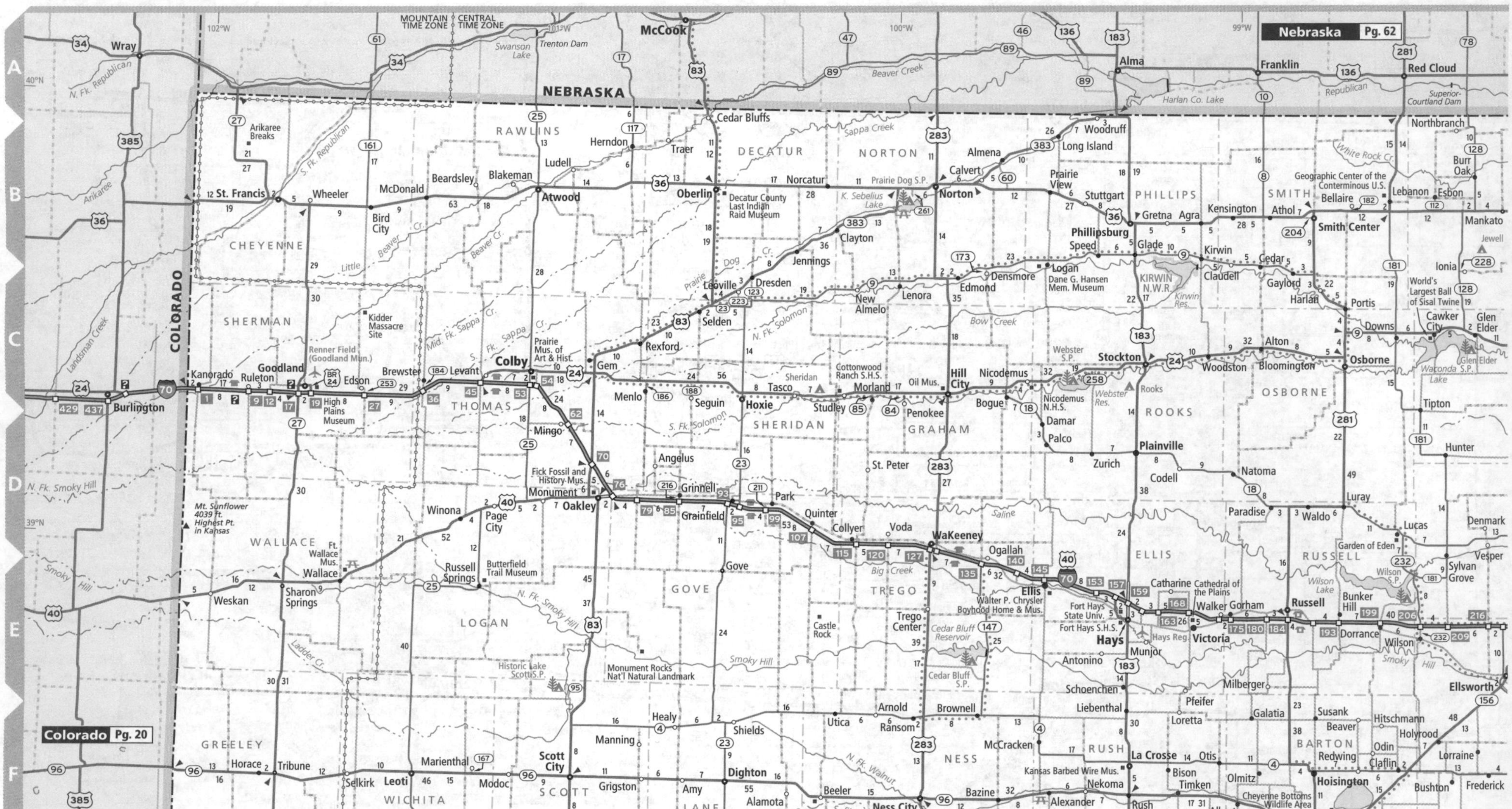

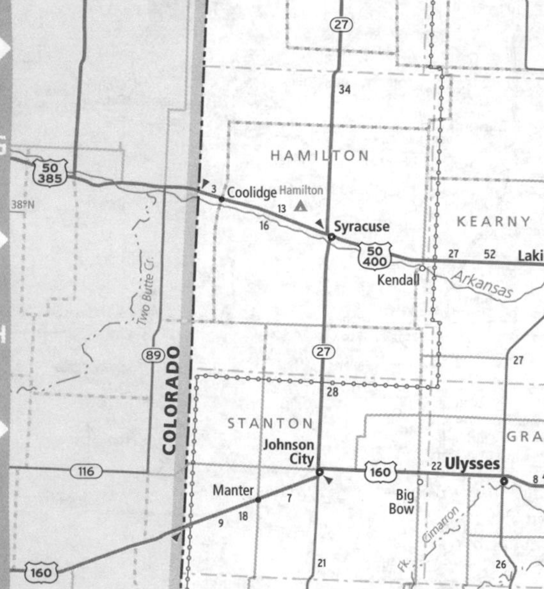

Monument Rocks

Mileages between cities	Arkansas City	Atchison	Coffeyville	Dodge City	Emporia	Fort Scott	Goodland	Hays	Hutchinson	Joplin, MO	Kansas City	Liberal	Manhattan	Salina	Topeka	Wichita
Dodge City	212	323	288		240	304	192	104	122	337	333	82	227	164	273	154
Goodland	384	395	455	192	349	472		144	268	505	406	209	299	235	344	323
Joplin, MO	150	196	65	337	177	60	505	366	233		154	395	252	274	196	183
Kansas City	228	58	172	333	109	94	406	266	220	154		406	117	173	62	196
Salina	151	160	224	164	117	238	235	96	65	274	173	246	65		109	90
Smith Center	266	213	338	195	231	342	175	91	155	387	263	277	150	117	206	205
Topeka	170	55	155	273	58	136	344	204	162	196	62	349	56	109		137
Wichita	61	188	134	154	85	149	323	183	51	183	196	212	130	90	137	

Total mileages through Kansas

- 35: 235 miles
- 56: 464 miles
- 70: 424 miles
- 81: 220 miles

More mileages at randmcnally.com/MC

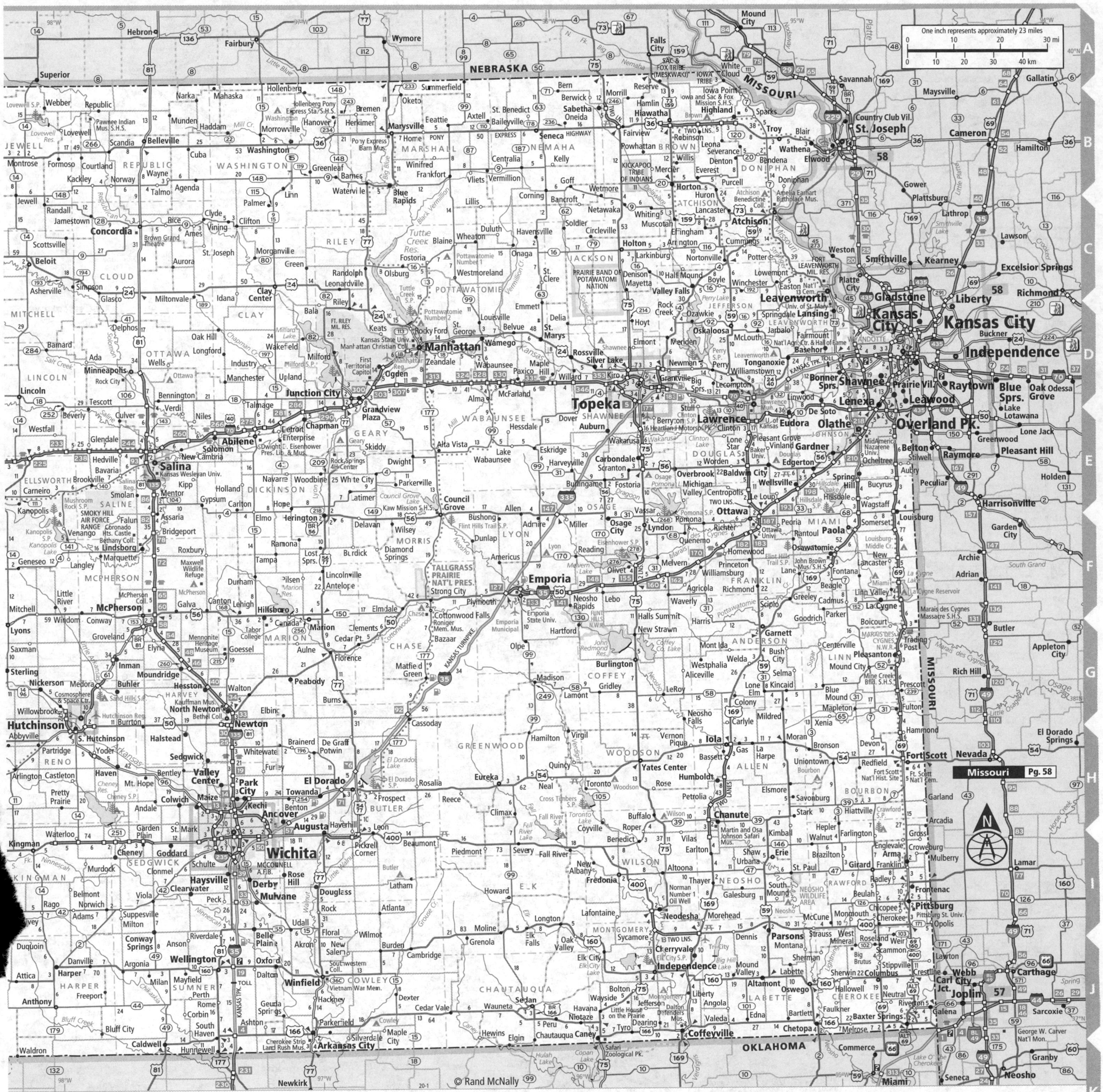

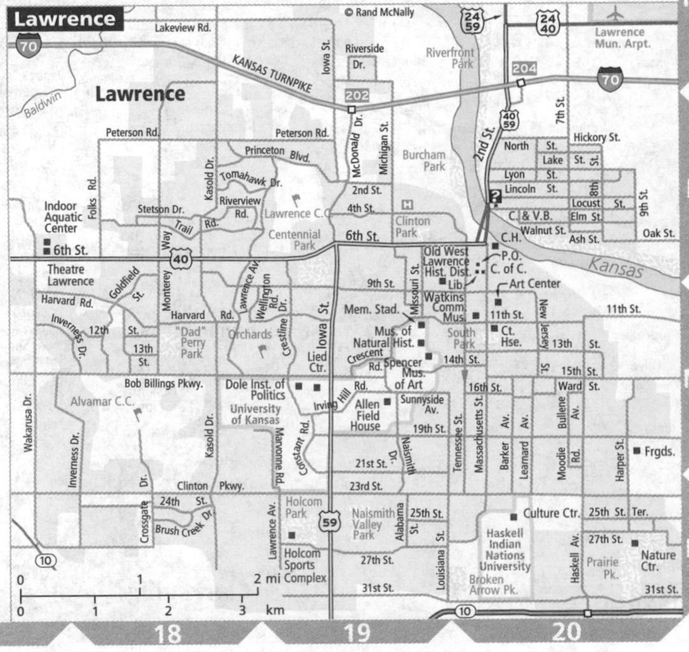

Nickname: The Bluegrass State
Capital: Frankfort, G-11
Land area: 39,486 sq. mi. (rank: 37th)
Population: 4,339,367 (rank: 26th)
Largest city: Louisville, 597,337, G-8

Index of places Pg. 131

Travel planning & on-the-road resources

Tourism Information
Kentucky Department of Tourism: (800) 225-8747, (502) 564-4930; www.kentuckytourism.com

Road Conditions & Construction
511, (866) 737-3767; drive.ky.gov, transportation.ky.gov

Toll Road Information
RiverLink (Louisville area toll bridges) ***(RiverLink or E-ZPass)***: (855) 748-5465; www.riverlink.com

Determining distances along roads

Highway distances (segments of one mile or less not shown):
Cumulative miles (red): the distance between red arrows
Intermediate miles (black): the distance between intersections & places

Interchanges and exit numbers
For most states, the mileage between interchanges may be determined by subtracting one number from the other.

Churchill Downs, Louisville

Mileages between cities	Ashland	Bowling Green	Cave City	Covington	Elizabethtown	Frankfort	Hopkinsville	Lexington	Louisville	Mayfield	Maysville	Middlesboro	Owensboro	Paducah	Pikeville	Somerset
Ashland		269	242	138	202	140	325	117	187	383	76	227	294	372	96	175
Bowling Green	269		31	209	70	147	64	151	113	160	216	198	71	151	265	109
Covington	138	209	181		140	78	265	81	97	322	59	208	203	312	216	157
Lexington	117	151	124	81	84	29	207		76	266	63	130	177	256	140	78
Louisville	187	113	85	97	44	50	170	76		227	133	203	106	216	211	124
Middlesboro	227	198	175	208	182	157	265	130	203	363	191		275	353	125	88
Owensboro	294	71	108	203	94	159	96	177	106	154	242	275		143	318	187
Paducah	372	151	186	312	172	250	72	256	216	24	319	353	143		396	265

Mileages © Rand McNally

Total mileages through Kentucky

64: 191 miles
71: 97 miles
65: 137 miles
75: 192 miles

More mileages at randmcnally.com/MC

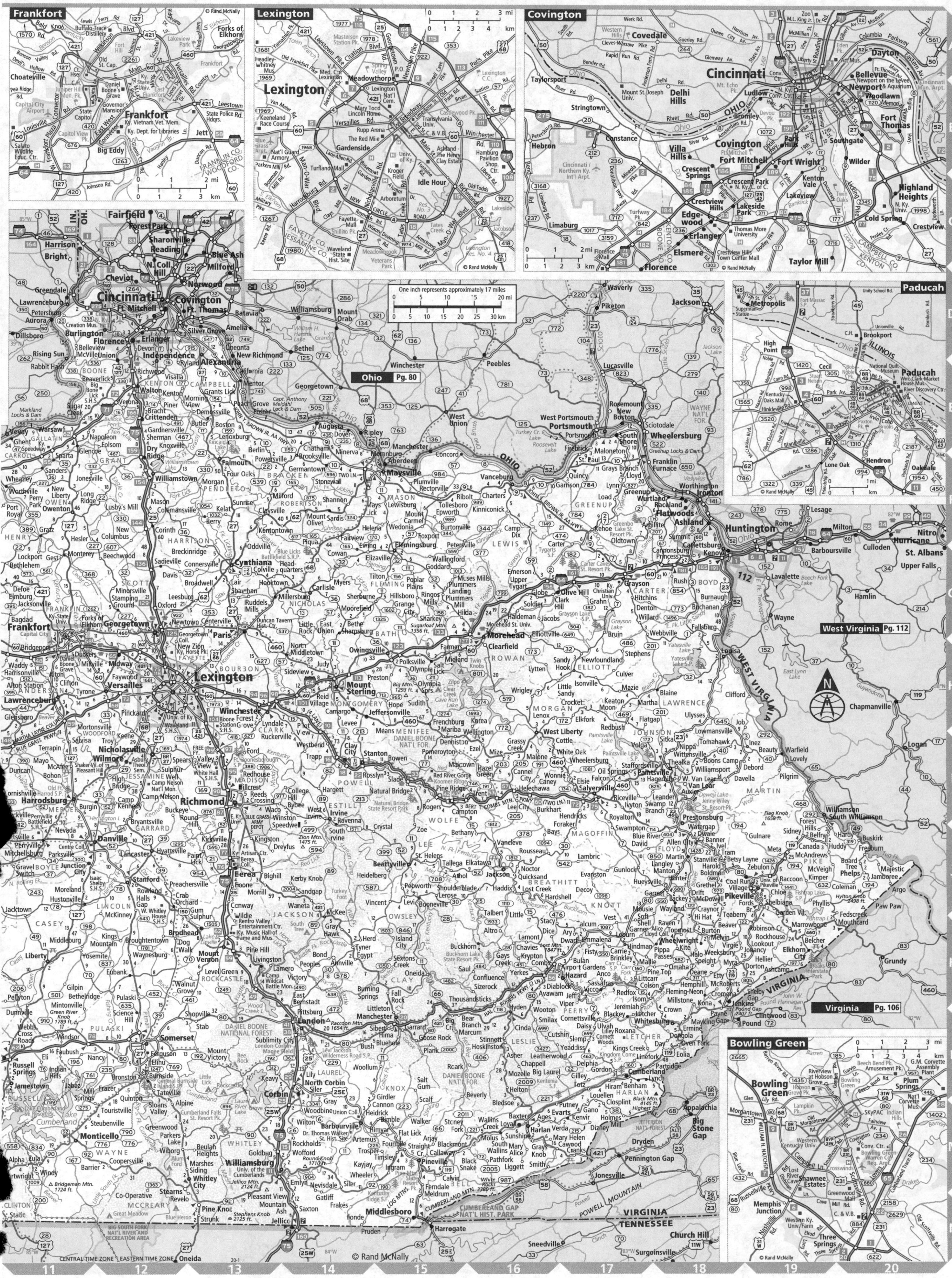

Louisiana

Nickname: The Pelican State
Capital: Baton Rouge, G-7
Land area: 43,204 sq. mi. (rank: 33rd)
Population: 4,533,372 (rank: 25th)
Largest city: New Orleans, 343,829, H-9

Index of places Pg. 131

Mileages between cities

	Baton Rouge	Beaumont, TX	Houma	Lake Charles	Monroe	New Orleans	Shreveport	Vicksburg, MS
Alexandria	125	155	190	97	95	218	123	147
Baton Rouge		183	85	124	186	79	250	157
Gulfport, MS	134	318	131	258	276	78	375	201
Lafayette	55	133	102	73	182	134	211	212
Lake Charles	124	60	177		190	203	184	243
New Orleans	79	262	56	203	281		340	207
Shreveport	250	206	314	184	98	340		171
Vicksburg, MS	157	301	234	243	74	207	171	

Mileages © Rand McNally

Total mileages through Louisiana

10: 274 miles
49: 208 miles
20: 190 miles
55: 66 miles

More mileages at randmcnally.com/MC

Travel planning & on-the-road resources

Tourism Information
Louisiana Office of Tourism: (800) 677-4082, (225) 635-0090; www.louisianatravel.com

Road Conditions & Construction
511, (888) 762-3511; www.511la.org, www.dotd.la.gov

Toll Bridges
Louisiana Dept. of Trans. & Development (La. Hwy. 1 Bridge) *(GeauxPass)*: (866) 662-8987; www.geauxpass.com
Lake Ponchartrain Causeway *(TollTag)*: (504) 835-3118; www.thecauseway.us

Travel planning & on-the-road resources

Tourism Information
Maine Office of Tourism:
(888) 624-6345
(207) 624-7483
visitmaine.com

Toll Road Information
Maine Turnpike Authority
(E-ZPass): (877) 682-9433
(207) 871-7771
www.maineturnpike.com

Road Conditions & Construction
511, (207) 624-3000; newengland511.org
www.maine.gov/mdot

Determining Distances
(segments of one mile or less not shown)
Cumulative miles (red): the distance between red arrows
Intermediate miles (black): the distance between intersections & places

Total mileages through Maine
95: 299 miles
2: 273 miles
1: 527 miles
201: 164 miles

More mileages at randmcnally.com/MC

Mileages between cities	Auburn	Bangor	Bar Harbor	Eastport	Houlton	Millinocket	Portland	Rangeley
Bangor	107		47	120	118	72	128	120
Eastport	226	120	118		115	125	247	242
Houlton	225	118	167	115		69	246	238
Madawaska	326	219	267	218	102	170	347	339
Portland	35	128	174	247	246	181		118
Portsmouth, NH	81	180	225	301	298	231	51	165
Rangeley	84	120	165	242	238	153	118	
Waterville	53	55	101	174	173	107	75	77

Mileages © Rand McNally

Nickname: The Pine Tree State
Capital: Augusta, F-4
Land area: 30,843 sq. mi. (rank: 39th)
Population: 1,328,361 (rank: 41st)
Largest city: Portland, 66,194, H-3

Index of places Pg. 131

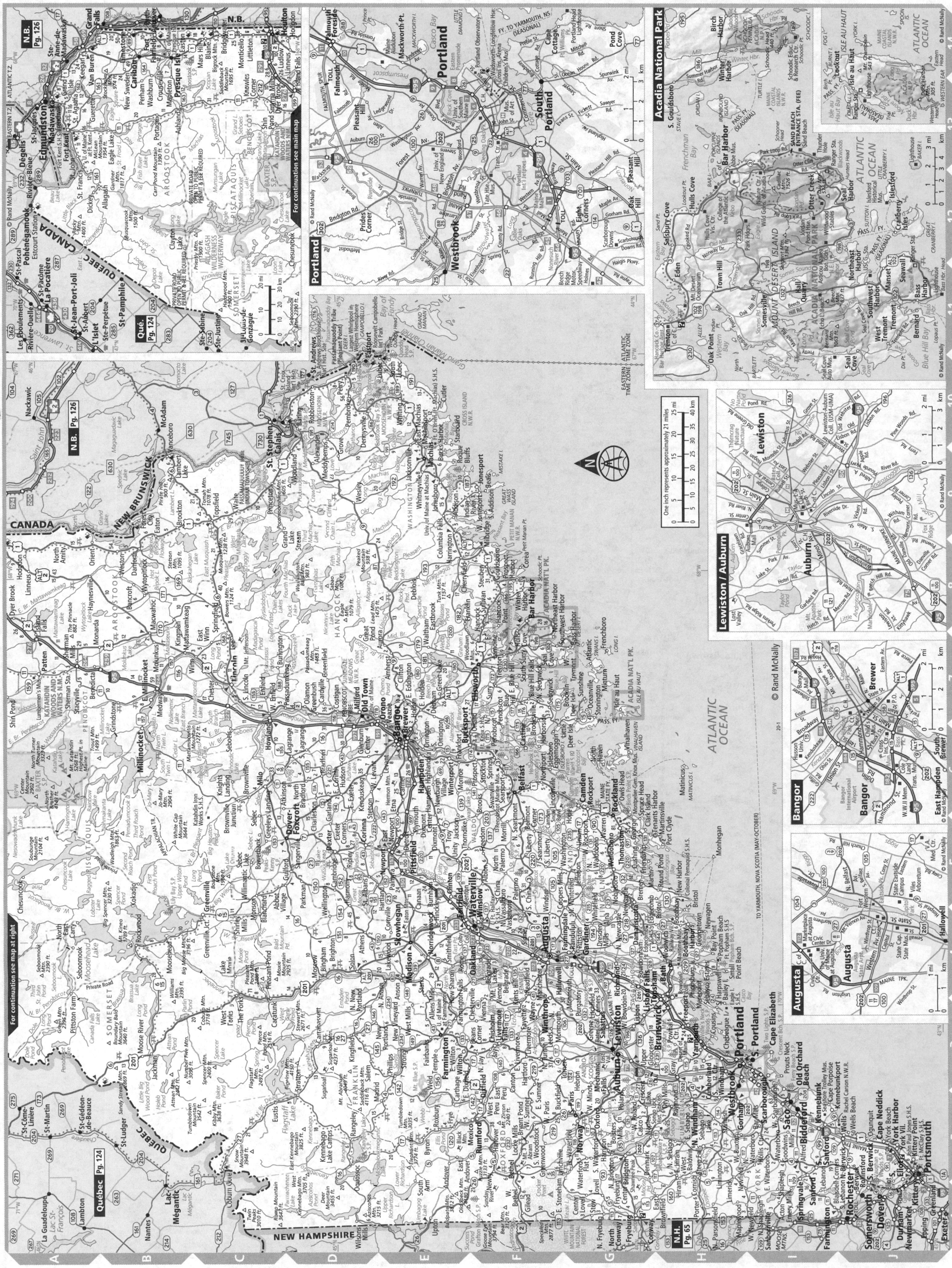

Maryland

Nickname: The Old Line State
Capital: Annapolis, E-14
Land area: 9,707 sq. mi. (rank: 42nd)
Population: 5,773,552 (rank: 19th)
Largest city: Baltimore, 620,961, C-13

Index of places Pg. 131

Travel planning & on-the-road resources

Tourism Information
Maryland Office of Tourism Development: (866) 639-3526; visitmaryland.org

Road Conditions & Construction
511, (855) 466-3511, (410) 582-5650; www.md511.org, www.roads.maryland.gov

Toll Road Information
Maryland Transportation Authority (*E-ZPass*): (866) 713-1596, In Maryland: (410) 537-1000; www.mdta.maryland.gov

Determining distances along roads

Highway distances (segments of one mile or less not shown):
Cumulative miles (red): the distance between red arrows
Intermediate miles (black): the distance between intersections & places

Interchanges and exit numbers
For most states, the mileage between interchanges may be determined by subtracting one number from the other.

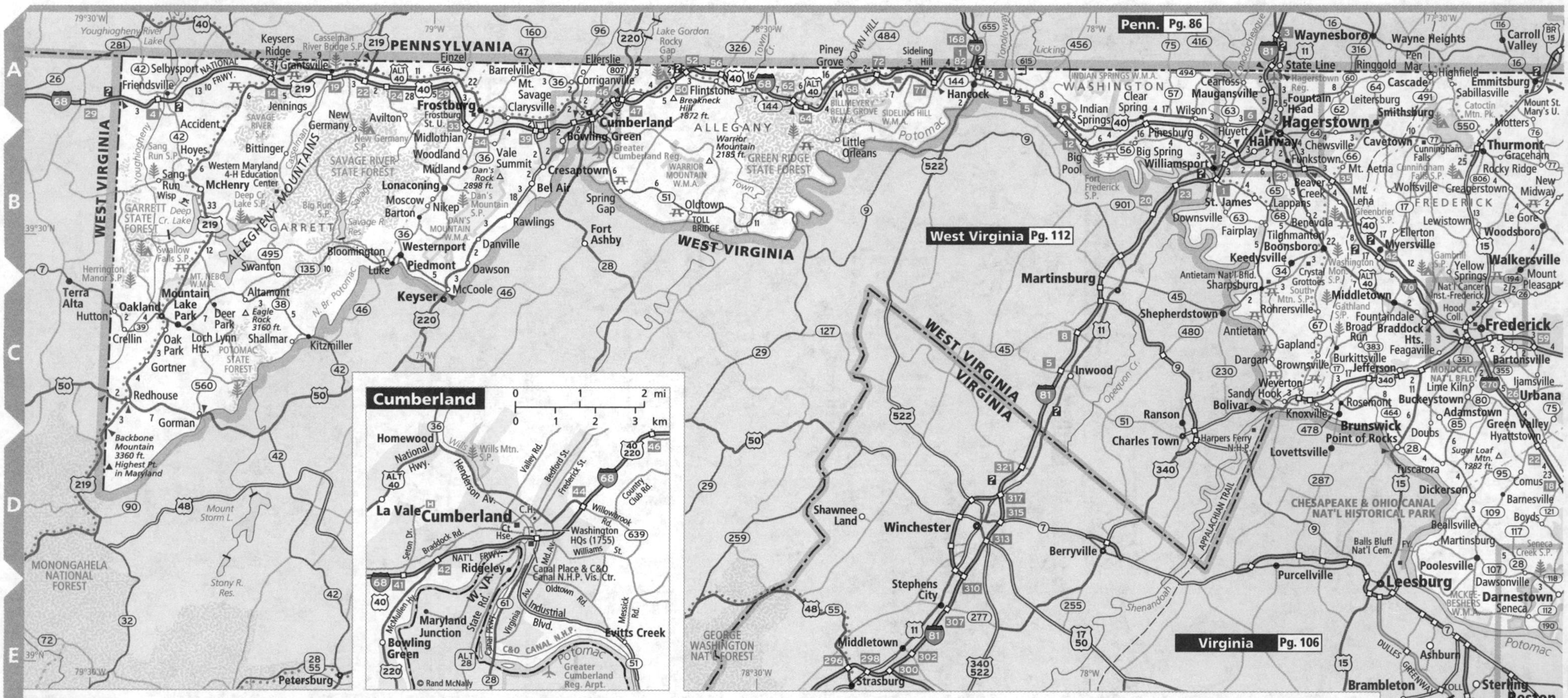

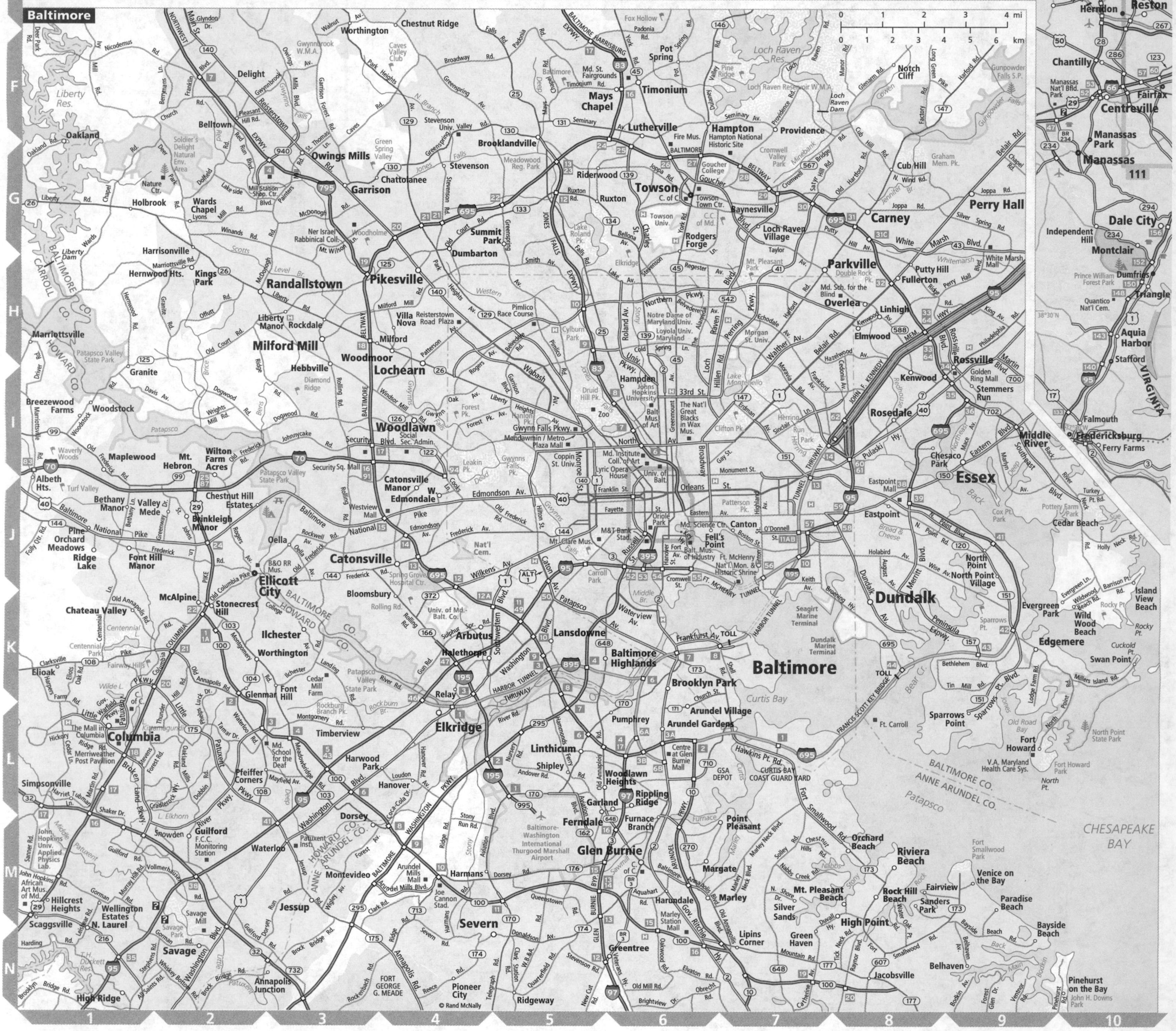

Wild horses at Assateague Island National Seashore

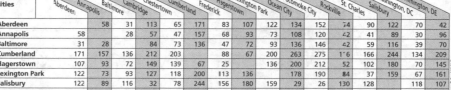

Mileages between cities	Aberdeen	Annapolis	Baltimore	Cambridge	Chestertown	Cumberland	Frederick	Hagerstown	Lexington Park	Ocean City	Pocomoke City	Rockville	St. Charles	Salisbury	Washington, DC	Wilmington, DE
Aberdeen		58	31	113	65	171	83	107	122	134	152	74	90	122	70	42
Annapolis	58		28	57	47	157	68	93	73	108	120	42	41	89	30	96
Baltimore	31	28		84	73	136	47	72	93	136	146	42	59	116	39	70
Cumberland	171	157	136	212	203		88	67	200	263	275	116	166	244	134	209
Hagerstown	107	93	72	149	139	67	25		136	200	212	52	102	180	70	145
Lexington Park	122	73	93	127	118	200	113	136		178	190	84	37	159	67	161
Salisbury	122	89	116	32	78	244	156	180	159	29	26	130	128		118	107
Washington, DC	70	30	39	86	76	134	48	70	67	139	148	19	30	118		109

Total mileages through Maryland

- I-68: 81 miles
- I-81: 12 miles
- I-70: 94 miles
- I-95: 110 miles

More mileages at randmcnally.com/MC

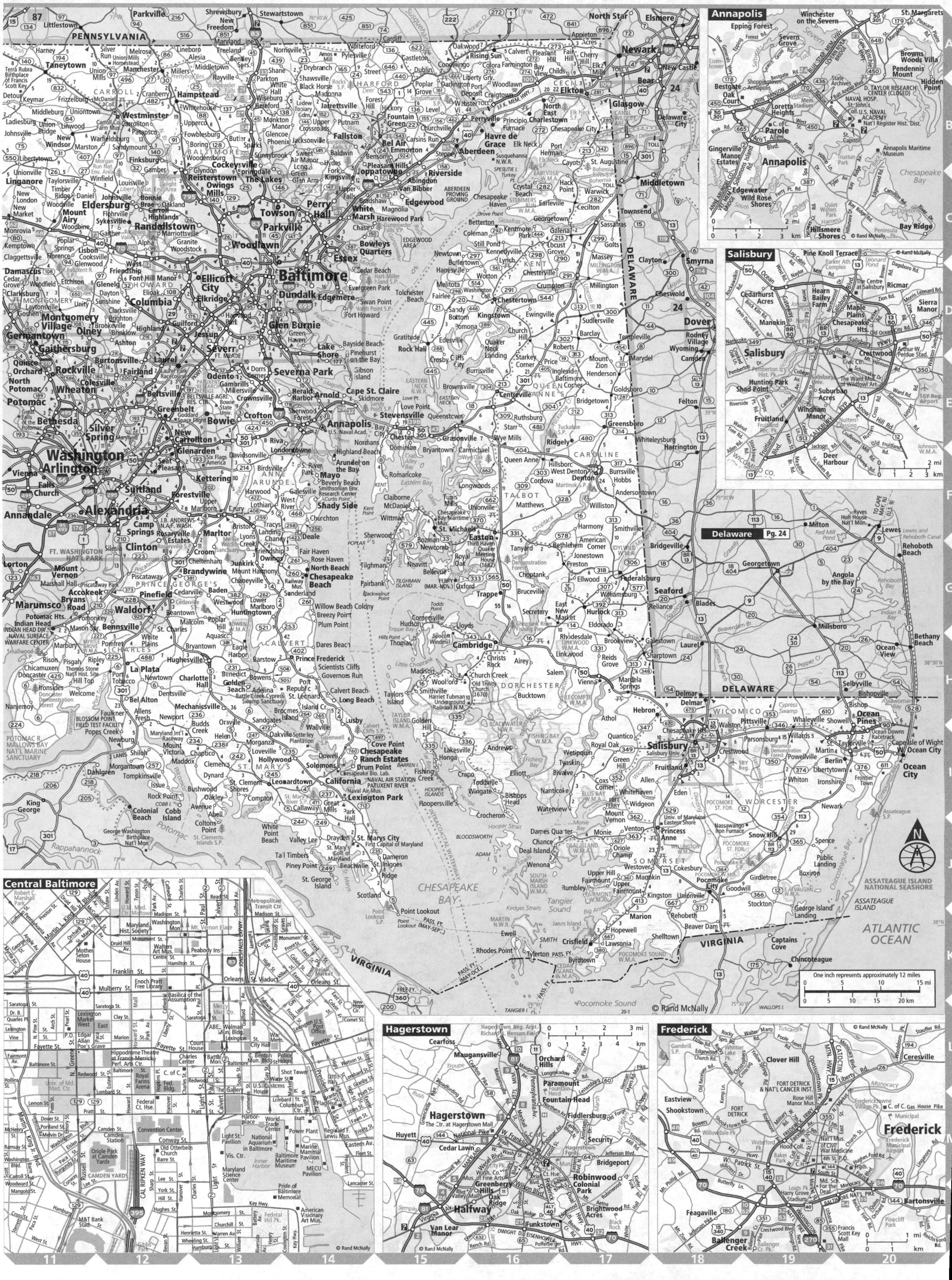

Massachusetts

Nickname: The Bay State
Capital: Boston, E-14
Land area: 7,800 sq. mi. (rank: 45th)
Population: 6,547,629 (rank: 14th)
Largest city: Boston, 617,594, E-14

Index of places Pg. 131

Travel planning & on-the-road resources

Tourism Information
Massachusetts Office of Travel & Tourism: (800) 227-6277, (617) 973-8500 www.massvacation.com

Road Conditions & Construction
511, Metro Boston: (617) 986-5511, Central: (508) 499-5511, Western: (413) 754-5511
www.mass511.com

Toll Road Information
Massachusetts Department of Transportation (*E-ZPass*): (877) 627-7745; www.mass.gov/ezdrivema

Determining distances along roads

Highway distances (segments of one mile or less not shown):
Cumulative miles (red): the distance between red arrows
Intermediate miles (black): the distance between intersections & places

Interchanges and exit numbers
For most states, the mileage between interchanges may be determined by subtracting one number from the other.

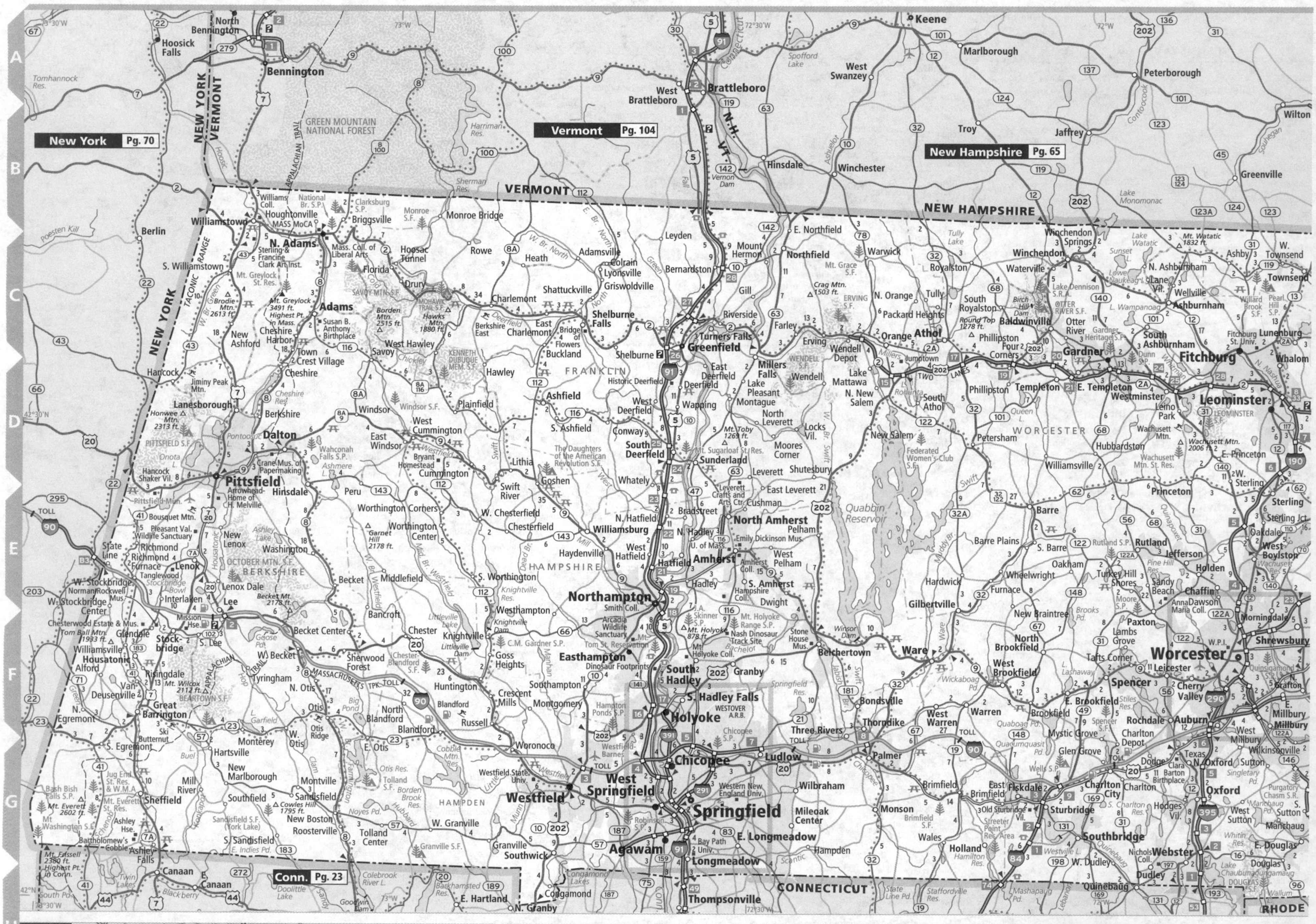

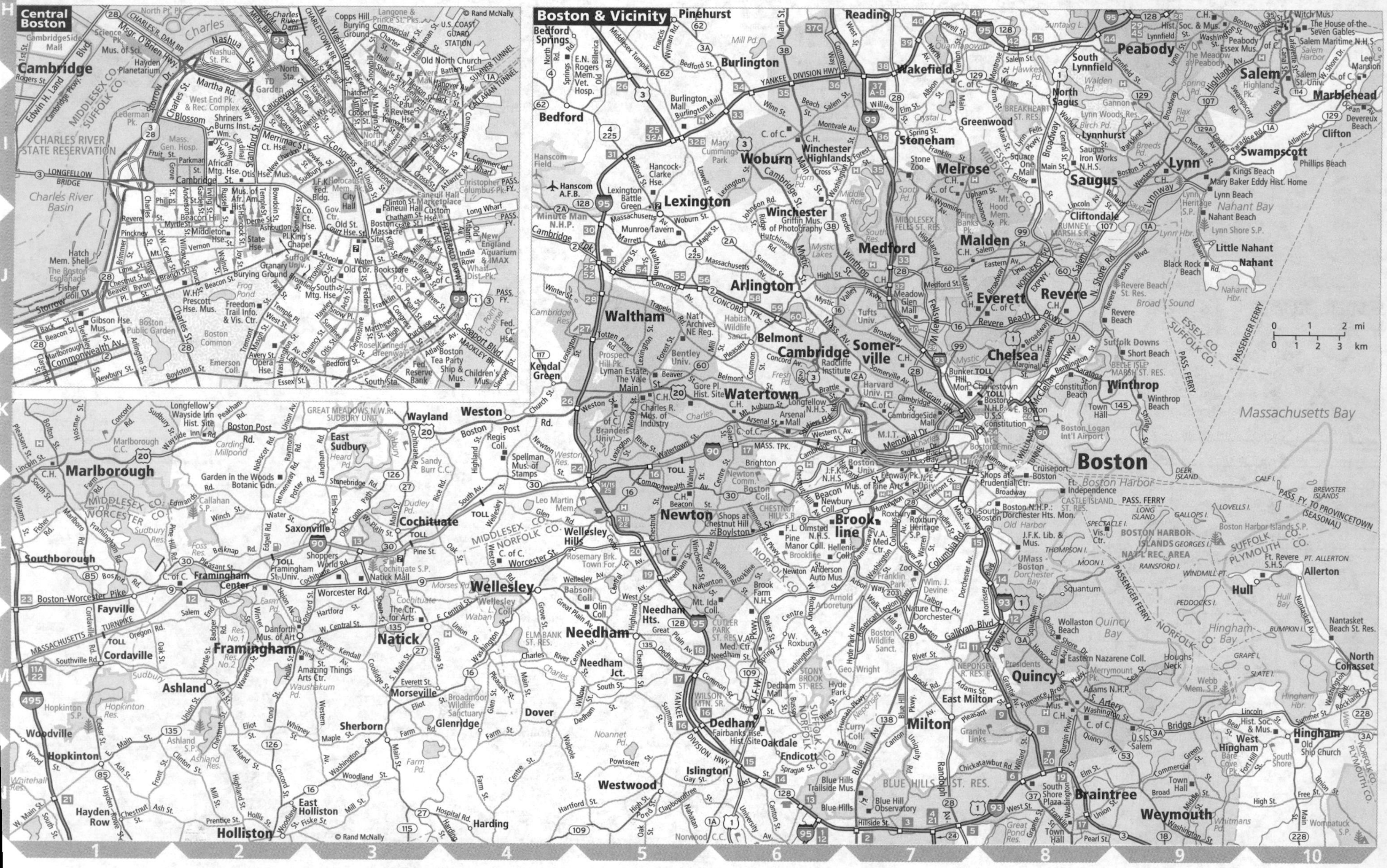

Faneuil Hall, Boston

Mileages between cities *Via ferry

	Boston	Brockton	Falmouth	Fitchburg	Gloucester	Greenfield	Lowell	Nantucket	New Bedford	North Adams	Pittsfield	Plymouth	Providence, RI	Provincetown	Springfield	Worcester
Boston		24	76	47	39	94	29	101*	58	157	136	40	50	116	90	43
Gloucester	39	63	114	74		120	47	140*	97	157	169	73	90	154	122	75
Lowell	29	50	102	32	47	78		130*	84	115	139	63	69	145	92	41
New Bedford	58	37	40	94	97	148	84	77*		182	161	37	31	91	114	71
Pittsfield	136	150	189	124	169	79	139	226*	161	22		167	130	240	51	98
Provincetown	116	106	69	162	154	208	145	78*	91	262	240	77	119		194	146
Springfield	90	103	143	77	122	38	92	180*	114	73	51	121	83	194		51
Worcester	43	56	96	26	75	72	41	133*	71	120	98	74	40	146	51	

Total mileages through Massachusetts

- 90: 136 miles
- 91: 55 miles
- 93: 47 miles
- 95: 92 miles

More mileages at randmcnally.com/MC

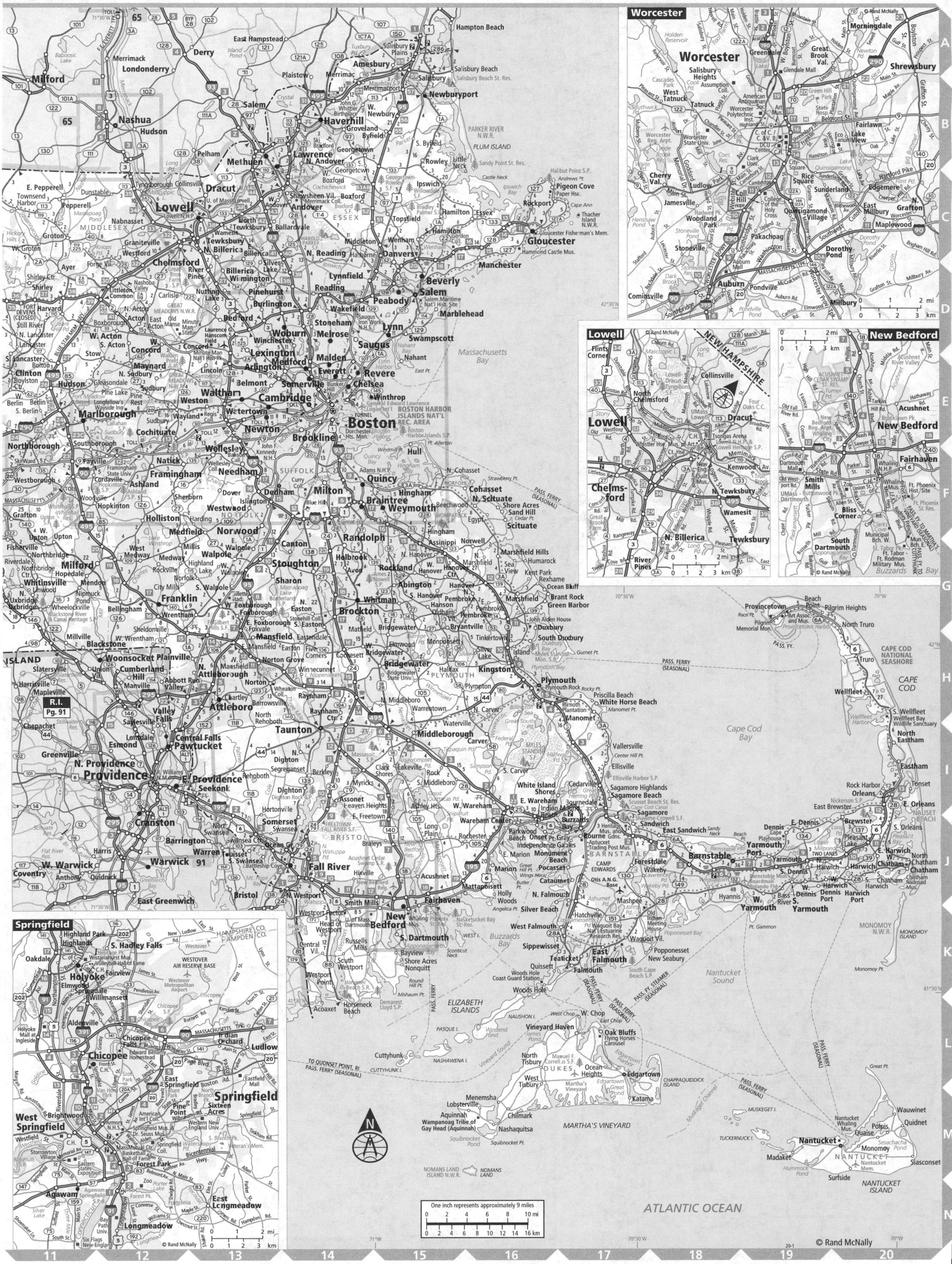

Michigan

Nickname: The Great Lake State
Capital: Lansing, Q-9
Land area: 56,539 sq. mi. (rank: 22nd)
Population: 9,883,640 (rank: 8th)
Largest city: Detroit, 713,777, R-12

Index of places Pg. 131

Travel planning & on-the-road resources

Tourism Information
Pure Michigan:
(888) 784-7328; www.michigan.org

Road Conditions & Construction
(517) 373-2090
www.michigan.gov/drive, www.michigan.gov/mdot

International Toll Bridge/Tunnel Information
Michigan Department of Transportation: Blue Water Bridge (Port Huron): (810) 984-3131; www.michigan.gov/mdot
Ambassador Bridge (Detroit): (800) 462-7434; www.ambassadorbridge.com
Detroit-Windsor Tunnel (*NEXPRESS*): (313) 567-4422 ext. 200, (519) 258-7424; www.dwtunnel.com
International Bridge Administration (Sault Ste. Marie): (906) 635-5255, (705) 942-4345; www.saultbridge.com

Michigan Toll Bridge/Tunnel Information
Mackinac Bridge Authority (*Mac Pass*): (906) 643-7600; www.mackinacbridge.org

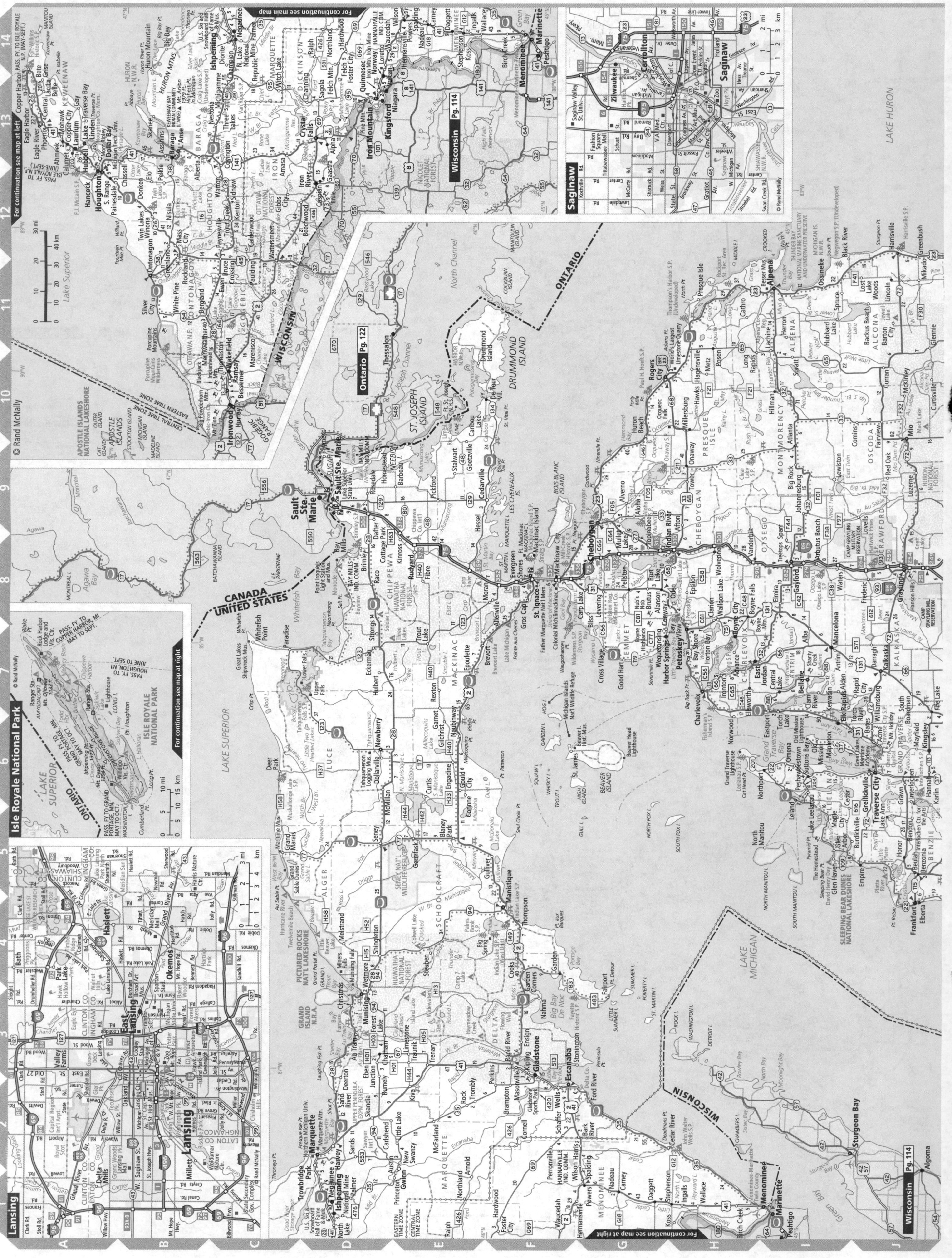

Eagle Harbor Lighthouse, Keweenaw Peninsula

Mileages between cities	Alpena	Chicago, IL	Detroit	Grand Rapids	Houghton	Ironwood	Kalamazoo	Ludington	Mackinaw City	Menominee	Muskegon	Port Huron	Saginaw	Sault Ste. Marie	Toledo, OH	Traverse City
Ann Arbor	227	240	43	132	538	584	98	228	272	473	172	102	86	329	51	238
Detroit	244	280		157	553	599	140	252	290	488	197	62	102	345	59	255
Flint	178	271	68	113	489	534	130	186	224	423	152	66	37	280	107	188
Grand Rapids	249	177	157		502	552	50	97	236	438	41	180	115	292	185	140
Ironwood	405	403	599	552	109		544	319	311	195	586	600	499	307	636	413
Kalamazoo	298	145	140	50	556	544		146	287	408	91	197	161	344	150	190
Lansing	228	216	90	68	494	539	75	162	228	429	107	122	88	284	118	180
Mackinaw City	94	412	290	236	266	311	287	218		200	251	250	188	56	327	102

Mileages © Rand McNally

Total mileages through Michigan

- 69: 199 miles
- 75: 396 miles
- 94: 275 miles
- 96: 192 miles

More mileages at randmcnally.com/MC

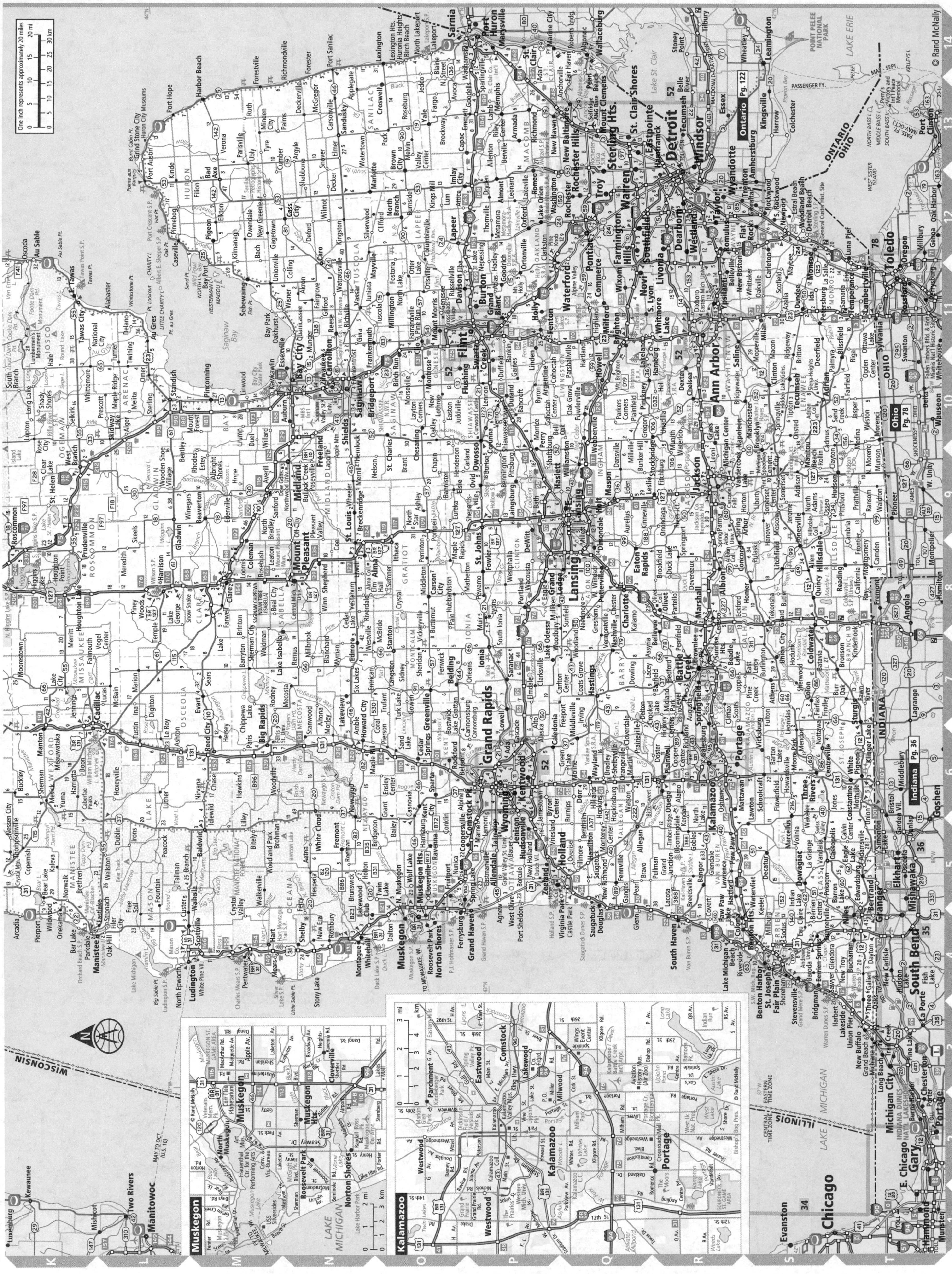

Detroit Institute of Art

Sights to see

- Cranbrook Art Museum, Bloomfield Hills D-5
- Detroit Zoo, Royal Oak E-6
- Edsel & Eleanor Ford House, Grosse Pointe Shores E-9
- Frederik Meijer Gardens, Grand Rapids. L-6
- Gerald R. Ford Museum, Grand Rapids L-5
- Gerald R. Ford Presidential Library, Ann Arbor M-10
- GM Renaissance Center, Detroit. K-10
- Henry Ford Mus. of American Innovation, Dearborn . . H-5
- Motown Historical Museum, Detroit G-6
- New Detroit Science Center, Detroit G-7
- Sloan Museum, Flint L-2
- University of Michigan, Ann Arbor M-9

Walker Art Center, Minneapolis

Sights to see

- Bell Museum of Natural History, Minneapolis F-6
- Cathedral of St. Paul, St. Paul. M-7
- Frederick R. Weisman Art Museum, Minneapolis. M-4
- Mall of America, Bloomington. I-5
- Mill City Museum, Minneapolis L-3
- Minneapolis Institute of the Arts, Minneapolis N-2
- Minneapolis Sculpture Garden, Minneapolis M-1
- Minnesota History Center, Minneapolis M-7
- Minnesota State Capitol, St. Paul. L-7
- Ordway Center for the Performing Arts, St. Paul. M-7
- Science Museum of Minnesota, St. Paul M-7
- Walker Art Center, Minneapolis M-1

Minneapolis / St. Paul & Vicinity

Central Minneapolis

Central St. Paul

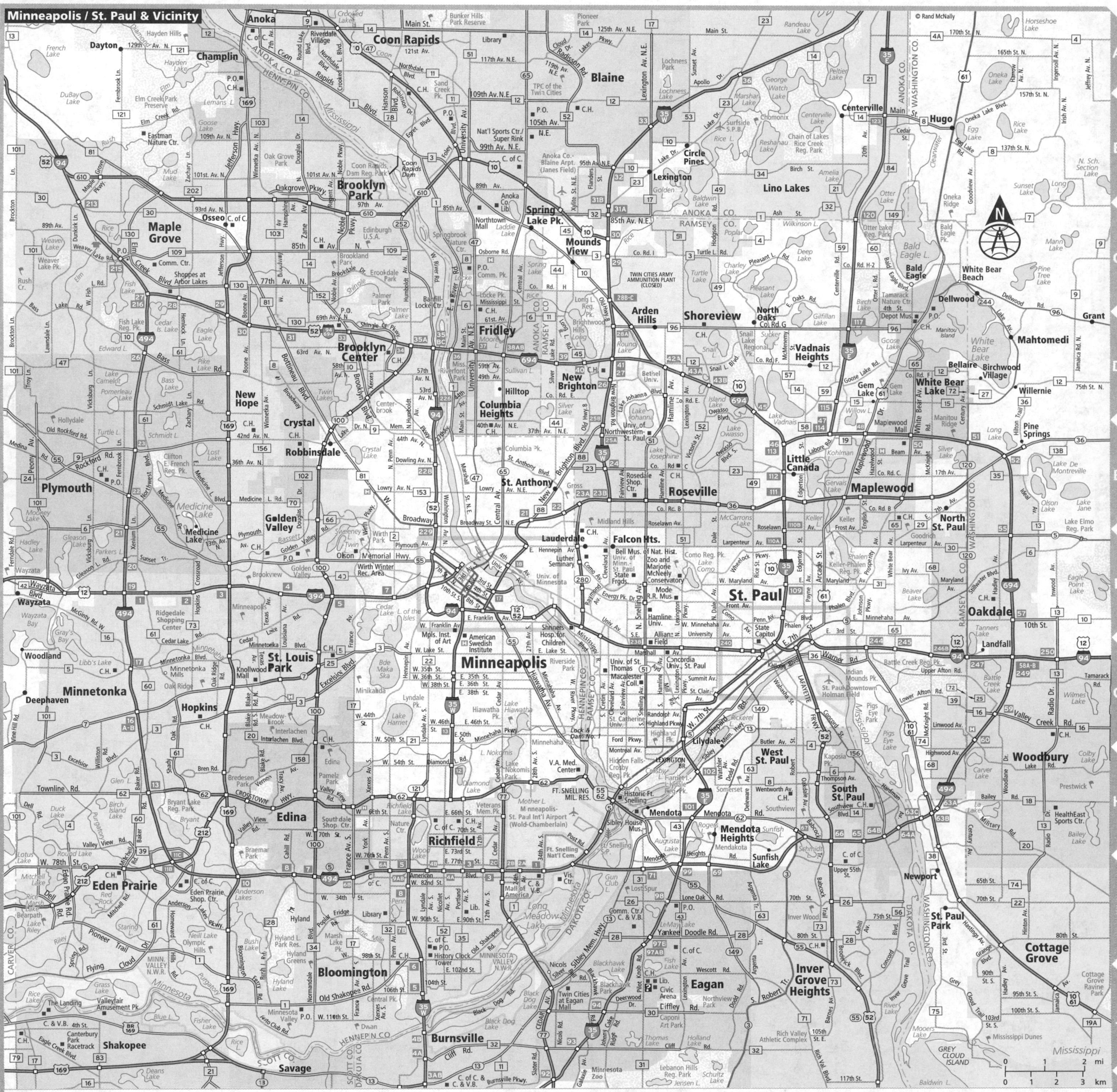

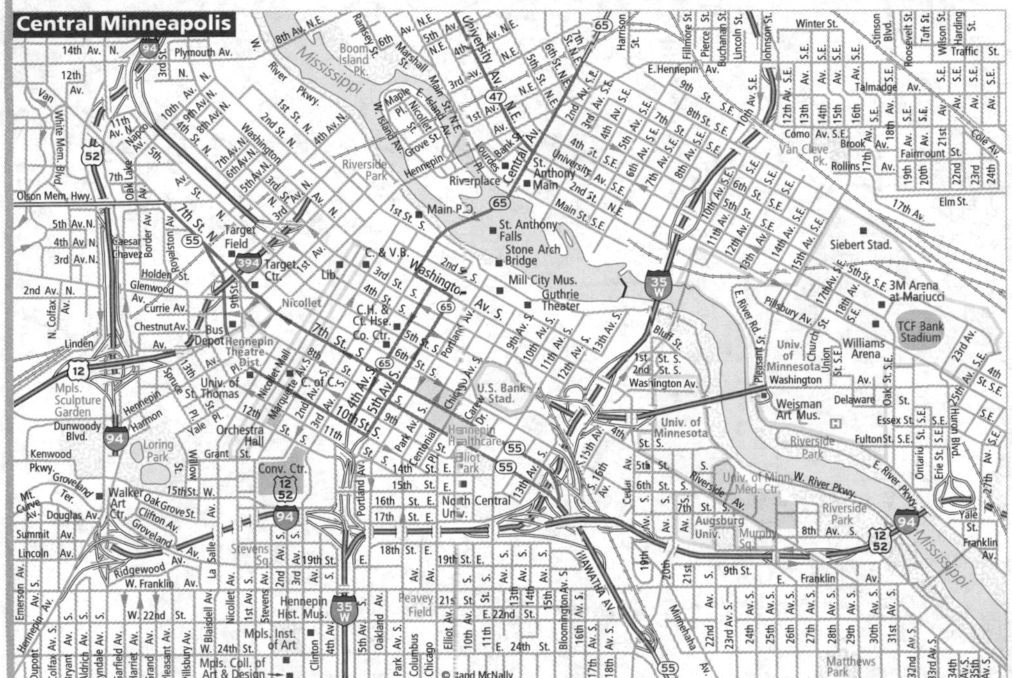

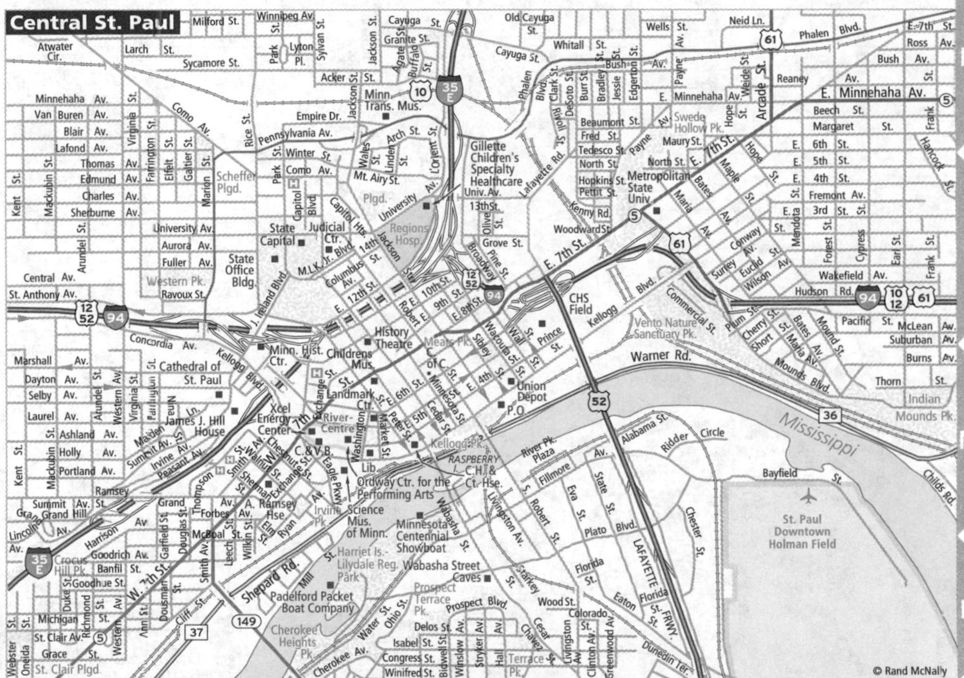

Nickname: The North Star State
Capital: St. Paul, O-10
Land area: 79,627 sq. mi. (rank: 14th)
Population: 5,303,925 (rank: 21st)
Largest city: Minneapolis, 382,578, O-9

Index of places Pg. 132

Travel planning & on-the-road resources

Tourism Information
Explore Minnesota:
(888) 847-4866, (651) 556-8465; www.exploreminnesota.com

Road Conditions & Construction
511, (800) 542-0220, (651) 296-3000, (800) 657-3774
www.511mn.org, www.dot.state.mn.us

Toll Bridge Information
Boise Inc./Resolute Forest Products (International Falls Bridge):
www.usborder.com/border-crossings/mn/international-falls-fort-frances/

Toll Road Information
Minnesota Dept. of Transportation (Twin Cities metro) *(MnPass)*:
(800) 657-3774; www.dot.state.mn.us/mnpass

Boundary Waters Canoe Area

Mileages between cities	Albert Lea	Bemidji	Brainerd	Duluth	Grand Forks, ND	Grand Marais	Hibbing	International Falls	Mankato	Marshall	Minneapolis	Moorhead	Rochester	St. Cloud	Sioux Falls, SD	Willmar
Bemidji	316		97	151	114	259	105	112	290	258	222	135	306	151	380	188
Duluth	247	151	113		266	110	76	162	233	273	152	250	226	141	390	204
Minneapolis	96	222	130	152	314	262	208	293	80	153		233	86	65	236	93
Moorhead	328	135	136	250	82	361	212	249	303	206	233		321	170	244	172
Rochester	62	306	213	226	401	338	280	366	86	194	86	321		153	236	178
St. Cloud	160	151	63	141	251	253	173	251	135	130	65	170	153		220	62
St. Paul	98	230	137	149	325	260	204	290	87	159	9	243	78	75	241	102
Sioux Falls, SD	176	380	281	390	319	500	456	494	155	91	236	244	236	220		158

Mileages © Rand McNally

Total mileages through Minnesota

35: 260 miles
94: 260 miles
90: 276 miles
2: 255 miles

More mileages at randmcnally.com/MC

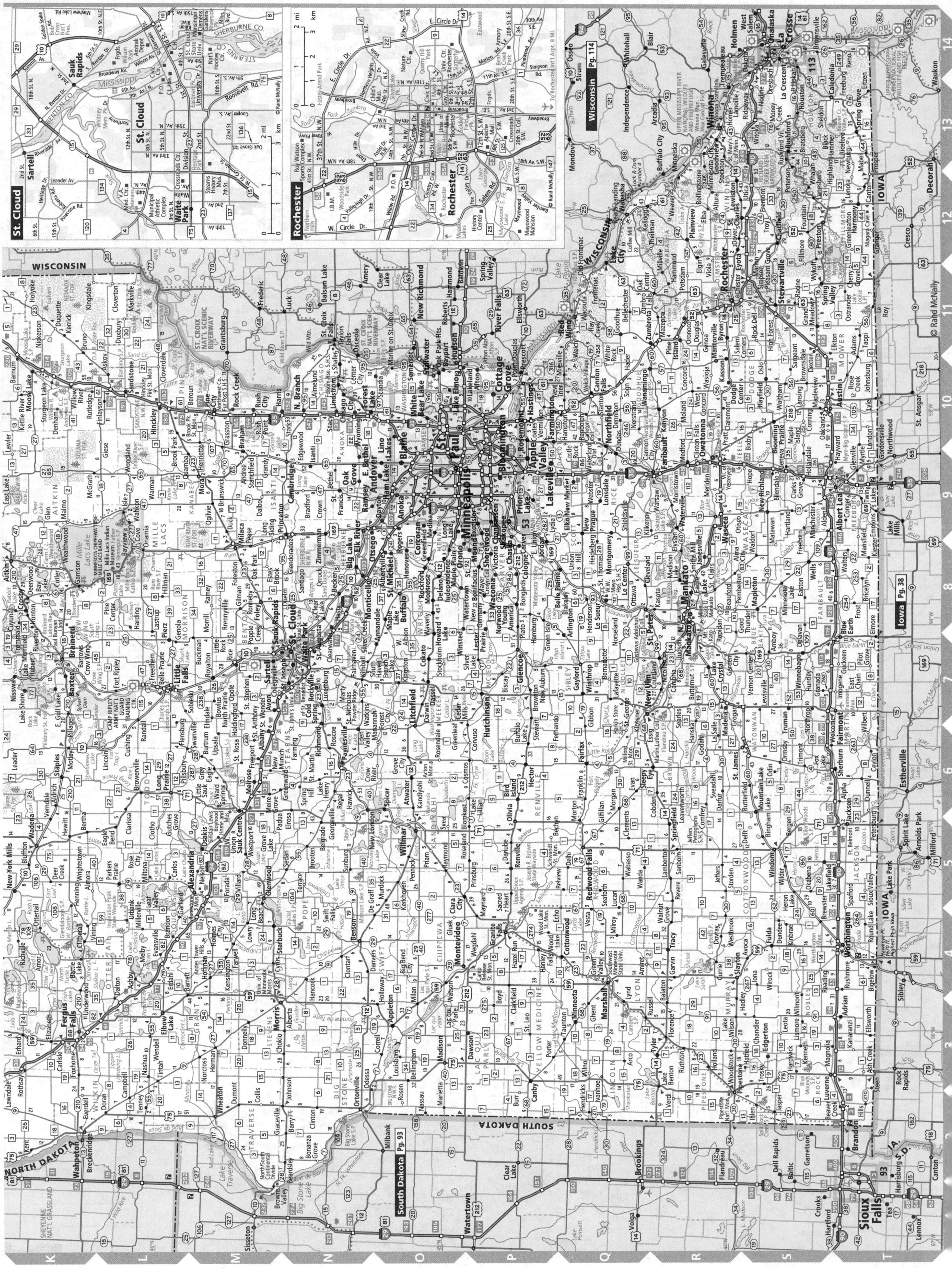

Mississippi

Nickname: The Magnolia State
Capital: Jackson, H-6
Land area: 46,923 sq. mi. (rank: 31st)
Population: 2,967,297 (rank: 31st)
Largest city: Jackson, 173,514, H-6

Index of places Pg. 132

Mileages between cities

	Batesville	Biloxi	Hattiesburg	Jackson	Memphis, TN	Natchez	Tupelo	Vicksburg
Biloxi	320		80	172	379	228	315	214
Greenville	112	293	210	121	152	152	177	91
Jackson	149	172	89		209	103	190	44
Memphis, TN	61	379	297	209		304	105	245
Meridian	176	172	89	91	234	194	142	134
New Orleans, LA	335	90	109	183	394	171	340	207
Tupelo	74	315	232	190	105	283		225
Vicksburg	188	214	131	44	245	70	225	

Total mileages through Mississippi

- I-10: 77 miles
- I-20: 169 miles
- I-55: 290 miles
- I-59: 172 miles

More mileages at randmcnally.com/MC

Travel planning & on-the-road resources

Tourism Information

Visit Mississippi:
(866) 733-6477, (601) 359-3297; visitmississippi.org

Road Conditions & Construction

511, (888) 672-4502
www.mdottraffic.com

Toll Road Information

No tolls on state or federal highways

Determining Distances

(segments of one mile or less not shown)

Cumulative miles (red): the distance between red arrows

Intermediate miles (black): the distance between intersections & places

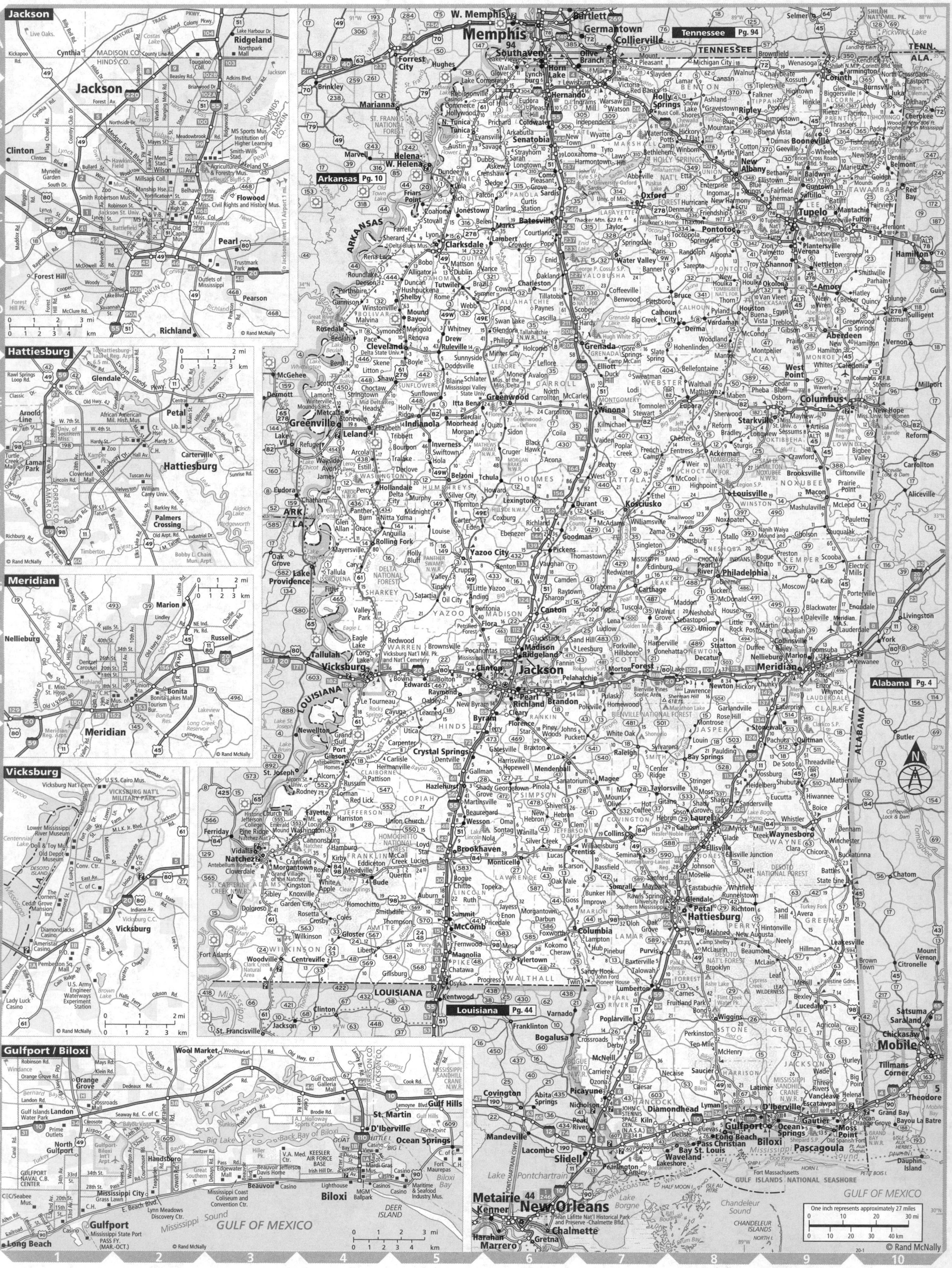

Sights to see

- Andy Williams Moon River Theatre, Branson M-8
- Anheuser-Busch Brewery, St. Louis ... I-7
- Dolly Parton's Stampede, Branson M-9
- Gateway Arch, St. Louis L-4
- Laumeier Sculpture Park, St. Louis ... J-4
- Magic House, Kirkwood I-4
- Missouri Botanical Garden, St. Louis . I-6
- Shoji Tabuchi Theatre, Branson L-7
- St. Louis Art Museum, St. Louis H-6
- St. Louis Science Center, St. Louis ... H-6
- St. Louis Zoo, St. Louis H-6
- Shepherd of the Hills, Branson K-6
- White Water, Branson M-7
- Wonders of Wildlife Nat'l Museum & Aquarium, Springfield C-3

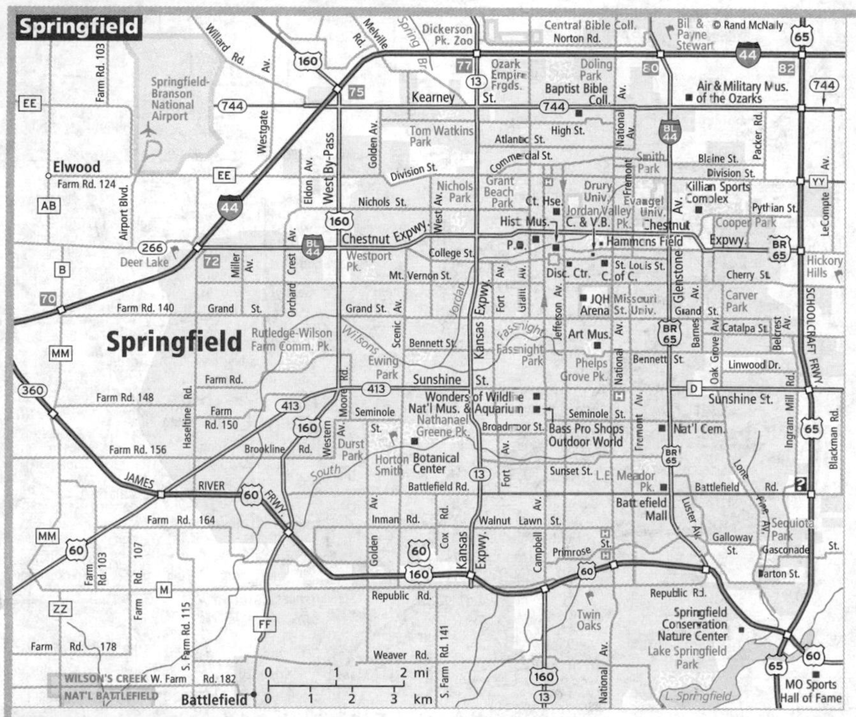

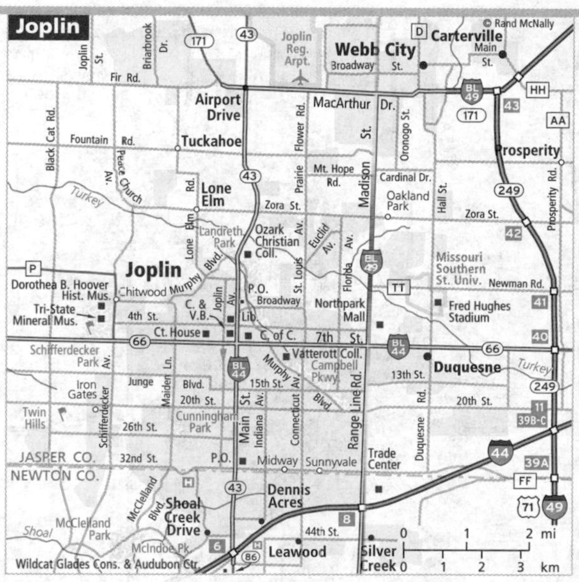

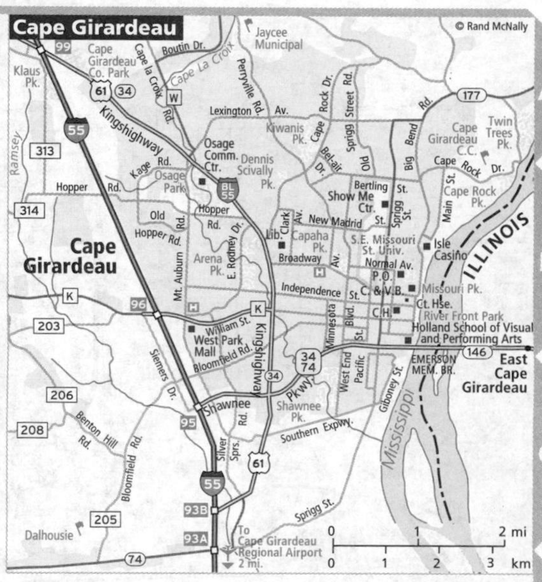

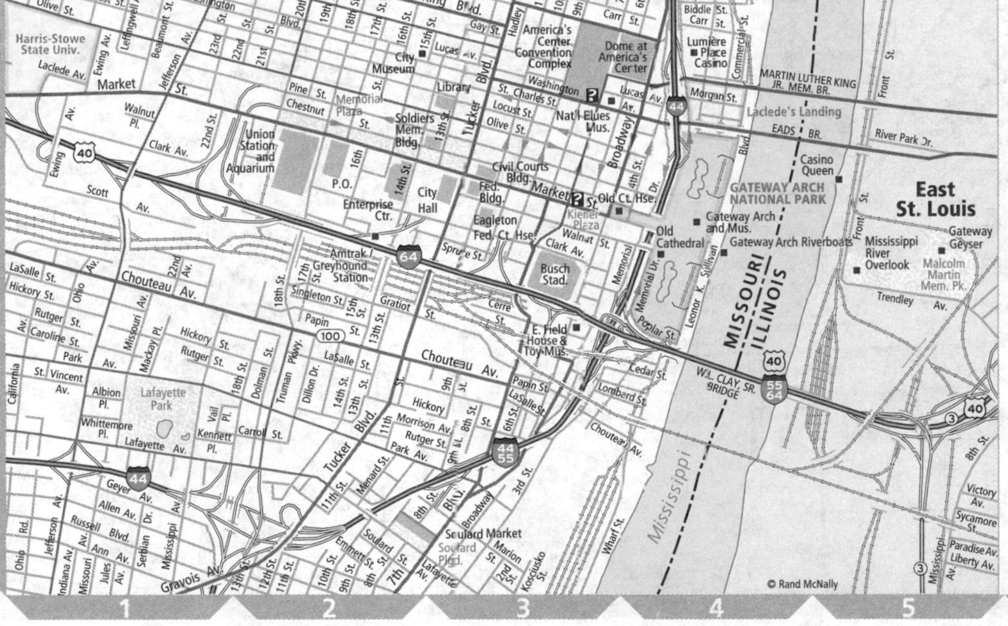

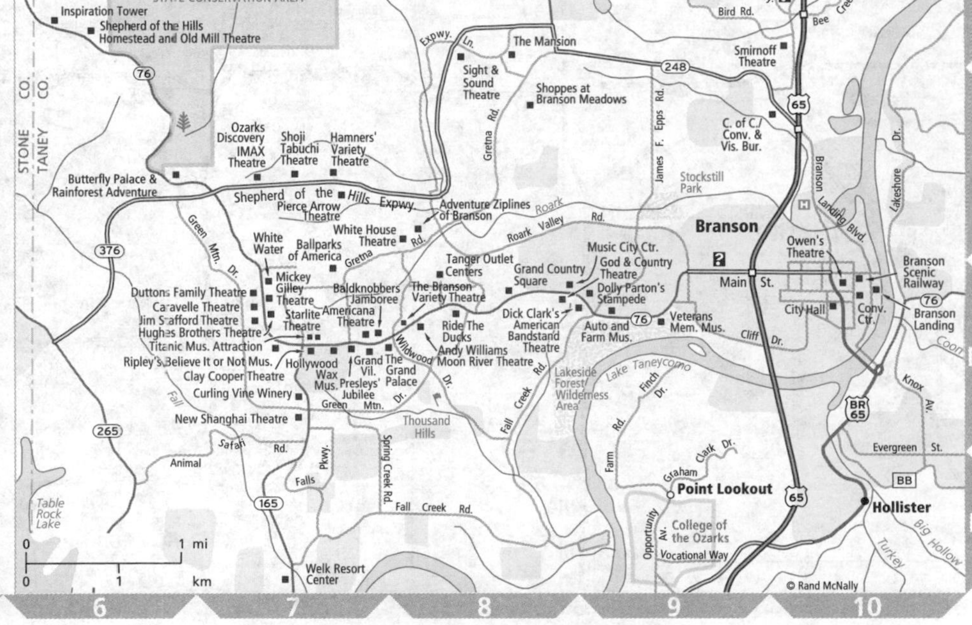

Missouri

Nickname: The Show Me State
Capital: Jefferson City, G-14
Land area: 68,741 sq. mi. (rank: 18th)
Population: 5,988,927 (rank: 18th)
Largest city: Kansas City, 459,787, F-9

Index of places Pg. 132

Travel planning & on-the-road resources

Tourism Information
Missouri Division of Tourism: (573) 751-4133; www.visitmo.com

Road Conditions & Construction
(888) 275-6636, (573) 751-2551; www.modot.org, traveler.modot.org/map

Toll Road Information
No tolls on state or federal highways

Determining distances along roads

Highway distances (segments of one mile or less not shown):
Cumulative miles (red): the distance between red arrows
Intermediate miles (black): the distance between intersections & places

Interchanges and exit numbers
For most states, the mileage between interchanges may be determined by subtracting one number from the other.

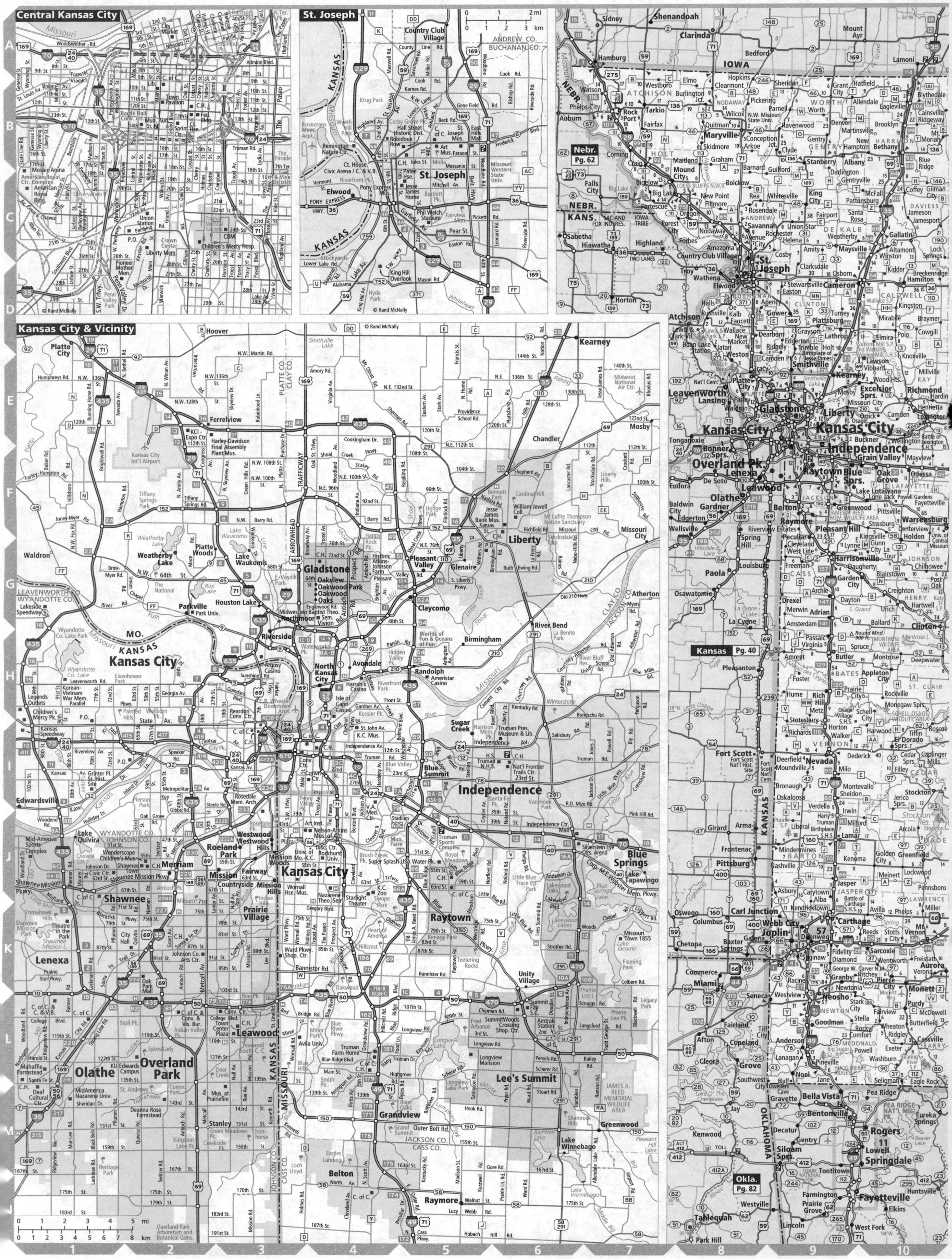

Country Club Plaza, Kansas City

Mileages between cities

	Branson	Cape Girardeau	Columbia	Hannibal	Hayti	Jefferson City	Joplin	Kansas City	Kirksville	Maryville	Osage Beach	Poplar Bluff	Rolla	St. Louis	Springfield	West Plains
Cape Girardeau	295		225	218	80	216	336	348	313	445	218	82	158	114	270	182
Columbia	205	225		97	301	32	236	124	91	222	76	261	93	126	168	191
Joplin	109	336	236	312	319	206		157	312	243	161	256	178	282	70	176
Kansas City	209	348	124	209	424	156	157		157	93	164	356	219	250	166	275
Poplar Bluff	215	82	261	255	62	223	256	356	300	457	224		147	151	191	98
St. Joseph	270	405	182	191	481	214	203	53	141	43	222	416	276	308	225	336
St. Louis	249	114	126	120	192	124	282	250	217	347	164	151	104		213	202
Springfield	42	270	168	242	253	136	70	166	259	266	91	191	108	213		108

Mileages © Rand McNally

Total mileages through Missouri

- 35: 115 miles
- 44: 290 miles
- 55: 210 miles
- 70: 252 miles

More mileages at randmcnally.com/MC

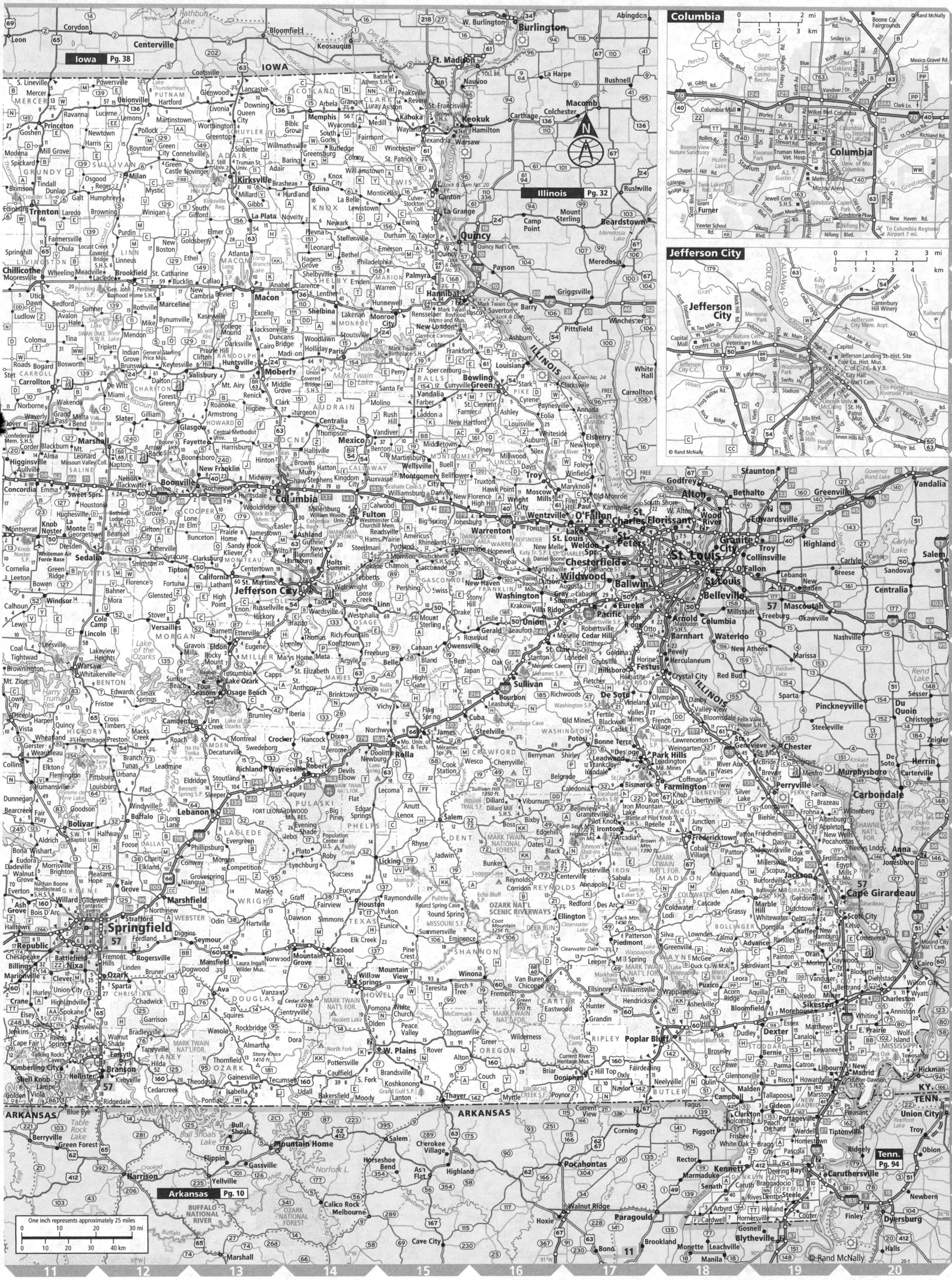

Montana

Nickname: The Treasure State
Capital: Helena, G-7
Land area: 145,546 sq. mi. (rank: 4th)
Population: 989,415 (rank: 44th)
Largest city: Billings, 104,170, I-13

Index of places Pg. 132

Travel planning & on-the-road resources

Tourism Information
Montana Office of Tourism: (800) 847-4868; www.visitmt.com

Road Conditions & Construction
511, (800) 226-7623, (406) 444-6200; www.mdt.mt.gov/travinfo

Toll Road Information
No tolls on state or federal highways

Determining distances along roads

Highway distances (segments of one mile or less not shown):
Cumulative miles (red): the distance between red arrows
Intermediate miles (black): the distance between intersections & places

Interchanges and exit numbers
For most states, the mileage between interchanges may be determined by subtracting one number from the other.

Glacier National Park

Mileages between cities

	Belle Fourche, SD	Billings	Bozeman	Butte	Dillon	Glasgow	Great Falls	Havre	Kalispell	Lewistown	Libby	Miles City	Missoula	St. Mary	Sidney	West Yellowstone
Billings	261		143	223	256	276	218	247	451	125	536	144	343	375	269	232
Butte	486	223	82		54	425	154	267	224	244	309	367	120	269	494	149
Great Falls	481	218	186	154	219	271		113	224	106	312	317	166	158	375	264
Helena	500	238	98	66	132	360	90	202	193	193	281	383	113	205	463	177
Kalispell	711	451	308	224	278	419	224	261		330	88	593	121	82	558	371
Miles City	174	144	285	367	399	195	317	333	593	211	678		487	473	126	375
Missoula	606	343	202	120	172	437	166	280	121	272	191	487		203	614	267
Sidney	298	269	411	494	524	140	375	298	558	270	646	126	614	490		501

Total mileages through Montana

15: 396 miles
94: 249 miles
90: 552 miles

More mileages at randmcnally.com/MC

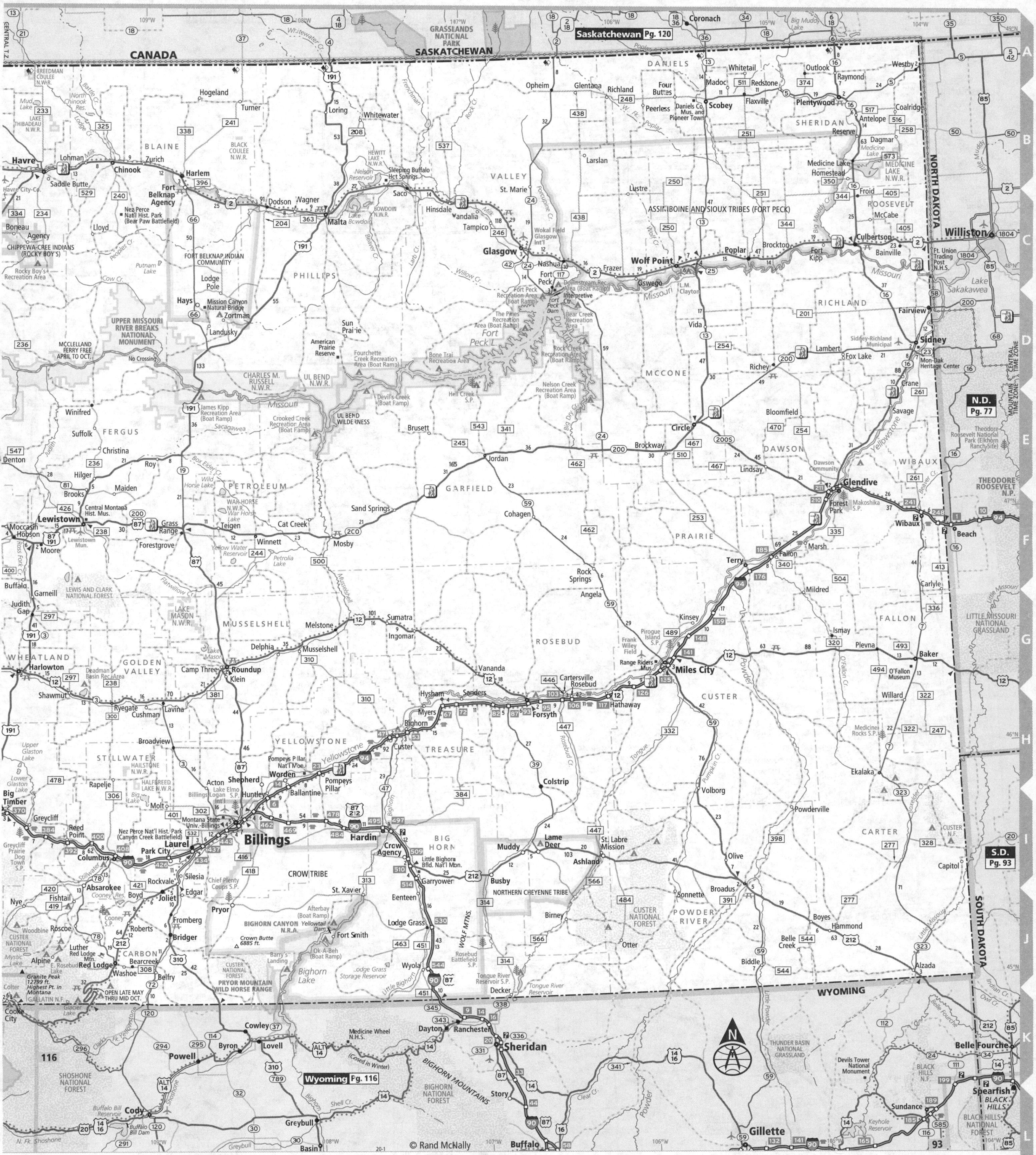

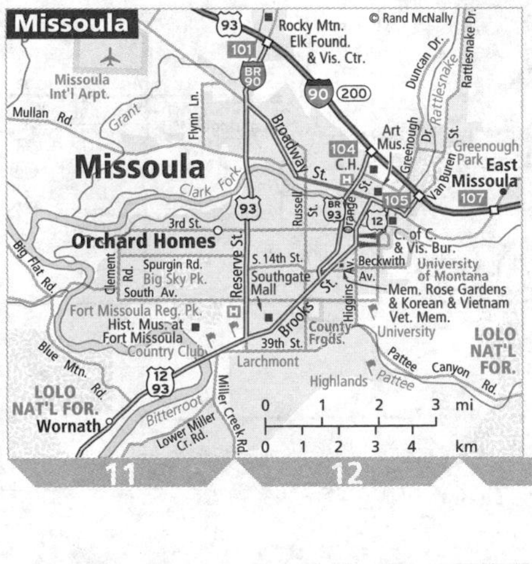

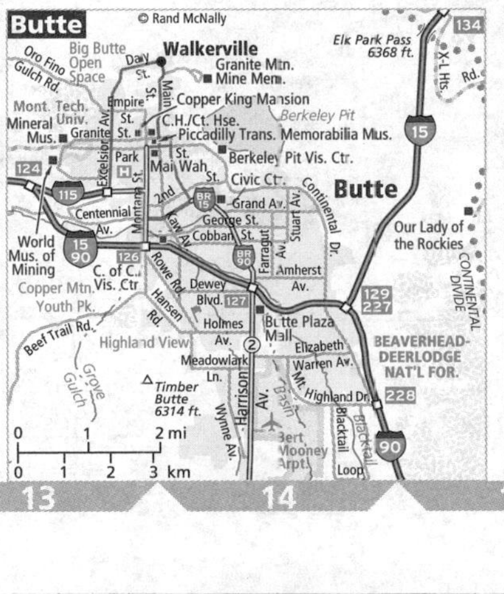

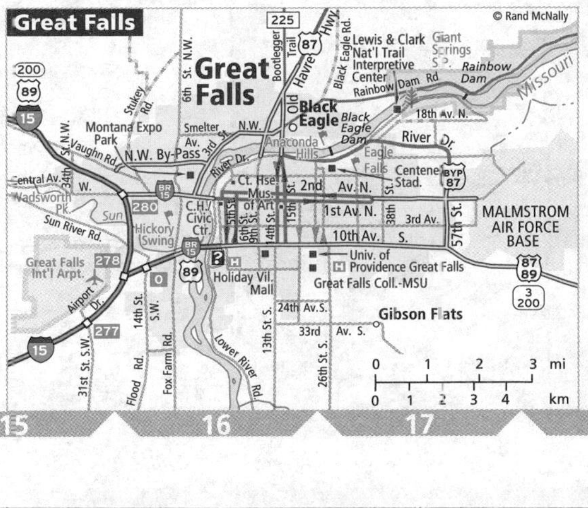

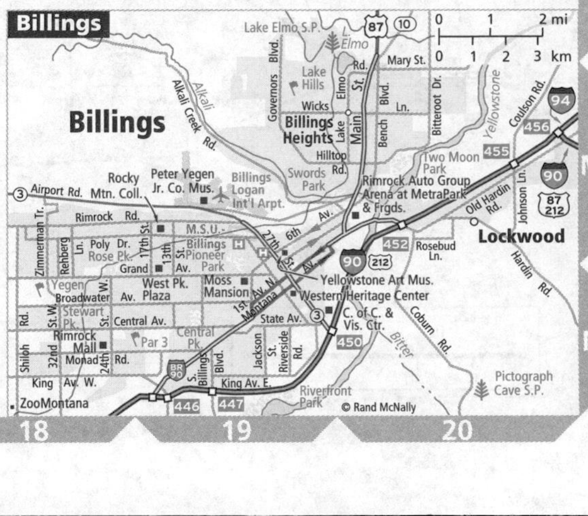

Nebraska

Nickname: The Cornhusker State
Capital: Lincoln, K-17
Land area: 76,824 sq. mi. (rank: 15th)
Population: 1,826,341 (rank: 38th)
Largest city: Omaha, 408,958, J-19

Index of places Pg. 132

Travel planning & on-the-road resources

Tourism Information
Nebraska Tourism Commission: (402) 471-3796; visitnebraska.com

Road Conditions & Construction
511, (800) 906-9069, (402) 471-4567; www.511.nebraska.gov, www.dot.nebraska.gov

Toll Road Information
No tolls on state or federal highways

Determining distances along roads

Highway distances (segments of one mile or less not shown):
Cumulative miles (red): the distance between red arrows
Intermediate miles (black): the distance between intersections & places

Interchanges and exit numbers
For most states, the mileage between interchanges may be determined by subtracting one number from the other.

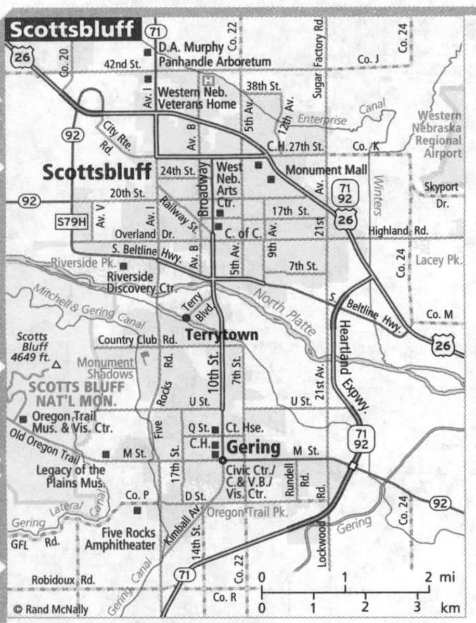

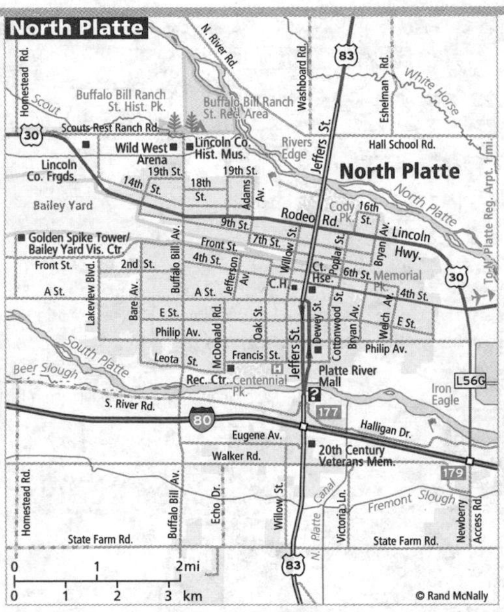

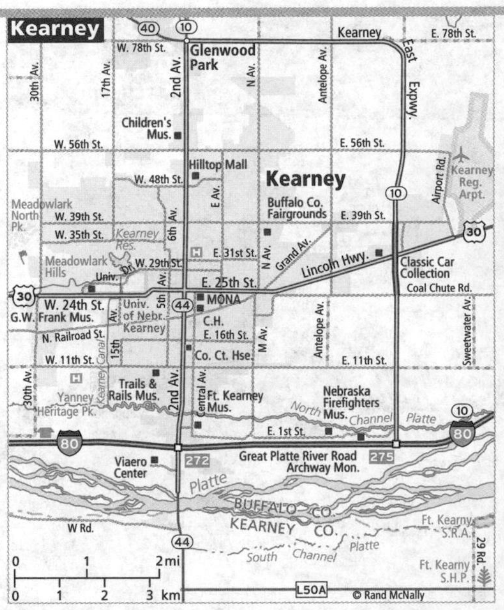

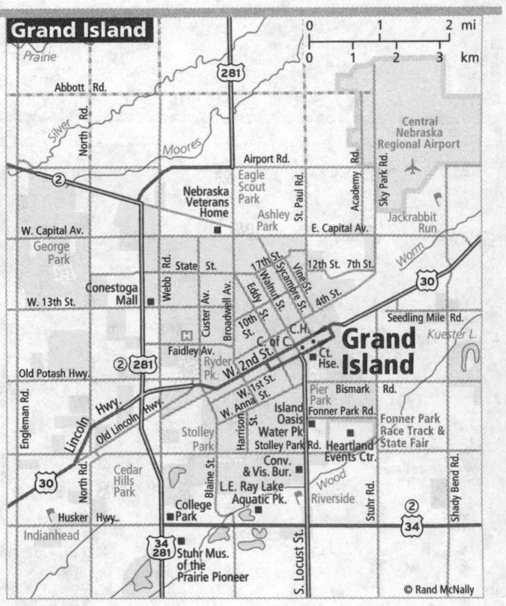

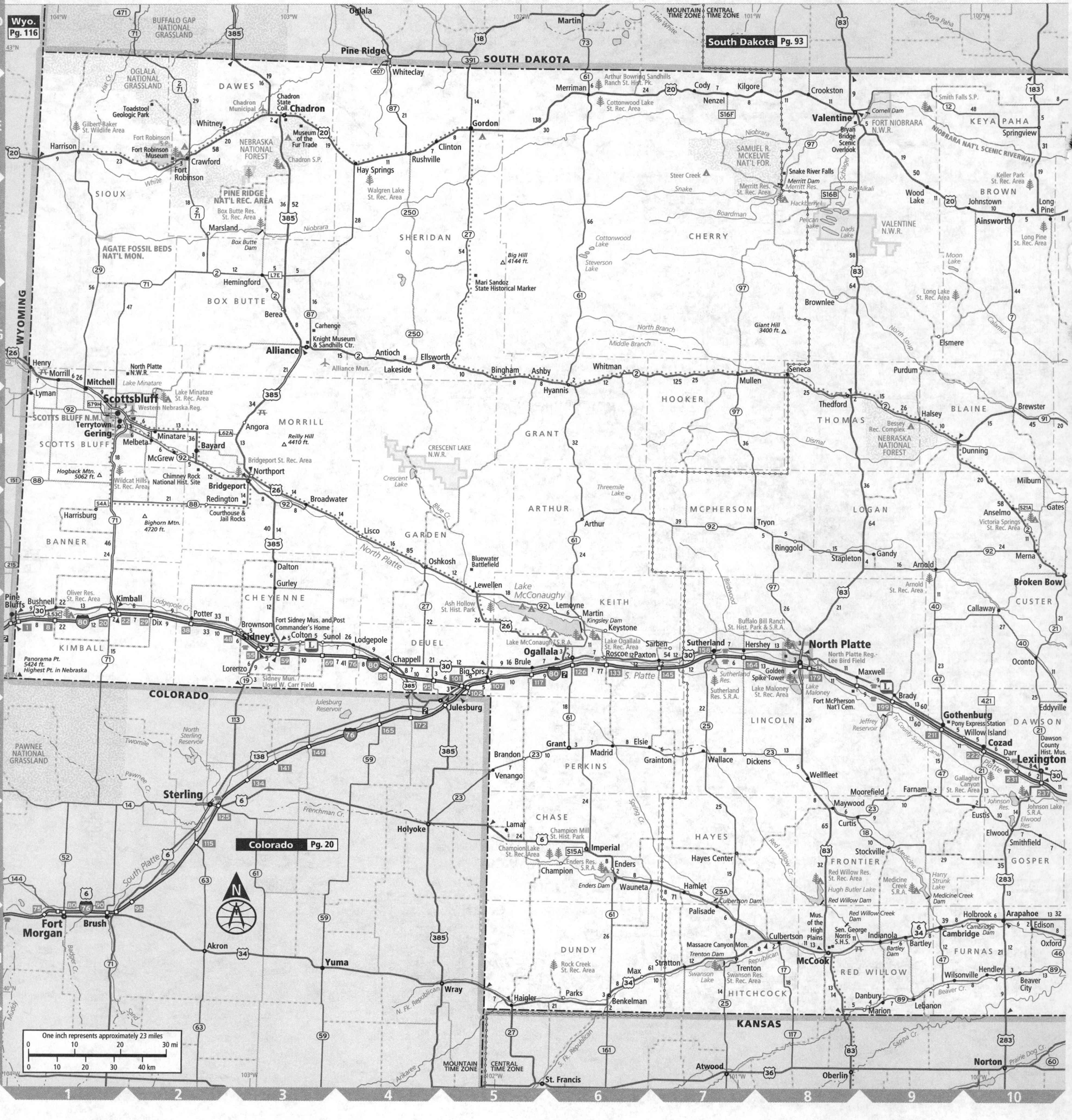

Scotts Bluff National Monument

Mileages between cities	Beatrice	Chadron	Columbus	Falls City	Grand Island	Kearney	Lincoln	McCook	Norfolk	North Platte	Ogallala	Omaha	O'Neill	Scottsbluff	Sioux City, IA	Valentine
Grand Island	131	326	64	196		50	93	152	105	145	194	147	112	323	187	210
Lincoln	41	450	79	102	93	129		232	124	224	274	55	208	402	151	304
Norfolk	162	322	45	218	105	155	124	259		250	300	109	75	417	82	186
North Platte	262	229	210	327	145	99	224	67	250		53	276	189	182	373	129
Omaha	95	431	83	104	147	181	55	283	109	276	325		184	458	97	294
Scottsbluff	440	99	388	505	323	277	402	245	417	182	129	458	322		467	216
Sidney	381	131	329	445	263	218	343	186	369	122	71	394	311	77	492	251
Valentine	342	137	230	406	210	195	304	197	186	129	182	294	111	216	236	

Total mileages through Nebraska

80: 455 miles
83: 226 miles
81: 219 miles
20: 436 miles

More mileages at randmcnally.com/MC

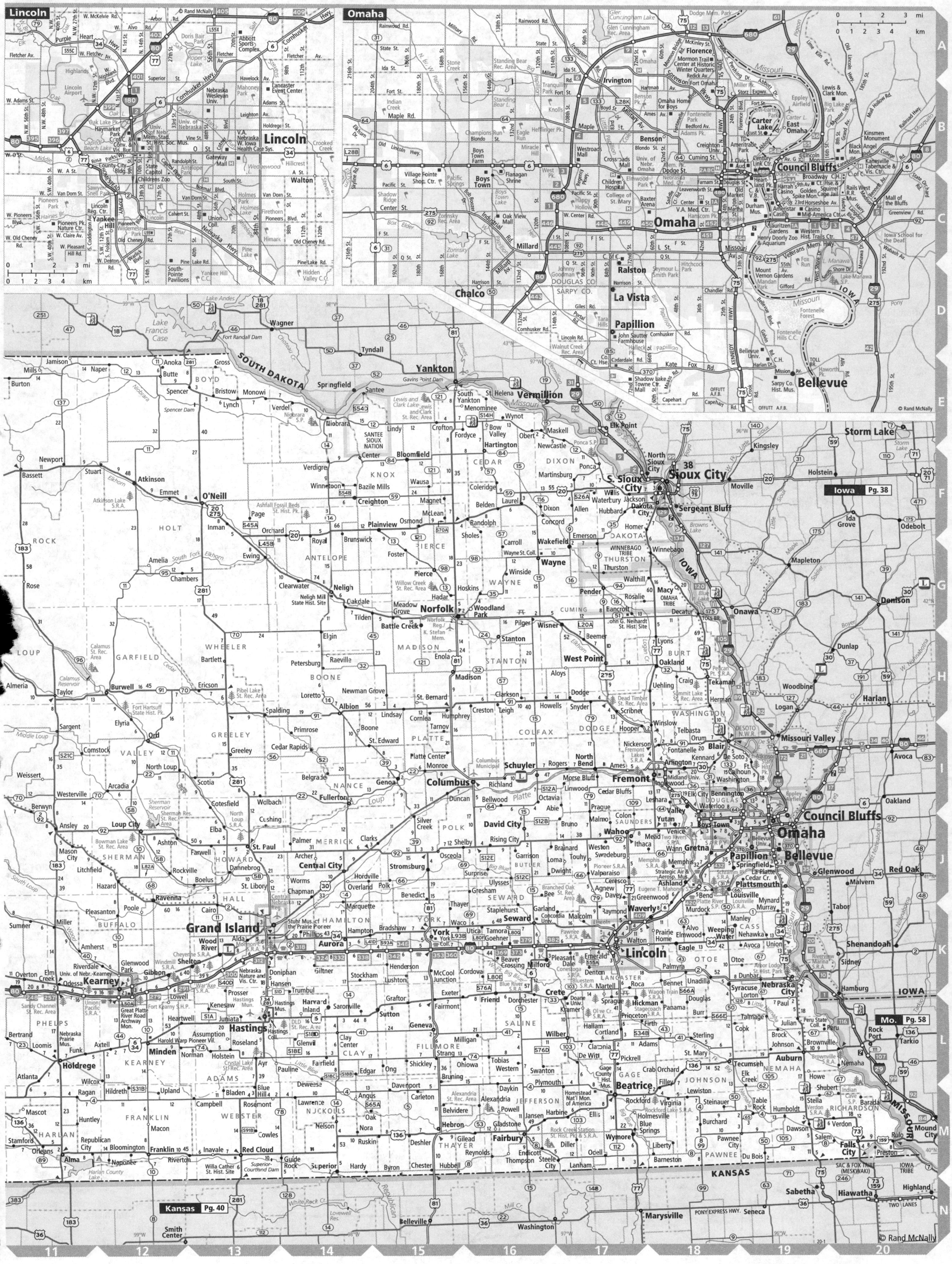

Nevada

Nickname: The Silver State
Capital: Carson City, F-2
Land area: 109,781 sq. mi. (rank: 7th)
Population: 2,700,551 (rank: 35th)
Largest city: Las Vegas, 583,756, L-8

Index of places Pg. 132

Mileages between cities	Carson City	Elko	Ely	Jackpot	Las Vegas	Reno	Tonopah	Winnemucca
Elko	304		188	117	429	288	252	125
Ely	319	188		205	241	319	167	271
Las Vegas	435	429	241	446		447	210	472
Reno	32	288	319	405	447		237	163
S. Lake Tahoe, CA	27	332	347	450	451	60	237	208
Tonopah	225	252	167	373	210	237		261
West Wendover	414	109	120	125	361	397	288	232
Winnemucca	179	125	271	240	472	163	261	

Mileages © Rand McNally

Total mileages through Nevada
15: 124 miles · 6: 307 miles
80: 411 miles · 95: 652 miles

More mileages at randmcnally.com/MC

Travel planning & on-the-road resources

Tourism Information
Travel Nevada:
(800) 638-2328, (775) 687-4322; travelnevada.com

Road Conditions & Construction
511, (877) 687-6237, (775) 888-7000
nvroads.com/511-home, www.nevadadot.com

Toll Road Information
No tolls on state or federal highways

Determining Distances
(segments of one mile or less not shown)
Cumulative miles (red): the distance between red arrows
Intermediate miles (black): the distance between intersections & places

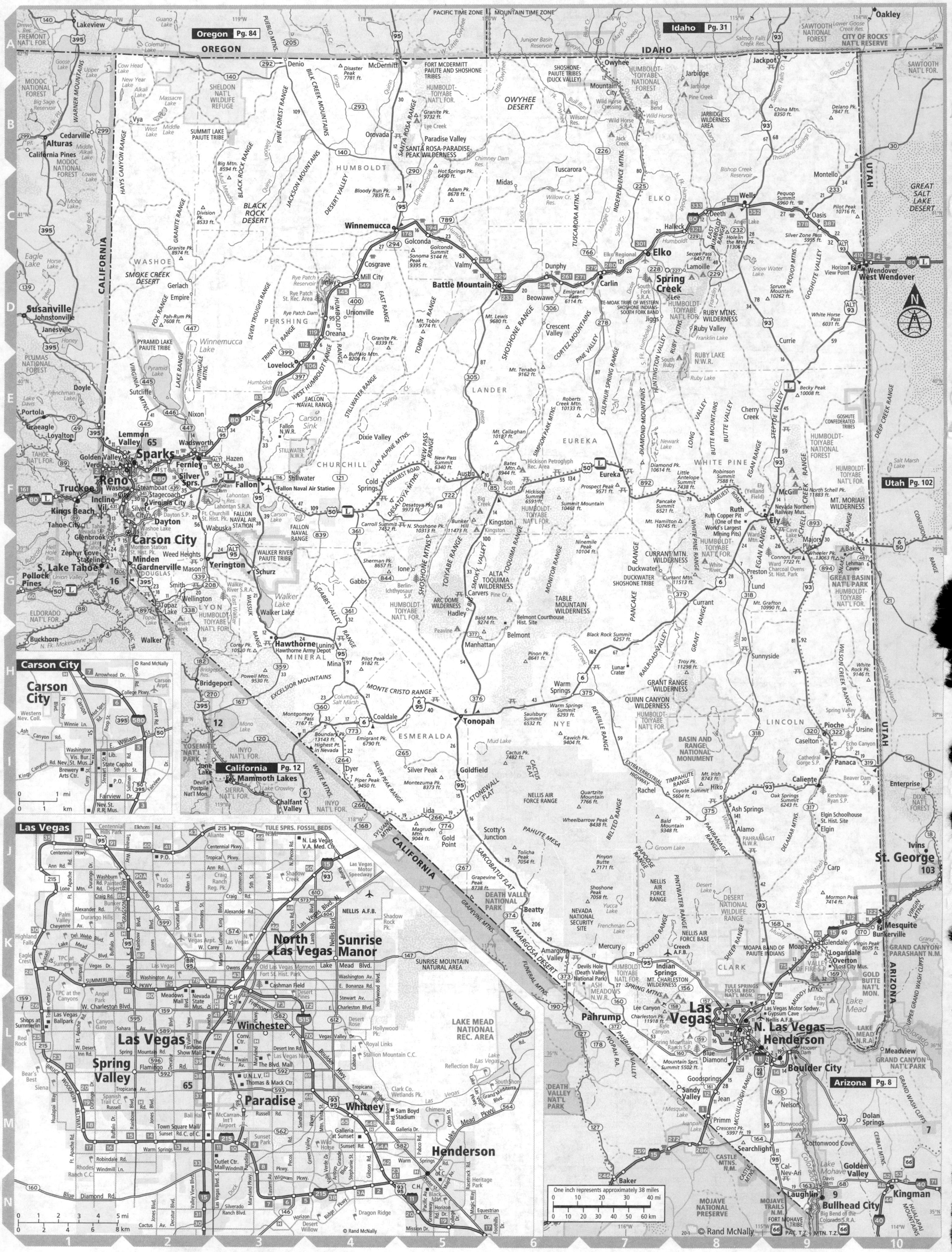

Travel planning & on-the-road resources

Tourism Information
New Hampshire Division of Travel and Tourism Development:
(603) 271-2665; www.visitnh.gov

Road Conditions & Construction
(603) 271-6862; newengland511.org, www.nhtmc.com

Toll Road Information
Bureau of Turnpikes (*E-ZPass*):
(603) 485-3806; www.nh.gov/dot/org/operations/turnpikes

Total mileages through New Hampshire

89: 61 miles
95: 16 miles
93: 132 miles
2: 36 miles

More mileages at randmcnally.com/MC

Mileages between cities	Colebrook	Concord	Conway	Keene	Laconia	Littleton	Nashua	Portsmouth
Berlin	49	115	40	168	97	42	151	117
Concord	137		77	51	27	37	36	44
Keene	181	51	130		80	136	50	99
Lebanon	128	57	88	64	58	32	89	111
Littleton	56	87	54	136	66		121	129
Manchester	155	18	95	55	45	105	18	43
Nashua	172	36	113	50	63	121		54
Portsmouth	180	44	77	99	57	129	54	

New Hampshire

Nickname: The Granite State
Capital: Concord, K-7
Land area: 8,953 sq. mi. (rank: 44th)
Population: 1,316,470 (rank: 42nd)
Largest city: Manchester, 109,565, L-7

Index of places Pg. 132

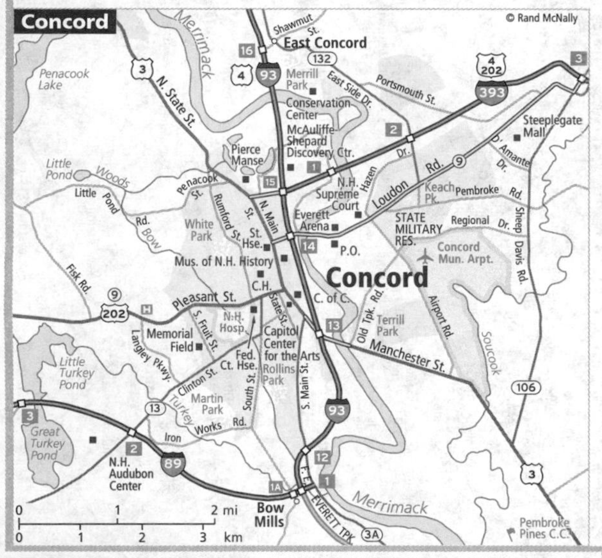

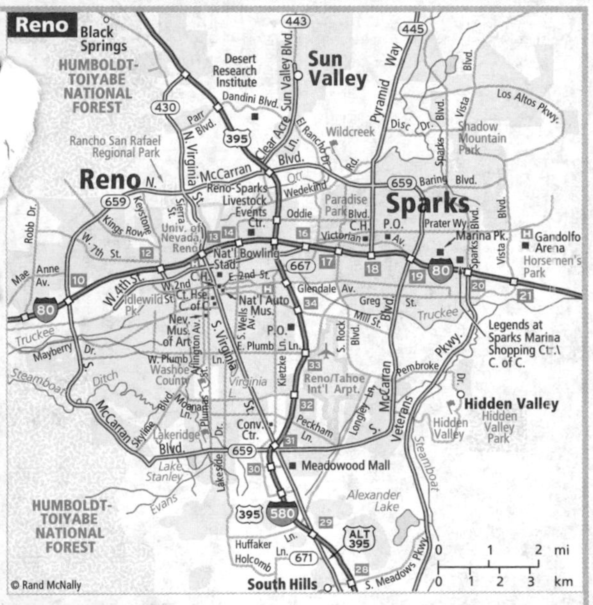

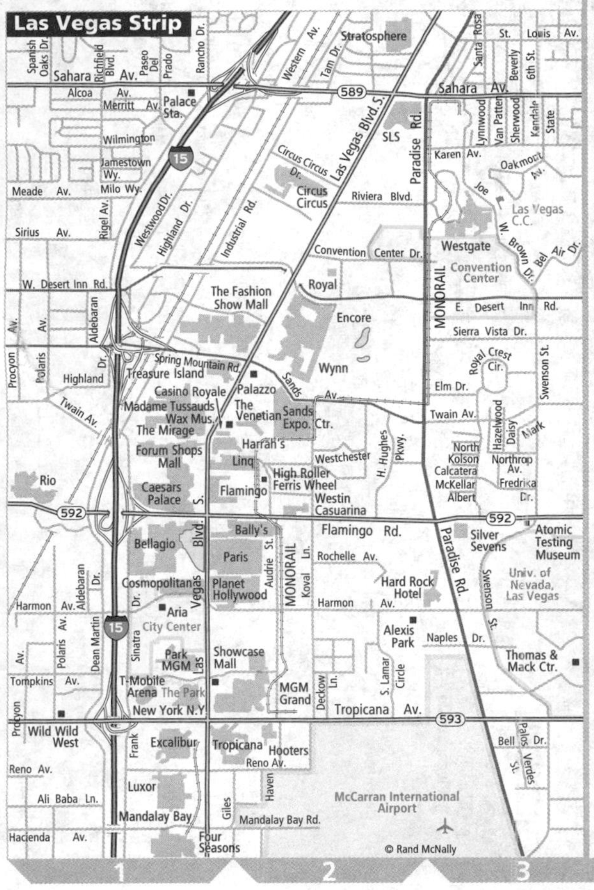

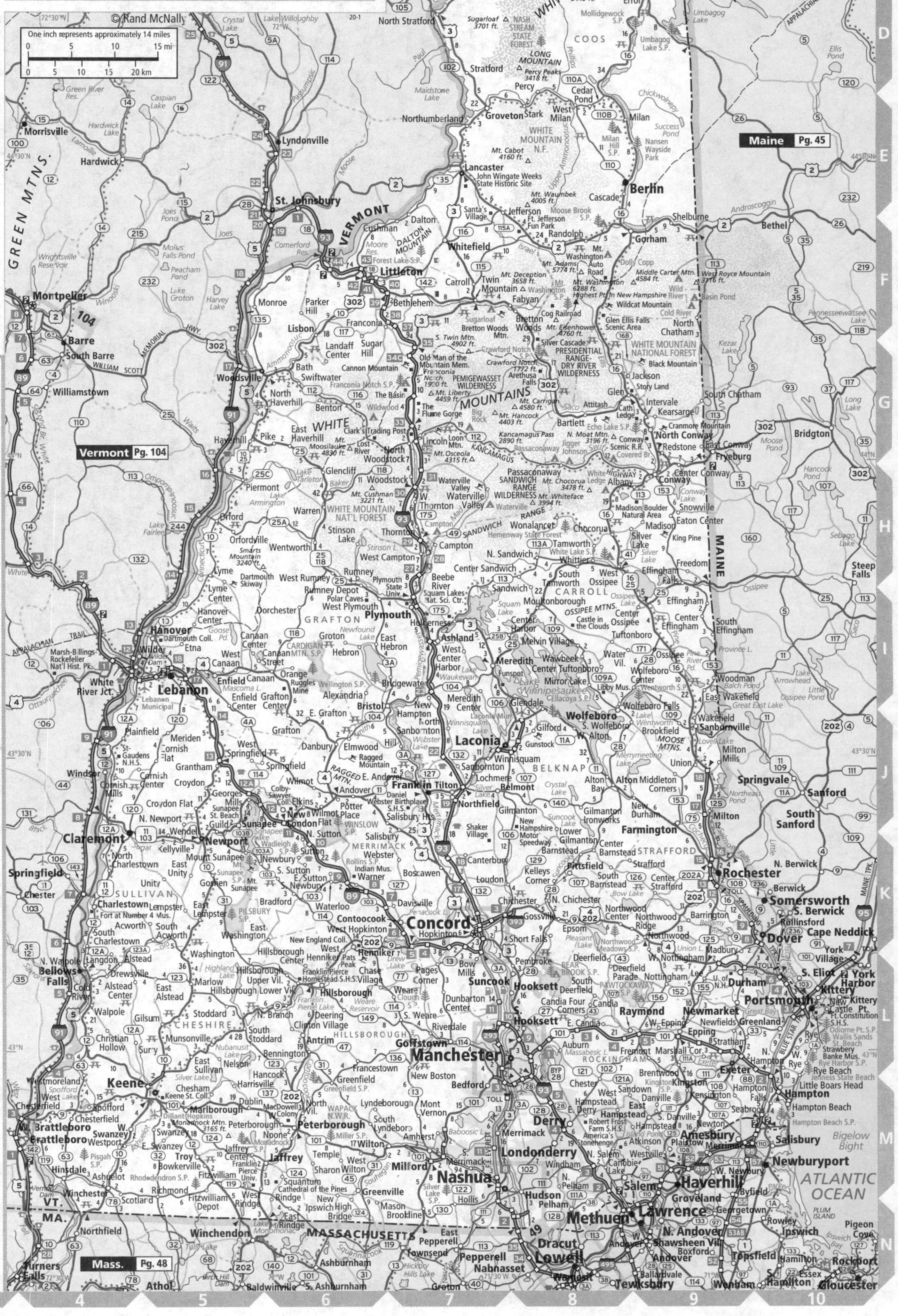

Nickname: The Garden State
Capital: Trenton, J-8
Land area: 7,354 sq. mi. (rank: 46th)
Population: 8,791,894 (rank: 11th)
Largest city: Newark, 277,140, F-12

Index of places Pg. 132

Travel planning & on-the-road resources

Tourism Information
New Jersey Div. of Travel and Tourism: (609) 599-6540; www.visitnj.org

Toll Road Information: *(all use E-ZPass)*
New Jersey Turnpike Authority (N.J. Turnpike, Garden St. Pkwy.): (732) 750-5300 ext. 8750; www.state.nj.us/turnpike
South Jersey Transportation Authority (Atlantic City Expressway): (609) 965-6060; www.sjta.com

Road Conditions & Construction
511, (866) 511-6538; www.511nj.org, www.state.nj.us/transportation

Toll Bridge/Tunnel Information: *(all use E-ZPass)*
Burlington County Bridge Commission: (856) 829-1900; www.bcbridges.org
Delaware R. & Bay Auth. (Del. Mem. Br., Cape May/Lewes Fy.): (302) 571-6300; www.drba.net
Delaware R. Port Auth. (Philadelphia area bridges): (877) 567-3772, (856) 968-2000; www.drpa.org
Delaware R. Joint Toll Br. Commission (other Delaware R. bridges): (800) 363-0049; www.drjtbc.org
Port Auth. of N.Y. & N.J. (NYC area inter-state bridges & tunnels): (800) 221-9903; www.panynj.gov

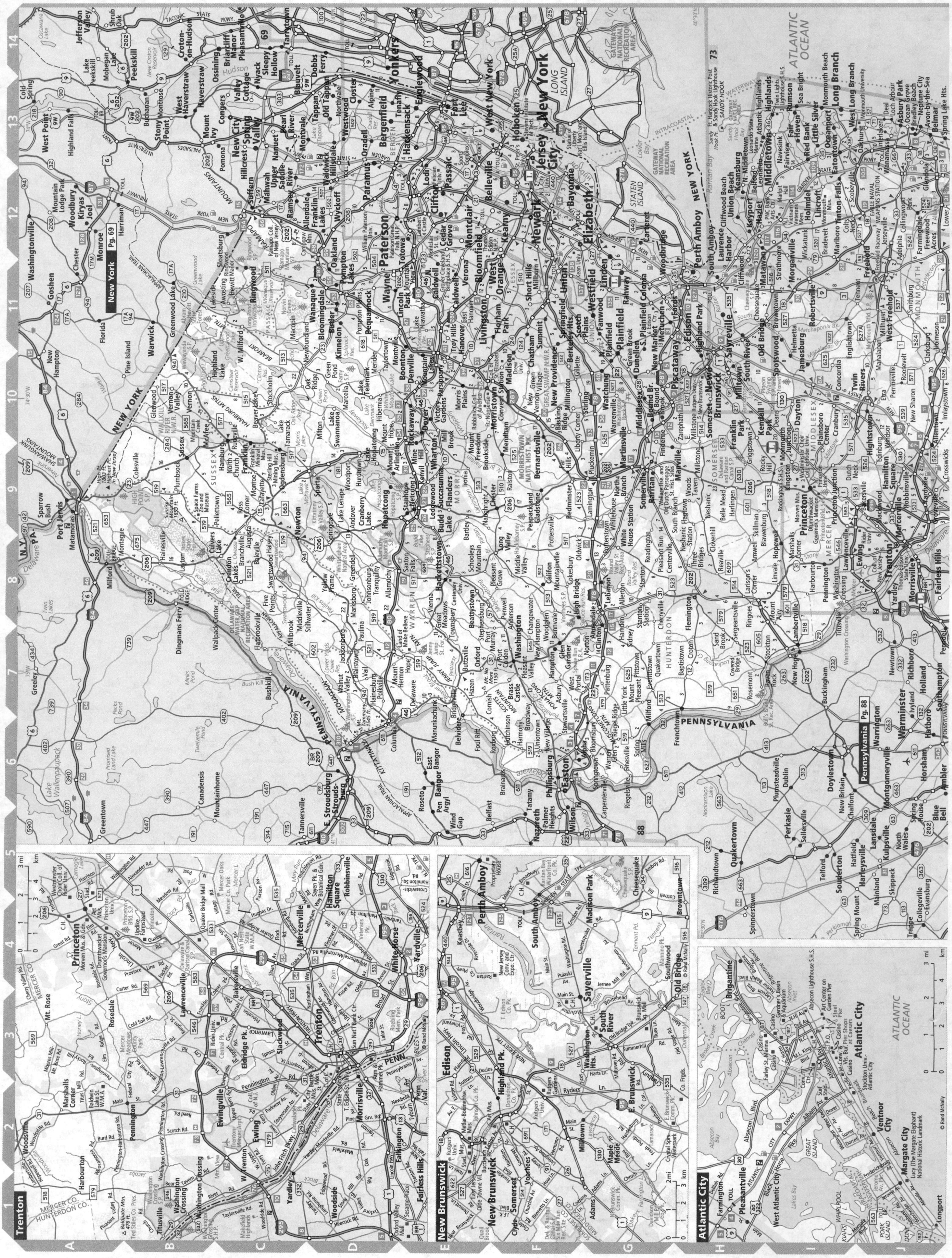

Victorians at Cape May

Mileages between cities

	Atlantic City	Camden	Cape May	Jersey City	Long Branch	Newark	New Brunswick	New York, NY	Paterson	Phillipsburg	Port Jervis, NY	Princeton	Toms River	Trenton	Vineland	Wilmington, DE
Atlantic City		58	47	120	82	115	94	126	129	138	182	99	52	90	36	82
Camden	58		88	86	76	80	61	96	94	80	143	45	55	34	36	31
Cape May	47	88		151	114	147	126	157	161	170	214	131	84	121	48	98
Newark	115	80	147	6	43		25	10	15	58	74	41	63	55	114	112
New Brunswick	94	61	126	30	34	25		36	39	48	92	16	43	26	95	93
Phillipsburg	138	80	170	64	81	58	48	68	67		74	54	101	54	118	95
Port Jervis, NY	182	143	214	89	110	74	92	95	73	74		94	130	122	180	158
Trenton	90	34	121	61	52	55	26	66	69	54	122	11	47		69	61

Total mileages through New Jersey

78 68 miles

95 78 miles

80 68 miles

More mileages at randmcnally.com/MC

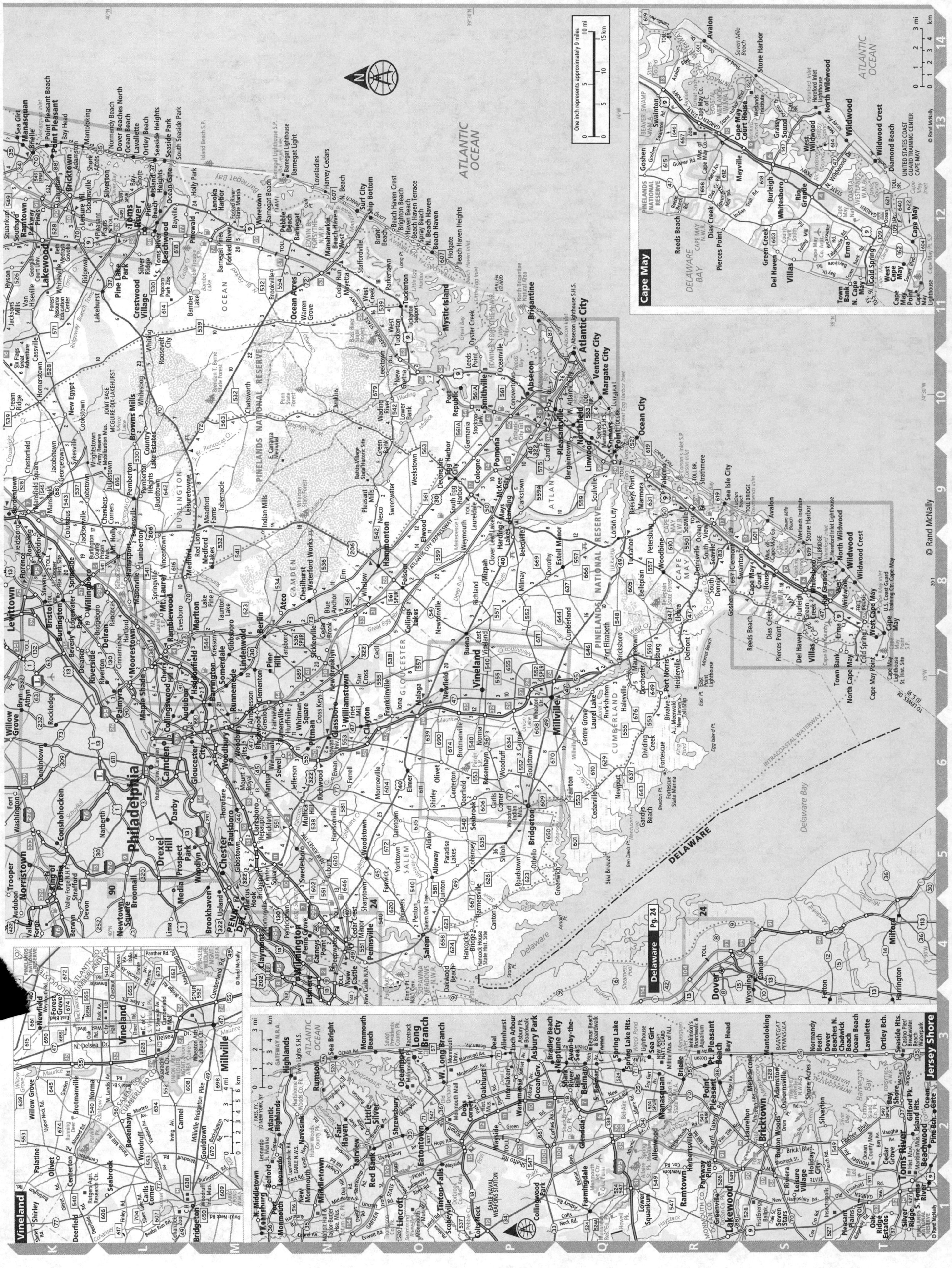

Nickname: Land of Enchantment
Capital: Santa Fe, D-6
Land area: 121,298 sq. mi. (rank: 5th)
Population: 2,059,179 (rank: 36th)
Largest city: Albuquerque, 545,852, E-4

Index of places Pg. 133

Mileages between cities

	Albuquerque	Carlsbad	Clayton	Gallup	Las Cruces	Socorro	Taos	Tucumcari
Albuquerque		277	270	137	222	78	128	173
Carlsbad	277		374	412	206	241	336	263
Clayton	270	374		407	415	347	163	111
Clovis	219	180	168	356	292	248	246	83
Farmington	180	455	418	121	404	258	202	354
Las Cruces	222	206	415	338		146	351	303
Roswell	199	76	293	336	184	165	260	182
Santa Fe	58	268	215	197	282	136	68	166

Total mileages through New Mexico

I-10: 164 miles
I-40: 374 miles
I-25: 462 miles

More mileages at randmcnally.com/MC

Travel planning & on-the-road resources

Tourism Information
New Mexico Tourism Department:
(505) 827-7336; www.newmexico.org

Road Conditions & Construction
511, (800) 432-4269, (505) 827-5100
www.nmroads.com, www.dot.state.nm.us

Toll Road Information
No tolls on state or federal highways

Determining Distances

Cumulative miles (red): the distance between red arrows
Intermediate miles (black): the distance between intersections & places
(segments of one mile or less not shown)

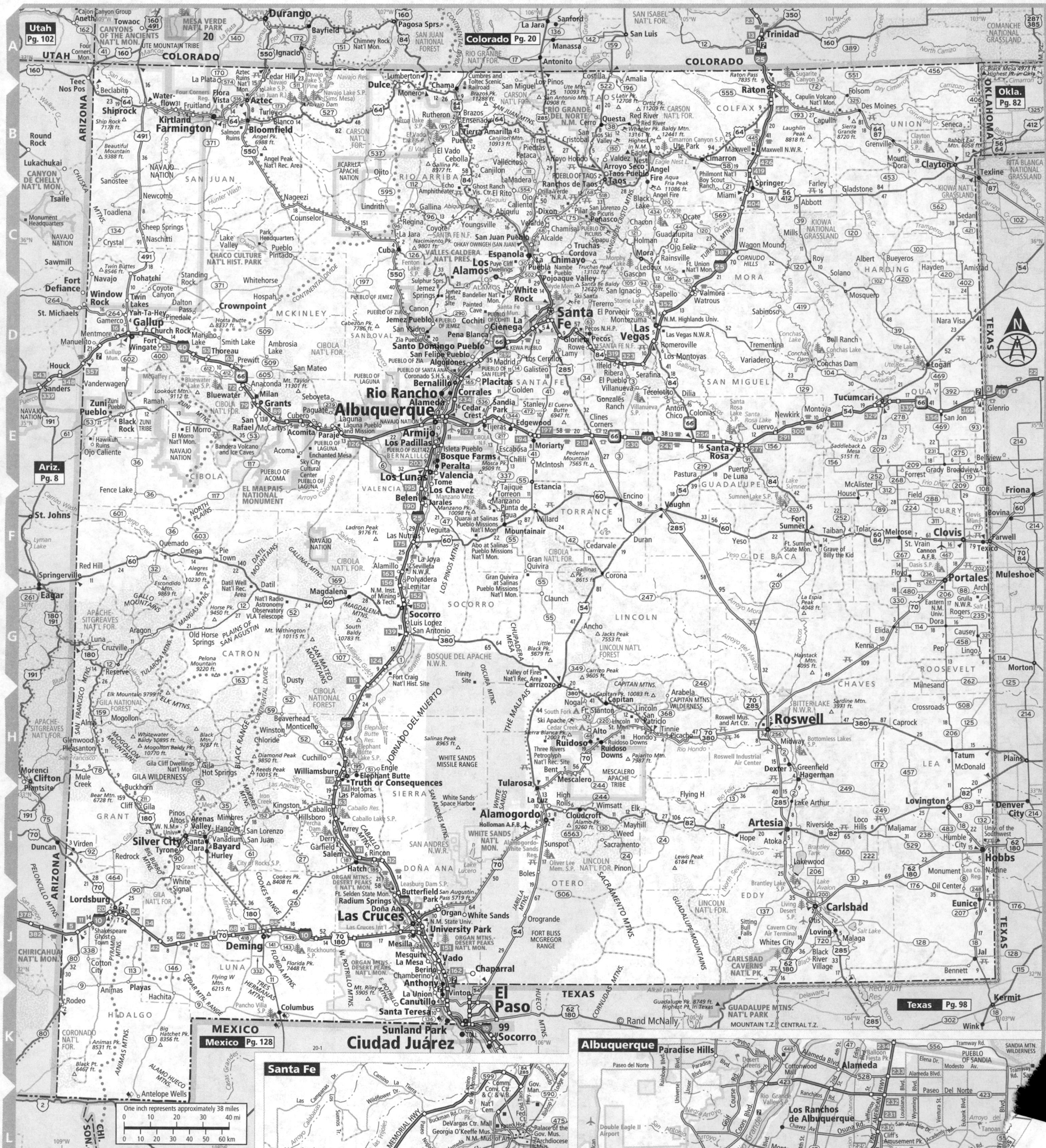

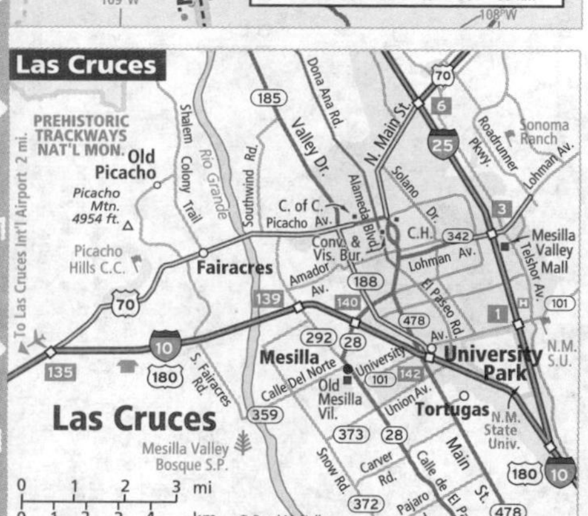

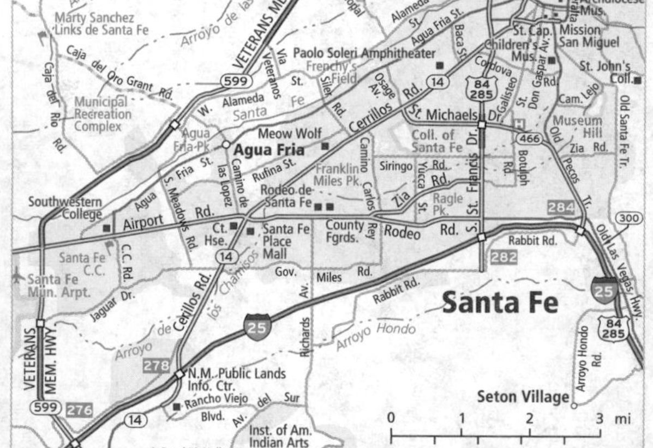

Travel planning & on-the-road resources

Tourism Information
N.Y. State Division of Tourism: (800) 225-5697; www.iloveny.com

Toll Road Info
see next page for listings

Road Conditions & Construction
511, (888) 465-1169, (877) 690-5110
511ny.org, www.dot.ny.gov
Thruway: (800) 847-8929; www.thruway.ny.gov

Determining Distances

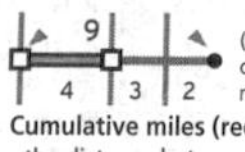

Cumulative miles (red): the distance between red arrows
Intermediate miles (black): the distance between intersections & places

Total mileages through New York
84: 72 miles
95: 24 miles
87: 334 miles
495: 66 miles

More mileages at randmcnally.com/MC

Mileages between cities

	Albany	Buffalo	Hempstead	Newburgh	New York	Poughkeepsie	Riverhead	White Plains
Albany		289	167	87	156	75	219	138
Buffalo	289		423	361	395	362	471	394
Hempstead	167	423		78	12	92	59	34
Kingston	55	339	116	37	106	19	168	87
Montauk	260	513	97	172	107	184	42	126
Newburgh	87	361	78		72	19	130	49
New York	156	395	12	72		84	66	26
Poughkeepsie	75	362	92	19	84		143	60

New York/Southern

Nickname: The Empire State
Capital: Albany, NK-19
Land area: 47,126 sq. mi. (rank: 30th)
Population: 19,378,102 (rank: 3rd)
Largest city: New York, 8,175,133, SF-6

Index of places Pg. 133

Nickname: The Empire State
Capital: Albany, NK-19
Land area: 47,126 sq. mi. (rank: 30th)
Population: 19,378,102 (rank: 3rd)
Largest city: New York, 8,175,133, SF-6

Index of places Pg. 133

Travel planning & on-the-road resources

Tourism Information
New York State Division of Tourism:
(800) 225-5697; www.iloveny.com

Road Conditions & Construction
511, (888) 465-1169; (877) 690-5110
511ny.org, www.dot.ny.gov
Thruway: (800) 847-8929; www.thruway.ny.gov

Toll Road Information: *(all use E-ZPass)*
New York State Thruway Authority:
(518) 436-2805; www.thruway.ny.gov
MTA (N.Y. City in-state bridges & tunnels):
(877) 690-5116, N.Y.C. only: 511 & say "bridges & tunnels"
www.mta.info/bandt
New York State Bridge Authority (Hudson River bridges):
(845) 691-7245; www.nysba.state.ny.us

International Toll Bridge Information:
Buffalo & Ft. Erie Public Br. Auth. (Peace Br.) *(E-ZPass)*:
(716) 884-6744; www.peacebridge.com
Niagara Falls Bridge Comm. *(E-ZPass or ExpressPass)*:
(716) 285-6322; www.niagarafallsbridges.com
Ogdensburg Br. & Port Auth.: (315) 393-4080; www.ogdensport.com
Seaway Int'l Bridge Corp. *(Seaway Transit Card)*: (613) 932-6601; www.sibc.ca
Thousand Islands Br. Auth. (Alexandria Bay): (315) 482-2501; www.tibridge.com

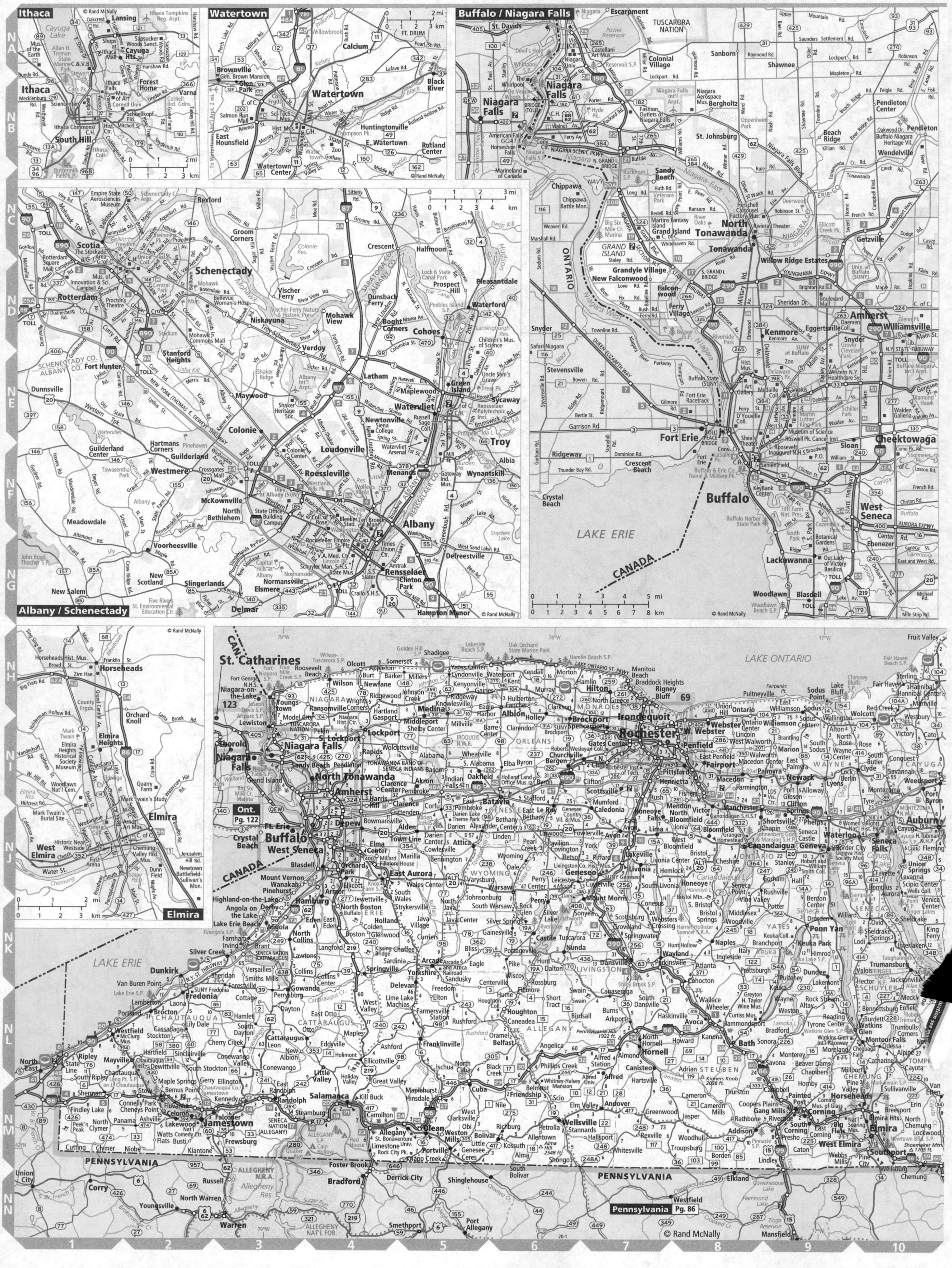

Niagara Falls

Mileages between cities

	Albany	Binghamton	Buffalo	Elmira	Glens Falls	Jamestown	Kingston	Lake Placid	Massena	New York	Niagara Falls	Plattsburgh	Rochester	Syracuse	Utica	Watertown
Albany		140	239	195	53	356	55	140	217	156	302	160	226	145	94	175
Binghamton	140		222	56	179	218	130	266	231	176	235	287	159	73	89	143
Buffalo	289	222		148	313	71	339	337	305	395	21	373	73	150	198	212
Jamestown	356	218	71	163	395		349	404	370	392	92	436	139	214	263	278
Plattsburgh	160	287	373	342	110	436	214	50	82	317	384		308	227	183	165
Rochester	226	159	73	120	248	139	277	275	242	332	87	308		86	135	149
Syracuse	145	73	150	90	160	214	195	195	159	246	162	227	86		53	70
Watertown	175	143	212	160	179	278	226	125	89	316	225	165	149	70	80	

Total mileages through New York

81: 184 miles
86: 176 miles
87: 334 miles
90: 385 miles

More mileages at randmcnally.com/MC

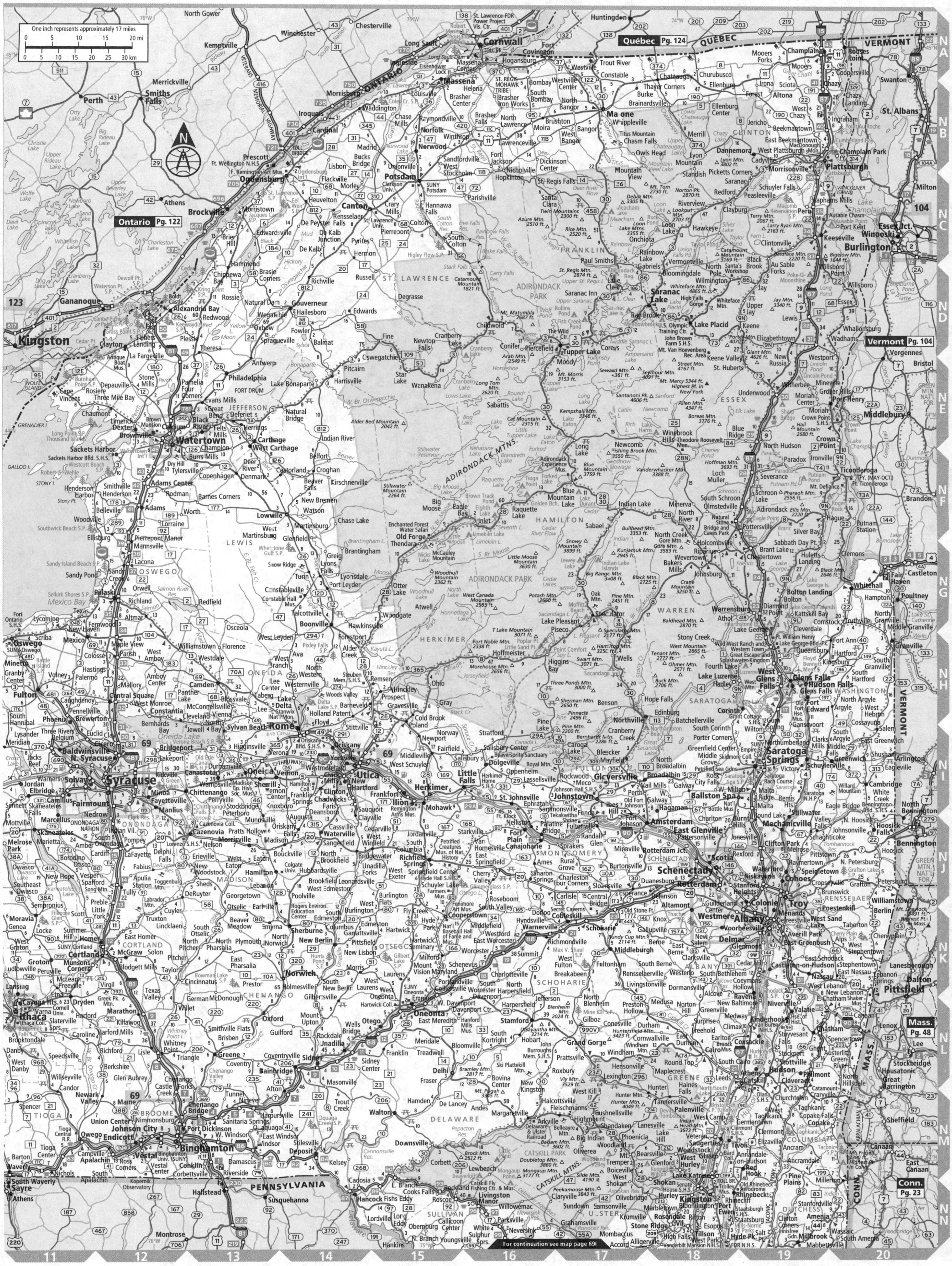

Sights to see

- American Museum of Natural History A-4
- Battery Park I-1
- Bronx Zoo E-12
- Brooklyn Bridge H-2
- Carnegie Hall C-4
- Central Park B-4
- Chrysler Building D-4
- Coney Island L-10
- Ellis Island I-9
- Empire State Building D-3
- Greenwich Village H-10
- Grand Central Terminal D-4

Ellis Island Museum

Brooklyn Bridge, New York City

Sights to see

- Guggenheim Museum A-5
- Intrepid Sea-Air Space Museum C-2
- Lincoln Center B-3
- Madison Square Garden D-2
- Metropolitan Museum of Art B-5
- National September 11 Memorial H-1
- New York Stock Exchange and Wall Street H-1
- Rockefeller Center C-4
- Staten Island Ferry .... I-2 and J-8
- Statue of Liberty I-9
- Times Square D-3
- Yankee Stadium E-11

North Carolina

Nickname: The Tar Heel State
Capital: Raleigh, E-12
Land area: 48,618 sq. mi. (rank: 29th)
Population: 9,535,483 (rank: 10th)
Largest city: Charlotte, 731,424, F-5

Index of places Pg. 133

Travel planning & on-the-road resources

Tourism Information
Visit North Carolina: (800) 847-4862; www.visitnc.com

Road Conditions & Construction
511, (877) 511-4662; www.ncdot.gov/travel-maps, www.ncdot.gov

Toll Road Information
I-77 Mobility Partners *(NC Quick Pass)*: (980) 337-2400; www.i77express.com
N.C. Turnpike Authority *(NC Quick Pass)*: (919) 707-2700; www.ncdot.gov/divisions/turnpike

Determining distances along roads

Highway distances (segments of one mile or less not shown):
Cumulative miles (red): the distance between red arrows
Intermediate miles (black): the distance between intersections & places

Interchanges and exit numbers
For most states, the mileage between interchanges may be determined by subtracting one number from the other.

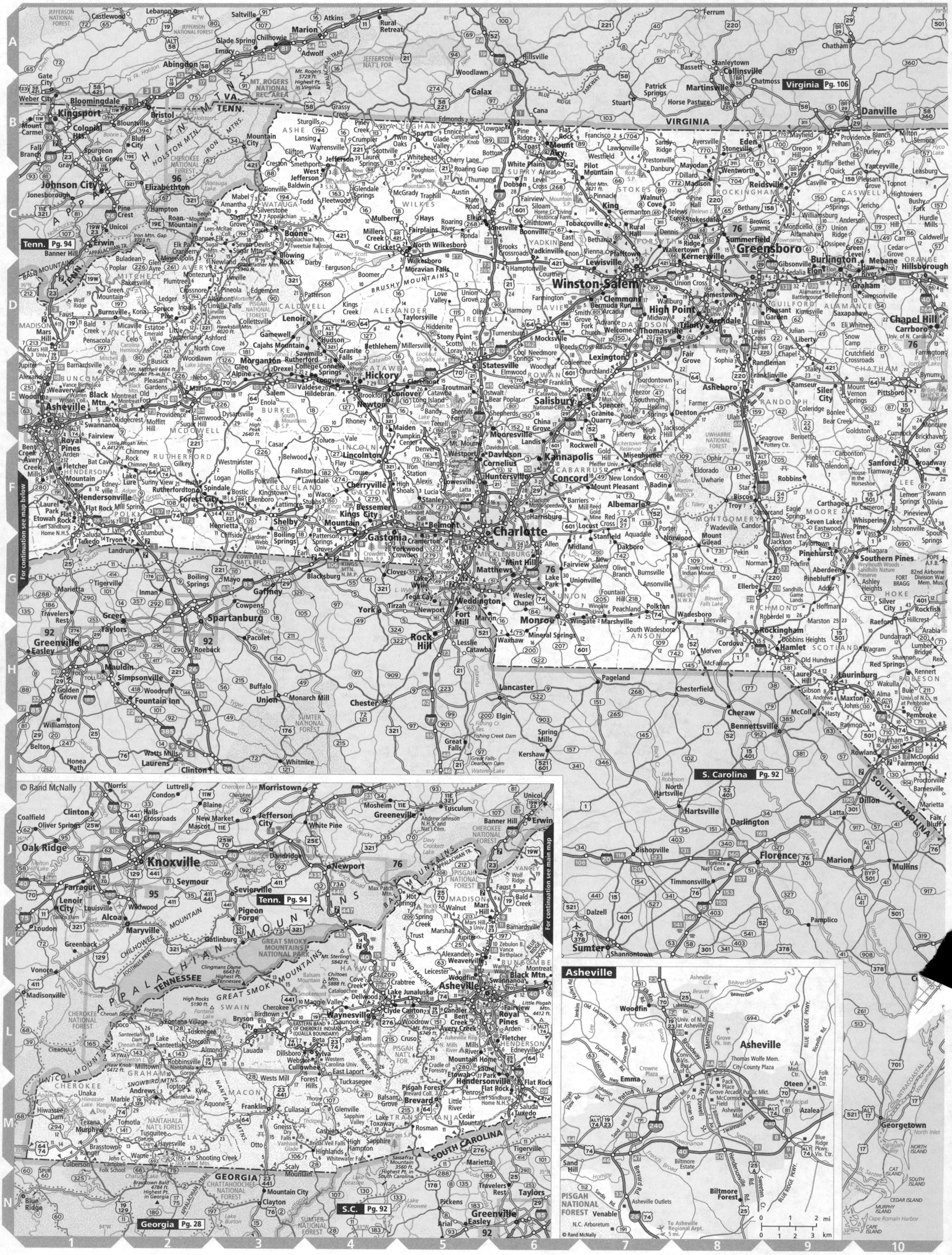

Linn Cove Viaduct

Mileages between cities	Asheville	Boone	Charlotte	Durham	Elizabeth City	Greensboro	Hickory	Morehead City	Murphy	Nags Head	New Bern	Raleigh	Roanoke Rapids	Rockingham	Wilmington	Winston-Salem
Asheville		94	128	224	412	172	77	393	110	444	358	251	308	200	327	145
Charlotte	128	100		144	332	93	57	313	223	364	278	168	231	71	197	77
Elizabeth City	412	354	332	185		241	338	152	520	56	119	164	97	259	208	269
Fayetteville	261	202	137	89	203	94	189	138	369	234	130	63	127	64	89	119
Greensboro	172	113	93	53	241		98	223	279	271	188	80	138	83	207	29
Greenville	332	273	250	101	97	156	258	79	440	129	44	82	86	176	116	188
Raleigh	251	192	168	22	164	80	177	146	358	195	111		89	98	130	107
Wilmington	327	319	197	156	208	207	259	91	428	230	90	130	178	127		236

Mileages © Rand McNally

Total mileages through North Carolina

- 40: 419 miles
- 85: 233 miles
- 77: 102 miles
- 95: 182 miles

More mileages at randmcnally.com/MC

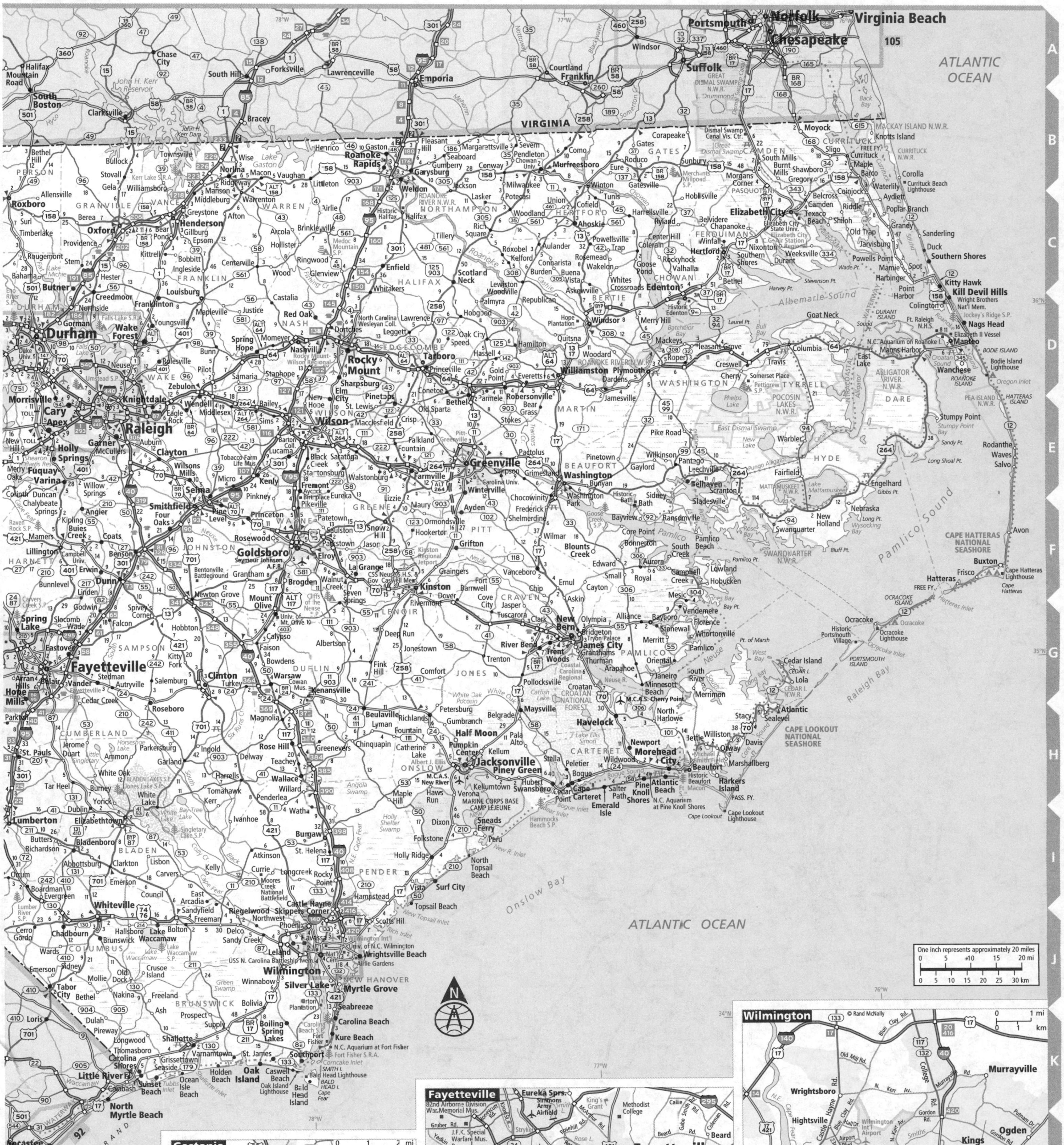

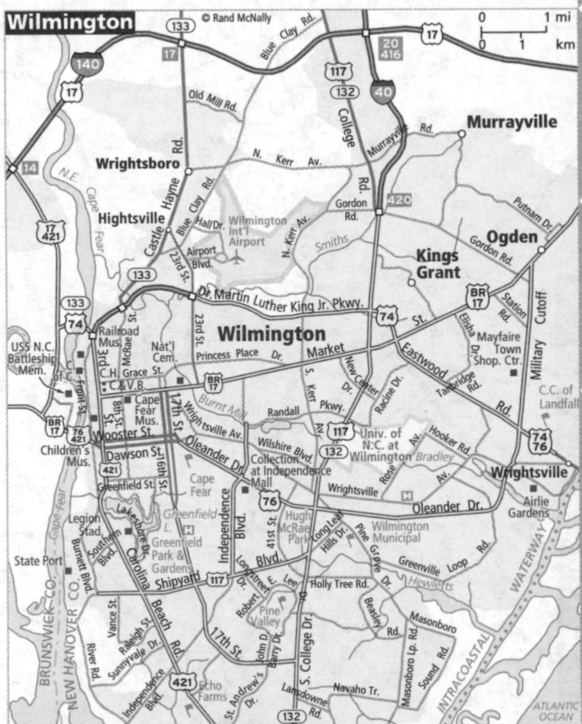

Sights to see

- Discovery Place, Charlotte H-4
- Duke Homestead State Historic Site & Tobacco Museum, Durham F-9
- Historic Bethabara Park, Winston-Salem A-1
- Mint Museum of Art, Charlotte H-5
- Morehead Planetarium & Science Center, Chapel Hill . . H-8
- North Carolina Museum of History, Raleigh I-12
- North Carolina Museum of Life & Science, Durham . . F-10
- North Carolina State Capitol, Raleigh I-13
- North Carolina State University, Raleigh I-13
- Old Salem, Winston-Salem B-2
- Reynolda House, Winston-Salem B-1

Great Smoky Mountains National Park

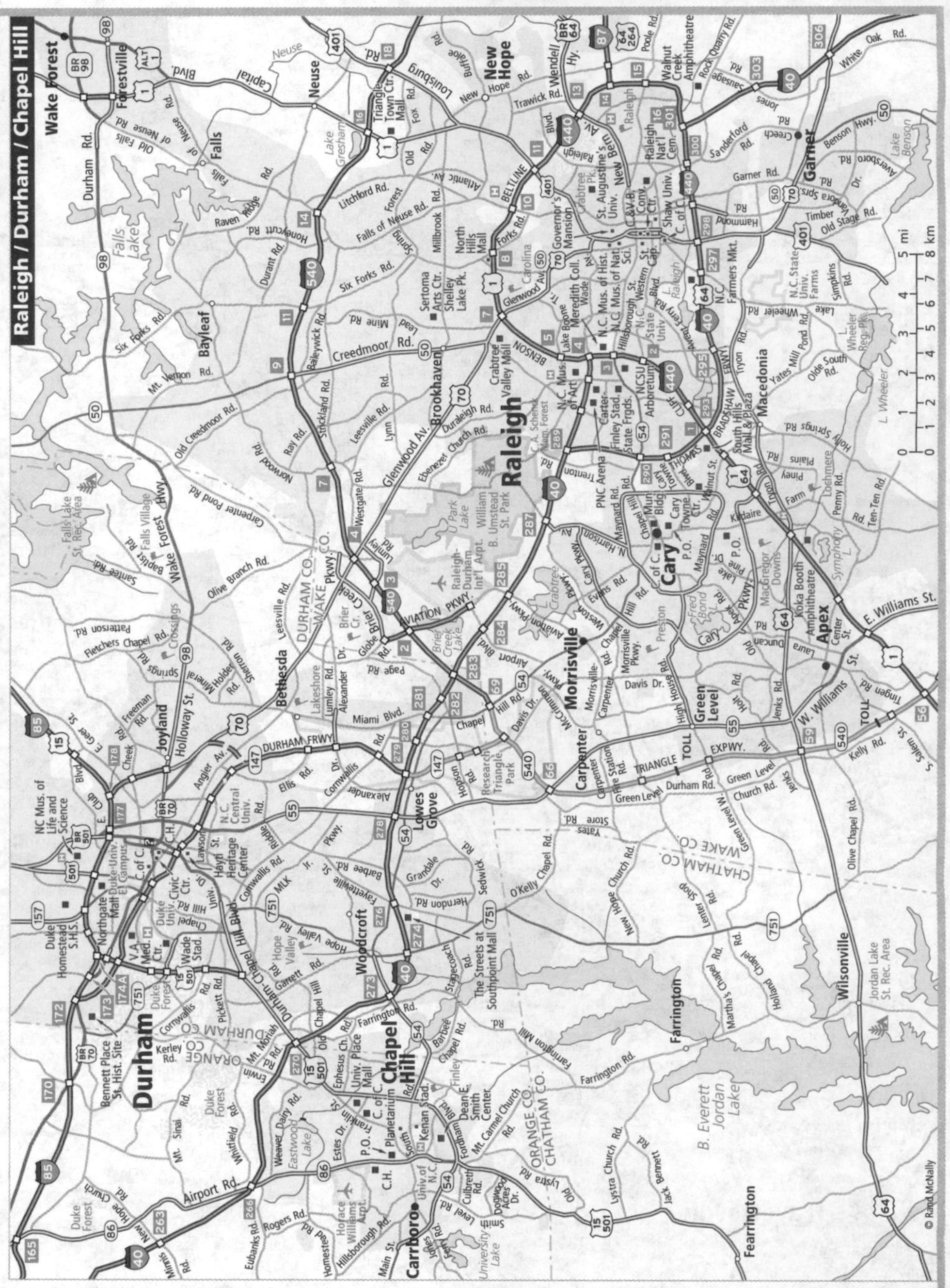

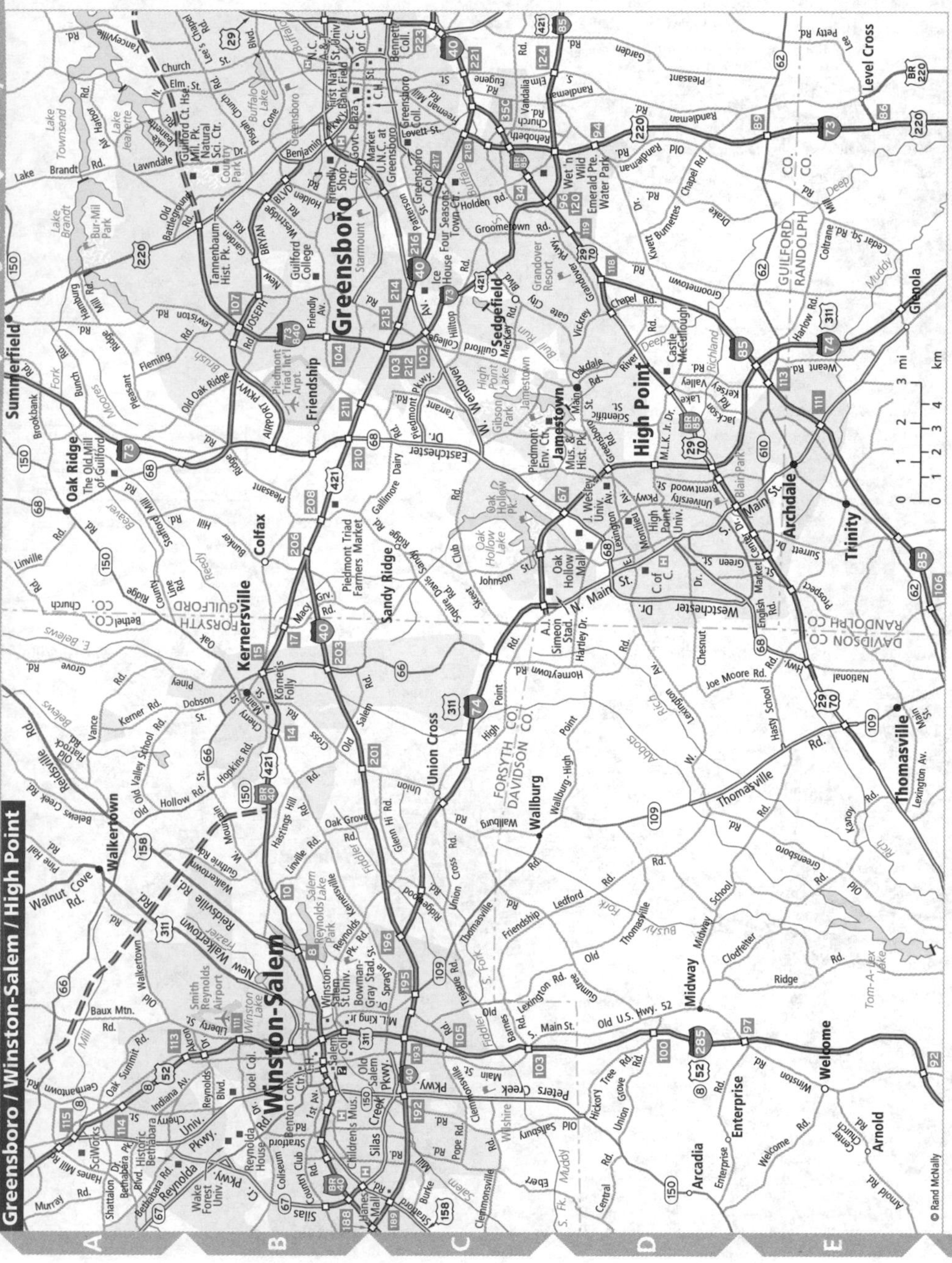

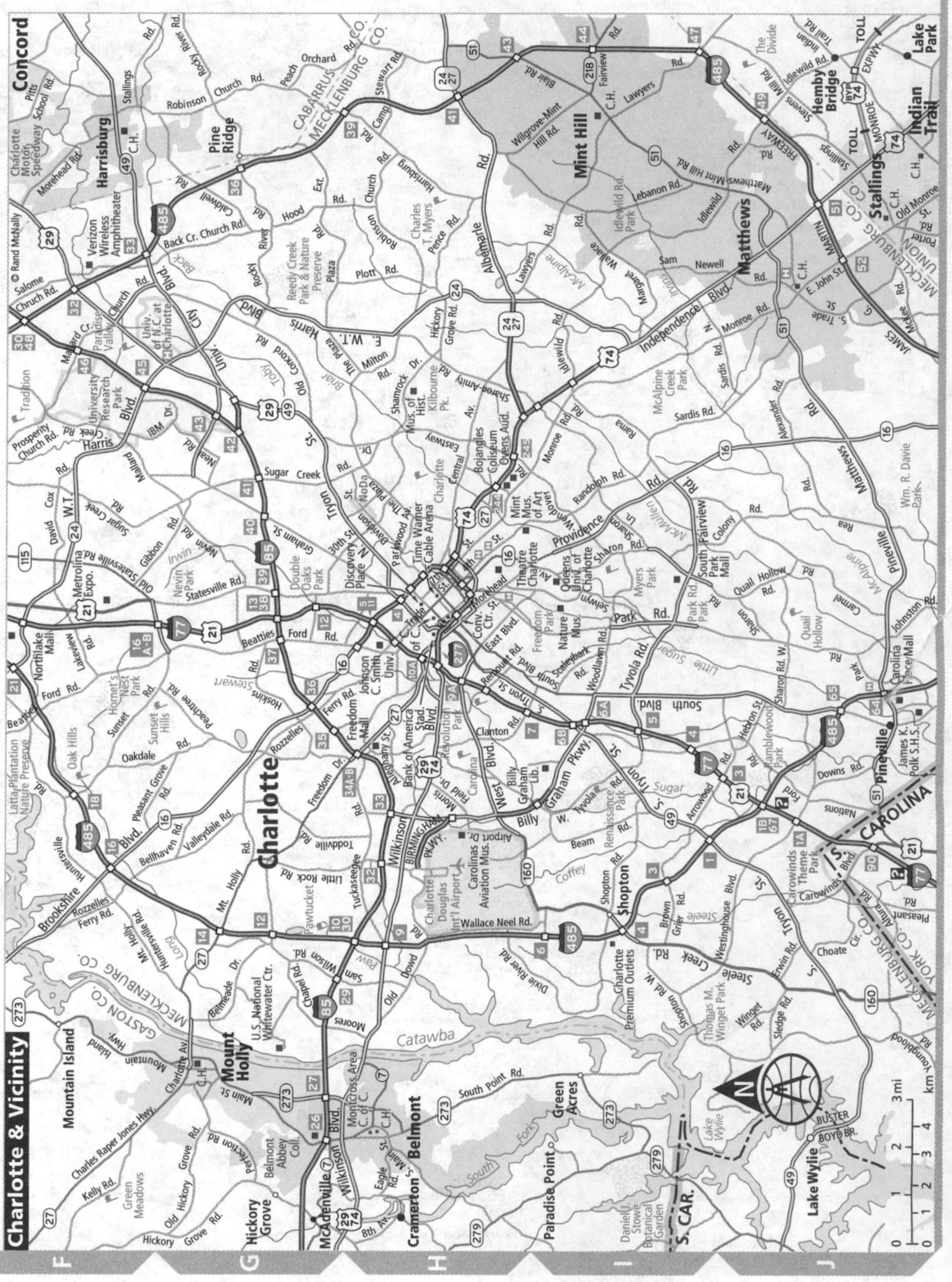

Travel planning & on-the-road resources

Tourism Information
North Dakota Tourism Division:
(800) 435-5663, (701) 328-2525; www.ndtourism.com

Road Conditions & Construction
511, (866) 696-3511
www.dot.nd.gov/travel, www.dot.nd.gov/travel-info-v2

Toll Road Information
No tolls on state or federal highways

Determining Distances
(segments of one mile or less not shown)
Cumulative miles (red): the distance between red arrows
Intermediate miles (black): the distance between intersections & places

Total mileages through North Dakota
29: 218 miles
94: 352 miles
2: 359 miles
83: 265 miles

More mileages at randmcnally.com/MC

Mileages between cities	Bismarck	Bowman	Fargo	Garrison	Grand Forks	Jamestown	Williston	Winnipeg, MB
Bismarck		174	195	75	272	102	228	413
Devils Lake	180	354	165	167	89	93	245	230
Dickinson	97	78	292	149	368	193	132	509
Fargo	195	368		266	80	94	422	222
Grand Forks	272	444	80	256		171	334	146
Minot	110	260	268	47	210	170	124	299
Wahpeton	243	416	54	315	131	142	470	273
Williston	228	170	422	144	334	293		424

North Dakota

Nickname: The Peace Garden State
Capital: Bismarck, H-7
Land area: 69,000 sq. mi. (rank: 17th)
Population: 672,591 (rank: 48th)
Largest city: Fargo, 105,549, H-13

Index of places Pg. 133

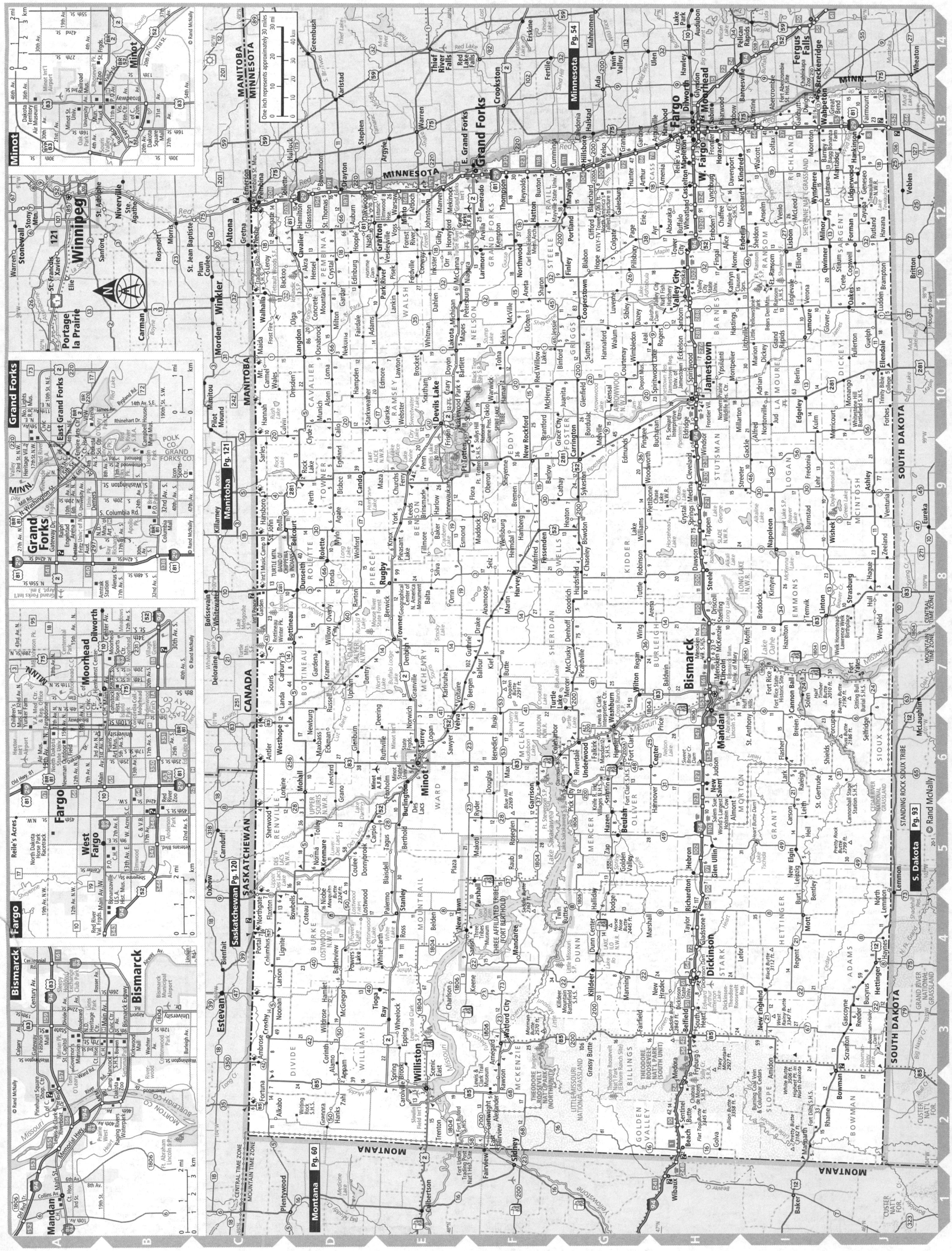

Nickname: The Buckeye State
Capital: Columbus, SB-9
Land area: 40,861 sq. mi. (rank: 35th)
Population: 11,536,504 (rank: 7th)
Largest city: Columbus, 787,033, SB-9

Index of places Pg. 133

Travel planning & on-the-road resources

Tourism Information
Tourism Ohio: (800) 282-5393; www.ohio.org

Road Conditions & Construction
511; (855) 511-6446; www.ohgo.com, www.dot.state.oh.us
Ohio Turnpike: (440) 234-2081, option 3; www.ohioturnpike.org

Toll Road Information
Ohio Turnpike and Infrastructure Commission (*E-ZPass*): (440) 234-2081; www.ohioturnpike.org

Determining distances along roads

Highway distances (segments of one mile or less not shown):
Cumulative miles (red): the distance between red arrows
Intermediate miles (black): the distance between intersections & places

Interchanges and exit numbers
For most states, the mileage between interchanges may be determined by subtracting one number from the other.

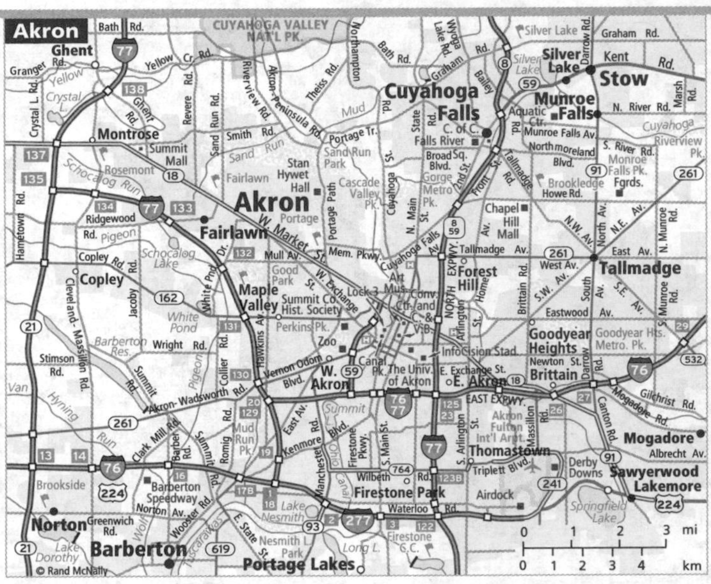

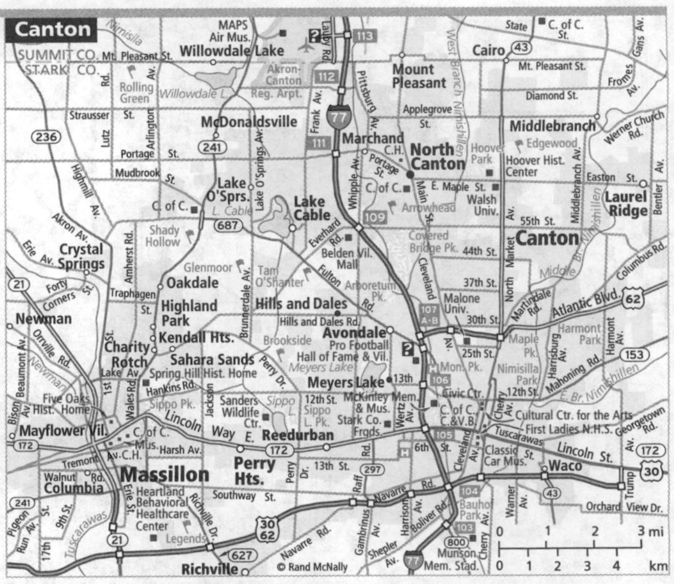

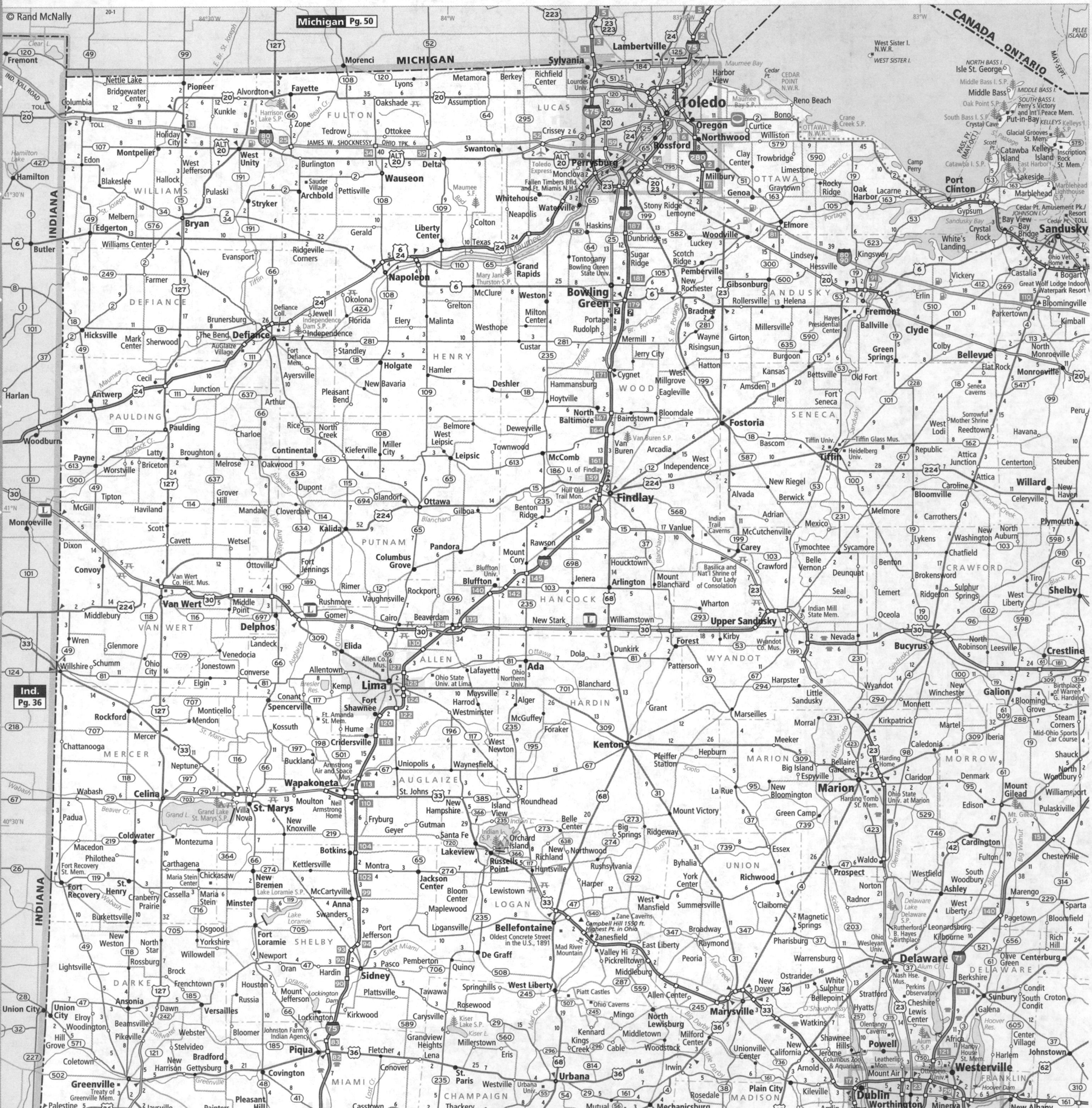

Cleveland's North Coast Harbor

Mileages between cities	Akron	Ashtabula	Canton	Cincinnati	Cleveland	Columbus	Coshocton	Findlay	Lima	Mansfield	New Philadelphia	Pittsburgh, PA	Sandusky	Steubenville	Toledo	Youngstown
Akron		81	20	232	39	124	80	132	154	62	47	107	85	[illegible]	133	48
Cleveland	39	58	58	248		142	102	121	156	80	85	131	62	[illegible]	111	72
Columbus	124	194	126	106	142		71	96	91	66	118	184	112	[illegible]	142	172
Defiance	180	[illegible]	185	169	157	135	177	51	44	123	190	274	98	[illegible]	57	214
Lima	154	216	156	124	156	91	134	34		94	162	261	96	[illegible]	77	202
Mansfield	62	132	64	172	80	66	62	72	94		67	170	53	[illegible]	99	110
Toledo	133	171	152	200	111	142	152	44	77	99	179	228	58	[illegible]		169
Youngstown	48	57	57	279	72	172	117	180	202	110	84	67	122	65	169	

Mileages © Rand McNally

Total mileages through Ohio

71: 248 miles
80: 237 miles
75: 211 miles
90: 245 miles

More mileages at randmcnally.com/MC

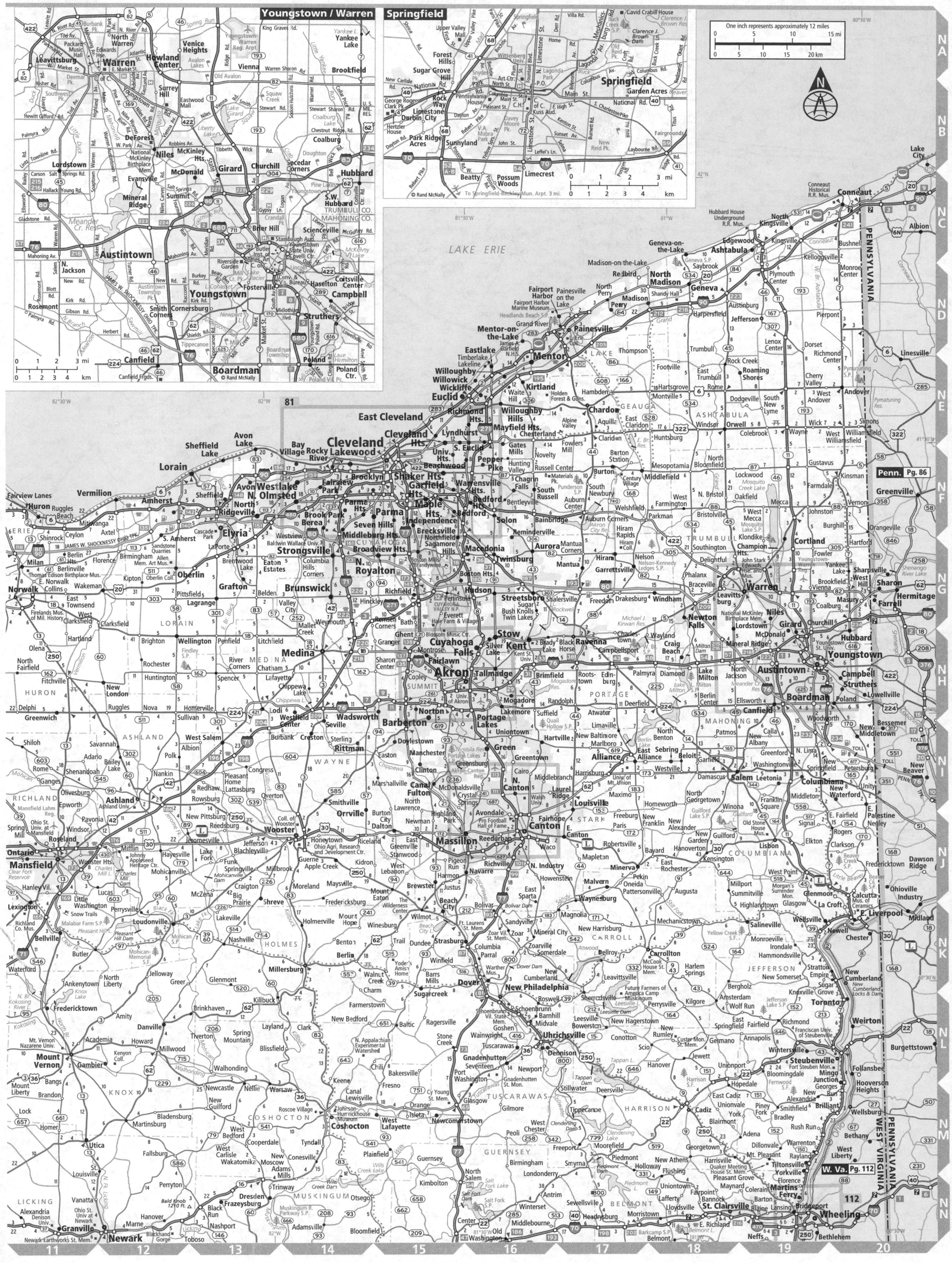

Nickname: The Buckeye State
Capital: Columbus, SB-9
Land area: 40,861 sq. mi. (rank: 35th)
Population: 11,536,504 (rank: 7th)
Largest city: Columbus, 787,033, SB-9

Index of places Pg. 133

Travel planning & on-the-road resources

Tourism Information
Tourism Ohio: (800) 282-5393; www.ohio.org

Road Conditions & Construction
511; (855) 511-6446; www.ohgo.com, www.dot.state.oh.us
Ohio Turnpike: (440) 234-2081, option 3; www.ohioturnpike.org

Toll Road Information
Ohio Turnpike and Infrastructure Commission (*E-ZPass*): (440) 234-2081; www.ohioturnpike.org

Determining distances along roads

Highway distances (segments of one mile or less not shown):
Cumulative miles (red): the distance between red arrows
Intermediate miles (black): the distance between intersections & places

Interchanges and exit numbers
For most states, the mileage between interchanges may be determined by subtracting one number from the other.

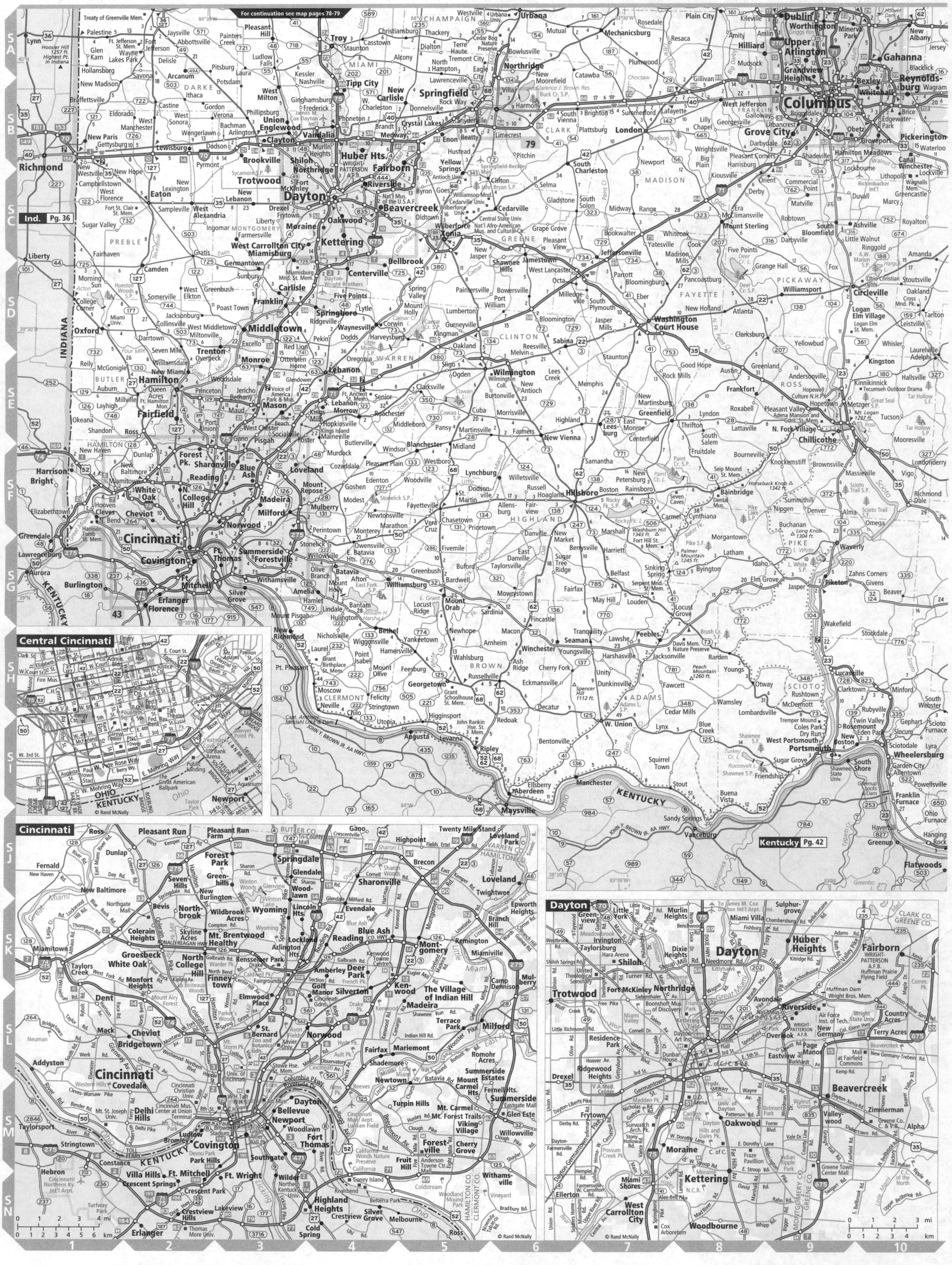

Hocking Hills State Park

Mileages between cities	Athens	Cambridge	Chillicothe	Cincinnati	Cleveland	Columbus	Dayton	Gallipolis	Huntington, WV	Lancaster	Marietta	Maysville, KY	Portsmouth	Wheeling, WV	Wilmington	Zanesville
Cincinnati	160	183	105		248	106	50	153	148	133	210	61	110	230	51	158
Columbus	74	79	47	106	142		71	106	137	30	124	112	91	126	62	55
Dayton	134	149	77	50	212	71		137	168	101	195	108	122	197	34	126
Gallipolis	42	114	60	153	235	106	137		39	86	66	111	55	162	112	94
Marietta	44	48	104	210	164	124	195	66	106	82		165	128	90	156	69
Portsmouth	81	162	44	110	233	91	122	55	46	80	128	52		210	79	138
Springfield	118	123	69	77	185	45	27	129	160	74	168	102	114	171	38	99
Zanesville	52	24	94	158	145	55	126	94	134	45	69	164	138	72	114	

Mileages © Rand McNally

Total mileages through Ohio

- 70: 226 miles
- 71: 248 miles
- 75: 211 miles
- 77: 160 miles

More mileages at randmcnally.com/MC

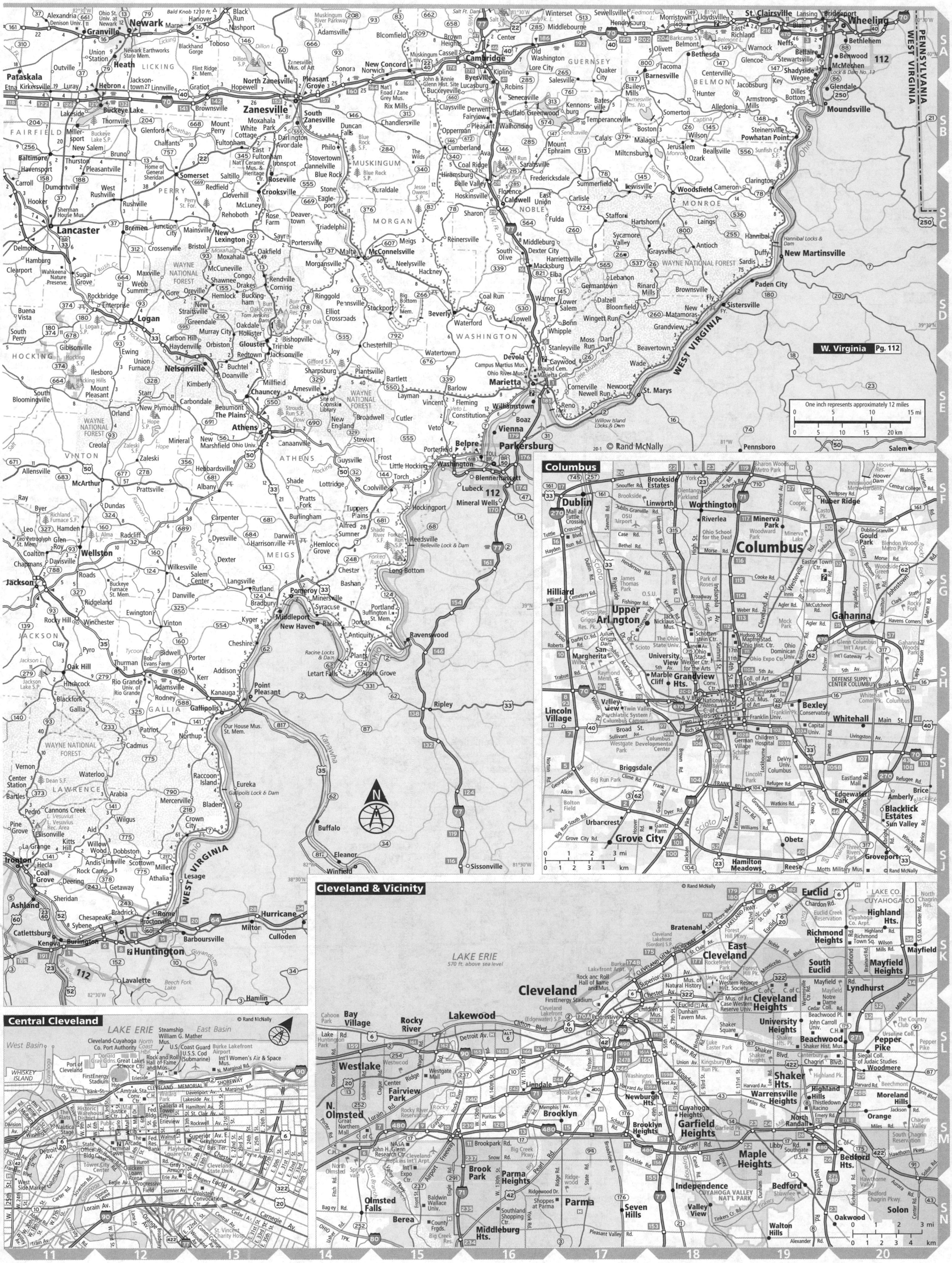

Oklahoma

Nickname: The Sooner State
Capital: Oklahoma City, F-13
Land area: 68,595 sq. mi. (rank: 19th)
Population: 3,751,351 (rank: 28th)
Largest city: Oklahoma City, 579,999, F-13

Index of places Pg. 134

Travel planning & on-the-road resources

Tourism Information
Oklahoma Tourism Department: (800) 652-6552; www.travelok.com

Road Conditions & Construction
(844) 465-4997, (405) 522-2800; www.okroads.org, www.okladot.state.ok.us

Toll Road Information
Oklahoma Turnpike Authority (*PIKEPASS*): (405) 425-3600; www.pikepass.com

Determining distances along roads

Highway distances (segments of one mile or less not shown):
Cumulative miles (red): the distance between red arrows
Intermediate miles (black): the distance between intersections & places

Interchanges and exit numbers
For most states, the mileage between interchanges may be determined by subtracting one number from the other.

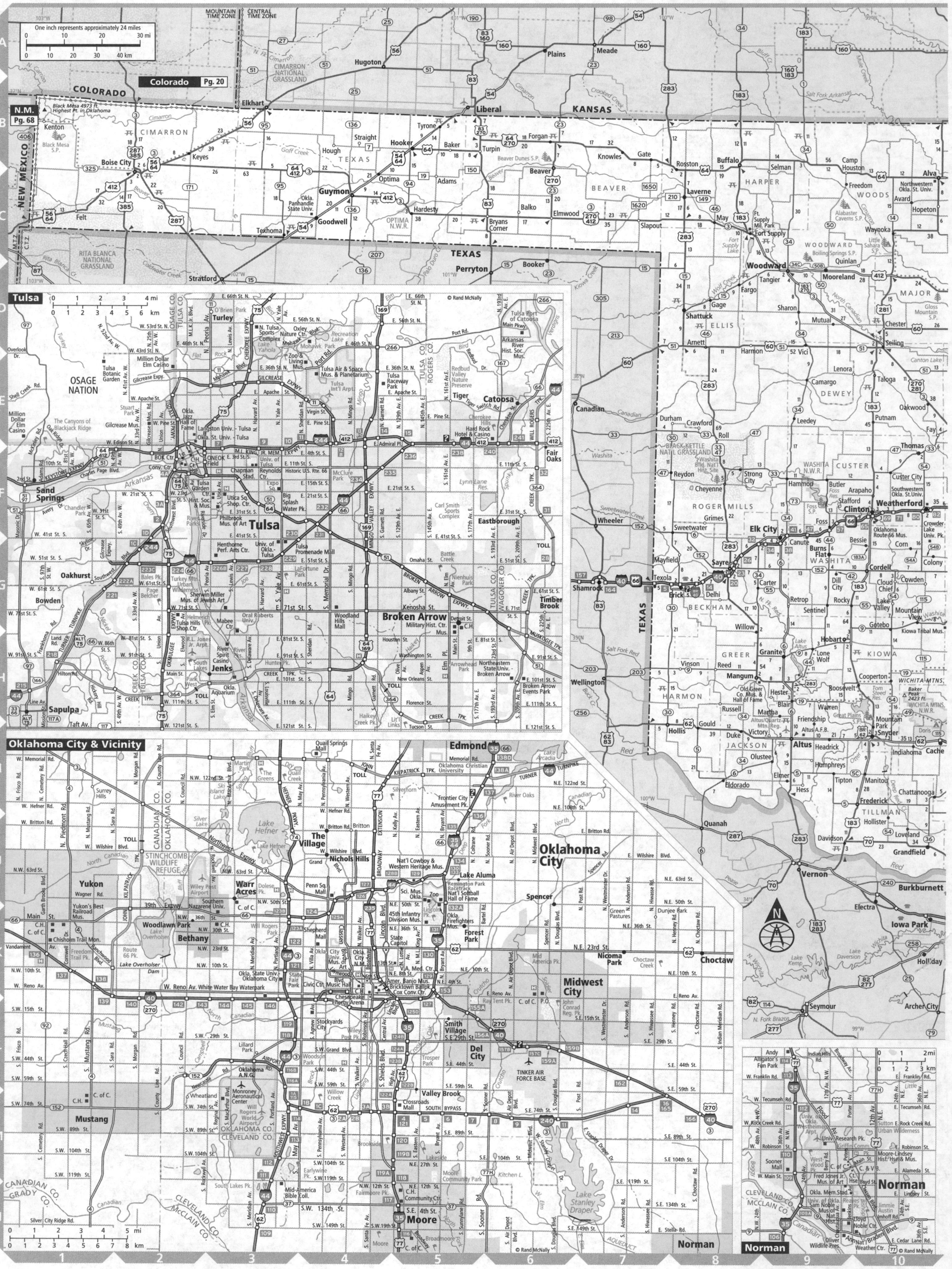

Buffalo

Mileages between cities	Ardmore	Bartlesville	Dallas, TX	Elk City	Enid	Ft. Smith, AR	Guymon	Joplin, MO	Lawton	McAlester	Muskogee	Oklahoma City	Ponca City	Tulsa	Wichita Falls, TX	Woodward
Ardmore		246	109	208	195	223	360	312	99	116	180	97	200	201	86	236
Elk City	208	260	303		148	292	184	327	108	240	249	112	216	215	143	77
Enid	195	134	302	148		232	211	227	142	204	164	99	67	114	196	87
Guymon	360	344	459	184	211	443		438	294	391	375	263	278	326	317	124
Idabel	149	248	171	352	316	136	504	295	245	116	180	240	293	203	238	380
Muskogee	180	91	236	249	164	70	375	117	218	65		137	142	50	272	251
Oklahoma City	97	149	204	112	99	180	263	216	86	128	137		105	104	140	139
Tulsa	201	45	258	215	114	118	326	113	191	91	50	104	91		244	202

Mileages © Rand McNally

Total mileages through Oklahoma

- I-35: 236 miles
- I-44: 329 miles
- I-40: 331 miles
- US 75: 227 miles

More mileages at randmcnally.com/MC

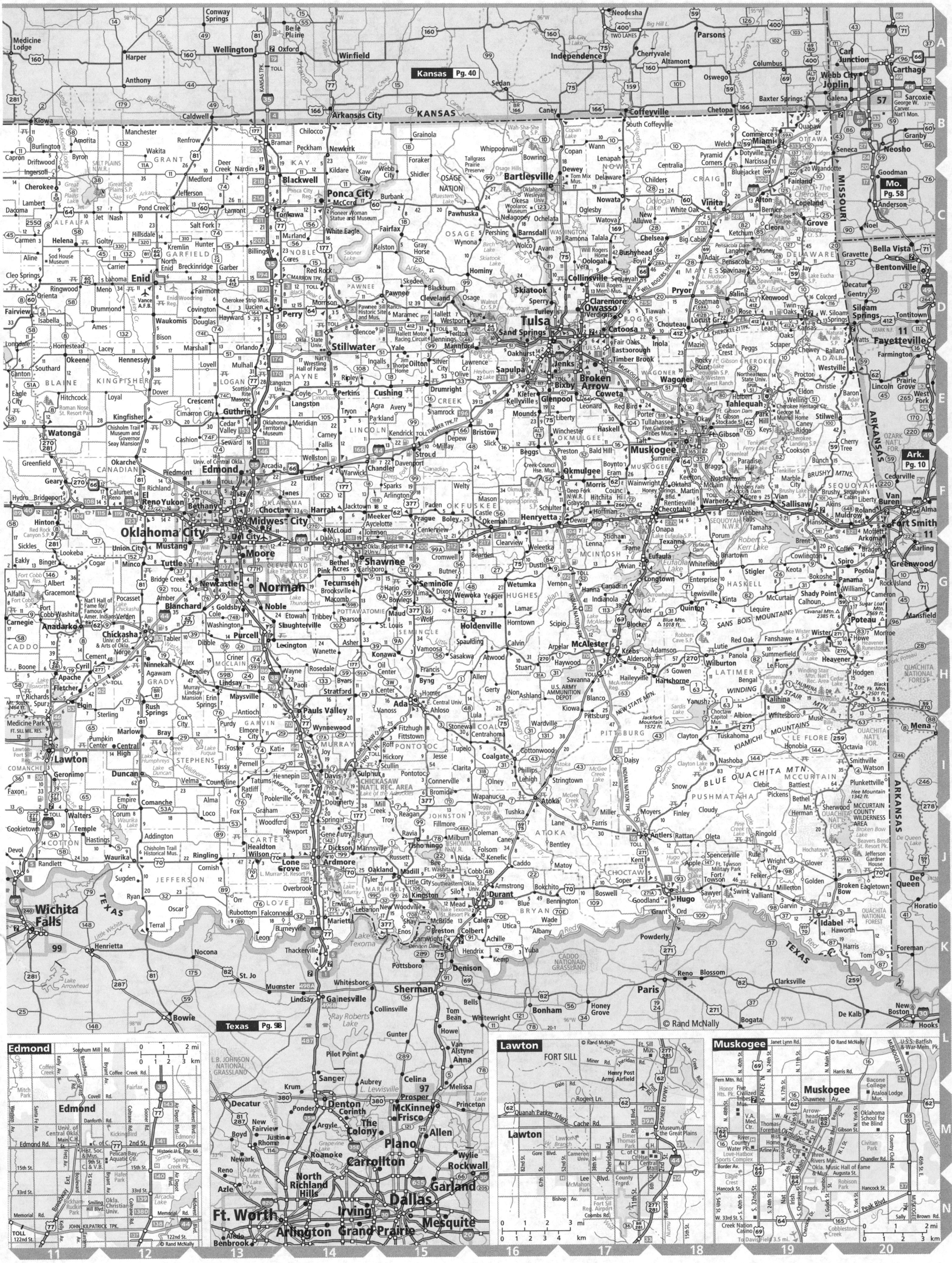

Nickname: The Beaver State
Capital: Salem, E-4
Land area: 95,988 sq. mi. (rank: 10th)
Population: 3,831,074 (rank: 27th)
Largest city: Portland, 583,776, C-5

Index of places Pg. 134

Travel planning & on-the-road resources

Tourism Information
Travel Oregon: (800) 547-7842
traveloregon.com

Road Conditions & Construction
511, (800) 977-6368, (503) 588-2941, (888) 275-6368, option 2
www.tripcheck.com; www.oregon.gov/odot

Toll Bridge Information
Bridge of the Gods (Cascade Locks): (541) 374-8619; portofcascadelocks.org/bridge-of-the-gods
Hood River Bridge (*BreezeBy*): (541) 386-1645; www.portofhoodriver.com/bridge

Determining distances along roads

Highway distances (segments of one mile or less not shown):
Cumulative miles (red): the distance between red arrows
Intermediate miles (black): the distance between intersections & places

Interchanges and exit numbers
For most states, the mileage between interchanges may be determined by subtracting one number from the other.

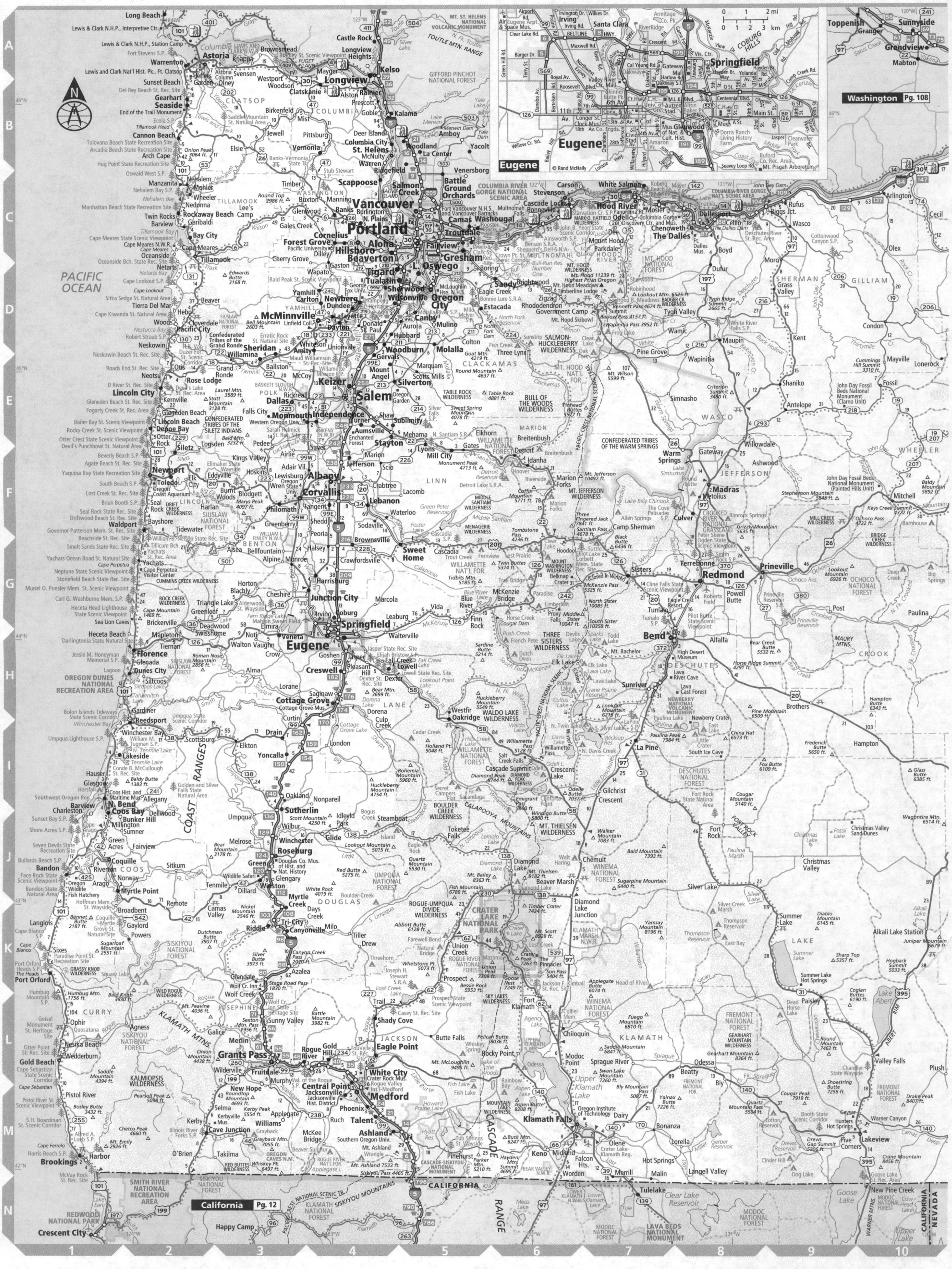

Cannon Beach

Mileages between cities	Astoria	Bend	Brookings	Burns	Coos Bay	Crater Lake N.P.	Eugene	Government Camp	John Day	Lakeview	Medford	Ontario	Pendleton	Portland	Salem	The Dalles
Bend	250		287	130	228	107	115	106	151	175	172	260	242	161	131	129
Corvallis	166	127	280	257	132	187	47	126	260	284	210	387	290	82	37	165
Eugene	193	115	234	245	109	142		154	249	241	166	375	318	110	66	193
McDermitt, NV	525	277	525	147	505	356	392	380	218	222	400	187	354	436	408	405
Medford	356	172	125	305	169	74	166	317	328	171		432	481	273	228	356
Ontario	464	260	547	130	488	367	375	354	131	269	432		167	374	420	291
Pendleton	298	242	550	196	428	349	318	188	126	335	481	167		208	254	125
Portland	96	161	342	281	220	250	110	55	265	336	273	374	208		47	83

Total mileages through Oregon

5: 308 miles
84: 375 miles
82: 11 miles
101: 348 miles

More mileages at randmcnally.com/MC

Nickname: The Keystone State
Capital: Harrisburg, EN-4
Land area: 44,743 sq. mi. (rank: 32nd)
Population: 12,702,379 (rank: 6th)
Largest city: Philadelphia, 1,526,006, EP-12

Index of places Pg. 134

Travel planning & on-the-road resources

Tourism Information
Visit PA: (800) 847-4872; visitpa.com

Road Conditions & Construction
511, (877) 511-7366; www.511pa.com, www.penndot.gov

Toll Road Information
Pennsylvania Turnpike Commission *(E-ZPass)*: (800) 331-3414; www.paturnpike.com

Determining distances along roads

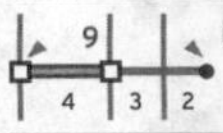

Highway distances (segments of one mile or less not shown):
Cumulative miles (red): the distance between red arrows
Intermediate miles (black): the distance between intersections & places

Interchanges and exit numbers
For most states, the mileage between interchanges may be determined by subtracting one number from the other.

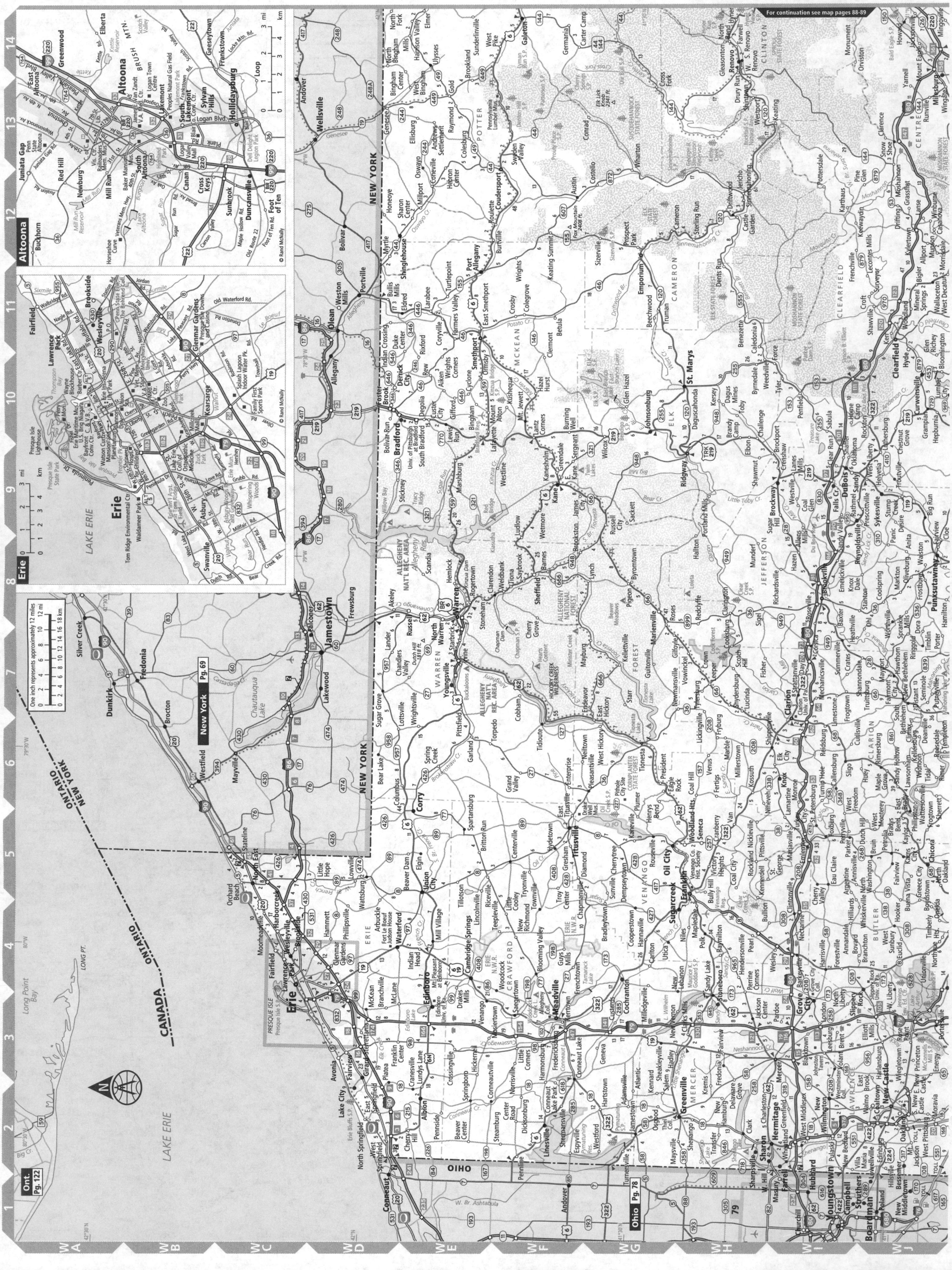

Allegheny National Forest

Mileages between cities	Altoona	Chambersburg	Cumberland, MD	Du Bois	Erie	Galeton	Harrisburg	Johnstown	Kittanning	Meadville	New Castle	Philadelphia	Pittsburgh	State College	Uniontown	Warren
Altoona		90	66	71	202	135	134	46	79	165	127	234	96	41	112	130
Chambersburg	90		87	153	282	215	54	94	160	246	206	157	160	101	149	218
Erie	202	282	232	148		159	297	177	123	41	88	419	127	208	184	66
Johnstown	46	94	70	77	177	179	137		53	141	102	238	67	85	80	135
New Castle	127	206	156	110	88	197	250	102	48	52		350	52	171	108	120
Pittsburgh	96	160	111	101	127	200	203	67	42	91	52	304		135	51	148
State College	41	101	106	61	208	100	87	85	120	173	171	193	135		152	119
Williamsport	100	132	166	110	257	72	83	146	168	220	219	176	196	63	212	171

Total mileages through Pennsylvania

- 70: 168 miles
- 79: 183 miles
- 80: 311 miles
- 90: 46 miles

More mileages at randmcnally.com/MC

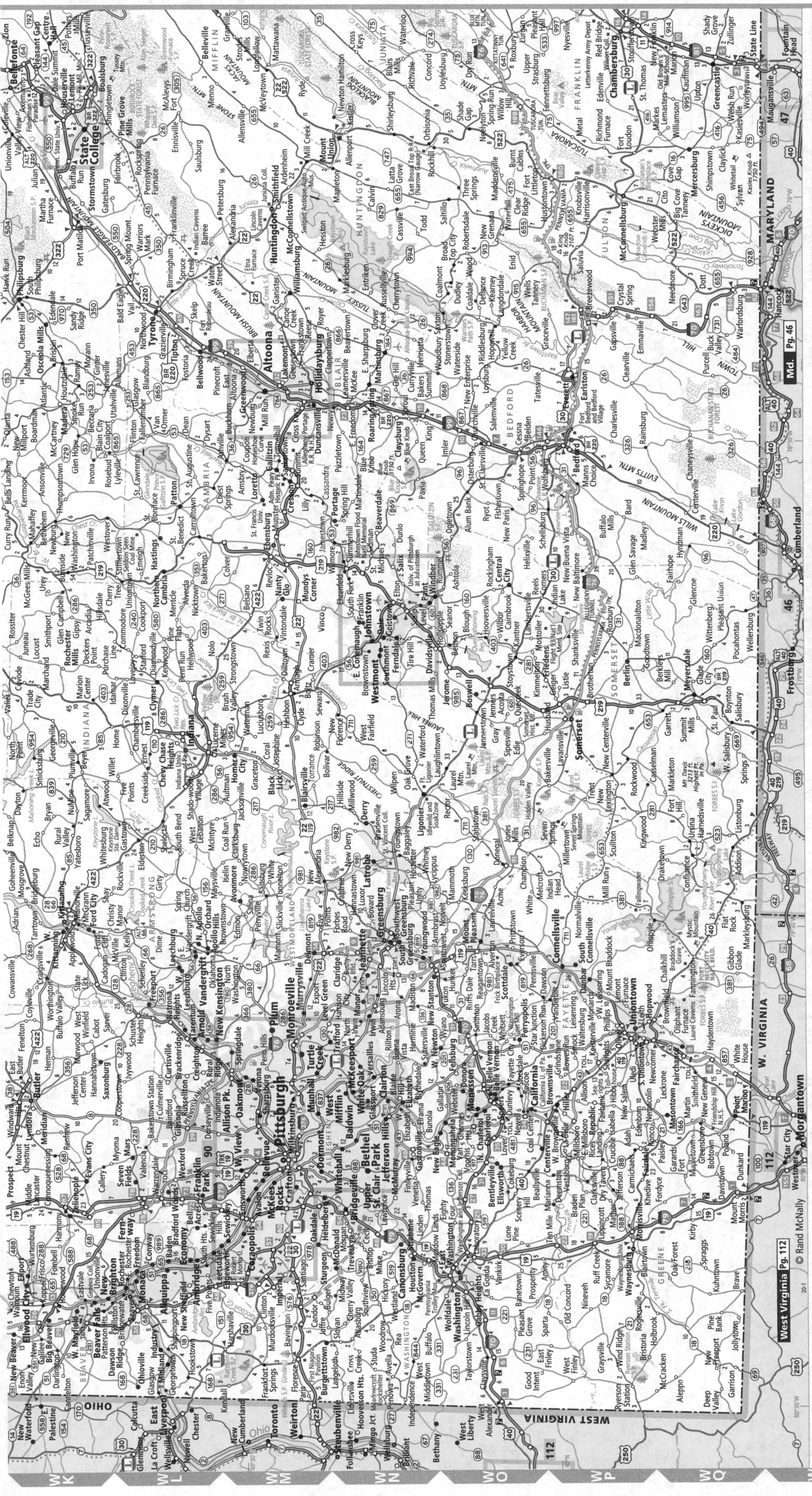

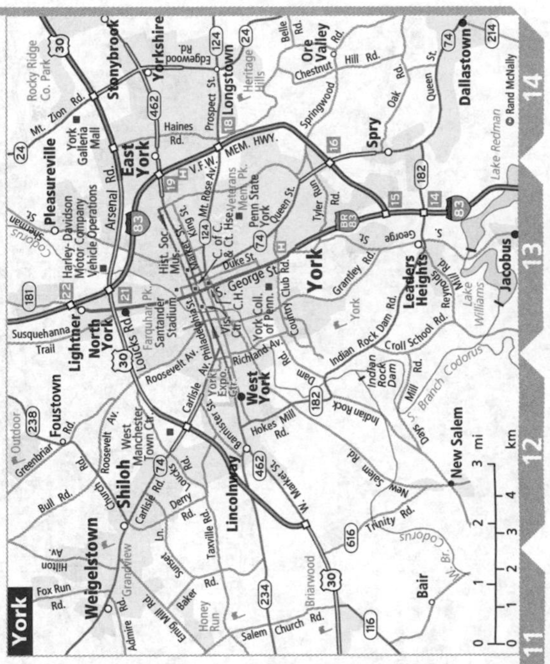

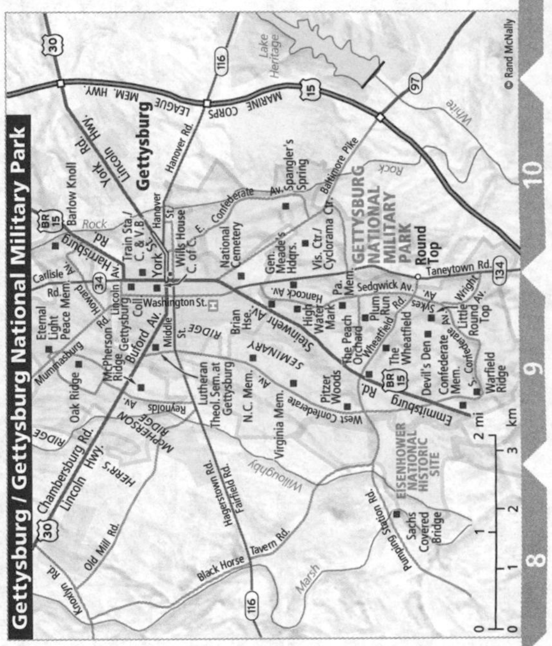

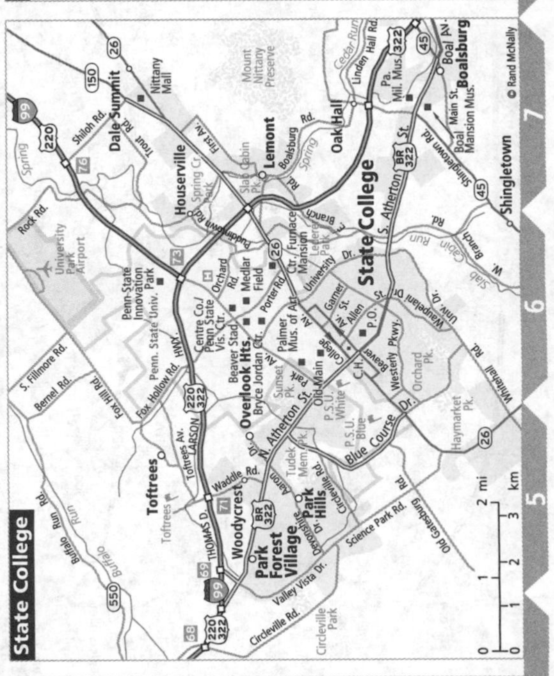

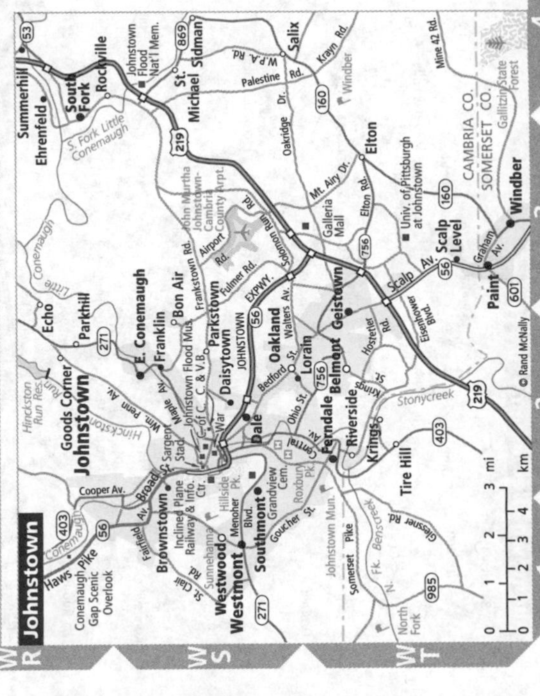

Nickname: The Keystone State
Capital: Harrisburg, EN-4
Land area: 44,743 sq. mi. (rank: 32nd)
Population: 12,702,379 (rank: 6th)
Largest city: Philadelphia, 1,526,006, EP-12

Index of places Pg. 134

Travel planning & on-the-road resources

Tourism Information
Visit PA: (800) 847-4872; visitpa.com

Road Conditions & Construction
511, (877) 511-7366; www.511pa.com; www.penndot.gov

Toll Road Information
Pennsylvania Turnpike Commission (*E-ZPass*): (800) 331-3414; www.paturnpike.com

Determining distances along roads

Highway distances (segments of one mile or less not shown):
Cumulative miles (red): the distance between red arrows
Intermediate miles (black): the distance between intersections & places

Interchanges and exit numbers
For most states, the mileage between interchanges may be determined by subtracting one number from the other.

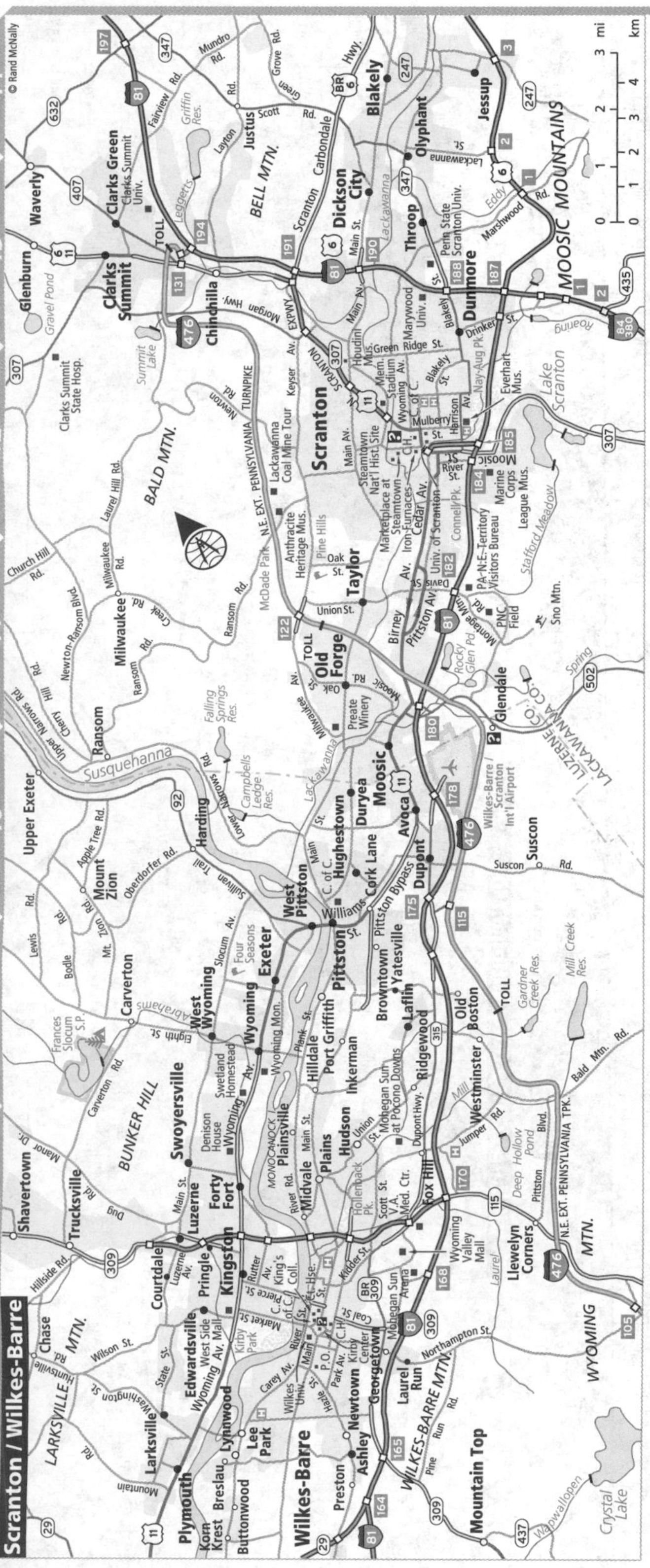

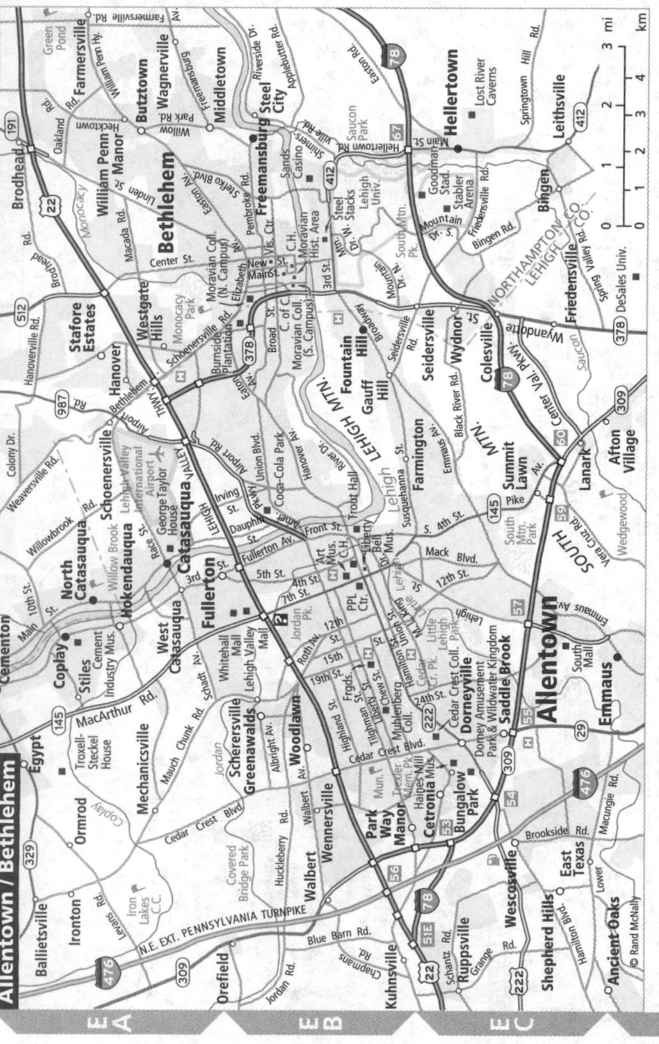

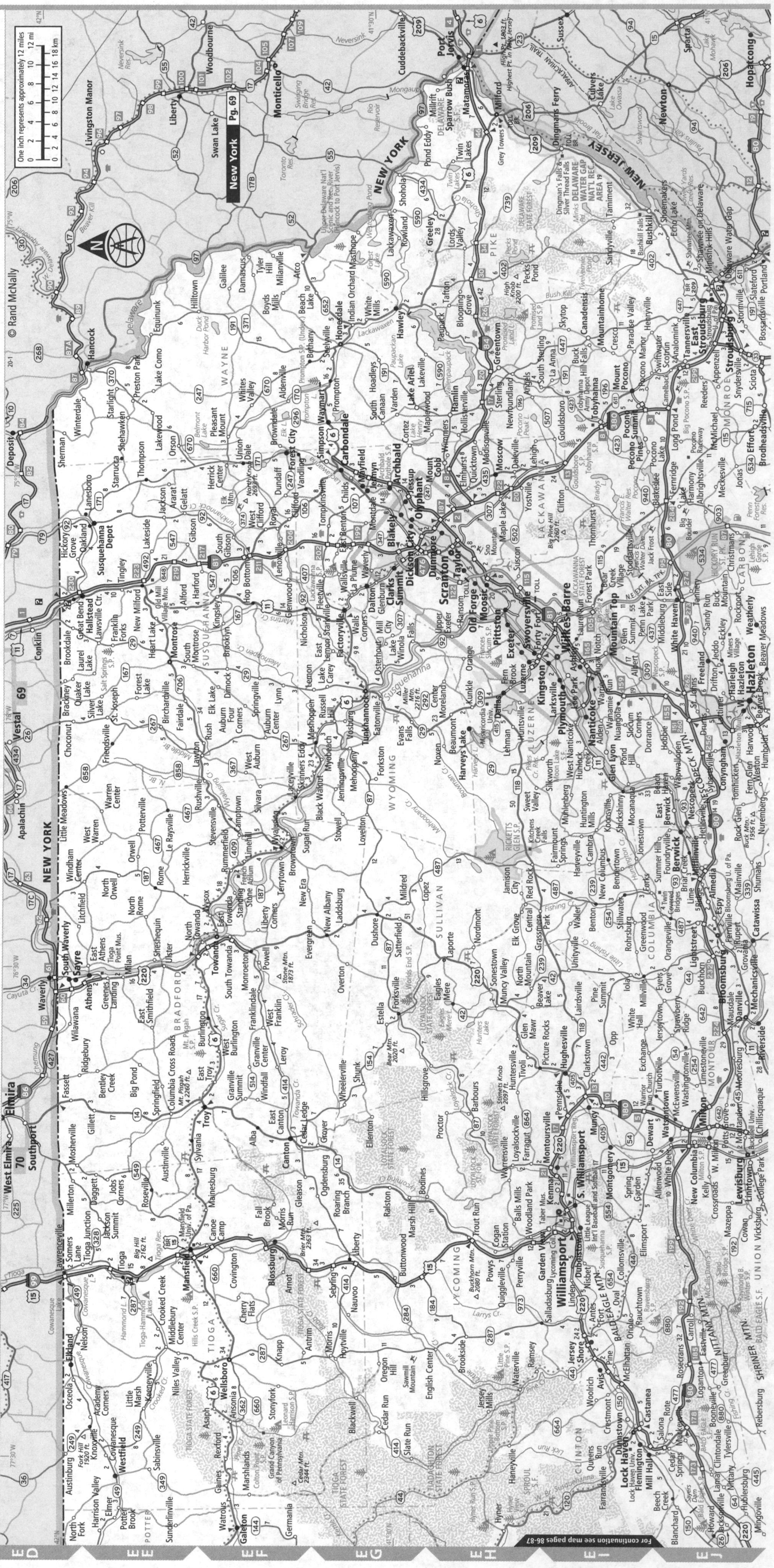

Ferry rides on the Delaware River

Mileages between cities	Allentown	Gettysburg	Harrisburg	Lancaster	Mansfield	Philadelphia	Pittsburgh	Port Jervis, NY	Scranton	State College	Stroudsburg	Towanda	Trenton, NJ	Wilkes Barre	Williamsport	York
Allentown		121	81	67	177	62	282	81	74	175	40	126	75	60	127	92
Chambersburg	132	25	54	91	182	157	160	227	171	101	170	188	177	154	132	74
Harrisburg	81	38		39	133	107	203	176	120	87	119	139	127	104	83	26
Philadelphia	62	138	107	78	226		304	140	124	193	100	175	32	109	176	101
Reading	37	96	64	34	175	62	261	118	100	150	76	152	82	86	126	56
Scranton	74	160	120	132	102	124	279	59		150	46	64	137	16	101	146
State College	175	129	87	126	107	193	135	205	150		162	134	213	132	63	118
Williamsport	127	126	83	123	50	176	196	157	101	63	113	67	189	84		115

Total mileages through Pennsylvania

- 76: 350 miles
- 81: 232 miles
- 80: 311 miles
- 95: 51 miles

More mileages at randmcnally.com/MC

Sights to see

- Adventure Aquarium, Camden E-5
- The Andy Warhol Museum, Pittsburgh L-2
- Betsy Ross House, Philadelphia F-10
- Carnegie Science Center, Pittsburgh L-1
- Duquesne Incline, Pittsburgh M-1
- Franklin Institute Science Museum, Philadelphia F-6
- Independence Hall, Philadelphia G-9
- Liberty Bell, Philadelphia G-9
- National Constitution Center, Philadelphia. F-9
- Philadelphia Museum of Art, Philadelphia E-4
- Point State Park, Pittsburgh M-1
- The Strip District, Pittsburgh. L-3

Independence National Historical Park

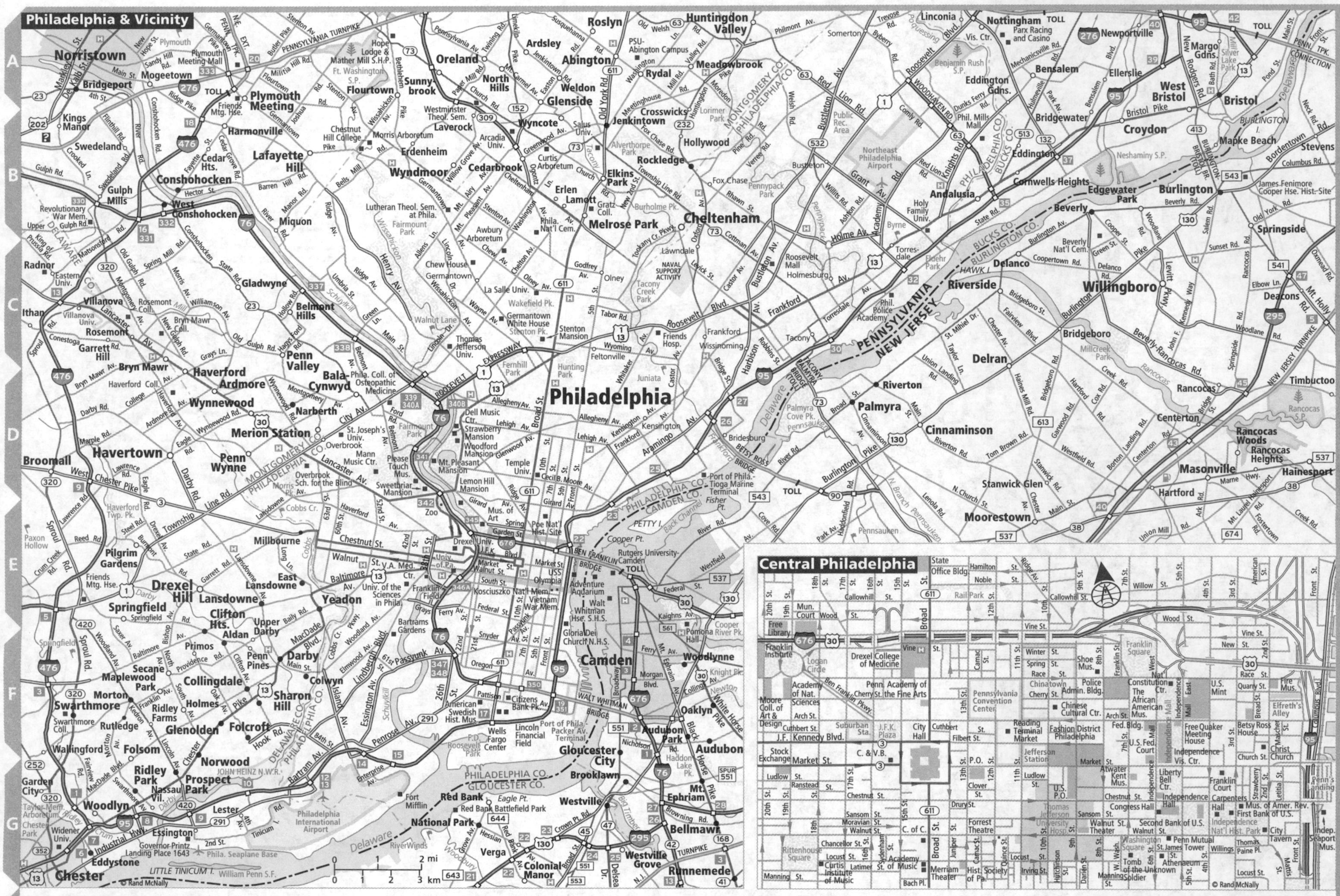

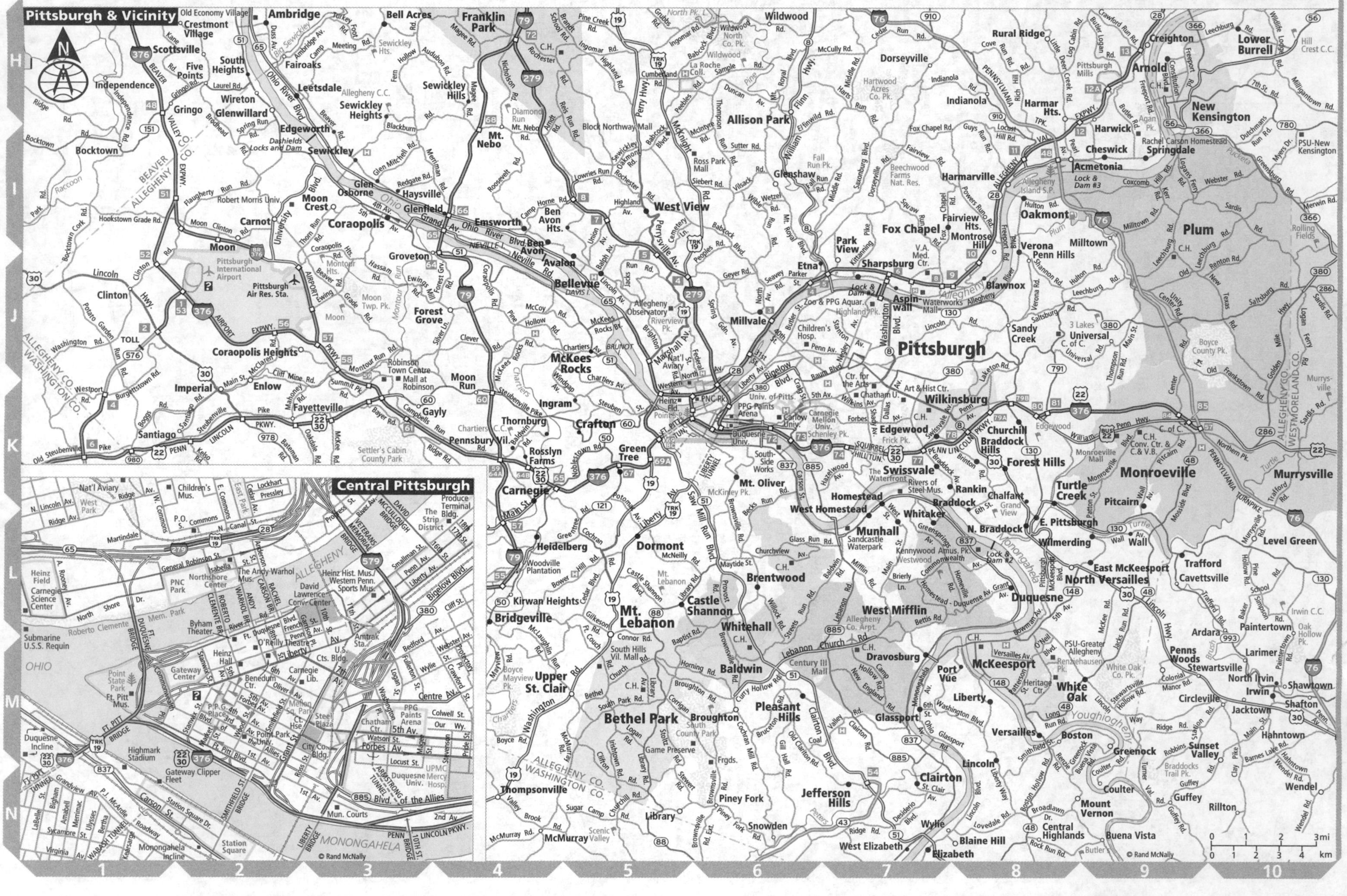

Travel planning & on-the-road resources

Tourism Information
Rhode Island Tourism Division:
(800) 556-2484
www.visitrhodeisland.com

Toll Bridge Info (*EZ-Pass*)
Rhode Island Turnpike & Bridge Authority:
(401) 423-0800
www.ritba.org

Road Conditions & Construction
(888) 401-4511, (401) 222-2450
www.dot.ri.gov/travel

Determining Distances

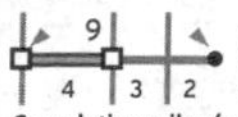

Cumulative miles (red): the distance between red arrows
Intermediate miles (black): the distance between intersections & places

Total mileages through Rhode Island
95: 42 miles
6: 31 miles
1: 60 miles

More mileages at randmcnally.com/MC

Mileages between cities	Fall River, MA	Kingston	Newport	Providence	Warwick	Westerly	Woonsocket	Worcester, MA
Chepachet	35	41	45	19	23	54	13	37
Fall River, MA		35	20	16	25	58	31	56
Newport	20	16		33	26	39	47	72
Providence	16	29	33		10	42	14	40
Warwick	25	23	26	10		37	24	50
Westerly	58	23	39	42	37		56	82
Woonsocket	31	43	47	14	24	56		27
Worcester, MA	56	68	72	40	50	82	27	

Rhode Island

Nickname: The Ocean State
Capital: Providence, D-6
Land area: 1,034 sq. mi. (rank: 50th)
Population: 1,052,567 (rank: 43rd)
Largest city: Providence, 178,042, D-6

Index of places Pg. 134

South Carolina

Nickname: The Palmetto State
Capital: Columbia, D-7
Land area: 30,061 sq. mi. (rank: 40th)
Population: 4,625,364 (rank: 24th)
Largest city: Columbia, 129,272, D-7

Index of places Pg. 134

Mileages between cities	Anderson	Augusta, GA	Charleston	Charlotte, NC	Columbia	Hilton Head I.	Myrtle Beach	Spartanburg
Augusta, GA	92		175	160	72	151	216	120
Charleston	238	175		207	112	104	95	201
Charlotte, NC	128	160	207		93	253	176	72
Columbia	117	72	112	93		158	148	93
Florence	206	148	130	104	81	177	67	169
Myrtle Beach	273	216	95	176	148	200		237
Savannah, GA	282	134	106	251	156	34	202	246
Spartanburg	60	120	201	72	93	247	237	

Total mileages through South Carolina

20: 142 miles
85: 106 miles
26: 221 miles
95: 199 miles

More mileages at randmcnally.com/MC

Travel planning & on-the-road resources

Tourism Information
South Carolina Department of Parks, Recreation and Tourism: (803) 734-0124; discoversouthcarolina.com

Road Conditions & Construction
511, (877) 511-4672, (855) 467-2368; www.511sc.org, www.scdot.org

Toll Road Information ***(all use Palmetto Pass)***
Cross Island Pkwy. (Hilton Head I.): (843) 342-6718; www.crossislandparkway.org
Southern Connector (Greenville Co.): (864) 527-2150; www.southernconnector.com

Travel planning & on-the-road resources

Tourism Information

South Dakota Department of Tourism: (800) 732-5682
www.travelsouthdakota.com

Road Conditions & Construction

511, (866) 697-3511
www.sddot.com, www.safetravelusa.com/sd

Toll Road Information

No tolls on state or federal highways

Determining Distances

(segments of one mile or less not shown)

Cumulative miles (red): the distance between red arrows

Intermediate miles (black): the distance between intersections & places

Total mileages through South Dakota

29: 253 miles
12: 317 miles
90: 413 miles
83: 242 miles

More mileages at randmcnally.com/MC

Mileages between cities

	Aberdeen	Mobridge	Pierre	Pine Ridge	Rapid City	Sioux Falls	Watertown	Yankton
Aberdeen		100	160	360	333	203	96	236
Belle Fourche	312	212	206	172	60	403	362	421
Mobridge	100		108	308	243	303	196	332
Pierre	160	108		200	173	224	138	242
Rapid City	333	243	173	111		347	403	365
Sioux City, IA	285	384	305	358	428	85	184	63
Sioux Falls	203	303	224	356	347		103	81
Watertown	96	196	188	415	403	103		155

Mileages © Rand McNally

South Dakota

Nickname: The Mount Rushmore State
Capital: Pierre, D-7
Land area: 75,811 sq. mi. (rank: 16th)
Population: 814,180 (rank: 46th)
Largest city: Sioux Falls, 153,888, F-13

Index of places Pg. 134

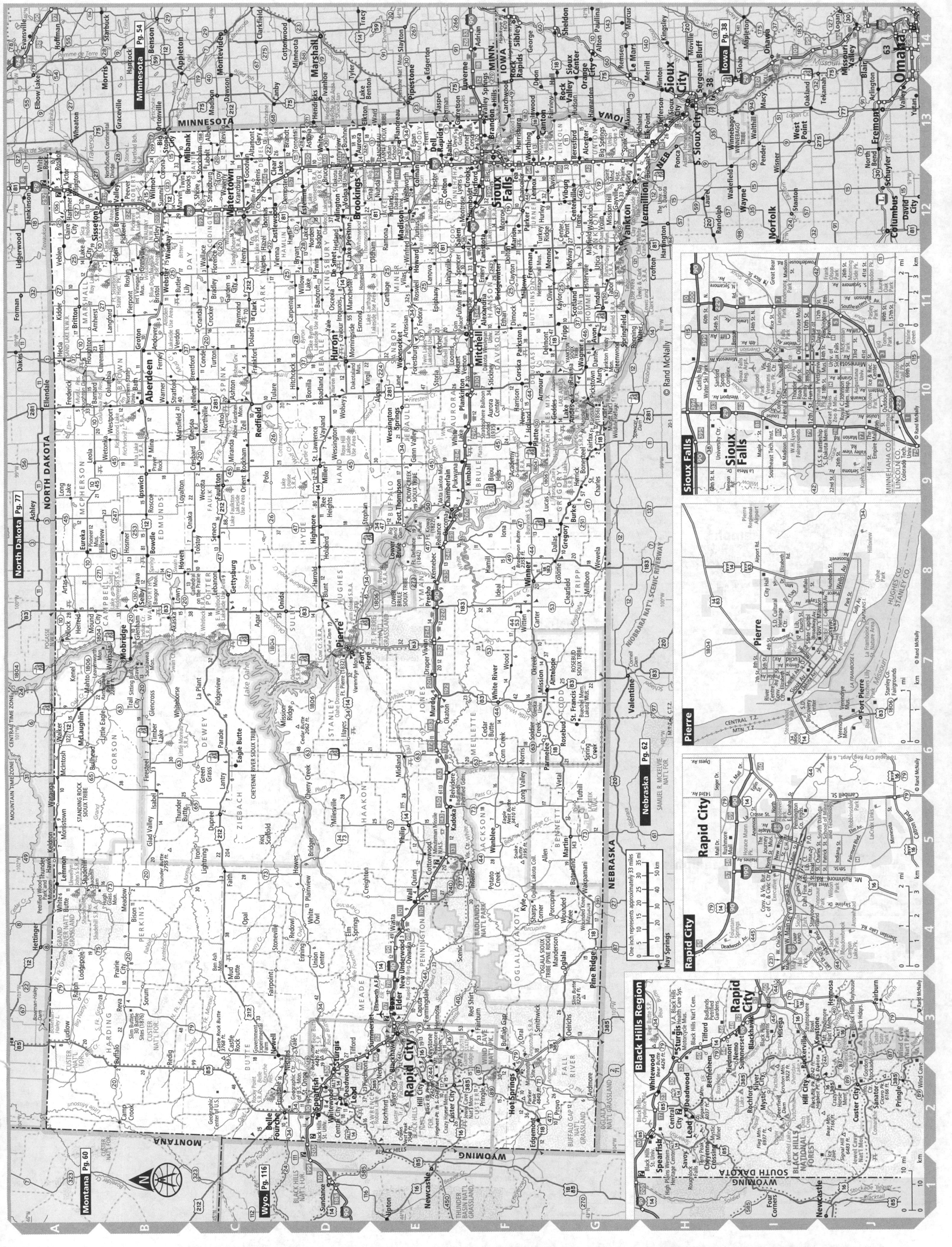

Nickname: The Volunteer State
Capital: Nashville, C-11
Land area: 41,235 sq. mi. (rank: 34th)
Population: 6,346,105 (rank: 17th)
Largest city: Memphis, 646,889, G-2

Index of places Pg. 134

Travel planning & on-the-road resources

Tourism Information
Tennessee Department of Tourist Development: (615) 741-2159; www.tnvacation.com

Road Conditions & Construction
511, (877) 244-0065; smartway.tn.gov, www.tn.gov/tdot/welcome-to-tennessee-511

Toll Road Information
No tolls on state or federal highways

Determining distances along roads

Highway distances (segments of one mile or less not shown):
Cumulative miles (red): the distance between red arrows
Intermediate miles (black): the distance between intersections & places

Interchanges and exit numbers
For most states, the mileage between interchanges may be determined by subtracting one number from the other.

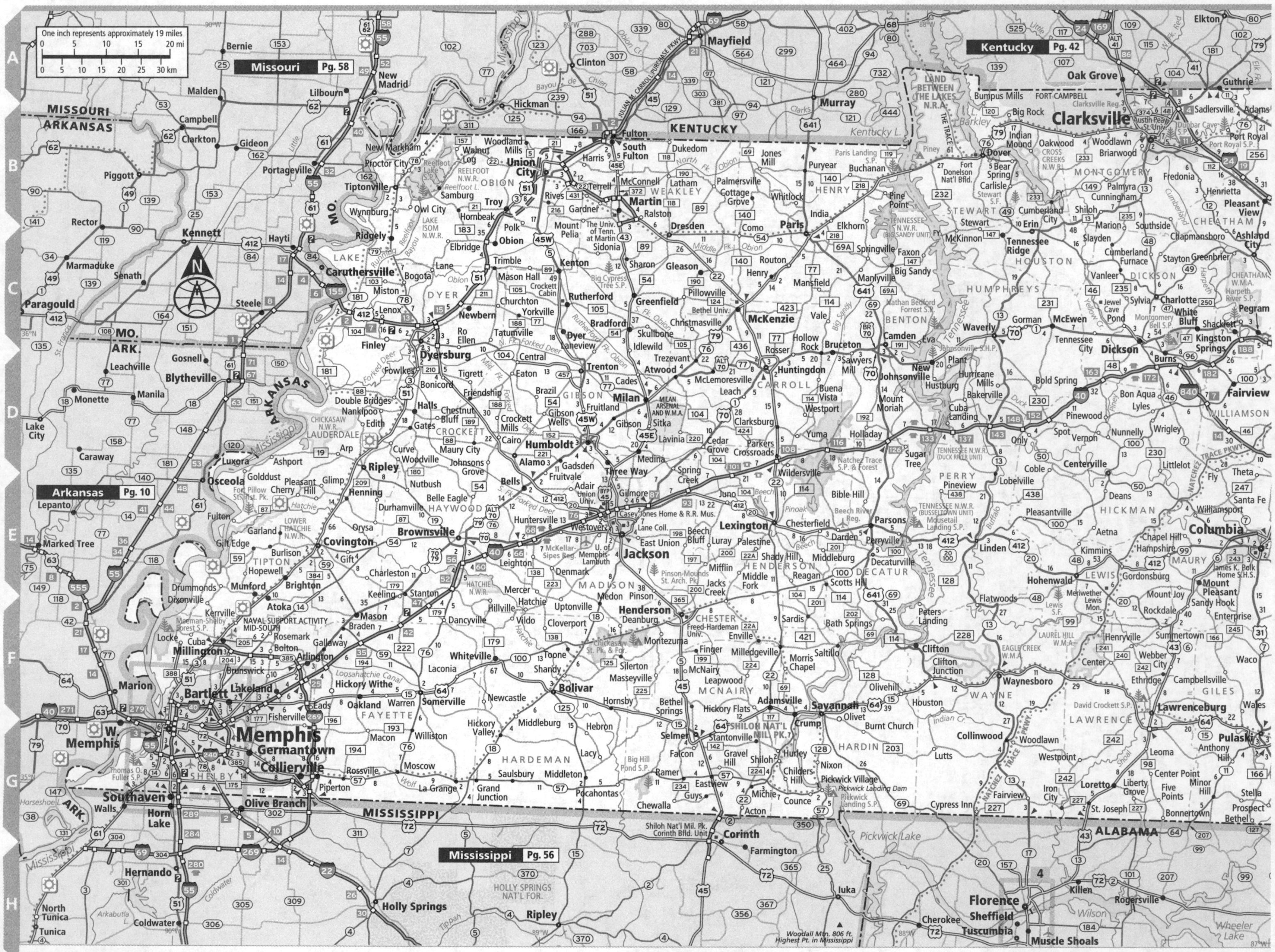

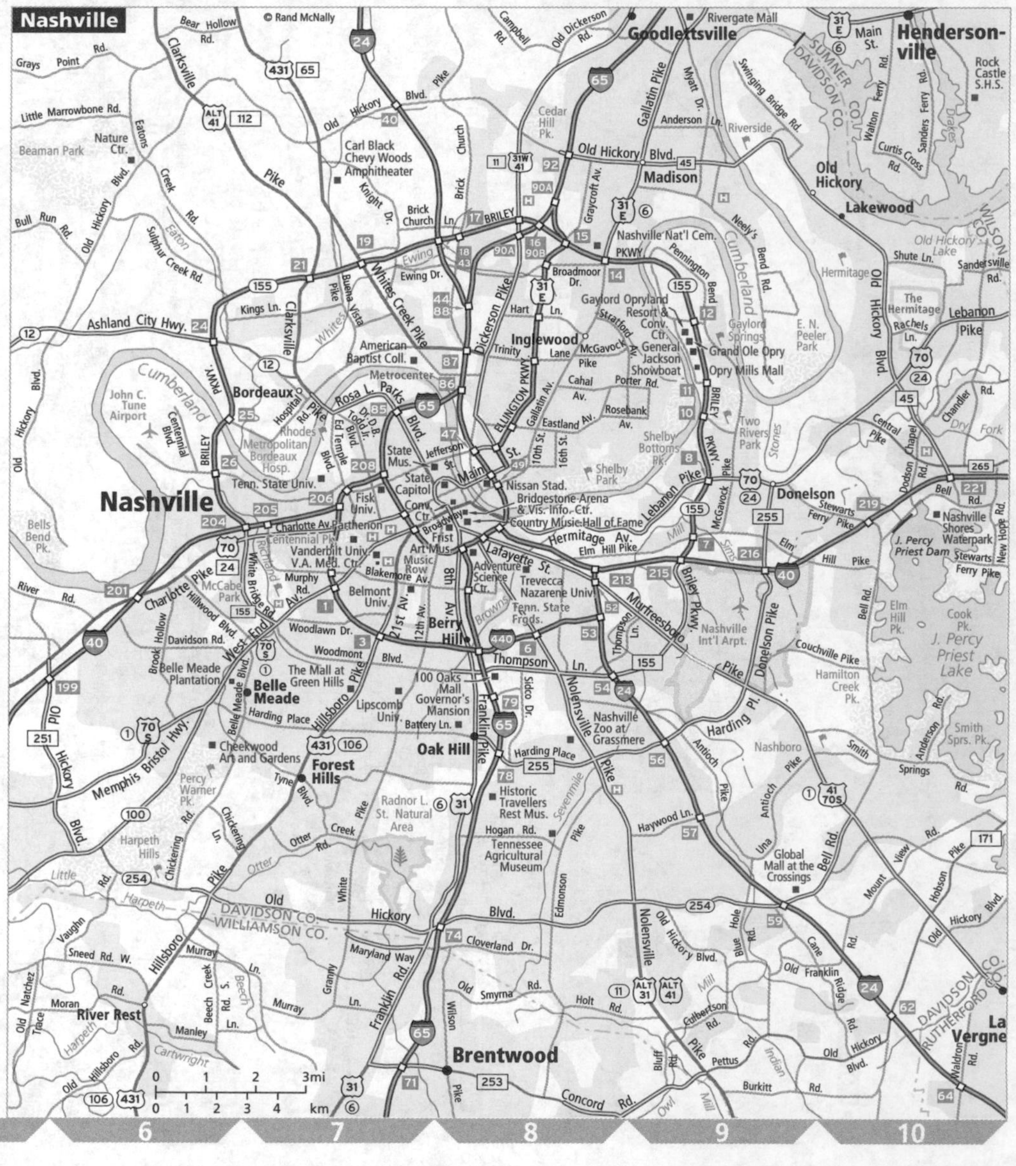

Beale Street, Memphis

Mileages between cities	Atlanta, GA	Bristol	Chattanooga	Clarksville	Cookeville	Dyersburg	Fayetteville	Gatlinburg	Jackson	Johnson City	Knoxville	Memphis	Morristown	Nashville	Oak Ridge	Union City
Chattanooga	117	223		177	98	303	94	151	260	215	110	314	158	131	103	311
Clarksville	293	337	177		125	173	136	265	123	329	224	201	271	47	207	138
Dyersburg	418	463	303	173	252		229	392	47	455	351	76	398	172	334	34
Fayetteville	211	317	94	136	109	229		246	167	308	204	243	252	90	189	224
Johnson City	256	24	215	329	206	455	308	106	412		104	495	65	283	128	463
Knoxville	202	113	110	224	102	351	204	41	308	104		390	48	179	24	358
Memphis	380	502	314	201	291	76	243	431	87	495	390		437	212	373	113
Nashville	249	292	131	47	80	172	90	220	129	283	179	212	226		162	168

Total mileages through Tennessee

- 40: 455 miles
- 75: 161 miles
- 65: 121 miles
- 81: 76 miles

More mileages at randmcnally.com/MC

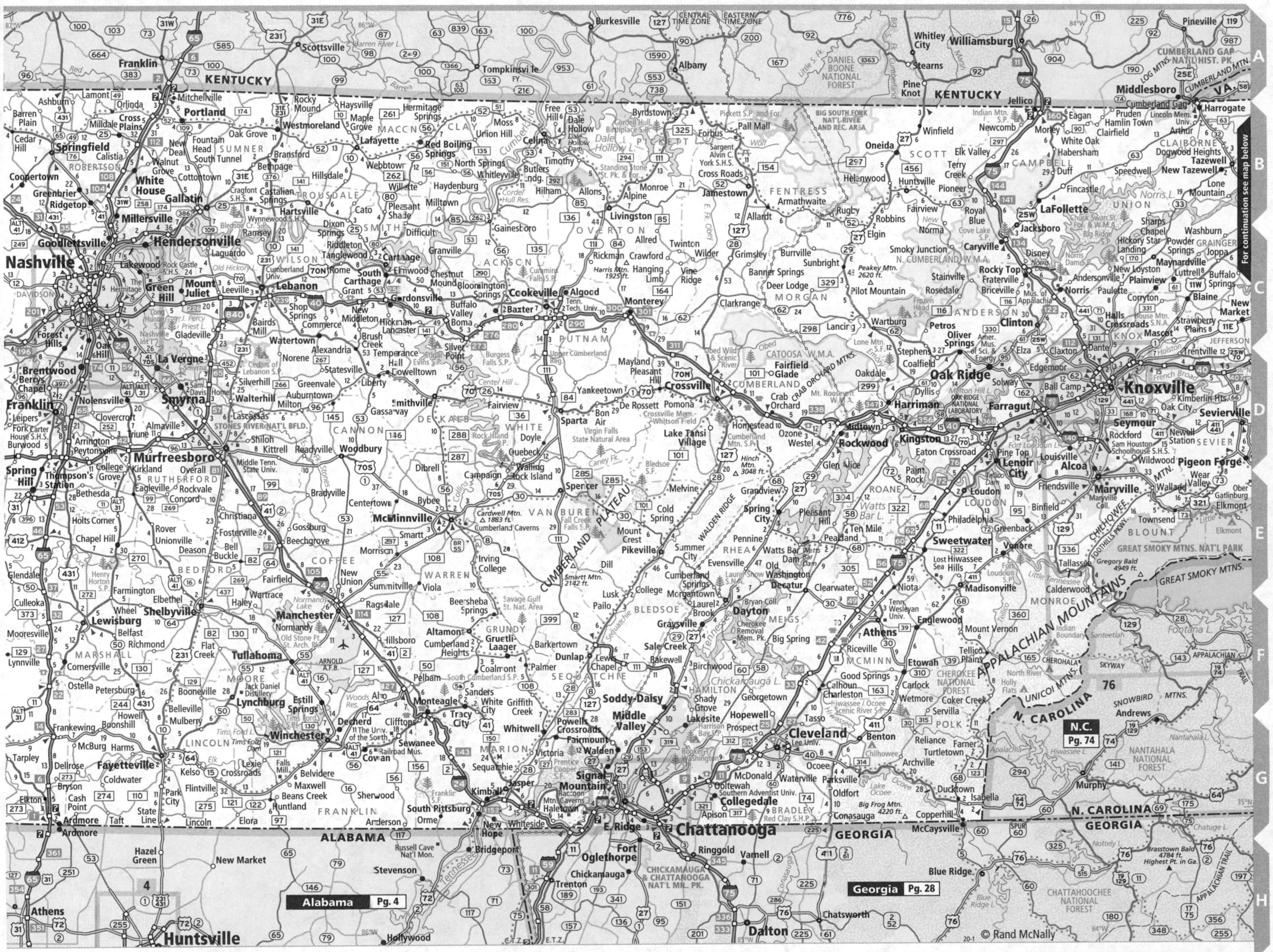

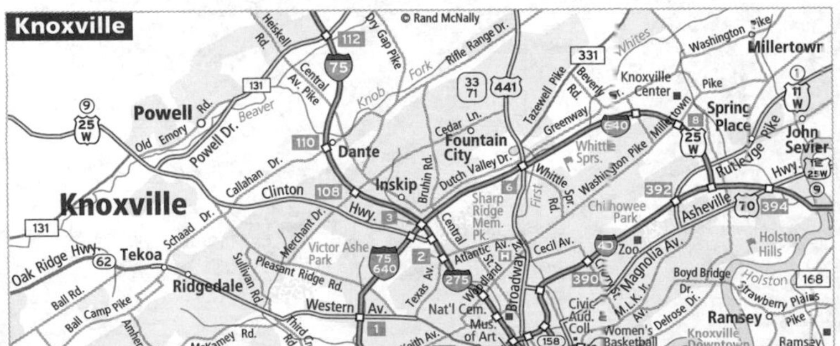

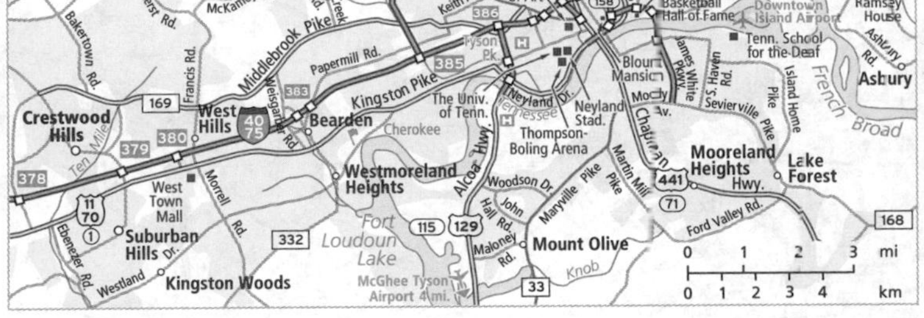

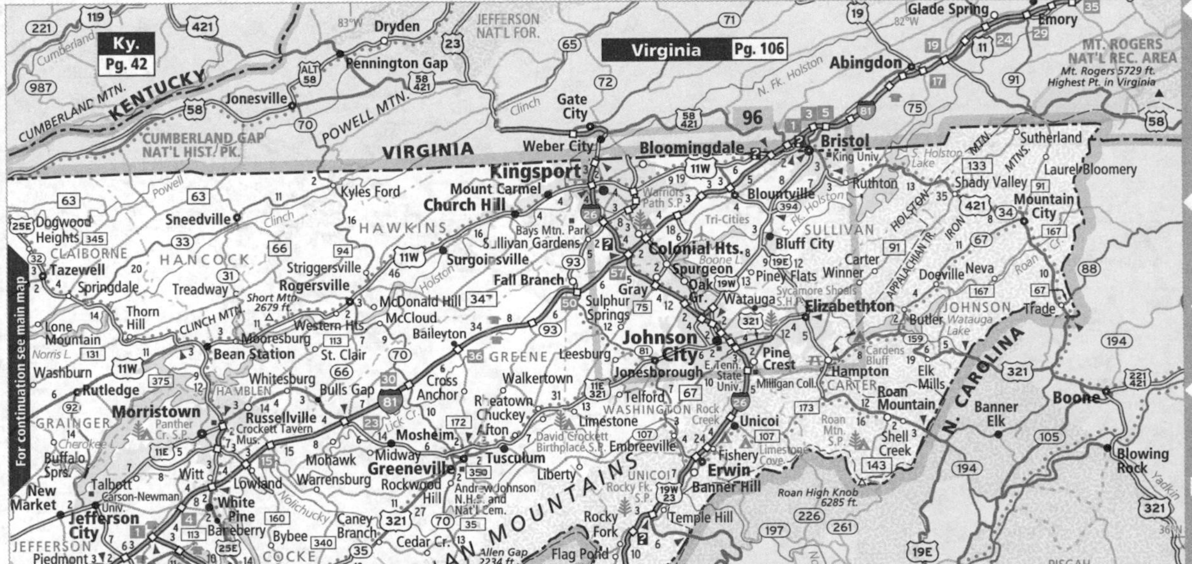

Sights to see

- Appalachian Caverns, Blountville K-3
- Battleship USS Texas, La Porte D-9
- Bayou Place, Houston K-8
- Bristol Caverns, Bristol J-6
- Bristol Motor Speedway, Bristol K-4
- Contemporary Arts Museum, Houston E-5
- Houston Fire Museum, Houston E-5
- Houston Zoo, Houston E-5
- Museum of Natural Science, Houston E-5
- Rocky Mount Museum, Piney Flats L-3
- Space Center Houston, Houston G-8
- Wortham Theatre Center, Houston K-8

Church Circle, Kingsport

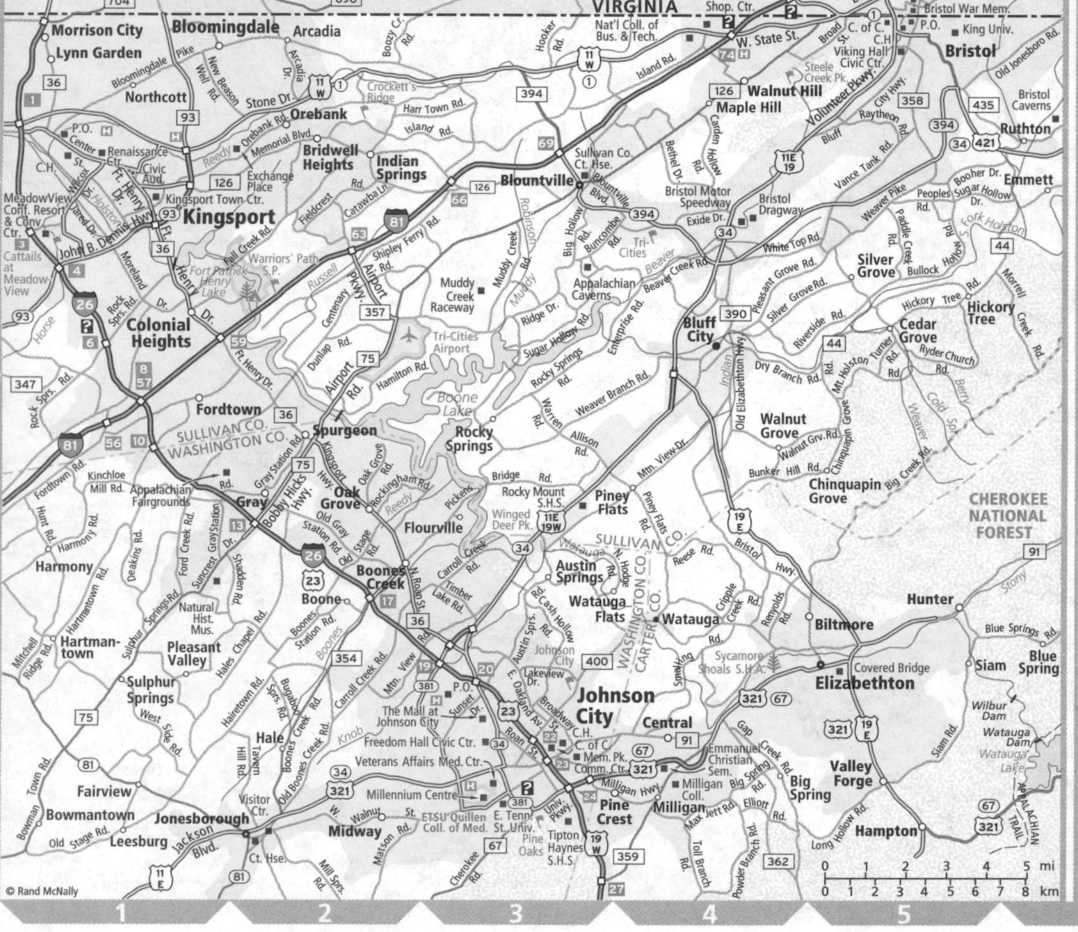

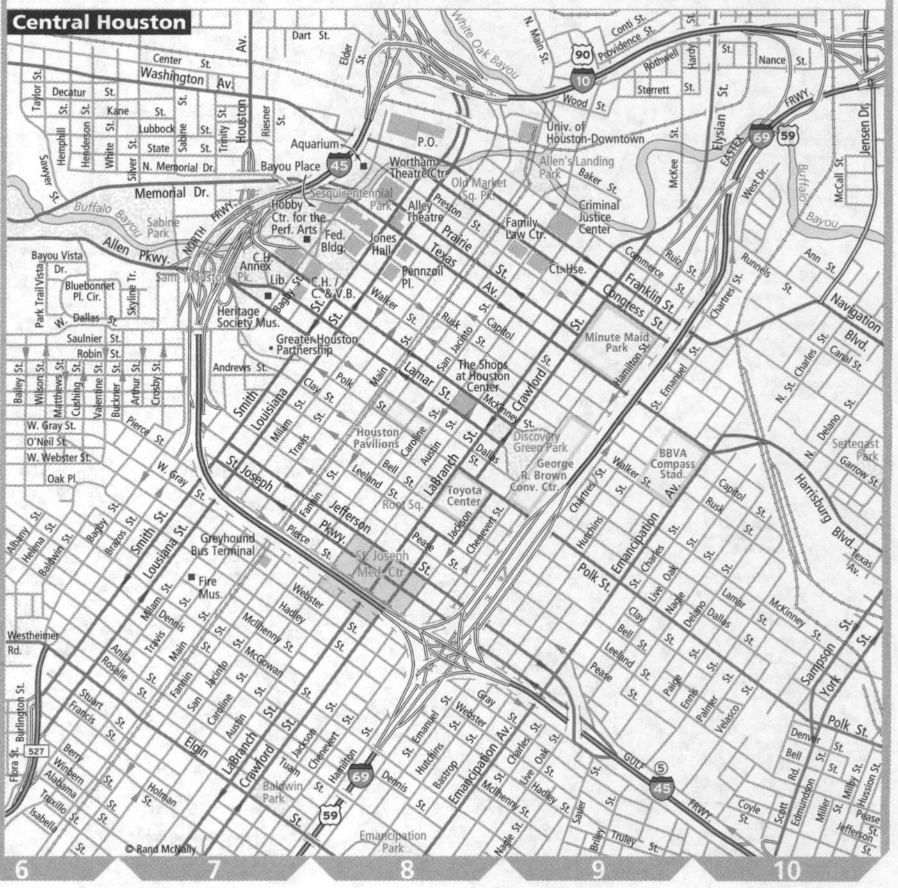

Fort Worth Historic Stockyards

Sights to see

- Dallas Museum of Art, Dallas B-2
- Dallas Zoo, Dallas H-10
- Fair Park, Dallas G-11
- Fort Worth Zoo, Fort Worth H-4
- Louis Tussaud's Palace of Wax & Ripley's Believe It or Not!, Grand Prairie G-8
- Old City Park, Dallas C-3
- Six Flags over Texas, Arlington H-7
- The Sixth Floor Museum at Dealey Plaza, Dallas B-1
- Stockyards Historic District, Fort Worth G-4
- Sundance Square, Fort Worth E-1
- Texas Civil War Museum, Fort Worth G-2

Nickname: The Lone Star State
Capital: Austin, EK-5
Land area: 261,231 sq. mi. (rank: 2nd)
Population: 25,145,561 (rank: 2nd)
Largest city: Houston, 2,099,451, EL-10

Index of places Pg. 135

Travel planning & on-the-road resources

Tourism Information
Texas Tourism: (800) 452-9292
www.traveltexas.com

Road Conditions & Construction
(800) 452-9292, (512) 463-8588,
Dallas Metroplex: (877) 511-3255
www.txdot.gov, www.drivetexas.org

Toll Road Information *(all use TxTag)*
Texas Department of Transportation: (888) 468-9824; www.txtag.org
Cameron County Reg. Mobility Authority (TX 550): (956) 621-5571; www.ccrma.org
Harris County Toll Road Authority (Houston area) *(also EZTAG)*:
(281) 875-3279; www.hctra.org
North Texas Tollway Authority (Dallas Metroplex) *(also TollTag)*:
(972) 818-6882; www.ntta.org

(list continued on page 100)

Toll Bridge Information
El Paso–Int'l Bridges: (912) 212-7500
www.elpasotexas.gov/international-bridges
Eagle Pass–Int'l Bridge System:
(830) 773-2622; www.eaglepasstx.us

(list continued on page 100)

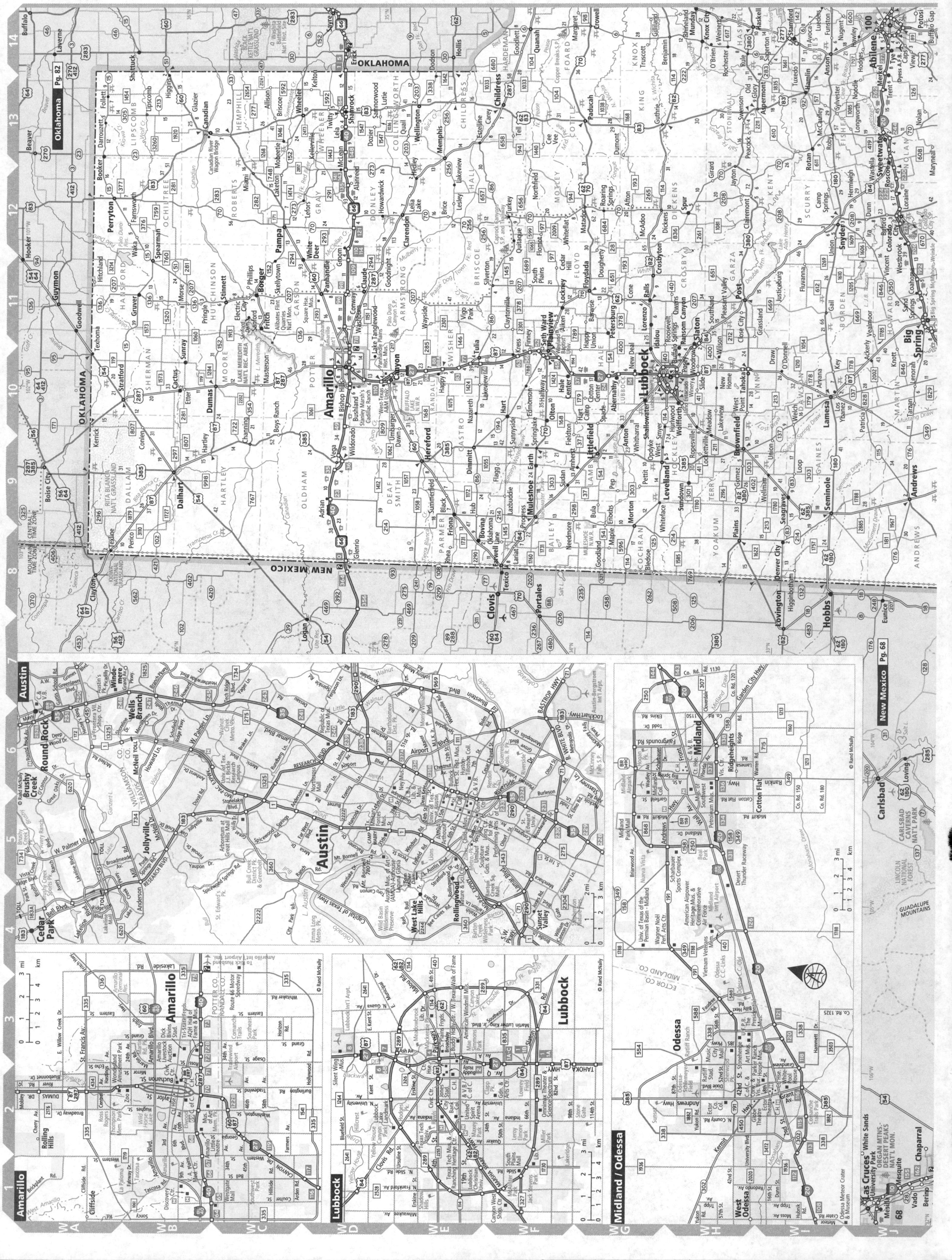

Rio Grande, Big Bend National Park

Mileages between cities

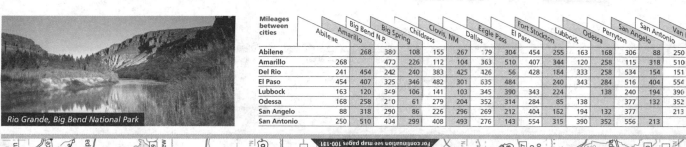

	Abilene	Amarillo	Big Bend N.P.	Big Spring	Childress	Clovis, NM	Dallas	Eagle Pass	El Paso	Fort Stockton	Lubbock	Odessa	Perryton	San Angelo	San Antonio	Van Horn
Abilene		268	380	108	155	267	179	304	454	255	163	168	306	88	250	332
Amarillo	268		470	226	112	104	363	510	407	344	120	258	115	318	510	423
Del Rio	241	454	242	240	383	425	426	56	428	184	333	258	534	154	151	303
El Paso	454	407	325	346	482	301	635	484		240	343	284	516	404	554	121
Lubbock	163	120	349	106	141	103	345	390	343	224		138	240	194	390	302
Odessa	168	258	210	61	279	204	352	314	284	85	138		377	132	352	164
San Angelo	88	318	290	86	226	296	269	212	404	162	194	132	377		213	282
San Antonio	250	510	404	299	408	493	276	143	554	315	390	352	556	213		434

Total mileages through Texas

- 10: 881 miles
- 40: 177 miles
- 20: 636 miles

More mileages at randmcnally.com/MC

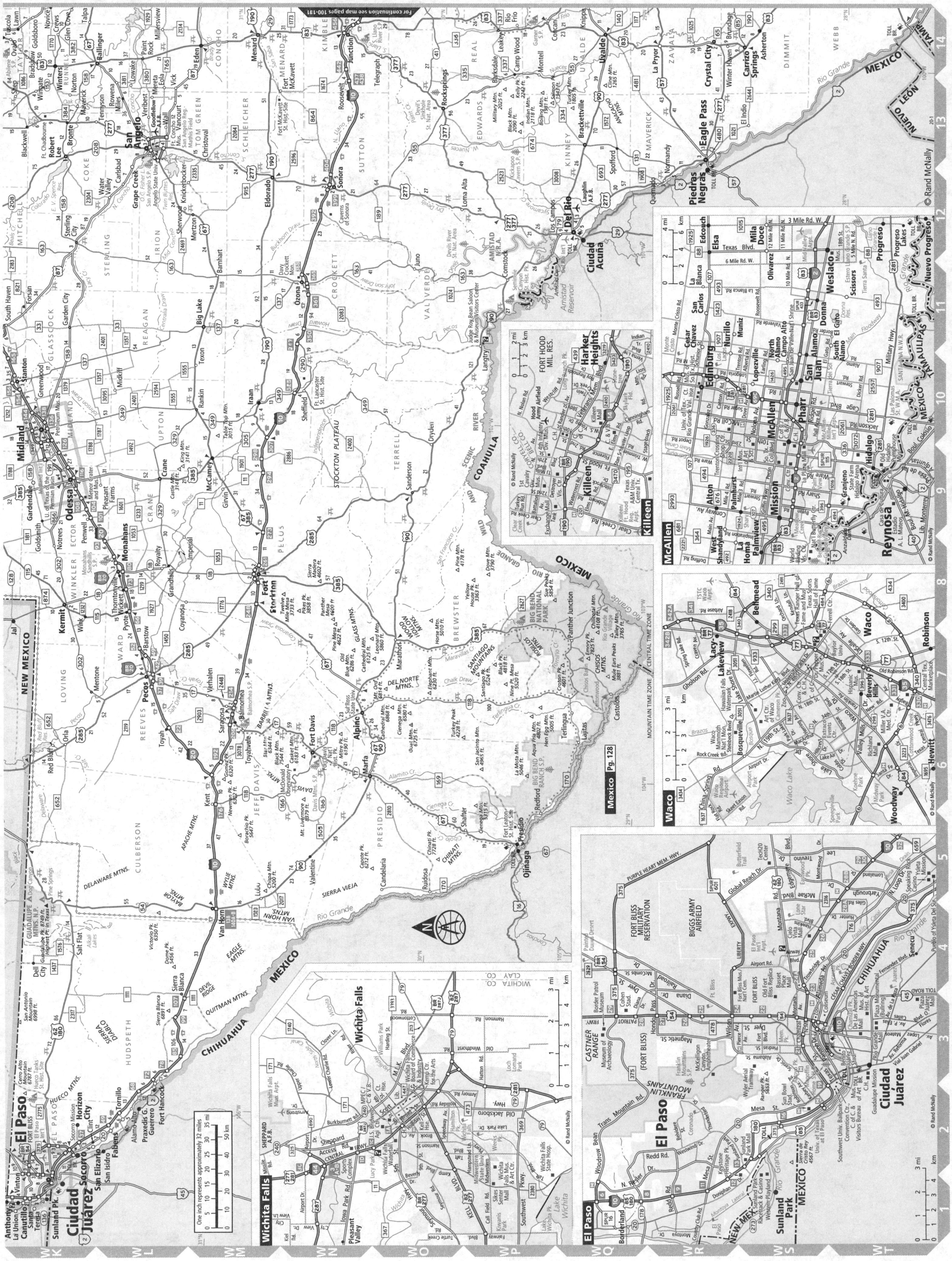

Nickname: The Lone Star State
Capital: Austin, EK-5
Land area: 261,231 sq. mi. (rank: 2nd)
Population: 25,145,561 (rank: 2nd)
Largest city: Houston, 2,099,451, EL-10

Index of places Pg. 135

Travel planning & on-the-road resources

Tourism Information
Texas Tourism: (800) 452-9292
www.traveltexas.com

Road Conditions & Construction
(800) 452-9292, (512) 463-8588,
Dallas Metroplex: (877) 511-3255
www.txdot.gov, www.drivetexas.org

Toll Road Information (cont. from p. 98) *(all use TxTag)*
Central Texas Regional Mobility Authority (Austin area):
(512) 996-9778; www.mobilityauthority.com
Ft. Bend County Toll Road Authority (Houston area):
(855) 999-2024, (832) 735-7385; www.fbctra.com
North East Regional Mobility Authority (TX 49):
(903) 630-7894; www.netrma.org
SH 130 Concession Co. (TX 130): (512) 371-4800; mysh130.com

Toll Bridge Info. (cont. from p. 98)
Cameron County–Int'l Bridge System:
(956) 574-8771; www.co.cameron.tx.us
Laredo–Int'l Bridge System: (956) 791-2200
www.cityoflaredo.com/bridgesys
McAllen–Bridge Dept: (956) 681-1800
www.mcallen.net/departments/bridge

Determining distances
(segments of one mile or less not shown)
Cumulative miles (red): the distance between red arrows
Intermediate miles (black): the distance between intersections & places

The Alamo, San Antonio

Mileages between cities	Abilene	Austin	Beaumont	Brownsville	Dallas	Houston	Laredo	Lufkin	Paris	San Angelo	San Antonio	Shreveport, LA	Texarkana	Tyler	Waco	Wichita Falls
Abilene		221	449	524	179	377	396	363	285	88	250	368	358	280	183	151
Austin	221		242	353	193	157	237	224	296	208	81	325	366	224	99	299
Brownsville	524	353	439		547	354	204	473	622	491	274	596	650	530	435	614
Corpus Christi	387	217	292	156	410	207	138	328	496	355	138	449	504	392	316	477
Dallas	179	193	282	547		228	428	183	106	269	276	187	177	100	96	139
Houston	377	157	85	354	228		348	118	299	368	197	242	295	199	184	375
San Antonio	250	81	280	274	276	197	154	314	380	213		406	451	309	180	341
Shreveport, LA	368	325	206	596	187	242	565	120	154	435	406		72	98	226	324

Mileages © Rand McNally

Total mileages through Texas

- 10: 881 miles
- 20: 636 miles
- 30: 223 miles
- 35: 504 miles

More mileages at randmcnally.com/MC

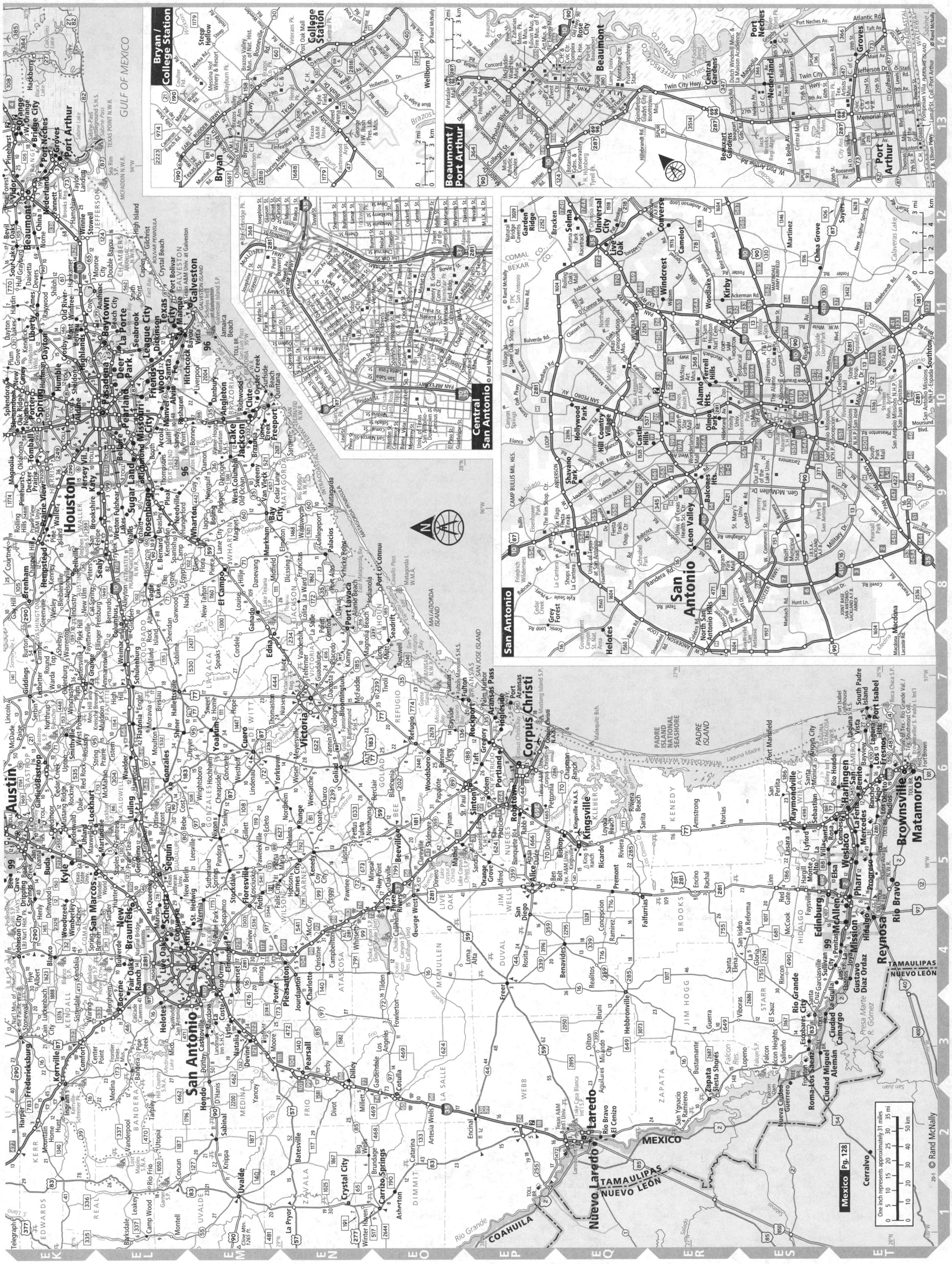

Utah

Nickname: The Beehive State
Capital: Salt Lake City, D-8
Land area: 82,169 sq. mi. (rank: 12th)
Population: 2,763,885 (rank: 34th)
Largest city: Salt Lake City, 186,440, D-8

Index of places Pg. 135

Travel planning & on-the-road resources

Tourism Information
Visit Utah: (800) 200-1160, (801) 538-1900
www.visitutah.com

Road Conditions & Construction
511, (866) 511-8824, (801) 887-3700
www.udot.utah.gov
www.utahcommuterlink.com

Toll Road Information
Adams Avenue Parkway, Inc.
(Washington Terrace) *(ExpressCard)*:
(801) 475-1909; www.adamsavenueparkway.com
ExpressLanes (Utah DOT) (I-15) *(Express Pass)*:
(855) 813-9127; www.udot.utah.gov/expresslanes

Determining distances along roads

Highway distances (segments of one mile or less not shown):
Cumulative miles (red): the distance between red arrows
Intermediate miles (black): the distance between intersections & places

Interchanges and exit numbers
For most states, the mileage between interchanges may be determined by subtracting one number from the other.

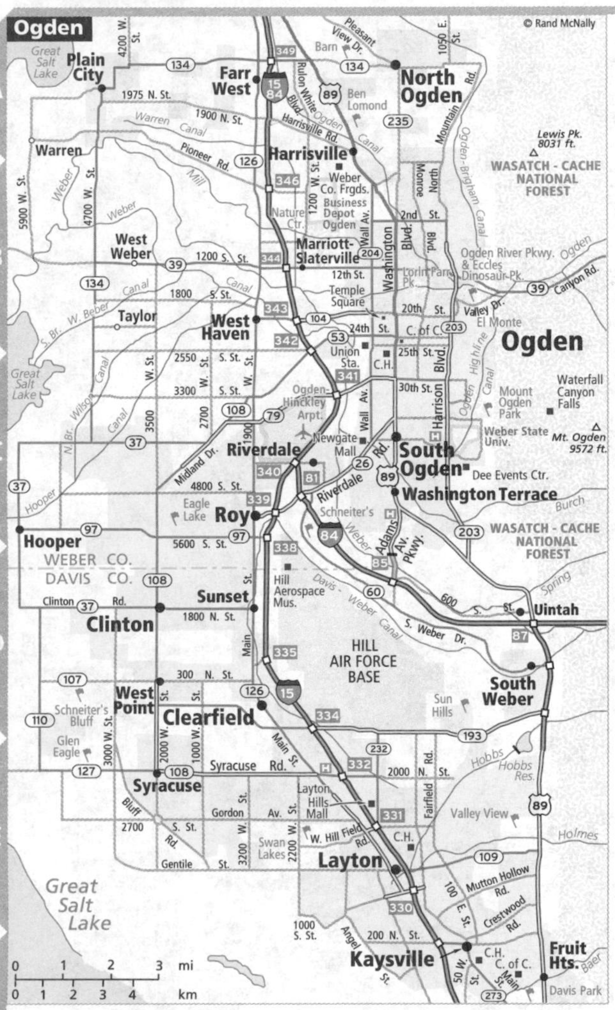

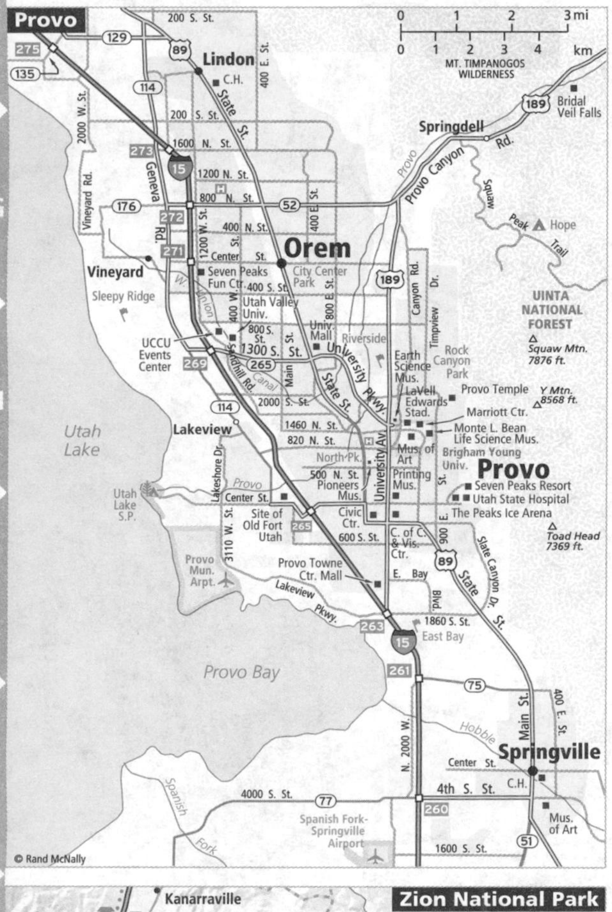

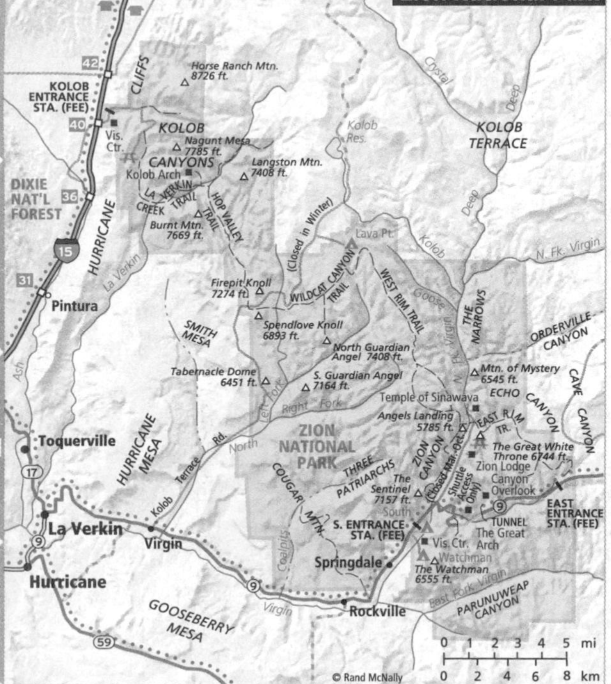

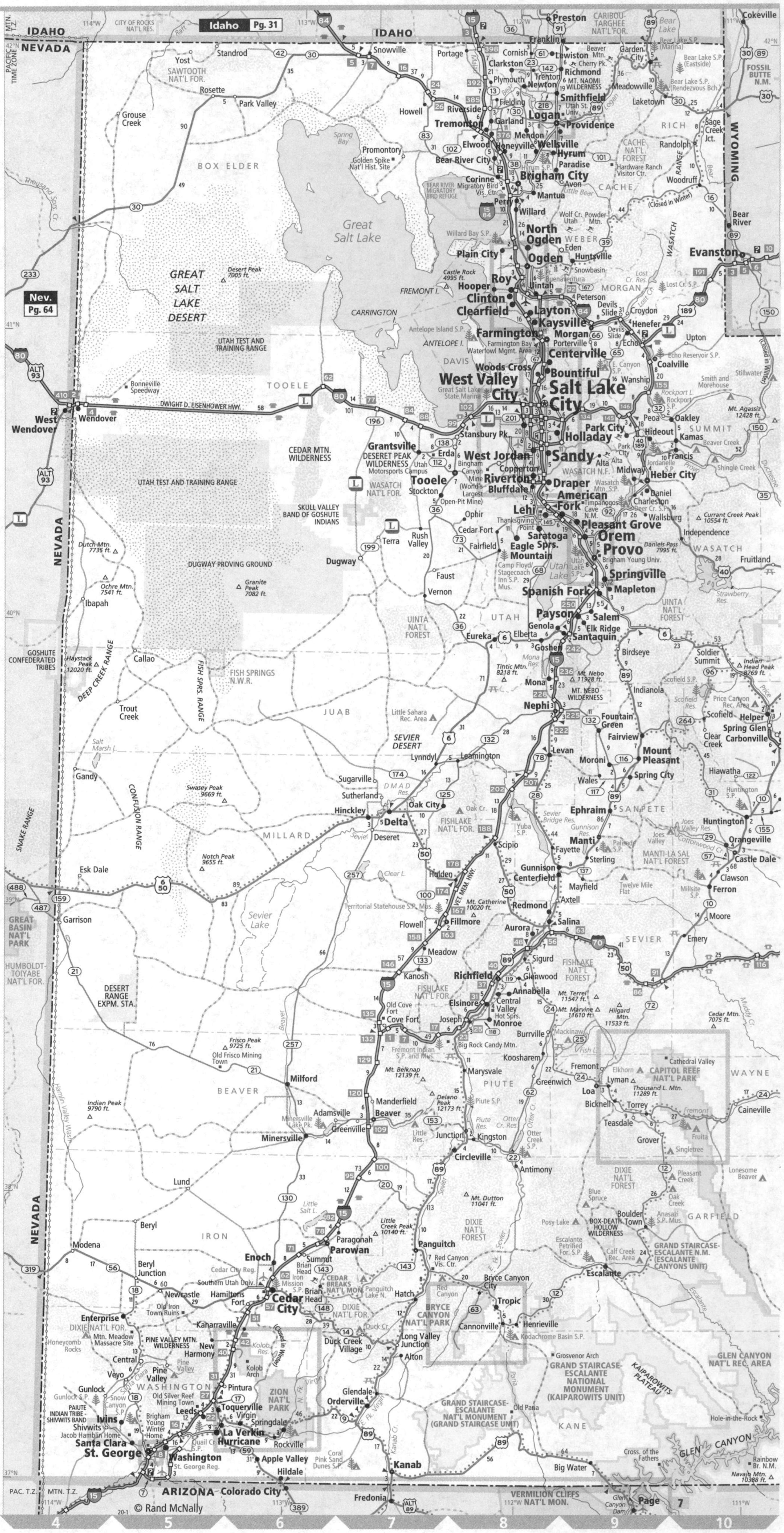

Delicate Arch

Mileages between cities	Blanding	Cedar City	Grand Jct., CO	Las Vegas, NV	Logan	Moab	Ogden	Page, AZ	Park City	Price	Provo	Richfield	St. George	Salt Lake City	Vernal	Wendover
Grand Junction, CO	186	335		506	363	112	319	380	286	164	240	224	389	283	40	401
Logan	388	330	363	499		313	46	457	113	199	124	239	385	82	252	199
Moab	74	287	112	456	313		269	268	238	115	190	174	341	234	207	352
Richfield	249	114	224	282	239	174	194	219	166	121	115		169	159	232	270
St. George	415	55	389	117	385	341	341	154	308	286	261	169		304	401	333
Salt Lake City	308	250	283	419	82	234	37	377	30	119	43	159	304		172	121
Vernal	281	345	140	514	252	207	207	450	145	112	154	232	401	172		291
Wendover	426	317	401	361	199	352	154	503	150	237	161	270	333	121	291	

Total mileages through Utah

- 15: 401 miles
- 70: 232 miles
- 80: 196 miles
- 84: 119 miles

More mileages at randmcnally.com/MC

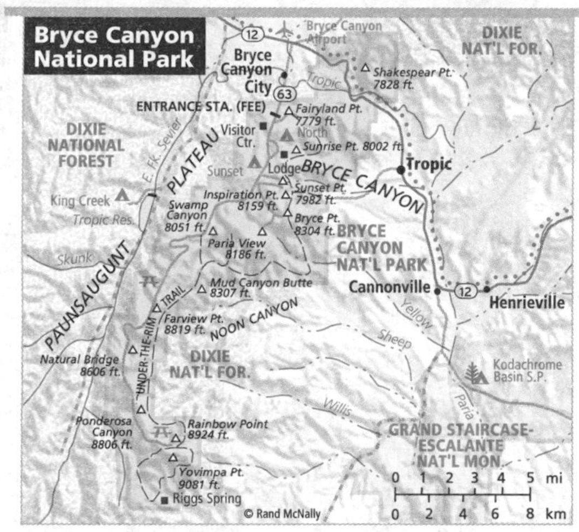

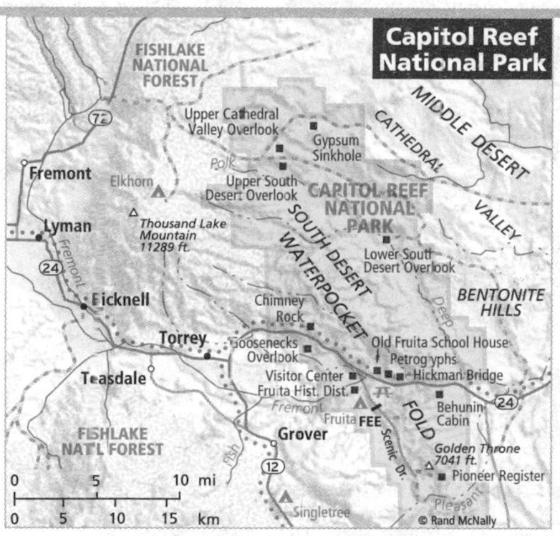

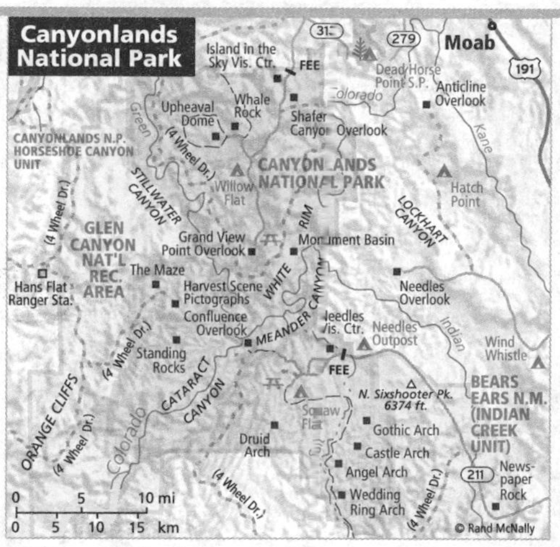

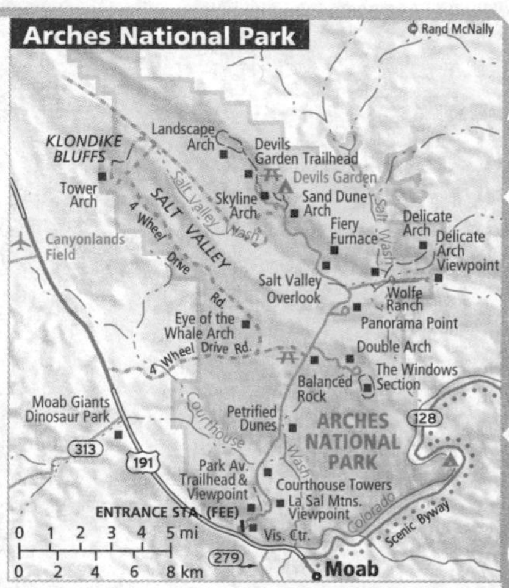

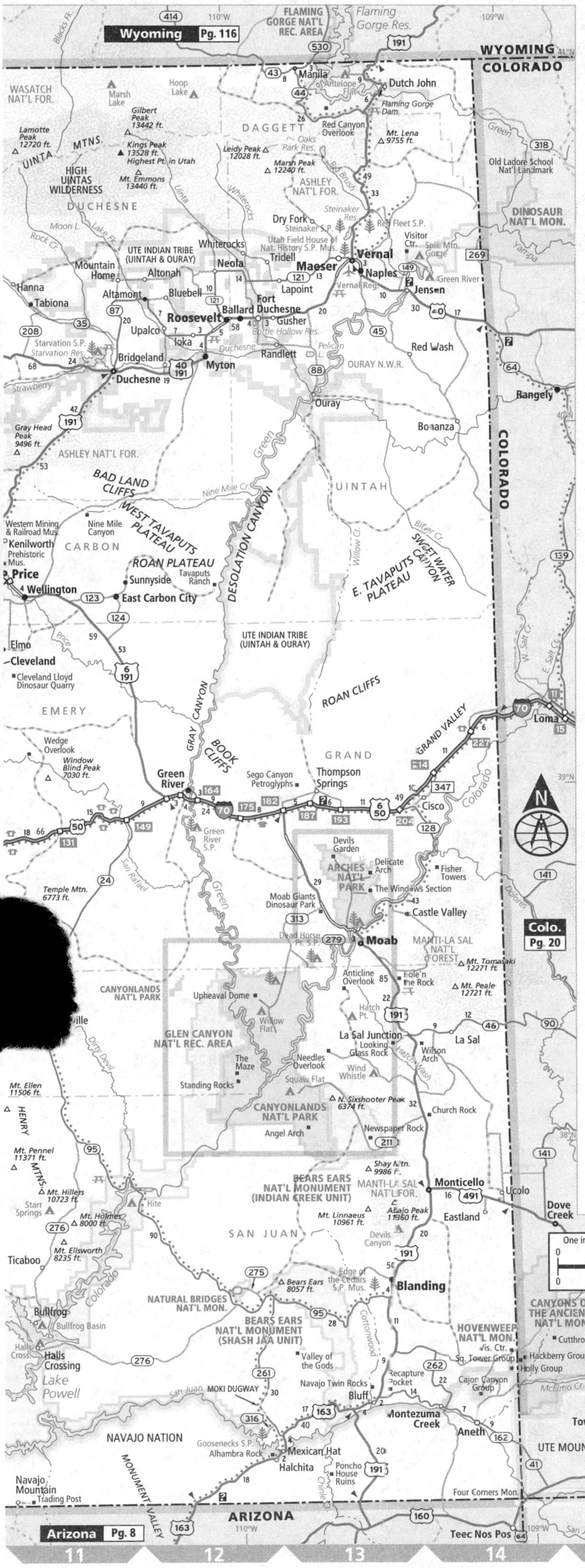

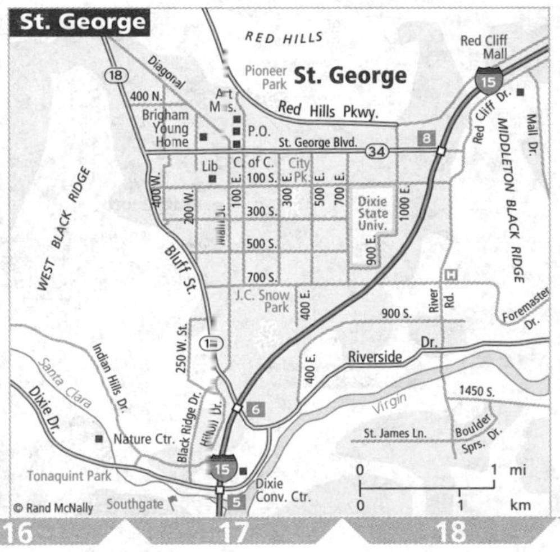

Nickname: The Green Mountain State
Capital: Montpelier, E-5
Land area: 9,217 sq. mi. (rank: 43rd)
Population: 625,741 (rank: 49th)
Largest city: Burlington, 42,417, D-2

Index of places Pg. 135

Mileages between cities

	Albany, NY	Brattleboro	Burlington	Montpelier	Newport	Rutland	St. Johnsbury	White River Jct.
Albany, NY		78	151	156	230	90	187	128
Brattleboro	78		151	115	164	73	121	62
Burlington	151	151		39	76	67	75	90
Montpelier	156	115	39		78	66	37	54
Newport	230	164	76	78		147	43	102
Rutland	90	73	67	66	147		105	45
St. Johnsbury	187	121	75	37	43	105		60
White River Jct.	128	62	90	54	102	45	60	

Total mileages through Vermont

89 130 miles
93 11 miles
91 177 miles
4 64 miles

More mileages at randmcnally.com/MC

Travel planning & on-the-road resources

Tourism Information

Vermont Department of Tourism & Marketing: (802) 828-3237; www.vermontvacation.com

Road Conditions & Construction

newengland511.org, www.vtrans.vermont.gov

Toll Road Information

No tolls on state or federal highways

Determining Distances

(segments of one mile or less not shown)

Cumulative miles (red): the distance between red arrows

Intermediate miles (black): the distance between intersections & places

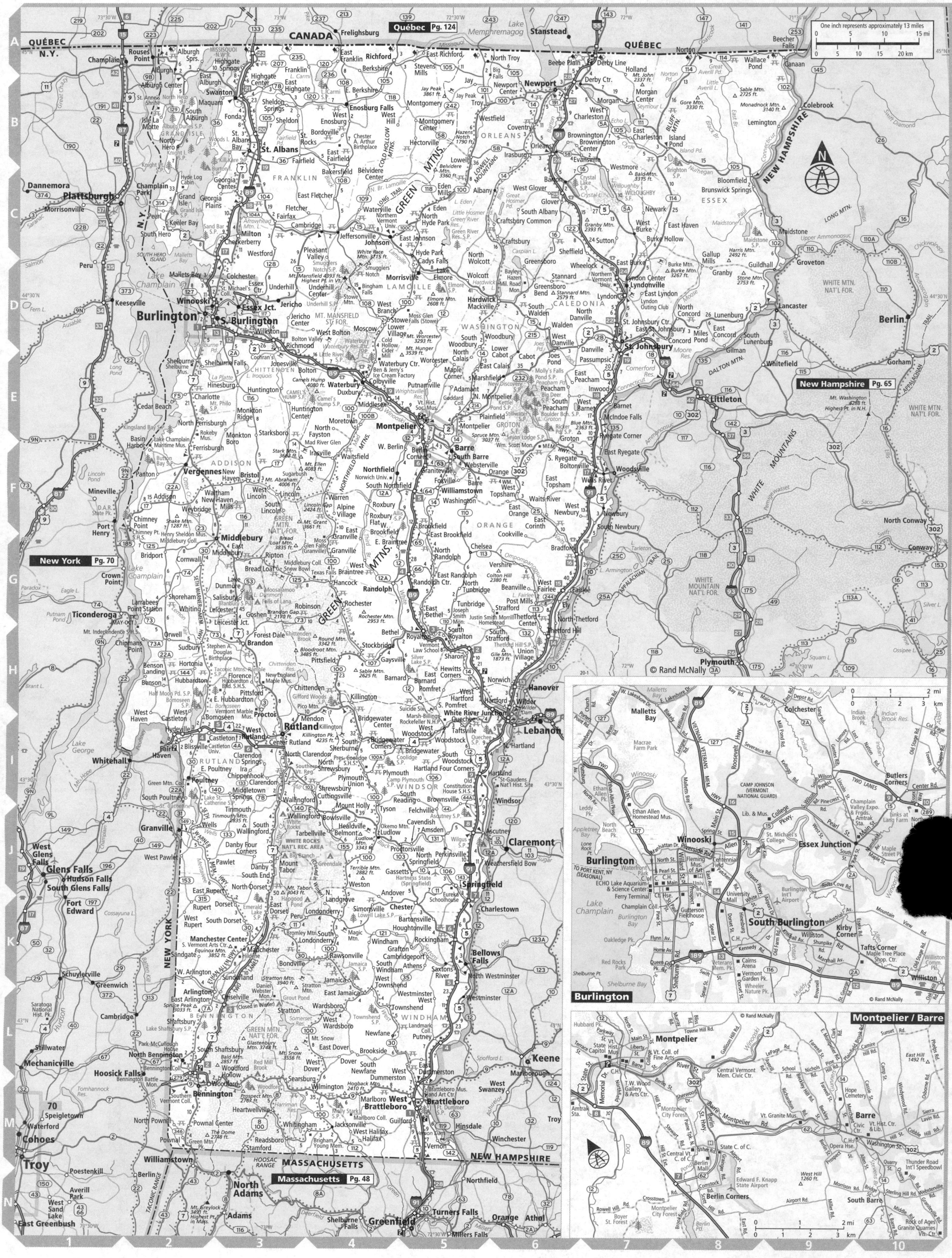

Historic Colonial Williamsburg

Sights to see

- Agecroft Hall and Gardens, Richmond C-7
- Children's Museum of Virginia, Portsmouth M-5
- Chrysler Museum of Art, Norfolk L-6
- Colonial Williamsburg, Williamsburg F-2
- Edgar Allan Poe Museum, Richmond C-8
- First Landing State Park, Virginia Beach L-9
- Hermitage Foundation Museum, Norfolk L-6
- Historic Jamestowne, Williamsburg G-1
- Nauticus, Norfolk L-6
- Ocean Breeze Waterpark, Virginia Beach M-10
- Old Cape Henry Lighthouse, Virginia Beach K-9
- Three Lakes Nature Center & Aquarium, Richmond B-8

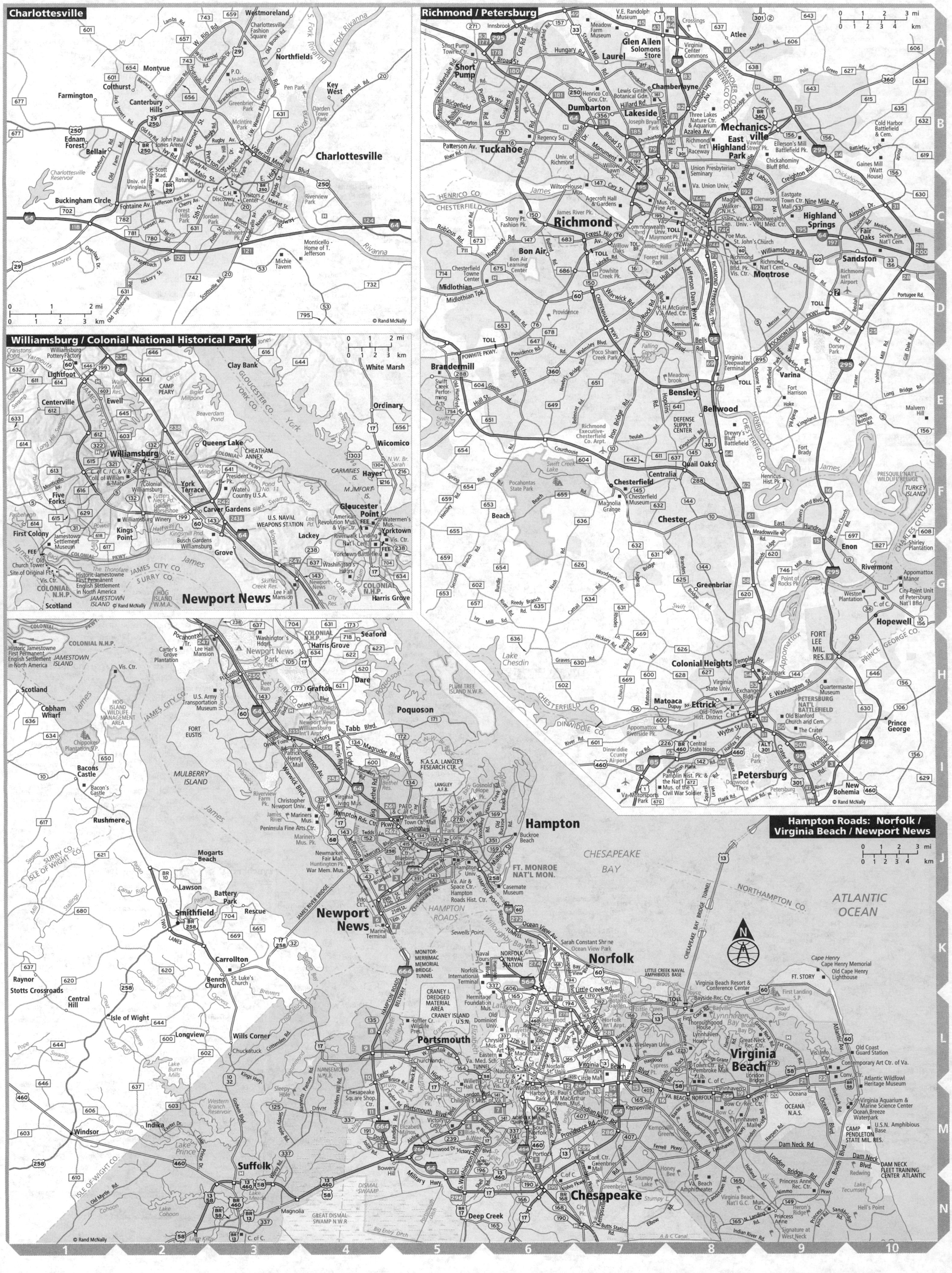

Nickname: Old Dominion
Capital: Richmond, J-14
Land area: 39,490 sq. mi. (rank: 36th)
Population: 8,001,024 (rank: 12th)
Largest city: Virginia Beach, 437,994, L-18

Index of places Pg. 135

Travel planning & on-the-road resources

Tourism Information
Virginia Tourism Corporation: (800) 847-4882; www.virginia.org

Road Conditions & Construction
511, (866) 695-1182, (800) 367-7623
www.511virginia.org
www.virginiadot.org/travel

Toll Road Information *(E-ZPass)*
Virginia Dept. of Transportation: (800) 367-7623; www.virginiadot.org/travel/faq-toll.asp
Chesapeake Expwy. (VA 168): (757) 204-0010; www.chesapeakeexpressway.com
Dulles Greenway: (703) 707-8870; www.dullesgreenway.com
ExpressLanes (Transurban Operations) (Wash. D.C. area): (855) 495-9777; www.expresslanes.com
Globalvia (Pocahontas Pkwy., Richmond): (866) 428-6339; www.pocahontas895.com
Metro. Wash. Airports Authority (Dulles Toll Rd.): (877) 762-7824; www.dullestollroad.com
Richmond Metro. Trans. Auth. (toll rds. within Richmond): (804) 523-3300; www.rmtaonline.org

Toll Bridge/Tunnel Info. *(E-ZPass)*
Chesapeake Bay Bridge-Tunnel: (757) 331-2960; www.cbbt.com
Elizabeth River Tunnels (Hampton Rds): (855) 378-7623; www.driveert.com
South Norfolk Jordan Bridge: (855) 690-7652; www.snjb.net

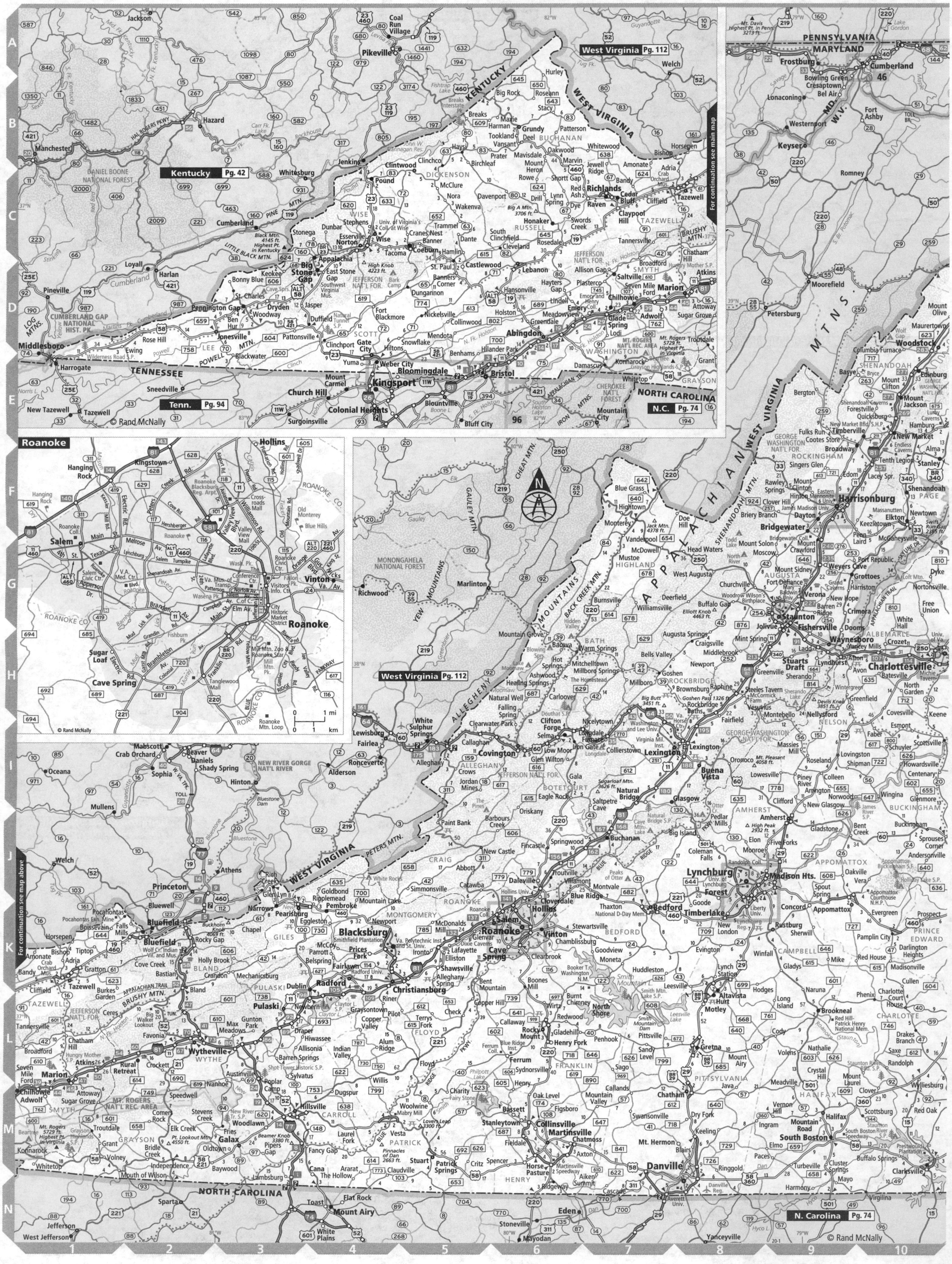

Lincoln Memorial, Washington, D.C.

Mileages between cities	Bristol	Chincoteague	Danville	Emporia	Fredericksburg	Harrisonburg	Lynchburg	Manassas	Norfolk	Richmond	Roanoke	Virginia Beach	Washington, DC	Williamsburg	Winchester	Wytheville
Bristol		510	192	341	323	242	200	347	407	321	145	423	377	370	310	67
Charlottesville	253	260	131	136	66	61	65	81	157	71	117	174	116	121	128	183
Danville	192	300		115	197	163	68	215	191	144	89	206	247	199	230	124
Norfolk	407	104	191	78	139	216	189	177		91	276	17	189	41	222	340
Richmond	321	190	144	66	56	130	114	96	91		187	105	107	50	135	253
Roanoke	145	378	89	176	192	111	53	214	276	187		292	241	238	178	77
Washington, DC	377	168	247	174	53	132	182	32	189	107	241	205		153	75	307
Winchester	310	244	230	200	83	68	164	54	222	135	178	236	76	181		244

Total mileages through Virginia

- 64: 298 miles
- 81: 325 miles
- 85: 69 miles
- 95: 179 miles

More mileages at randmcnally.com/MC

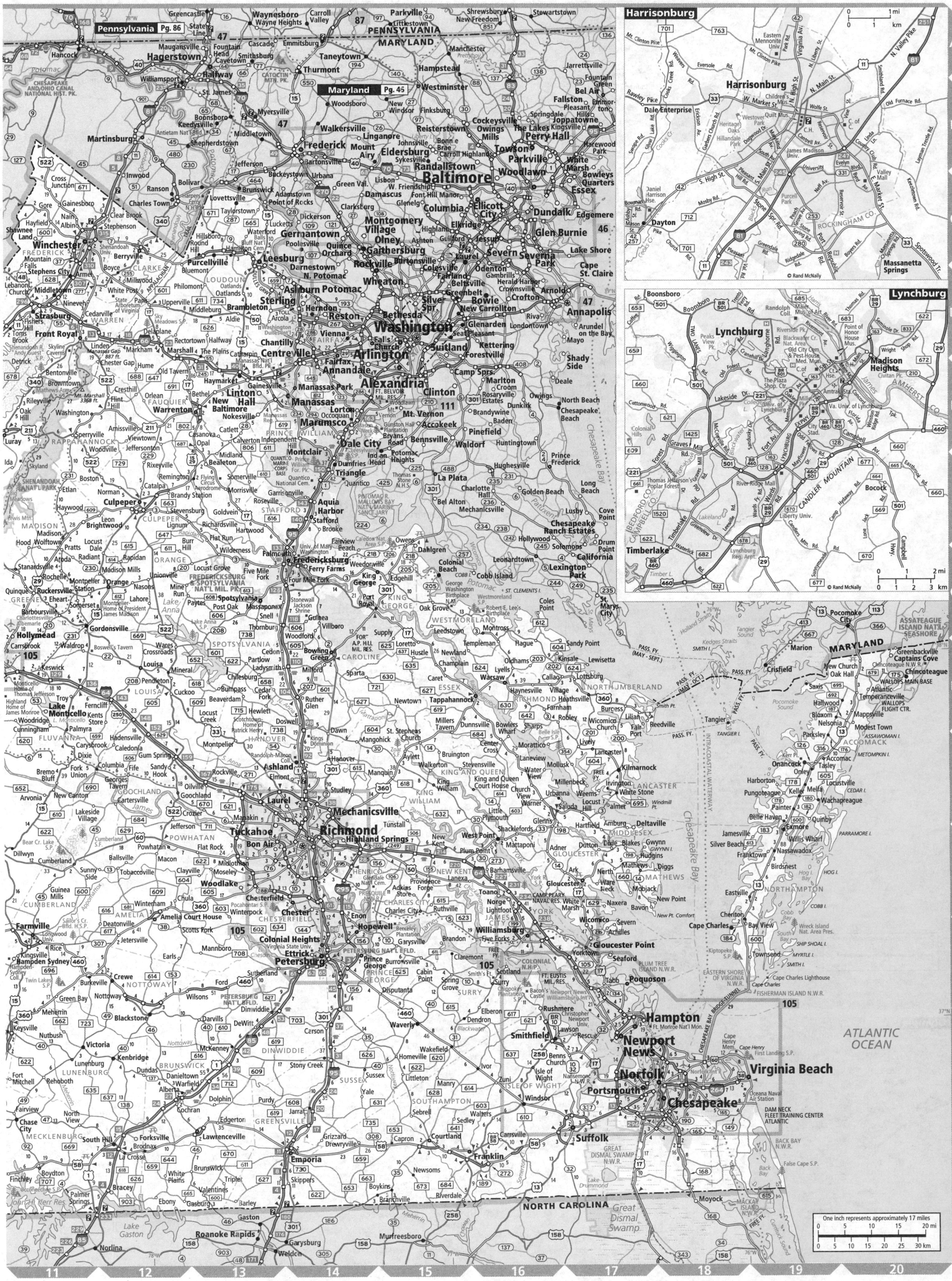

Nickname: The Evergreen State
Capital: Olympia, H-6
Land area: 66,455 sq. mi. (rank: 20th)
Population: 6,724,540 (rank: 13th)
Largest city: Seattle, 608,660, F-7

Index of places Pg. 135

Travel planning & on-the-road resources

Tourism Information
Washington Tourism Alliance: (800) 544-1800; www.experiencewa.com

Road Conditions & Construction
511, (800) 695-7623; www.wsdot.com/traffic

Toll Bridge/Tunnel Information
Wash. St. Dept. of Trans. *(Good to Go!)*: (360) 705-7000, (360) 705-7438; www.wsdot.wa.gov/tolling

Determining distances along roads

Highway distances (segments of one mile or less not shown):
Cumulative miles (red): the distance between red arrows
Intermediate miles (black): the distance between intersections & places

Interchanges and exit numbers
For most states, the mileage between interchanges may be determined by subtracting one number from the other.

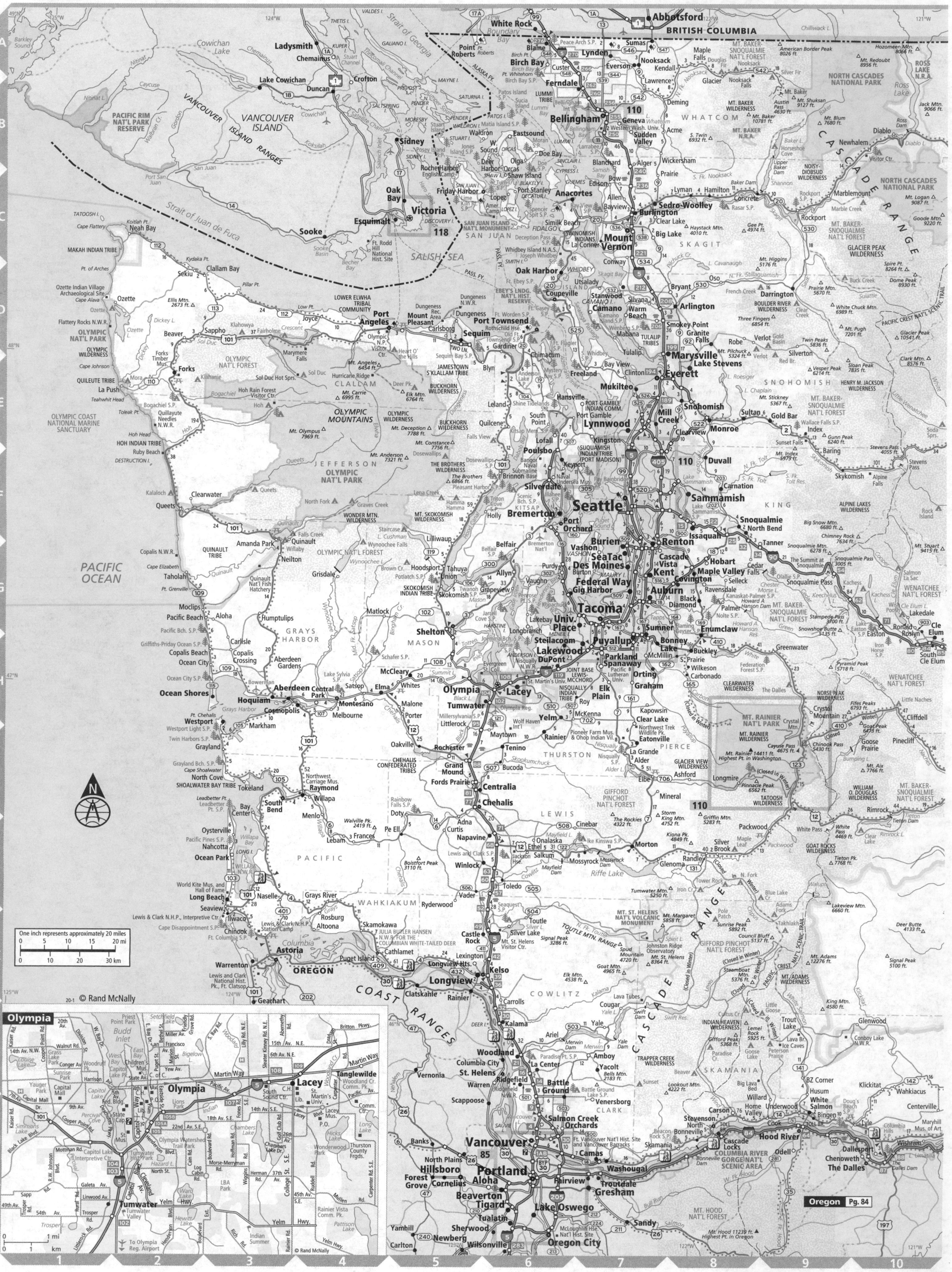

North Cascades National Park

Mileages between cities	Aberdeen	Bellingham	Colville	Kennewick	Longview	Olympia	Omak	Port Angeles	Portland, OR	Seattle	Spokane	Tacoma	The Dalles, OR	Vancouver, BC	Wenatchee	Yakima
Bellingham	198		317	306	216	149	201	118	261	89	361	121	326	52	182	224
Kennewick	312	306	209		254	263	189	340	213	223	138	235	130	359	132	82
Lewiston, ID	402	396	173	124	381	353	237	431	339	313	102	325	256	449	223	204
Portland, OR	141	261	422	213	48	113	377	228		172	351	141	83	313	251	185
Seattle	108	89	350	223	127	60	236	83	172		278	32	249	141	148	141
Spokane	367	361	71	138	386	319	139	396	351	278		291	268	413	169	201
Tacoma	77	121	362	235	96	28	248	106	141	32	291		217	174	140	153
Yakima	230	224	272	82	166	181	192	259	185	141	201	153	102	276	196	

Total mileages through Washington

- 5: 277 miles
- 90: 297 miles
- 82: 133 miles
- 101: 373 miles

More mileages at randmcnally.com/MC

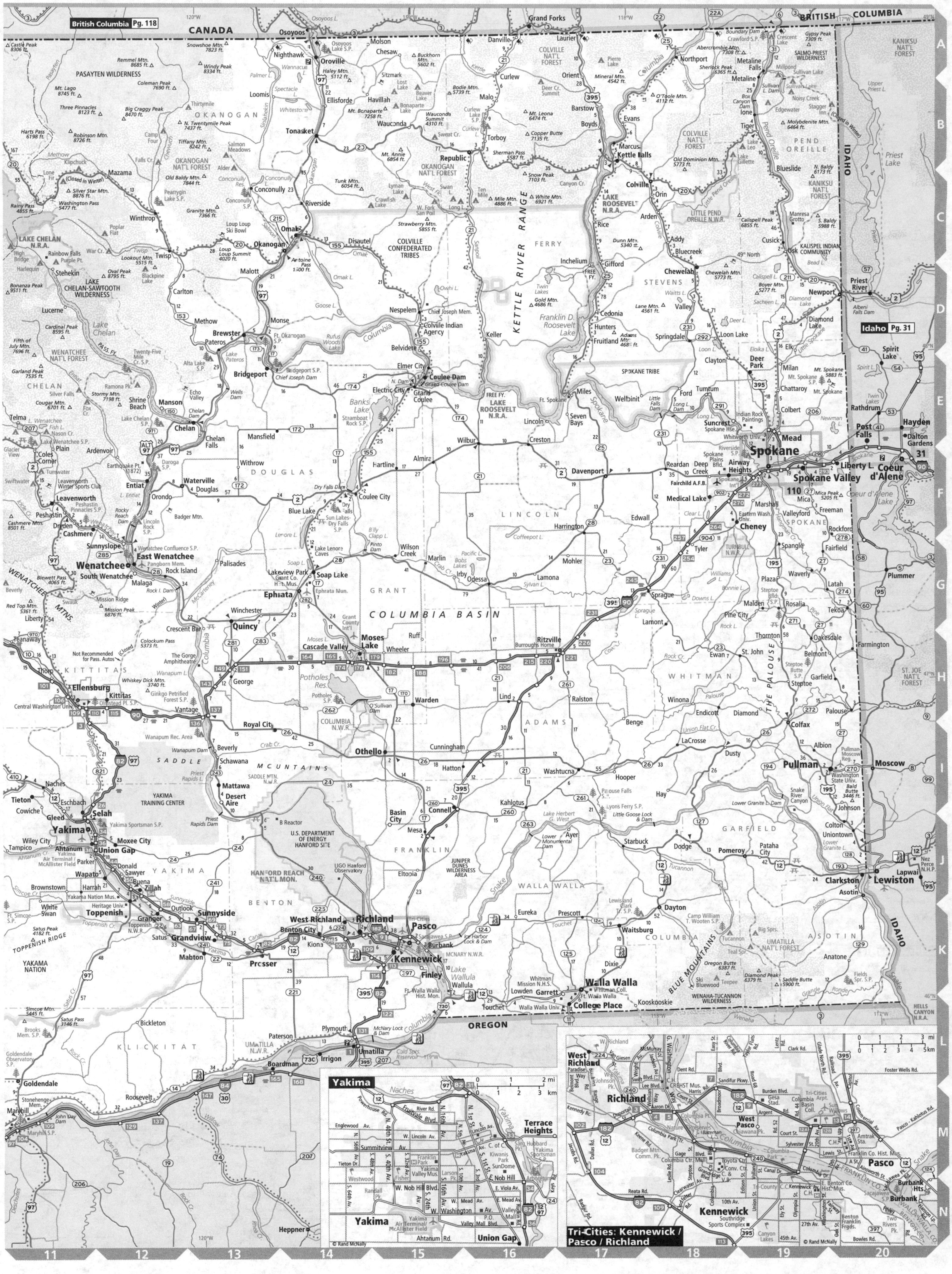

Sights to see

- Frye Art Museum, Seattle J-3
- Klondike Gold Rush National Historical Park, Seattle .. K-2
- Museum of Glass, Tacoma........................ L-6
- Museum of Pop Culture, Seattle H-1
- Nordic Heritage Museum, Seattle C-7
- Pacific Science Center, Seattle.................... H-1
- Pike Place Market, Seattle J-2
- Point Defiance Zoo & Aquarium, Tacoma........... K-5
- Seattle Aquarium, Seattle......................... J-1
- Space Needle, Seattle H-1
- Washington State History Museum, Tacoma L-6
- Woodland Park Zoo, Seattle........................ C-7

Mount Rainier National Park

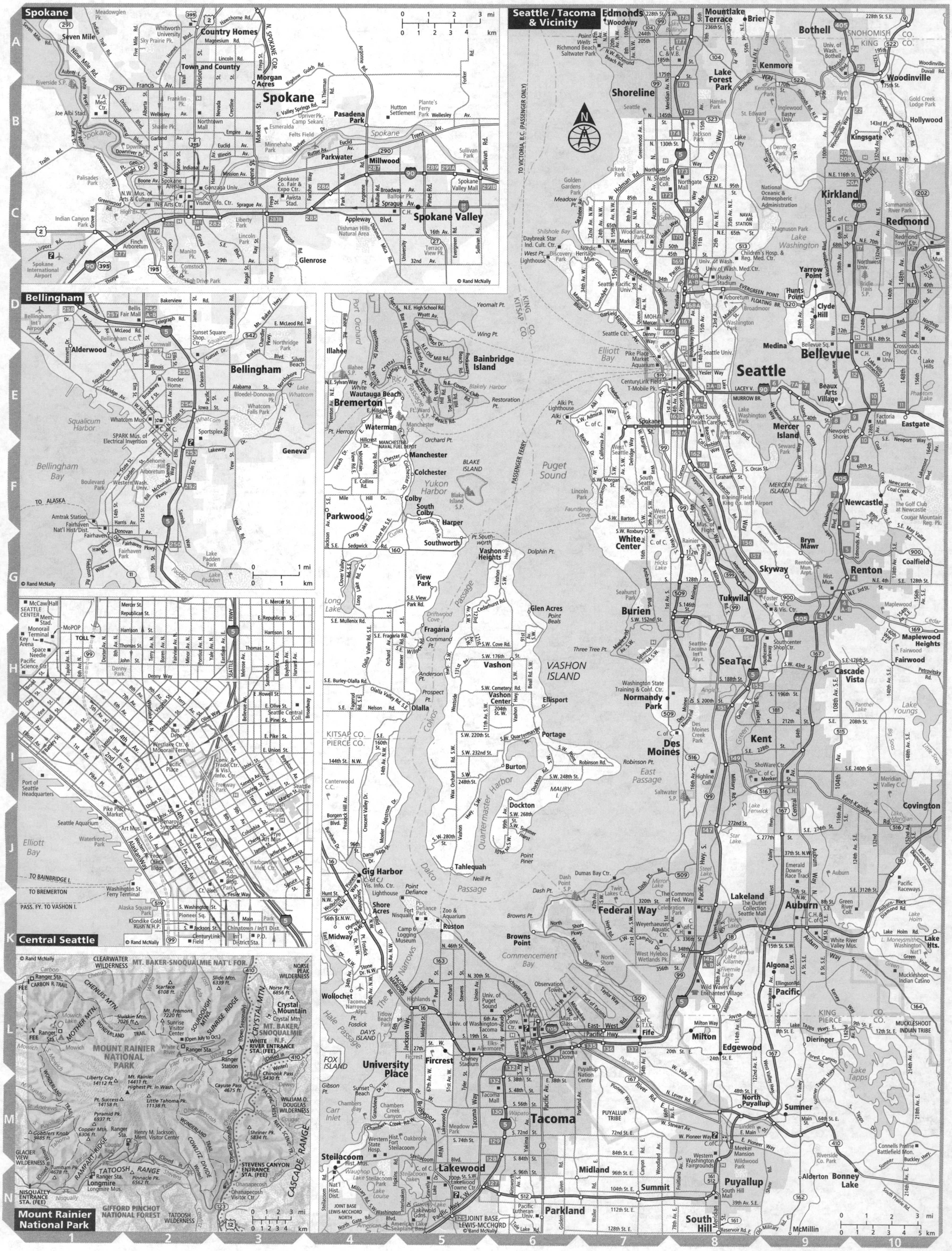

Land area: 61 sq. mi. | Population: 601,723

On-the-road resources

Tourism Information
Destination DC: (202) 789-7000; washington.org

Road Conditions & Construction
311, (202) 673-6813; ddot.dc.gov

Toll Road Information
No toll roads in District of Columbia
see Maryland or Virginia pages for toll road information

Sights to see

- Arlington National Cemetery, Arlington, VA N-1
- Frederick Douglass National Historic Site .. G-7
- John F. Kennedy Center for the Performing Arts L-3
- Martin Luther King Jr. Memorial M-4
- National African American Museum .. L-6
- National Arboretum F-7
- National Mall M-7
- National Zoological Park F-6
- The Pentagon, Arlington, VA G-6
- The Supreme Court of the United States M-9
- United States Botanic Garden M-8
- The White House K-5
- Wolf Trap National Park for the Performing Arts, Vienna, VA E-2

Washington, D.C. & Vicinity

Central Washington, D.C.

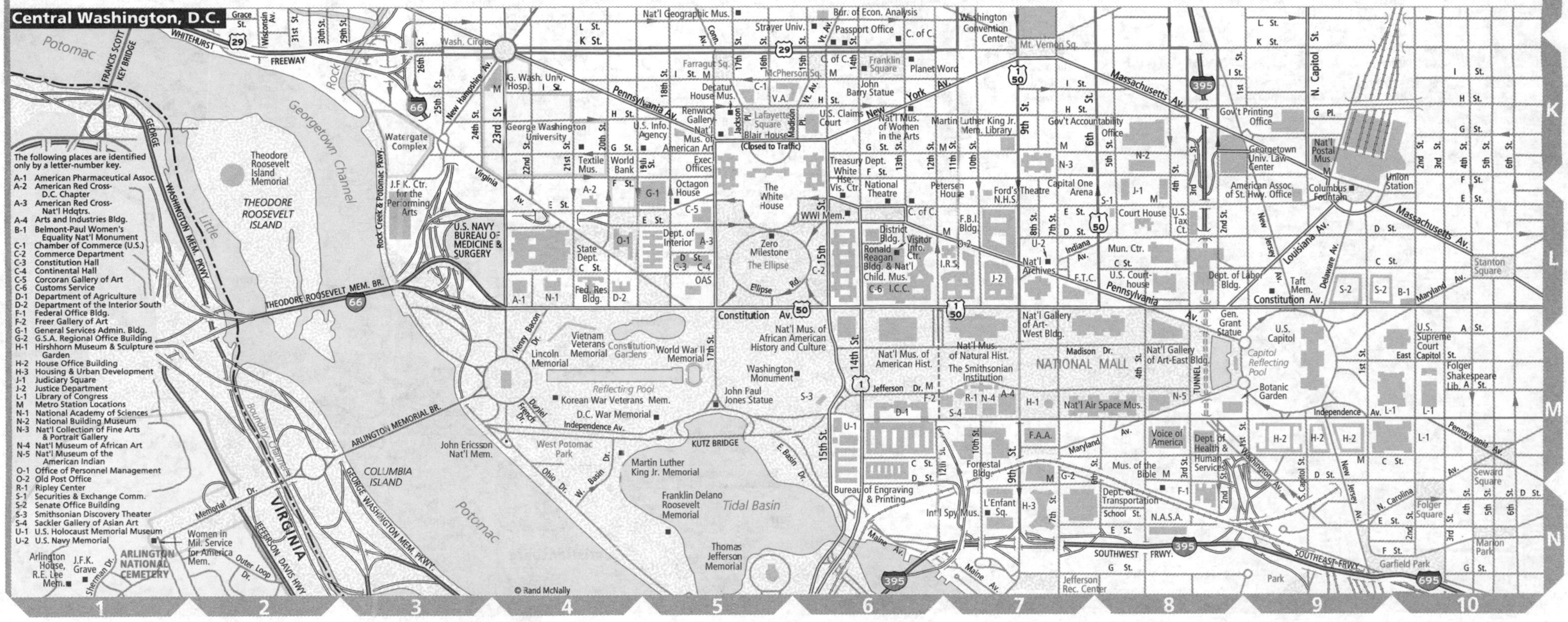

West Virginia

Nickname: The Mountain State
Capital: Charleston, J-3
Land area: 24,038 sq. mi. (rank: 41st)
Population: 1,852,994 (rank: 37th)
Largest city: Charleston, 51,400, J-3

Index of places Pg. 135

Mileages between cities	Bluefield	Charleston	Clarksburg	Cumberland, MD	Martinsburg	Petersburg	Wheeling	Wh. Sulphur Sprs.
Beckley	50	59	136	239	267	184	236	59
Charleston	106		123	225	304	193	177	120
Cumberland, MD	288	225	109		79	66	155	194
Huntington	158	51	174	276	355	244	228	172
Morgantown	218	154	38	73	151	103	78	187
Parkersburg	183	76	72	181	259	172	104	198
Wheeling	283	177	114	155	225	179		262
White Sulphur Sprs.	79	120	155	194	208	125	262	

Mileages © Rand McNally

Total mileages through West Virginia

I-64: 189 miles
I-77: 187 miles
I-70: 14 miles
I-79: 161 miles

More mileages at randmcnally.com/MC

Travel planning & on-the-road resources

Tourism Information
West Virginia Tourism Office:
(800) 225-5982, (304) 558-2200; www.wvtourism.com

Road Conditions & Construction
511, (855) 699-8511; www.wv511.org, transportation.wv.gov

Toll Road Information *(E-ZPass)*
W.V. Parkways Authority: (304) 926-1900; www.transportation.wv.gov/turnpike

HarborPark promenade, Kenosha

Sights to see

- Angel Museum, Beloit N-5
- Betty Brinn Children's Museum, Milwaukee L-9
- Golden Rondelle Theatre, Racine J-3
- Harley Davidson Museum, Milwaukee M-8
- Henry Maier Festival Park, Milwaukee M-9
- Kenosha History Center, Kenosha L-3
- Miller Brewery, Milwaukee E-9
- Milwaukee Art Museum, Milwaukee L-9
- Milwaukee Public Museum, Milwaukee L-8
- Mitchell Park Horticultural Conservatory, Milwaukee F-9
- Paul Bunyan Logging Camp, Eau Claire D-1
- Petit National Ice Center, Milwaukee F-8

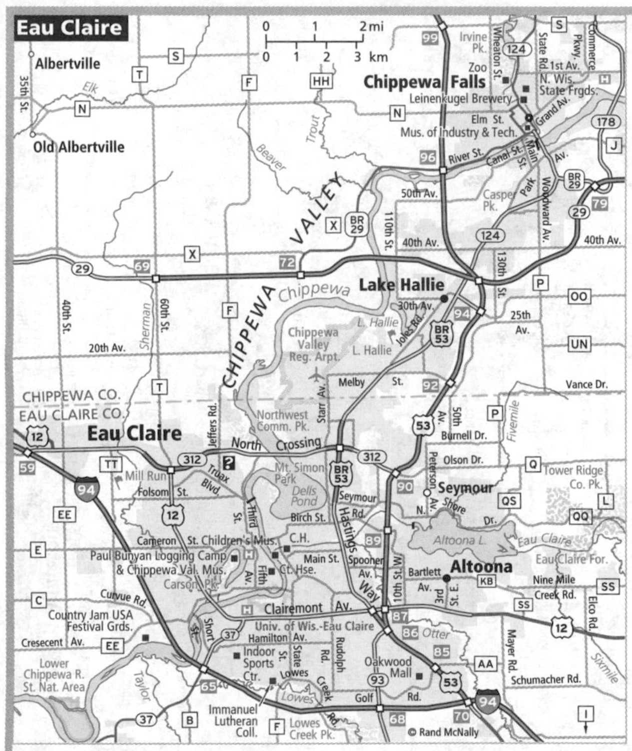

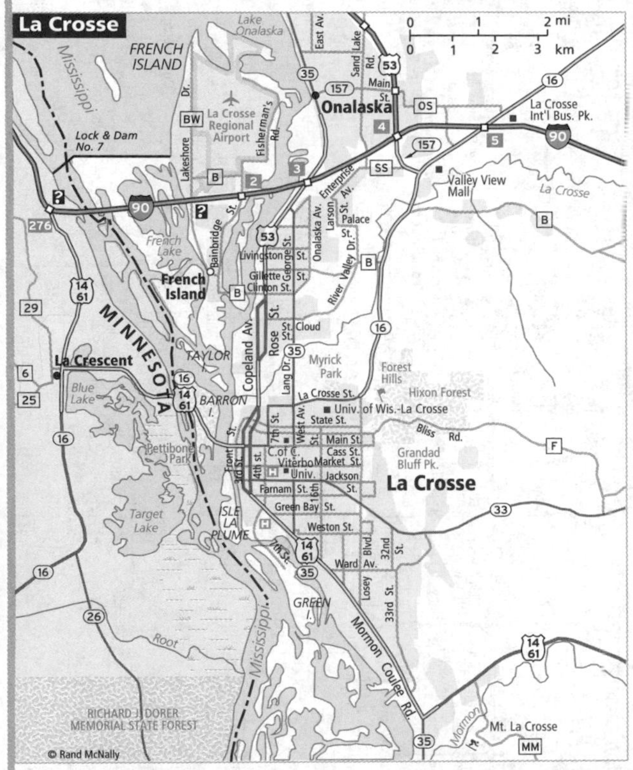

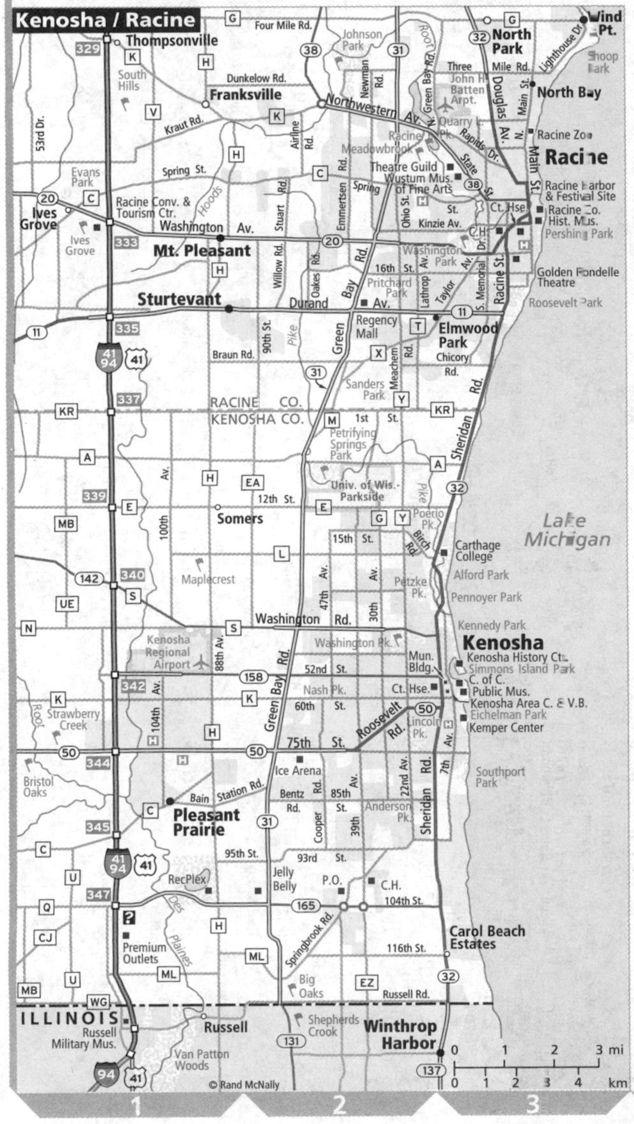

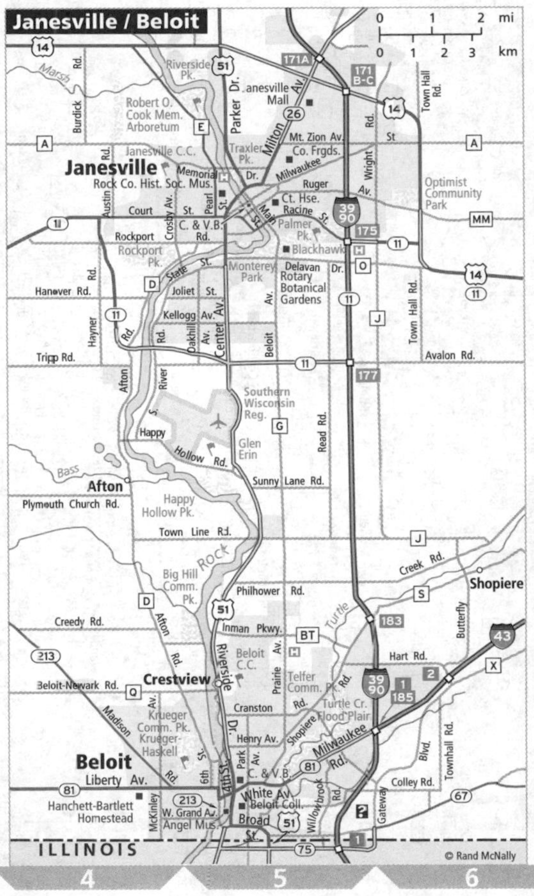

Nickname: The Badger State
Capital: Madison, N-9
Land area: 54,158 sq. mi. (rank: 25th)
Population: 5,686,986 (rank: 20th)
Largest city: Milwaukee, 594,833, N-13

Index of places Pg. 136

Travel planning & on-the-road resources

Tourism Information
Wisconsin Department of Tourism: (800) 432-8747, (608) 266-2161; www.travelwisconsin.com

Road Conditions & Construction
511, (866) 511-9472; 511wi.gov

Toll Road Information
No tolls on state or federal highways

Determining distances along roads

Highway distances (segments of one mile or less not shown):
Cumulative miles (red): the distance between red arrows
Intermediate miles (black): the distance between intersections & places

Interchanges and exit numbers
For most states, the mileage between interchanges may be determined by subtracting one number from the other.

Lighthouse, Sand Island

Mileages between cities	Beloit	Chicago, IL	Dubuque, IA	Eau Claire	Green Bay	Hayward	La Crosse	Madison	Milwaukee	Oshkosh	Rhinelander	Sheboygan	Sturgeon Bay	Superior	Wausau	Wisconsin Dells
Chicago, IL	96		177	315	206	420	281	146	90	175	338	145	245	462	281	195
Eau Claire	223	315	192		192	106	86	177	243	181	155	228	237	149	98	124
Green Bay	184	206	233	192		283	203	138	116	52	136	64	44	326	96	132
La Crosse	188	281	119	86	203	190		143	209	153	214	195	248	233	170	90
Madison	54	146	93	177	138	282	143		78	87	200	117	185	325	143	57
Milwaukee	74	90	171	243	116	348	209	78		86	244	54	155	390	187	123
Superior	370	462	339	149	326	70	233	325	390	332	182	388	370		232	271
Wausau	189	281	239	98	96	189	170	143	187	103	59	158	141	232		112

Total mileages through Wisconsin

39 182 miles
90 189 miles
43 192 miles
94 341 miles

More mileages at randmcnally.com/MC

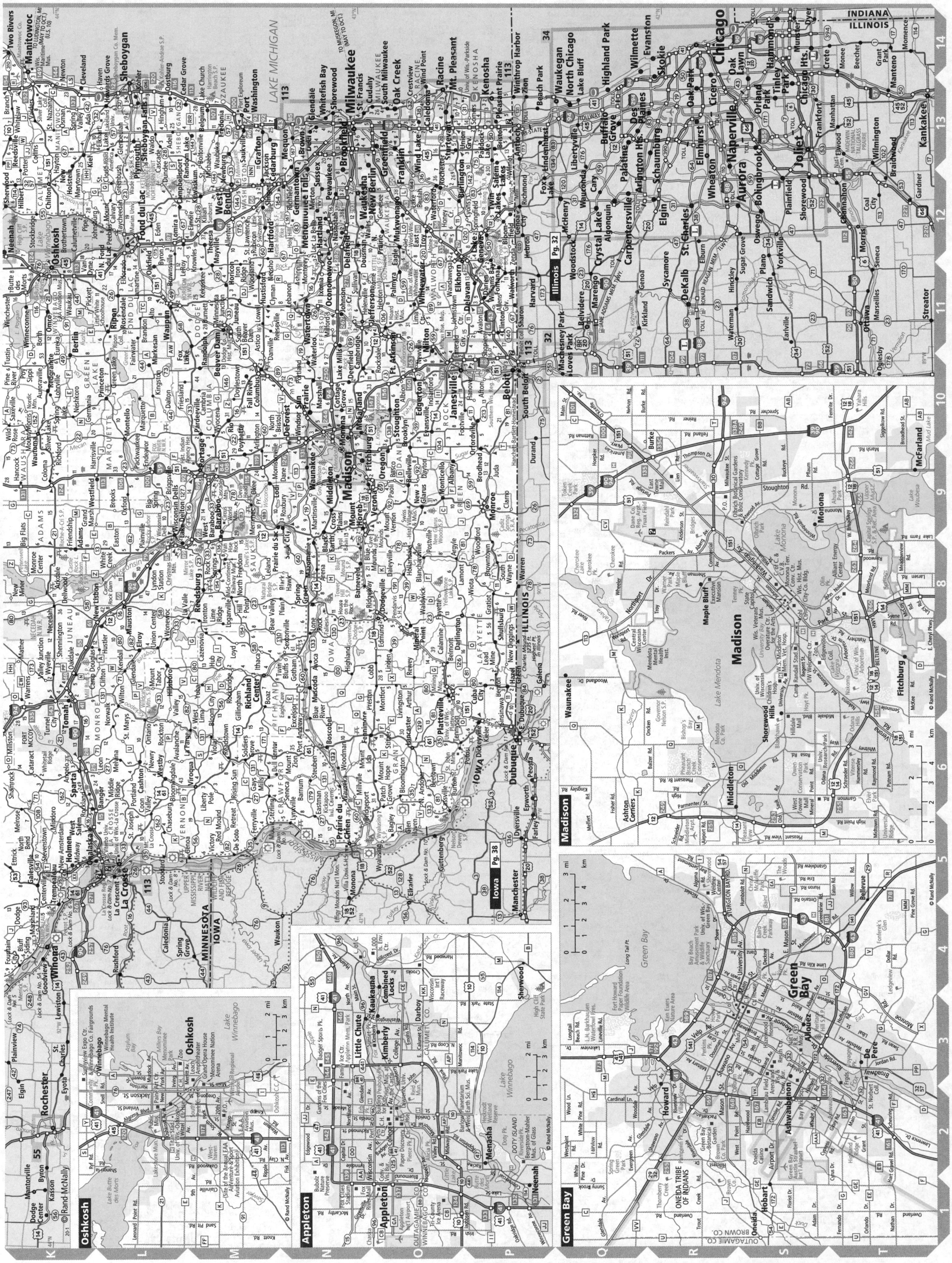

Wyoming

Nickname: The Equality State
Capital: Cheyenne, M-9
Land area: 97,093 sq. mi. (rank: 9th)
Population: 563,626 (rank: 50th)
Largest city: Cheyenne, 59,466, M-9

Index of places Pg. 136

Mileages between cities	Casper	Cheyenne	Cody	Evanston	Gillette	Laramie	Sheridan	Spearfish, SD
Casper		178	213	325	126	147	148	219
Cheyenne	178		392	357	244	49	324	290
Cody	213	392		376	250	363	148	344
Jackson	283	432	177	190	411	383	325	504
Riverton	119	272	138	238	248	222	213	341
Rock Springs	225	257	278	100	351	207	373	444
Sheridan	148	324	148	473	103	294		196
Spearfish, SD	219	290	344	544	93	296	196	

Total mileages through Wyoming
25: 301 miles
90: 209 miles
80: 403 miles
20: 505 miles

More mileages at randmcnally.com/MC

Travel planning & on-the-road resources

Tourism Information
Wyoming Office of Tourism: (800) 225-5996
(307) 777-7777; www.wyomingtourism.org

Road Conditions & Construction
511, (888) 996-7623; www.wyoroad.info

Toll Road Information
No tolls on state or federal highways

Determining Distances
(segments of one mile or less not shown)
Cumulative miles (red): the distance between red arrows
Intermediate miles (black): the distance between intersections & places

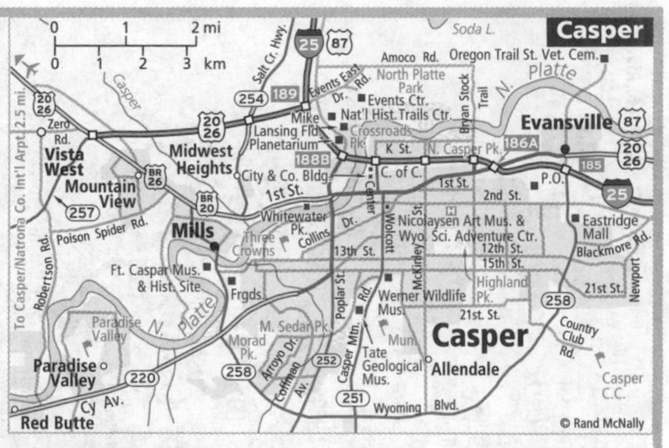

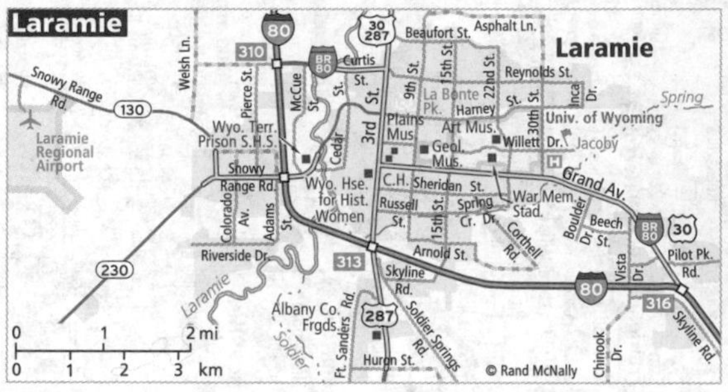

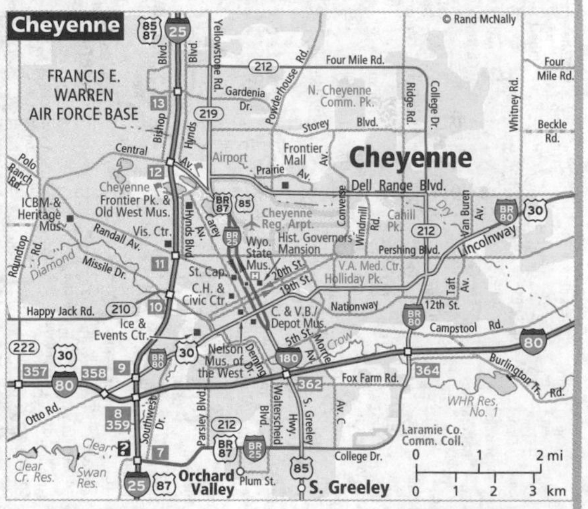

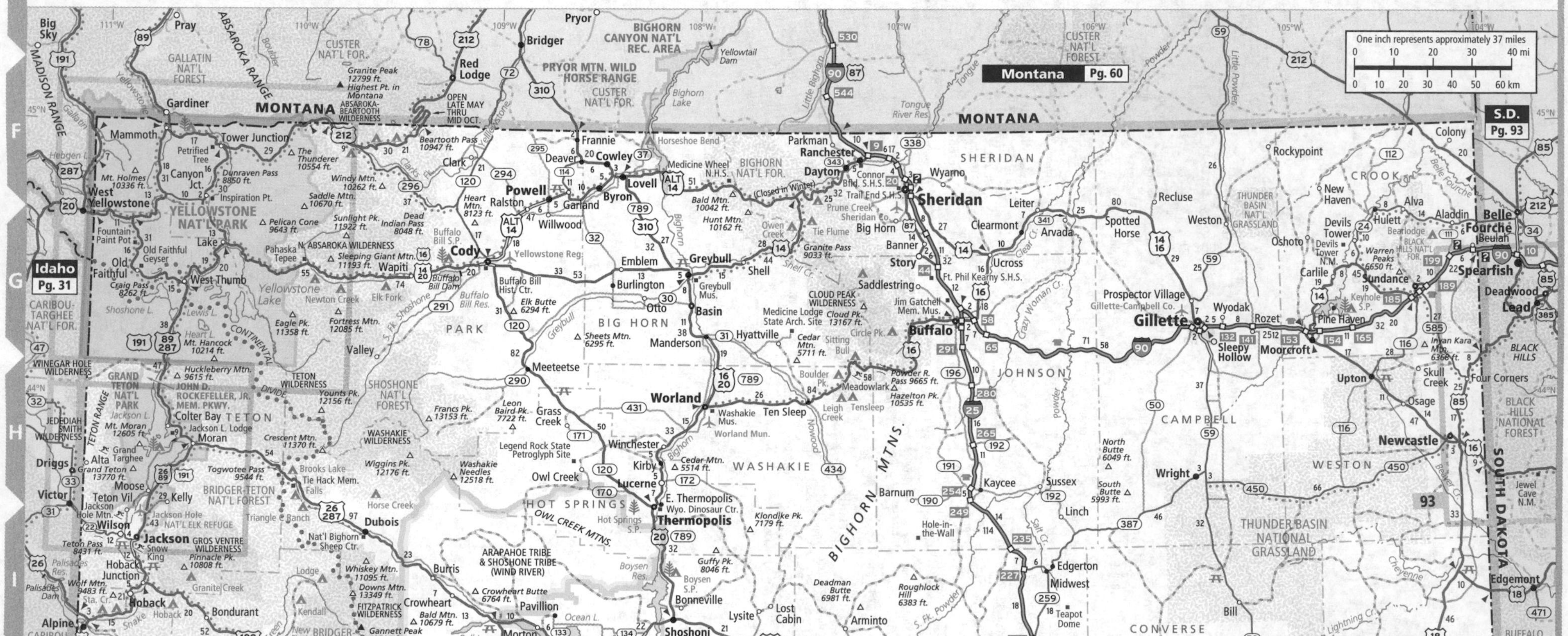

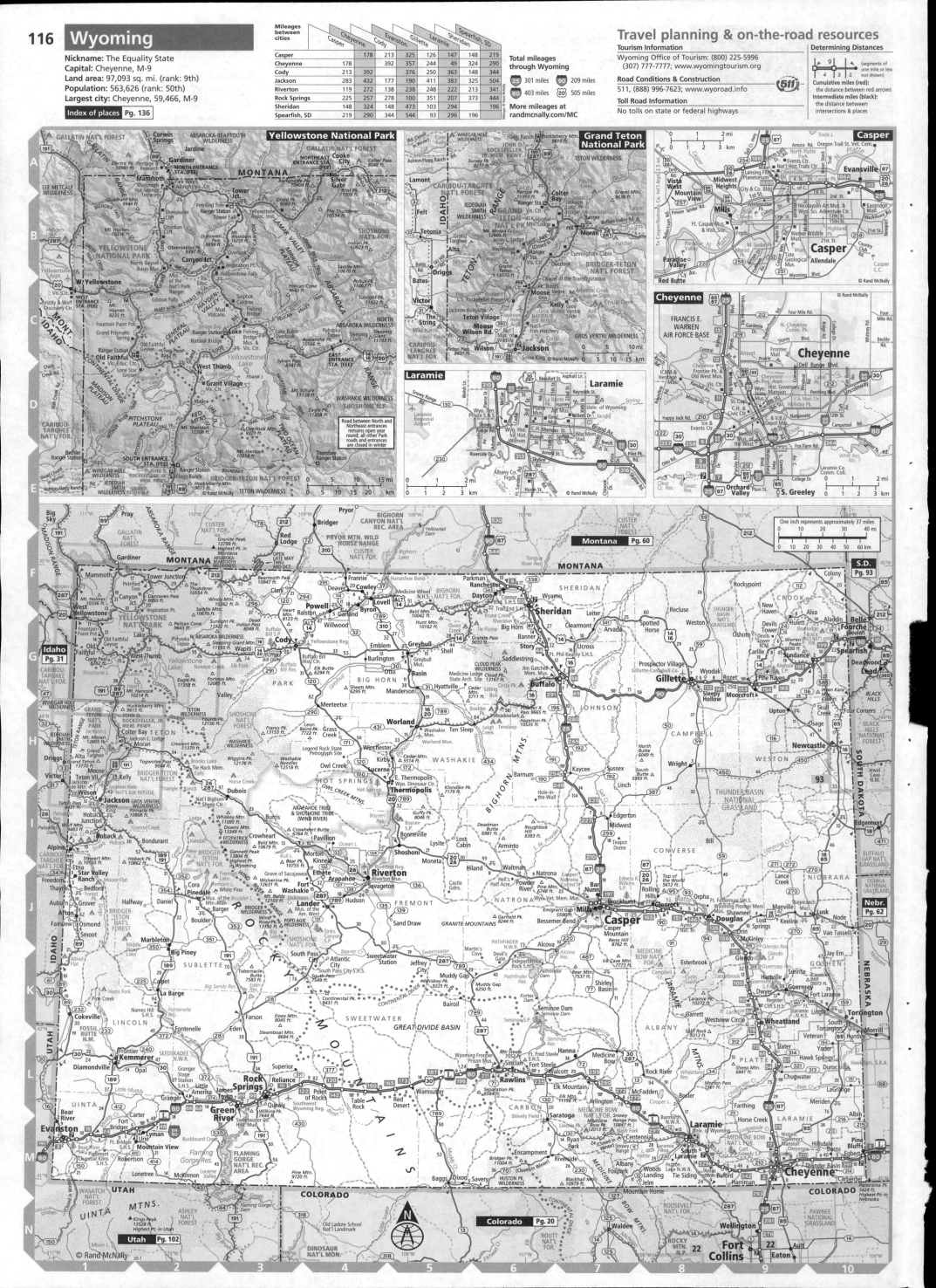

Selected National Park locations

- Banff National Park G-3
- Cape Breton Highlands Nat'l Park. . G-13
- Fundy National Park H-12
- Glacier National Park G-3
- Gros Morne National Park F-13
- Jasper National Park F-3
- Kejimkujik National Park H-12
- Kluane National Park & Reserve C-2
- Kootenay National Park G-3
- Mount Revelstoke National Park. . . . G-3
- Parc National de la Maurice. H-11
- Prince Albert National Park F-5
- Prince Edward Island Nat'l Park. . . . H-12
- Pukaskwa National Park. H-8
- Riding Mountain National Park. H-6
- St. Lawrence Islands National Park . . I-10

Capital: Ottawa, I-10
Land area: 3,511,023 sq. mi.
Population: 33,476,688
Largest city: Toronto, 2,615,060, I-10

Index of places Pg. 136

Glossary of French terms

- Áeroport .... Airport
- Arrondissement .... District
- Baie .... Bay
- Barrage .... Dam
- Basilique .... Basilica
- Bibliothèque .... Library
- Bois .... Woods
- Cap .... Cape
- Centre de recherches .... Research centre (or center)
- Centre des congrès .... Convention centre (or center)
- Chemin .... Road
- Chenal .... Channel
- Chutes .... Falls
- Débarquement .... Landing
- Détroit .... Strait
- Fleuve ...... Major river (that flows to the sea)
- Hippodrome .... Race track
- Hôtel de Ville .... City or town hall
- Hôtel du Parlement .... Parliament building
- Île .... Island
- Jardin .... Garden
- Jardin botanique .... Botanical garden
- Jardin zoologique . . Zoological garden (or Zoo)
- Lac .... Lake
- Lieu historique .... Historic site
- Lieu historique national . . National historic site
- Lieu natal .... Birthplace
- Mont .... Mountain
- Musée .... Museum
- Oratoire .... Oratory
- Parc .... Park
- Parc marin .... Marine park
- Parc national .... National park (or provincial park in Québec)
- Pont .... Bridge
- Promenade .... Boulevard
- Réserve faunique .... Wildlife reserve
- Réserve indienne .... Indian reserve (or Reservation)
- Rivière .... River
- Rue .... Street
- Stade .... Stadium
- Tribunal .... Court house
- Université .... University

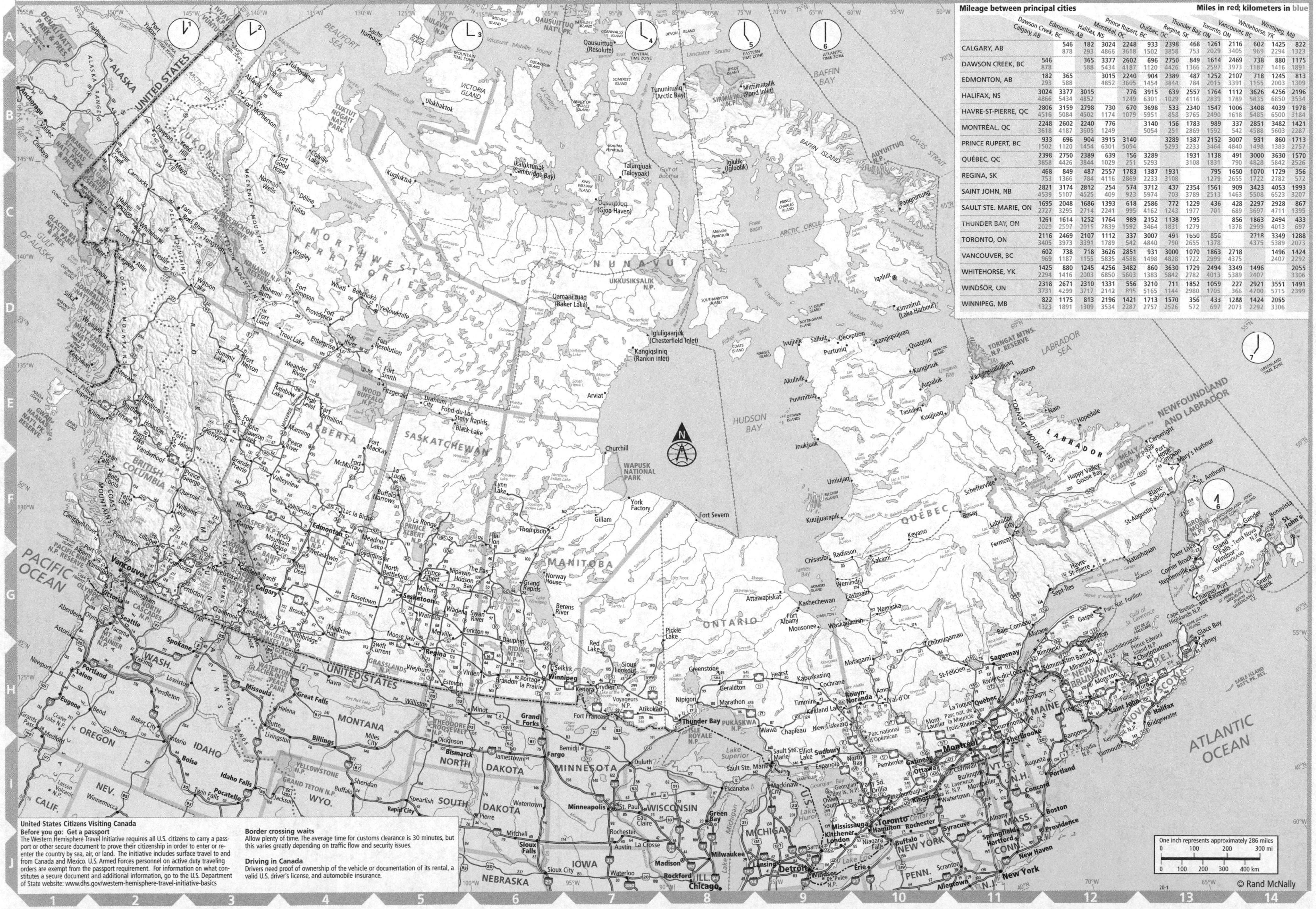

Mileage between principal cities

Miles in red; kilometers in blue

	Calgary, AB	Dawson Creek, BC	Edmonton, AB	Halifax, NS	Montréal, QC	Prince Rupert, BC	Québec, QC	Regina, SK	Thunder Bay, ON	Toronto, ON	Vancouver, BC	Whitehorse, YK	Winnipeg, MB
CALGARY, AB		546 / 878	182 / 293	3024 / 4866	2248 / 3618	933 / 1502	2398 / 3858	468 / 753	1261 / 2029	2116 / 3405	602 / 969	1425 / 2294	822 / 1323
DAWSON CREEK, BC	546 / 878		365 / 588	3377 / 5434	2602 / 4187	696 / 1120	2750 / 4426	849 / 1366	1614 / 2597	2469 / 3973	738 / 1187	880 / 1416	1175 / 1891
EDMONTON, AB	182 / 293	365 / 588		3015 / 4852	2240 / 3605	904 / 1454	2389 / 3844	487 / 784	1252 / 2015	2107 / 3391	718 / 1155	1245 / 2003	813 / 1309
HALIFAX, NS	3024 / 4866	3377 / 5434	3015 / 4852		776 / 1249	3915 / 6301	639 / 1029	2557 / 4116	1764 / 2839	1112 / 1789	3626 / 5835	4256 / 6850	2196 / 3534
HAVRE-ST-PIERRE, QC	2806 / 4516	3159 / 5084	2798 / 4502	730 / 1174	670 / 1079	3698 / 5951	533 / 858	2340 / 3765	1547 / 2490	1006 / 1618	3408 / 5485	4039 / 6500	1978 / 3184
MONTRÉAL, QC	2248 / 3618	2602 / 4187	2240 / 3605	776 / 1249		3140 / 5054	156 / 251	1783 / 2869	989 / 1592	337 / 542	2851 / 4588	3482 / 5603	1421 / 2287
PRINCE RUPERT, BC	933 / 1502	696 / 1120	904 / 1454	3915 / 6301	3140 / 5054		3289 / 5293	1387 / 2233	2152 / 3464	3007 / 4840	931 / 1498	860 / 1383	1713 / 2757
QUÉBEC, QC	2398 / 3858	2750 / 4426	2389 / 3844	639 / 1029	156 / 251	3289 / 5293		1931 / 3108	1138 / 1831	491 / 790	3000 / 4828	3630 / 5842	1570 / 2526
REGINA, SK	468 / 753	849 / 1366	487 / 784	2557 / 4116	1783 / 2869	1387 / 2233	1931 / 3108		795 / 1279	1650 / 2655	1070 / 1722	1729 / 2782	356 / 572
SAINT JOHN, NB	2821 / 4539	3174 / 5107	2812 / 4525	254 / 409	574 / 923	3712 / 5974	437 / 703	2354 / 3789	1561 / 2513	909 / 1463	3423 / 5508	4053 / 6523	1993 / 3207
SAULT STE. MARIE, ON	1695 / 2727	2048 / 3295	1686 / 2714	1393 / 2241	618 / 995	2586 / 4162	772 / 1243	1229 / 1977	436 / 701	428 / 689	2297 / 3697	2928 / 4711	867 / 1395
THUNDER BAY, ON	1261 / 2029	1614 / 2597	1252 / 2015	1764 / 2839	989 / 1592	2152 / 3464	1138 / 1831	795 / 1279		856 / 1378	1863 / 2999	2494 / 4013	433 / 697
TORONTO, ON	2116 / 3405	2469 / 3973	2107 / 3391	1112 / 1789	337 / 542	3007 / 4840	491 / 790	1650 / 2655	856 / 1378		2718 / 4375	3349 / 5389	1288 / 2073
VANCOUVER, BC	602 / 969	738 / 1187	718 / 1155	3626 / 5835	2851 / 4588	931 / 1498	3000 / 4828	1070 / 1722	1863 / 2999	2718 / 4375		1496 / 2407	1424 / 2292
WHITEHORSE, YK	1425 / 2294	880 / 1416	1245 / 2003	4256 / 6850	3482 / 5603	860 / 1383	3630 / 5842	1729 / 2782	2494 / 4013	3349 / 5389	1496 / 2407		2055 / 3306
WINDSOR, ON	2318 / 3731	2671 / 4299	2310 / 3717	1331 / 2142	556 / 895	3210 / 5165	711 / 1144	1852 / 2980	1059 / 1705	227 / 366	2921 / 4700	3551 / 5715	1491 / 2399
WINNIPEG, MB	822 / 1323	1175 / 1891	813 / 1309	2196 / 3534	1421 / 2287	1713 / 2757	1570 / 2526	356 / 572	433 / 697	1288 / 2073	1424 / 2292	2055 / 3306	

United States Citizens Visiting Canada

Before you go: Get a passport

The Western Hemisphere Travel Initiative requires all U.S. citizens to carry a passport or other secure document to prove their citizenship in order to enter or re-enter the country by sea, air, or land. The initiative includes surface travel to and from Canada and Mexico. U.S. Armed Forces personnel on active duty traveling orders are exempt from the passport requirement. For information on what constitutes a secure document and additional information, go to the U.S. Department of State website: www.dhs.gov/western-hemisphere-travel-initiative-basics

Border crossing waits

Allow plenty of time. The average time for customs clearance is 30 minutes, but this varies greatly depending on traffic flow and security issues.

Driving in Canada

Drivers need proof of ownership of the vehicle or documentation of its rental, a valid U.S. driver's license, and automobile insurance.

One inch represents approximately 286 miles

British Columbia
Capital: Victoria, M-7
Land area: 357,216 sq. mi. (rank: 4th)
Population: 4,400,057 (rank: 3rd)
Largest city: Vancouver, 603,502, L-7

Index of places Pg. 136

Mileages between cities	Banff, AB	Dawson Creek	Jasper, AB	Port Hardy	Prince Rupert	Vancouver	Victoria	Williams Lake
Banff, AB		503	178	808*	855	524	578*	483
Cranbrook	173	638	312	806*	989	521	575*	553
Dawson Creek	503		326	1022*	696	738	791*	399
Kamloops	307	576	275	502*	769	217	271*	177
Kelowna	299	671	376	526*	865	242	295*	272
Prince George	408	250	231	772*	447	488	542*	149
Prince Rupert	855	696	677	307*		931	985*	592
Vancouver	524	738	492	285*	931		72*	339

*Via ferry

Mileages © Rand McNally

Total mileages through British Columbia
1: 538 miles
16: 658 miles

More mileages at randmcnally.com/MC

Travel planning & on-the-road resources

Tourism Information
Destination British Columbia:
(800) 822-7899, (604) 660-2861; www.hellobc.com

Road Conditions & Construction
(800) 550-4997; www.drivebc.ca
www2.gov.bc.ca/gov/content/transportation

Toll Road Information
No tolls on provincial or federal highways

Determining Distances
(segments of one mile or less not shown)
Cumulative miles (red), km (blue): the distance between red arrows
Intermediate miles (black): the distance between intersections & places

Travel planning & on-the-road resources

Tourism Information
Travel Alberta: (800) 252-3782; www.travelalberta.us

Road Conditions & Construction
511, (855) 391-9743; 511.alberta.ca

Toll Road Information
No tolls on provincial or federal highways

Determining Distances

(segments of one mile or less not shown)

Cumulative miles (red), km (blue): the distance between red arrows
Intermediate miles (black): the distance between intersections & places

Total mileages through Alberta

1: 332 miles
16: 397 miles

More mileages at randmcnally.com/MC

Mileages between cities	Calgary	Dawson Creek, BC	Edmonton	Fort McMurray	Grande Prairie	Jasper	Lethbridge	Red Deer
Banff	78	503	260	544	423	178	217	167
Calgary		546	182	465	463	256	139	89
Grande Prairie	463	32	283	467		246	602	376
Edmonton	182	355		281	283	226	321	95
Lethbridge	139	684	321	604	602	395		227
Medicine Hat	178	724	360	563	641	434	102	267
Peace River	480	146	299	421	123	354	618	392
Vermilion	299	481	120	321	399	342	338	211

Alberta
Capital: Edmonton, E-16
Land area: 248,000 sq. mi. (rank: 6th)
Population: 3,645,257 (rank: 4th)
Largest city: Calgary, 1,096,833, I-16

Index of places Pg. 136

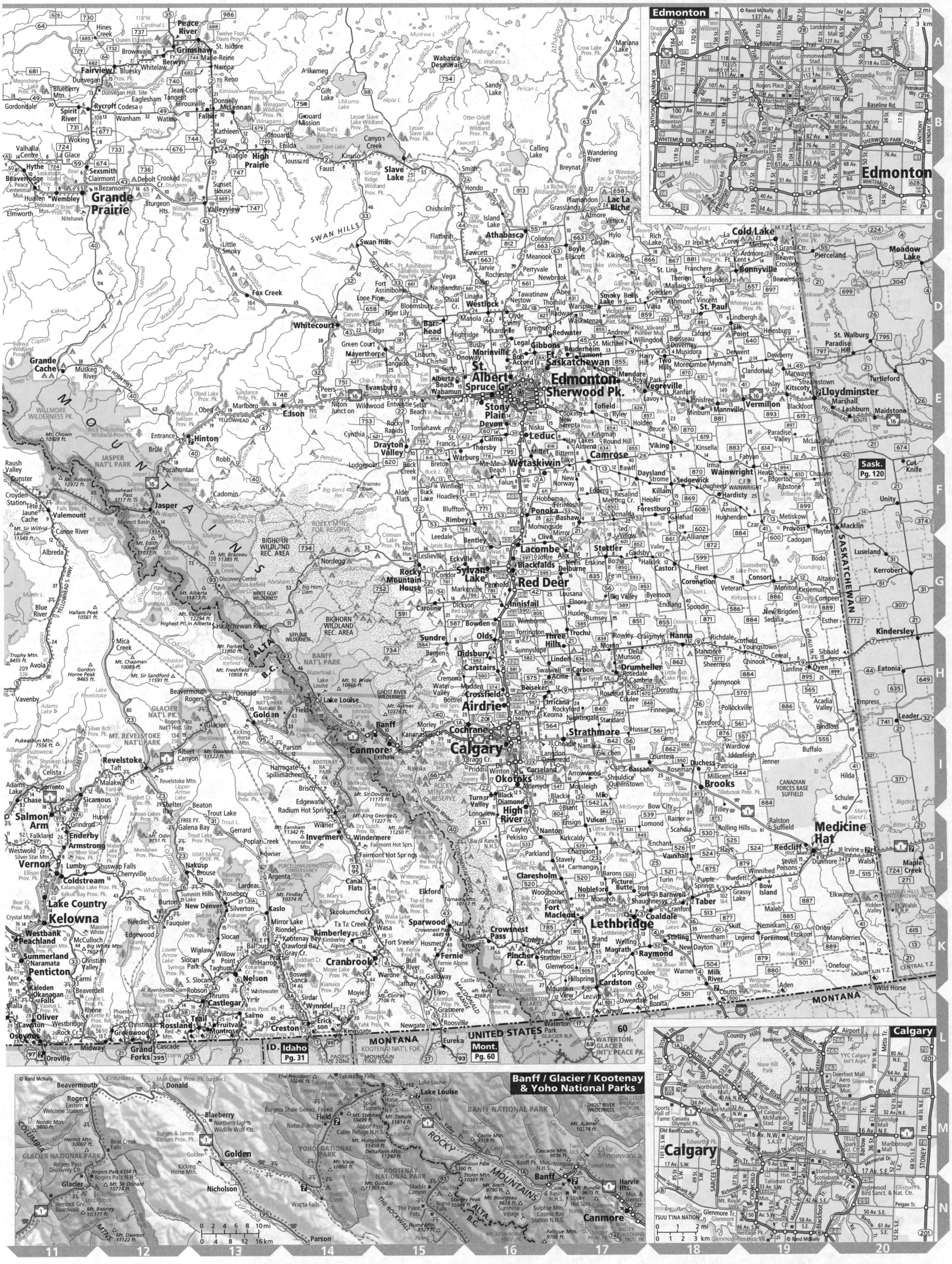

Saskatchewan
Capital: Regina, K-8
Land area: 228,445 sq. mi. (rank: 7th)
Population: 1,033,381 (rank: 6th)
Largest city: Saskatoon, 222,189, G-6

Index of places Pg. 136

Mileages between cities	La Loche	La Ronge	Medicine Hat, AB	N. Battleford	Prince Albert	Regina	Saskatoon	Yorkton
Estevan	668	498	391	371	350	125	285	159
Lloydminster	331	347	289	85	214	331	171	375
Meadow Lake	217	232	370	98	162	343	183	388
Prince Albert	318	148	365	129		225	88	233
Regina	543	373	289	246	225		160	116
Saskatoon	379	236	277	86	88	160		205
Swift Current	505	403	139	190	255	151	167	266
Yorkton	551	382	405	290	233	116	205	

Total mileages through Saskatchewan
1: 413 miles
16: 437 miles
More mileages at randmcnally.com/MC

Travel planning & on-the-road resources

Tourism Information
Tourism Saskatchewan: (877) 237-2273, (306) 787-9600
www.tourismsaskatchewan.com, www.sasktourism.com

Road Conditions & Construction
(888) 335-7623, Saskatoon area: (306) 933-8333, Regina area: (306) 787-7623
www.saskatchewan.ca/residents/transportation/highways/highway-hotline

Toll Road Info
No tolls on provincial or federal highways

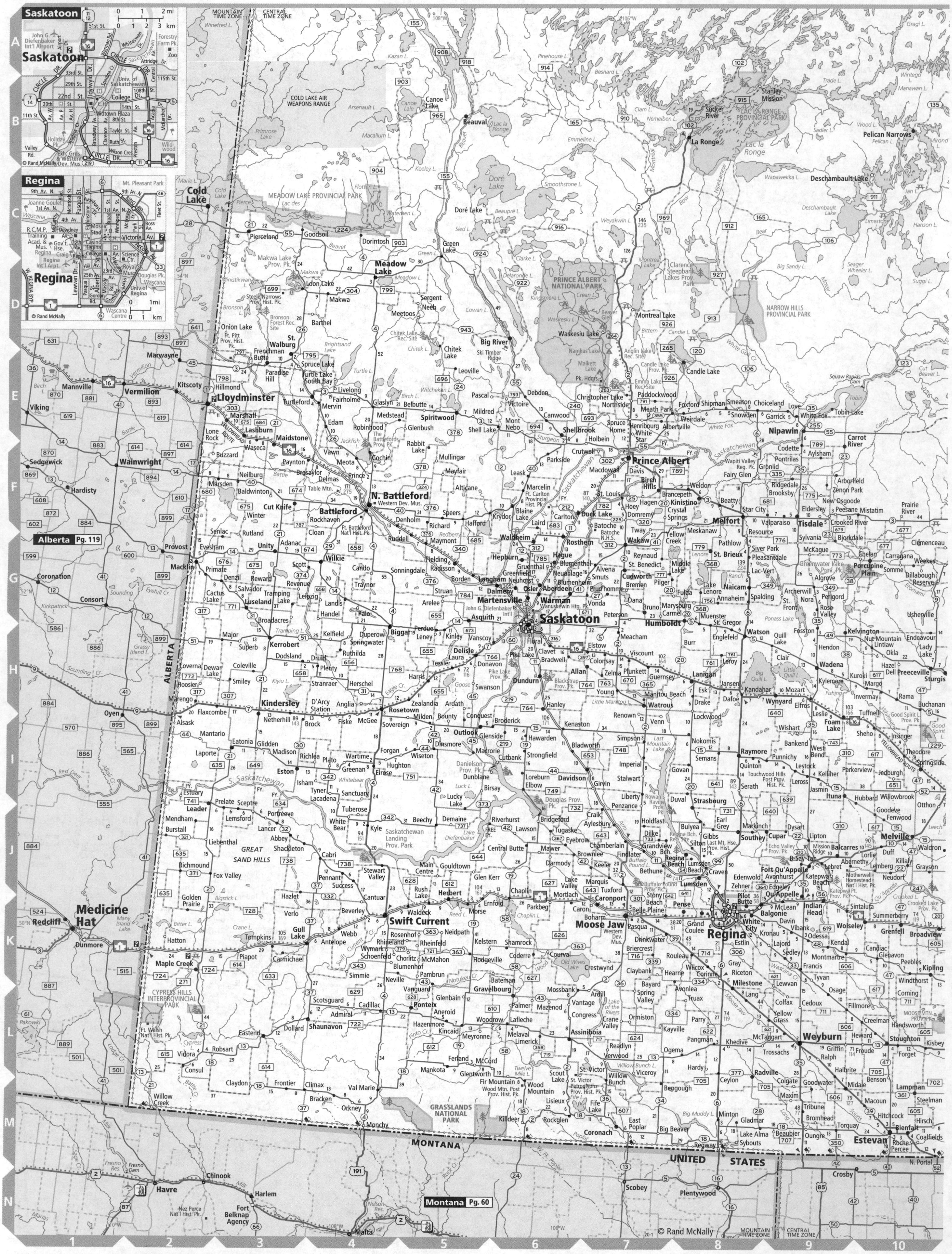

Travel planning & on-the-road resources

Tourism Information
Travel Manitoba: (800) 665-0040, (204) 927-7800
www.travelmanitoba.com

Road Conditions & Construction
511, In MB, ON, SK and ND only: (877) 627-6237
www.manitoba511.ca/en

Toll Road Information
No tolls on provincial or federal highways

Determining Distances
(segments of one mile or less not shown)
Cumulative miles (red), km (blue): the distance between red arrows
Intermediate miles (black): the distance between intersections & places

Total mileages through Manitoba
1: 306 miles
16: 166 miles

More mileages at randmcnally.com/MC

Mileages between cities	Ashern	Brandon	Dauphin	Flin Flon	Grand Rapids	Pine Falls	Thompson	Winnipeg
Brandon	200		104	444	355	217	558	134
Dauphin	127	104		342	282	267	485	198
Flin Flon	368	444	342		255	546	244	483
Morden	184	129	216	552	338	167	542	87
Portage la Prairie	119	80	144	485	274	136	477	53
Swan River	233	208	106	236	211	372	385	303
Virden	245	47	148	419	399	262	568	178
Winnipeg	114	134	198	483	269	81	472	

Mileages © Rand McNally

Manitoba

Capital: Winnipeg, L-17
Land area: 213,729 sq. mi. (rank: 8th)
Population: 1,208,268 (rank: 5th)
Largest city: Winnipeg, 663,617, L-17

Index of places Pg. 136

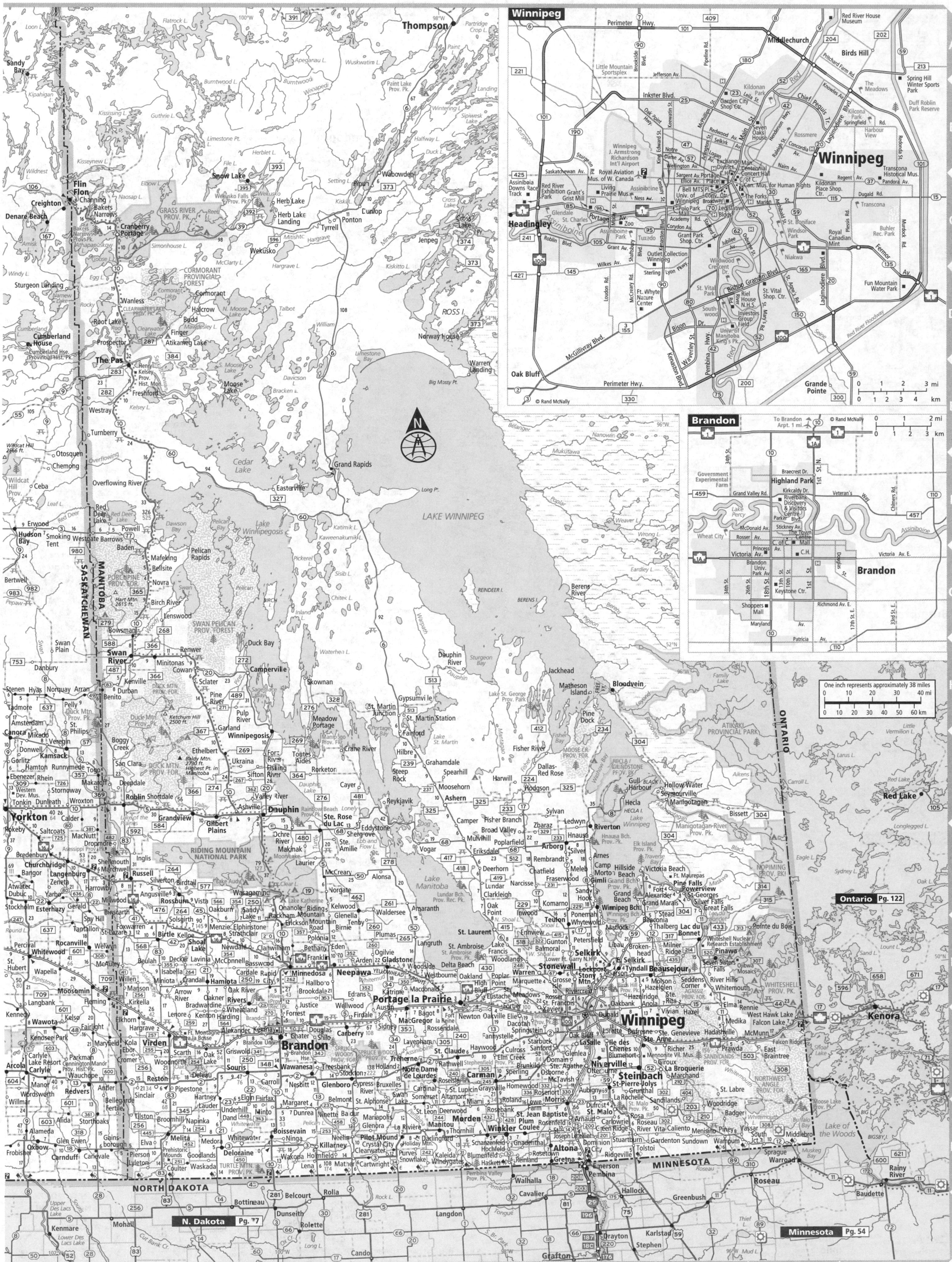

Capital: Toronto, I-10
Land area: 354,342 sq. mi. (rank: 5th)
Population: 12,851,821 (rank: 1st)
Largest city: Toronto, 2,615,060, I-10

Glossary of common French terms found on these maps: pg. 117

Index of places Pg. 136

Travel planning & on-the-road resources

Tourism Information
Ontario T.M.P.C.: (800) 668-2746; www.ontariotravel.net

Road Conditions & Construction
511, (800) 268-4686, Toronto area: (416) 235-4686
511on.ca, www.mto.gov.on.ca/english/traveller

Toll Road Information:
407 ETR (Toronto): (888) 407-0407; www.407etr.com

Ontario–Michigan Toll Bridge/Tunnel Information
Ambassador Bridge (Windsor) ***(A-Pass)***:
(800) 462-7434; www.ambassadorbridge.com
Federal Bridge Corp. (Blue Water Bridge, Sarnia):
(866) 422-6346; www.bluewaterbridge.ca
Detroit-Windsor Tunnel ***(NEXPRESS)***:
(313) 567-4422 ext. 200, (519) 258-7424 ext. 200; www.dwtunnel.com
International Bridge Administration (Sault Ste. Marie):
(705) 942-4345, (906) 635-5255; www.saultbridge.com

Ontario–New York Toll Bridge Information
Buffalo & Ft. Erie Public Br. Authority
(Peace Bridge) ***(E-ZPass)***:
(716) 884-6744; www.peacebridge.com
Niagara Falls Bridge Commission:
(E-ZPass or ExpressPass): (716) 285-6322;
www.niagarafallsbridges.com

For St. Lawrence River crossings, see New York, p. 70

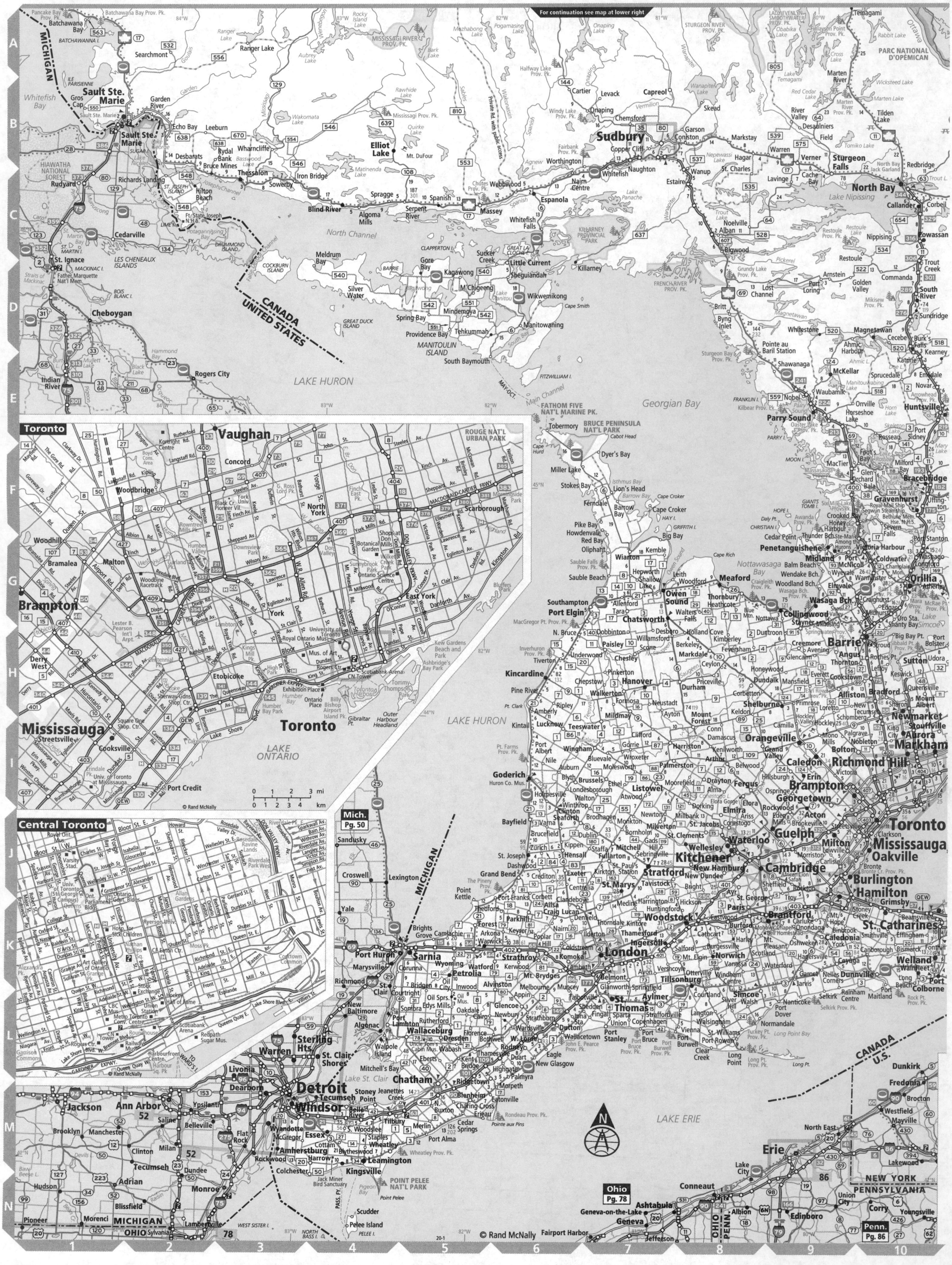

Nathan Phillips Square winter skating, Toronto

Mileages between cities	Bracebridge	Hamilton	Kenora	Kingston	Montréal, QC	Niagara Falls	Ottawa	Owen Sound	Pembroke	Sarnia	Sault Ste. Marie	Sudbury	Thunder Bay	Timmins	Toronto	Windsor
Kingston	223	204	1285		180	243	120	269	154	335	555	369	983	509	161	381
London	213	81	1255	274	450	127	360	143	360	58	525	339	953	535	121	116
Niagara Falls	185	47	1227	243	419		329	163	328	188	497	311	925	507	83	233
Ottawa	237	290	1207	120	124	329		338	91	421	494	300	905	445	247	467
Sudbury	153	272	925	369	424	311	300	238	209	401	195		623	182	242	446
Thunder Bay	767	886	303	983	989	925	905	852	814	1015	436	623		517	856	1060
Toronto	116	44	1158	161	337	83	247	118	246	182	428	242	856	438		227
Windsor	319	187	1361	381	556	233	467	259	466	96	631	445	1059	641	227	

Total mileages through Ontario

69 & 400 & QEW 323 miles

401 513 miles

17 & 417 1358 miles

More mileages at randmcnally.com/MC

Capital: Québec, J-11
Land area: 527,079 sq. mi. (rank: 2nd)
Population: 7,903,001 (rank: 2nd)
Largest city: Montréal, 1,649,519, M-8

Glossary of common French terms found on these maps: pg. 117

Index of places Pg. 136

Travel planning & on-the-road resources

Tourism Information
Tourisme Québec: (877) 266-5687, (514) 873-2015
www.quebecoriginal.com

Road Conditions & Construction
511, (888) 355-0511
www.quebec511.info/en

Toll Bridge Information
Concession A25 (Pont Olivier-Charbonneau, Montréal) ***(A25 Smart Link)***: (855) 766-8225, (514) 766-8225; www.a25.com
A30Express (near Montréal) ***(A30 Express)***: (855) 783-3030, (514) 782-0800; www.a30express.com

Determining distances along roads
Highway distances (segments of one mile or less not shown):
Cumulative miles (red): the distance between red arrows
Cumulative kilometers (blue): the distance between red arrows
Intermediate miles (black): the distance between intersections & places

Comparative distance: 1 mile = 1.609 kilometers 1 kilometer = 0.621 mile

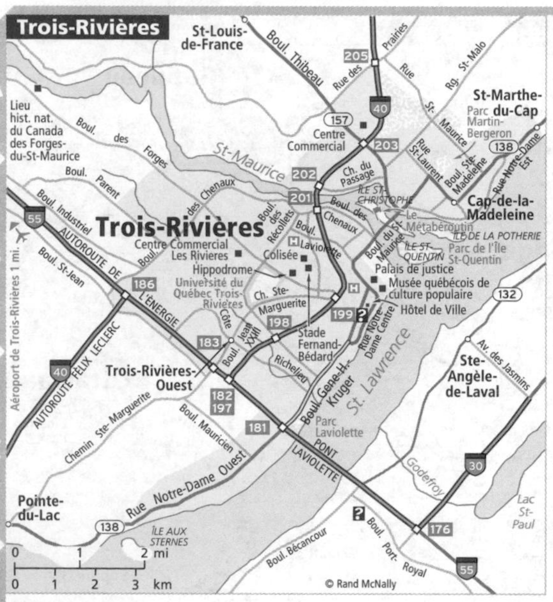

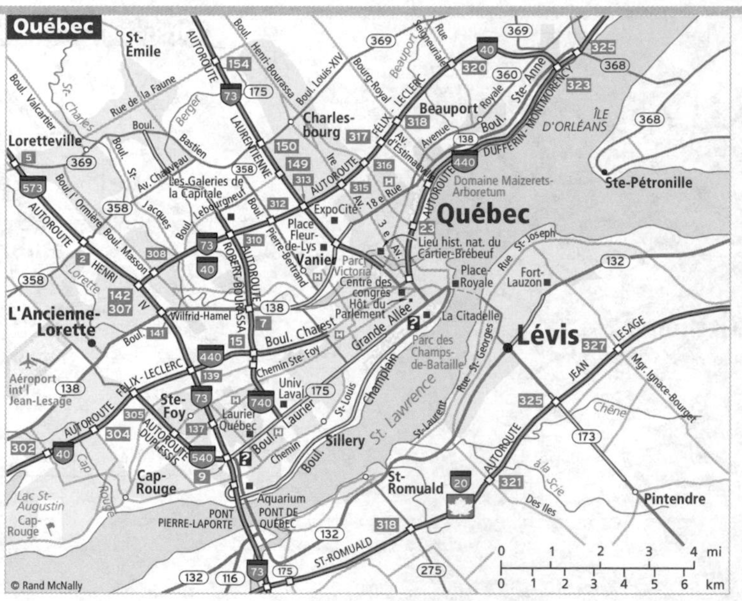

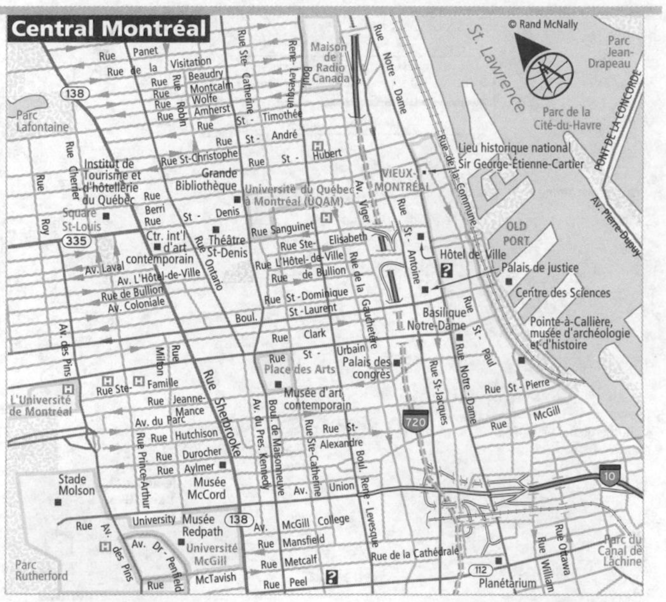

Québec

Mileages between cities	Baie-Comeau	Edmundston, NB	Gaspé	Mont-Laurier	Montréal	North Bay, ON	Ottawa, ON	Québec	Rimouski	Rivière-du-Loup	Rouyn-Noranda	Saguenay	Sept-Îles	Sherbrooke	Thetford Mines	Trois-Rivières
Montréal	410	336	565	145		346	124	156	331	266	389	289	534*	93	143	88
Ottawa, ON	533	459	683	122	124	222		279	454	389	323	411	657*	213	266	205
Québec	253	199	429	294	156	501	279		195	129	537	135	397*	146	72	78
Rouyn-Noranda	706	723	953	243	389	181	323	537	719	653		517	921*	481	530	461
Saguenay	196	186*	390*	427	289	634	411	135	156*	108*	517		339	279	205	211
Sept-Îles	143	306*	319*	678*	534*	879*	657*	397*	206*	268*	921*	339		524*	450*	465*
Sherbrooke	400	326	556	237	93	435	213	146	321	256	481	279	524*		65	94
Trois-Rivières	342	268	497	217	89	427	205	78	263	137	461	211	465*	94	88	

*Via ferry

Total mileages through Québec

20 132 937 miles
40 138 765 miles
15 117 412 miles

More mileages at randmcnally.com/MC

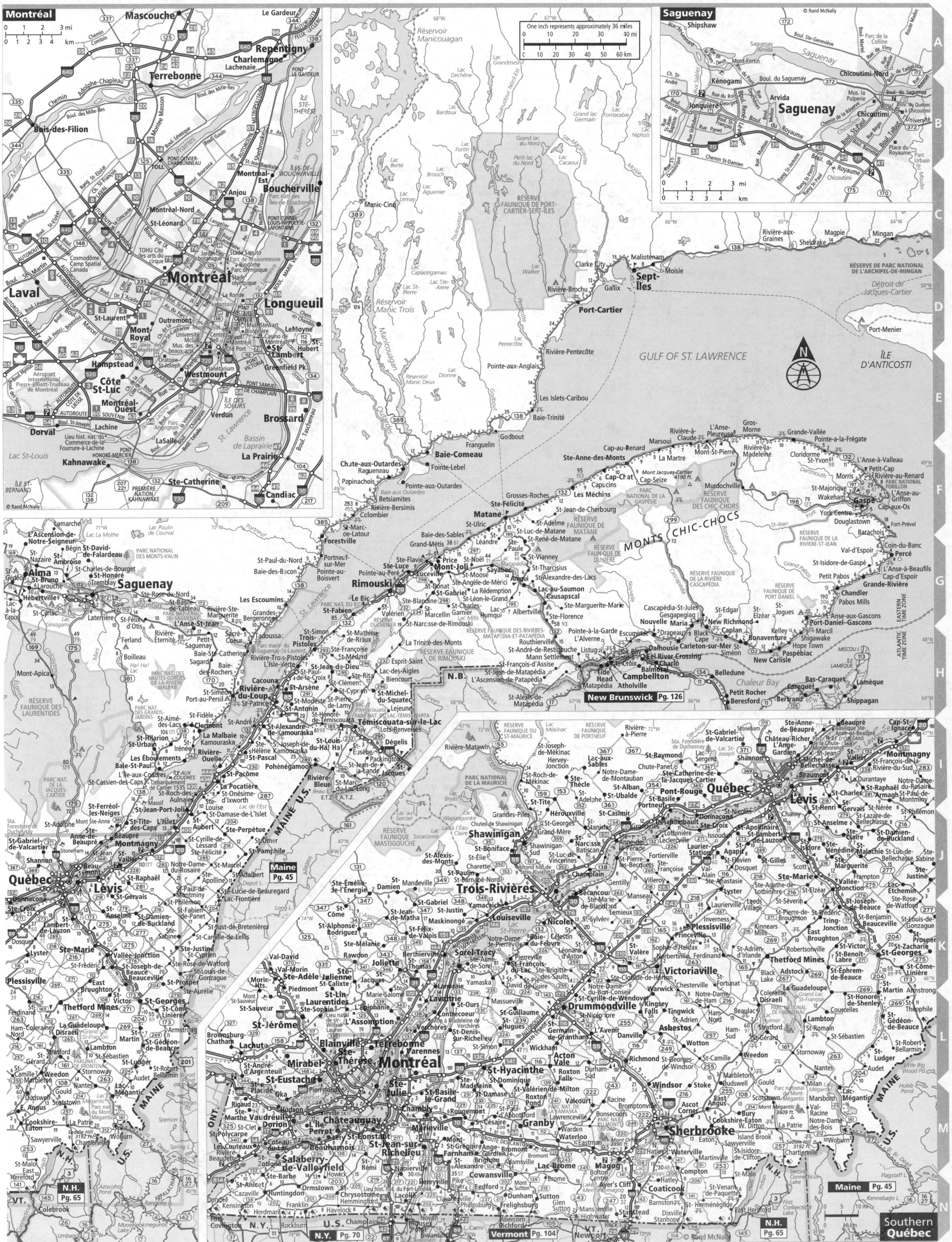

New Brunswick
Capital: Fredericton, H-4
Land area: 27,587 sq. mi. (rank: 11th)
Population: 751,171 (rank: 8th)
Largest city: Saint John, 70,063, J-5

Index of places Pg. 136

Travel planning & on-the-road resources

Tourism Information

Tourism New Brunswick:
(800) 561-0123
www.tourismnewbrunswick.ca

Tourism Nova Scotia:
(800) 565-0000, (902) 742-0511
www.novascotia.com

Prince Edward Island Tourism:
(800) 463-4734, (902) 437-8570
www.tourismpei.com

Newfoundland and Labrador Tourism:
(800) 563-6353, (709) 729-2830
www.newfoundlandlabrador.com

Road Conditions & Construction

New Brunswick:
511, (800) 561-4063
(506) 453-3939
www.gnb.ca/roads

Nova Scotia:
511, (902) 424-3933
In Canada: (888) 780-4440
511.novascotia.ca

Prince Edward Island:
511, (902) 368-4770
In Canada: (855) 241-2680
511.gov.pe.ca/en

Newfoundland & Labrador:
(709) 729-2300
www.roads.gov.nl.ca

Toll Road Information

Strait Crossing Bridge Ltd:
(Confederation Bridge) *(StraitPass)*:
(888) 437-6565; www.confederationbridge.com

Atlantic Hwy. Management Corp. Ltd.
(Cobequid Pass, N.S. (Hwy 104)) *(E-Pass)*:
(877) 727-7104, (902) 668-2211; www.cobequidpass.com

Halifax Harbor Bridges: *(MACPASS)*:
(902) 463-2800; www.hdbc.ca

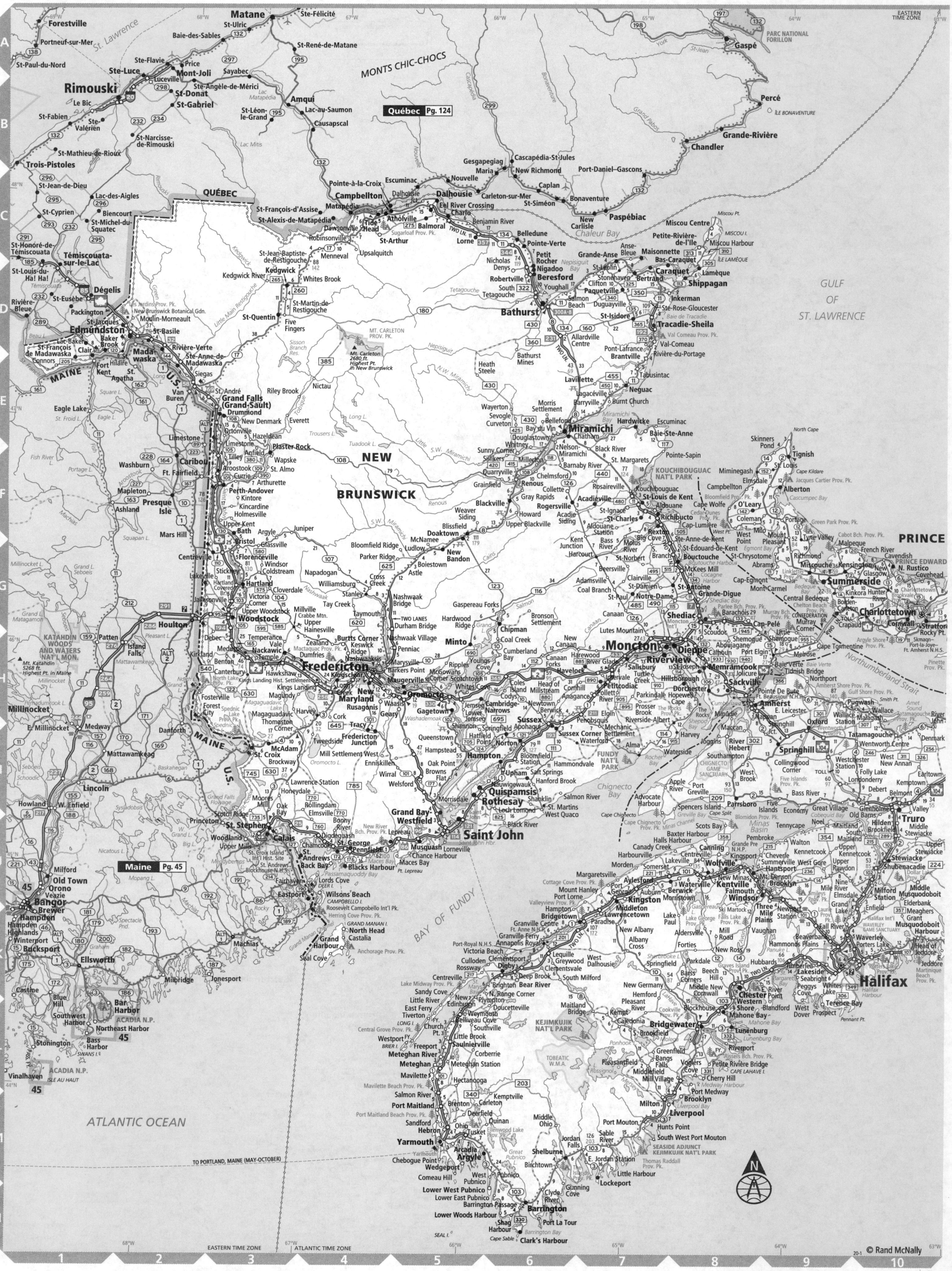

Mileages between cities	Amherst, NS	Bathurst, NB	Campbellton, NB	Charlottetown, PE	Corner Brook, NL	Edmundston, NB	Fredericton, NB	Grand Falls, NB	Halifax, NS	Moncton, NB	New Glasgow, NS	Saint John, NB	St. John's, NL	St. Stephen, NB	Sydney, NS	Yarmouth, NS
Charlottetown, PE	82	214	280		461*	392	222	354	205	112	63	204	888*	274	215	389
Edmundston, NB	319	160	125	392	817*		176	39	442	283	419	239	1244*	215	571	353
Fredericton, NB	149	160	248	222	647*	176		138	272	113	249	69	1074*	80	401	183
Halifax, NS	122	286	353	205	496*	442	272	403		162	98	254	923*	323	250	188
Moncton, NB	39	137	203	112	537*	283	113	244	162		139	95	964*	164	291	346
Saint John, NB	131	229	295	204	629*	239	69	201	254	95	237		1056*	69	383	114
St. John's, NL	925*	1088*	1155*	888*	433	1244*	1074*	1205*	923*	964*	825*	1056*		1125*	688*	1107*
Sydney, NS	252	415	482	215	261*	571	401	532	250	291	152	383	688*	452		434

*Via ferry

Mileages © Rand McNally

Nova Scotia
Capital: Halifax, K-9
Land area: 20,594 sq. mi. (rank: 12th)
Population: 921,727 (rank: 7th)
Largest city: Halifax, 390,096, K-9

Prince Edward Island
Capital: Charlottetown, G-10
Land area: 2,185 sq. mi. (rank: 13th)
Population: 140,204 (rank: 10th)
Largest city: Charlottetown, 34,562, G-10

Newfoundland & Labrador
Capital: St. John's, F-20
Land area: 144,353 sq. mi. (rank: 10th)
Population: 514,536 (rank: 9th)
Largest city: St. John's, 106,172, F-20

More mileages at randmcnally.com/MC

Glossary of common French terms found on these maps: pg. 117

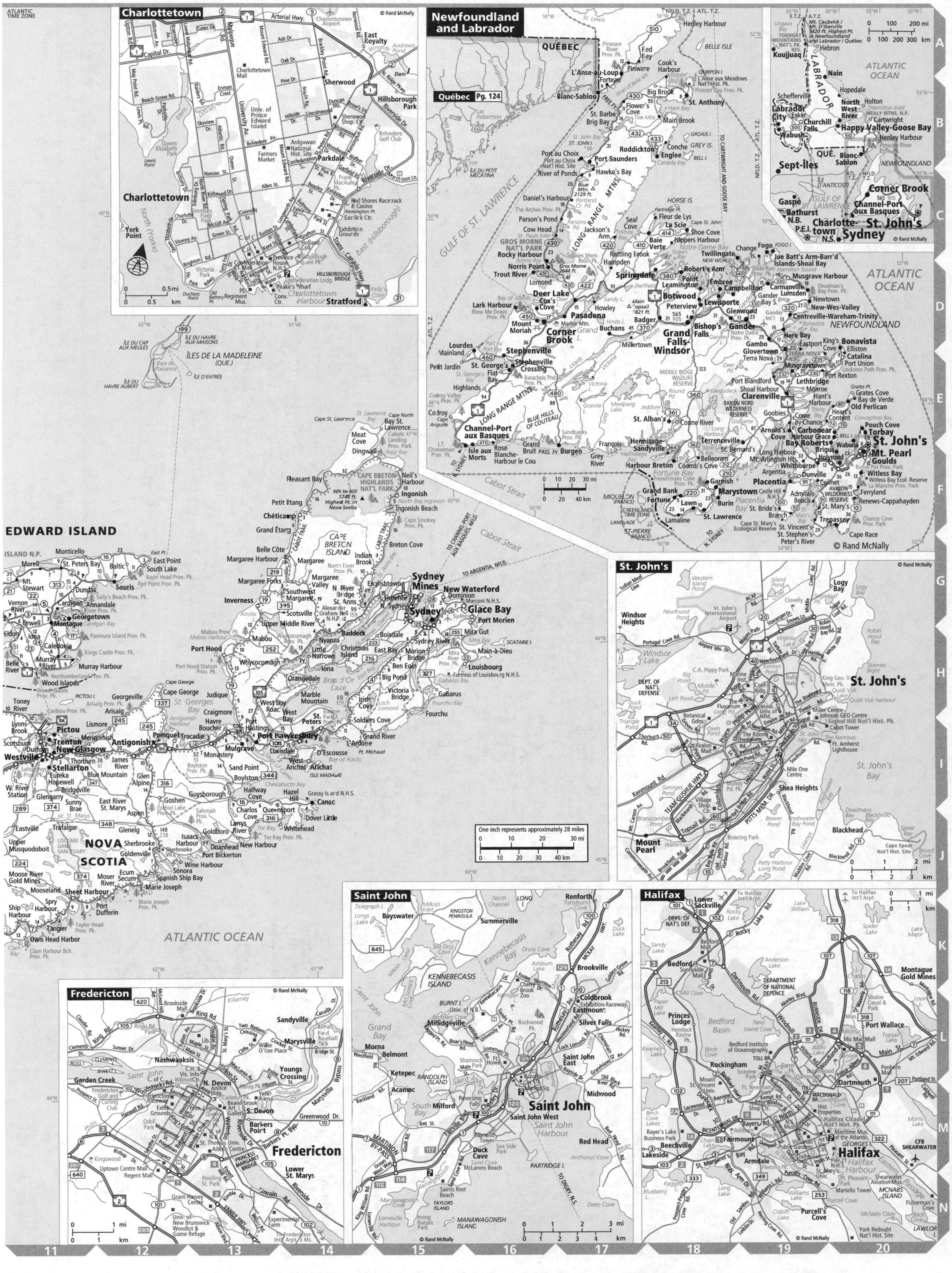

Mexico
Capital: Mexico City, G-8
Land area: 758,450 sq. mi.
Population: 112,336,538
Largest city: Mexico City, 8,851,080, G-8

Puerto Rico (U.S.)
Capital: San Juan, A-13
Land area: 3,425 sq. mi.
Population: 3,725,789
Largest city: San Juan, 381,931, A-13

Index of places Mexico: Pg. 136; Puerto Rico: Pg. 134

Sights to see

Mexico
- Chichen Itza Ruinas G-13
- Barranca del Cobre C-4
- Grutas de Cacahuamilpa H-8
- Parque Ecológico de Xochimilco I-3
- Parque Internacional del Río Bravo C-7
- Plaza de la Constitucion G-2
- Teotihuacán Ruinas G-8
- Tulum Ruinas G-14

Puerto Rico
- Bahía Fosforescente B-10
- Castillo del Morró A-13
- Museo de Arte de Ponce B-11
- Submarine Gardens A-13

On-the-road resources

Tourism Information
Mexico Tourism Board: +52 (800) 262-9128; www.visitmexico.com/en
Discover Puerto Rico: (800) 866-7827; www.discoverpuertorico.com

Toll Information, Road Conditions, & Construction
Mexico: www.gob.mx/carreteras (In Spanish)
Puerto Rico: (800) 981-3021, (787) 977-2200; its.dtop.gov.pr/en; www.dtop.gov.pr/carretera (In Spanish)

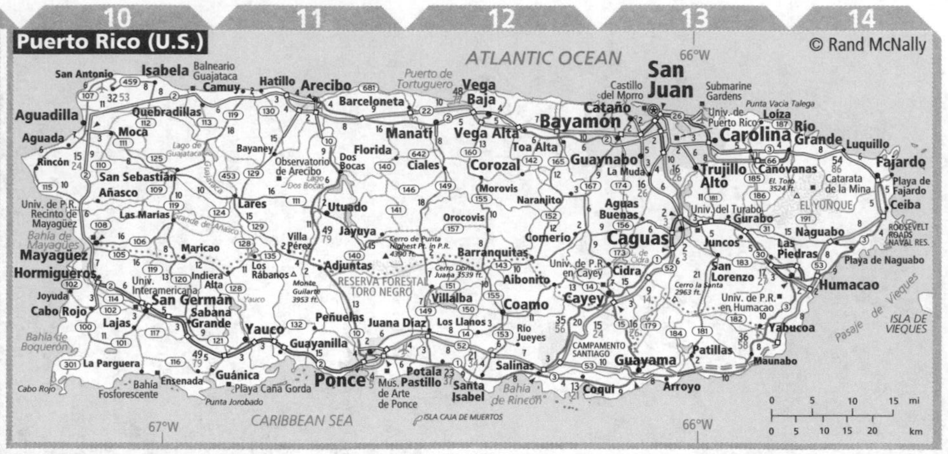

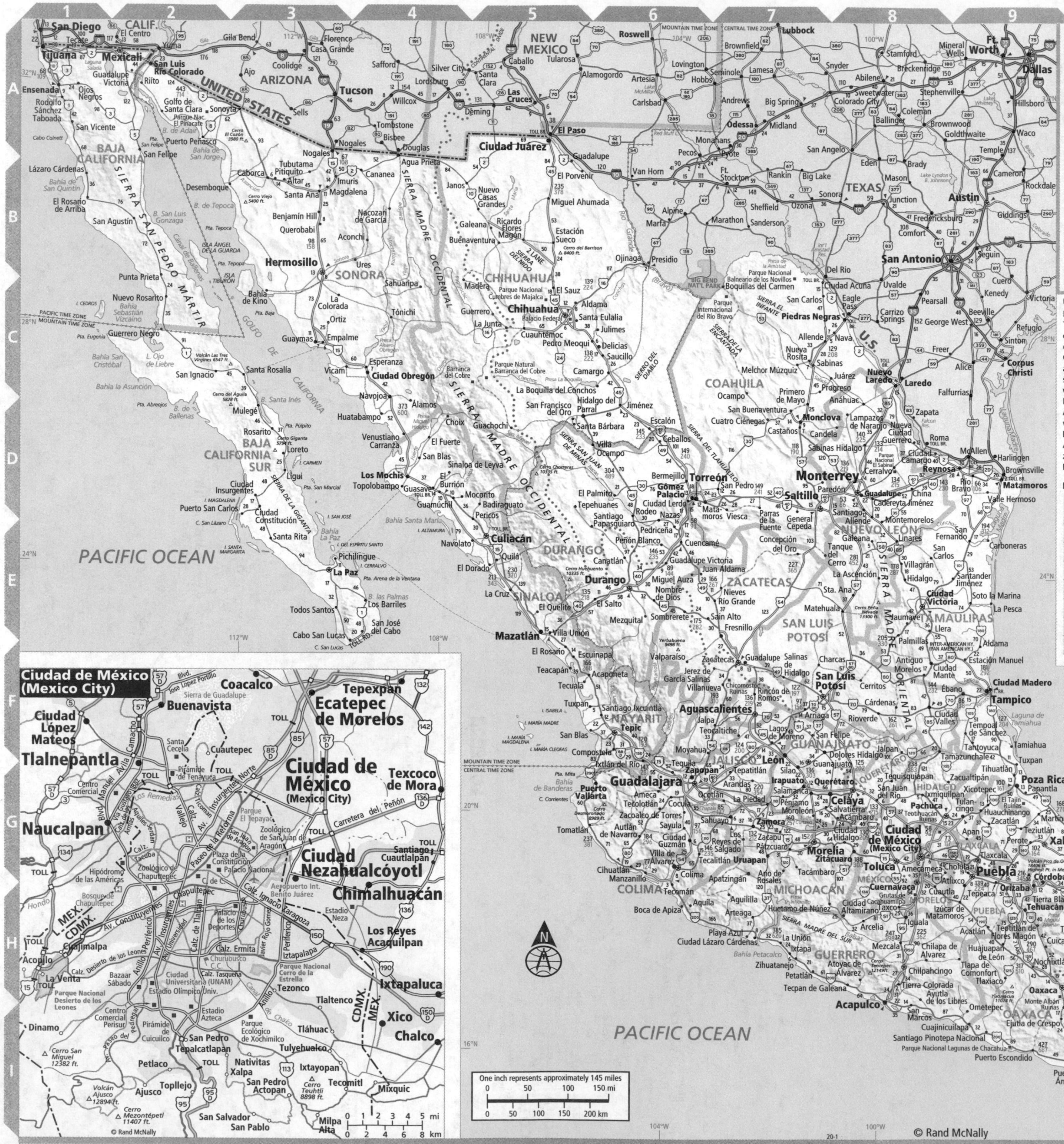

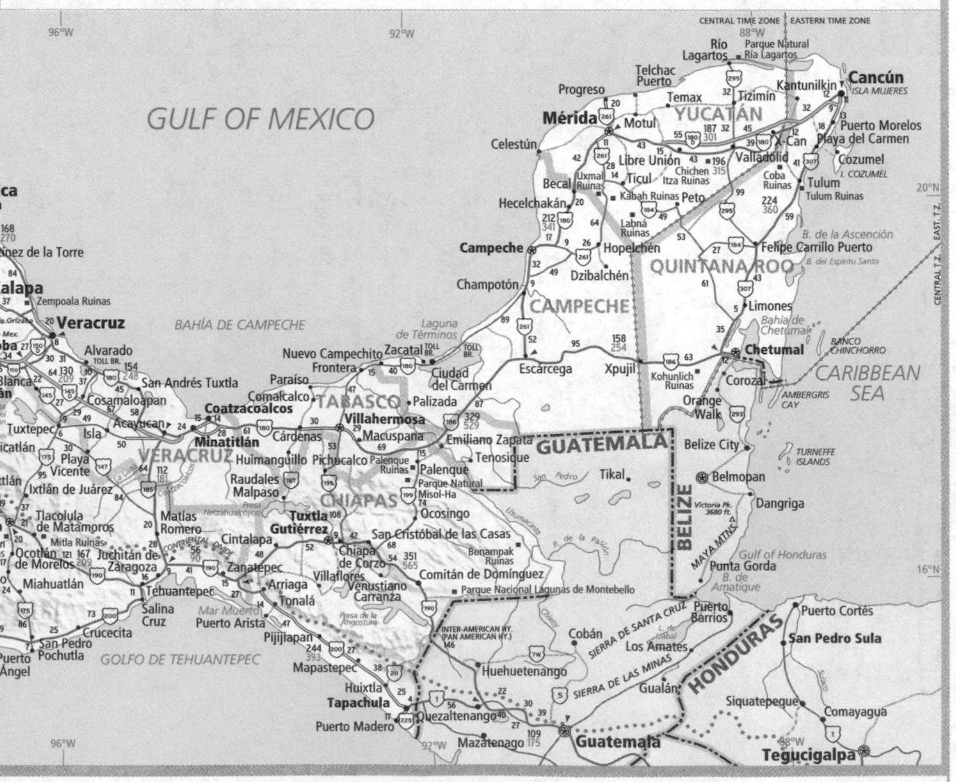

United States Citizens Visiting Mexico

Before you go: Get a passport
The Western Hemisphere Travel Initiative requires all U.S. citizens to carry a passport or other secure document to prove their citizenship in order to enter or re-enter the country by sea, air, or land. The initiative includes surface travel to and from Canada and Mexico. U.S. Armed Forces personnel on active duty traveling orders are exempt from the passport requirement. For information on what constitutes a secure document and additional information, go to the U.S. Department of State website: www.dhs.gov/western-hemisphere-travel-initiative-basics

Border crossing waits
Allow plenty of time. The average time for customs clearance is 30 minutes, but this varies greatly depending on traffic flow and security issues.

Driving in Mexico
According to the U.S. Department of State, tourists traveling beyond the border zone must obtain a temporary import permit or risk having their car confiscated by Mexican customs officials. To acquire a permit, submit evidence of citizenship, title for the car, a car registration certificate, driver's license, and a processing fee to either a Banjercito (Mexican Army Bank) branch located at a Mexican Customs office at the port of entry, or at one of the Mexican consulates in the U.S. Mexican law also requires posting a bond at a Banjercito office to guarantee departure of the car from Mexico within a period determined at the time of application. Carry proof of car ownership (the current registration card or a letter of authorization from the finance or leasing company). Auto insurance policies, other than Mexican, are not valid in Mexico. A short-term liability policy is obtainable at the border.

Tourist cards
Tourist cards are valid up to six months, require a fee, and are required for all persons, regardless of age, to visit the interior of Mexico. Cards may be obtained from Mexican border authorities, Consuls of Mexico, or Federal Delegates in major cities. Cards are also distributed to passengers en route to Mexico by air.

Mileage between principal cities

Miles in red; kilometers in blue

	Acapulco, GR	Chihuahua, CH	Cuidad Juárez, CH	Guadalajara, JA	Hermosillo, SO	La Paz, BS	Matamoros, TM	Mazatlan, SI	Mérida, YU	Mexico City, DF	Monterrey, NL	Nogales, SO	Nuevo Laredo, TM	Oaxaca, OA	San Luis Potosí, SL	Tampico, TM	Tijuana, BC	Torreón, CO	Tuxtlas Gutierrez, CS	Veracruz, VE
CUIDAD JUÁREZ, CH	1323 2129	233 375		910 1465	468 753	988 1590	933 1502	807 1299	1943 3127	1121 1804	739 1188	374 602	874 1406	1394 2243	855 1375	1058 1703	782 1259	518 834	1700 2735	1357 2183
GUADALAJARA, JA	509 819	678 1090	910 1465		864 1391	587 945	612 985	301 484	1140 1834	318 511	457 735	1034 1664	592 952	590 950	207 333	429 691	1392 2240	409 658	896 1442	553 891
MÉRIDA, YU	1027 1652	1710 2752	1943 3127	1140 1834	2004 3225	1727 2779	1255 2020	1440 2318		822 1323	1270 2044	2174 3499	1409 2268	691 1111	1088 1751	947 1525	2529 4070	1442 2320	486 782	649 1045
MEXICO CITY, DF	217 349	888 1429	1121 1804	318 511	1182 1902	905 1457	568 914	618 995	822 1323		551 887	1352 2176	678 1091	273 439	266 429	260 419	1710 2752	620 997	579 931	236 379
MONTERREY, NL	768 1236	506 814	739 1188	457 735	882 1419	813 1308	195 314	526 846	1270 2044	551 887		979 1576	135 218	790 1272	336 541	323 520	1387 2232	220 355	1027 1653	621 1000
TIJUANA, BC	1872 3013	882 1419	782 1259	1392 2240	528 850	891 1434	1582 2546	1092 1757	2529 4070	1710 2752	1387 2232	484 779	1522 2449	1981 3188	1503 2419	1726 2778		1167 1878	2284 3676	1943 3127
TUXTLAS GUTIERREZ, CS	560 901	1467 2360	1700 2735	896 1442	1760 2833	1484 2388	1012 1628	1197 1926	486 782	579 931	1027 1653	1931 3107	1166 1876	303 487	845 1360	704 1133	2284 3676	1198 1928		406 653

Glossary of Spanish terms

- Avenida (Av.) ..... Avenue
- Bahía (B.) .... Bay
- Barranca .... Canyon
- Cabo (C.) .... Cape
- Calzada (Calz.) .... Highway
- Canal .... Canal, strait
- Carretera .... Highway
- Castillo .... Fort
- Centro Comercial .. Shopping center
- Cerro .... Mountain
- Ciudad .... City
- Deportes .... Sports
- Estadio .... Stadium
- Golfo .... Gulf
- Grutas .... Caves
- Hipódromo .... Race track
- Isla (I.) .... Island
- Lago (L.) .... Lake
- Parque Nacional (Nac.) .... National park
- Parque Natural .... Wildlife park
- Paseo .... Drive
- Playa .... Beach
- Presa .... Reservoir
- Punta (Pta.) .... Point, headland
- Sierra .... Mountain
- Via .... Road

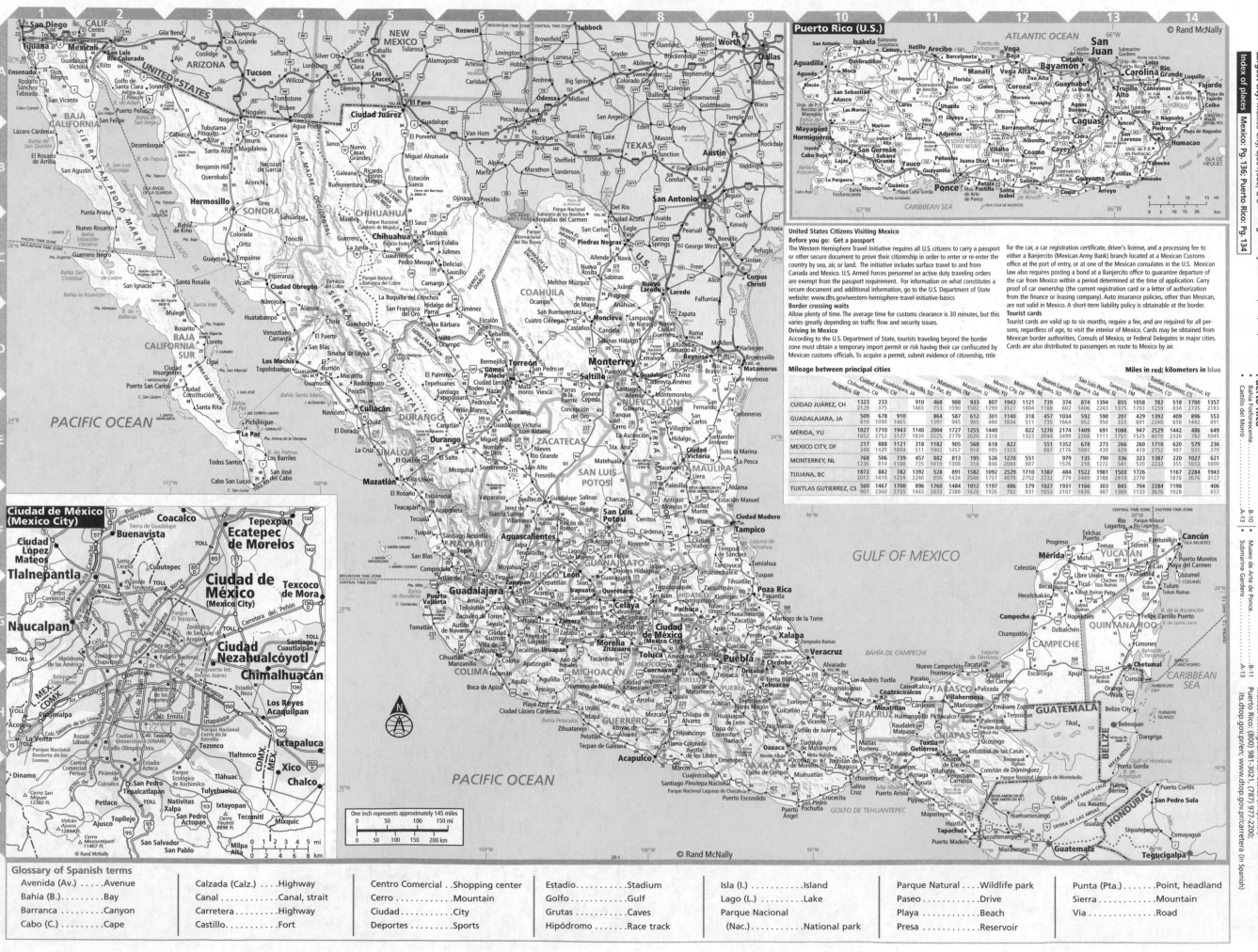

Index

United States Counties, cities, towns & places

Populations are from the 2010 U.S. Census or Rand McNally estimates

Index to Canada and Mexico cities and towns, page 136

Alabama
Map pp. 4 – 5

Abbeville, 2688 M-11
Adamsville, 4522 F-6
Addison, 758 D-5
Alabaster, 30352 G-6
Albertville, 21160 C-8
Alexander City, 14875 H-9
Alexandria, 3917 E-9
Aliceville, 2486 G-3
Altoona, 933 D-8
Andalusia, 9015 N-7
Anniston, 23106 E-9
Arab, 8050 C-7
Ardmore, 1194 A-6
Argo, 4071 E-7
Ariton, 764 M-10
Ashford, 2148 N-11
Ashland, 2037 G-9
Ashville, 2212 E-8
Athens, 21897 A-6
Atmore, 10194 O-4
Attalla, 6048 D-9
Auburn, 53380 I-10
AUTAUGA CO., 54571 J-7
Autaugaville, 870 J-7
Axis, 757 O-3
BALDWIN CO., 182265 O-4
Ballplay, 1580 D-9
BARBOUR CO., 27457 K-11
Bay Minette, 8044 O-4
Bayou La Batre, 2558 Q-2
Bear Creek, 1070 C-4
Berry, 1148 E-4
Bessemer, 27456 F-6
BIBB CO., 22915 H-6
Birmingham, 212237 F-7
BLOUNT CO., 57322 D-7
Blountsville, 1684 D-7
Boaz, 9551 D-8
Bon Secour, 900 Q-4
Brantley, 809 M-8
Brantleyville, 884 G-6
Brent, 4947 H-5
Brewton, 5408 N-6
Bridgeport, 2418 A-10
Brighton, 2945 S-10
Brilliant, 900 D-4
Brookside, 1363 P-10
Brookwood, 1828 G-5
Brundidge, 2076 L-9
BULLOCK CO., 10914 K-10
Butler, 1894 K-2
BUTLER CO., 20947 L-6
Cahaba Hts., 5203 S-13
Calera, 11620 G-7
CALHOUN CO., 118572 E-9
Camden, 2020 K-5
Camp Hill, 1014 H-10
Carbon Hill, 2021 E-4
Carrollton, 1019 G-3
Cedar Bluff, 1820 C-10
Center Pt., 16921 F-7
Centre, 3489 D-10
Centreville, 2778 H-6
CHAMBERS CO., 34215 H-11
Chatom, 1288 M-2
Chelsea, 10183 G-7
Cherokee, 1048 B-3
CHEROKEE CO., 25989 C-10
Chickasaw, 6106 P-3
Childersburg, 5175 G-8
CHILTON CO., 43643 I-7
CHOCTAW CO., 13859 K-2
Citronelle, 3905 N-2
Clanton, 8619 H-7
CLARKE CO., 25833 L-3
Clay, 9708 E-7
CLAY CO., 13932 G-9
Clayton, 3008 L-11
CLEBURNE CO., 14972 E-10
Cleveland, 1303 D-7
Clio, 1399 L-10
Coaling, 1657 G-5
COFFEE CO., 49948 M-9
Coker, 979 G-4
COLBERT CO., 54428 B-3
Collinsville, 1983 C-9
Columbiana, 4197 G-7
Concord, 1837 F-6
CONECUH CO., 13228 M-6
COOSA CO., 11539 H-8
Coosada, 1224 J-8
Cordova, 2095 E-5
Cottonwood, 1289 O-11
COVINGTON CO., 37765 N-7
Cowarts, 1871 N-11
CRENSHAW CO., 13906 L-8
Creola, 1926 O-3
Crossville, 1862 C-9
Crumley Chapel, 1630 Q-10
Cullman, 14775 D-6
CULLMAN CO., 80406 D-6
Dadeville, 3230 H-10
DALE CO., 50251 M-10
Daleville, 5295 N-10
DALLAS CO., 43820 J-5
Daphne, 21570 P-3
Dauphin Island, 1238 Q-3
DE KALB CO., 71109 C-9
Deatsville, 1154 I-8
Decatur, 55683 B-6
Demopolis, 7483 I-3
Docena, 1000 Q-10
Dora, 2025 E-6
Dothan, 65496 N-11
Double Sprs., 1083 D-5
E. Brewton, 2478 O-6
Eastern Valley, 2000 T-10
Eclectic, 1001 I-9
Edgewater, 883 R-10
Elba, 3940 M-9
Elberta, 1498 Q-4
Elmore, 1262 I-8
ELMORE CO., 79303 J-9
Enterprise, 26562 N-9
ESCAMBIA CO., 38319 N-5
ETOWAH CO., 104430 D-9
Eufaula, 13137 L-11
Eutaw, 2934 H-3
Evergreen, 3944 M-6
Fairfield, 11117 R-10
Fairhope, 15326 P-3
Falkville, 1279 C-6
Fayette, 4619 E-3
FAYETTE CO., 17241 E-4
Fayetteville, 1284 G-8
Flomaton, 1440 O-5
Florala, 1980 O-8
Florence, 39319 B-4
Foley, 14618 Q-4
Forestdale, 10162 F-6
Ft. Deposit, 1344 K-7
Ft. Mitchell, 750 J-12
Ft. Payne, 14012 C-10
FRANKLIN CO., 31704 C-3
Frisco City, 1309 M-5
Fultondale, 8380 F-7
Fyffe, 1018 C-9
Gadsden, 36856 D-9
Gallant, 855 D-8
Gardendale, 13893 E-6
Geneva, 4452 O-9
GENEVA CO., 26790 O-10
Georgiana, 1738 M-7
Geraldine, 896 C-9
Glencoe, 5160 D-9
Good Hope, 2264 D-6
Goodwater, 1475 H-9
Gordo, 1750 G-3
Grand Bay, 3672 Q-2
Grant, 896 B-8
Graysville, 2165 F-6
GREENE CO., 9045 H-3
Greensboro, 2497 I-4
Greenville, 8135 L-7
Grove Hill, 1570 L-4
Guin, 2376 D-3
Gulf Shores, 9741 Q-4
Guntersville, 8197 C-8
Gurley, 801 B-8
Hackleburg, 1516 C-4
HALE CO., 15760 H-4
Haleyville, 4173 D-4
Hamilton, 6885 D-3
Hanceville, 2982 D-7
Harpersville, 1637 G-8
Hartford, 2624 N-10
Hartselle, 14255 C-6
Harvest, 5281 A-7
Hayneville, 932 K-7
Hazel Green, 3630 A-7
Headland, 4510 N-11
Heflin, 3480 F-10
Helena, 16793 G-6
Henagar, 2344 B-10
HENRY CO., 17302 M-11
Hillview, 3080 Q-11
Hobson City, 771 F-9
Hokes Bluff, 4286 D-9
Holly Pond, 798 D-7
Hollywood, 1000 B-9
Holt, 3638 G-4
Holtville, 4096 I-8
Homewood, 25167 F-7
Hoover, 81619 F-6
HOUSTON CO., 101547 N-11
Hueytown, 16105 F-6
Huguley, 2540 H-11
Huntsville, 180105 B-7
Indian Sprs. Vil., 2363 G-7
Irondale, 12349 F-7
Irvington, 1000 Q-2
Jackson, 5228 M-3
JACKSON CO., 53227 A-8
Jacksons Gap, 828 H-9
Jacksonville, 12548 E-10
Jasper, 14352 E-5
JEFFERSON CO., 658466 F-5
Jemison, 2585 H-7
Killen, 1108 A-4
Kimberly, 2711 E-6
Kinsey, 2198 N-11
Ladonia, 3142 J-12
LaFayette, 3003 H-11
LAMAR CO., 14564 E-3
Lanett, 6468 H-11
LAUDERDALE CO., 92709 A-4
LAWRENCE CO., 34339 B-5
LEE CO., 140247 I-11
Leeds, 11773 F-7
Leesburg, 1027 D-10
Leroy, 911 M-3
Level Plains, 2085 N-10
Lillian, 900 Q-5
LIMESTONE CO., 82782 A-6
Lincoln, 6266 F-9
Linden, 2123 J-4
Lineville, 2395 G-10
Lipscomb, 2210 S-10
Littleville, 1011 B-4
Livingston, 3485 I-2
Locust Fork, 1186 E-7
LOWNDES CO., 11299 K-6
Loxley, 1632 P-4
Luverne, 2800 L-8
MACON CO., 21452 J-9
Madison, 42938 B-7
MADISON CO., 334811 A-7
Malvern, 1448 N-10
Marbury, 1418 I-8
MARENGO CO., 21027 J-4
Margaret, 4428 E-7
Marion, 3686 I-5
MARION CO., 30776 D-3
MARSHALL CO., 93019 C-7
McCalla, 1000 G-6
Meridianville, 6021 A-7
Midfield, 5365 F-6
Midland City, 2344 N-10
Millbrook, 14640 J-8
Millertown, 1700 O-2
Millport, 1049 F-3
Minor, 1094 Q-10
Mobile, 195111 P-3
MOBILE CO., 412992 O-2
MONROE CO., 23068 M-5
Monroeville, 6519 M-5
Montevallo, 6323 G-6
Montgomery, 205764 J-8
MONTGOMERY CO., 229363 K-8
Moody, 11726 F-7
Moores Mill, 5682 A-7
MORGAN CO., 119490 C-7
Morris, 1859 E-6
Mosses, 1029 K-7
Moulton, 3471 C-5
Moundville, 2427 H-4
Mt. Olive, 4079 E-6
Mt. Vernon, 1574 O-3
Mountain Brook, 20413 R-13
Mulga, 836 Q-9
Munford, 1292 F-9
Muscle Shoals, 13146 B-4
New Brockton, 1146 M-9
New Hope, 2810 B-8
New Market, 1597 A-8
New Site, 773 H-10
Newton, 1511 N-10
Northport, 23330 G-4
Notasulga, 965 I-10
Oakman, 789 E-5
Odenville, 3585 E-8
Ohatchee, 1170 E-9
Oneonta, 6567 D-7
Opelika, 26477 I-11
Opp, 6659 N-8
Orange Bch., 5441 Q-4
Owens Cross Roads, 1521 B-8
Oxford, 21348 F-9
Ozark, 14907 M-10
Parrish, 982 E-5
Pea Ridge, 800 G-6
Pelham, 21352 G-6
Pell City, 12695 F-8
Perdido, 1200 O-4
PERRY CO., 10591 I-5
Peterson, 950 G-5
Petersville, 1400 D-13
Phenix City, 32822 J-12
Phil Campbell, 1148 C-4
PICKENS CO., 19746 G-2
Piedmont, 4878 E-10
PIKE CO., 32899 L-9
Pike Road, 5406 J-9
Pine Hill, 975 K-4
Pinedale Shores, 800 E-8
Pinson, 7163 E-7
Plantersville, 750 I-6
Pleasant Grove, 10110 F-6
Point Clear, 2125 Q-3
Powell, 955 C-9
Prattville, 33960 J-8
Priceville, 2658 B-6
Prichard, 22659 P-3
Ragland, 1639 E-8
Rainbow City, 9602 D-9
Rainsville, 4948 C-9
RANDOLPH CO., 22913 G-10
Red Bay, 3158 C-3
Reform, 1702 F-3
Rehobeth, 1297 N-11
Riverside, 2208 F-8
Roanoke, 6074 G-11
Robertsdale, 5276 P-4
Rockford, 477 H-8
Rogersville, 1257 A-5
RUSSELL CO., 52947 J-11
Russellville, 9830 C-4
ST. CLAIR CO., 83593 E-8
St. Elmo, 1050 Q-2
Saks, 10744 E-9
Samson, 1940 N-9
Saraland, 13405 O-3
Sardis City, 1704 D-9
Satsuma, 6168 O-3
Scottsboro, 14770 B-9
Section, 770 B-9
Selma, 20756 J-6
Semmes, 2350 P-2
Shannon, 1000 T-11
Sheffield, 9039 B-4
Shelby, 1044 G-7
SHELBY CO., 195085 F-7
Skyline, 851 A-8
Slocomb, 1980 N-10
Smiths Sta., 4926 I-12
Snead, 835 D-8
Southside, 8412 E-9
Spanish Fort, 6798 P-3
Springville, 4080 E-7
Stapleton, 1300 P-4
Steele, 1043 E-8
Stevenson, 2046 A-9
Stewartsville, 1767 H-8
Sulligent, 1927 E-3
Sumiton, 2520 E-6
Summerdale, 862 Q-4
SUMTER CO., 13763 I-2
Susan Moore, 763 D-8
Sycamore, 1000 G-8
Sylacauga, 12749 G-8
Sylvan Sprs., 1542 R-9
Sylvania, 1837 B-9
Talladega, 15676 F-9
TALLADEGA CO., 82291 F-8
TALLAPOOSA CO., 41616 I-9
Tallassee, 4819 I-9
Tanner, 750 B-6
Tarrant City, 6397 Q-12
Taylor, 2375 N-11
Theodore, 6130 P-2
Thomasville, 4209 L-4
Thorsby, 1980 H-7
Tillmans Cor., 17398 P-2
Town Creek, 1100 B-5
Trinity, 2095 B-6
Troy, 18033 L-9
Trussville, 19933 F-7
Tuscaloosa, 90468 G-4
TUSCALOOSA CO., 194656 G-4
Tuscumbia, 8423 B-4
Tuskegee, 9865 J-10
Union Sprs., 3980 K-10
Uniontown, 1775 J-4
Valley, 9524 H-11
Valley Grande, 4020 J-6
Vance, 1529 G-5
Vernon, 2000 E-3
Vestavia Hills, 34033 F-7
Vincent, 1988 F-8
Wadley, 751 G-10
WALKER CO., 67023 F-5
Warrior, 3176 E-6
WASHINGTON CO., 17581 N-2
Weaver, 3038 E-9
Webb, 1430 N-11
Wedowee, 823 G-10
W. Blocton, 1240 G-6
W. End Anniston, 2760 F-9
Westover, 1275 G-7
Westwood, 1630 Q-10
Wetumpka, 6528 I-8
White Hall, 858 J-7
White Plains, 811 E-10
WILCOX CO., 11670 L-5
Wilsonville, 1827 G-7
Winfield, 4717 E-4
WINSTON CO., 24484 D-5
Woodstock, 1428 G-5
York, 2538 J-2

Alaska
Map p. 6

Akiachak, 627 G-4
Akutan, 1027 J-1
Alakanuk, 677 E-3
Anchor Pt., 1930 H-7
Anchorage, 291826 G-7
Angoon, 459 I-12
Aniak, 501 F-4
Bethel, 6080 G-4
Big Delta, 591 E-8
Big Lake, 3350 G-7
Chevak, 938 F-3
College, 12964 A-1
Cordova, 2239 G-8
Craig, 1201 J-13
Delta Jct., 958 E-8
Dillingham, 2329 H-4
Emmonak, 762 E-3
Fairbanks, 31535 E-8
Ft. Yukon, 583 D-8
Galena, 470 E-5
Gambell, 681 D-2
Glennallen, 483 F-8
Haines, 1713 H-12
Healy, 1021 E-8
Homer, 5003 H-7
Hoonah, 760 H-12
Hooper Bay, 1093 F-3
Houston, 1912 G-7
Juneau, 31275 H-12
Kake, 557 I-12
Kasigluk, 569 G-4
Kasilof, 549 G-7
Kenai, 7100 G-7
Ketchikan, 8050 J-13
King Cove, 938 J-3
Kipnuk, 639 G-3
Klawock, 755 J-13
Kodiak, 6130 I-6
Kotlik, 577 E-4
Kotzebue, 3201 C-4
Kwethluk, 721 G-4
Metlakatla, 1405 J-13
Mountain Vil., 813 F-3
Naknek, 544 H-5
New Stuyahok, 510 H-5
Nikiski, 4493 G-7
Ninilchik, 883 H-7
Noatak, 514 C-4
Nome, 3598 D-3
Noorvik, 668 C-5
N. Pole, 2117 E-8
Nunapitchuk, 496 G-4
Palmer, 5937 G-7
Petersburg, 2948 I-13
Pilot Station, 568 F-4
Point Hope, 674 B-4
Prudhoe Bay, 2174 A-8
Quinhagak, 669 G-4
St. Marys, 507 F-4
St. Paul, 479 I-10
Sand Pt., 976 J-3
Savoonga, 671 D-2
Scammon Bay, 474 F-3
Selawik, 829 C-5
Seward, 2693 H-7
Shishmaref, 563 C-3
Sitka, 8881 I-12
Skagway, 920 H-12
Soldotna, 4163 G-7
Stebbins, 556 E-4
Sutton, 1447 G-7
Talkeetna, 876 F-7
Thorne Bay, 471 J-13
Togiak, 817 H-4
Tok, 1258 F-9
Toksook Bay, 590 G-3
Trapper Creek, 481 F-7
Unalakleet, 688 E-4
Unalaska, 4376 J-1
Utqiagvik (Barrow), 4212 A-6
Valdez, 3976 G-8
Wainwright, 556 A-5
Wasilla, 7831 G-7
Willow, 2102 G-7
Wrangell, 2369 I-13
Yakutat, 662 H-10

Arizona
Map pp. 8 – 9

* City keyed to p. 7

Aguila, 798 I-5
Ajo, 3304 M-6
Anthem, 21700 I-7
APACHE CO., 71518 D-13
Apache Jct., 35840 J-9
Arivaca, 695 O-9
Arivaca Jct., 1090 N-10
Arizona City, 10475 L-8
Arizona Vil., 946 F-2
Avondale, 76238 J-7
Avra Valley, 6050 M-9
Bagdad, 1876 G-5
Beaver Dam, 1962 *A-3
Benson, 5105 N-11
Bisbee, 5575 O-12
Black Canyon City, 2837 H-7
Bouse, 996 I-3
Buckeye, 50876 J-6
Bullhead City, 39540 F-2
Bylas, 1962 K-12
Cameron, 885 D-9
Camp Verde, 10873 G-8
Carefree, 3363 I-8
Casa Grande, 48571 K-8
Casas Adobes, 66795 O-3
Catalina, 7569 L-10
Cave Creek, 5015 I-8
Central Hts., 2000 J-10
Chandler, 236123 J-8
Chilchinbito, 506 B-12
Chinle, 4518 C-13
Chino Valley, 10817 G-7
Cibecue, 1713 H-11
Citrus Pk., 4028 *H-2
Clarkdale, 4097 G-8
Claypool, 1538 J-10
Clifton, 3311 K-13
COCHISE CO., 131346 M-12
COCONINO CO., 134421 C-8
Colorado City, 4821 A-6
Congress, 1975 H-6
Coolidge, 11825 K-9
Cordes Lakes, 2633 H-7
Cornville, 3280 G-8
Cottonwood, 11265 G-8
Dennehotso, 746 A-12
Desert Hills, 2245 S-10
Dewey-Humboldt, 3894 G-7
Dilkon, 1184 E-11
Dolan Sprs., 2033 D-3
Douglas, 17378 O-13
Dreamland Villa, 4800 *J-8
Drexel Hts., 27749 S-2
Dudleyville, 959 K-10
Duncan, 696 L-14
Eagar, 4885 H-13
E. Fork, 699 I-12
Ehrenberg, 1470 I-2
El Mirage, 31797 *H-3
Eloy, 16631 L-9
Flagstaff, 65870 E-8
Florence, 25536 K-9
Flowing Wells, 16419 P-2
Ft. Defiance, 3624 D-14
Fortuna Foothills, 26265 L-2
Fountain Hills, 22489 J-8
Fredonia, 1314 A-7
Gadsden, 678 L-2
Ganado, 1210 D-13
Gila Bend, 1922 K-6
GILA CO., 53597 I-11
Gila Crossing, 621 *K-4
Gilbert, 208453 *K-8
Gisela, 570 H-9
Glendale, 226721 J-7
Globe, 7532 J-10
Gold Canyon, 10159 J-9
Golden Valley, 8370 E-3
Goodyear, 65275 J-7
GRAHAM CO., 37220 K-12
Grand Canyon Vil., 2004 C-7
Greasewood, 547 E-12
Green Valley, 21391 N-10
GREENLEE CO., 8437 J-13
Guadalupe, 5523 *J-6
Hayden, 662 K-10
Holbrook, 5053 F-11
Hotevilla-Bacavi, 957 D-10
Houck, 1024 E-13
Huachuca City, 1853 O-11
Joseph City, 1386 F-11
Kaibito, 1522 B-10
Kayenta, 5189 B-11
Kearny, 1950 K-10
Kingman, 28068 E-3
Komatke, 821 J-7
Kykotsmovi Vil., 746 D-10
LA PAZ CO., 20489 H-4
L. Havasu City, 52527 G-3
L. Montezuma, 4706 G-8
Leupp, 951 E-10
Linden, 2597 H-12
Litchfield Pk., 5476 *I-3
Lukachukai, 1701 B-13
Mammoth, 1426 L-11
Many Farms, 1348 C-13
Marana, 34961 L-9
Maricopa, 43482 K-8
MARICOPA CO., 3817117 I-6
Martinez Lake, 798 K-2
Mayer, 1497 H-7
McNary, 528 H-12
Meadview, 1224 C-3
Mesa, 439041 J-8
Miami, 1837 J-10
Moenkopi, 964 C-9
MOHAVE CO., 200186 F-4
Morenci, 1489 K-13
Mountainaire, 1119 F-8
Munds Pk., 631 F-8
Naco, 1046 O-12
NAVAJO CO., 107449 E-11
New River, 14952 I-7
Nogales, 20837 O-10
Oracle, 3686 L-10
Oro Valley, 41011 M-10
Page, 7247 A-9
Paradise Valley, 12820 *H-6
Parker, 3083 H-3
Parks, 1188 E-8
Patagonia, 913 O-10
Paulden, 5231 F-7
Payson, 15301 H-9
Peach Sprs., 1090 E-5
Peoria, 154065 J-7
Peridot, 1350 J-11
Phoenix, 1445632 J-7
Picture Rocks, 9563 M-9
Pima, 2387 K-12
PIMA CO., 980263 M-8
PINAL CO., 375770 L-9
Pine, 1963 H-9
Pinetop-Lakeside, 4282 H-12
Pinon, 904 C-11
Pirtleville, 1744 O-13
Plantsite, 600 K-13
Polacca, 700 D-11
Prescott, 39843 G-7
Prescott Valley, 38822 G-7
Quartzsite, 3677 I-3
Queen Creek, 26361 J-8
Queen Valley, 788 J-9
Red Rock, 2169 L-9
Rio Rico, 18962 O-10
Rio Verde, 1811 *G-9
Rock Pt., 642 B-13
Round Rock, 789 B-13
Sacaton, 2672 K-8
Safford, 9566 K-13
Sahuarita, 25259 N-10
St. David, 1699 N-11
St. Johns, 3480 G-13
St. Michaels, 1443 D-14
Salome, 1530 I-4
San Carlos, 4038 J-11
San Luis, 25505 L-2
San Manuel, 3551 L-11
San Tan Valley, 81321 K-9
Sanders, 630 E-13
SANTA CRUZ CO., 47420 O-11
Santa Rosa, 628 M-8
Santan, 650 K-8
Sawmill, 748 D-14
Scottsdale, 217385 J-8
Second Mesa, 962 D-11
Sedona, 10031 F-8
Sells, 2495 N-8
Shongopovi, 831 D-11
Shonto, 591 B-10
Show Low, 10660 H-12
Sierra Vista, 43888 O-11
Snowflake, 5590 G-12
Somerton, 14287 L-2
Sonoita, 818 N-11
S. Tucson, 5652 R-3
Springerville, 1961 H-13
Stanfield, 740 K-8
Star Valley, 2310 H-9
Strawberry, 961 G-9
Summit, 5372 T-3
Sun City, 37499 J-7
Sun City West, 24535 I-7
Sun Lakes, 13975 K-8
Superior, 2837 J-10
Surprise, 117517 I-7
Swift Trail Jct., 2935 L-13
Tacna, 602 L-3
Tanque Verde, 16901 Q-7
Taylor, 4112 G-12
Teec Nos Pos, 730 A-14
Tempe, 161719 J-8
Thatcher, 4865 K-12
Three Points, 5581 M-9
Tolleson, 6545 *J-3
Tombstone, 1380 N-12
Tortolita, 3740 N-2
Tsaile, 1205 C-13
Tuba City, 8611 C-9
Tubac, 1191 O-10
Tucson, 520116 M-10
Tucson Estates, 12192 M-10
Tusayan, 558 D-7
Vail, 10208 M-10
Valle, 832 *E-8
Verde Vil., 11605 G-8
Vicksburg, 597 I-4
Waddell, 500 *H-2
Wellton, 2882 L-3
Wenden, 728 I-4
Whiteriver, 4104 I-12
Wickenburg, 6363 I-6
Wilhoit, 868 G-6
Willcox, 3757 M-12
Williams, 3023 E-7
Window Rock, 2712 D-14
Winslow, 9655 F-10
Wittmann, 763 I-7
Yarnell, 649 H-6
YAVAPAI CO., 211033 F-6
Young, 666 H-10
Youngtown, 6156 *H-3
Yuma, 93064 L-2
YUMA CO., 195751 K-4

Arkansas
Map pp. 10 – 11

Alexander, 2901 H-7
Alma, 5419 E-2
Altheimer, 984 I-9
Altus, 758 E-3
Arkadelphia, 10714 J-5
Arkansas City, 366 K-10
ARKANSAS CO., 19019 I-10
Ash Flat, 1082 B-9
Ashdown, 4723 K-2
ASHLEY CO., 21853 L-9
Atkins, 3016 F-5
Augusta, 2199 E-10
Austin, 2038 G-8
Bald Knob, 2897 E-9
Barling, 4649 E-1
Batesville, 10248 D-9
BAXTER CO., 41513 B-7
Bay, 1801 D-13
Bearden, 966 K-5
Beebe, 7315 F-8
Bella Vista, 26461 A-2
Benton, 30681 H-5
BENTON CO., 221339 B-1
Bentonville, 35301 B-2
Berryville, 5356 B-4
Bethel Hts., 2372 D-10
Blytheville, 15620 C-14
Bono, 2131 C-11
BOONE CO., 36903 E-5
Booneville, 3990 [illegible]-3
Bradford, 759 E-10
BRADLEY CO., 11508 [illegible]-7
Brinkley, 3188 G-10
Brookland, 1642 C-12
Bryant, 16688 H-7
Bull Shoals, 1950 B-6
Cabot, 23776 G-8
CALHOUN CO., 5368 K-6
Calico Rock, 1545 C-8
Camden, 12183 K-6
Cammack Vil., 768 [illegible]-14
Caraway, 1279 [illegible]-13
Carlisle, 2214 G-9
CARROLL CO., 27446 B-4
Cave City, 1904 C-9
Cave Sprs., 1729 B-2
Cedarville, 1394 D-1
Centerton, 9515 B-2
Charleston, 2494 E-2
Cherokee Vil., 4671 B-9
CHICOT CO., 11800 M-10
Clarendon, 1664 H-10
CLARK CO., 22995 J-5
Clarksville, 9178 E-4
CLAY CO., 16083 B-12
CLEBURNE CO., 25970 D-8
CLEVELAND CO., 868[illegible] J-7
Clinton, 2602 D-7
Coal Hill, 1012 E-3
COLUMBIA CO., 24552 M-5
Conway, 58908 F-7
CONWAY CO., 2127[illegible] F-6
Corning, 3377 B-12
Cotter, 970 B-7
CRAIGHEAD CO., 96443 C-12
CRAWFORD CO., 61948 D-1
CRITTENDEN CO., 50902 F-13
CROSS CO., 17870 E-11
Crossett, 5507 M-8
DALLAS CO., 8116 J-6
Danville, 2409 F-4
Dardanelle, 4745 F-5
De Queen, 6594 J-1
De Valls Bluff, 619 G-10
De Witt, 3292 I-10
Decatur, 1699 B-1
Dermott, 2316 L-10
Des Arc, 1717 G-10
Desha, 750 D-9
DESHA CO., 1300[illegible] K-10
Diamond City, 782 A-5
Diaz, 1318 D-10
Dierks, 1133 J-2
Dover, 1378 E-5
DREW CO., 1850[illegible] L-9
Dumas, 4706 J-10
Dyer, 876 E-2
Earle, 2414 F-12
E. Camden, 931 K-6
E. End, 6998 H-7
El Dorado, 18884 M-6
Elkins, 2648 C-2
Elm Sprs., 1535 B-2
England, 2825 H-8
Eudora, 2269 M-10
Eureka Sprs., 20[illegible] B-3
Fairfield Bay, 23[illegible] D-7
Farmington, 597[illegible] C-2
FAULKNER CO., 113237 F-7
Fayetteville, 73580 C-2
Flippin, 1355 B-6
Fordyce, 4300 K-7
Foreman, 1011 K-1
Forrest City, 15371 F-12
Ft. Smith, 8620[illegible] E-1
Fouke, 859 M-3
FRANKLIN CO., 18125 D-3
FULTON CO., 12245 B-8
GARLAND CO., 96024 G-5
Gassville, 207[illegible] B-7
Gentry, 3158 B-1
Gibson, 3543 J-16
Glenwood, 22[illegible]8 I-4
Goshen, 1071 C-2
Gosnell, 3548 C-14
Gould, 837 J-9
GRANT CO., [illegible]7853 I-7
Gravel Ridge, 3232 J-16
Gravette, 23[illegible] A-1
Green Forest, 2761 B-4
Greenbrier, 4[illegible]06 F-7
GREENE CO., 42090 C-12
Greenland, 1[illegible]59 C-2
Greenwood, 3952 F-2
Greers Ferry, 891 E-8
Gurdon, 22[illegible] J-5
Hackett, 81[illegible] F-1
Hamburg, 2[illegible]57 M-9
Hampton, 1[illegible]24 L-7
Hardy, 772 B-10
Harrisburg, [illegible]288 E-12
Harrison, 1[illegible]943 B-5
Haskell, 39[illegible]0 H-6
Hazen, 14[illegible] G-9
Heber Sprs., 7165 E-8
Helena-West Helena, 12282 H-12
HEMPSTEAD CO., 22609 K-3
Hermitage, 830 L-8
Highland, [illegible]045 B-9
Hope, 10[illegible]5 K-3
Horatio, [illegible]044 J-1
Horseshoe Bend, 2184 B-9
HOT SPRING CO., 32923 I-5
Hot Sprs., 35193 H-5
Hot Sprs. Vil., 12807 H-5
HOWARD CO., 13789 I-2
Hoxie, 2[illegible]80 C-11
Hughes, [illegible]441 G-12
Huntsville, 2346 C-3
INDEPENDENCE CO., 3664[illegible] C-9
IZARD CO., 13696 C-8
JACKSON CO., 17997 E-10
Jacksonville, 28364 G-8
Jasper, [illegible]66 C-5
JEFFERSON CO., 77435 I-8
Johnson, 3354 F-19
JOHNSON CO., 25540 E-4
Jonesboro, 67263 D-12
Judsonia, 2019 F-9
Keiser, 759 D-13
Kensett, 1648 F-9
Kibler, 961 E-2
Kirby, 786 I-3
LAFAYETTE CO., 7645 M-3
L. Catherine, 870 H-5
Lake City, 2082 D-13
L. Hamilton, 2135 H-5
Lake Vil., 2575 L-10
Lamar, 1605 E-4
Lavaca, 2289 E-2
LAWRENCE CO., 17[illegible]15 C-10
Leachville, 1993 C-13
LEE CO., 10424 G-11
Lepanto, 1893 D-13
Lewisville, 1280 L-3
Lincoln, 2249 C-1
LINCOLN CO., 14134 J-9
Little Flock, 2585 B-2
LITTLE RIVER CO., 13171 K-1
Little Rock, 193524 G-7
LOGAN CO., 22353 F-3
London, 1039 E-4
Lonoke, 4245 G-8
LONOKE CO., 68356 G-8
Lowell, 7327 B-2
Luxora, 1178 D-14
Macon, 960 G-8
Madison, 769 F-12
MADISON CO., 15717 C-3
Magazine, 847 F-3
Magnolia, 11577 M-4
Malvern, 10318 I-6
Mammoth Spr., 977 A-9
Manila, 3342 C-13
Mansfield, 1139 F-2
Marianna, 4115 G-12
Marion, 12345 F-13
MARION CO., 16653 B-6
Marked Tree, 2566 E-13
Marmaduke, 1111 B-13
Marshall, 1355 C-6
Marvell, 1186 H-11
Maumelle, 17163 G-7
Mayflower, 2234 G-7
McAlmont, 1873 K-16
McCrory, 1729 F-10
McGehee, 4219 K-10
Melbourne, 1848 C-8
Mena, 5737 H-2
MILLER CO., 43462 L-3
Mineral Sprs., 1208 J-2
MISSISSIPPI CO., 46480 D-13
Monette, 1501 C-13
MONROE CO., 8149 [illegible]-10
MONTGOMERY CO., 9487 H-3
Monticello, 9467 K-9
Morrilton, 6767 F-6
Mt. Ida, 1076 H-3
Mountain Home, 12448 B-7
Mountain Pine, 770 H-5
Mountain View, 2748 D-8
Mulberry, 1655 E-2
Murfreesboro, 1641 J-3
Nashville, 4627 J-3
NEVADA CO., 8997 K-4
Newark, 1176 D-10
Newport, 7879 D-10
NEWTON CO., 8330 C-4
Norphlet, 844 L-6
N. Crossett, 3119 M-8
N. Little Rock, 62304 G-7
Oak Grv. Hts., 889 C-12
Ola, 1281 F-5
Oppelo, 781 F-6
Osceola, 7757 D-14
OUACHITA CO., 26120 K-6
Ozark, 3684 E-3
Ozark Acres, 760 B-10
Paragould, 26113 C-12
Paris, 3532 E-3
Parkin, 1105 F-12
Pea Ridge, 4794 A-2
PERRY CO., 10445 G-5
Perryville, 1460 F-6
PHILLIPS CO., 21757 H-11
Piggott, 3849 B-13
PIKE CO., 11291 I-4
Pine Bluff, 49083 I-8
Piney, 4699 E-15
Plumerville, 826 F-6
Pocahontas, 6608 B-11
POINSETT CO., 24583 E-12
POLK CO., 20662 H-2
POPE CO., 61754 E-5
Pottsville, 2838 F-5
PRAIRIE CO., 8715 G-9
Prairie Grv., 4380 C-2
Prescott, 3296 K-4
PULASKI CO., 382748 H-8
Quitman, 762 E-7
RANDOLPH CO., 17969 B-11
Rector, 1977 B-13
Redfield, 1297 H-8
Rison, 1344 J-7
Rogers, 55964 B-2
Russellville, 27920 F-5
ST. FRANCIS CO., 28258 F-11
Salem, 2607 H-6
Salem, 1635 B-9
SALINE CO., 107118 G-6
SCOTT CO., 11233 G-2
Searcy, 22858 F-9
SEARCY CO., 8195 D-6
SEBASTIAN CO., 125744 F-1
SEVIER CO., 17058 J-1
Shannon Hills, 3143 H-7
SHARP CO., 17264 C-9
Sheridan, 4603 I-7
Sherwood, 29523 G-7
Siloam Sprs., 15039 B-1
Smackover, 1865 L-6
Springdale, 69797 B-2
Stamps, 1693 L-4
Star City, 2274 J-9
Stephens, 891 L-5
STONE CO., 12394 D-8
Stuttgart, 9326 H-9
Sulphur Sprs., 1101 I-8
Sweet Home, 849 H-7
Swifton, 798 D-11
Texarkana, 29919 L-2
Tontitown, 2460 B-2
Trumann, 7243 D-12
Tuckerman, 1362 D-10
Tumbling Shoals, 978 E-8
Tyronza, 762 E-13
UNION CO., 41639 M-6
Van Buren, 22791 E-1
VAN BUREN CO., 17295 D-5
Vilonia, 3815 F-8
Waldo, 1372 L-4
Waldron, 3618 G-2
Walnut Ridge, 4890 C-11
Ward, 4067 F-8
Warren, 6003 K-8
WASHINGTON CO., 203065 C-1
W. Crossett, 1256 M-8
W. Fork, 2317 C-2
W. Memphis, 26245 F-13
WHITE CO., 77076 E-8
White Hall, 5526 I-8
Wickes, 754 I-1
Wilson, 903 D-14
WOODRUFF CO., 7260 F-10
Wooster, 860 F-7
Wrightsville, 2114 H-7
Wynne, 8367 E-12
YELL CO., 22185 F-4
Yellville, 1204 B-6

California
Map pp. 12 – 15

Map keys	Atlas pages
NA – NN	12 – 13
SA – SN	14 – 15

* City keyed to p. 16
† City keyed to p. 17
‡ City keyed to pp. 18 – 19

Aberdeen, 100 SJ-4
Acton, 7596 SI-11
Adelanto, 31765 SH-13
Agoura Hills, 20330 SJ-10
Agua Dulce, 3342 ‡N-6
Ahwahnee, 2246 NN-11
Alameda, 73812 NM-5
ALAMEDA CO., 1510271 NM-6
Alamo, 14570 NE-17
Alberhill, 200 ‡J-18
Alhambra, 83089 ‡E-8
Aliso Viejo, 47823 ‡L-13
Allendale, 1506 NK-6
Alpine, 14236 SM-15
ALPINE CO., 1175 NK-11
Alta Sierra, 6911 NI-8
Altadena, 42777 ‡C-9
Alturas, 2827 NC-9
Alum Rock, 15536 NL-20
Amador City, 185 NK-8
AMADOR CO., 38091 NK-10
Ambler Pk., 600 *N-4
American Canyon, 19454 NL-5
Anaheim, 336265 SK-12
Anderson, 9932 NE-5
Angels Camp, 3836 NL-9
Angwin, 3051 NK-5
Antelope, 45770 *F-4
Antioch, 102372 NL-6
Anza, 3014 SK-15
Apple Valley, 69135 SI-13
Aptos, 6220 SB-3
Arbuckle, 3028 NI-6
Arcade, 42000 *G-4
Arcadia, 56364 ‡D-10
Arcata, 17231 ND-2
Arden Town, 55000 *H-4
Armona, 4156 SD-8
Arnold, 3843 NL-9
Arrowhead Highlands, 1900 ‡C-19
Arroyo Grande, 17252 SG-6
Artesia, 16522 ‡H-9
Arvin, 19304 SG-10
Ashland, 21925 NG-16
Atascadero, 28310 SF-6
Atherton, 6914 NK-15
Atwater, 28168 NN-9
Aubery, 2359 SB-8
Auburn, 13330 NJ-8
August, 8390 *L-10
Avalon, 3728 SL-11
Avenal, 15505 SE-7
Avila Bch., 1627 SG-5
Avocado Hts., 15411 ‡E-10
Azusa, 46361 ‡D-11
Bakersfield, 347483 SF-9
Baldwin Pk., 75390 ‡D-10
Banning, 29603 SJ-14
Barstow, 22639 SH-14
Bay Pt., 21349 NC-18
Bayview, 2510 ND-2
Baywood Pk., 6000 SF-5
Beaumont, 36877 SJ-14
Bel Marin Keys, 1650 NB-12
Bell, 35477 ‡F-8
Bell Gdns., 42072 ‡F-8
Bella Vista, 2781 NE-6
Bellflower, 76616 ‡H-9
Belmont, 25835 NJ-14
Belvedere, 2068 NE-12
Ben Lomond, 6234 SA-2
Benicia, 26997 NL-6
Berkeley, 112580 NM-5
Bermuda Dunes, 7282 SH-2
Berry Creek, 1424 NH-7
Bethel Island, 2137 NL-7
Beverly Hills, 34109 SJ-11
Big Bear City, 12304 SI-14
Big Bear Lake, 5019 SI-14
Big Pine, 1756 SA-11
Biggs, 1707 NH-7
Biola, 1623 SB-7
Bishop, 3879 NN-14
Black Pt., 470 NA-12
Blackhawk, 9354 NF-19
Bloomington, 23851 ‡E-17
Blue Jay, 700 ‡B-20
Blue Lake, 1253 ND-2
Blythe, 20817 SK-19
Bodfish, 1956 SF-10
Bolinas, 1620 NL-4
Bolsa Knolls, 1950 SB-3
Bonita, 12538 †L-4
Bonsall, 3982 SL-13
Bootjack, 960 NN-1
Boron, 2253 SG-12
Borrego Sprs., 3429 SL-15
Bostonia, 15379 †H-6
Boulder Creek, 4923 SA-2
Boyes Hot Sprs., 6656 NK-5
Bradbury, 1048 ‡D-11
Brawley, 24953 SM-17
Brea, 39282 ‡G-11
Brentwood, 51481 NL-7
Bridgeport, 575 NL-12
Brisbane, 4282 NH-13
Broadmoor, 4176 NG-12
Brockway, 370 *F-9
Brooktrails, 3235 NH-3
Buckhorn, 2429 NK-9
Buellton, 4828 SH-7
Buena Pk., 80530 ‡H-10
Burbank, 103340 SJ-11
Burbank, 4926 NM-19
Burlingame, 28806 NI-14
Burney, 3154 ND-7
BUTTE CO., 220000 NH-7
Buttonwillow, 1508 SF-8
Cabazon, 2535 SJ-14
Calabasas, 23058 ‡D-2
CALAVERAS CO., 45578 NK-10
Calexico, 38572 SN-18
California City, 14120 SG-12
Calimesa, 7879 SJ-14
Calipatria, 7705 SL-17
Calistoga, 5155 NK-5
Camarillo, 65201 SI-9
Cambria, 6032 SF-5
Cambrian Pk., 3282 NN-19
Cameron Pk., 18228 NJ-8
Camino, 1750 NJ-9
Camino Tassajara, 2197 NF-19
Campbell, 39349 SA-3
Campo, 2684 SN-15
Canyon Lake, 10561 SK-13
Carlsbad, 105328 SL-13
Carmel Pt., 500 *N-1
Carmel Valley Vil., 4407 SC-3
Carmel-by-the-Sea, 3722 SC-3
Carmichael, 61762 NK-7
Carpinteria, 13040 SI-8
Carson, 91714 ‡H-7
Caruthers, 2497 SC-7
Casa de Oro, 12000 †J-6
Castaic, 19015 SI-10
Castro Valley, 61388 NM-6
Castroville, 6481 SB-3
Cathedral City, 51200 SK-15
Cayucos, 2592 SF-5
Cedar Glen, 2100 ‡B-20
Cedarpines Pk., 850 ‡B-18
Ceres, 45417 NM-8
Cerritos, 49041 ‡H-9
Charter Oak, 9310 ‡D-12
Chatsworth Lake Manor, 1100 ‡C-2
Cherryland, 14728 NG-17
Chester, 2144 NF-8
Chico, 86187 NG-6
Chino, 77983 ‡F-14
Chino Hills, 74799 SJ-12
Chowchilla, 18720 SA-7
Chula Vista, 243916 SN-14
Citrus, 10866 ‡D-11
Citrus Hts., 83301 NJ-7
Claremont, 34926 ‡D-13
Clayton, 10897 NL-6
Clearlake, 15250 NJ-5
Clearlake Oaks, 2359 NI-5
Cloverdale, 8618 NJ-4
Clovis, 95631 SB-8
Clyde, 678 NC-17
Coachella, 40704 SK-16
Coalinga, 13380 SD-6
Coarsegold, 1840 SA-8
Cobb, 1778 NJ-4
Colfax, 1963 NI-8
Collierville, 1934 NL-7
Colma, 1792 NH-12
Colton, 52154 SJ-13
Columbia, 2297 NL-9
Colusa, 5971 NI-6
COLUSA CO., 21419 NI-5
Commerce, 12823 ‡F-8
Compton, 96455 ‡H-7
Concord, 122067 NL-6
CONTRA COSTA CO., 1049025 NM-6
Copperopolis, 3671 NL-9
Corcoran, 24813 SD-8
Corning, 7663 NG-6
Corona, 152374 SJ-13
Coronado, 18912 SN-14
Coronita, 2608 ‡H-15
Corte Madera, 9253 ND-12
Costa Mesa, 109960 ‡K-11
Cotati, 7265 NK-4
Coto de Caza, 14866 ‡L-15
Cottonwood, 3316 NF-6
Country Club, 9379 *L-9
Covina, 47796 ‡E-12
Cowan Hts., 4000 ‡I-13
Crescent City, 7643 NB-2
Crest Pk., 600 ‡B-20
Crestline, 10770 ‡B-19
Crestmore, 4500 ‡E-17
Crockett, 3094 NB-15
Cudahy, 23805 ‡G-8
Culver City, 38883 ‡F-5
Cupertino, 58302 NM-17
Cutler, 5000 SC-9
Cypress, 47802 ‡I-9
Daly City, 101123 NG-12
Dana Pt., 33351 ‡N-14
Danville, 42039 NM-6
Davis, 65622 NK-7
Del Aire, 10001 ‡G-6
Del Dios, 355 †C-3
Del Mar, 4161 SM-13
Del Monte Forest, 4514 *M-1
DEL NORTE CO., 28610 NB-2
Del Rey, 1639 SC-8
Del Rey Oaks, 1624 SC-3
Delano, 53041 SE-9
Delhi, 10755 NN-8
Denair, 4404 NN-8
Desert Hot Sprs., 25938 SJ-15
Desert View Highlands, 2360 SH-11
Diablo, 1158 NE-18
Diamond Bar, 55544 ‡F-12
Diamond Sprs., 11037 NJ-8
Dinuba, 21453 SC-8
Dixon, 18351 NK-6
Dollar Pt., 1215 *F-8
Dorris, 939 NA-6
Dos Palos, 4950 SB-6
Downey, 111772 SJ-11
Downieville, 282 NH-8
Duarte, 21321 ‡D-11
Dublin, 46036 NM-6
Dunsmuir, 1650 NC-6
Durham, 5518 NH-6
Earlimart, 8537 SE-9
E. Foothills, 8269 NL-20
E. La Mirada, 9757 ‡G-10
E. Los Angeles, 126496 ‡F-8
E. Palo Alto, 28155 NK-16
E. Pasadena, 6144 ‡D-9
E. Quincy, 2489 NG-8
E. Richmond Hts., 3280 ND-14
Easton, 2083 SC-8
El Cajon, 99478 SM-14
El Centro, 42598 SM-17
El Cerrito, 23549 NL-5
El Cerrito, 5100 ‡H-16
EL DORADO CO., 181058 NK-9
El Granada, 5467 NJ-12
El Monte, 113475 ‡E-10
El Rio, 7198 SI-9
El Segundo, 16654 ‡G-5
El Sobrante, 12669 NC-14
El Sueno, 2000 †B-3
Elk Grv., 153015 NK-7
Ellwood, 7800 †B-1
Elverta, 5492 *F-2
Emerald Bay, 1100 ‡L-13
Emerald L. Hills, 4278 NK-15
Emeryville, 10080 NE-14
Empire, 4189 NM-8
Encinitas, 59518 SM-13
Escalon, 7132 NM-8
Escondido, 143911 SL-14
Esparto, 3108 NJ-6
Etna, 737 NC-4
Eucalyptus Hills, 5313 †G-6
Eureka, 27191 ND-2
Exeter, 10334 SD-9
Fair Oaks, 30912 *G-5
Fairbanks Ranch, 3148 †E-2
Fairfax, 7441 NL-5
Fairfax, 991 SM-8
Fairfield, 105321 NL-6
Fairmead, 1447 SB-7
Fairmont Ter., 4000 NG-16
Fairview, 10003 NH-17
Fallbrook, 30534 SL-13
Farmersville, 10588 SD-9
Felton, 4057 SB-3
Ferndale, 1371 NE-1
Fernwood, 500 ‡E-3
Fillmore, 15002 SI-10
Firebaugh, 7549 SB-6
Florence, 25000 ‡G-7
Florin, 47513 *I-3
Folsom, 72203 NJ-8
Fontana, 196069 ‡D-17
Foothill Farms, 33121 *F-4
Ford City, 4278 SG-8
Foresthill, 1483 NI-8
Forestville, 3293 NK-4
Ft. Bragg, 7273 NH-2
Ft. Jones, 839 NB-4
Fortuna, 11926 NE-2
Foster City, 30567 NI-15
Fountain Valley, 55313 ‡J-10
Fowler, 5570 SC-8
Frazier Pk., 2691 SH-9
Freedom, 3070 SB-3
Freeport, 38 *J-2
Fremont, 214089 NM-6
French Camp, 3376 NM-7
Fresno, 494665 SC-8
FRESNO CO., 930450 SC-7
Fullerton, 135161 SJ-12
Galt, 23647 NL-7
Garden Acres, 10648 *L-10
Garden Grv., 170883 SK-12
Gardena, 58829 ‡H-6
Georgetown, 2367 NJ-8
Gilroy, 48821 SB-4
Glendale, 191719 SJ-11
Glendora, 50073 ‡D-12
GLENN CO., 28122 NH-5
Glenview, 160 ‡D-3
Gold River, 7912 *G-5
Golden Hills, 8656 SG-10
Goleta, 29888 SI-7
Gonzales, 8187 SC-4
Goshen, 3006 SD-8
Grand Ter., 12040 ‡E-18
Granite Bay, 20402 *E-6
Granite Hills, 3035 †I-7
Grass Valley, 12860 NI-8
Graton, 1707 NK-4
Green Brae, 3400 ND-12
Greenacres, 5566 SL-5
Greenfield, 16330 SD-4
Gridley, 6584 NH-7
Grover Bch., 13156 SG-6
Guadalupe, 7080 SG-6
Gualala, 1500 NJ-3
Guerneville, 4534 NK-4
Gustine, 5520 SA-5
Hacienda Hts., 54038 ‡F-10
Half Moon Bay, 11324 NN-5
Hamilton City, 1759 NG-6
Hanford, 53967 SD-8
Hawaiian Gdns., 14254 ‡H-9
Hawthorne, 84293 ‡G-6
Hayfork, 2368 NE-4
Hayward, 144186 NM-6
Healdsburg, 11254 NJ-4
Heber, 4275 SM-17
Hemet, 78657 SK-14
Hercules, 24060 NC-15
Hermosa Bch., 19506 ‡H-5
Hesperia, 90173 SI-13
Hidden Hills, 1856 ‡D-2
Hidden Valley Lake, 5579 NJ-5
Highgrove, 3988 ‡F-18
Highland, 53104 SJ-13
Hillsborough, 10825 NI-14
Hollister, 34928 SB-4
Holtville, 5939 SM-18
Home Gdns., 11570 ‡H-16
Hope Ranch, 1600 †B-3
Hughson, 6640 NM-8
HUMBOLDT CO., 134623 NE-2
Humboldt Hill, 3414 NE-2
Huntington Bch., 189992 SK-12
Huntington Pk., 58114 ‡F-7
Huron, 6754 SD-7
Idyllwild, 2200 SK-15
Imperial, 14758 SM-17
Imperial Bch., 26324 SN-14
IMPERIAL CO., 174528 SM-18
Incline, 60 NM-1
Independence, 669 SB-11
Indian Wells, 4958 SK-16
Indio, 76036 SK-16
Indio Hills, 972 SG-2
Industry, 219 ‡F-11
Inglewood, 109673 SJ-11
INYO CO., 18546 SC-13
Ione, 7918 NK-8
Irvine, 212375 SK-12
Irwindale, 1422 ‡D-11
Isla Vista, 23096 SI-7
Isleton, 804 NL-7
Ivanhoe, 4495 SD-9
Jackson, 4651 NK-9
Jamestown, 3433 NL-9
Jamul, 6163 SN-14
Joshua Tree, 7414 SJ-16
Julian, 1502 SM-15
Jurupa Valley, 94235 ‡F-16
Kelseyville, 3353 NI-4
Kennedy, 3254 *M-10
Kensington, 5077 ND-14
Kentfield, 6485 ND-11
Kerman, 13544 SC-7
KERN CO., 839631 SF-10
Kettleman City, 1439 SE-7
Keyes, 5601 NM-8
King City, 12874 SD-5
Kings Bch., 3795 NI-10
KINGS CO., 152982 SD-7
Kingsburg, 11382 SC-8
Knightsen, 1568 NL-7
La Cañada Flintridge, 20246 ‡C-7
La Crescenta, 13000 ‡C-7
La Habra, 60239 ‡G-11
La Habra Hts., 5325 ‡G-11
La Mesa, 57065 †I-5
La Mirada, 48527 ‡G-10
La Palma, 15568 ‡H-10
La Presa, 34169 †J-5
La Puente, 39816 ‡E-10
La Quinta, 37467 SK-16
La Riviera, 10802 *H-4
La Verne, 31063 SJ-12
Ladera, 1426 NL-16
Ladera Hts., 6498 ‡F-6
Ladera Ranch, 350 ‡L-15
Lafayette, 23893 ND-16
Laguna Bch., 22723 SK-12
Laguna Hills, 30344 ‡L-14
Laguna Niguel, 62979 ‡M-14
Laguna Woods, 16192 ‡L-13
L. Arrowhead, 12424 ‡B-20
LAKE CO., 64665 NI-4
L. Elsinore, 51821 SK-13
L. Forest, 77264 SK-12
L. Isabella, 3466 SF-11
L. Los Angeles, 12328 SH-12
L. Nacimiento, 2411 SE-5
Lake of the Pines, 3917 NI-8
L. Wildwood, 4991 NI-8
Lakeland Vil., 11541 ‡K-18
Lakeport, 4753 NI-4
Lakeside, 20648 SM-14
Lakeview, 2104 SJ-14
Lakewood, 80048 ‡H-9
Lamont, 15120 SG-10
Lancaster, 156633 SH-11
Landers, 2300 SI-15
Larkspur, 11926 ND-11
Las Flores, 5971 ‡L-15
LASSEN CO., 34895 NE-9
Lathrop, 18023 NM-7
Laton, 1824 SC-8
Lawndale, 32769 ‡H-5
Le Grand, 1659 SA-7
Lebec, 1468 SH-10
Lemon Grv., 25320 †J-5
Lemon Hts., 2800 ‡I-13
Lemoore, 24531 SD-8
Lennox, 22753 ‡G-6
Lenwood, 3543 SH-14
Leona Valley, 1607 ‡M-6
Lincoln, 42819 NJ-7
Lincoln Acres, 1650 †K-4
Lincoln Vil., 4381 *K-9
Linda, 17773 NI-7
Linden, 1784 NL-8
Lindsay, 11768 SD-9
Live Oak, 8392 NI-7
Livermore, 80968 NM-6
Livingston, 13058 NN-9
Lockeford, 3233 NL-8
Lodi, 62134 NL-7
Loma Linda, 23261 SJ-13
Loma Rica, 2368 NI-7
Lomita, 20256 ‡I-6
Lompoc, 42434 SH-6
London, 1869 SC-8
Lone Pine, 2035 SC-11
Long Bch., 462257 SK-11
Loomis, 6430 NJ-8
Los Alamitos, 11449 ‡I-9
Los Alamos, 1890 SH-6
Los Altos, 28976 NN-6
Los Altos Hills, 7922 NL-16
Los Angeles, 3792621 SJ-11
LOS ANGELES CO., 9818605 SI-12
Los Banos, 35972 SB-5
Los Gatos, 29413 SA-3
Los Molinos, 2037 NG-6
Los Nietos, 8200 ‡F-9
Los Osos, 14276 SF-5
Los Ranchitos, 425 NC-11
Lost Hills, 2412 SF-8
Loyalton, 769 NH-10
Loyola, 3261 NL-17
Lucas Valley, 4000 NC-11
Lucerne, 3067 NI-4
Lucerne Valley, 5811 SI-14
Lynwood, 69772 ‡G-7
Lytle Creek, 701 ‡B-16
Madera, 61416 SB-7
Madera Acres, 9163 SB-7
MADERA CO., 150865 SB-7
Magalia, 11310 NG-7
Malibu, 12645 SJ-10
Mammoth Lakes, 8234 NM-12
Manhattan Bch., 35135 SJ-11
Manteca, 67096 NM-8
Maricopa, 1154 SG-8
Marin City, 2666 NE-12
MARIN CO., 252409 NL-4
Marina, 19718 SC-3
Marina del Rey, 8866 ‡F-5
Marinwood, 2300 NB-11
Mariposa, 2173 NN-10
MARIPOSA CO., 18251 SA-7
Markleeville, 210 NJ-11
Martinez, 35824 NL-6
Marysville, 12072 NI-7
Maywood, 27395 ‡F-8
McFarland, 12707 SE-9
McKinleyville, 15177 ND-2
Mead Valley, 18510 ‡H-19
Meadow Vista, 3217 NI-8
Mecca, 8577 SK-16
Meiners Oaks, 3571 SI-9
MENDOCINO CO., 87841 NH-3
Mendota, 11014 SB-6
Menifee, 77519 SK-14
Menlo Pk., 32026 NN-5
Merced, 78958 SA-6
MERCED CO., 255793 SA-6
Midway City, 8485 ‡J-10
Mill Valley, 13903 NL-5
Millbrae, 21532 NI-13
Milpitas, 66790 NN-6
Mira Monte, 6854 SI-9
Mission Viejo, 93305 SK-12
Modesto, 201165 NM-8
Modjeska, 500 ‡J-15
MODOC CO., 9686 NB-8
Mojave, 4238 SG-11
MONO CO., 14202 NL-13
Monrovia, 36590 ‡D-10
Montague, 1443 NB-5
Montalvin Manor, 2876 NC-14
Montara, 2909 NJ-12
Montclair, 36664 ‡E-14
Monte Nido, 850 ‡E-2
Monte Sereno, 3341 NN-18
Montebello, 62500 ‡F-9
Montecito, 8965 SI-8
Monterey, 27810 SC-3
MONTEREY CO., 415057 SD-4
Monterey Pk., 60269 ‡E-8
Montrose, 4100 ‡C-7
Moorpark, 34421 SI-10
Morada, 3828 *K-10
Moraga, 16016 NE-16
Moreno Valley, 193365 SJ-14
Morgan Hill, 37882 SA-3
Morongo Valley, 3552 SJ-15
Morro Bay, 10234 SF-5
Moss Bch., 3103 NJ-12
Mt. Baldy, 200 ‡B-14
Mt. Helix, 6400 †I-6
Mt. Shasta, 3394 NC-6
Mountain Ranch, 1628 NL-9
Mountain View, 74066 NL-17
Mountain View, 1500 NC-16
Murphys, 2213 NL-9
Murrieta, 103466 SK-14
Murrieta Hot Sprs., 2948 ‡L-20
Muscoy, 10644 ‡D-18
Napa, 76915 NK-5
NAPA CO., 136484 NK-5
National City, 58582 SN-14
Needles, 4844 SH-19
Nevada City, 3068 NI-8
NEVADA CO., 98764 NH-9
Newark, 42573 NM-6
Newberry Sprs., 1500 SH-15
Newman, 10224 SA-5
Newport Bch., 85186 SK-12
Nice, 2731 NI-4
Nipomo, 16714 SG-6
Norco, 27063 SJ-13
N. Fair Oaks, 14687 NK-15
N. Highlands, 42694 *F-4
N. Richmond, 3717 ND-13
N. Shore, 3477 SK-16
N. Tustin, 24044 ‡I-13
Norwalk, 105549 ‡H-9
Novato, 51904 NL-5
Nuevo, 6447 ‡I-20
Nyland, 2200 †B-9
Oak Hills, 8879 SI-13
Oak Pk., 13811 ‡C-1
Oak View, 4066 SI-9
Oakdale, 20675 NM-8
Oakhurst, 2829 NN-11
Oakland, 390724 NM-5
Oakley, 35432 NL-6
Oasis, 6890 SK-16
Oceano, 7286 SG-6
Oceanside, 167086 SL-13
Oildale, 32684 SF-9
Ojai, 7461 SI-9
Olivehurst, 13656 NI-7
Ontario, 163924 SJ-12
Orange, 136416 ‡I-12
ORANGE CO., 3010232 SK-12
Orange Cove, 9078 SC-9
Orangevale, 33960 *F-6
Orcutt, 28905 SH-6
Orinda, 17643 NE-16
Orland, 7291 NG-6
Orosi, 8770 SC-9
Oroville, 15546 NH-7
Oxnard, 197899 SJ-9
Pacheco, 3685 NC-17
Pacific Grv., 15041 SC-3
Pacifica, 37234 NM-5
Pajaro, 3070 SB-3
Palermo, 5382 NH-7
Palm Desert, 48445 SK-15
Palm Sprs., 44552 SJ-15
Palmdale, 152750 SH-11
Palo Alto, 64403 NN-5
Palomar Pk., 530 NJ-15
Palos Verdes Estates, 13438 ‡I-5
Paradise, 26218 NG-7
Paramount, 54098 ‡H-8
Parkway, 14670 *I-2
Parkwood, 2268 SB-7
Parlier, 14494 SC-8
Pasadena, 137122 SJ-11
Paso Robles, 29793 SF-6
Patterson, 20413 NN-8
Penn Valley, 1621 NI-8
Penngrove, 2522 NK-4
Perris, 68386 SK-13
Petaluma, 57941 NL-4
Phelan, 14304 SI-13
Pico Rivera, 62942 ‡F-9
Piedmont, 10667 NE-15
Pine Grv., 2219 NK-9
Pine Hills, 3131 ND-2
Pine Mtn. Club, 2315 SH-9
Pine Valley, 1510 SM-15
Pinole, 18390 NC-14
Piñon Hills, 7272 SI-12
Piru, 2063 SI-10
Pismo Bch., 7655 SG-6
Pittsburg, 63264 NL-6
Pixley, 3310 SE-9
Placentia, 50533 ‡H-12
PLACER CO., 348432 NI-9
Placerville, 10389 NJ-9
Planada, 4584 SA-6
Pleasant Hill, 33152 NL-6
Pleasanton, 70285 NM-6
PLUMAS CO., 20007 NF-9
Plymouth, 1005 NK-8
Point Arena, 449 NJ-2
Pollock Pines, 6871 NJ-9
Pomona, 149058 SJ-12
Port Costa, 190 NB-16
Port Hueneme, 21723 SJ-9
Porterville, 54165 SD-9
Portola, 2104 NG-9
Portola Hills, 6391 ‡K-15
Portola Valley, 4353 NL-15
Poway, 47811 SM-14
Prunedale, 17560 SB-3
Quartz Hill, 10912 SH-11
Quincy, 1728 NG-8
Rainbow, 1832 SL-14
Ramona, 20292 SM-14
Rancho Calaveras, 5325 NL-8
Rancho Cordova, 64776 NK-7
Rancho Cucamonga, 165269 ‡D-15
Rancho Mirage, 17218 SK-15
Rancho Murieta, 5488 NK-8
Rancho Palos Verdes, 41643 ‡J-6
Rancho San Diego, 21208 †J-6
Rancho Santa Fe, 3117 SM-14
Rancho Santa Margarita, 47853 ‡K-16
Red Bluff, 14076 NF-6
Red Hill, 2800 ‡J-13
Redding, 89861 NE-5
Redlands, 68747 SJ-14
Redondo Bch., 66748 SJ-11
Redwood City, 76815 NN-5
Redwood Valley, 1729 NI-3
Reedley, 24194 SC-8
Rialto, 99171 SJ-13
Richgrove, 2882 SE-9
Richmond, 103701 ND-13
Ridgecrest, 27616 SF-12
Rimforest, 700 ‡B-19
Rio del Mar, 9216 SB-3
Rio Dell, 3368 NE-2
Rio Linda, 15106 *F-3
Rio Vista, 7360 NL-7
Ripon, 14297 NM-8
Riverbank, 22678 NM-8
Riverdale, 3153 SC-7
Riverdale Pk., 1128 *J-8
Riverside, 303871 SJ-13
RIVERSIDE CO., 2189641 SJ-16
Rocklin, 56974 NJ-8
Rodeo, 8679 NB-15
Rohnert Pk., 40971 NK-4
Rolling Hills, 1860 ‡I-5
Rolling Hills Estates, 8067 ‡I-6
Rollingwood, 2969 NC-14
Romoland, 1684 ‡I-20
Rosamond, 18150 SH-11
Rosedale, 14058 SF-9
Roseland, 6325 *I-6
Rosemead, 53764 ‡E-9
Rosemont, 22681 *H-4
Rosemont, 800 †E-6
Roseville, 118788 NI-7
Ross, 2415 NC-11
Rossmoor, 10244 ‡I-9
Rowland Hts., 48993 ‡F-11
Running Sprs., 4862 SI-14
Sacramento, 466488 NK-7
SACRAMENTO CO., 1418788 NK-8
St. Helena, 5814 NK-5
Salida, 13722 NM-8
Salinas, 150441 SC-3
Salton City, 3763 SL-16
San Andreas, 2783 NL-9
San Anselmo, 12336 NC-11
San Antonio Hts., 3371 ‡D-14
SAN BENITO CO., 55269 SC-5
San Bernardino, 209924 SJ-13
SAN BERNARDINO CO., 2035210 SG-16
San Bruno, 41114 NM-5
San Carlos, 28406 NN-5
San Clemente, 63522 SL-13
San Diego, 1307402 SN-14
SAN DIEGO CO., 3095313 SM-15
San Dimas, 33371 ‡D-12
San Fernando, 23645 SI-11
San Francisco, 805235 NM-5
SAN FRANCISCO CO., 805235 NE-12
San Gabriel, 39718 ‡E-9
San Jacinto, 44199 SK-14
San Joaquin, 4001 SC-7
SAN JOAQUIN CO., 685306 NL-8
San Jose, 945942 NN-6
San Juan Bautista, 1862 SB-4
San Juan Capistrano, 34593 SK-12
San Leandro, 84950 NM-6
San Lorenzo, 23452 NH-16
San Luis Obispo, 45119 SG-6
SAN LUIS OBISPO CO., 269637 SG-6
San Marcos, 83781 SL-14
San Marino, 13147 ‡D-9
San Martin, 7027 SB-4
San Mateo, 97207 NI-14
SAN MATEO CO., 718451 SA-2
San Miguel, 2336 SE-6
San Pablo, 29139 NL-5
San Quentin, 100 ND-12
San Rafael, 57713 NL-5
San Ramon, 72148 NM-6
Sand City, 334 *M-2
Sanger, 24270 SC-8
Santa Ana, 324528 SK-12
Santa Barbara, 88410 SI-8
SANTA BARBARA CO., 423895 SH-8
Santa Clara, 116468 NL-18
SANTA CLARA CO., 1781642 SA-4
Santa Clarita, 176320 SI-10
Santa Cruz, 59946 SB-3
SANTA CRUZ CO., 262382 SB-3
Santa Fe Sprs., 16223 ‡G-9
Santa Maria, 99553 SG-6
Santa Monica, 89736 SJ-11
Santa Paula, 29321 SI-9
Santa Rosa, 167815 NK-4
Santa Susana, 1037 ‡B-2
Santa Venetia, 4292 NC-12
Santa Ynez, 4418 SH-7
Santee, 53413 SM-14
Saranap, 5202 NE-17
Saratoga, 29926 SA-3
Saticoy, 1029 †A-9
Sausalito, 7061 NE-12
Scotland, 285 ‡B-16
Scotts Valley, 11580 SB-3
Seal Bch., 24168 ‡J-9
Searles Valley, 1739 SE-13
Seaside, 33025 SC-3
Sebastopol, 7379 NK-4
Sedco Hills, 3078 ‡K-19
Seeley, 1739 SM-17
Selma, 23219 SC-8
Shackelford, 3371 *J-9
Shafter, 16988 SF-9
Shasta, 1771 NE-5
SHASTA CO., 177223 NE-6
Shasta Lake, 10164 NE-5
Sherwood Forest, 2600 ND-14
Shingle Sprs., 4432 NJ-8
Shingletown, 2283 NE-6
Shore Acres, 4000 NB-18
SIERRA CO., 3240 NH-9
Sierra Madre, 10917 ‡D-9
Signal Hill, 11016 ‡I-8
Silver Strand, 1200 †C-8
Silverado, 800 ‡J-15
Simi Valley, 124237 SI-10
SISKIYOU CO., 44900 NC-5
Sky Valley, 2406 SG-1
Skyforest, 750 ‡B-20
Solana Bch., 12867 SM-13
SOLANO CO., 413344 NK-6
Soledad, 25738 SC-4
Solvang, 5245 SH-7
Sonoma, 10648 NK-5
SONOMA CO., 483878 NJ-3
Sonora, 4903 NL-9
Soquel, 9644 SB-3
Soulsbyville, 2215 NL-10
S. Dos Palos, 1620 SB-6
S. El Monte, 20116 ‡E-10
S. Gate, 94396 ‡G-8
S. L. Tahoe, 21403 NJ-10
S. Pasadena, 25619 ‡D-8
S. San Francisco, 63632 NM-5
S. San Gabriel, 8070 ‡E-9
S. San Jose Hills, 20551 ‡F-11
S. Taft, 2169 SG-8
S. Whittier, 57156 ‡G-10
Spreckels, 673 *N-5
Spring Valley, 28205 SN-14
Squaw Valley, 3162 SC-9
Stallion Sprs., 2488 SG-10
STANISLAUS CO., 514453 SA-4
Stanton, 38186 ‡I-10
Stockton, 291707 NL-7
Strathmore, 2819 SD-9
Strawberry, 5393 ND-12
Suisun City, 28111 NL-6
Summerland, 1448 SI-8
Sunnyside, 4235 SC-20
Sunnyside, 1000 †K-5
Sunnyvale, 140081 NL-17
Sunol, 913 NI-19
Sunset Bch., 971 ‡J-9
Susanville, 17947 NF-9
Sutter, 2904 NI-6
SUTTER CO., 94737 NI-6
Sutter Creek, 2501 NK-8
Sylvia Pk., 600 ‡D-3
Taft, 9327 SG-8
Taft Hts., 1949 SG-8
Tahoe Vista, 1433 NI-10
Tamalpais Valley, 7000 NE-12
Tara Hills, 5126 NC-14
Tarpey Vil., 3888 SB-20
Tehachapi, 14414 SG-11
Tehama, 418 NG-6
TEHAMA CO., 63463 NG-5
Temecula, 100097 SK-14
Temescal Valley, 22535 ‡I-16
Temple City, 35558 ‡E-9
Templeton, 7674 SF-6
Terra Bella, 3310 SE-9
Thermal, 2865 SK-16
Thermalito, 6646 NH-7
Thousand Oaks, 126683 SJ-10
Thousand Palms, 7715 SJ-15
Three Rivers, 2182 SC-10
Tiburon, 8962 NM-5
Tipton, 2543 SD-9
Topanga, 8289 ‡E-3
Topanga Pk., 600 ‡D-2
Torrance, 145438 SK-11
Trabuco Canyon, 800 ‡K-15
Tracy, 82922 NM-7
Trinidad, 367 ND-2
TRINITY CO., 13786 NE-4
Truckee, 16180 NI-10
Tulare, 59278 SD-9
TULARE CO., 442179 SD-9
Tulelake, 1010 NA-7
Tuolumne, 1779 NL-10
TUOLUMNE CO., 55365 NM-9
Turlock, 68549 NN-8
Tustin, 75540 ‡J-12
Twain Harte, 2226 NL-10
Twentynine Palms, 25048 SJ-16
Twin Peaks, 2100 ‡B-19
Ukiah, 16075 NI-3
Union City, 69516 NI-16
Upland, 73732 SJ-12
Vacaville, 92428 NK-6
Valinda, 22822 ‡E-11
Valle Vista, 14578 SK-14
Vallejo, 115942 NL-5
Valley Ctr., 9277 SL-14
Valley Sprs., 3553 NL-8
Vandenberg Vil., 6497 SH-6
Ventura, 106433 SI-9
VENTURA CO., 823318 SH-9
Vernon, 112 ‡F-7
Victorville, 115903 SI-13
View Pk., 5500 ‡F-6
Villa Pk., 5812 ‡I-12
Vincent, 15922 SI-11
Vine Hill, 3761 NC-16
Vineyard, 24836 *J-4
Visalia, 124442 SD-9
Vista, 93834 SL-13
Walnut, 29172 ‡E-12
Walnut Creek, 64173 NL-6
Walnut Grv., 1542 NL-7
Walnut Pk., 15966 ‡F-7
Wasco, 25545 SF-9
Waterford, 8456 NM-9
Watsonville, 51199 SB-3
Weaverville, 3600 NE-4
Weed, 2967 NC-5
Weldon, 2642 SE-11
W. Athens, 8729 ‡G-7
W. Carson, 21699 ‡I-7
W. Covina, 106098 ‡E-11
W. Hollywood, 34399 ‡E-6
W. Menlo Pk., 3659 NK-15
West Park, 1157 SC-18
W. Puente Valley, 22636 ‡E-11
W. Sacramento, 48744 NK-7
Westlake Vil., 8270 SJ-10
Westminster, 89701 ‡J-10
Westmorland, 2225 SM-17
Westwood, 1647 NF-8
Wheatland, 3456 NI-7
Whittier, 85331 SJ-12
Wildomar, 32176 SK-13
Williams, 5123 NI-6
Willits, 4888 NH-3
Willow Creek, 1710 ND-3
Willows, 6166 NH-6
Wilsonia, 5 SK-1
Wilton, 5363 NK-7
Winchester, 2534 SK-14
Windsor, 26801 NK-4
Windsor Hills, 5000 ‡F-6
Winter Gdns., 20631 †H-6
Winters, 6624 NK-6
Winton, 10613 NN-9
Wofford Hts., 2200 SE-11
Woodcrest, 14347 ‡H-18
Woodlake, 7279 SC-9
Woodland, 55468 NJ-6
Woodside, 5287 NK-15
Woodville, 1740 SD-9
Wrightwood, 4525 SI-12
YOLO CO., 200849 NJ-6
Yorba Linda, 64234 ‡G-13
Yosemite Lakes, 4952 SA-8
Yountville, 2933 NK-5
Yreka, 7765 NB-5
Yuba City, 64925 NI-7
YUBA CO., 72155 NI-7
Yucaipa, 51367 SJ-14
Yucca Valley, 20700 SJ-15

Colorado
Map pp. 20 – 21

* City keyed to p. 22

Acequia, 950 *M-4
Acres Green, 3007 *L-5
ADAMS CO., 441603 E-15
Akron, 1702 D-17
ALAMOSA CO., 15445 L-11
Alamosa, 8780 L-11
Antonito, 781 M-11
Applewood, 7160 *I-2
ARAPAHOE CO., 572003 F-14
ARCHULETA CO., 12084 M-8
Arvada, 106433 E-13
Aspen, 6658 G-9
Ault, 1519 C-14
Aurora, 325078 E-14
Avon, 6447 F-10
Avondale, 674 J-15
BACA CO., 3788 L-19
Basalt, 3857 F-8
Bayfield, 2333 M-7
Bennett, 2308 E-15
BENT CO., 6499 K-18
Berkley, 11207 *H-4
Berthoud, 5105 D-13
Black Forest, 13116 H-14
Blende, 878 J-14
Blue River, 849 F-11
BOULDER CO., 294567 D-12
Boulder, 97385 D-13
Bow Mar, 866 *K-3
Breckenridge, 4540 F-11
Brighton, 33352 E-14
Brookridge, 800 *K-4
BROOMFIELD CO., 55889 *E-3
Broomfield, 55889 E-13
Brush, 5463 D-16
Buena Vista, 2617 H-11
Burlington, 4254 G-20
Byers, 1160 E-15
Calhan, 780 H-15
Campion, 1830 D-13
Cañon City, 16400 I-13
Carbondale, 6427 F-8
Castle Pines Vil., 3614 *N-5
Castle Pines, 10360 *N-5
Castle Rock, 48231 F-14
Cattle Creek, 641 F-8
Cedaredge, 2253 H-6
Centennial, 100377 F-13
Center, 2230 K-11
Central City, 663 E-12
CHAFFEE CO., 17809 I-10
Cherry Hills Vil., 5987 *K-4
CHEYENNE CO., 1836 H-19
Cheyenne Wells, 846 H-20
CLEAR CREEK CO., 9088 F-12
Clifton, 19889 G-5
Collbran, 708 G-6
Colorado City, 2193 K-14
Colorado Sprs., 416427 H-14
Columbine Valley, 1256 *L-3
Columbine, 24280 *L-3
Commerce City, 45913 *G-6
CONEJOS CO., 8256 M-10
Conejos, 58 M-11
Cortez, 8482 L-5
COSTILLA CO., 3524 M-12
Craig, 9464 C-7
Creede, 290 K-9
Crested Butte, 1487 H-8
Cripple Creek, 1189 H-13
CROWLEY CO., 5823 J-16
CUSTER CO., 4255 K-12
Dacono, 4152 D-13
Del Norte, 1686 L-10
DELTA CO., 30952 H-6
Delta, 8915 H-6
DENVER CO., 600158 *J-5
Denver, 600158 E-13
Derby, 7685 *H-5
Dillon, 904 F-11
DOLORES CO., 2064 K-5
Dolores, 936 L-5
DOUGLAS CO., 285465 G-13
Dove Creek, 735 K-4
Durango, 16887 M-6
Eads, 609 I-19
EAGLE CO., 52197 E-9
Eagle, 6508 F-9
Eaton, 4365 C-14
Edgewater, 5170 *I-3
Edwards, 10266 F-9
El Jebel, 3801 F-8
EL PASO CO., 622263 H-14
ELBERT CO., 23086 F-15
Elizabeth, 1358 G-14
Ellicott, 1131 H-15
Englewood, 30255 F-13
Erie, 18135 D-13
Estes Park, 5858 C-12
Evans, 18537 C-14
Evergreen, 9038 F-12
Fairplay, 679 G-11
Federal Hts., 11467 *G-4
Firestone, 10147 D-13
Florence, 3881 I-13
Ft. Collins, 143986 C-13
Ft. Lupton, 7377 D-14
Ft. Morgan, 11315 D-16
Fountain, 25846 I-14
Fowler, 1182 J-16
Foxfield, 685 F-14
Fraser, 1224 E-11
Frederick, 8679 D-13
FREMONT CO., 46824 I-12
Frisco, 2683 F-11
Fruita, 12646 G-4
Fruitvale, 7675 H-3
GARFIELD CO., 56389 F-6
Genesee, 3609 *J-1
Georgetown, 1034 E-12
Gilcrest, 1034 D-14
GILPIN CO., 5441 E-12
Glendale, 4184 *J-5
Glenwood Sprs., 9614 F-8
Golden, 18867 E-13
Goodnight, 1400 M-1
Granby, 1864 D-11
GRAND CO., 14843 D-10
Grand Jct., 58566 G-5
Greeley, 92889 C-14
Green Mtn. Falls, 640 H-13
Greenwood Vil., 13925 *K-5
Gunbarrel, 9263 *D-2
GUNNISON CO., 15324 H-8
Gunnison, 5854 I-9
Gypsum, 6477 F-9
Haxtun, 946 C-19
Hayden, 1810 C-8
Henderson, 600 *G-6
Highlands Ranch, 96713 *M-4
HINSDALE CO., 843 K-7
Holly, 802 J-20
Holyoke, 2313 C-19
Hot Sulphur Sprs., 663 D-11
Hotchkiss, 944 H-7
Howard, 723 I-11
Hudson, 2356 D-14
HUERFANO CO., 6711 L-13
Hugo, 730 G-17
Idaho Sprs., 1717 E-12
Ignacio, 697 M-7
Indian Hills, 1280 F-13
JACKSON CO., 1394 B-10
JEFFERSON CO., 534543 F-12
Johnstown, 9887 D-13
Julesburg, 1225 B-20
Keenesburg, 1127 D-14
Ken Caryl, 32438 *L-3
Kersey, 1454 C-14
KIOWA CO., 1398 I-18
Kiowa, 723 G-14
KIT CARSON CO., 8270 F-19
Kremmling, 1444 D-10
Lake City, 408 K-8
LAKE CO., 7310 G-10
La Jara, 818 M-11
La Junta, 7077 K-17
LA PLATA CO., 51334 L-6
La Salle, 1955 D-14
La Veta, 800 L-13
Lafayette, 24453 *E-2
Lakewood, 142980 *J-2
Lamar, 7804 J-19
Laporte, 2450 C-13
LARIMER CO., 299630 C-12
LAS ANIMAS CO., 15507 M-15
Las Animas, 2410 J-17
Leadville, 2602 G-10
Limon, 1880 G-16
LINCOLN CO., 5467 H-17
Lincoln Park, 3546 I-13
Littleton, 41737 F-13
Lochbuie, 4726 *E-7
Log Lane Vil., 873 D-16
LOGAN CO., 22709 B-17
Loma, 1293 G-4
Lombard Vil., 600 N-2
Lone Tree, 10218 *M-5
Longmont, 86270 D-13
Louisville, 18376 E-13
Loveland, 66859 C-13
Lyons, 2033 D-13
Manassa, 991 M-11
Mancos, 1336 M-5
Manitou Sprs., 4992 H-13
Mead, 3405 D-13
Meeker, 2475 D-6
Meridian, 2970 *M-6
MESA CO., 146723 H-5
Milliken, 5610 D-14
MINERAL CO., 712 L-8
Minturn, 1027 F-10
MOFFAT CO., 13795 C-6
Monte Vista, 4444 L-10
MONTEZUMA CO., 25535 M-4
MONTROSE CO., 41276 I-6
Montrose, 19132 I-6
Monument, 5530 G-13
MORGAN CO., 28159 D-16
Mt. Crested Butte, 801 H-9
Mountain View, 1700 *E-8
Mountain Vil., 1320 K-6
Nederland, 1445 E-12
New Castle, 4518 F-7
Niwot, 4006 D-13
N. Cherry Creek Valley, 1550 *J-5
Northglenn, 35789 *G-4
Nucla, 711 J-5
Oak Creek, 884 D-9
Olathe, 1849 I-6
Orchard City, 3119 H-6
Orchard Mesa, 6836 G-5
Ordway, 1080 J-16
OTERO CO., 18831 K-16
OURAY CO., 4436 J-6
Ouray, 1000 K-7
Pagosa Sprs., 1727 M-8
Palisade, 2692 G-5
Palmer Lake, 2420 G-13
Paonia, 1451 H-7
Parachute, 1085 F-6
Paragon Estates, 928 *E-2
PARK CO., 16206 G-11
Parker, 45297 F-14
Penrose, 3582 I-13
PHILLIPS CO., 4442 C-19
Pierce, 834 C-14
PITKIN CO., 17148 G-9
Platteville, 2485 D-14
Pleasant View, 4100 *J-2
Poncha Sprs., 737 I-11
Ponderosa Hills, 900 *M-7
PROWERS CO., 12551 K-19
PUEBLO CO., 159063 J-14
Pueblo West, 29637 J-14
Pueblo, 106595 J-14
Rangely, 2365 D-4
Redlands, 8685 G-5
Ridgway, 924 J-7
Rifle, 9172 F-7
RIO BLANCO CO., 6666 E-6
RIO GRANDE CO., 11982 L-10
Rocky Ford, 3957 J-16
ROUTT CO., 23509 C-8
Roxborough Park, 9099 *N-3
SAGUACHE CO., 6108 K-9
Saguache, 485 J-10
Salida, 5236 I-11
SAN JUAN CO., 699 L-7
San Luis, 629 M-12
SAN MIGUEL CO., 7359 K-5
Sanford, 879 M-11
Security, 4400 *N-10
SEDGWICK CO., 2379 B-19
Severance, 3165 C-14
Shaw Hts., 5116 *H-3
Sheridan, 5664 *K-4
Sherrelwood, 18287 *H-4
Silt, 2930 F-7
Silverthorne, 3887 F-11
Silverton, 637 K-7
Simla, 618 G-15
Snowmass Vil., 2826 G-9
Springfield, 1451 L-19
Steamboat Sprs., 12088 C-9
Sterling, 14777 C-17
Stonegate, 8962 *M-6
Strasburg, 2447 E-15
Stratmoor, 6900 *M-10
Stratton, 658 G-19
SUMMIT CO., 27994 F-11
Superior, 12483 E-13
Swink, 617 K-17
TELLER CO., 23350 H-13
Telluride, 2325 K-6
The Pinery, 10517 *N-7
Thornton, 118772 E-13
Timnath, 625 C-13
Todd Creek, 3768 *F-6
Towaoc, 1087 M-4
Trinidad, 9096 M-14
Twin Lakes, 6101 *H-4
Vail, 5305 F-10
Walden, 608 B-10
Walsenburg, 3068 L-14
WASHINGTON CO., 4814 D-17
Watkins, 653 E-14
Welby, 14846 *H-4
WELD CO., 252825 B-15
Wellington, 6289 B-13
Westcliffe, 568 J-12
Westminster, 106114 E-13
Wheat Ridge, 30166 *I-2
Widefield, 4200 *N-10
Wiggins, 893 D-15
Williamsburg, 662 J-13
Windsor, 18644 C-13
Winter Park, 999 E-11
Woodland Park, 7200 H-13
Wray, 2342 D-20
YUMA CO., 10043 D-19
Yuma, 3524 D-19

Connecticut
Map p. 23

Abington, 750 B-13
Addison, 800 C-9
Amston, 780 D-11
Ansonia, 19249 F-6
Attawaugan, 660 B-13
Avon, 1800 C-8
Ball Pond, 2400 E-3
Ballouville, 660 B-14
Baltic, 1250 D-12
Bantam, 759 C-5
Beacon Falls, 1650 E-6
Berlin, 1230 D-8
Bethany, 1280 F-7
Bethel, 9549 F-4
Bethlehem, 2021 D-5
Bloomfield, 7500 B-8
Blue Hills, 2901 H-13
Branford, 5819 G-8
Branford Ctr., 5819 J-11
Bridgeport, 144229 H-5
Bristol, 60477 D-7
Broad Brook, 4069 B-9
Brookfield, 1650 E-4
Brookfield Ctr., 1550 E-4
Brooklyn, 981 C-13
Byram, 4146 I-3
Canaan, 1212 A-5
Candlewood Isle, 1260 E-4
Candlewood Shores, 1800 E-4
Centerbrook, 1000 F-10
Central Vil., 1800 C-13
Cheshire, 5786 E-7
Chester, 1558 F-10
Clinton, 3368 G-10
Colchester, 4781 D-11
Collinsville, 3746 C-7
Columbia, 800 C-11
Cos Cob, 6770 E-1
Cromwell, 2500 D-9
Crystal Lake, 1945 B-10
Danbury, 80893 F-4
Danielson, 4051 C-13
Darien, 20732 H-4
Dayville, 1650 B-13
Deep River, 1700 F-10
Derby, 12902 F-6
Double Bch., 1100 G-8
Durham, 2933 E-9
E. Berlin, 1100 D-8
E. Brooklyn, 1638 C-13
E. Canaan, 1000 A-5
E. Granby, 1300 A-8
E. Haddam, 800 E-10
E. Hampton, 2691 D-10
E. Hartford, 51252 C-9
E. Hartland, 1200 A-7
E. Haven, 29257 G-7
E. River, 3800 G-9
Eastford, 1020 B-12
Ellington, 1700 B-10
Essex, 1270 F-10
Fairfield, 57300 H-5
FAIRFIELD CO., 916829 F-4
Farmington, 3100 C-8
Flanders, 1330 F-11
Gales Ferry, 1162 F-12
Gaylordsville, 730 D-4
Georgetown, 1805 G-4
Giants Neck, 1330 G-11
Glastonbury, 7387 C-9
Goshen, 890 B-5
Granby, 700 A-8
Greenwich, 12942 I-3
Grosvenor Dale, 850 A-13
Groton, 10389 F-12
Guilford, 2597 G-9
Haddam, 1300 E-10
Hamden, 56900 F-7
Hartford, 124775 C-9
HARTFORD CO., 894014 B-7
Hazardville, 4599 A-9
Hebron, 800 D-11
Higganum, 1698 E-9
Honeypot Glen, 1200 E-7
Indian Neck, 2500 G-8
Ivoryton, 2600 F-10
Jewett City, 3487 D-13
Kensington, 8459 D-8
Kent, 1050 C-4
Lakeside, 1340 F-5
Lakeville, 928 A-4
Litchfield, 1258 C-6
LITCHFIELD CO., 189927 A-5
Long Hill, 4205 F-3
Madison, 2290 G-9
Manchester, 30577 C-10
Mansfield Ctr., 947 C-12
Marion, 850 E-7
Meriden, 60868 E-8
Middlebury, 4200 E-6
Middlefield, 1250 E-8
MIDDLESEX CO., 165676 F-9
Middletown, 47648 E-9
Milford, 51271 G-6
Milldale, 900 E-7
Mixville, 1400 E-7
Monroe, 8500 F-5
Moodus, 1413 E-10
Moosup, 3231 C-13
Mystic, 4205 F-13
Naugatuck, 31862 E-6
New Britain, 73206 D-8
New Canaan, 17900 H-4
New Fairfield, 5200 E-4
New Haven, 129779 G-7
NEW HAVEN CO., 862477 E-7
New London, 27620 F-12
NEW LONDON CO., 274055 E-13
New Milford, 6523 D-4
New Preston, 1182 D-5
Newington, 30562 C-8
Newtown, 1941 F-5
Niantic, 3114 F-12
Noank, 1796 F-13
N. Branford, 7400 F-8
N. Granby, 1944 A-8
N. Grosvenor Dale, 1530 A-13
N. Haven, 24093 F-8
N. Windham, 1000 C-12
Northfield, 710 C-6
Northford, 3600 F-8
Norwalk, 85603 H-4
Norwich, 40493 E-12
Oakdale, 910 E-12
Oakville, 9047 D-6
Old Greenwich, 6611 I-3
Old Mystic, 3554 F-13
Old Saybrook, 2039 G-10
Oneco, 750 C-14
Orange, 13956 G-7
Oxford, 2100 F-6
Pawcatuck, 5624 F-14
Pine Br., 1000 F-6
Pine Orchard, 950 G-8
Plainfield, 2557 D-13
Plainville, 17400 D-8
Plantsville, 6000 D-7
Plymouth, 1200 D-6
Point O'Woods, 740 G-11
Pomfret, 670 B-13
Poquonock, 1100 B-9
Poquonock Br., 1727 F-13
Portland, 5862 D-9
Prospect, 7770 E-7
Putnam, 7214 B-13
Quinebaug, 1133 A-13
Redding, 1500 G-4
Ridgefield, 7645 G-4
Riverside, 8416 I-3
Rockfall, 980 E-9
Rockville, 7474 B-10
Rocky Hill, 16500 D-9
Rogers, 660 B-13
Sandy Hook, 1200 F-5
Saybrook Manor, 1052 G-10
Scotland, 900 C-12
Seymour, 14300 F-6
Sharon, 729 B-4
Shelton, 39559 G-6
Simsbury, 5836 B-8
Somers, 1789 A-10
Somersville, 1300 A-10
S. Britain, 1060 E-5
S. Glastonbury, 2000 D-9
S. Windham, 1421 D-12
S. Windsor, 14000 B-9
S. Woodstock, 1291 A-13
Southbury, 3400 E-5
Southport, 1585 H-5
Stafford, 720 A-11
Stafford Sprs., 4988 A-11
Staffordville, 720 A-11
Stamford, 122643 I-3
Stepney, 750 G-5
Sterling, 660 C-14
Stevenson, 1150 F-6
Stonington, 929 F-13
Stony Creek, 830 G-8
Storrs, 15344 C-11
Stratford, 51384 G-6
Suffield Depot, 1325 A-9
Tariffville, 1324 B-8
Terryville, 5387 D-7
Thomaston, 1910 D-6
Thompson, 960 A-14
Thompsonville, 8577 A-9
Tolland, 1350 B-11
TOLLAND CO., 152691 B-10
Torrington, 36383 C-6
Trumbull, 36018 G-5
Uncasville, 1420 F-12
Unionville, 4400 C-7
Upper Stepney, 1000 F-5
Vernon, 28100 B-10
Wallingford, 18209 E-8
Warehouse Pt., 2100 B-9
Washington, 700 D-5
Washington Depot, 700 D-5
Waterbury, 110366 E-6
Watertown, 3574 D-6
Wauregan, 1205 C-13
Wequetequock, 850 F-14
W. Goshen, 700 B-5
W. Granby, 700 A-8
W. Hartford, 63268 C-8
W. Haven, 55564 G-7
W. Simsbury, 2447 B-8
W. Suffield, 860 A-9
Westbrook, 2413 G-10
Weston, 1460 G-4
Westport, 26391 H-4
Wethersfield, 26668 C-9
Willimantic, 17737 C-11
Wilton, 732 G-4
Windham, 1150 C-12
WINDHAM CO., 118428 C-13
Windsor, 18800 B-9
Windsor Locks, 12498 B-9
Winsted, 7712 B-6
Wolcott, 6400 D-7
Woodbridge, 7860 F-7
Woodbury, 1294 E-5
Woodmont, 1488 G-7
Woodtick, 740 D-7

Delaware
Map p. 24

Angola by the Bay, 1200 K-5
Arden, 439 C-3
Bear, 19371 D-2
Bellefonte, 1193 C-3
Bethany Bch., 1060 L-5
Blades, 1241 K-2
Bowers Bch., 335 H-3
Boxwood, 500 C-8
Brandywine, 3600 A-9
Bridgeville, 2048 K-2
Brookside, 14353 D-6
Camden, 3464 H-2
Capitol Pk., 600 G-9
Carpenter, 1300 A-10
Centerville, 500 B-2
Cheswold, 1380 G-2
Christiana, 500 D-2
Claymont, 8253 C-3
Clayton, 2918 F-2
Dagsboro, 805 L-4
Delaware City, 1695 D-2
Delmar, 1597 M-2
Dewey Bch., 341 K-5
Dover, 36047 G-2
Dupont Manor, 300 G-2
Edgemoor, 5677 B-9
Ellendale, 381 J-3
Elsmere, 6131 C-2
Fairfax, 3200 B-9
Fairfield Farms, 700 H-8
Faulkland, 1500 C-7
Felton, 1298 I-2
Fenwick Island, 379 M-5
Frankford, 847 L-4
Frederica, 774 I-3
Georgetown, 6422 K-3
Glasgow, 14303 D-1
Greenville, 2326 C-2
Greenwood, 973 J-2
Harbeson, 400 K-4
Harrington, 3562 I-2
Hockessin, 13527 C-2
Houston, 374 I-3
Iron Hill, 500 E-5
Keen-Wik, 400 M-5
Kent Acres, 1890 H-8
KENT CO., 162310 H-2
Kitts Hummock, 300 H-3
Laurel, 3708 L-2
Lewes, 2747 J-5
Lincoln, 500 J-3
Loveville, 500 B-7
Marshallton, 1800 C-7
Middletown, 18871 E-1
Midway, 600 K-5
Milford, 9559 I-3
Millsboro, 3877 L-4
Milltown, 800 C-7
Millville, 544 L-5
Milton, 2576 J-4
Montchanin, 300 B-8
New Castle, 5285 D-2
NEW CASTLE CO., 538479 E-2
Newark, 31454 C-1
Newport, 1055 C-2
N. Star, 7980 C-1
Oak Orchard, 500 L-5
Ocean View, 1882 L-5
Odessa, 364 E-2
Ogletown, 600 C-2
Pike Creek, 7898 C-6
Pike Creek Valley, 11217 C-6
Rehoboth Bch., 1327 K-5
Riverdale, 500 L-4
Rodney Vil., 1487 H-2
St. Georges, 350 D-2
Seaford, 6928 K-2
Selbyville, 2167 M-4
Shawnee Acres, 450 I-3
Smyrna, 10023 F-2
S. Bethany, 449 L-5
Stanton, 3100 C-7
SUSSEX CO., 197145 K-3
Talleyville, 800 C-2
Townsend, 2049 F-2
Ways Corner, 800 A-9
Wilmington, 70851 C-2
Wilmington Manor, 7889 D-8
Wyoming, 1313 H-2
Yorklyn, 300 C-2

District of Columbia
Map p. 111

Washington, 601723 E-6

Florida
Map pp. 26 – 27

* City keyed to p. 24
† City keyed to p. 25

Alachua, 9059 D-7
ALACHUA CO., 247336 E-7
Alafaya, 78113 H-10
Allentown, 894 Q-3
Altamonte Sprs., 41496 H-10
Alturas, 4185 J-9
Alva, 2596 N-9
Anglers Pk., 980 R-13
Anna Maria, 1503 K-6
Anthony, 1150 F-8
Apalachicola, 2231 T-8
Apopka, 41542 H-10
Arcadia, 7637 L-9
Archer, 1118 E-7
Asbury Lake, 8700 C-9
Astatula, 1810 G-9
Astor, 1556 F-9
Atlantic Bch., 12655 C-10
Atlantis, 2005 N-14
Auburndale, 13507 I-9
Aventura, 35762 P-14
Avon Pk., 8836 K-10
Azalea Pk., 12556 N-4
Babson Pk., 1356 J-10
Bagdad, 3761 R-3
BAKER CO., 27115 B-7
Bal Harbour, 2513 †K-9
Baldwin, 1425 C-8
Balm, 1457 J-8
Barefoot Bay, 3000 J-12
Bartow, 17298 J-9
BAY CO., 168852 S-6
Bay Hbr. Islands, 5628 †K-9
Bay Pines, 2931 †D-1
Bayshore Gdns., 16323 †G-3
Baywood Vil., 1300 †A-1
Bee Ridge, 9598 L-7
Belle Glade, 17467 N-12
Belle Isle, 5988 O-4
Belleair, 3869 J-6
Belleair Bch., 1560 J-6
Belleair Bluffs, 2031 †C-1
Belleview, 4492 F-8
Bellview, 23355 R-2
Beverly Hills, 8445 G-7
Big Coppitt Key, 2458 T-9
Big Pine Key, 4252 T-10
Biscayne Pk., 3055 †K-9
Bithlo, 8268 H-11
Bloomingdale, 22711 †C-5
Blountstown, 2514 R-7
Boca Del Mar, 21800 †F-9
Boca Pointe, 3300 †F-9
Boca Raton, 84392 O-14
Boca West, 2100 †E-9
Bokeelia, 1780 N-8
Bonifay, 2793 Q-6
Bonita Sprs., 43914 O-9
Bowling Green, 2930 K-9
Boyette, 5890 †D-5
Boynton Bch., 68217 N-14
Bradenton, 49546 K-7
Bradenton Bch., 1171 K-6
BRADFORD CO., 28520 D-8
Brandon, 103483 J-7
Brent, 21804 *I-9
BREVARD CO., 543376 J-12
Bristol, 996 R-8
Broadview Pk., 7125 †I-8
Bronson, 1113 E-7
Brookridge, 4420 H-7
Brooksville, 7719 H-7
BROWARD CO., 1748066 O-12
Buckhead Ridge, 1450 L-11
Buckingham, 4036 N-9
Buenaventura Lakes, 26079 I-10
Bunnell, 2676 E-10
Bushnell, 2418 H-8
CALHOUN CO., 14625 S-7
Callahan, 1123 B-9
Callaway, 14405 S-6
Campbell, 2479 I-10
Cantonment, 2800 R-2
Cape Canaveral, 9912 H-12
Cape Coral, 154305 N-8
Carrabelle, 2778 D-1
Carrollwood, 33365 †B-3
Casselberry, 26241 L-4
Cedar Grv., 3397 S-6
Center Hill, 988 H-8
Century, 1698 Q-2
CHARLOTTE CO., 159978 M-9
Charlotte Hbr., 3714 M-8
Chassahowitzka, 850 G-7
Chattahoochee, 3652 R-8
Chiefland, 2245 E-6
Chipley, 3605 Q-6
Christmas, 1146 H-11
Chuluota, 2483 H-11
Chumuckla, 850 Q-2
Citra, 950 E-8
CITRUS CO., 141236 G-7
Citrus Pk., 24252 †B-3

*, †, ‡, § See explanation under state title in this index. County and parish names are listed in capital letters and in boldface type. Independent cities (not in any county) are shown in italics.

Citrus Ridge, 12015.....P-1
Citrus Sprs., 8622.....G-7
Clair-Mel City, 7500.....†C-4
Clarcona, 2990.....M-2
CLAY CO., 190865.....D-9
Clearwater, 107685.....J-6
Clermont, 28742.....H-9
Cleveland, 2990.....M-8
Clewiston, 7155.....M-11
Cocoa, 17140.....I-12
Cocoa Bch., 11231.....I-12
Coconut Creek, 52909.....†F-8
COLLIER CO., 321520.....O-10
COLUMBIA CO., 67531.....B-7
Conway, 13467.....H-10
Cooper City, 28547.....†I-8
Coral Cove, 1160.....L-7
Coral Gables, 46780.....Q-13
Coral Sprs., 121096.....O-13
Coral Ter., 24376.....†M-7
Cortez, 4241.....†G-2
Cottage Hill, 1050.....R-2
Cottondale, 933.....Q-7
Crawfordville, 3702.....C-2
Crescent Bch., 931.....D-10
Crescent City, 1577.....E-10
Crestview, 20978.....Q-4
Cross City, 1728.....E-5
Crystal Bch., 1350.....†A-1
Crystal River, 3108.....G-7
Crystal Sprs., 1327.....I-8
Cudjoe Key, 1763.....T-10
Curlew, 780.....†B-1
Cutler Bay, 40286.....Q-13
Cypress Gdns., 8917.....†K-5
Cypress Quarters, 1215.....L-12
Dade City, 6437.....I-8
Dania Bch., 29639.....P-13
Davenport, 2888.....I-9
Davie, 91992.....P-13
Daytona Bch., 61005.....F-11
Daytona Bch. Shores, 4247.....A-14
De Funiak Sprs., 5177.....R-5
De Leon Sprs., 2614.....F-10
DE SOTO CO., 34862.....L-9
DeBary, 19320.....G-10
Deerfield Bch., 75018.....O-14
DeLand, 27031.....F-10
Delray Bch., 60522.....N-14
Deltona, 85182.....G-10
Destin, 12305.....R-4
DIXIE CO., 16422.....E-5
Doctors Inlet, 1800.....C-9
Doral, 45704.....†L-7
Dover, 3702.....J-8
Dundee, 3717.....J-9
Dunedin, 35321.....J-6
Dunnellon, 1733.....F-7
DUVAL CO., 864263.....B-8
Eagle Lake, 2255.....J-9
E. Naples, 2050.....O-9
E. Palatka, 1654.....E-9
E. Tampa, 750.....†C-4
Eastpoint, 2337.....T-8
Eaton Pk., 900.....†K-2
Eatonville, 2159.....M-3
Edgewater, 20750.....G-11
Edgewood, 2503.....N-4
Egypt Lake, 3500.....†B-3
El Portal, 2325.....†K-8
Elfers, 13986.....I-6
Ellenton, 4275.....K-7
Eloise Woods, 1900.....†K-5
Englewood, 14863.....M-7
Ensley, 20602.....R-2
Enterprise, 2000.....G-10
ESCAMBIA CO., 297619.....Q-2
Estero, 22612.....N-9
Eustis, 18558.....G-9
Fairview Shores, 10239.....M-3
Fanning Sprs., 764.....E-6
Fellsmere, 5197.....J-12
Fern Pk., 7704.....L-4
Fernandina Bch., 11487.....B-10
Ferry Pass, 28921.....R-2
Five Points, 1265.....C-7
Flagler Bch., 4484.....E-11
FLAGLER CO., 95696.....E-10
Flamingo Bay, 880.....N-8
Floral City, 5217.....G-7
Florida City, 11245.....Q-13
Florosa, 1000.....R-4
Forest City, 13854.....L-3
Ft. Lauderdale, 165521.....O-13
Ft. Meade, 5626.....J-9
Ft. Myers, 62298.....N-9
Ft. Myers Bch., 6277.....N-8
Ft. Myers Villas, 5600.....†N-2
Ft. Pierce, 41590.....K-13
Ft. Walton Bch., 19507.....R-4
Fountainbleau, 59764.....†L-7
FRANKLIN CO., 11549.....D-1
Franklin Pk., 2400.....†M-2
Freeport, 1787.....R-5
Frostproof, 2992.....J-10
Fruit Cove, 29362.....C-9
Fruitland Pk., 4078.....G-8
Fruitville, 13224.....L-7
Fuller Hts., 8758.....J-8
GADSDEN CO., 46389.....B-1
Gainesville, 124354.....E-7
Gateway, 8401.....N-9
Geneva, 2940.....G-11
Gibsonia, 4507.....†I-1
Gibsonton, 14234.....J-7
Gifford, 9590.....K-13
GILCHRIST CO., 16939.....E-6
GLADES CO., 12884.....M-10
Gladeview, 11535.....†L-8
Glenvar Hts., 16898.....†M-7
Golden Bch., 919.....†J-9
Golden Gate, 23961.....O-9
Golden Gate, 2650.....L-13
Golden Glades, 33145.....†K-8
Goldenrod, 12039.....M-4
Gonzalez, 13273.....R-2
Gordonville, 1500.....†K-4
Gotha, 1915.....N-2
Goulding, 4102.....*J-9
Graceville, 2278.....Q-6
Grand Island, 1200.....G-9
Grand Ridge, 892.....R-7
Grant-Valkaria, 3850.....J-12
Green Cove Sprs., 6908.....D-9
Greenacres, 37573.....N-13
Greenville, 843.....B-4
Gretna, 1460.....B-1
Grove City, 1804.....M-7
Groveland, 8729.....H-9
Gulf Bch. Hts., 1600.....*K-7
Gulf Breeze, 5763.....R-3
GULF CO., 15863.....T-7
Gulf Harbors, 3300.....I-6
Gulf Stream, 786.....†D-10
Gulfport, 12029.....J-6
Haines City, 20535.....I-9
Hallandale Bch., 37113.....P-13
HAMILTON CO., 14799.....B-6
Hamptons at Boca Raton, 11300.....†E-9
Harbinwood Estates, 1900.....*L-7
HARDEE CO., 27731.....K-8
Harlem, 2658.....M-11
Harold, 823.....R-3
Havana, 1754.....B-2
Haverhill, 1873.....†B-9
Hawthorne, 1417.....E-8
Heathrow, 5896.....G-10
Hedges, 800.....B-9
HENDRY CO., 39140.....N-10
Hernando, 9054.....G-7
HERNANDO CO., 172778.....H-7
Hialeah, 224669.....P-13
Hialeah Gdns., 21744.....†K-7
High Sprs., 5350.....D-7
Highland Bch., 3539.....N-14
Highland City, 10834.....J-9
Highland Lakes, 3700.....†A-2
Highland Lakes, 850.....K-10
HIGHLANDS CO., 98786.....L-10
Highlands Pk. Estates, 1100.....L-10
Highpoint, 2300.....†C-2
Hilliard, 3086.....A-8
Hillsboro Bch., 1875.....†F-10
HILLSBOROUGH CO., 1229226.....J-8
Hobe Sound, 11521.....L-13
Holiday, 22403.....I-6
Holley, 1630.....R-3
Holly Hill, 11659.....F-11
Hollywood, 140768.....P-13
Holmes Bch., 3836.....K-6
HOLMES CO., 19927.....Q-6
Homestead, 60512.....Q-13
Homosassa, 2578.....G-7
Homosassa Sprs., 13791.....G-7
Howey-in-the-Hills, 1098.....G-9
Hudson, 12158.....I-6
Hypoluxo, 2588.....†C-10
Immokalee, 24154.....N-10
Indialantic, 2720.....I-12
Indian Harbour Bch., 8225.....I-12
INDIAN RIVER CO., 138028.....K-12
Indian River Shores, 3901.....J-13
Indian Rocks Bch., 4113.....J-6
Indian Shores, 1420.....†C-1
Indiantown, 6083.....M-12
Inglis, 1325.....G-6
Interlachen, 1403.....E-9
Inverness, 7210.....G-7
Inwood, 6403.....J-9
Islamorada, 6119.....S-12
Ives Estates, 19525.....†J-9
JACKSON CO., 49746.....Q-7
Jacksonville, 821784.....C-9
Jacksonville Bch., 21362.....C-10
Jan Phyl Vil., 5573.....†K-4
Jasper, 4546.....B-6
JEFFERSON CO., 14761.....C-3
Jennings, 878.....B-5
Jensen Bch., 11707.....L-13
June Pk., 4094.....I-12
Juno Bch., 3176.....M-14
Jupiter, 55156.....M-14
Jupiter Island, 817.....M-14
Kathleen, 6332.....I-8
Kendale Lakes, 56148.....Q-13
Kendall, 75371.....Q-13
Kenneth City, 4980.....J-6
Key Biscayne, 12344.....Q-13
Key Colony Bch., 797.....T-11
Key Haven, 850.....T-9
Key Largo, 10433.....R-13
Key West, 24649.....T-9
Keystone, 24039.....†A-2
Keystone Hts., 1350.....D-8
Kings Pt., 12200.....†D-9
Kissimmee, 59682.....I-10
LaBelle, 4640.....M-10
Lacoochee, 1714.....H-8
Lady Lake, 13926.....G-8
LAFAYETTE CO., 8870.....D-5
Laguna Bch., 3932.....S-5
L. Alfred, 5015.....I-9
L. Brantley, 3000.....L-3
L. Butler, 1897.....D-7
L. Cain Hills, 1600.....N-3
Lake City, 12046.....C-7
L. Clarke Shores, 3376.....†B-10
LAKE CO., 297052.....H-9
L. Geneva, 1200.....D-8
L. Hamilton, 1231.....J-9
L. Helen, 2624.....G-10
L. Mary, 13822.....G-10
L. Panasoffkee, 3551.....G-8
Lake Pk., 8155.....M-14
L. Placid, 2223.....L-10
L. Suzy, 1040.....M-8
L. Wales, 14225.....J-9
L. Worth, 34910.....N-14
Lakeland, 97422.....I-8
Lakewood Pk., 11323.....K-13
Land O' Lakes, 31996.....I-7
Lantana, 10423.....N-14
Largo, 77648.....J-6
Lauderdale Lakes, 32593.....†H-8
Lauderdale-by-the-Sea, 6056.....†G-9
Lauderhill, 66887.....†H-8
Laurel, 8171.....L-7
Lealman, 19879.....†D-2
Lecanto, 5882.....G-7
LEE CO., 618754.....N-9
Leesburg, 20117.....G-9
Lehigh Acres, 86784.....N-9
Leisure City, 22655.....Q-13
LEON CO., 275487.....B-3
LEVY CO., 40801.....E-6
LIBERTY CO., 8365.....S-8
Lighthouse Pt., 10344.....O-14
Live Oak, 6850.....C-6
Lochmoor, 1200.....†M-1
Lockhart, 13060.....M-3
Longboat Key, 6888.....K-6
Longwood, 13657.....L-4
Loughman, 2680.....I-9
Loxahatchee Groves, 3180.....N-13
Lutz, 19344.....I-7
Lynn Haven, 18493.....S-6
Macclenny, 6374.....C-8
Madeira Bch., 4263.....J-6
Madison, 2843.....B-4
MADISON CO., 19224.....C-4
Maitland, 15751.....M-4
Malabar, 2757.....J-12
Malone, 2088.....Q-7
MANATEE CO., 322833.....K-7
Mango, 11313.....†B-5
Mangonia Pk., 1888.....†A-10
Marathon, 8297.....T-11
Marco Island, 16413.....P-9
Margate, 53284.....O-13
Marianna, 6102.....Q-7
MARION CO., 331298.....F-7
Marion Oaks, 4200.....G-8
MARTIN CO., 146318.....L-13
Mary Esther, 3851.....R-4
Masaryktown, 1040.....H-7
Mascotte, 5101.....H-9
Mayo, 1237.....C-5
Medley, 838.....†L-7
Medulla, 8892.....†K-1
Melbourne, 76068.....I-12
Melbourne Bch., 3101.....I-12
Melrose, 1100.....D-8
Memphis, 7848.....†F-3
Merritt Island, 34743.....I-12
Mexico Bch., 1072.....T-7
Miami, 399457.....P-13
Miami Bch., 87779.....P-14
Miami Gdns., 107167.....P-13
Miami Lakes, 29361.....†K-7
Miami Shores, 10493.....†K-8
Miami Sprs., 13809.....†L-7
MIAMI-DADE CO., 2496435.....R-12
Micco, 9052.....J-12
Middleburg, 13008.....C-9
Midway, 3004.....B-2
Midway, 1705.....G-10
Millview, 1100.....*J-7
Milton, 8826.....R-3
Mims, 7058.....H-11
Minneola, 9403.....H-9
Miramar, 122041.....†J-7
Miramar Bch., 6146.....R-4
Mission Bay, 2900.....†E-8
Mission City, 1700.....F-11
Molino, 1277.....Q-2
MONROE CO., 73090.....Q-11
Monticello, 2506.....B-3
Montverde, 1463.....M-1
Moore Haven, 1680.....M-11
Morse Shores, 3300.....†L-3
Mt. Dora, 12370.....G-9
Mt. Plymouth, 4011.....G-9
Mulberry, 3817.....J-8
Myrtle Grv., 15870.....R-2
Naples, 19537.....O-9
Naples Manor, 5562.....P-9
Naples Pk., 5967.....O-9
Naranja, 8303.....Q-13
NASSAU CO., 73314.....B-9
Nassauville, 1900.....B-9
Navarre, 31378.....R-3
Neptune Bch., 7037.....C-10
New Port Richey, 14911.....I-6
New Smyrna Bch., 22464.....F-11
Newberry, 4950.....E-7
Niceville, 12749.....R-4
Nocatee, 4524.....L-9
Nokomis, 3167.....L-7
N. Bay Vil., 7137.....†K-9
N. Fort Myers, 39407.....N-9
N. Key Largo, 1244.....R-13
N. Lauderdale, 41023.....†G-8
N. Miami, 58786.....P-13
N. Miami Bch., 41523.....P-13
N. Palm Bch., 12015.....M-14
N. Port, 57357.....M-8
N. Redington Bch., 1417.....†D-1
N. River Shores, 3079.....L-13
Northdale, 22079.....I-7
Oak Hill, 1792.....G-11
Oakland, 2538.....N-1
Oakland Pk., 41363.....O-14
Ocala, 56315.....F-8
Ocean Ridge, 1786.....†C-10
Ocklawaha, 860.....F-8
Ocoee, 35579.....M-2
Odessa, 7267.....I-7
Ojus, 18036.....†J-9
OKALOOSA CO., 180822.....R-4
Okeechobee, 5621.....L-11
OKEECHOBEE CO., 39996.....K-11
Oldsmar, 13591.....J-6
Olympia Hts., 13488.....†M-7
Oneco, 3200.....K-7
Opa-locka, 15219.....P-13
Orange City, 10599.....G-10
ORANGE CO., 1145956.....H-11
Orange Pk., 8412.....C-9
Orangetree, 4406.....O-9
Oriole Bch., 1420.....*J-10
Orlando, 238300.....H-10
Orlovista, 6123.....N-3
Ormond Bch., 38137.....F-11
Ormond-By-The-Sea, 7406.....F-11
OSCEOLA CO., 268685.....I-11
Osprey, 6100.....L-7
Oviedo, 33342.....H-10
Ozona, 1900.....I-6
Pace, 20039.....R-3
Pahokee, 5649.....M-12
Paisley, 818.....G-9
Palatka, 10558.....E-9
Palm Bay, 103190.....I-12
PALM BEACH CO., 1320134.....N-12
Palm Bch., 8348.....N-14
Palm Bch. Gdns., 48452.....M-13
Palm City, 23120.....L-13
Palm Coast, 75180.....E-10
Palm Hbr., 57439.....I-6
Palm Shores, 900.....I-12
Palm Sprs., 18928.....†B-10
Palm Sprs. North, 5253.....†J-7
Palm Valley, 20019.....C-10
Palma Sola, 3100.....†F-2
Palmetto, 12606.....K-7
Palmetto Bay, 23410.....Q-13
Palmetto Estates, 13535.....†N-7
Panacea, 816.....C-2
Panama City, 36484.....S-6
Panama City Bch., 12018.....S-5
Parker, 4317.....S-6
Parkland, 23962.....†F-8
PASCO CO., 464697.....I-7
Pebble Creek, 7622.....†A-4
Pelican Bay, 6346.....O-9
Pembroke Pk., 6102.....†J-9
Pembroke Pines, 154750.....P-13
Pensacola, 51923.....R-2
Pensacola Bch., 1200.....R-3
Perry, 7017.....C-4
Pierson, 1736.....F-10
Pine Castle, 10805.....N-4
Pine Forest, 2500.....*I-8
Pine Hills, 60076.....H-10
Pinecrest, 18223.....†N-7
PINELLAS CO., 916542.....J-6
Pinellas Pk., 49079.....J-6
Pinewood, 16520.....†K-8
Plant City, 34721.....J-8
Plantation, 84955.....†H-8
Pleasant Grv., 1000.....*J-8
Plymouth, 1250.....L-2
Poinciana, 53193.....I-10
Poincianna Pl., 1100.....N-13
Polk City, 1562.....I-9
POLK CO., 602095.....J-9
Pomona Pk., 912.....E-9
Pompano Bch., 99845.....O-14
Ponce Inlet, 3032.....F-11
Ponte Vedra Bch., 3000.....C-10
Port Charlotte, 54392.....M-8
Port LaBelle, 3530.....M-10
Port Orange, 56048.....F-11
Port Richey, 2671.....I-6
Port St. Joe, 3445.....T-7
Port St. John, 12267.....E-12
Port St. Lucie, 164603.....L-13
Port Salerno, 10091.....L-13
Princeton, 22038.....Q-13
Progress Vil., 5392.....†C-4
Punta Gorda, 16641.....M-8
Punta Rassa, 1750.....N-8
PUTNAM CO., 74364.....E-9
Quincy, 7972.....B-1
Rainbow Lakes, 1550.....†C-9
Rainbow Lakes Estates, 1050.....F-7
Ratliff, 2000.....B-9
Redington Bch., 1427.....†D-1
Redington Shores, 2121.....J-6
Richmond Hts., 8541.....Q-13
Ridge Manor, 4513.....H-8
River Pk., 5222.....L-13
Riverview, 71050.....J-7
Riviera Bch., 32488.....M-14
Rockledge, 24926.....I-12
Roseland, 1472.....J-12
Rotonda, 8759.....M-8
Royal Palm Bch., 34140.....N-13
Royal Palm Estates, 3025.....†B-9
Ruskin, 17208.....K-7
Safety Hbr., 16884.....J-6
St. Augustine, 12975.....D-10
St. Augustine Bch., 6176.....D-10
St. Augustine Shores, 7359.....D-10
St. Cloud, 35183.....I-10
St. James City, 3784.....N-8
St. Joe Bch., 850.....T-7
ST. JOHNS CO., 190039.....D-9
St. Leo, 1340.....I-8
ST. LUCIE CO., 277789.....L-12
St. Pete Bch., 9346.....K-6
St. Petersburg, 244769.....J-7
Samoset, 3854.....K-7
Samsula, 1260.....G-11
San Antonio, 1138.....I-8
San Carlos Pk., 16824.....N-9
San Mateo, 1100.....E-9
Sandalfoot Cove, 16600.....†F-8
Sanford, 53570.....G-10
Sanibel, 6469.....N-8
SANTA ROSA CO., 151372.....Q-3
Sarasota, 51917.....L-7
SARASOTA CO., 379448.....L-8
Satellite Bch., 10109.....I-12
Satsuma, 1000.....E-9
Schall Circle, 1117.....†A-9
Scottsmoor, 1340.....G-11
Seaglades, 900.....*K-7
Sebastian, 21929.....J-12
Sebring, 10491.....K-10
Seffner, 7579.....†B-5
Seminole, 17233.....J-6
SEMINOLE CO., 422718.....H-11
Seven Sprs., 2000.....I-6
Sewall's Pt., 1996.....L-13
Shady, 800.....F-8
Sharpes, 3411.....H-12
Siesta Key, 6565.....†H-3
Siesta Lago, 1800.....P-3
Silver Sprs., 1050.....F-8
Silver Sprs. Shores, 6539.....F-8
Sky Lake, 6153.....O-3
Slavia, 1000.....M-5
Sneads, 1849.....R-8
Sorrento, 861.....G-9
S. Apopka, 5728.....L-2
S. Bay, 4876.....N-12
S. Daytona, 12252.....F-11
S. Miami, 11657.....†M-7
S. Miami Hts., 35696.....Q-13
S. Palm Bch., 1171.....†C-10
S. Pasadena, 4964.....†D-1
S. Punta Gorda Hts., 940.....M-8
S. Venice, 13949.....M-7
Southport, 1500.....S-6
Southwest Ranches, 7345.....†I-6
Southwood, 1700.....N-3
Spring Hill, 98621.....H-7
Spring Lake, 1100.....K-10
Springfield, 8903.....S-6
Starke, 5449.....D-8
Steinhatchee, 1047.....E-4
Stuart, 15593.....L-13
Summerland Key, 950.....T-10
SUMTER CO., 93420.....H-8
Sun City Ctr., 19258.....K-7
Sun Valley, 1300.....†C-9
Sunland Gdns., 1600.....K-13
Sunny Isles Bch., 20832.....†K-9
Sunrise, 84439.....†H-8
Sunset, 16389.....†M-7
Surfside, 5744.....†K-9
SUWANNEE CO., 41551.....C-6
Sweetwater, 13499.....P-13
Sweetwater Creek, 6600.....†B-3
Sweetwater Oaks, 1100.....L-3
Switzerland, 2900.....C-9
Taft, 2205.....H-10
Tallahassee, 181376.....B-2
Tamarac, 60427.....O-13
Tampa, 335709.....J-7
Tangelo Pk., 2231.....O-3
Tangerine, 2865.....G-9
Tarpon Lake Villages, 1200.....†A-2
Tarpon Sprs., 23484.....I-6
Tavares, 13951.....G-9
Tavernier, 2136.....S-13
TAYLOR CO., 22570.....D-3
Temple Ter., 24541.....J-7
Tequesta, 5629.....M-14
The Villages, 51442.....G-8
Thonotosassa, 13014.....I-7
Three Lakes, 15047.....†N-6
Tice, 4470.....N-9
Tierra Verde, 3721.....†E-2
Tiger Pt., 3090.....R-3
Titusville, 43761.....H-11
Treasure Island, 6705.....J-6
Trenton, 1999.....E-6
Tropical Gulf Acres, 8200.....M-8
Uleta, 2300.....†J-9
Umatilla, 3456.....G-9
UNION CO., 15535.....C-7
Union Pk., 9765.....M-5
Valparaiso, 5036.....R-4
Vamo, 4727.....L-7
Venice, 20748.....L-7
Venice Gdns., 7104.....L-7
Vero Bch., 15220.....K-13
Vero Lake Estates, 1600.....J-12
Vilano Bch., 2678.....D-10
Villas, 11569.....N-9
Vineyards, 3375.....O-9
Virginia Gdns., 2375.....†L-7
VOLUSIA CO., 494593.....G-11
Wahneta, 5091.....†L-4
WAKULLA CO., 30776.....C-1
Waldo, 1015.....D-8
Wallace, 1785.....R-3
WALTON CO., 55043.....R-5
Warm Mineral Sprs., 5061.....M-8
Warrington, 14531.....R-2
WASHINGTON CO., 24896.....R-6
Watertown, 2829.....C-7
Wauchula, 5001.....K-9
Waverly, 767.....J-9
Webster, 785.....H-8
Weirsdale, 840.....G-8
Wellington, 56508.....N-13
Wesley Chapel, 44092.....I-7
W. Little River, 34699.....†K-8
W. Melbourne, 18355.....I-12
W. Miami, 5965.....†L-7
W. Palm Bch., 99919.....N-14
W. Park, 14156.....†J-8
W. Pensacola, 21339.....R-2
Westchester, 29862.....†M-7
Weston, 65333.....O-13
Westview, 9650.....†K-8
Westwood Lakes, 11838.....†M-7
Wewahitchka, 1981.....S-7
Whisper Walk, 5100.....†E-9
White City, 3719.....K-13
White Sprs., 777.....C-6
Wilbur-By-The-Sea, 1300.....F-11
Wildwood, 6709.....G-8
Williston, 2768.....E-7
Williston Highlands, 2275.....F-7
Wilton Mnr.s, 11632.....†H-9
Wimauma, 6373.....K-7
Windermere, 2462.....H-9
Winston, 9024.....†J-1
Winter Bch., 2067.....J-13
Winter Gdn., 34568.....H-9
Winter Haven, 33874.....J-9
Winter Pk., 27852.....M-4
Winter Sprs., 33282.....G-10
Woodville, 2978.....C-2
Wright, 23127.....R-4
Yalaha, 1364.....G-9
Yulee, 11491.....B-9
Zellwood, 2817.....G-9
Zephyrhills, 13288.....I-8
Zolfo Sprs., 1827.....K-9

Georgia

Map pp. 28 – 29

* City keyed to p. 30
† City keyed to p. 95

Abbeville, 2908.....K-7
Acworth, 20425.....D-3
Adairsville, 4648.....C-3
Adel, 5334.....N-7
Alamo, 2797.....J-8
Albany, 77434.....L-5
Alma, 3466.....L-9
Alpharetta, 57551.....D-5
Alto, 1172.....C-6
Americus, 17041.....K-5
Appling, 500.....F-10
APPLING CO., 18236.....K-10
Aragon, 1249.....D-3
Arcade, 1786.....D-6
Arlington, 1479.....M-3
Ashburn, 4152.....L-6
Athens, 115452.....E-7
ATKINSON CO., 8375.....M-8
Atlanta, 420003.....E-4
Auburn, 6887.....E-6
Augusta, 195844.....F-11
Austell, 6581.....E-4
Avondale Estates, 2960.....*E-5
BACON CO., 11096.....L-9
Baconton, 915.....M-5
Bainbridge, 12697.....N-4
BAKER CO., 3451.....M-4
Baldwin, 3279.....C-6
BALDWIN CO., 45720.....G-7
Ball Ground, 1433.....D-4
BANKS CO., 18395.....C-6
Barnesville, 6755.....H-5
BARROW CO., 69367.....D-6
BARTOW CO., 100157.....D-3
Baxley, 4400.....L-10
Belvedere Pk., 6000.....*E-5
BEN HILL CO., 17634.....L-7
BERRIEN CO., 19286.....M-7
Beverly Hills, 1000.....†N-12
BIBB CO., 155547.....H-6
Blackshear, 3445.....M-10
Blackwells, 5000.....E-4
Blairsville, 652.....B-5
Blakely, 5068.....M-3
BLECKLEY CO., 13063.....J-7
Bloomingdale, 2713.....J-12
Blue Ridge, 1290.....B-4
Bogart, 1034.....E-6
Bonaire, 900.....I-6
Bonanza, 3135.....F-4
Boston, 1315.....O-6
Bowdon, 2040.....F-2
Bowman, 862.....D-8
BRANTLEY CO., 18411.....N-10
Braselton, 7511.....D-6
Bremen, 6227.....E-2
Briar Wood Estates, 750.....*A-1
Brookhaven, 7000.....E-4
Brooklet, 1395.....J-11
BROOKS CO., 16243.....N-6
Broxton, 1189.....L-8
Brunswick, 15383.....N-12
BRYAN CO., 30233.....K-12
Buchanan, 1104.....E-2
Buena Vista, 2173.....J-4
Buford, 12225.....D-5
BULLOCH CO., 70217.....J-11
BURKE CO., 23316.....G-10
Butler, 1972.....I-5
BUTTS CO., 23655.....G-5
Byron, 4512.....I-6
Cairo, 9607.....N-5
Calhoun, 15650.....C-3
CALHOUN CO., 6694.....L-4
CAMDEN CO., 50513.....N-12
Camilla, 5360.....M-5
CANDLER CO., 10998.....J-10
Canon, 804.....D-8
Canton, 22958.....D-4
Carnesville, 577.....C-7
CARROLL CO., 110527.....F-3
Carrollton, 24388.....F-2
Cartersville, 19731.....D-3
CATOOSA CO., 63942.....B-2
Cave Spr., 1200.....D-2
Cedar Grv., 2000.....*G-5
Cedartown, 9750.....E-2
Centerville, 7148.....I-6
Chamblee, 9892.....*B-5
CHARLTON CO., 12171.....N-10
CHATHAM CO., 265128.....K-13
Chatsworth, 4299.....B-3
CHATTAHOOCHEE CO., 11267.....J-3
Chattahoochee Hills, 2378.....F-3
Chattanooga Valley, 3846.....B-2
CHATTOOGA CO., 26015.....C-1
CHEROKEE CO., 214346.....D-4
Chester, 1596.....J-7
Chickamauga, 3101.....B-2
Chicopee, 750.....D-6
CLARKE CO., 116714.....E-7
Clarkesville, 1733.....C-7
Clarkston, 7554.....*D-6
Claxton, 2746.....J-11
CLAY CO., 3183.....L-3
Clayton, 2047.....B-7
CLAYTON CO., 259424.....F-4
Clermont, 875.....C-6
Cleveland, 3410.....C-6
CLINCH CO., 6798.....O-9
COBB CO., 688078.....E-4
Cochran, 5150.....J-7
COFFEE CO., 42356.....M-8
College Pk., 13942.....*G-2
Colquitt, 1992.....N-3
COLQUITT CO., 45498.....N-6
COLUMBIA CO., 124053.....F-10
Columbus, 189885.....I-3
Comer, 1126.....D-8
Commerce, 6544.....D-7
Conley, 6228.....*G-4
Conyers, 15195.....F-5
COOK CO., 17212.....N-6
Cordele, 11147.....K-6
Cornelia, 4160.....C-7
Country Club Estates, 8545.....R-13
Covington, 13118.....F-6
COWETA CO., 127317.....G-3
Crawford, 832.....E-7
CRAWFORD CO., 12630.....I-5
Crawfordville, 534.....F-8
CRISP CO., 23439.....K-6
Crystal Sprs., 1300.....R-7
Cumming, 5430.....D-5
Cusseta, 11267.....J-3
Cuthbert, 3873.....L-3
Dacula, 4442.....E-6
DADE CO., 16633.....B-1
Dahlonega, 5242.....C-5
Dallas, 11544.....E-3
Dalton, 33128.....B-3
Danielsville, 560.....D-7
Darien, 1975.....M-12
Dasher, 912.....O-7
Davisboro, 2010.....H-9
Dawson, 4540.....L-4
DAWSON CO., 22330.....C-5
Dawsonville, 2536.....C-5
DE KALB CO., 691893.....F-5
De Soto Pk., 1200.....D-2
Decatur, 19335.....E-4
DECATUR CO., 27842.....N-3
Deenwood, 2146.....M-10
Deerwood Pk., 3000.....*E-5
Demorest, 1823.....C-6
Dock Jct., 7721.....R-13
DODGE CO., 21796.....J-7
Doerun, 774.....M-5
Donalsonville, 2650.....N-3
DOOLY CO., 14918.....K-5
Doraville, 8330.....*B-5
DOUGHERTY CO., 94565.....L-4
Douglas, 11589.....L-8
DOUGLAS CO., 132403.....F-3
Douglasville, 30961.....E-3
Druid Hills, 14568.....*E-4
Dublin, 16201.....I-8
Duluth, 26600.....E-5
Dunwoody, 46267.....*A-4
Dutch Island, 1257.....T-12
EARLY CO., 11008.....M-2
E. Dublin, 2441.....I-8
E. Newnan, 1321.....G-3
East Point, 33712.....*G-2
Eastman, 4962.....J-7
Eatonton, 6480.....G-7
ECHOLS CO., 4034.....O-8
Eden, 750.....J-12
Edison, 1531.....L-3
EFFINGHAM CO., 52250.....I-12
ELBERT CO., 20166.....D-8
Elberta, 950.....I-6
Elberton, 4653.....D-8
Ellaville, 1812.....J-4
Ellijay, 1619.....B-4
EMANUEL CO., 22598.....I-10
Embry Hills, 1600.....*C-5
Emerson, 1470.....D-3
Enigma, 1278.....M-7
Eton, 910.....B-3
Euharlee, 4136.....D-3
Evans, 29011.....F-10
EVANS CO., 11000.....K-11
Experiment, 2894.....G-5
Fair Oaks, 8225.....*B-1
Fairburn, 12950.....F-4
FANNIN CO., 23682.....B-4
FAYETTE CO., 106567.....F-4
Fayetteville, 15945.....F-4
Fitzgerald, 9053.....L-7
Flowery Branch, 5679.....D-5
FLOYD CO., 96317.....D-2
Folkston, 2502.....O-11
Forest Pk., 18468.....*H-4
Forsyth, 3788.....H-5
FORSYTH CO., 175511.....D-5
Ft. Gaines, 1107.....L-2
Ft. Oglethorpe, 9263.....B-2
Ft. Valley, 9815.....I-6
Franklin, 993.....G-2
FRANKLIN CO., 22084.....C-7
Franklin Sprs., 952.....D-8
FULTON CO., 920581.....D-5
Gainesville, 33804.....D-6
Garden City, 8778.....K-13
Garden Lakes, 4000.....D-2
Georgetown, 11823.....T-8
Georgetown, 2513.....K-2
Gibson, 663.....G-9
GILMER CO., 28292.....B-4
GLASCOCK CO., 3082.....G-9
Glen Haven, 3000.....*E-6
Glennville, 3569.....K-11
Glenwood, 1500.....D-2
Glenwood Hills, 5200.....*E-5
GLYNN CO., 79626.....M-11
Gordon, 2017.....H-7
GORDON CO., 55186.....C-3
GRADY CO., 25011.....N-4
Grantville, 3041.....G-3
Gray, 3276.....H-6
Grayson, 2666.....E-5
GREENE CO., 15994.....F-7
Greensboro, 3359.....F-7
Greenville, 876.....H-3
Gresham Pk., 7432.....*F-5
Griffin, 23643.....G-5
Grovetown, 11216.....F-10
Gumlong, 2146.....C-8
Guyton, 1684.....J-12
GWINNETT CO., 805321.....E-5
HABERSHAM CO., 43041.....C-6
Haddock, 750.....H-7
Hahira, 2737.....N-7
HALL CO., 179684.....C-5
Hamilton, 1016.....H-3
Hampton, 6987.....G-5
HANCOCK CO., 9429.....G-8
Hannahs Mill, 3298.....H-4
Hapeville, 6373.....*G-3
HARALSON CO., 28780.....E-2
Harlem, 2666.....F-10
HARRIS CO., 32024.....I-3
HART CO., 25213.....D-8
Hartwell, 4469.....D-8
Hawkinsville, 4589.....J-7
Hazlehurst, 4226.....K-9
HEARD CO., 11834.....G-2
Helena, 2883.....K-8
HENRY CO., 203922.....F-5
Hephzibah, 4011.....G-10
Hiawassee, 880.....B-6
Hinesville, 33437.....K-12
Hiram, 3546.....E-3
Hogansville, 3060.....G-3
Holly Sprs., 9189.....D-4
Homeland, 910.....O-11
Homer, 1141.....D-7
Homerville, 2456.....N-9
Honey Creek, 1060.....F-5
Hoschton, 1377.....D-6
HOUSTON CO., 139900.....J-6
Industrial City, 800.....C-3
IRWIN CO., 9538.....L-7
Irwinton, 589.....H-7
Isle of Hope, 2402.....K-13
Ivey, 981.....H-7
Jackson, 5045.....G-5
JACKSON CO., 60485.....D-7
Jasper, 3684.....C-4
JASPER CO., 13900.....G-6
JEFF DAVIS CO., 15068.....K-9
Jefferson, 9432.....D-6
JEFFERSON CO., 16930.....H-9
Jeffersonville, 1035.....I-7
JENKINS CO., 8340.....H-10
Jesup, 10214.....L-11
Johns Creek, 76728.....D-5
JOHNSON CO., 9980.....I-9
JONES CO., 28669.....G-6
Jonesboro, 4724.....F-4
Kennesaw, 29783.....D-4
Kingsland, 15946.....O-11
Knoxville, 69.....I-5
La Vista, 5000.....*D-4
LaFayette, 7121.....B-2
LaGrange, 29588.....H-3
Lake City, 2612.....*H-4
L. Lucerne, 900.....E-5
Lakeland, 3366.....N-8
Lakeview, 4839.....†N-13
LAMAR CO., 18317.....H-5
LANIER CO., 10078.....N-8
LAURENS CO., 48434.....I-8
Lavonia, 2156.....C-8
Lawrenceville, 28546.....E-5
LEE CO., 28298.....K-5
Leesburg, 2896.....L-5
Lenox, 873.....M-7
Lexington, 228.....E-8
LIBERTY CO., 63453.....K-11
Lilburn, 11596.....E-5
LINCOLN CO., 7996.....E-9
Lincoln Pk., 833.....H-4
Lincolnton, 1566.....E-9
Lindale, 4191.....D-2
Lithia Sprs., 15491.....E-4
Lithonia, 1924.....E-5
Locust Grv., 5402.....G-5
Loganville, 10458.....E-6
LONG CO., 14464.....L-12
Lookout Mtn., 1602.....A-2
Louisville, 2493.....H-9
Lovejoy, 6422.....F-4
LOWNDES CO., 109233.....O-7
Ludowici, 1703.....L-11
Lula, 2758.....C-6
Lumber City, 1328.....K-9
Lumpkin, 2741.....K-3
LUMPKIN CO., 29966.....C-5
Luthersville, 874.....G-3
Lyons, 4367.....J-10
Mableton, 37115.....E-4
Macon, 91351.....H-6
MACON CO., 14740.....J-5
Madison, 3979.....F-7
MADISON CO., 28120.....D-7
Manchester, 4230.....H-4
Marietta, 56579.....E-4
MARION CO., 8742.....J-4
Marlborough, 1600.....F-4
Marshallville, 1448.....I-5
Martinez, 35795.....F-10
Maysville, 1798.....D-6
McCaysville, 1056.....B-4
McDonough, 22084.....F-5
MCDUFFIE CO., 21875.....G-9
MCINTOSH CO., 14333.....L-12
McRae, 5740.....K-8
Mechanicsville, 1600.....*A-6
Meigs, 1035.....N-5
MERIWETHER CO., 21992.....H-3
Metter, 4130.....J-10
Midway, 2121.....L-12
Milledgeville, 17715.....H-7
Millen, 3120.....H-11
MILLER CO., 6125.....M-3
Milstead, 1500.....F-5
Milton, 32661.....D-5
MITCHELL CO., 23498.....M-5
Monroe, 13234.....E-6
MONROE CO., 26424.....H-5
Montezuma, 3460.....J-5
MONTGOMERY CO., 9123.....J-9
Monticello, 2657.....G-6
Morgan, 240.....L-4
MORGAN CO., 17868.....F-7
Morrow, 6445.....F-4
Moultrie, 14268.....N-6
Mt. Airy, 1284.....C-7
Mt. Vernon, 2451.....J-9
Mt. Zion, 1696.....F-2
Mountain City, 1088.....B-7
Mountain View, 1100.....*G-3
MURRAY CO., 39628.....B-3
Murrayville, 800.....C-6
MUSCOGEE CO., 189885.....I-3
Nahunta, 1053.....M-11
Nashville, 4939.....M-7
Nelson, 1314.....C-4
New Holland, 1200.....D-6
Newnan, 33039.....G-3
Newton, 654.....M-4
NEWTON CO., 99958.....F-6
Nicholls, 2798.....L-9
Nicholson, 1696.....D-7
Norcross, 9116.....E-5
Norman Pk., 972.....M-6
N. Atlanta, 40456.....*C-4
N. Decatur, 16698.....*D-5
N. Druid Hills, 18947.....*D-5
Oak Grv., 2850.....*D-5
Oakwood, 3970.....D-6
Ocilla, 3414.....L-7
OCONEE CO., 32808.....E-7
Oglethorpe, 1328.....J-5
OGLETHORPE CO., 14899.....E-7
Omega, 1221.....M-6
Oxford, 2134.....F-6
Palmetto, 4488.....F-3
Panthersville, 9749.....*F-5
Parkersburg, 1000.....T-11
PAULDING CO., 142324.....E-3
PEACH CO., 27695.....I-6
Peachtree City, 34364.....F-4
Pearson, 2117.....M-8
Pelham, 3898.....N-5
Pembroke, 2196.....J-12
Perry, 13839.....I-6
PICKENS CO., 29431.....C-4
PIERCE CO., 18758.....M-10
PIKE CO., 17869.....G-4
Pine Mtn., 1304.....H-3
Pine Mtn. Valley, 950.....H-3
Plains, 776.....K-4
POLK CO., 41475.....E-2
Pooler, 19140.....K-13
Port Wentworth, 5359.....J-13
Porterdale, 1429.....F-6
Poulan, 851.....L-6
Powder Sprs., 13940.....E-3
Preston, 2799.....K-4
PULASKI CO., 12010.....J-7
PUTNAM CO., 21218.....G-7
Putney, 2898.....M-5
Quitman, 3850.....O-6
QUITMAN CO., 2513.....K-2
RABUN CO., 16276.....B-7
Radium Sprs., 1400.....L-5
RANDOLPH CO., 7719.....L-3
Raoul, 2558.....C-6
Ray City, 1090.....N-7
Reed Creek, 2604.....C-8
Rehoboth, 1300.....*D-5
Reidsville, 4944.....K-10
Remerton, 1123.....O-7
Reynolds, 1086.....I-5
Riceboro, 809.....L-12
Richland, 1473.....K-3
RICHMOND CO., 200549.....G-10
Richmond Hill, 9281.....K-12
Rincon, 8836.....J-13
Ringgold, 3580.....B-2
Riverdale, 15134.....F-4
Roberta, 1007.....I-5
Rochelle, 1174.....K-7
ROCKDALE CO., 85215.....F-5
Rockmart, 4199.....E-3
Rocky Face, 1000.....B-3
Rome, 36303.....D-2
Rossville, 4105.....A-2
Roswell, 88346.....D-4
Royston, 2582.....D-8
Russell, 1203.....E-6
Rutledge, 781.....F-6
St. Marys, 17121.....O-12
St. Simons, 12743.....N-12
Sandersville, 5912.....H-8
Sandfly, 1200.....T-11
Sandy Sprs., 93853.....E-4
Sardis, 999.....H-11
Sargent, 900.....F-3
Savannah, 136286.....K-13
SCHLEY CO., 5010.....J-4
Scottdale, 10631.....*D-5
Screven, 766.....M-11
SCREVEN CO., 14593.....H-11
SEMINOLE CO., 8729.....N-3
Senoia, 3307.....G-4
Shannon, 1862.....C-2
Shellman, 1083.....L-4
Skidaway Island, 8341.....K-13
Smyrna, 51271.....E-4
Snellville, 18242.....E-5
Social Circle, 4262.....F-6
Soperton, 3115.....J-9
S. Fulton, 87000.....F-4
SPALDING CO., 64073.....G-4
Sparks, 2052.....N-7
Sparta, 1400.....G-8
Springfield, 2852.....J-12
Statenville, 1040.....O-8
Statesboro, 28422.....I-11
Statham, 2408.....E-6
STEPHENS CO., 26175.....C-7
STEWART CO., 6058.....J-3
Stockbridge, 25636.....F-5
Stone Mtn., 5802.....E-5
Stonecrest, 52000.....F-5
Sugar Hill, 18522.....D-5
Summerville, 4534.....C-2
SUMTER CO., 32819.....K-5
Sunnyside, 1303.....M-10
Sunset Vil., 846.....H-4
Suwanee, 15355.....D-5
Swainsboro, 7277.....I-10
Sylvania, 2956.....I-12
Sylvester, 6188.....L-6
TALBOT CO., 6865.....I-4
Talbotton, 970.....I-4
TALIAFERRO CO., 1717.....F-8
Tallapoosa, 3170.....E-2
Tate, 1000.....C-4
TATTNALL CO., 25520.....J-10
TAYLOR CO., 8906.....I-5
TELFAIR CO., 16500.....K-8
Temple, 4228.....E-3
Tennille, 1539.....H-8
TERRELL CO., 9315.....K-4
THOMAS CO., 44720.....O-5
Thomaston, 9170.....H-4
Thomasville, 18413.....O-5
Thomson, 6778.....F-9
Thunderbolt, 2668.....S-11
TIFT CO., 40118.....M-6
Tifton, 16350.....M-7
Toccoa, 8491.....C-7
Toccoa Falls, 900.....C-7
TOOMBS CO., 27223.....K-10
TOWNS CO., 10471.....B-6
Trenton, 2301.....B-1
TREUTLEN CO., 6885.....J-9
Trion, 1827.....C-2
TROUP CO., 67044.....G-3
Tucker, 27581.....*C-6
Tunnel Hill, 856.....B-3
TURNER CO., 8930.....L-6
TWIGGS CO., 9023.....H-7
Twin City, 1742.....I-10
Twin Lakes, 950.....O-7
Tybee Island, 2990.....K-14
Tyrone, 6879.....F-4
Unadilla, 3796.....J-6
Union City, 19456.....F-4
UNION CO., 21356.....B-5
Union Pt., 1617.....F-8
Unionville, 1845.....M-7
UPSON CO., 27153.....H-5
Valdosta, 54518.....O-7
Varnell, 1744.....B-3
Vidalia, 10473.....J-9
Vienna, 4011.....K-6
Villa Rica, 13956.....E-3
Vinings, 9734.....*C-2
Vista Grv., 3000.....*D-5
Wadley, 2061.....H-9
WALKER CO., 68756.....C-2
Walnut Grv., 1330.....E-6
Walthourville, 4111.....L-12
WALTON CO., 83768.....E-6
WARE CO., 36312.....N-9
Warner Robins, 66588.....I-6
WARREN CO., 5834.....G-9
Warrenton, 1937.....F-9
Washington, 4134.....E-9
WASHINGTON CO., 21187.....H-8
Watkinsville, 2832.....E-7
Waycross, 14649.....M-10
WAYNE CO., 30099.....L-10
Waynesboro, 5766.....G-11
WEBSTER CO., 2799.....K-4
West Pt., 3474.....H-2
WHEELER CO., 7421.....K-8
WHITE CO., 27144.....C-6
WHITFIELD CO., 102599.....B-3
WILCOX CO., 9255.....K-6
WILKES CO., 10593.....E-8
WILKINSON CO., 9563.....I-7
Willacoochee, 1391.....M-8
Wilmington Island, 15138.....K-13
Winder, 14099.....E-6
Winterville, 1122.....E-7
Woodbine, 1412.....N-11
Woodbury, 961.....H-4
Woodstock, 23896.....D-4
WORTH CO., 21679.....M-6
Wrens, 2187.....G-10
Wrightsville, 2195.....I-9
Young Harris, 899.....B-6
Zebulon, 1174.....G-4

Hawaii

Map p. 30

'Aiea, 9019.....M-4
Anahola, 2223.....H-2
Captain Cook, 3429.....M-8
'Ewa Bch., 14955.....N-3
'Ewa Villages, 6108.....M-3
Haiku, 1150.....I-9
Hālawa Hts., 4000.....M-4
Hale'iwa, 3970.....I-4
Hali'imaile, 964.....I-9
Hāna, 1235.....K-8
Hanamā'ulu, 3835.....I-2
Hanapepe, 2638.....I-2
Hau'ula, 4148.....K-4
Hawai'i Kai, 1150.....N-6
HAWAII CO., 185079.....L-10
Hāwī, 1081.....L-8
Hilo, 43263.....M-10
Hōlualoa, 8538.....M-8
Honoka'a, 2258.....L-9
Honokowai, 2200.....K-7
Honolulu, 337256.....J-5
HONOLULU CO., 953207.....I-5
Honomu, 509.....L-9
Honouliuli, 520.....M-3
Ka'a'awa, 1379.....K-4
Kahala, 800.....H-10
Kahalu'u, 4738.....L-4
Kahuku, 2614.....I-5
Kahului, 26337.....K-7
Kailua, 38635.....J-5
Kailua, 11975.....M-8
Kaimuki, 6800.....G-10
Kalāheo, 4595.....I-2
Kalihi, 1900.....G-7
Kamehameha Hts., 1100.....G-8
Kāne'ohe, 34597.....J-5
Kapa'a, 10699.....I-2
Kapolei, 15186.....M-2
KAUAI CO., 67091.....I-2
Kaunakakai, 3425.....J-6
Kea'au, 2253.....M-10
Kealakekua, 2019.....M-8
Kekaha, 3537.....I-2
Keokea, 1612.....K-7
Kīhei, 20881.....K-7
Kīlauea, 2803.....H-2
Koloa, 2144.....I-2
Kualapu'u, 2027.....J-6
Kunia Camp, 580.....L-2
Kurtistown, 1298.....M-10
Lā'ie, 6138.....J-4
Lahaina, 11704.....K-7
Lāna'i City, 3102.....K-6
Laupāhoehoe, 581.....L-9
Līhu'e, 6455.....I-2
Mā'ili, 9488.....M-1
Mākaha, 8278.....L-1
Makakilo City, 18248.....M-2
Makawao, 7184.....I-9
MAUI CO., 154834.....J-7
Maunalani Hts., 700.....G-10
Maunawili, 2040.....M-5
Mililani Town, 27629.....L-3
Mountain View, 3924.....M-9
Nā'ālehu, 866.....N-9
Nānākuli, 12666.....J-4
Niu, 570.....N-5
Pa'auilo, 595.....L-9
Pauwela, 500.....K-7
Pacific Hts., 650.....F-8
Pacific Palisades, 5600.....M-3
Pāhala, 1356.....N-9
Pāhoa, 945.....M-10
Pā'ia, 2668.....I-9
Pāpa'ikou, 1314.....M-10
Pearl City, 47698.....J-5
Pepe'ekeo, 1789.....M-10
Pukalani, 7574.....K-7
Punalu'u, 1164.....K-4
St. Louis Hts., 1000.....G-10
Sunset Bch., 660.....J-3
Volcano, 2575.....M-9
Wahiawā, 17821.....J-5
Wai'anae, 13177.....J-4
Waiakoa, 900.....J-9
Waialua, 3860.....J-7
Waiehu, 600.....I-8
Waikapu, 2965.....K-7
Waikīkī, 3000.....H-9
Wailua, 2254.....I-2
Wailuku, 15313.....K-7
Waimānalo, 5451.....J-5
Waimānalo Bch., 4481.....M-6
Waimea, 9212.....L-9
Waimea, 1855.....I-2
Waimea, 650.....J-2
Waipahu, 38216.....M-3
Whitmore Vil., 4499.....L-3
Woodlawn, 1200.....F-9

Idaho

Map p. 31

Aberdeen, 1994.....L-6
ADA CO., 392365.....K-2
ADAMS CO., 3976.....H-1
American Falls, 4457.....L-6
Ammon, 13816.....K-7
Arco, 995.....K-6
Ashton, 1127.....J-8
BANNOCK CO., 82839.....M-7
BEAR LAKE CO., 5986.....N-9
Bellevue, 2287.....K-4
BENEWAH CO., 9285.....E-1
BINGHAM CO., 45607.....L-6
Blackfoot, 11899.....L-7
BLAINE CO., 21376.....K-5
Boise, 205671.....K-2
BOISE CO., 7028.....J-2
BONNER CO., 40877.....C-2
Bonners Ferry, 2543.....B-2
BONNEVILLE CO., 104234.....K-8
BOUNDARY CO., 10972.....B-2
Buhl, 4122.....M-4
Burley, 10345.....M-5
BUTTE CO., 2891.....K-6
Caldwell, 46237.....K-1
CAMAS CO., 1117.....K-4
CANYON CO., 188923.....K-1
CARIBOU CO., 6963.....L-7
Cascade, 939.....I-2
CASSIA CO., 22952.....M-5
Challis, 1081.....I-4
Chubbuck, 13922.....L-7
CLARK CO., 982.....J-7
CLEARWATER CO., 8761.....E-3
Coeur d'Alene, 44137.....D-1
Cottonwood, 900.....G-2
Council, 839.....I-2
CUSTER CO., 4368.....J-4
Dalton Gdns., 2335.....C-1
Driggs, 1660.....K-9
Dubois, 677.....J-7
Eagle, 19908.....K-2
ELMORE CO., 27038.....L-3
Emmett, 6557.....J-2
Fairfield, 416.....K-4
Filer, 2508.....M-4
FRANKLIN CO., 12786.....M-8
FREMONT CO., 13242.....J-8
Fruitland, 4684.....J-1
Garden City, 10972.....B-6
GEM CO., 16719.....J-2
Genesee, 955.....F-1
Glenns Ferry, 1319.....L-3
Gooding, 3567.....L-4
GOODING CO., 15464.....L-4
Grace, 915.....M-8
Grangeville, 3141.....G-2
Greenleaf, 846.....K-1
Hagerman, 872.....L-4
Hailey, 7960.....K-4
Hansen, 1144.....M-4
Hayden, 13294.....C-1
Hazelton, 753.....M-5
Heyburn, 3089.....M-5
Homedale, 2633.....K-1
Horseshoe Bend, 707.....J-2
Idaho City, 485.....K-2
IDAHO CO., 16267.....G-2
Idaho Falls, 56813.....K-7
Inkom, 854.....L-7
Iona, 1803.....K-7
JEFFERSON CO., 26140.....K-7
Jerome, 10890.....M-4
JEROME CO., 22374.....L-4
Kamiah, 1295.....F-2
Kellogg, 2120.....D-2
Ketchum, 2689.....K-4
Kimberly, 3264.....M-4
Kingston, 800.....D-2
KOOTENAI CO., 138494.....C-1
Kuna, 15210.....K-2
Lapwai, 1137.....F-1
LATAH CO., 37244.....E-2
LEMHI CO., 7936.....H-4
LEWIS CO., 3821.....F-2
Lewiston, 31894.....F-1
Lincoln, 3647.....K-7
LINCOLN CO., 5208.....L-5
MADISON CO., 37536.....K-8
Malad City, 2095.....M-7
Marsing, 1031.....K-1
McCall, 2991.....I-2
McCammon, 809.....M-7
Menan, 741.....K-7
Meridian, 75092.....K-2
Middleton, 5524.....K-1
MINIDOKA CO., 20069.....L-5
Montpelier, 2597.....M-8
Moreland, 1278.....L-7
Moscow, 23800.....E-1
Mountain Home, 14206.....L-3
Moyie Sprs., 718.....B-2
Murphy, 97.....L-1
Nampa, 81557.....K-1
New Plymouth, 1538.....J-1
NEZ PERCE CO., 39265.....F-1
Nezperce, 466.....F-2
Oakley, 763.....M-5
ONEIDA CO., 4286.....N-6
Orofino, 3142.....F-2
Osburn, 1555.....D-2
OWYHEE CO., 11526.....M-2
Paris, 513.....M-8
Parma, 1983.....K-1
Paul, 1169.....M-5
Payette, 7433.....J-1
PAYETTE CO., 22623.....J-1
Pinehurst, 1619.....D-2
Plummer, 1044.....D-1
Pocatello, 54255.....L-7
Ponderay, 1137.....B-2
Post Falls, 27574.....C-1
Potlatch, 804.....E-1
POWER CO., 7817.....M-6
Preston, 5204.....N-8
Priest River, 1751.....C-1
Rathdrum, 6826.....C-1
Rexburg, 25484.....K-8
Rigby, 3945.....K-7
Riverside, 838.....L-7
Rupert, 5554.....M-5
St. Anthony, 3542.....J-8
St. Maries, 2402.....D-2
Salmon, 3112.....H-5
Sandpoint, 7365.....C-2
Shelley, 4409.....K-7
Shoshone, 1461.....L-4
SHOSHONE CO., 12765.....D-2
Soda Sprs., 3058.....M-8
Spirit Lake, 1945.....C-1
Star, 5793.....K-2
Sugar City, 1514.....J-8
Sun Valley, 1406.....K-4
Teton, 735.....J-8
TETON CO., 10170.....K-8
Troy, 862.....E-1
Twin Falls, 44125.....M-4
TWIN FALLS CO., 77230.....M-4
Tyhee, 1123.....L-7
Ucon, 1108.....K-7
VALLEY CO., 9862.....I-3
Victor, 1928.....K-9
Wallace, 784.....D-2
WASHINGTON CO., 10198.....I-1
Weiser, 5507.....J-1
Wendell, 2782.....L-4
Wilder, 1533.....K-1

Illinois

Map pp. 32 – 33

* City keyed to pp. 34 – 35
† City keyed to p. 57

Abingdon, 3319.....G-6
ADAMS CO., 67103.....J-3
Addison, 36942.....*H-5
Albany, 891.....C-6
Albers, 1190.....O-8
Albion, 1988.....P-12
Aledo, 3640.....E-5
ALEXANDER CO., 8238.....T-8
Alexis, 831.....F-5
Algonquin, 30046.....B-11
Alorton, 2002.....†I-8
Alsip, 19277.....*K-8
Altamont, 2319.....M-10
Alton, 27865.....N-6
Amboy, 2500.....D-9
Andalusia, 1178.....E-5
Anna, 4442.....S-9
Annawan, 878.....E-7
Antioch, 14430.....A-12
Arbury Hills, 1770.....*M-7
Arcola, 2916.....K-11
Argenta, 947.....J-10
Arlington Hts., 75101.....B-12
Arthur, 2288.....K-11
Ashkum, 761.....G-12
Ashland, 1333.....J-7
Ashmore, 785.....K-12
Ashton, 972.....C-9
Assumption, 1168.....K-9
Astoria, 1141.....I-6
Athens, 1988.....J-7
Atkinson, 972.....E-7
Atlanta, 1692.....I-9
Atwood, 1224.....J-11
Auburn, 4771.....K-7
Aurora, 197899.....C-11
Aviston, 1945.....O-8
Avon, 799.....G-6
Bannockburn, 1583.....*D-7
Barrington, 10327.....B-12
Barrington Hills, 4209.....*E-3
Barry, 1318.....K-4
Bartlett, 41208.....*G-3
Bartonville, 6471.....H-8
Batavia, 26045.....C-11
Beach Pk., 13638.....A-12
Beardstown, 6123.....J-6
Beecher, 4359.....E-13
Belleville, 44478.....O-7
Bellevue, 1978.....G-8
Bellwood, 19071.....*H-7
Belvidere, 25585.....B-10
Bement, 1730.....J-11
Benld, 1556.....M-7
Bensenville, 18352.....*G-6
Benton, 7087.....Q-10
Berkeley, 5209.....*H-6
Berwyn, 56657.....*I-8
Bethalto, 9521.....N-7
Bethany, 1352.....K-10
Big Rock, 1126.....C-11
Bloomingdale, 22018.....C-12
Bloomington, 76610.....H-9
Blue Island, 23706.....*K-9
Blue Mound, 1158.....K-9
Bolingbrook, 73366.....D-12
BOND CO., 17768.....N-8
BOONE CO., 54165.....B-10
Bourbonnais, 18631.....F-12
Braceville, 793.....E-11
Bradford, 768.....F-8
Bradley, 15895.....F-13
Braidwood, 6191.....E-12
Breese, 4442.....O-8
Bridgeport, 1886.....N-13
Bridgeview, 16446.....*J-7
Brighton, 2254.....M-6
Brimfield, 868.....G-7
Broadview, 7932.....*I-7
Brookfield, 18978.....*I-7
Brookport, 984.....T-10
BROWN CO., 6937.....J-5
Brownstown, 759.....M-10
Buffalo Grv., 41496.....B-12
Bull Valley, 1077.....*B-2
Bunker Hill, 1774.....M-7
Burbank, 28925.....*J-8
BUREAU CO., 34978.....E-8
Burnham, 4206.....*L-10
Burr Ridge, 10559.....*J-6
Bushnell, 3117.....H-5
Butterfield, 3750.....*I-5
Byron, 3753.....B-9
Cahokia, 15241.....O-6
Cairo, 2831.....T-9
CALHOUN CO., 5089.....L-5
Calumet City, 37042.....*L-10
Calumet Pk., 7835.....*L-9
Cambria, 1228.....R-9
Cambridge, 2160.....E-6
Camp Pt., 1132.....J-4
Campton Hills, 11131.....*H-1
Canton, 14704.....H-7
Capron, 1376.....A-10
Carbon Cliff, 2134.....S-5
Carbondale, 25902.....R-9
Carlinville, 5917.....L-7
Carlyle, 3281.....O-8
Carmi, 5240.....Q-12
Carol Stream, 39711.....*H-4
Carpentersville, 37691.....B-11
Carrier Mills, 1653.....R-10
CARROLL CO., 15387.....C-7
Carrollton, 2484.....L-6
Carterville, 5496.....R-9
Carthage, 2605.....H-4
Cary, 18271.....B-11
Casey, 2769.....L-12
Caseyville, 4245.....†H-9
CASS CO., 13642.....J-6
Catlin, 2040.....I-13
Central City, 1172.....O-9
Centralia, 13032.....O-9
Centreville, 5309.....†I-8
Cerro Gordo, 1403.....J-10
Champaign, 81055.....I-11
CHAMPAIGN CO., 201081.....J-12
Channahon, 12560.....E-11
Charleston, 21838.....L-12
Chatham, 11500.....K-7
Chatsworth, 1205.....G-11
Chebanse, 1062.....F-12
Chenoa, 1785.....G-10
Cherry Valley, 3162.....B-10
Chester, 8586.....Q-7
Chicago, 2695598.....C-13
Chicago Hts., 30276.....D-13
Chicago Ridge, 14305.....*K-8
Chillicothe, 6097.....F-8
Chrisman, 1343.....J-13
CHRISTIAN CO., 34800.....K-8
Christopher, 2382.....Q-9
Cicero, 83891.....C-13
Cissna Pk., 846.....H-12
Clarendon Hills, 8427.....*I-6
CLARK CO., 16335.....L-13
Clay City, 959.....N-11
CLAY CO., 13815.....N-11
Clifton, 1468.....F-12
Clinton, 7225.....I-10
CLINTON CO., 37762.....N-8
Coal City, 5587.....E-11
Coal Valley, 3743.....E-6
Cobden, 1157.....S-9
Colchester, 1401.....H-5
COLES CO., 53873.....K-11
Colfax, 1061.....H-10
Collinsville, 25579.....N-7
Colona, 5099.....T-6
Columbia, 9707.....O-6
COOK CO., 5194675.....C-13
Cortland, 4270.....C-10
Cottage Hills, 980.....†D-8
Coulterville, 945.....P-8
Country Club Hills, 16541.....*M-8
Countryside, 5895.....*J-7
CRAWFORD CO., 19817.....M-13
Crest Hill, 20837.....*M-4
Crestwood, 10950.....*L-8
Crete, 8259.....E-13
Creve Coeur, 5451.....G-8
Crystal Lake, 40743.....B-11
Cuba, 1294.....H-6
CUMBERLAND CO., 11048.....L-11
Dallas City, 945.....G-4
Danvers, 1154.....H-9
Danville, 33027.....I-13
Darien, 22086.....*J-5
Davis Jct., 2373.....B-9
De Soto, 1590.....R-9
DE WITT CO., 16561.....I-9
Decatur, 76122.....J-10
Deer Pk., 3200.....*D-4
Deerfield, 18225.....*D-7
DeKalb, 43862.....C-10
DEKALB CO., 105160.....B-10
Delavan, 1689.....H-8
Depue, 1838.....E-9
Des Plaines, 58364.....B-12
Diamond, 2527.....E-11
Diamond Lake, 1500.....*C-5
Divernon, 1172.....K-8
Dixmoor, 3644.....*L-9
Dixon, 15733.....C-8
Dolton, 23153.....*L-10
DOUGLAS CO., 19980.....K-12
Downers Grv., 47833.....C-12
Downs, 1005.....H-10
Du Quoin, 6109.....Q-9
Dunlap, 1386.....G-8
DUPAGE CO., 916924.....C-12
Dupo, 4138.....O-6
Durand, 1443.....A-9
Dwight, 4260.....F-11
Earlville, 1701.....D-10
E. Alton, 6301.....N-6
E. Dubuque, 1704.....A-5
E. Dundee, 2860.....*E-2
E. Galesburg, 812.....F-6
E. Hazel Crest, 1543.....*M-9
E. Moline, 21302.....D-6
E. Peoria, 23402.....G-8
E. St. Louis, 27006.....O-6
Eastwood Mnr., 950.....*A-3
EDGAR CO., 18576.....K-13
Edinburg, 1078.....K-8
EDWARDS CO., 6721.....O-12
Edwardsville, 24293.....N-7
Effingham, 12328.....M-11
EFFINGHAM CO., 34242.....M-11
El Paso, 2810.....G-9
Elburn, 5602.....C-11
Eldorado, 4122.....R-11
Elgin, 108188.....B-11
Elizabeth, 761.....A-6
Elizabethtown, 299.....S-11
Elk Grove Vil., 33127.....*F-5
Elkville, 928.....Q-9
Elmhurst, 44121.....C-12
Elmwood, 2097.....G-7
Elmwood Pk., 24883.....*H-7
Elwood, 2279.....E-12
Energy, 1146.....R-9
Erie, 1602.....D-7
Essex, 802.....F-12
Eureka, 5295.....G-9
Evanston, 74486.....B-13
Evergreen Pk., 19852.....*K-8
Fairbury, 3757.....G-11
Fairfield, 5154.....P-11
Fairmont, 2459.....*M-4
Fairmont City, 2635.....†H-8
Fairview Hts., 17078.....†I-9
Farmer City, 2037.....I-10
Farmington, 2448.....G-7
FAYETTE CO., 22140.....M-9
Fisher, 1881.....I-11
Flanagan, 1110.....G-10
Flora, 5070.....N-11
Flossmoor, 9464.....*M-9
FORD CO., 14081.....H-12
Ford Hts., 2763.....*N-10
Forest Homes, 1700.....†D-8
Forest Lake, 1659.....*C-5
Forest Pk., 14167.....*I-7
Forrest, 1220.....G-11
Forreston, 1446.....B-8
Forsyth, 3490.....J-10
Fox Lake, 10579.....A-12
Fox River Grv., 4854.....B-11
Frankfort, 17782.....D-12
FRANKLIN CO., 39561.....Q-10
Franklin Grv., 1021.....C-9
Franklin Pk., 18333.....*G-7
Freeburg, 4354.....O-7
Freeport, 25638.....B-8
Fulton, 3481.....C-6
FULTON CO., 37069.....H-6
Galatia, 933.....Q-11
Galena, 3429.....A-6
Galesburg, 32195.....F-6
GALLATIN CO., 5589.....R-12
Galva, 2589.....F-7
Gardner, 1463.....F-11
Geneseo, 6586.....E-6
Geneva, 21495.....C-11
Genoa, 5193.....B-10
Georgetown, 3474.....J-13
Germantown, 1269.....O-8
Germantown Hills, 3438.....G-8
Gibson City, 3407.....H-11
Gifford, 975.....I-12
Gilberts, 6879.....*E-1
Gillespie, 3319.....M-7
Gilman, 1814.....G-12
Girard, 2103.....L-7
Glasford, 1022.....H-7
Glen Carbon, 12934.....†F-9
Glen Ellyn, 27450.....*H-5
Glencoe, 8723.....B-13
Glendale Hts., 34208.....*G-4
Glenview, 44692.....*E-7
Glenwood, 8969.....*M-9
Godfrey, 17982.....M-6
Golconda, 668.....S-11
Goodfield, 860.....G-9
Goreville, 1049.....R-9
Grandview, 1441.....*L-17
Granite City, 29849.....N-6
Grant Pk., 1331.....E-13
Granville, 1427.....E-9
Grayslake, 20957.....*B-5
Grayville, 1666.....P-12
Green Oaks, 3866.....*B-6
GREENE CO., 13886.....L-5
Greenfield, 1071.....L-6
Greenup, 1513.....L-12
Greenview, 778.....I-7
Greenville, 7000.....N-8
Gridley, 1432.....G-10
Griggsville, 1226.....K-5
GRUNDY CO., 50063.....E-11
Gurnee, 31295.....*A-6
Hainesville, 3597.....*A-5
Hamel, 816.....N-7
Hamilton, 2951.....H-3
HAMILTON CO., 8457.....P-11
Hampshire, 5563.....B-11
Hampton, 1863.....R-5
HANCOCK CO., 19104.....H-3
Hanna City, 1225.....G-7
Hanover, 844.....B-6
Hanover Pk., 37973.....*F-4
Hardin, 967.....M-5
HARDIN CO., 4320.....S-11
Harrisburg, 9017.....R-11
Harristown, 1367.....J-9
Hartford, 1429.....†E-8
Harvard, 9447.....A-10
Harvey, 25282.....D-13
Harwood Hts., 8612.....*G-7
Havana, 3301.....I-7
Hawthorn Woods, 7663.....*C-5
Hazel Crest, 14100.....*M-9
Hebron, 1216.....A-11
Hegeler, 1900.....I-13
HENDERSON CO., 7331.....G-4
Hennepin, 757.....E-9
Henry, 2464.....F-8
HENRY CO., 50486.....E-6
Herrin, 12501.....R-9
Herscher, 1591.....F-12
Heyworth, 2841.....I-9
Hickory Hills, 14049.....*J-7
Highland, 9919.....N-8
Highland Pk., 29763.....B-13
Highwood, 5405.....B-13
Hillcrest, 1326.....C-9
Hillsboro, 6207.....M-8
Hillside, 8157.....*H-6
Hinckley, 2070.....C-10
Hinsdale, 16816.....*J-6
Hodgkins, 1897.....*J-7
Hoffman Estates, 51895.....*F-4
Hollywood Hts., 1060.....†H-9
Homer, 1193.....J-12
Homer Glen, 24220.....*L-6
Hometown, 4349.....*J-8
Homewood, 19323.....*M-9
Hoopeston, 5351.....H-13
Hopedale, 865.....H-8
Hudson, 1838.....H-9
Huntley, 24291.....B-11
Hurst, 795.....Q-9
Illiopolis, 891.....J-9
Ina, 2338.....P-10
Indian Head Pk., 3809.....*J-6
Ingalls Pk., 3314.....*N-5
Ingleside, 1700.....*A-4
Inverness, 7399.....*E-5
IROQUOIS CO., 29718.....G-12
Island Lake, 8080.....*B-3
Itasca, 8649.....*G-5
JACKSON CO., 60218.....Q-8
Jacksonville, 19446.....K-6
JASPER CO., 9698.....M-12
JEFFERSON CO., 38827.....O-10
Jerome, 1656.....*M-16
JERSEY CO., 22985.....M-6
Jerseyville, 8465.....M-6
JO DAVIESS CO., 22678.....B-6
JOHNSON CO., 12582.....S-10
Johnston City, 3543.....R-10
Joliet, 147433.....D-12
Jonesboro, 1821.....S-9
Justice, 12926.....*J-7
KANE CO., 515269.....C-11
Kankakee, 27537.....F-12
KANKAKEE CO., 113449.....F-12
Kansas, 787.....K-12
KENDALL CO., 114736.....D-11
Kenilworth, 2513.....*E-8
Kewanee, 12916.....E-7
Kildeer, 3968.....*D-5
Kincaid, 1505.....K-8
Kingston, 1164.....B-10
Kinmundy, 796.....N-10
Kirkland, 1744.....B-10
Knollwood, 1747.....*B-7
KNOX CO., 52919.....F-6
Knoxville, 2911.....F-6
La Grange, 15550.....*I-7
La Grange Highlands, 3650.....*J-6
La Grange Pk., 13579.....*I-7
La Harpe, 1235.....H-4
La Salle, 9609.....E-9
LA SALLE CO., 113924.....E-10
Lacon, 1937.....F-8
Ladd, 1295.....E-9
L. Barrington, 4973.....*C-4
L. Bluff, 5722.....B-12
LAKE CO., 703462.....B-12
L. Forest, 19375.....B-13
L. Holiday, 4761.....D-10
L. in the Hills, 28965.....*D-2
L. Mattoon, 1000.....L-11
L. Summerset, 2048.....A-8
L. Villa, 8741.....A-12
L. Zurich, 19631.....B-12
Lakemoor, 6017.....A-11
Lakewood, 3811.....*C-1
Lanark, 1457.....B-7
Lansing, 28331.....*M-10
LAWRENCE CO., 16833.....N-13
Lawrenceville, 4348.....N-13
Le Roy, 3560.....H-10
Lebanon, 4418.....O-7
LEE CO., 36031.....D-8
Leland, 977.....D-10
Leland Grv., 1503.....*M-16
Lemont, 16000.....*K-5
Lena, 2912.....A-7
Lewistown, 2384.....H-6
Lexington, 2060.....G-10
Libertyville, 20315.....B-12
Lily Lake, 993.....C-11
Lincoln, 14504.....I-8
Lincolnshire, 7275.....*D-6
Lincolnwood, 12590.....*F-8
Lindenhurst, 14462.....A-12
Lisle, 22390.....C-12
Litchfield, 6939.....M-8
Livingston, 858.....M-7
LIVINGSTON CO., 38950.....F-11
Lockport, 24839.....D-12
LOGAN CO., 30305.....I-8
Lombard, 43165.....*H-5
Long Creek, 1328.....J-10
Long Grv., 8043.....*D-5
Long Lake, 3515.....*A-4
Louisville, 1139.....N-11
Loves Pk., 23996.....A-9
Lovington, 1130.....K-10
Lynwood, 9007.....*M-10
Lyons, 10729.....*I-7
Machesney Pk., 23499.....A-9
Mackinaw, 1950.....H-8
Macomb, 19288.....H-5
Macon, 1138.....K-9
MACON CO., 110768.....J-9
MACOUPIN CO., 47765.....L-7
Madison, 3891.....†G-7
MADISON CO., 269282.....N-7
Mahomet, 7258.....I-11
Malta, 1164.....C-10
Manhattan, 7051.....E-12
Manito, 1642.....H-7
Mansfield, 906.....I-11
Manteno, 9204.....E-13
Maple Pk., 1310.....C-10
Marengo, 7648.....B-10
Marine, 960.....N-7
Marion, 17193.....R-10
MARION CO., 39437.....O-10
Marissa, 1979.....P-7
Markham, 12508.....*L-9
Maroa, 1801.....J-10
Marseilles, 5094.....E-10
Marshall, 3933.....L-13
MARSHALL CO., 12640.....F-9
Martinsville, 1167.....L-13
Maryville, 7487.....†G-10
Mascoutah, 7483.....O-7
Mason City, 2343.....I-8
MASON CO., 14666.....I-7
MASSAC CO., 15429.....T-10
Matteson, 19009.....*N-8
Mattoon, 18555.....L-11
Maywood, 24090.....*H-7
Mazon, 1015.....E-11
McCullom Lake, 1049.....*A-2
MCDONOUGH CO., 32612.....I-5
McHenry, 26992.....A-11
MCHENRY CO., 308760.....A-11
McLean, 830.....I-9
MCLEAN CO., 169572.....H-10
McLeansboro, 2883.....Q-11
Meadowbrook, 1000.....†D-9
Melrose Pk., 25411.....*H-7
MENARD CO., 12705.....I-7
Mendon, 953.....I-3
Mendota, 7372.....D-9
MERCER CO., 16434.....E-5
Meredosia, 1044.....J-5
Merrionette Pk., 1900.....*K-9
Metamora, 3636.....G-8
Metropolis, 6537.....T-10
Midlothian, 14819.....*L-8
Milan, 5099.....T-3
Milford, 1306.....G-13
Milledgeville, 1032.....C-7
Millstadt, 4011.....O-6
Minier, 1252.....H-9
Minonk, 2078.....G-9
Minooka, 10924.....E-11
Mitchell, 1356.....†F-8
Mokena, 18740.....*M-7
Moline, 43483.....D-5
Momence, 3310.....F-13
Monee, 5148.....E-13
Monmouth, 9444.....F-5
MONROE CO., 32957.....P-6
Montgomery, 18438.....D-11
MONTGOMERY CO., 30104.....L-8
Monticello, 5548.....J-11
MORGAN CO., 35547.....J-6
Morris, 13636.....E-11
Morrison, 4188.....C-7
Morrisonville, 1056.....L-8
Morton, 16267.....H-8
Morton Grv., 23270.....*F-7
MOULTRIE CO., 14846.....K-10
Mound City, 588.....T-9
Mounds, 810.....T-9
Mt. Carmel, 7284.....O-13
Mt. Carroll, 1717.....B-7
Mt. Morris, 2998.....B-8
Mt. Olive, 2099.....M-7
Mt. Prospect, 54167.....*E-6
Mt. Pulaski, 1566.....J-9
Mt. Sterling, 2025.....J-5
Mt. Vernon, 15277.....P-10
Mt. Zion, 5833.....K-10
Moweaqua, 1831.....K-9
Mundelein, 31064.....*C-5
Murphysboro, 7970.....R-8
Naperville, 141853.....C-12
Nashville, 3258.....P-8
Nauvoo, 1149.....H-3
Neoga, 1636.....L-11
New Athens, 2054.....P-7
New Baden, 3349.....O-7
New Berlin, 1346.....K-7
New Lenox, 24394.....D-12
Newark, 992.....D-11
Newman, 865.....J-12
Newton, 2849.....M-12
Niles, 29803.....*F-7
Nokomis, 2256.....L-9
Normal, 52497.....H-9
Norridge, 14572.....*G-7
Norris City, 1275.....Q-11
N. Aurora, 16760.....C-11
N. Barrington, 3047.....*C-4
N. Chicago, 32574.....A-12
N. Dupo, 1380.....†J-7
N. Glen Ellyn, 1400.....*H-5
N. Riverside, 6672.....*I-7
Northbrook, 33170.....*E-7
Northfield, 5420.....*E-8
Northlake, 12323.....*H-6
O'Fallon, 28281.....O-7
Oak Brook, 7883.....*I-6
Oak Forest, 27962.....*L-8
Oak Hills, 1150.....†H-9
Oak Lawn, 56690.....D-13
Oak Pk., 51878.....C-13
Oakbrook Ter., 2134.....*I-6
Oakland, 880.....K-12
Oakwood, 1595.....I-13
Oakwood Hills, 2083.....*C-3
Oblong, 1466.....M-12
Odell, 1046.....F-11
Odin, 1076.....O-9
Ogden, 810.....I-12
OGLE CO., 53497.....B-8
Oglesby, 3791.....E-9
Okawville, 1434.....O-8
Olive Branch, 864.....T-8
Olney, 9115.....N-12
Olympia Fields, 4988.....*N-9
Onarga, 1368.....G-12
Oquawka, 1371.....F-4
Orangeville, 793.....A-8
Oreana, 875.....J-10
Oregon, 3721.....C-9
Orion, 1861.....E-6
Orland Hills, 7149.....*M-7
Orland Pk., 56767.....D-12
Oswego, 30355.....D-11
Ottawa, 18768.....E-10
Palatine, 68557.....B-12
Palestine, 1369.....M-13
Palos Hts., 12515.....*L-8
Palos Hills, 17484.....*K-7
Palos Pk., 4847.....*K-7
Pana, 5847.....L-9
Paris, 8837.....K-13
Park City, 7570.....*A-7
Park Forest, 21975.....D-13
Park Ridge, 37480.....*F-7
Paw Paw, 870.....D-9
Pawnee, 2739.....K-8
Paxton, 4473.....H-12
Payson, 1026.....J-3
Pearl City, 838.....B-7
Pecatonica, 2195.....A-8
Pekin, 34094.....H-8
Peoria, 115007.....G-8
PEORIA CO., 186494.....G-7
Peoria Hts., 6156.....G-8
Peotone, 4142.....E-13
Percy, 970.....Q-8
PERRY CO., 22350.....P-8
Peru, 10295.....E-9
Petersburg, 2260.....J-7
Philo, 1466.....J-12
Phoenix, 1964.....*L-9
PIATT CO., 16729.....J-10
PIKE CO., 16430.....K-4
Pinckneyville, 5648.....Q-8
Pingree Grv., 4532.....B-11
Piper City, 826.....G-12
Pittsfield, 4576.....K-4
Plainfield, 39581.....D-12
Plano, 10856.....D-11
Pleasant Hill, 966.....L-4
Pleasant Plains, 802.....J-7
Pocahontas, 784.....N-8
Polo, 2355.....C-8
Pontiac, 11931.....G-10
Pontoon Bch., 5836.....†G-8
POPE CO., 4470.....S-11
Poplar Grv., 5023.....A-10
Port Barrington, 1517.....*C-3
Port Byron, 1647.....D-6
Posen, 5987.....*L-9
Potomac, 750.....I-13
Prairie Grv., 1904.....*C-3
Preston Hts., 2575.....*N-4
Princeton, 7660.....E-8
Princeville, 1738.....F-7
Prophetstown, 2080.....D-7
Prospect Hts., 16256.....*E-6
PULASKI CO., 6161.....T-9
PUTNAM CO., 6006.....E-8
Quincy, 40633.....J-3
Ramsey, 1037.....M-9
RANDOLPH CO., 33476.....Q-7
Rantoul, 12941.....I-12
Rapids City, 959.....D-6
Raymond, 1006.....L-8
Red Bud, 3698.....P-7
RICHLAND CO., 16233.....N-12
Richmond, 1874.....A-11
Richton Pk., 13646.....*N-8
Ridge Farm, 882.....J-13
Ridgway, 869.....R-12
Ringwood, 836.....A-11
River Forest, 11172.....*H-7
River Grv., 10227.....*H-7
Riverdale, 13549.....*L-9
Riverside, 8875.....*I-7
Riverton, 3455.....J-8
Riverwoods, 3660.....*D-7
Roanoke, 2065.....G-9
Robbins, 5337.....*L-9
Robinson, 7713.....M-13
Rochelle, 9574.....C-9
Rochester, 3689.....K-8
Rock Falls, 9266.....C-8
Rock Island, 39018.....D-5
ROCK ISLAND CO., 147546.....E-4
Rockdale, 1976.....*N-4
Rockford, 152871.....B-9
Rockton, 7685.....A-9
Rolling Meadows, 24099.....*E-5
Rome, 1738.....G-8
Romeoville, 39680.....D-12
Roodhouse, 1814.....L-6
Roscoe, 10785.....A-9
Roselle, 22763.....C-12
Rosemont, 4202.....*G-7
Roseville, 989.....G-5
Rosewood Hts., 4038.....†D-8
Rosiclare, 1160.....S-11
Rossville, 1331.....H-13
Round Lake, 18289.....*A-4
Round Lake Bch., 28175.....*A-4
Round Lake Hts., 2676.....*A-4
Round Lake Pk., 7505.....*A-4
Roxana, 1542.....N-6
Royalton, 1151.....Q-9
Rushville, 3192.....I-5
St. Anne, 1257.....F-13
St. Charles, 32974.....C-11
ST. CLAIR CO., 270056.....O-7
St. Elmo, 1426.....M-10
St. Jacob, 1098.....N-7
St. Joseph, 3967.....I-12
Salem, 7485.....O-10
SALINE CO., 24913.....R-11
Sandoval, 1274.....O-9
Sandwich, 7421.....D-10
SANGAMON CO., 197465.....K-7
Sauk Vil., 10506.....*N-10
Savanna, 3062.....B-6
Savoy, 7280.....J-11
Schaumburg, 74227.....B-12
Schiller Pk., 11793.....*G-7
SCHUYLER CO., 7544.....I-5
SCOTT CO., 5355.....K-5
Seneca, 2371.....E-10
Sesser, 1931.....Q-9
Shabbona, 925.....C-10
Shannon, 757.....B-7
Shawneetown, 1239.....R-12
Sheffield, 926.....E-7
SHELBY CO., 22363.....K-10
Shelbyville, 4700.....L-10
Sheldon, 1070.....G-13
Sheridan, 2137.....D-10
Sherman, 4148.....J-8
Shiloh, 12651.....†I-10
Shorewood, 15615.....D-12
Sidney, 1233.....J-12
Silver Lake, 800.....*C-3
Silvis, 7479.....S-5
Skokie, 64784.....B-13
Sleepy Hollow, 3304.....*E-2
Smithton, 3693.....O-7
Somonauk, 1893.....D-10
S. Barrington, 4565.....*E-4
S. Beloit, 7892.....A-9
S. Chicago Hts., 4139.....*N-9
S. Elgin, 21985.....*G-2
S. Holland, 22030.....*M-10
S. Jacksonville, 3331.....K-6
S. Pekin, 1146.....H-8
S. Roxana, 2053.....†E-8
Southern View, 1642.....*M-16
Sparta, 4302.....P-7
Spaulding, 873.....J-8
Spring Grv., 5778.....A-11
Spring Valley, 5558.....E-9
Springfield, 116250.....J-8
STARK CO., 5994.....F-7
State Park Pl., 2600.....†H-9
Staunton, 5139.....M-7
Steeleville, 2083.....Q-8
Steger, 9570.....D-13
STEPHENSON CO., 47711.....A-8
Sterling, 15370.....C-8
Stickney, 6786.....*I-8
Stillman Valley, 1120.....B-9
Stockton, 1862.....A-7
Stone Pk., 4946.....*H-7
Stonington, 932.....K-9
Streamwood, 39858.....*F-3
Streator, 13710.....F-10
Stronghurst, 883.....G-4
Sugar Grv., 8997.....C-11
Sullivan, 4440.....K-10
Summit, 11054.....*J-7
Sumner, 3174.....N-13
Swansea, 13430.....O-7
Sycamore, 17519.....C-10
Tampico, 790.....D-7
Taylorville, 11246.....K-9
TAZEWELL CO., 135394.....H-8
Teutopolis, 1530.....M-11
Third Lake, 1182.....*A-5
Thomasboro, 1126.....I-12
Thornton, 2338.....*M-10
Tilden, 934.....P-7
Tilton, 2724.....I-13
Timberlane, 934.....A-10
Tinley Pk., 56703.....D-13
Tiskilwa, 829.....E-8
Toledo, 1238.....L-12
Tolono, 3447.....J-11
Toluca, 1414.....F-9
Tonica, 768.....E-9
Toulon, 1292.....F-7
Tower Lake, 1283.....*C-4
Tremont, 2236.....H-8
Trenton, 2715.....O-8
Troy, 9888.....N-7
Tuscola, 4480.....J-11
UNION CO., 17808.....S-9
University Pk., 7129.....E-13
Urbana, 41250.....I-12
Utica, 1352.....E-9
Valley View, 2100.....*G-2
Valmeyer, 1263.....P-6
Vandalia, 7042.....M-9
Venice, 1890.....†H-7
VERMILION CO., 81625.....J-13
Vernon Hills, 25113.....*C-6
Vienna, 1434.....S-10
Villa Grv., 2537.....J-12
Villa Hills, 1410.....†J-8
Villa Pk., 21904.....*H-5
Viola, 955.....E-5
Virden, 3425.....L-7
Virginia, 1611.....J-6
Volo, 2929.....A-12
WABASH CO., 11947.....O-13
Wadsworth, 3815.....A-12
Walnut, 1416.....D-8
Wamac, 1185.....O-9
Warren, 1428.....A-7
WARREN CO., 17707.....G-5
Warrensburg, 1210.....J-9
Warrenville, 13140.....*I-3
Warsaw, 1607.....H-3
Washburn, 1155.....F-9
Washington, 15134.....G-8
WASHINGTON CO., 14716.....P-8
Washington Pk., 4196.....†H-8
Wataga, 843.....F-6
Waterloo, 9811.....P-6
Waterman, 1506.....C-10
Watseka, 5255.....G-13
Watson, 754.....M-11
Wauconda, 13603.....B-12
Waukegan, 89078.....A-12
Waverly, 1307.....K-7
Wayne, 2431.....*G-3
Wayne City, 1032.....P-11
WAYNE CO., 16760.....O-11
Wenona, 1056.....F-9
W. Chicago, 27086.....*H-3
W. Dundee, 7331.....*E-2
W. Frankfort, 8182.....Q-10
W. Peoria, 4458.....*I-15
W. Salem, 897.....O-12
Westchester, 16718.....*I-7
Western Sprs., 12975.....*I-6
Westmont, 24685.....*J-5
Westville, 3202.....J-13
Wheaton, 52894.....C-12
Wheeling, 37648.....*E-6
WHITE CO., 14665.....P-11
White Hall, 2520.....L-6
WHITESIDE CO., 58498.....C-7
WILL CO., 677560.....E-12
WILLIAMSON CO., 66357.....R-10
Williamsville, 1476.....J-8
Willow Sprs., 5524.....*J-7
Willowbrook, 8540.....*J-6
Wilmette, 27087.....B-13
Wilmington, 5724.....E-12
Winchester, 1593.....K-5
Windsor, 1187.....L-11
Winfield, 9080.....*H-4
Winnebago, 3101.....B-9
WINNEBAGO CO., 295266.....A-9
Winnetka, 12187.....B-13
Winthrop Hbr., 6742.....A-13
Witt, 903.....L-8
Wonder Lake, 4026.....A-11
Wood Dale, 13770.....*G-6
Wood River, 10657.....N-6
WOODFORD CO., 38664.....G-9
Woodhull, 811.....F-6
Woodridge, 32971.....*J-5
Woodstock, 24770.....A-11
Worden, 1044.....N-7
Worth, 10789.....*K-8
Wyanet, 991.....E-8
Wyoming, 1429.....F-7
Yorkville, 16921.....D-11
Zeigler, 1801.....Q-9
Zion, 24413.....A-13

Indiana

Map pp. 36 – 37

* City keyed to p. 35

ADAMS CO., 34387.....E-13
Akron, 1167.....D-9
Albany, 2165.....H-12
Albion, 2349.....B-11
Alexandria, 5145.....H-10
ALLEN CO., 355329.....D-12
Anderson, 56129.....I-10
Andrews, 1149.....E-11
Angola, 8612.....A-13
Arcadia, 1666.....H-9
Ardmore, 2200.....*I-18
Argos, 1691.....C-8
Ashley, 983.....B-13
Atlanta, 725.....H-9
Attica, 3245.....H-5
Auburn, 12731.....C-13
Aurora, 3750.....N-13
Austin, 4295.....O-10
Avilla, 2401.....C-12
Avon, 12446.....J-8
Bainbridge, 746.....J-6
Barbee, 900.....C-10
Bargersville, 4013.....L-9
BARTHOLOMEW CO., 76794.....M-9
Bass Lake, 1195.....C-7
Batesville, 6520.....M-12
Battle Ground, 1334.....G-6
Bedford, 13413.....O-7
Beech Grove, 14192.....K-9
BENTON CO., 8854.....F-4
Berne, 3999.....F-13
Bicknell, 2915.....O-4
BLACKFORD CO., 12766.....G-12
Bloomfield, 2405.....N-6
Bloomington, 80405.....M-7
Bluffton, 9897.....F-12
BOONE CO., 56640.....I-8
Boonville, 6246.....S-4
Borden, 808.....Q-9
Boswell, 778.....G-4
Bourbon, 1810.....C-9
Brazil, 7912.....L-5
Bremen, 4588.....B-9
Bright, 5693.....M-14
Bristol, 1602.....A-10
Brook, 997.....E-4
Brooklyn, 1598.....L-8
Brookston, 1554.....F-6
Brookville, 2596.....L-13
BROWN CO., 15242.....M-8
Brownsburg, 21285.....J-8
Brownstown, 2947.....O-9
Buffalo, 692.....E-6
Bunker Hill, 888.....F-9
Burlington Bch., 900.....B-5
Burns Harbor, 1156.....A-5
Butler, 2684.....B-13
Cambridge City, 1870.....J-12
Cannelton, 1563.....T-6
Carlisle, 692.....N-4
Carmel, 79191.....I-9
CARROLL CO., 20155.....G-7
Carthage, 927.....K-11
CASS CO., 38966.....F-8
Cayuga, 1162.....J-4
Cedar Lake, 11560.....C-4
Centerville, 2552.....J-13
Chandler, 2887.....S-4
Charlestown, 7585.....Q-11
Chesterfield, 2547.....I-11
Chesterton, 13068.....A-5
Churubusco, 1796.....C-12
Cicero, 4812.....I-9
CLARK CO., 110232.....Q-10
Clarksville, 21724.....R-10
Clay City, 861.....M-5
CLAY CO., 26890.....L-5
Clayton, 972.....K-7
Clear Creek, 1200.....N-7
Clermont, 1356.....J-8
Clinton, 4893.....K-4
CLINTON CO., 33224.....H-7
Cloverdale, 2172.....L-6
Colfax, 691.....H-7
Columbia City, 8750.....D-11
Columbus, 44061.....M-10
Connersville, 13481.....K-12
Converse, 1265.....F-10
Corydon, 3122.....R-9
Country Vil., 1100.....H-11
Covington, 2645.....I-4
CRAWFORD CO., 10713.....Q-7
Crawfordsville, 15915.....I-6
Crothersville, 1591.....O-10
Crown Pt., 27317.....B-4
Culver, 1353.....C-8
Cumberland, 5169.....J-9
Dale, 1593.....R-5
Daleville, 1647.....I-11
Danville, 9001.....J-7
Darlington, 843.....I-6
Darmstadt, 1407.....S-3
DAVIESS CO., 31648.....O-5
Dayton, 1420.....G-6
DE KALB CO., 42223.....B-13
DEARBORN CO., 50047.....M-13
Decatur, 9405.....E-13
DECATUR CO., 25740.....M-11
DELAWARE CO., 117671.....H-11
Delphi, 2893.....F-7
DeMotte, 3814.....C-5
Dillsboro, 1327.....N-13
Dublin, 790.....J-12
DUBOIS CO., 41889.....Q-6
Dugger, 920.....N-4
Dunkirk, 2362.....G-12
Dunlap, 6235.....A-10
Dyer, 16390.....B-4
E. Chicago, 29698.....A-4
Eaton, 1805.....H-12
Edgewood, 1913.....I-10
Edinburgh, 4480.....L-9
Elkhart, 50949.....A-9
ELKHART CO., 197559.....B-9
Ellettsville, 6378.....M-7
Elwood, 8614.....H-10
English, 645.....Q-7
Evansville, 117429.....S-3
Fairmount, 2954.....G-11
Fairview Pk., 1386.....K-4
Farmersburg, 1118.....M-4
Farmland, 1333.....H-13
FAYETTE CO., 24277.....K-12
Ferdinand, 2157.....R-6
Fish Lake, 1016.....B-7
Fishers, 76794.....J-9
Flora, 2036.....G-7
FLOYD CO., 74578.....Q-9
Floyds Knobs, 800.....Q-10
Ft. Branch, 2771.....R-3
Ft. Wayne, 253691.....D-12
Fortville, 3929.....J-10
Fountain City, 796.....J-13
FOUNTAIN CO., 17240.....I-4
Fowler, 2317.....F-4
Francesville, 879.....E-6
Frankfort, 16422.....H-7
Franklin, 23712.....L-9
FRANKLIN CO., 23087.....L-13
Frankton, 1862.....H-10
Fremont, 2138.....A-13
French Lick, 1807.....P-7
FULTON CO., 20836.....D-8
Galena, 1818.....Q-10
Galveston, 1311.....F-9
Garden Vil., 4000.....A-10
Garrett, 6286.....C-12
Gary, 80294.....B-4
Gas City, 5965.....G-11
Gaston, 871.....H-11
Geneva, 1293.....F-13
Georgetown, 2876.....R-9
GIBSON CO., 33503.....R-3
Goodland, 1043.....F-4
Goshen, 31719.....B-10
Gosport, 826.....L-7
Grabill, 1053.....C-13
Grandview, 749.....S-5
Granger, 30465.....A-9
GRANT CO., 70061.....G-10
Greencastle, 10326.....K-6
Greendale, 4520.....N-14
GREENE CO., 33165.....N-6
Greenfield, 20602.....J-10
Greensburg, 11492.....M-11
Greentown, 2415.....G-9
Greenwood, 49791.....K-9
Griffith, 16893.....B-4
Hagerstown, 1787.....J-12
Hamilton, 1532.....B-13
HAMILTON CO., 274569.....I-9
Hamlet, 800.....C-7
Hammond, 80830.....A-4
HANCOCK CO., 70002.....J-10
Hanover, 3546.....P-11
Harlan, 1634.....C-13
HARRISON CO., 39364.....R-9
Harrodsburg, 691.....N-7
Hartford City, 6220.....G-12
Hatfield, 813.....T-5
Haubstadt, 1577.....R-3
Hebron, 3724.....C-5
HENDRICKS CO., 145448.....K-7
HENRY CO., 49462.....J-11
Henryville, 1905.....P-10
Heritage Lake, 2880.....K-7
Highland, 4489.....S-12
Hoagland, 821.....E-13
Home Place, 1300.....J-9
Hope, 2102.....M-10
HOWARD CO., 82752.....G-8
Howe, 807.....A-11
Hudson Lake, 1297.....A-7
Huntertown, 4810.....C-12
Huntingburg, 6057.....R-6
Huntington, 17391.....E-11
HUNTINGTON CO., 37124.....E-11
Hymera, 801.....M-4
Indian Hts., 3011.....G-9
Indianapolis, 820445.....J-9
Ingalls, 2394.....J-10
JACKSON CO., 42376.....O-9
Jamestown, 958.....J-7
Jasonville, 2222.....M-5
Jasper, 15038.....Q-6
JASPER CO., 33478.....D-5
JAY CO., 21253.....G-13
JEFFERSON CO., 32428.....O-11
Jeffersonville, 44953.....R-10
JENNINGS CO., 28525.....N-10
Jewell Vil., 700.....M-10
JOHNSON CO., 139654.....L-9
Jonesboro, 1756.....G-11
Kendallville, 9862.....B-12
Kentland, 1748.....F-4
Kingsford Hts., 1435.....B-7
Kirklin, 788.....H-8
Knightstown, 2182.....J-11
Knightsville, 872.....L-5
Knox, 3704.....C-7
KNOX CO., 38440.....P-4
Kokomo, 45468.....G-9
Koontz Lake, 1557.....B-7
KOSCIUSKO CO., 77358.....C-10
Kouts, 1879.....C-5
La Fontaine, 875.....F-10
La Porte, 22053.....A-7
Ladoga, 985.....J-6
Lafayette, 67140.....G-6
Lagrange, 2625.....A-11
LAGRANGE CO., 37128.....B-11
LAKE CO., 496005.....C-4
L. Dalecarlia, 1355.....C-4
L. Holiday, 750.....I-6
L. James, 800.....A-13
Lake of the Woods, 700.....B-8
Lake Village, 765.....D-4
Lakes of the Four Seasons, 7033.....B-5
Lakeville, 786.....B-8
Lapel, 2068.....I-10
LAPORTE CO., 111467.....B-7
Lawrence, 46001.....J-9
LAWRENCE CO., 46134.....O-8
Lawrenceburg, 5042.....N-14
Lebanon, 15792.....I-7
Leo-Cedarville, 3603.....C-13
Liberty, 2133.....K-13
Ligonier, 4405.....B-11
Linden, 759.....H-6
Linton, 5413.....N-5
Logansport, 18396.....F-8
Long Bch., 1179.....A-6
Loogootee, 2751.....P-6
Lowell, 9276.....C-4
Lydick, 800.....A-8
Lynn, 1097.....I-13
Lynnville, 888.....R-4
Lyons, 742.....N-5
Madison, 11967.....O-12
MADISON CO., 131636.....H-10
Marengo, 828.....Q-8
Marion, 29948.....G-11
MARION CO., 903393.....J-9
Markle, 1095.....E-12
MARSHALL CO., 47051.....C-8
MARTIN CO., 10334.....P-6
Martinsville, 11828.....L-8
Maryland, 800.....M-2
McCordsville, 4797.....J-10
Medora, 693.....O-9
Melody Hill, 3628.....S-13
Mentone, 1001.....D-9
Meridian Hills, 1616.....*B-18
Merrillville, 35246.....B-4
Mexico, 836.....E-9
MIAMI CO., 36903.....F-9
Michigan City, 31479.....A-6
Middlebury, 3420.....A-10
Middletown, 2322.....I-11
Middletown Pk., 850.....J-1
Milan, 1899.....N-13
Milford, 1562.....B-10
Millersburg, 903.....B-10
Milltown, 818.....Q-8
Mishawaka, 48252.....A-9
Mitchell, 4350.....P-7
Monon, 1777.....E-6
Monroe, 842.....F-13
MONROE CO., 137974.....M-7
Monroeville, 1235.....E-13
Monrovia, 1063.....K-7
Montezuma, 1022.....J-4
MONTGOMERY CO., 38124.....I-6
Monticello, 5378.....F-6
Montpelier, 1805.....G-12
Mooresville, 9326.....K-8
MORGAN CO., 68894.....L-7
Morgantown, 986.....L-8
Morocco, 1129.....E-4
Morristown, 1218.....K-10
Mt. Vernon, 6687.....S-2
Mulberry, 1254.....H-7
Muncie, 70085.....H-12
Munster, 23603.....B-4
Nappanee, 6648.....B-9
Nashville, 803.....M-8
New Albany, 36372.....R-10
New Carlisle, 1861.....A-7
New Castle, 18114.....J-12
New Harmony, 789.....R-2
New Haven, 14794.....D-13
New Palestine, 2055.....K-10
New Paris, 1494.....B-10
New Pekin, 1401.....Q-9
New Whiteland, 5472.....K-9
Newburgh, 3325.....S-4
Newport, 515.....J-4
NEWTON CO., 14244.....D-4
NOBLE CO., 47536.....C-12
Noblesville, 51969.....I-9
N. Judson, 1772.....C-6
N. Liberty, 1896.....B-8
N. Manchester, 6112.....D-10
N. Terre Haute, 4305.....L-4
N. Vernon, 6728.....N-11
N. Webster, 1146.....C-10
Notre Dame, 5973.....*I-19
Oakland City, 2429.....Q-4
Odon, 1354.....O-5
OHIO CO., 6128.....N-13
Oolitic, 1184.....O-7
ORANGE CO., 19840.....P-7
Orleans, 2142.....P-8
Osceola, 2463.....A-9
Osgood, 1624.....N-12
Ossian, 3289.....E-12
Otterbein, 1262.....G-5
OWEN CO., 21575.....M-6
Owensville, 1284.....R-3
Oxford, 1162.....G-5
Palmyra, 930.....Q-9
Paoli, 3677.....P-7
PARKE CO., 17339.....J-5
Parker City, 1419.....H-12
Patoka, 735.....Q-3
Pendleton, 4253.....I-10
Pennville, 701.....G-12
PERRY CO., 19338.....S-7
Peru, 11417.....F-9
Petersburg, 2383.....Q-4
Pheasant Run, 1200.....D-12
Pierceton, 1015.....C-10
PIKE CO., 12845.....Q-5
Pine Lake, 1700.....A-7
Pittsboro, 2928.....J-8
Plainfield, 27631.....K-8
Plymouth, 10033.....C-8
Portage, 36828.....B-5
Porter, 4858.....A-5
PORTER CO., 164343.....C-5
Portland, 6223.....G-13
POSEY CO., 25910.....S-2
Poseyville, 1045.....R-2
Princes Lakes, 1312.....L-9
Princeton, 8644.....Q-3
PULASKI CO., 13402.....D-7
PUTNAM CO., 37963.....K-6
RANDOLPH CO., 26171.....I-13
Redkey, 1353.....H-12
Remington, 1185.....F-5
Rensselaer, 5859.....E-5
Richmond, 36812.....J-13
Ridgeville, 803.....H-13
RIPLEY CO., 28818.....M-12
Rising Sun, 2304.....N-14
Roachdale, 926.....J-6
Roanoke, 1722.....E-12
Rochester, 6218.....D-8
Rockport, 2270.....T-5
Rockville, 2607.....J-5
Rome City, 1361.....B-12
Rosedale, 725.....K-4
Roselawn, 4131.....D-4
Ross, 1100.....B-4
Rossville, 1653.....G-7
Royal Ctr., 861.....E-7
Royerton, 900.....H-12
RUSH CO., 17392.....K-11
Rushville, 6341.....K-11
Russiaville, 1094.....G-8
St. John, 14850.....B-4
ST. JOSEPH CO., 266931.....B-8
St. Leon, 678.....M-13
St. Mary-of-the-Woods, 797.....L-4
St. Meinrad, 706.....R-6
St. Paul, 1031.....L-11
Salem, 6319.....P-9
Santa Claus, 2481.....S-6
Schererville, 29243.....B-4
SCOTT CO., 24181.....P-10
Scottsburg, 6747.....P-10
Seelyville, 1029.....L-4
Sellersburg, 6128.....Q-10
Selma, 866.....H-12
Seymour, 17503.....N-10
Shadeland, 1610.....G-6
Shelburn, 1252.....M-4
SHELBY CO., 44436.....L-10
Shelbyville, 19191.....L-10
Sheridan, 2665.....I-8
Shirley, 830.....J-11
Shoals, 756.....P-6
Silver Lake, 915.....D-10
Simonton Lake, 4678.....A-9
Smith Valley, 1800.....K-8
S. Bend, 101168.....A-8
S. Whitley, 1751.....D-11
Southport, 1712.....K-9
Speedway, 11812.....J-8
Spencer, 2217.....M-6
SPENCER CO., 20952.....S-5
Spiceland, 890.....J-11
STARKE CO., 23363.....C-7
STEUBEN CO., 34185.....B-13
Sullivan, 4249.....N-4
SULLIVAN CO., 21475.....N-4
Summitville, 967.....H-11
Sunman, 1049.....M-13
Swayzee, 981.....G-10
Sweetser, 1229.....G-10
SWITZERLAND CO., 10613.....O-13
Syracuse, 2810.....B-10
Taylorsville, 919.....M-9
Tell City, 7272.....S-6
Terre Haute, 60785.....L-4
Thorntown, 1520.....I-7
TIPPECANOE CO., 172780.....H-6
Tipton, 5106.....H-9
TIPTON CO., 15936.....H-9
Topeka, 1153.....B-11
Town of Pines, 708.....A-6
Trafalgar, 1101.....L-9
Trail Creek, 2052.....A-6
Tri-Lakes, 1421.....C-11
Union City, 3584.....H-14
UNION CO., 7516.....K-13
Upland, 3845.....G-11
Utica, 776.....Q-11
Valparaiso, 31730.....B-5
Van Buren, 864.....F-11
Van Buren Pk., 700.....N-7
VANDERBURGH CO., 179703.....R-3
Veedersburg, 2180.....I-5
VERMILLION CO., 16212.....J-4
Vernon, 318.....N-11
Versailles, 2113.....N-12
Vevay, 1683.....O-13
VIGO CO., 107848.....M-4
Vincennes, 18423.....P-3
Wabash, 10666.....E-10
WABASH CO., 32888.....E-10
Wakarusa, 1758.....B-9
Waldron, 804.....L-10
Walkerton, 2144.....B-7
Walton, 1049.....F-8
Wanatah, 1048.....B-6
Warren, 1239.....F-11
WARREN CO., 8508.....G-4
Warren Pk., 1480.....*D-20
WARRICK CO., 59689.....R-4
Warsaw, 13559.....C-10
Washington, 11509.....P-5
WASHINGTON CO., 28262.....P-9
Waterloo, 2242.....B-13
WAYNE CO., 68917.....J-13
Waynetown, 958.....I-5
WELLS CO., 27636.....F-12
W. College Cor., 676.....K-14
W. Lafayette, 29596.....G-6
W. Lebanon, 723.....H-4
W. Terre Haute, 2236.....L-4
Westfield, 30068.....I-9
Westlawn, 700.....D-12
Westport, 1379.....M-11
Westville, 5853.....B-6
Wheatfield, 853.....C-5
WHITE CO., 24643.....F-6

*, †, ‡, § See explanation under state title in this index. County and parish names are listed in capital letters and in boldface type. Independent cities (not in any county) are shown in italics.

Iowa

Map pp. 38 – 39

† City keyed to p. 63

Kansas

Map pp. 40 – 41

* City keyed to p. 58

Kentucky

Map pp. 42 – 43

† City keyed to p. 112

Louisiana

Map p. 44

Maine

Map p. 45

Maryland

Map pp. 46 – 47

* City keyed to p. 111

Massachusetts

Map pp. 48 – 49

Michigan

Map pp. 50 – 51

* City keyed to p. 52

Clio, 2646 O-11
Cloverville, 1950 O-5
Coldwater, 10945 S-8
Coleman, 1243 M-9
Coloma, 1483 S-4
Colon, 1173 S-7
Columbiaville, 787 O-12
Commerce, 4800 Q-11
Comstock Pk., 10088 P-6
Concord, 1050 R-8
Constantine, 2076 T-6
Coopersville, 4275 P-5
Corunna, 3497 P-10
CRAWFORD CO., 14074 J-8
Croswell, 2447 O-13
Crystal Falls, 1469 D-13
Cutlerville, 14370 *N-5
Davison, 5173 P-11
Dearborn, 98153 R-12
Dearborn Hts., 57774 *G-4
Decatur, 1819 S-5
Deckerville, 830 N-13
Deerfield, 898 S-11
DELTA CO., 37069 F-3
Delton, 872 Q-7
Detroit, 713777 R-12
Detroit Bch., 2087 S-12
DeWitt, 4507 P-9
Dexter, 4067 R-10
DICKINSON CO., 26168 C-13
Dimondale, 1234 Q-8
Dollar Bay, 1082 A-13
Dorr, 1600 Q-6
Douglas, 1232 Q-5
Dowagiac, 5879 S-5
Dryden, 951 P-12
Dundee, 3957 S-11
Durand, 3446 P-10
Eagle Lake, 1160 T-5
Eagle River, 71 A-13
E. Grand Rapids, 10694 *L-6
E. Jordan, 2351 H-7
E. Lansing, 48579 Q-9
E. Tawas, 2808 K-11
Eastpointe, 32442 Q-13
EATON CO., 107759 Q-8
Eaton Rapids, 5214 Q-8
Ecorse, 9512 *H-6
Edmore, 1201 N-7
Edwardsburg, 1259 T-5
Elk Rapids, 1642 I-6
Elkton, 808 M-12
Elsie, 966 O-9
EMMET CO., 32694 G-7
Escanaba, 12616 F-2
Essexville, 3478 N-10
Evart, 1903 M-7
Fair Plain, 7631 S-4
Farmington, 10372 *E-3
Farmington Hills, 79740 Q-12
Farrandville, 820 O-11
Farwell, 871 M-8
Fennville, 1398 Q-5
Fenton, 11756 P-11
Ferndale, 19900 *E-6
Ferrysburg, 2892 O-4
Flat Rock, 9878 S-12
Flint, 102434 P-11
Flushing, 8389 O-10
Forest Hills, 25867 *L-6
Fowler, 1208 P-8
Fowlerville, 2886 Q-10
Frankenmuth, 4944 O-11
Frankfort, 1286 J-4
Franklin, 3150 *D-4
Fraser, 14480 *D-8
Freeland, 6969 N-10
Fremont, 4081 N-5
Fruitport, 1093 O-5
Galesburg, 2009 R-7
Garden City, 27692 *G-4
Gaylord, 3645 I-8
Genesee, 2500 O-11
GENESEE CO., 425790 O-10
Gibraltar, 4656 S-12
Gladstone, 4973 F-3
Gladwin, 2933 L-9
GLADWIN CO., 25692 L-9
Gobles, 829 R-5
GOGEBIC CO., 16427 C-11
Goodrich, 1860 P-11
Grand Blanc, 8276 P-11
Grand Haven, 10412 P-4
Grand Ledge, 7786 Q-8
Grand Rapids, 188040 P-6
GRAND TRAVERSE CO., 86986 J-6
Grandville, 15378 *M-4
Grant, 894 O-6
Grass Lake, 1173 R-10
GRATIOT CO., 42476 O-8
Grawn, 772 J-6
Grayling, 1884 J-8
Greenville, 8481 O-7
Greilickville, 1530 J-6
Grosse Ile, 10300 *J-6
Grosse Pte., 5421 *F-8
Grosse Pte. Farms, 9479 *F-9
Grosse Pte. Pk., 11555 *F-8
Grosse Pte. Shores, 2823 *F-9
Grosse Pte. Woods, 16135 *E-9
Gwinn, 1917 E-2
Hamburg, 1050 R-11
Hamilton, 1170 Q-5
Hamtramck, 22423 R-12
Hancock, 4634 A-12
Harbor Bch., 1703 M-13
Harbor Sprs., 1194 G-7
Harper Woods, 14236 *F-8
Harrison, 24600 *C-10
Harrison, 2114 L-8
Harrisville, 493 J-12
Hart, 2126 M-4
Hartford, 2688 R-5
Harvey, 1393 D-2
Haslett, 19220 Q-9
Hastings, 7350 Q-7
Hazel Pk., 16422 *E-7
Hemlock, 1466 N-9
Hesperia, 954 N-5
Highland, 4000 Q-11
Highland Pk., 11776 *F-6
Hillman, 701 I-10
Hillsdale, 8305 S-9
HILLSDALE CO., 46688 T-8
Holland, 33051 P-5
Holly, 6086 P-11
Holt, 23973 Q-9
Homer, 1668 S-8
Houghton, 7708 A-12
HOUGHTON CO., 36628 B-12
Houghton Lake, 3427 K-8
Howard City, 1808 N-6
Howell, 9489 Q-10
Hubbell, 946 A-13
Hudson, 2307 T-9
Hudsonville, 7116 P-5
Huntington Woods, 6238 *E-6
HURON CO., 33118 M-12
Ida, 1020 S-11
Imlay City, 3597 P-12
Indian River, 1959 G-8
INGHAM CO., 280895 Q-9
Inkster, 25369 *G-4
Ionia, 11394 P-7
IONIA CO., 63905 P-7
IOSCO CO., 25887 K-11
IRON CO., 11817 C-12
Iron Mtn., 7624 D-13
Iron River, 3029 D-12
Ironwood, 5387 C-10
ISABELLA CO., 70311 N-8
Ishpeming, 6470 D-1
Ithaca, 2910 O-8
Jackson, 33534 R-9
JACKSON CO., 160248 R-9
Jenison, 16538 P-6
Jonesville, 2258 S-8
Kalamazoo, 74262 R-6
KALAMAZOO CO., 250331 S-6
Kalkaska, 2020 J-7
KALKASKA CO., 17153 J-7
Keego Hbr., 2970 *C-4
Kent City, 1057 O-6
KENT CO., 602622 O-6
Kentwood, 48707 P-6
KEWEENAW CO., 2156 A-13
Kingsford, 5133 D-13
Kingsley, 1480 J-6
Klinger Lake, 1000 T-6
L'Anse, 2011 B-13
Laingsburg, 1283 P-9
Lake City, 836 K-7
LAKE CO., 11539 L-6
Lake Isabella, 1681 N-8
Lake Linden, 1007 A-13
L. Michigan Bch., 1216 R-4
Lake Odessa, 2018 P-7
Lake Orion, 2973 P-12
Lakeland, 1050 Q-10
Lakeside, 1100 T-3
Lakeview, 1007 N-7
Lakewood Club, 1291 N-4
Lambertville, 9953 T-11
Lansing, 114297 Q-9
Lapeer, 8841 O-12
LAPEER CO., 88319 O-12
Lathrup Vil., 4075 *E-5
Laurium, 1977 A-13
Lawrence, 996 R-5
Lawton, 1900 S-5
LEELANAU CO., 21708 I-6
Leland, 377 I-6
LENAWEE CO., 99892 S-10
Leslie, 1851 R-9
Level Pk., 3490 R-7
Lewiston, 1392 I-9
Lexington, 1178 O-14
Lincoln Pk., 38144 *H-5
Linden, 3991 P-11
Litchfield, 1369 S-8
Little Lake, 800 E-2
LIVINGSTON CO., 180967 Q-10
Livonia, 96942 R-12
Lowell, 3783 P-7
LUCE CO., 6631 D-6
Ludington, 8076 M-4
Luna Pier, 1436 T-12
Lyons, 789 P-8
MACKINAC CO., 11113 E-7
Mackinaw City, 806 F-8
MACOMB CO., 840978 P-13
Madison Hts., 29694 *D-6
Mancelona, 1390 I-7
Manchester, 2091 S-10
Manistee, 6226 L-4
MANISTEE CO., 24733 K-5
Manistique, 3097 F-4
Manitou Bch., 1400 S-9
Manton, 1287 K-6
Marcellus, 1198 S-6
Marine City, 4248 P-14
Marion, 872 L-7
Marlette, 1875 N-12
Marquette, 21355 D-2
MARQUETTE CO., 67077 E-1
Marshall, 7088 R-8
Marysville, 9959 P-14
Mason, 8252 Q-9
MASON CO., 28705 L-4
Mattawan, 1997 R-6
Mayville, 950 N-12
MECOSTA CO., 42798 N-7
Melvindale, 10715 *H-5
Memphis, 1183 P-13
Mendon, 870 S-6
Menominee, 8599 I-1
MENOMINEE CO., 24029 G-1
Merrill, 778 N-9
Michigan Ctr., 4672 R-9
Middleville, 3319 Q-6
Midland, 41863 N-9
MIDLAND CO., 83629 N-9
Milan, 5836 S-11
Milford, 6175 Q-11
Millett, 770 Q-8
Millington, 1072 O-11
Mio, 1826 J-10
MISSAUKEE CO., 14849 K-7
Moline, 750 Q-6
Monroe, 20733 S-12
MONROE CO., 152021 S-11
Montague, 2361 N-4
MONTCALM CO., 63342 O-7
MONTMORENCY CO., 9765 I-9
Montrose, 1657 O-10
Morenci, 2220 T-10
Morrice, 927 P-10
Mt. Clemens, 16314 Q-13
Mt. Morris, 3086 O-11
Mt. Pleasant, 26016 N-8
Munising, 2355 D-3
Muskegon, 38401 O-4
MUSKEGON CO., 172188 O-5
Muskegon Hts., 10856 O-4
Napoleon, 1258 S-9
Nashville, 1628 Q-7
Negaunee, 4568 D-1
New Baltimore, 12084 Q-13
New Boston, 1300 R-12
New Buffalo, 1883 T-3
New Haven, 4642 P-13
Newaygo, 1976 N-6
NEWAYGO CO., 48460 N-5
Newberry, 1519 D-6
Newport, 1070 S-12
Niles, 11600 T-4
N. Branch, 1033 O-12
N. Muskegon, 3786 O-4
Northville, 5970 *F-2
Norton Shores, 23994 O-4
Norway, 2845 D-13
Novi, 55224 Q-11
Oak Pk., 29319 *E-5
OAKLAND CO., 1202362 P-12
OCEANA CO., 26570 N-5
OGEMAW CO., 21699 K-9
Olivet, 1605 R-8
Onaway, 880 H-9
Onsted, 917 S-10
Ontonagon, 1494 B-11
ONTONAGON CO., 6780 B-11
Orchard Lake Vil., 2375 *C-4
Ortonville, 1442 P-11
OSCEOLA CO., 23528 L-7
Oscoda, 903 K-12
OSCODA CO., 8640 J-9
Oshtemo, 7600 R-6
Ossineke, 938 I-11
Otisville, 864 O-11
Otsego, 3956 R-6
OTSEGO CO., 24164 I-8
OTTAWA CO., 263801 P-5
Ovid, 1603 P-9
Owosso, 15194 P-10
Oxford, 3436 P-12
Parkdale, 704 K-4
Parma, 769 R-9
Paw Paw, 3534 R-5
Paw Paw Lake, 3511 R-4
Pearl Bch., 2829 Q-14
Pellston, 822 G-8
Pentwater, 857 M-4
Perry, 2188 P-9
Petersburg, 1146 S-11
Petoskey, 5670 H-7
Pigeon, 1208 M-12
Pinckney, 2427 Q-10
Pinconning, 1307 M-10
Plainwell, 3804 R-6
Pleasant Ridge, 2526 *E-6
Plymouth, 9132 *F-2
Pontiac, 59515 Q-12
Port Huron, 30184 P-14
Portage, 46292 R-6
Portland, 3883 P-8
Potterville, 2617 Q-8
PRESQUE ISLE CO., 13376 H-9
Prudenville, 1682 K-8
Quincy, 1652 S-8
Quinnesec, 1191 D-13
Ramsay, 1080 C-10
Rapid City, 1352 J-7
Rapid River, 800 F-3
Ravenna, 1219 O-5
Reading, 1078 T-8
Redford, 48300 *F-4
Reed City, 2425 M-6
Reese, 1454 N-11
Richland, 751 R-6
Richmond, 5735 P-13
River Rouge, 7903 *H-6
Riverview, 12486 *I-6
Rochester, 12711 Q-12
Rochester Hills, 70995 Q-12
Rockford, 5719 O-6
Rockwood, 3289 S-12
Rogers City, 2827 G-10
Romeo, 3596 P-12
Romulus, 23989 R-12
Roosevelt Pk., 3831 O-4
Roscommon, 1075 K-8
ROSCOMMON CO., 24449 K-8
Roseville, 47299 *E-8
Royal Oak, 57236 *D-6
Rudyard, 1100 E-8
Saginaw, 51508 N-10
SAGINAW CO., 200169 O-10
St. Charles, 2054 O-10
St. Clair, 5485 P-14
ST. CLAIR CO., 163040 P-14
St. Clair Shores, 59715 Q-13
St. Helen, 2668 K-9
St. Ignace, 2452 F-8
St. Johns, 7865 P-9
St. Joseph, 8365 S-4
ST. JOSEPH CO., 61295 T-6
St. Louis, 7482 N-8
Saline, 8810 R-11
Sandusky, 2679 N-13
Sanford, 859 M-9
SANILAC CO., 43114 N-13
Saranac, 1325 P-7
Saugatuck, 925 Q-5
Sault Ste. Marie, 14144 D-9
Schoolcraft, 1525 S-6
SCHOOLCRAFT CO., 8485 E-4
Scottville, 1214 M-4
Sebewaing, 1759 M-11
Seven Hbr.s, 4700 *B-1
Shelby, 16700 *B-7
Shelby, 2065 N-4
Shepherd, 1515 N-8
SHIAWASSEE CO., 70648 P-10
Shields, 6587 N-10
Shoreham, 862 S-4
Skidway Lake, 3392 L-10
S. Haven, 4403 R-4
S. Lyon, 11327 Q-11
S. Range, 758 A-12
S. Rockwood, 1675 S-12
Southfield, 71739 Q-12
Southgate, 30047 *I-5
Sparta, 4140 O-6
Spring Arbor, 2881 R-9
Spring Lake, 2323 O-5
Springfield, 5260 R-7
Springfield, 4000 *A-2
Springport, 800 R-8
Standish, 1509 L-10
Stanton, 1417 O-7
Stephenson, 862 H-1
Sterling Hts., 129699 Q-12
Stevensville, 1142 S-4
Stockbridge, 1218 R-10
Sturgis, 10994 T-7
Sunrise Hts., 1350 R-7
Swartz Creek, 5758 P-10
Sylvan Lake, 1720 *C-4
Tawas City, 1827 K-11
Taylor, 63131 R-12
Tecumseh, 8521 S-10
Tekonsha, 717 S-8
Temperance, 8517 T-11
Three Oaks, 1622 T-4
Three Rivers, 7811 S-6
Traverse City, 14674 J-6
Trenton, 18853 S-12
Trowbridge Pk., 2176 D-2
Troy, 80980 Q-12
TUSCOLA CO., 55729 N-11
Twin Lake, 1720 O-5
Ubly, 858 M-13
Union City, 1599 S-7
Union Lake, 8500 *C-3
Union Pier, 1100 T-3
Utica, 4757 *C-7
VAN BUREN CO., 76258 R-5
Vandercook Lake, 4721 R-9
Vassar, 2697 N-11
Vermontville, 759 Q-7
Vernon, 783 P-10
Vicksburg, 2906 S-6
Virginia Pk., 1800 Q-5
Wacousta, 1440 P-8
Wakefield, 1851 C-10
Walker, 23537 *L-4
Walled Lake, 6999 *D-2
Warren, 134056 Q-13
Washington, 1850 Q-12
WASHTENAW CO., 344791 R-10
Waterford, 17600 Q-12
Watervliet, 1735 R-4
Wayland, 4079 Q-6
Wayne, 17593 *H-3
WAYNE CO., 1820584 R-12
Webberville, 1272 Q-10
Weidman, 959 M-8
Wells, 1000 F-2
W. Bloomfield, 64700 *D-4
W. Branch, 2139 K-9
Westland, 84094 R-12
Westphalia, 923 P-8
WEXFORD CO., 32735 K-6
White Cloud, 1408 N-6
White Lake, 5200 *B-2
White Pigeon, 1522 T-6
Whitehall, 2706 N-4
Whitmore Lake, 6423 R-11
Williamston, 3854 Q-9
Wixom, 13498 Q-11
Wolf Lake, 4104 O-5
Wolverine Lake, 4312 *D-2
Woodhaven, 12875 *J-5
Woodland Bch., 2049 S-12
Wyandotte, 25883 R-12
Wyoming, 72125 P-6
Yale, 1955 O-13
Ypsilanti, 19435 R-11
Zeeland, 5504 P-5
Zilwaukee, 1658 N-10

Minnesota
Map pp. 54 – 55
* City keyed to p. 53
Ada, 1707 H-2
Adams, 787 T-10
Adrian, 1209 T-3
Afton, 2886 P-10
Aitkin, 2165 K-8
AITKIN CO., 16202 K-9
Albany, 2561 M-6
Albert Lea, 18016 T-9
Albertville, 7044 O-8
Alexandria, 11070 M-5
Andover, 30598 O-9
Annandale, 3228 O-7
Anoka, 17142 O-9
ANOKA CO., 330844 N-9
Apple Valley, 49084 P-9
Appleton, 1412 O-3
Arden Hills, 9552 *D-6
Arlington, 2233 Q-7
Arnold, 2960 J-12
Atwater, 1133 O-6
Aurora, 1682 G-11
Austin, 24718 T-10
Avon, 1396 M-7
Babbitt, 1475 G-12
Bagley, 1392 G-5
Bald Eagle, 1800 *C-9
Barnesville, 2563 J-2
Battle Lake, 875 K-4
Baudette, 1106 D-6
Baxter, 7610 K-7
Bayport, 3471 O-10
Becker, 4538 N-8
BECKER CO., 32504 I-4
Belgrade, 740 N-5
Bellaire, 1900 *D-9
Belle Plaine, 6661 Q-8
BELTRAMI CO., 44442 E-5
Bemidji, 13431 H-6
Benson, 3240 N-4
BENTON CO., 38451 M-7
Big Lake, 10060 N-8
BIG STONE CO., 5269 N-2
Birchwood Vil., 870 *D-9
Bird Island, 1042 P-6
Biwabik, 969 G-11
Blackduck, 785 G-6
Blaine, 57186 O-9
Blooming Prairie, 1996 S-10
Bloomington, 82893 P-9
Blue Earth, 3353 T-7
BLUE EARTH CO., 64013 S-7
Bovey, 804 H-9
Braham, 1793 M-9
Brainerd, 13590 K-7
Breckenridge, 3386 K-2
Breezy Pt., 2346 J-7
Brooklyn Ctr., 30104 *D-3
Brooklyn Park, 75781 *B-3
Brooten, 743 N-5
Browerville, 790 L-6
BROWN CO., 25893 R-6
Brownton, 762 P-7
Buffalo, 15453 O-8
Buffalo Lake, 733 P-6
Buhl, 1000 H-10
Burnsville, 60306 *J-4
Byron, 4914 R-11
Caledonia, 2868 T-13
Cambridge, 8111 N-9
Canby, 1795 P-3
Cannon Falls, 4083 Q-10
Carlton, 862 J-11
CARLTON CO., 35386 J-10
Carver, 3724 P-8
CARVER CO., 91042 P-8
CASS CO., 28567 I-7
Cass Lake, 770 H-6
Center City, 628 N-10
Centerville, 3792 *B-8
Champlin, 23089 *A-2
Chanhassen, 22952 P-9
Chaska, 23770 P-9
Chatfield, 2779 S-12
CHIPPEWA CO., 12441 O-4
Chisago City, 4967 N-10
CHISAGO CO., 53887 N-10
Chisholm, 4976 H-10
Circle Pines, 4918 *B-7
Clara City, 1360 P-5
Clarkfield, 863 P-4
Clarks Grove, 706 S-9
CLAY CO., 58999 I-2
Clearwater, 1735 N-8
CLEARWATER CO., 8695 G-5
Cleveland, 719 Q-8
Cloquet, 12124 J-11
Cohasset, 2698 H-8
Cokato, 2694 O-7
Cold Spring, 4025 N-7
Coleraine, 1970 H-9
Cologne, 1519 P-8
Columbia Hts., 19496 *D-5
COOK CO., 5176 F-14
Coon Rapids, 61476 *A-4
Corcoran, 5379 O-9
Cottage Grove, 34589 P-10
Cottonwood, 1212 Q-4
COTTONWOOD CO., 11687 S-5
Crookston, 7891 G-2
Crosby, 2386 K-8
Crosslake, 2141 J-7
CROW WING CO., 62500 K-7
Crystal, 22151 *E-3
DAKOTA CO., 398552 Q-9
Dassel, 1469 O-7
Dawson, 1540 P-3
Dayton, 4671 O-9
Deephaven, 3642 *G-1
Deer River, 930 H-8
Delano, 5464 O-8
Dellwood, 1063 *C-9
Detroit Lakes, 8569 J-4
Dilworth, 4024 I-2
Dodge Ctr., 2670 R-10
DODGE CO., 20087 S-10
DOUGLAS CO., 36009 L-4
Dover, 735 R-12
Duluth, 86265 J-12
Dundas, 1367 Q-9
Eagan, 64206 *J-7
Eagle Lake, 2422 R-8
E. Bethel, 11626 N-9
E. Grand Forks, 8601 F-1
E. Gull Lake, 1004 K-7
Eden Prairie, 60797 *I-1
Eden Valley, 1042 N-6
Edgerton, 1189 S-3
Edina, 47941 *H-3
Elbow Lake, 1176 L-3
Elgin, 1089 R-12
Elk River, 22974 N-9
Elko New Market, 4110 Q-9
Ely, 3460 F-12
Emily, 813 J-8
Esko, 1869 J-11
Eveleth, 3718 H-11
Excelsior, 2188 P-9
Eyota, 1977 R-12
Fairfax, 1235 Q-6
Fairmont, 10666 T-7
Falcon Hts., 5321 *F-6
Faribault, 23352 R-9
FARIBAULT CO., 14553 S-8
Farmington, 21086 P-10
Fergus Falls, 13138 K-3
Fertile, 842 G-3
FILLMORE CO., 20866 T-12
Foley, 2603 M-8
Forest Lake, 18375 O-10
Fosston, 1527 G-4
Frazee, 1350 J-4
FREEBORN CO., 31255 T-9
Fridley, 27208 *D-5
Fulda, 1318 S-4
Gaylord, 2305 Q-7
Gibbon, 772 Q-6
Gilbert, 1799 H-11
Glencoe, 5631 P-7
Glenwood, 2564 M-5
Glyndon, 1394 I-2
Golden Valley, 20371 *E-3
Goodhue, 1176 Q-11
GOODHUE CO., 46183 Q-10
Goodview, 4036 R-13
Grand Marais, 1351 B-12
Grand Meadow, 1139 S-11
Grand Rapids, 10869 H-9
Granite Falls, 2897 P-4
Grant, 4096 *D-10
GRANT CO., 6018 M-3
Greenbush, 719 D-3
Greenfield, 2777 O-8
Hallock, 981 C-2
Ham Lake, 15296 O-9
Hancock, 765 N-4
Hanover, 2938 O-8
Harmony, 1020 T-12
Harris, 1132 N-10
Hastings, 22172 P-10
Hawley, 2067 I-3
Hayfield, 1340 S-10
Hector, 1151 P-6
Henderson, 886 Q-8
Hendricks, 713 Q-2
HENNEPIN CO., 1152425 O-8
Henning, 802 K-5
Hermantown, 9414 J-11
Hibbing, 16361 H-10
Hilltop, 744 *D-5
Hinckley, 1800 L-10
Holdingford, 708 M-7
Hopkins, 17591 *G-2
Houston, 979 S-13
HOUSTON CO., 19027 S-13
Howard Lake, 1962 O-7
Hoyt Lakes, 2017 G-12
HUBBARD CO., 20428 I-5
Hugo, 13332 *B-9
Hutchinson, 14178 P-7
Independence, 3504 O-8
International Falls, 6424 D-9
Inver Grove Hts., 33880 *J-8
Isanti, 5251 N-9
ISANTI CO., 37816 M-9
Isle, 751 L-9
ITASCA CO., 45058 G-9
Ivanhoe, 559 Q-3
Jackson, 3299 T-5
JACKSON CO., 10266 T-5
Janesville, 2256 R-8
Jordan, 5470 P-8
KANABEC CO., 16239 M-9
KANDIYOHI CO., 42239 O-5
Karlstad, 760 D-2
Kasson, 5931 R-10
Keewatin, 1068 H-10
Kenyon, 1815 R-10
Kerkhoven, 759 O-5
Kimball, 762 N-7
KITTSON CO., 4552 D-2
KOOCHICHING CO., 13311 E-7
La Crescent, 4830 S-14
LAC QUI PARLE CO., 7259 P-3
Lake City, 5063 Q-12
LAKE CO., 10866 G-13
Lake Crystal, 2549 R-7
Lake Elmo, 8069 O-10
LAKE OF THE WOODS CO., 4045 D-5
Lake Park, 783 I-3
Lake Shore, 1004 K-7
Lakefield, 1694 S-5
Lakeland, 1796 P-10
Lakeville, 55954 P-9
Lamberton, 824 R-5
Lanesboro, 754 S-12
Lauderdale, 2379 *F-6
Le Center, 2499 Q-8
Le Roy, 929 T-11
Le Sueur, 4058 Q-8
LE SUEUR CO., 27703 Q-8
Lester Prairie, 1730 P-8
Lewiston, 1620 R-12
Lexington, 2049 *B-6
LINCOLN CO., 5896 Q-3
Lindstrom, 4442 N-10
Lino Lakes, 20216 O-10
Litchfield, 6726 O-6
Little Canada, 9773 *E-8
Little Falls, 8343 L-7
Long Lake, 1768 O-9
Long Prairie, 3458 L-6
Lonsdale, 3674 Q-9
Luverne, 4745 S-3
LYON CO., 25857 Q-4
Mabel, 780 T-13
Madelia, 2308 R-7
Madison, 1551 O-3
Madison Lake, 1017 R-8
Mahnomen, 1214 H-3
MAHNOMEN CO., 5413 H-4
Mahtomedi, 7676 *D-10
Mankato, 39309 R-8
Mantorville, 1197 R-10
Maple Grove, 61567 *B-1
Maple Lake, 2059 O-8
Maple Plain, 1768 O-8
Mapleton, 1756 S-8
Maplewood, 38018 *E-8
Marble, 701 H-9
Marshall, 13680 Q-4
MARSHALL CO., 9439 E-2
MARTIN CO., 20840 T-6
Mayer, 1749 P-8
Mazeppa, 842 R-11
MCLEOD CO., 36651 P-7
Medford, 1239 R-9
Medina, 4892 O-9
MEEKER CO., 23300 O-7
Melrose, 3598 M-6
Menahga, 1306 J-5
Mendota Hts., 11071 *H-7
Milaca, 2946 M-8
MILLE LACS CO., 26097 L-8
Minneapolis, 382578 O-9
Minneota, 1392 Q-3
Minnetonka, 49734 *G-1
Montevideo, 5383 O-4
Montgomery, 2956 Q-9
Monticello, 12759 N-8
Montrose, 2847 O-8
Moorhead, 38065 I-2
Moose Lake, 2751 K-10
Mora, 3571 M-9
Morgan, 896 Q-6
Morris, 5286 N-3
MORRISON CO., 33198 L-8
Morristown, 987 R-9
Mound, 9052 P-8
Mounds View, 12155 *C-6
Mountain Iron, 2869 H-11
Mountain Lake, 2104 S-6
MOWER CO., 39163 T-10
MURRAY CO., 8725 R-3
Nashwauk, 983 H-9
New Brighton, 21456 *D-6
New Hope, 20339 *D-3
New London, 1251 N-6
New Prague, 7321 Q-9
New Richland, 1203 S-9
New Ulm, 13522 Q-7
New York Mills, 1199 K-5
Newport, 3435 *I-9
Nicollet, 1093 R-7
NICOLLET CO., 32727 Q-7
Nisswa, 1971 K-7
NOBLES CO., 21378 S-3
NORMAN CO., 6852 H-2
N. Branch, 10125 N-10
N. Mankato, 13394 R-8
N. Oaks, 4469 *D-7
N. St. Paul, 11460 *E-9
Northfield, 20007 Q-10
Norwood Young America, 3549 P-8
Oak Grove, 8031 N-9
Oak Park Hts., 4339 O-10
Oakdale, 27378 *F-9
Olivia, 2484 P-5
OLMSTED CO., 144248 R-11
Onamia, 878 L-8
Orono, 7437 P-8
Oronoco, 1300 R-11
Ortonville, 1916 N-2
Osakis, 1740 M-5
Osseo, 2430 *C-2
Otsego, 13571 O-9
OTTER TAIL CO., 57303 L-4
Owatonna, 25599 R-9
Park Rapids, 3709 I-5
Parkers Prairie, 1011 L-5
Paynesville, 2432 N-6
Pelican Rapids, 2464 J-3
Pengilly, 850 H-9
PENNINGTON CO., 13930 F-3
Pequot Lakes, 2162 J-7
Perham, 2985 J-4
Pierz, 1393 L-7
Pine City, 3123 M-10
PINE CO., 29750 L-10
Pine Island, 3263 R-11
Pine River, 944 J-7
Pipestone, 4317 R-2
PIPESTONE CO., 9596 R-2
Plainview, 3340 R-12
Plymouth, 70576 *E-1
POLK CO., 31600 G-3
Ponemah, 724 F-6
POPE CO., 10995 N-4
Preston, 1325 S-12
Princeton, 4698 N-9
Prior Lake, 22796 P-9
Proctor, 3057 J-11
Ramsey, 23668 O-9
RAMSEY CO., 508640 O-10
Raymond, 764 O-5
Red Lake, 1731 F-6
RED LAKE CO., 4089 F-3
Red L. Falls, 1427 F-3
Red Wing, 16459 Q-11
Redby, 1334 F-6
REDWOOD CO., 16059 Q-5
Redwood Falls, 5254 Q-5
Renville, 1287 P-5
RENVILLE CO., 15730 P-6
Rice, 1275 M-7
RICE CO., 64142 Q-9
Richfield, 35228 *H-4
Richmond, 1422 N-7
Robbinsdale, 13953 *E-3
Rochester, 106769 R-11
ROCK CO., 9687 S-3
Rock Creek, 1628 M-10
Rockford, 4316 O-8
Rockville, 2448 N-7
Rogers, 8597 O-9
Roseau, 2633 C-4
ROSEAU CO., 15629 D-4
Rosemount, 21874 P-10
Roseville, 33660 *E-7
Royalton, 1242 M-7
Rush City, 3079 M-10
Rushford, 1731 S-13
Rushford Vil., 807 S-13
St. Anthony, 8226 *E-5
St. Augusta, 3317 N-7
St. Bonifacius, 2283 P-8
St. Charles, 3735 S-12
St. Clair, 868 R-8
St. Cloud, 65842 N-7
St. Francis, 7218 N-9
St. James, 4605 S-6
St. Joseph, 6534 N-7
ST. LOUIS CO., 200226 G-11
St. Louis Park, 45250 *G-3
St. Michael, 16399 O-8
St. Paul, 285068 O-10
St. Paul Park, 5279 *I-9
St. Peter, 11196 Q-8
St. Stephen, 851 M-7
Sandstone, 2849 L-10
Sartell, 15876 M-7
Sauk Centre, 4317 M-6
Sauk Rapids, 12773 N-7
Savage, 26911 *J-3
Scandia, 3936 O-10
Scanlon, 991 J-11
SCOTT CO., 129928 Q-8
Sebeka, 711 J-5
Shafer, 1045 N-10
Shakopee, 37076 P-9
Sherburn, 1137 T-6
SHERBURNE CO., 88499 N-8
Shoreview, 25043 *D-7
Shorewood, 7307 P-9
SIBLEY CO., 15226 Q-7
Silver Bay, 1887 H-13
Silver Lake, 837 P-7
Slayton, 2153 R-4
Sleepy Eye, 3599 R-6
S. St. Paul, 20160 *H-8
Spicer, 1167 O-6
Spring Grove, 1330 T-13
Spring L. Park, 6412 *C-5
Spring Valley, 2479 S-11
Springfield, 2152 R-5
Stacy, 1456 N-10
Staples, 2981 K-6
Starbuck, 1302 M-4
STEARNS CO., 150642 N-6
STEELE CO., 36576 S-9
STEVENS CO., 9726 M-3
Stewartville, 5916 S-11
Stillwater, 18225 O-10
SWIFT CO., 9783 O-4
Taylors Falls, 976 N-11
Thief River Falls, 8573 F-3
TODD CO., 24895 L-6
Tracy, 2163 R-4
TRAVERSE CO., 3558 M-2
Trimont, 747 S-6
Truman, 1115 S-7
Twin Valley, 821 H-3
Two Harbors, 3745 I-13
Tyler, 1143 R-3
Vadnais Hts., 12302 *D-8
Victoria, 7345 P-8
Virginia, 8712 G-11
Wabasha, 2521 Q-12
WABASHA CO., 21676 R-12
Waconia, 10697 P-8
Wadena, 4088 K-5
WADENA CO., 13843 J-5
Waite Park, 6715 N-7
Walker, 941 I-6
Walnut Grove, 871 R-4
Wanamingo, 1086 R-10
Warren, 1563 E-2
Warroad, 1781 C-5
Waseca, 9410 R-9
WASECA CO., 19136 S-8
WASHINGTON CO., 238136 O-10
Watertown, 4205 O-8
Waterville, 1868 R-9
Watkins, 962 N-7
WATONWAN CO., 11211 S-6
Waverly, 1357 O-8
Wayzata, 3688 *F-1
Wells, 2343 S-8
W. Concord, 782 R-10
W. St. Paul, 19540 *H-7
Westbrook, 739 R-4
Wheaton, 1424 M-2
White Bear Lake, 23797 O-10
WILKIN CO., 6576 K-2
Willmar, 19610 O-5
Windom, 4646 S-5
Winnebago, 1437 S-7
Winona, 27592 R-13
WINONA CO., 51461 R-12
Winsted, 2355 P-8
Winthrop, 1399 Q-7
Woodbury, 61961 *H-10
Worthington, 12764 T-4
WRIGHT CO., 124700 O-8
Wyoming, 7791 N-10
YELLOW MEDICINE CO., 10438 P-3
Zimmerman, 5228 N-9
Zumbrota, 3252 R-11

Mississippi
Map p. 56
Aberdeen, 5612 D-9
Ackerman, 1510 F-8
ADAMS CO., 32297 J-3
Alcorn, 1000 I-4
ALCORN CO., 37057 B-9
AMITE CO., 13131 K-4
Amory, 7316 D-9
Arnold Line, 1719 E-1
Ashland, 569 B-8
ATTALA CO., 19564 F-7
Baldwyn, 3297 B-9
Batesville, 7463 C-6
Bay St. Louis, 9260 M-8
Bay Sprs., 1786 I-8
Beaumont, 951 K-8
Belmont, 2021 B-10
Belzoni, 2235 F-5
BENTON CO., 8729 B-8
Biloxi, 44054 M-9
Blue Mtn., 920 B-8
Bogue Chitto, 887 G-8
BOLIVAR CO., 34145 D-4
Booneville, 8743 B-9
Brandon, 21705 H-6
Brookhaven, 12513 J-5
Brooklyn, 900 K-8
Brooksville, 1223 F-9
Bruce, 1939 D-8
Bude, 1063 J-4
Burnsville, 936 B-10
Byhalia, 1302 B-7
Byram, 11489 H-6
Caledonia, 1041 E-10
Calhoun City, 1774 D-8
CALHOUN CO., 14962 D-8
Canton, 13189 G-6
Carriere, 880 L-7
CARROLL CO., 10597 E-6
Carrollton, 190 E-6
Carthage, 5075 G-7
Centreville, 1684 K-4
Charleston, 2193 D-6
CHICKASAW CO., 17392 D-8
CHOCTAW CO., 8547 F-8
CLAIBORNE CO., 9604 I-4
CLARKE CO., 16732 H-9
Clarksdale, 17962 C-5
CLAY CO., 20634 E-8
Cleary, 1544 H-6
Cleveland, 12334 D-5
Clinton, 25216 H-5
COAHOMA CO., 26151 D-5
Coffeeville, 905 D-7
Coldwater, 1677 B-6
Collins, 2586 J-7
Collinsville, 1948 H-9
Columbia, 6582 K-6
Columbus, 23640 E-9
Como, 1279 C-6
Conehatta, 1342 H-8
COPIAH CO., 29449 I-5
Corinth, 14573 A-9
COVINGTON CO., 19568 J-7
Crenshaw, 885 C-6
Crystal Sprs., 5044 I-5
D'Iberville, 9486 M-9
De Kalb, 1164 G-9
DE SOTO CO., 161252 B-6
Decatur, 1841 H-8
DeLisle, 1147 M-8
Derma, 1025 D-8
Diamondhead, 8425 M-8
Drew, 1927 D-5
Durant, 2673 F-6
Ecru, 895 C-8
Edwards, 1034 H-5
Elliott, 990 E-7
Ellisville, 4448 J-8
Escatawpa, 3722 M-9
Eupora, 2197 E-8
Farmington, 2186 A-9
Fayette, 1614 J-4
Flora, 1886 G-5
Florence, 4141 H-6
Flowood, 7823 C-3
Forest, 5684 H-7
FORREST CO., 74934 K-8
FRANKLIN CO., 8118 J-4
Friars Pt., 1200 C-5
Fulton, 3961 C-9
Gautier, 18572 M-9
GEORGE CO., 22578 L-9
Glendale, 1657 J-8
Gloster, 960 K-4
Goodman, 1386 F-6
GREENE CO., 14400 K-9
Greenville, 34400 E-4
Greenwood, 15205 E-6
Grenada, 13092 D-7
GRENADA CO., 21906 D-7
Gulf Hills, 7144 M-5
Gulfport, 67793 M-8
Guntown, 2083 C-9
HANCOCK CO., 43929 M-7
HARRISON CO., 187105 L-8
Hattiesburg, 45989 K-8
Hazlehurst, 4009 I-5
Helena, 1184 M-9
Hernando, 14090 B-6
Hillsboro, 1130 H-7
HINDS CO., 245285 I-5
Hollandale, 2702 F-4
Holly Sprs., 7699 B-7
HOLMES CO., 19198 F-6
Horn Lake, 26066 A-6
Houston, 3623 D-8
HUMPHREYS CO., 9375 F-5
Hurley, 1551 L-9
Indianola, 10683 E-5
Inverness, 1019 E-5
ISSAQUENA CO., 1406 G-4
ITAWAMBA CO., 23401 C-9
Itta Bena, 2049 E-5
Iuka, 3028 B-10
Jackson, 173514 H-6
JACKSON CO., 139668 L-9
JASPER CO., 17062 I-8
JEFFERSON CO., 7726 I-4
JEFFERSON DAVIS CO., 12487 J-6
JONES CO., 67761 J-8
Jonestown, 1298 C-5
KEMPER CO., 10456 G-9
Kiln, 2238 M-7
Kosciusko, 7402 F-7
LAFAYETTE CO., 47351 C-7
Lakeshore, 1200 M-7
LAMAR CO., 55658 K-7
Lambert, 1638 C-6
Latimer, 6079 M-9
LAUDERDALE CO., 80261 H-9
Laurel, 18540 J-8
LAWRENCE CO., 12929 J-6
LEAKE CO., 23805 G-7
Leakesville, 898 K-9
LEE CO., 82910 C-9
LEFLORE CO., 32317 E-6
Leland, 4481 E-4
Lexington, 1731 F-6
Liberty, 728 K-4
LINCOLN CO., 34869 J-5
Long Bch., 14792 M-8
Louisville, 6631 F-8
LOWNDES CO., 59779 E-9
Lucedale, 2923 L-9
Lumberton, 2086 K-7
Lyman, 1277 M-8
Lynchburg, 2437 A-6
Maben, 871 E-8
Macon, 2768 F-9
Madison, 24149 H-6
MADISON CO., 95203 G-6
Magee, 4408 I-7
Magnolia, 2420 K-5
Mantachie, 1144 C-9
Marion, 1479 H-9
MARION CO., 27088 K-7
Marks, 1735 C-6
MARSHALL CO., 37144 B-7
Mayersville, 547 G-4
McComb, 12790 K-5
McNeill, 1050 L-7
Meadville, 449 J-4
Mendenhall, 2504 I-6
Meridian, 41148 H-9
Metcalfe, 1067 E-4
MONROE CO., 36989 E-9
MONTGOMERY CO., 10925 E-7
Monticello, 1571 J-6
Moorhead, 2405 E-5
Morgantown, 1412 J-3
Morton, 3462 H-7
Moss Pt., 13704 M-9
Mound Bayou, 1533 D-5
Mt. Olive, 982 I-7
Natchez, 15792 J-3
Nellieburg, 1414 H-9
NESHOBA CO., 29676 G-8
Nettleton, 1992 D-9
New Albany, 8034 C-8
New Augusta, 644 K-8
New Hope, 3193 E-10
Newton, 3373 H-8
NEWTON CO., 21720 H-8
Nicholson, 3092 M-7
N. Tunica, 1035 B-5
NOXUBEE CO., 11545 F-9
Ocean Sprs., 17442 M-9
Okolona, 2692 D-9
OKTIBBEHA CO., 47671 E-9
Olive Branch, 33484 A-7
Oxford, 18916 C-7
PANOLA CO., 34707 C-6
Pascagoula, 22392 M-9
Pass Christian, 4613 M-8
Paulding, 150 I-8
Pearl, 25092 H-6
Pearl River, 3601 G-8
PEARL RIVER CO., 55834 L-7
Pearlington, 1332 M-7
Pelahatchie, 1334 H-7
PERRY CO., 12250 K-8
Petal, 10454 J-8
Philadelphia, 7477 G-8
Picayune, 10878 M-7
Pickens, 1157 G-6
PIKE CO., 40404 K-5
Pittsboro, 202 D-8
Plantersville, 1155 C-9
Polkville, 833 H-7
Pontotoc, 5625 C-8
PONTOTOC CO., 29957 D-8
Poplarville, 2894 L-7
Port Gibson, 1567 I-4
Prentiss, 1081 J-6
PRENTISS CO., 25276 B-9
Purvis, 2175 K-7
Quitman, 2323 I-9
QUITMAN CO., 8223 C-5
Raleigh, 1462 I-7
RANKIN CO., 141617 H-6
Rawls Sprs., 1254 J-7
Raymond, 1933 H-5
Richland, 6912 H-6
Richton, 1068 J-8
Ridgeland, 24047 H-6
Ripley, 5395 B-8
Rolling Fork, 2143 G-4
Rosedale, 1873 D-4
Ruleville, 3007 D-5
Saltillo, 4752 C-9
Sardis, 1703 C-6
Saucier, 1342 L-8
SCOTT CO., 28264 H-7
Senatobia, 8165 B-6
Shannon, 1753 C-9
SHARKEY CO., 4916 G-4
Sharon, 1406 I-8
Shaw, 1952 E-5
Shelby, 2229 D-5
SIMPSON CO., 27503 I-6
SMITH CO., 16491 I-7
Smithville, 942 D-10
Southaven, 48982 A-6
St. Martin, 7730 M-5
Starkville, 23888 E-9
STONE CO., 17786 L-8
Stonewall, 1088 H-9
Stratton, 1250 H-8
Summit, 1705 K-5
Sumner, 316 D-5
Sumrall, 1421 J-7
Sunflower, 1159 E-5
SUNFLOWER CO., 29450 E-5
TALLAHATCHIE CO., 15378 D-6
TATE CO., 28886 B-6
Taylorsville, 1353 I-7
Tchula, 2096 F-6
Terry, 1063 I-6
TIPPAH CO., 22232 B-8
TISHOMINGO CO., 19593 B-10
Tunica, 1030 B-5
TUNICA CO., 10778 C-5
Tupelo, 34546 C-9
Tutwiler, 3550 D-5
Tylertown, 1609 K-6
Union, 1988 G-8
UNION CO., 27134 C-8
Utica, 820 I-5
Vaiden, 734 E-7
Vancleave, 5886 L-9
Vardaman, 1316 D-8
Verona, 3006 C-9
Vicksburg, 23856 H-4
Wade, 1074 L-9
Walls, 1162 A-6
Walnut Grove, 1911 G-7
Walthall, 144 E-8
WALTHALL CO., 15443 K-6
WARREN CO., 48773 H-5
WASHINGTON CO., 51137 F-4
Water Valley, 3392 C-7
Waveland, 6435 M-7
WAYNE CO., 20747 J-9
Waynesboro, 5043 J-9
WEBSTER CO., 10253 E-7
Wesson, 1925 J-5
West Point, 11307 E-9
Wiggins, 4390 L-8
WILKINSON CO., 9878 K-3
Winona, 5043 E-7
WINSTON CO., 19198 F-8
Woodville, 1096 K-3
YALOBUSHA CO., 12678 D-7
Yazoo City, 11403 G-5
YAZOO CO., 28065 G-5

Missouri
Map pp. 58 – 59
* City keyed to p. 57
ADAIR CO., 25607 B-13
Adrian, 1677 G-9
Advance, 1347 K-19
Affton, 20307 *J-5
Albany, 1730 B-9
Alton, 871 L-16
Anderson, 1961 L-9
ANDREW CO., 17291 C-8
Appleton City, 1127 H-10
Archie, 1170 G-9
Arnold, 20808 G-18
Ash Grove, 1472 J-11
Ashland, 3707 F-14
ATCHISON CO., 5685 B-7
AUDRAIN CO., 25529 E-14
Aurora, 7508 K-10
Auxvasse, 983 F-14
Ava, 2993 K-13
Ballwin, 30404 G-17
Barnhart, 5682 G-18
BARRY CO., 35597 L-10
BARTON CO., 12402 J-9
BATES CO., 17049 H-9
Battlefield, 5590 K-11
Bel-Nor, 1499 *G-5
Bel-Ridge, 2737 *G-5
Bella Villa, 729 *J-6
Belle, 1545 H-15
Bellefontaine Neighbors, 10860 *F-6
Belton, 23116 F-9
Benbush, 2000 *G-3
Benton, 863 K-19
BENTON CO., 19056 H-12
Berkeley, 8978 *F-5
Bernie, 1958 L-19
Bertrand, 821 K-20
Bethany, 3292 B-10
Bevier, 718 D-13
Billings, 1035 K-11
Bismarck, 1546 I-17
Black Jack, 6929 *F-6
Bloomfield, 1933 K-19
Blue Sprs., 52575 F-9
Blue Summit, 1200 I-5
Bolivar, 10325 J-11
BOLLINGER CO., 12363 K-18
Bonne Terre, 6864 I-17
BOONE CO., 162642 E-13
Boonville, 8319 F-13
Bourbon, 1632 H-16
Bowling Green, 5334 E-16
Branson, 10520 L-12
Braymer, 878 D-10
Breckenridge Hills, 4746 *G-5
Brentwood, 8055 *I-5
Bridgeton, 11550 *F-4
Brookfield, 4542 D-12
Brunswick, 858 E-12
BUCHANAN CO., 89201 D-8
Buckner, 3076 E-10
Buffalo, 3084 I-12
Butler, 4219 H-9
BUTLER CO., 42794 L-18
Cabool, 2146 K-14
CALDWELL CO., 9424 D-10
California, 4278 G-13
CALLAWAY CO., 44332 F-14
Calverton Pk., 1293 *F-5
CAMDEN CO., 44002 I-13
Camdenton, 3718 H-13
Cameron, 9933 D-9
Campbell, 1992 L-18
Canton, 2377 C-15
Cape Girardeau, 37941 J-20
CAPE GIRARDEAU CO., 75674 J-19
Cardwell, 713 N-18
Carl Jct., 7445 K-9
CARROLL CO., 9295 E-11
Carrollton, 3784 E-11
Carsonville, 2000 *G-5
CARTER CO., 6265 K-16
Carterville, 1891 *A-7
Carthage, 14378 K-9
Caruthersville, 6168 M-19
CASS CO., 99478 G-9
Cassville, 3266 L-10
CEDAR CO., 13982 I-10
Cedar Hill, 1721 G-17
Centerville, 191 J-16
Centralia, 4027 E-14
Chaffee, 2955 K-19
CHARITON CO., 7831 E-12
Charlack, 1363 *G-5
Charleston, 5947 K-20
Chesterfield, 47484 G-17
Chillicothe, 9515 D-11
CHRISTIAN CO., 77422 K-12
Clarence, 813 D-14
CLARK CO., 7139 B-14
Clarkson Valley, 2632 *I-2
Clarkton, 1288 M-19
CLAY CO., 221939 E-9
Claycomo, 1430 G-5
Clayton, 15939 *H-5
Clever, 2139 K-11
Clinton, 9008 G-10
CLINTON CO., 20743 D-9
Cole Camp, 1121 G-12
COLE CO., 75990 G-13
Columbia, 108500 F-13
Concord, 16421 *J-5
Concordia, 2450 F-11
Conway, 788 J-12
Cool Valley, 1196 *G-5
COOPER CO., 17601 F-13
Country Club Hills, 1274 *G-6
Country Club Vil., 2449 C-8
Crane, 1462 K-11
CRAWFORD CO., 24696 I-16
Crestwood, 11912 *I-5
Creve Coeur, 17833 *H-4
Crocker, 1110 I-14
Crystal City, 4855 H-18
Cuba, 3356 H-15
DADE CO., 7883 J-10
DALLAS CO., 16777 J-12
DAVIESS CO., 8433 C-10
DE KALB CO., 12892 C-9
De Soto, 6400 H-17
Dellwood, 5025 *F-6
DENT CO., 15657 J-15
Des Peres, 8373 *I-4
Desloge, 5054 I-17
Dexter, 7864 L-19
Diamond, 902 K-9
Dixon, 1549 I-14
Doe Run, 915 I-17
Doniphan, 1997 L-17
DOUGLAS CO., 13684 K-13
Drexel, 965 G-9
Duenweg, 1121 K-9
DUNKLIN CO., 31953 M-18
Duquesne, 1763 *C-7
E. Prairie, 3176 L-20
Edina, 1176 C-14
Edmundson, 834 *G-5
El Dorado Sprs., 3593 I-10
Eldon, 4567 H-13
Ellington, 987 K-16
Ellisville, 9133 *I-2
Elsberry, 1934 E-17
Eminence, 600 K-16
Eureka, 10189 G-17
Excelsior Sprs., 11084 E-9
Exeter, 772 L-10
Fair Grove, 1393 J-12
Farmington, 16240 I-18
Fayette, 2688 E-13
Fenton, 4022 *J-4
Ferguson, 21203 *G-5
Festus, 11602 H-18
Flordell Hills, 822 *G-6
Florissant, 52158 F-18
Fordland, 800 K-12
Forsyth, 2255 L-12
Four Seasons, 2217 H-13
FRANKLIN CO., 101492 G-16
Fredericktown, 3985 J-18
Fremont Hills, 826 K-12
Frontenac, 3482 *H-4
Fulton, 12790 F-14
Gainesville, 773 L-13
Galena, 440 L-11
Gallatin, 1786 C-10
Garden City, 1642 G-10
GASCONADE CO., 15222 G-15
GENTRY CO., 6738 B-9
Gerald, 1345 G-16
Gideon, 1093 M-19
Gladstone, 25410 E-9
Glasgow, 1103 E-12
Glasgow Vil., 5429 *F-7
Glendale, 5925 *I-5
Golden City, 765 J-10
Goodman, 1248 L-9
Gower, 1526 D-9
Grain Valley, 12854 F-10
Granby, 2134 K-9
Grandview, 24475 M-4
Grant City, 859 B-9
Grantwood Vil., 863 *J-5
Gray Summit, 2701 G-17
Green Pk., 2622 *J-5
GREENE CO., 275174 J-11
Greenfield, 1371 J-10
Greenville, 511 K-18
Greenwood, 5221 F-9
GRUNDY CO., 10261 B-11
Hallsville, 1491 E-14
Hamilton, 1809 D-10
Hanley Hills, 2101 *H-5
Hannibal, 17916 D-15
HARRISON CO., 8957 B-10
Harrisonville, 10019 G-9
Hartville, 613 K-13
Hayti, 2939 M-19
Hazelwood, 25703 *F-4
HENRY CO., 22272 G-10
Herculaneum, 3468 H-18
Hermann, 2431 G-15
Hermitage, 467 I-11
HICKORY CO., 9627 H-11
Higginsville, 4797 F-11
High Ridge, 4305 G-17
Highlandville, 911 K-11
Hillsboro, 2821 H-17
Hillsdale, 1478 *G-6
Holden, 2252 G-10
Hollister, 4426 L-12
HOLT CO., 4912 B-7
Holts Summit, 3247 G-14
Horine, 821 H-18
Houston, 2081 J-14
HOWARD CO., 10144 E-13
HOWELL CO., 40400 K-14
Humansville, 1048 I-11
Huntsville, 1564 E-13
Iberia, 736 H-14
Independence, 116830 E-9
IRON CO., 10630 J-17
Iron Mtn. Lake, 737 I-17
Ironton, 1460 J-17
Jackson, 13758 J-19
JACKSON CO., 674158 F-9
Jasper, 931 J-9
JASPER CO., 117404 J-9
Jefferson City, 43079 G-14
JEFFERSON CO., 218733 H-17
Jennings, 14712 *G-6
JOHNSON CO., 52595 G-10
Jonesburg, 768 F-16
Joplin, 50150 K-9
Kahoka, 2078 B-15
Kansas City, 459787 F-9
Kearney, 8381 E-9
Kennett, 10932 M-18
Keytesville, 471 E-12
Kimberling City, 2400 L-11
King City, 1013 C-9
Kingston, 348 D-10
Kirksville, 17505 C-13
Kirkwood, 27540 *I-4
Knob Noster, 2709 F-11
KNOX CO., 4131 C-14
La Grange, 931 C-15
La Monte, 1140 F-11
La Plata, 1366 C-13
LACLEDE CO., 35571 J-13
Ladue, 8521 *H-5
LAFAYETTE CO., 33381 F-10
Lake Lotawana, 1939 F-9
Lake Ozark, 1586 H-13
Lake St. Louis, 14545 F-17
Lake Tapawingo, 730 J-7
Lake Waukomis, 870 G-3
Lake Winnebago, 1131 M-6
Lakeshire, 1432 *J-5
Lamar, 4532 J-9
Lancaster, 728 B-13
Lathrop, 2086 D-9
LAWRENCE CO., 38634 J-10
Lawson, 2473 E-10
Leadwood, 1282 I-17
Lebanon, 14474 I-13
Lees Summit, 91364 L-6
Lemay, 16645 *J-6
LEWIS CO., 10211 C-15
Lexington, 4726 E-10
Liberal, 759 J-9
Liberty, 29149 E-9
Licking, 3124 J-15
Lilbourn, 1190 L-19
Lincoln, 1190 G-11
LINCOLN CO., 52566 F-16
Linn, 1459 G-15
LINN CO., 12761 C-12
Linneus, 278 C-12
LIVINGSTON CO., 15195 C-11
Lockwood, 936 J-10
Lone Jack, 1050 F-10
Louisiana, 3364 E-16
Macon, 5471 D-13
MACON CO., 15566 C-13
MADISON CO., 12226 J-18
Malden, 4275 L-19
Manchester, 18094 *I-3
Mansfield, 1296 K-13
Maplewood, 8046 *I-5
Marble Hill, 1477 J-19
Marceline, 2233 D-12
MARIES CO., 9176 H-14
MARION CO., 28781 D-15
Marionville, 2225 K-11
Marlborough, 2179 *I-5
Marshall, 13065 E-12
Marshfield, 6633 J-12
Marthasville, 1136 G-16
Maryland Hts., 27472 *G-4
Maryville, 11972 B-8
Mattese, 2500 *K-5
Maysville, 1114 C-9
MCDONALD CO., 23083 L-9
Mehlville, 28380 *J-5
Memphis, 1822 B-14
MERCER CO., 3785 B-11
Mexico, 11543 E-14
Milan, 1960 C-12
MILLER CO., 24748 H-13
Miner, 984 K-20
MISSISSIPPI CO., 14358 L-20
Moberly, 13974 E-13
Moline Acres, 2442 *G-6
Monett, 8873 K-10
MONITEAU CO., 15607 G-13
Monroe City, 2531 D-15
MONROE CO., 8840 D-14
Montgomery City, 2834 F-15
MONTGOMERY CO., 12236 F-15
Monticello, 98 C-15
Morehouse, 973 L-19
MORGAN CO., 20565 G-12
Moscow Mills, 2509 F-16
Mound City, 1159 C-7
Mt. Vernon, 4575 K-10
Mountain Grove, 4789 K-14
Mountain View, 2719 K-15
Murphy, 8690 *K-3
Neosho, 11835 L-9
Nevada, 8386 I-9
New Florence, 769 F-15
New Franklin, 1089 F-13
New Haven, 2089 G-16
New London, 974 D-15
New Madrid, 3116 L-20
NEW MADRID CO., 18956 M-19
NEWTON CO., 58114 L-9
Nixa, 19022 K-11
NODAWAY CO., 23370 B-8
Noel, 1832 L-9
Norborne, 708 E-11
Normandy, 5008 *G-6
N. Kansas City, 4208 H-4
Northwoods, 4227 *G-6
O'Fallon, 79329 F-17
Oak Grove, 7795 F-10
Oakland, 1381 *I-5
Oakville, 36143 *K-6
Odessa, 5300 F-10
Olivette, 7737 *H-5
Olympian Vil., 774 H-17
Oran, 1294 K-19
Oregon, 857 C-8
OREGON CO., 10881 L-16
Orrick, 837 E-10
Osage Bch., 4351 H-13
OSAGE CO., 13878 G-14
Osceola, 947 H-11
Overland, 16062 *G-4
Owensville, 2676 H-15
Ozark, 17820 K-12
OZARK CO., 9723 L-13
Ozark View, 1000 *I-4
Pacific, 7002 G-17
Pagedale, 3304 *H-5
Palmyra, 3595 D-15
Paris, 1220 D-14
Park Hills, 8759 I-17
Parkville, 5554 G-2
Parma, 713 L-19
Pasadena Hills, 930 *G-6
Peculiar, 4608 F-9
PEMISCOT CO., 18296 M-19
PERRY CO., 18971 I-19
Perryville, 8225 I-19
PETTIS CO., 42201 G-11
Pevely, 5484 H-18
PHELPS CO., 45156 J-14
Piedmont, 1977 K-17
Pierce City, 1292 K-10
PIKE CO., 18516 E-16
Pilot Grove, 768 F-12
Pilot Knob, 746 I-17
Pine Lawn, 3275 *G-6
Pineville, 791 L-9
Platte City, 4691 E-8
PLATTE CO., 89322 E-8
Plattsburg, 2319 D-9
Pleasant Hill, 8113 F-9
Pleasant Valley, 2961 G-5
Point Lookout, 1200 *N-9
POLK CO., 31137 I-11
Poplar Bluff, 17023 L-18
Portageville, 3228 M-19
Potosi, 2660 I-17
Princeton, 1166 B-11
PULASKI CO., 52274 I-14
Purdy, 1098 L-10
PUTNAM CO., 4979 B-12
Puxico, 881 K-18
RALLS CO., 10167 E-15
RANDOLPH CO., 25414 D-13
RAY CO., 23494 E-10
Raymore, 19206 F-9
Raytown, 29526 F-9
Reeds Spring, 913 L-11
Republic, 14751 K-11
REYNOLDS CO., 6696 J-16
Rich Hill, 1396 H-9
Richland, 1863 I-13
Richmond, 5797 E-10
Richmond Hts., 8603 *H-5
RIPLEY CO., 14100 L-17
Riverside, 2937 H-3
Riverview, 2856 *F-7
Rock Hill, 4635 *I-5
Rock Port, 1318 B-7
Rogersville, 3073 K-12
Rolla, 19559 I-15
Russellville, 807 G-13
St. Ann, 13020 *G-4
St. Charles, 65794 F-17
SAINT CHARLES CO., 360485 G-16
St. Clair, 4724 H-16
ST. CLAIR CO., 9805 H-10
ST. FRANCOIS CO., 65359 I-18
St. George, 1337 *J-5
St. James, 4216 H-15
St. John, 6517 *G-5
St. Joseph, 76780 D-8
St. Louis, 319294 G-18
ST. LOUIS CO., 998954 G-17
St. Martins, 1140 G-13
St. Paul, 1829 F-17
St. Peters, 52575 F-17
St. Robert, 4340 I-14
Ste. Genevieve, 4410 H-18
STE. GENEVIEVE CO., 18145 I-18
Salem, 4950 I-15
SALINE CO., 23370 F-11
Salisbury, 1618 E-12
Sappington, 7580 *J-5
Sarcoxie, 1330 K-10
Savannah, 5057 C-8
SCHUYLER CO., 4431 B-13
SCOTLAND CO., 4843 B-14
Scott City, 4565 J-20
SCOTT CO., 39191 K-20
Sedalia, 21387 G-12
Seligman, 851 L-10
Senath, 1767 M-18
Seneca, 2336 L-9
Seymour, 1921 K-13
SHANNON CO., 8441 K-15
Shelbina, 1704 D-14
SHELBY CO., 6373 D-14
Shelbyville, 552 D-14
Shell Knob, 1379 L-11
Shrewsbury, 6254 *I-5
Sikeston, 16318 K-19
Slater, 1856 E-12
Smithville, 8425 E-9
Southwest City, 970 L-9
Spanish Lake, 19650 *F-6
Sparta, 1756 K-12
Springfield, 159498 K-11
Stanberry, 1185 B-9
Steele, 2172 N-19
Steelville, 1642 I-16
Stewartsville, 750 D-9
Stockton, 1819 I-10
STODDARD CO., 29968 L-19
STONE CO., 32202 L-11
Stover, 1094 G-12
Strafford, 2358 J-12
Sturgeon, 872 E-14
Sugar Creek, 3345 I-5
Sullivan, 7081 H-16
SULLIVAN CO., 6714 B-12
Sunset Hills, 8496 *J-4
Sweet Sprs., 1484 F-11
TANEY CO., 51675 L-12
Taos, 878 G-14
Tarkio, 1583 B-7
TEXAS CO., 26008 K-14
Thayer, 2243 L-15
Tipton, 3262 G-13
Town and Country, 10815 *H-3
Trenton, 6001 C-11
Troy, 10540 F-16
Tuscumbia, 203 H-13
Union, 10204 G-16
Unionville, 1865 B-12
University City, 35371 *H-5
Valley Pk., 6942 *J-3
Van Buren, 819 K-16
Vandalia, 3899 E-15
Velda Vil., 1420 *G-6
Velda Vil. Hills, 1055 *G-6
VERNON CO., 21159 I-9
Versailles, 2482 G-12
Vienna, 610 H-14
Villa Ridge, 2636 G-17
Vinita Pk., 1880 *G-5
Wardsville, 1506 G-14
WARREN CO., 32513 F-16
Warrensburg, 18838 F-10
Warrenton, 7880 F-16
Warsaw, 2127 H-11
Warson Woods, 1962 *I-4
Washington, 13982 G-16
WASHINGTON CO., 25195 H-16
Waverly, 849 E-11
WAYNE CO., 13521 K-18
Waynesville, 4830 I-14
Weatherby Lake, 1723 G-2
Webb City, 10996 K-9
WEBSTER CO., 36202 J-12
Webster Groves, 22995 *I-5
Weldon Spring, 5443 F-17
Wellington, 812 E-10
Wellston, 2313 *H-6
Wellsville, 1217 F-15
Wentzville, 29070 F-17
W. Plains, 11986 L-15
Weston, 1641 E-8
Wildwood, 35517 G-17
Willard, 5288 J-11
Willow Sprs., 2184 K-14
Winchester, 1547 *I-3
Windsor, 2901 G-11
Winfield, 1404 F-17
Winona, 1335 K-16
Wood Hts., 717 E-10
Woodson Ter., 4063 *G-5
WORTH CO., 2171 B-9
Wright City, 3119 F-16
WRIGHT CO., 18815 J-13

Montana
Map pp. 60 – 61
Absarokee, 1150 I-11
Anaconda, 9298 H-6
Arlee, 636 E-4
Ashland, 824 I-17
Baker, 1741 G-20
BEAVERHEAD CO., 9246 K-6
Belgrade, 7389 I-8
Belt, 597 E-9
BIG HORN CO., 12865 I-15
Big Sandy, 598 C-10
Big Sky, 2308 J-8
Big Timber, 1641 I-10
Bigfork, 4270 C-4
Billings, 104170 I-13
Billings Hts., 6000 M-20
Black Eagle, 904 E-8
BLAINE CO., 6491 B-12
Boulder, 1183 H-7
Bozeman, 37280 I-9
Bridger, 708 J-12
Broadus, 468 I-18
BROADWATER CO., 5612 G-8
Browning, 1016 B-6
Busby, 745 I-15
Butte, 33525 H-6
CARBON CO., 10078 J-12
Carlton, 694 G-4
CARTER CO., 1160 I-19
Cascade, 685 E-8
CASCADE CO., 81327 F-8
Chester, 847 B-9
Chinook, 1203 B-12
Choteau, 1684 D-7
CHOUTEAU CO., 5813 D-10
Churchill, 902 I-8
Circle, 615 E-17
Clancy, 1661 G-7
Clinton, 1052 F-4
Colstrip, 2214 H-16
Columbia Falls, 4688 C-4
Columbus, 1893 I-12
Conrad, 2570 C-7
Coram, 539 C-4
Corvallis, 976 G-4
Crow Agency, 1616 I-15
Culbertson, 714 C-19
CUSTER CO., 11699 H-18
Cut Bank, 2869 B-7
DANIELS CO., 1751 A-17
Darby, 720 H-4
DAWSON CO., 8966 E-18
Deer Lodge, 3111 G-6
DEER LODGE CO., 9298 H-5
Dillon, 4134 J-6
E. Helena, 1984 G-7
Ekalaka, 332 H-19
Ennis, 838 J-8
Eureka, 1037 A-3
Evergreen, 7616 C-4
Fairfield, 708 E-7
Fairview, 840 D-20
FALLON CO., 2890 G-19
FERGUS CO., 11586 E-12
FLATHEAD CO., 90928 D-5
Florence, 765 G-4
Forsyth, 1777 H-16
Ft. Belknap Agency, 1293 C-12
Ft. Benton, 1464 D-9
Four Cors., 3146 I-8
Frenchtown, 1825 F-4
GALLATIN CO., 89513 J-8
Gallatin Gateway, 856 I-8
Gardiner, 875 K-9
GARFIELD CO., 1206 F-15
GLACIER CO., 13399 B-6
Glasgow, 3250 C-16
Glendive, 4935 F-19
GOLDEN VALLEY CO., 884 G-12
GRANITE CO., 3079 G-5
Great Falls, 58505 E-8
Hamilton, 4348 H-4
Hardin, 3505 I-14
Harlem, 808 B-12
Harlowton, 997 G-11
Havre, 9310 B-11
Hays, 843 D-12
Heart Butte, 582 C-6
Helena, 28190 G-7
HILL CO., 16096 B-10
Hot Sprs., 544 D-3
Hungry Horse, 826 C-4
Hysham, 312 H-15
JEFFERSON CO., 11406 H-7
Joliet, 595 J-12
Jordan, 343 E-15
JUDITH BASIN CO., 2072 F-10
Kalispell, 19927 C-4
LAKE CO., 28746 D-3
Lakeside, 2669 C-4
Lame Deer, 2052 I-16
Laurel, 6718 I-12
LEWIS & CLARK CO., 63395 E-6
Lewistown, 5901 F-11
Libby, 2628 B-2
LIBERTY CO., 2339 B-9
Lincoln, 1013 F-6
LINCOLN CO., 19687 B-2
Livingston, 7044 I-9
Lockwood, 6797 M-20
Lolo, 3892 F-4
MADISON CO., 7691 J-7
Malta, 1997 C-14
Manhattan, 1520 I-8
Marion, 886 C-3
Martin City, 500 C-4
MCCONE CO., 1734 D-17
MEAGHER CO., 1891 F-8
Miles City, 8410 G-17
MINERAL CO., 4223 F-3
Missoula, 66788 F-4
MISSOULA CO., 109299 F-3
Montana City, 2715 G-7
Muddy, 617 I-16
MUSSELSHELL CO., 4538 G-13
Orchard Homes, 5197 M-11
Pablo, 2254 D-4
Park City, 983 I-12
PARK CO., 15636 J-10
PETROLEUM CO., 494 E-13
Philipsburg, 820 G-5
PHILLIPS CO., 4253 C-13
Pinesdale, 917 G-4
Plains, 1048 E-3
Plentywood, 1734 B-19
Polson, 4488 D-4
PONDERA CO., 6153 C-8
Poplar, 810 C-18
POWDER RIVER CO., 1743 J-17
POWELL CO., 7027 G-6
PRAIRIE CO., 1179 F-17
Pray, 681 J-9
Pryor, 618 J-13
RAVALLI CO., 40212 I-4
Red Lodge, 2125 J-12
RICHLAND CO., 9746 D-19
Ronan, 1871 E-4
ROOSEVELT CO., 10425 C-19
ROSEBUD CO., 9233 G-16
Roundup, 1788 G-13
Ryegate, 245 H-12
St. Ignatius, 842 E-4
SANDERS CO., 11413 D-2
Scobey, 1017 B-18
Seeley Lake, 1659 E-5
Shelby, 3376 B-8
Shepherd, 516 H-13
Sheridan, 642 J-7
SHERIDAN CO., 3384 B-19
Sidney, 5191 D-20
SILVER BOW CO., 34200 I-6
Somers, 1109 C-4
Stanford, 401 F-10
Stevensville, 1809 G-4
STILLWATER CO., 9117 H-12
Superior, 812 E-3
SWEET GRASS CO., 3651 J-10
Terry, 605 F-18
TETON CO., 6073 D-6
Thompson Falls, 1313 D-2
Three Forks, 1869 I-8
TOOLE CO., 5324 B-8
Townsend, 1878 H-8
TREASURE CO., 718 H-15
Trego, 541 B-3
Troy, 938 B-1
Ulm, 738 E-8
Valier, 509 C-7
VALLEY CO., 7369 B-15
Vaughn, 658 E-8
Victor, 745 G-4
Virginia City, 190 J-7
Walkerville, 675 H-6
W. Riverside, 800 F-4
W. Yellowstone, 1271 K-9
WHEATLAND CO., 2168 G-11
White Haven, 577 C-2
White Sulphur Sprs., 939 G-9
Whitefish, 6357 C-4
Whitehall, 1038 I-7
Wibaux, 589 F-20
WIBAUX CO., 1017 E-20
Winnett, 182 F-13
Wolf Pt., 2621 C-17
Woods Bay, 661 D-4
Worden, 577 H-13
Wornath, 5197 N-11
YELLOWSTONE CO., 147972 H-13

Nebraska
Map pp. 62 – 63
ADAMS CO., 31364 L-13
Ainsworth, 1728 F-10
Albion, 1650 H-14
Alliance, 8491 G-3
Alma, 1133 M-11
ANTELOPE CO., 6685 G-14
Arapahoe, 1026 M-10
Arlington, 1243 I-18
Arthur, 117 I-6
ARTHUR CO., 460 I-5
Ashland, 2453 J-18
Atkinson, 1245 F-12
Auburn, 3460 L-19
Aurora, 4479 K-14
BANNER CO., 690 I-1
Bartlett, 117 H-13
Bassett, 619 F-11
Battle Creek, 1207 G-15
Bayard, 1209 H-2
Beatrice, 12459 M-17
Beaver City, 609 M-10
Bellevue, 50137 J-19
Benkelman, 953 M-6
Bennington, 1458 I-18
Bertrand, 750 L-11
BLAINE CO., 478 H-9
Blair, 7990 I-18
Bloomfield, 1028 F-15
Blue Hill, 936 M-13
BOONE CO., 5505 H-14
BOX BUTTE CO., 11308 G-2
BOYD CO., 2099 E-13
Boys Town, 745 J-18
Brewster, 17 H-10
Bridgeport, 1545 H-3
Broken Bow, 3559 I-10
BROWN CO., 3145 F-10
BUFFALO CO., 46102 K-12
BURT CO., 6858 H-18
Burwell, 1210 H-12
BUTLER CO., 8395 J-16
Butte, 326 E-12
Cairo, 785 K-13
Cambridge, 1063 M-9
CASS CO., 25241 K-19
CEDAR CO., 8852 F-16
Center, 94 F-14
Central City, 2934 J-14
Ceresco, 889 J-17
Chadron, 5851 E-3
Chalco, 10994 D-16
Chappell, 929 J-4
CHASE CO., 3966 L-5
CHERRY CO., 5713 F-7
CHEYENNE CO., 9998 J-3
Clay Ctr., 760 L-14
CLAY CO., 6542 L-14
COLFAX CO., 10515 I-16
Columbus, 22111 I-16
Cozad, 3977 K-10
Crawford, 997 E-2
Creighton, 1154 F-14
Crete, 6960 L-17
CUMING CO., 9139 G-17
Curtis, 939 L-8
CUSTER CO., 10939 J-10
Dakota City, 1919 F-18
DAKOTA CO., 21006 F-17
David City, 2906 J-16
DAWES CO., 9182 E-2
DAWSON CO., 24326 K-10
Deshler, 747 M-15
DEUEL CO., 1941 J-4
DIXON CO., 6000 F-16
DODGE CO., 36691 I-17
Doniphan, 829 K-13
DOUGLAS CO., 517110 I-18
DUNDY CO., 2008 M-6
Eagle, 1024 K-18
Elm Creek, 901 K-11
Elwood, 707 L-10
Emerson, 840 G-17
Fairbury, 3942 M-16
Falls City, 4325 M-20
FILLMORE CO., 5890 L-15
Ft. Calhoun, 908 I-19
Franklin, 1000 M-12
FRANKLIN CO., 3225 M-12
Fremont, 26397 I-18
Friend, 1027 K-16
FRONTIER CO., 2756 L-8
Fullerton, 1307 I-14
FURNAS CO., 4959 M-9
GAGE CO., 22311 L-17
GARDEN CO., 2057 I-4
GARFIELD CO., 2049 H-12
Geneva, 2217 L-15
Genoa, 1003 I-15
Gering, 8500 H-1
Gibbon, 1833 K-12
Gordon, 1612 E-5
GOSPER CO., 2044 L-10
Gothenburg, 3574 K-9
Grand Island, 48520 K-13
Grant, 1165 K-6
GRANT CO., 614 H-5
Greeley, 466 I-13
GREELEY CO., 2538 I-13
Gretna, 4441 J-18
HALL CO., 58607 J-13
HAMILTON CO., 9124 K-14
HARLAN CO., 3423 M-11
Harrisburg, 100 I-1
Harrison, 251 E-1
Hartington, 1554 F-16
Harvard, 1013 L-14
Hastings, 24907 L-13
Hayes Ctr., 214 L-7
HAYES CO., 967 L-7
Hebron, 1579 M-15
Hemingford, 803 F-3
Henderson, 991 K-15
Hickman, 1657 L-17
HITCHCOCK CO., 2908 M-7
Holdrege, 5495 L-11
HOLT CO., 10435 F-12
HOOKER CO., 736 H-7
Hooper, 830 I-17
HOWARD CO., 6274 J-13
Humboldt, 877 M-19
Humphrey, 760 H-15
Hyannis, 182 G-6
Imperial, 2071 L-6
JEFFERSON CO., 7547 M-16
JOHNSON CO., 5217 L-18
Juniata, 755 L-13
Kearney, 30787 K-12
KEARNEY CO., 6489 L-12
KEITH CO., 8368 J-6
Kenesaw, 880 L-13
KEYA PAHA CO., 824 E-10
Kimball, 2496 J-1
KIMBALL CO., 3821 J-1
KNOX CO., 8701 F-15
La Vista, 15758 D-17
LANCASTER CO., 285407 K-17
Laurel, 964 F-16
Lexington, 10230 K-10
Lincoln, 258379 K-17
LINCOLN CO., 36288 K-8
LOGAN CO., 763 I-8
Louisville, 1106 J-18
Loup City, 1029 J-12
LOUP CO., 632 H-11
Lyons, 851 H-18
Macy, 1023 G-18
Madison, 2438 H-15
MADISON CO., 34876 H-15
McCook, 7698 M-8
MCPHERSON CO., 539 I-7
MERRICK CO., 7845 J-14
Milford, 2090 K-16
Minatare, 816 H-2
Minden, 2923 L-12
Mitchell, 1702 H-1
Morrill, 921 G-1
MORRILL CO., 5042 H-3
Mullen, 509 G-7
NANCE CO., 3735 I-14
Nebraska City, 7289 K-19
Neligh, 1599 G-14
Nelson, 488 M-14
NEMAHA CO., 7248 L-19
Norfolk, 24210 G-15
N. Bend, 1177 I-17
N. Platte, 24733 J-8
NUCKOLLS CO., 4500 M-14
O'Neill, 3705 F-13
Oakland, 1244 H-18
Ogallala, 4737 J-6
Omaha, 408958 J-19
Ord, 2112 I-12
Osceola, 880 J-15
Oshkosh, 884 I-4
Osmond, 783 F-15
OTOE CO., 15740 K-18
Oxford, 779 M-10
Papillion, 18894 J-19
Pawnee City, 878 M-19
PAWNEE CO., 2773 M-18
Pender, 1002 G-17
PERKINS CO., 2970 K-6
Peru, 865 L-19
PHELPS CO., 9188 L-11
Pierce, 1767 G-15
PIERCE CO., 7266 G-15
Plainview, 1246 F-15
PLATTE CO., 32237 I-15
Plattsmouth, 6502 J-19
POLK CO., 5406 J-15
Ponca, 961 F-17
Ralston, 5943 C-17
Randolph, 944 F-16
Ravenna, 1360 J-12
Red Cloud, 1020 M-13
RED WILLOW CO., 11055 M-8
RICHARDSON CO., 8363 M-20
ROCK CO., 1526 G-11
Rushville, 890 E-4
St. Paul, 2290 J-13
SALINE CO., 14200 L-16
SARPY CO., 158840 J-18
SAUNDERS CO., 20780 J-17
Schuyler, 6211 I-16
SCOTTS BLUFF CO., 36970 H-1
Scottsbluff, 15039 H-1
Scribner, 857 H-17
Seward, 6964 K-16
SEWARD CO., 16750 J-16
Shelton, 1059 K-13
SHERIDAN CO., 5469 F-4
SHERMAN CO., 3152 J-12
Sidney, 6757 J-3
SIOUX CO., 1311 F-1
S. Sioux City, 13353 F-18
Springfield, 1529 J-18
Springview, 242 E-10
Stanton, 1577 H-16
STANTON CO., 6129 H-16
Stapleton, 305 I-8
Stockville, 25 L-9
Stromsburg, 1171 J-15
Superior, 1957 M-14
Sutherland, 1286 J-7
Sutton, 1502 L-15
Syracuse, 1942 K-18
Taylor, 190 H-11
Tecumseh, 1677 L-18
Tekamah, 1736 H-18
Terrytown, 1198 H-1
THAYER CO., 5228 M-15
Thedford, 188 H-8
THOMAS CO., 647 H-8
THURSTON CO., 6940 G-17
Tilden, 953 G-15
Trenton, 560 M-7
Tryon, 157 I-7
Utica, 861 K-16
Valentine, 2737 E-8
Valley, 1875 I-18
VALLEY CO., 4260 I-12
Wahoo, 4508 J-17
Wakefield, 1451 G-17
Walthill, 780 G-18
WASHINGTON CO., 20234 H-18
Waterloo, 848 I-18
Waverly, 3277 K-18
Wayne, 5660 G-16
WAYNE CO., 9595 G-16
WEBSTER CO., 3812 M-13
Weeping Water, 1050 K-18
West Point, 3364 H-17
WHEELER CO., 818 H-13
Wilber, 1855 L-17
Winnebago, 774 G-18
Wisner, 1170 G-17
Wood River, 1325 K-13
Woodland Pk., 1866 G-16
Wymore, 1457 M-17
York, 7766 K-15
YORK CO., 13665 K-15
Yutan, 1174 J-18

Nevada
Map p. 64
* City keyed to p. 16
† City keyed to p. 65
Alamo, 1080 J-8
Battle Mtn., 3635 D-6
Beatty, 1010 K-6
Boulder City, 15023 L-9
Bunkerville, 1303 K-10
Caliente, 1130 I-9
Carlin, 2368 D-7
Carson City, 55274 F-2
CHURCHILL CO., 24877 F-4
CLARK CO., 1951269 K-8
Dayton, 8964 F-2
DOUGLAS CO., 46997 G-2
Elko, 18297 C-7
ELKO CO., 48818 C-7
Ely, 4255 F-9
ESMERALDA CO., 783 I-5
Eureka, 610 F-7
EUREKA CO., 1987 E-6
Fallon, 8606 F-3
Fernley, 19368 F-2
Gardnerville, 5656 G-2
Genoa, 939 *G-10
Golden Valley, 1556 F-2
Goldfield, 268 I-5
Hawthorne, 3269 H-3
Henderson, 257729 L-8
Hidden Valley, 1000 †I-3
HUMBOLDT CO., 16528 B-4
Incline Vil., 8777 F-1
Indian Sprs., 991 K-7
Jackpot, 1195 A-9
Kingsbury, 2152 *G-10
LANDER CO., 5775 E-5
Las Vegas, 583756 L-8
Laughlin, 7323 N-9
Lemmon Valley, 5040 F-1
LINCOLN CO., 5345 I-9
Lovelock, 1894 E-3
LYON CO., 51980 G-2
McGill, 1148 F-9
Mesquite, 15276 K-10
Minden, 3001 G-2
MINERAL CO., 4772 H-3
Moapa, 1025 K-9
N. Las Vegas, 216961 L-8
NYE CO., 43946 H-6
Owyhee, 953 A-7
Pahrump, 36441 L-7
Panaca, 963 I-9
Paradise, 223167 M-2
PERSHING CO., 6753 D-3
Pioche, 1002 I-9
Reno, 225221 F-2
Sandy Valley, 2051 M-8
Schurz, 658 G-3
Searchlight, 539 M-9
Silver Sprs., 5296 F-2
S. Hills, 1100 †J-2
Sparks, 90264 F-2
Spring Creek, 12361 D-7
Spring Valley, 178395 M-1
Stagecoach, 1874 F-2
Stateline, 842 G-1
STOREY CO., 4010 F-2
Sun Valley, 19299 †G-2
Sunrise Mnr., 189372 L-3
Tonopah, 2478 H-5
Verdi, 1415 F-1
Virginia City, 855 F-2
Wadsworth, 834 F-2
Washoe City, 500 F-2
WASHOE CO., 421407 D-2
Wells, 1292 C-8
W. Wendover, 4410 D-10
WHITE PINE CO., 10030 F-8
Whitney, 38585 M-3
Winchester, 27978 K-3
Winnemucca, 7396 C-4
Yerington, 3048 G-2
Zephyr Cove, 565 G-1

New Hampshire
Map p. 65
Alton Bay, 900 J-8
Amherst, 613 M-7
Antrim, 1397 L-6
Ashland, 1244 I-7
Atkinson, 900 M-9
Bedford, 1800 M-7
BELKNAP CO., 60088 J-8
Belmont, 1301 J-7
Berlin, 10051 E-8
Bethlehem, 972 F-7
Bow Mills, 700 L-7
Bristol, 1688 I-7
Brookline, 700 N-7
Campton, 700 H-7
Canobie Lake, 700 M-8
CARROLL CO., 47818 I-8
Center Hbr., 650 I-7
Charlestown, 1152 K-4
CHESHIRE CO., 77117 L-5
Chester, 600 M-8
Claremont, 13355 J-4
Colebrook, 1394 C-7
Concord, 42695 K-7
Contoocook, 1444 K-7
Conway, 1823 H-9
COOS CO., 33055 D-8
Danville, 700 M-9
Derry, 22015 M-8
Dover, 29987 K-10
Dublin, 650 M-5
Durham, 10345 L-9
E. Derry, 850 M-8
E. Hampstead, 1400 M-9
Enfield, 1540 I-5
Epping, 1681 L-9
Exeter, 9242 L-9
Farmington, 3885 J-9
Fitzwilliam, 650 M-5
Franconia, 600 F-6
Franklin, 8477 J-7
Fremont, 900 L-9
Gilford, 600 J-8
Gilmanton, 700 J-8
Gilmanton Ironworks, 600 J-8
Goffstown, 3196 L-7
Gorham, 1600 F-8
GRAFTON CO., 89118 I-6
Greenfield, 900 M-6
Greenland, 1400 L-10
Greenville, 1108 M-6
Groveton, 1118 E-7
Hampstead, 900 M-8
Hampton, 9656 M-10
Hampton Bch., 2275 M-10
Hanover, 8636 I-5
Henniker, 1747 K-6
Hillsborough, 1976 L-6
HILLSBOROUGH CO., 400721 L-6
Hinsdale, 1548 M-4
Hollis, 600 N-7
Hooksett, 4147 L-8
Hudson, 7336 N-8
Jaffrey, 2757 M-6
Keene, 23409 M-5
Kingston, 700 M-9
Laconia, 15951 J-7
Lancaster, 1725 E-7
Lebanon, 13151 I-5
Lincoln, 993 G-7
Lisbon, 980 F-6
Littleton, 4412 F-6
Londonderry, 11037 M-8
Manchester, 109565 L-7
Marlborough, 1094 M-5
Meredith, 1718 I-7
Merrimack, 2400 M-7
MERRIMACK CO., 146445 K-6
Milford, 8835 M-7
Mont Vernon, 600 M-7
Nashua, 86494 M-7
New Boston, 850 L-7
New Castle, 840 L-10
New Ipswich, 800 M-6
New London, 1415 J-6
Newmarket, 5297 L-9
Newport, 4769 K-5
Newton, 650 M-9
N. Conway, 2349 G-9
N. Walpole, 828 L-4
Northfield, 1500 J-7
Northwood, 650 K-9
Ossipee, 250 I-9
Pelham, 1200 N-8
Peterborough, 3103 M-6
Pinardville, 4780 B-4
Pittsfield, 1576 K-8
Plaistow, 2200 M-9
Plymouth, 4456 I-7
Portsmouth, 20779 L-10
Raymond, 2855 L-8
Rochester, 29752 K-9
ROCKINGHAM CO., 295223 L-8
Rollinsford, 1500 K-10
Rye, 850 L-10
Salem, 12000 M-8
Sanbornville, 1056 J-9
Sandown, 600 M-8
Seabrook, 900 M-10
Somersworth, 11766 K-10
S. Hooksett, 5418 L-8
STRAFFORD CO., 123143 K-9
Stratham, 800 L-9
SULLIVAN CO., 43742 K-4
Sunapee, 1000 J-5
Suncook, 5379 L-8
Swanzey, 900 M-5
Tamworth, 600 H-8
Tilton, 1300 J-7
Troy, 1221 M-5
Walpole, 605 L-4
W. Swanzey, 1308 M-4
Whitefield, 1142 F-7
Wilton, 1163 M-7
Winchester, 1733 M-4
Winnisquam, 650 J-7
Wolfeboro, 2838 I-8
Wolfeboro Falls, 600 I-8
Woodsville, 1126 G-5

New Jersey
Map pp. 66 – 67
† City keyed to pp. 72 – 73
‡ City keyed to p. 90
Absecon, 8411 P-10
Allendale, 6505 C-12
Allentown, 1828 J-10
Allenwood, 925 R-2
Alloway, 3467 O-5
Almonesson, 800 M-6
Alpha, 2369 F-6
Alpine, 1849 D-13
Annandale, 1695 G-8
Asbury Pk., 16116 J-13
Atco, 5700 N-8
Atlantic City, 39558 Q-10
ATLANTIC CO., 274549 P-9
Atlantic Highlands, 4385 H-13
Audubon, 8819 M-7
Audubon Pk., 1023 ‡F-5
Avalon, 1334 S-9
Avenel, 17011 †L-4
Avon-by-the-Sea, 1901 J-13
Bargaintown, 1600 Q-10
Barnegat, 2817 N-12
Barrington, 6983 M-7
Basking Ridge, 4000 F-10
Bay Head, 968 K-13
Bayonne, 63024 F-12
Bayville, 900 L-12
Beach Haven, 1170 O-12
Beach Haven West, 3896 N-12
Beachwood, 11045 L-12
Beattystown, 4554 E-8
Bedminster, 3000 F-9
Beesleys Pt., 850 Q-9
Belford, 1768 H-12
Belleville, 36000 E-12
Bellmawr, 11262 ‡G-6
Belmar, 5794 J-13
Belvidere, 2681 E-7
BERGEN CO., 905116 D-13
Bergenfield, 26764 D-13
Berkeley Hts., 13100 F-10
Berlin, 7588 M-7
Bernardsville, 7707 F-10
Beverly, 2577 K-7
Blackwood, 4545 M-7
Bloomfield, 37800 E-12
Bloomingdale, 7656 D-11
Bloomsbury, 870 G-6
Bogota, 8187 †D-9
Boonton, 8347 E-11
Bordentown, 3924 K-9
Bound Brook, 10402 G-10
Bradley Bch., 4298 J-13
Branchville, 841 C-8
Brass Castle, 1555 F-7
Bricktown, 25900 K-12
Bridgeton, 25349 P-6
Brielle, 4774 K-13
Brigantine, 9450 P-11
Brookdale, 9239 †E-6
Brooklawn, 1955 ‡G-5
Brookside, 1800 E-10
Browns Mills, 11223 L-10
Browntown, 2400 I-11
Brownville, 2383 H-4
Budd Lake, 8968 E-9
Buena, 4603 P-7
Burlington, 9920 K-8
BURLINGTON CO., 448734 L-9
Butler, 7539 D-11
Caldwell, 7822 E-11
Califon, 1076 F-8
Camden, 77344 L-6
CAMDEN CO., 513657 N-8
Cape May, 3607 T-7
CAPE MAY CO., 97265 R-8
Cape May Court House, 5338 S-8
Carlls Cor., 900 P-6
Carlstadt, 6127 †E-8
Carneys Pt., 7382 N-4
Carteret, 22844 G-12
Cassville, 800 K-11
Cedar Brook, 800 N-8
Cedar Grove, 12300 E-12
Cedarville, 776 Q-6
Chadwick Bch., 1200 T-3
Chatham, 8962 F-11
Cherry Hill, 4000 L-7
Chesilhurst, 1634 N-8
Chester, 1649 F-9
Clark, 14597 †K-3
Clarksboro, 1700 M-6
Clayton, 8179 N-6
Clementon, 4999 M-7
Cliffside Pk., 23594 †F-10
Cliffwood, 1500 H-12
Cliffwood Bch., 3194 H-12
Clifton, 84136 E-12
Clinton, 2719 G-8
Closter, 8373 D-13
Clover Leaf Lakes, 900 P-9
Collings Lakes, 1706 O-8
Collingswood, 13926 L-7
Cologne, 1100 P-9
Colonia, 17795 G-11
Colonial Manor, 2000 ‡G-4
Colts Neck, 800 I-12
Concordia, 3092 I-10
Convent Sta., 1800 F-10
Country Lake Estates, 3943 L-10
Cranberry Lake, 1000 D-9
Cranbury, 2181 I-10
Crandon Lakes, 1178 C-8
Cranford, 22578 †J-4
Cresskill, 8573 †B-11
Crestwood Vil., 7907 L-11
Crosswicks, 800 K-9
Culvers Lake, 1100 C-8
CUMBERLAND CO., 156898 Q-6
Dayton, 7063 I-10
Deal, 750 J-13
Del Haven, 1200 S-7
Delanco, 4200 K-7
Delran, 10300 L-7
Demarest, 4881 †B-11
Denville, 5600 E-10
Dogs Cor., 1100 P-2
Dorothy, 900 P-8
Dover, 18157 E-10
Dover Beaches North, 1239 L-13
Dumont, 17479 †B-10
Dunellen, 7227 G-10
E. Brunswick, 10700 G-3
E. Newark, 2406 †G-7
E. Orange, 64270 †G-6
E. Rutherford, 8913 †E-8
Eatontown, 12709 I-13
Edgewater, 11513 †E-10
Edgewater Pk., 2000 K-8
Edison, 40500 H-11
Egg Hbr. City, 4243 O-9
Eldridge Pk., 3000 C-3
Elizabeth, 124969 F-12
Elmer, 1395 O-6
Elmwood Pk., 19403 †C-7
Elwood, 1437 O-9
Emerson, 7401 †A-9
Englewood, 27147 E-13
Englewood Cliffs, 5281 †D-11
Englishtown, 1847 I-11
Erma, 2134 T-8
ESSEX CO., 783969 F-11
Estell Manor, 1735 Q-8
Ewing, 22800 J-8
Ewingville, 9300 C-2
Fair Haven, 6121 I-13
Fair Lawn, 32457 †B-7
Fairton, 1264 Q-6
Fairview, 13835 †F-10
Fairview, 3806 I-12
Fanwood, 7318 G-11
Far Hills, 919 F-9
Farmingdale, 1329 J-12
Finderne, 5600 G-10
Flanders, 6200 E-9
Flemington, 4581 H-8
Florence, 4426 K-8
Florham Pk., 11696 E-11
Folsom, 1885 O-8
Fords, 15187 G-11
Forked River, 5244 M-12
Ft. Lee, 35345 E-13
Franklin, 5045 C-10
Franklin Lakes, 10590 D-12
Franklin Pk., 13295 H-10
Franklinville, 1500 O-7
Freehold, 12052 J-11
Freewood Acres, 1900 J-12
Frenchtown, 1373 H-7
Garfield, 30487 †D-8
Garwood, 4226 †J-3
Gibbsboro, 2274 M-7
Gibbstown, 3739 M-5
Gillette, 900 F-10
Glassboro, 18579 N-6
Glen Gardner, 1704 F-7
Glen Ridge, 7527 †F-6
Glen Rock, 11601 †B-7
Glendola, 2400 J-13
Gloucester City, 11456 M-6
GLOUCESTER CO., 288288 O-7
Green Brook, 2400 G-10
Green Creek, 900 S-8
Green Pond, 900 D-10
Griggstown, 819 H-9
Groveville, 2945 J-9
Guttenberg, 11176 †F-10
Hackensack, 43010 E-13
Hackettstown, 9724 E-8
Haddonfield, 11593 M-7
Hainesport, 1200 L-8
Haledon, 8318 †B-6
Hamburg, 3277 C-10
Hamilton Sq., 12784 J-9
Hammonton, 14791 O-8
Hampton, 1401 F-7
Hanover, 13700 E-10
Harding Lakes, 1000 P-8
Harrington Pk., 4664 †A-10
Harrison, 27472 †G-7
Hasbrouck Hts., 11842 †D-8
Haworth, 3382 †B-10
Hawthorne, 18791 †B-7
Hazlet, 12000 H-12
Helmetta, 2178 I-10
High Bridge, 3648 F-8
Highland Lake, 4933 B-10
Highland Pk., 13982 H-10
Highlands, 5005 I-13
Hightstown, 5494 J-10
Hillsdale, 10219 D-13
Hillside, 21747 †I-5
Hoboken, 50005 F-13
Holmdel, 16773 I-12
Hopatcong, 15147 D-9
Hopelawn, 800 †M-4
Hopewell, 1922 I-8
HUDSON CO., 634266 F-12
HUNTERDON CO., 128349 G-7
Hyson, 2000 K-11
Interlaken, 820 J-13
Ironia, 800 E-9
Irvington, 60695 †H-5
Iselin, 18695 †L-3
Island Hts., 1673 L-12
Jamesburg, 5915 I-10
Jersey City, 247597 F-13
Keansburg, 10105 H-12
Kearny, 40684 F-12
Kendall Pk., 9339 H-10
Kenilworth, 7914 †I-4
Kenvil, 3009 E-9
Keyport, 7240 H-12
Kingston, 1493 I-9
Kinnelon, 10248 D-11
Lake Como, 1759 Q-3
Lake Hopatcong, 3000 D-9
Lake Swannanoa, 1600 D-10
Lake Tamarack, 800 C-10
Lake Telemark, 1255 D-10
Lakehurst, 2654 L-11
Lakewood, 53805 K-12
Lambertville, 3906 I-7
Lanoka Hbr., 2500 M-12
Laurel Lake, 2989 Q-7
Laurence Hbr., 6536 H-12
Lavallette, 1875 L-13
Lawrenceville, 3887 I-9
Lebanon, 1358 G-8
Ledgewood, 1200 E-9
Leesburg, 750 R-7
Leisure Vil., 4400 K-12
Leisuretowne, 3582 M-9
Leonardo, 2757 H-13
Leonia, 8937 †D-10
Liberty Cor., 800 F-10
Lincoln Pk., 10521 D-11
Lincroft, 6135 I-12
Linden, 40499 G-12
Lindenwold, 17613 M-7
Linwood, 7092 Q-10
Little Ferry, 10626 †E-9
Little Silver, 5950 I-13
Livingston, 29300 E-11
Lodi, 24136 E-13
Long Branch, 30719 I-13
Long Valley, 1879 F-8
Longport, 895 Q-10
Lumberton, 5100 L-8
Lyndhurst, 19383 †F-7
Madison, 15845 F-10
Madison Park, 7144 G-4
Mahwah, 15000 C-12
Malaga, 2100 O-7
Manahawkin, 2303 N-12
Manasquan, 5897 K-13
Mantua, 2400 M-6
Manville, 10344 G-9
Maple Shade, 18700 L-7
Maplewood, 23868 †H-4
Margate City, 6354 Q-10
Marlboro, 1100 I-12
Marlton, 10133 M-7
Marmora, 1700 R-9
Martinsville, 11980 G-10
Masonville, 6600 L-8
Matawan, 8810 H-12
Mays Lndg., 2135 P-9
Maywood, 9555 †C-9
McAfee, 1400 B-10
McKee City, 1200 P-9
Medford, 2400 L-8
Medford Lakes, 4146 M-8
Mendham, 4981 F-9
Menlo Pk., 8100 †L-3
MERCER CO., 366513 I-8
Mercerville, 13230 J-9
Metuchen, 13574 G-11
Mickleton, 1200 M-6
Middlesex, 13635 G-10
MIDDLESEX CO., 809858 I-10
Middletown, 66522 I-12
Middletown, 24000 N-1
Milford, 1233 G-6
Mill Brook, 1700 E-10
Millburn, 6900 F-11
Millington, 2500 F-10
Milltown, 6893 H-10
Millville, 28400 P-7
Mine Hill, 2800 E-9
Mizpah, 1000 P-8
Monmouth Bch., 3279 I-13
MONMOUTH CO., 630380 J-11
Monmouth Jct., 2887 I-10
Montclair, 27500 E-12

*, †, ‡, § See explanation under state title in this index. County and parish names are listed in capital letters and in boldface type. Independent cities (not in any county) are shown in italics.

Montvale, 7844....C-13
Montville, 3600....D-11
Moonachie, 2708....*E-9
Moorestown, 12300....L-7
Morganville, 5040....I-12
MORRIS CO., 492276....E-9
Morris Plains, 5532....E-10
Morristown, 18411....E-10
Mt. Arlington, 5050....D-9
Mt. Ephraim, 4676....*G-6
Mt. Freedom, 1900....E-10
Mt. Holly, 6400....L-8
Mt. Laurel, 19000....L-8
Mt. Royal, 900....M-6
Mountain Lakes, 4160....E-10
Mullica Hill, 3982....N-6
Mystic Island, 8493....Q-11
National Pk., 3036....*G-4
Navesink, 2020....I-13
Neptune City, 4869....J-13
Netcong, 3232....E-9
New Brooklyn, 4000....N-7
New Brunswick, 55181....H-10
New Egypt, 2512....K-10
New Market, 21100....G-10
New Milford, 16341....*B-10
New Providence, 12171....F-11
Newark, 277140....F-12
Newfield, 1553....O-7
Newton, 7997....C-8
N. Arlington, 15392....*F-7
N. Beach Haven, 2235....O-12
N. Branch, 1300....G-9
N. Caldwell, 6183....E-11
N. Cape May, 3226....T-7
N. Haledon, 8417....*B-6
N. Middletown, 3295....H-12
N. Plainfield, 21936....G-10
N. Stelton, 3000....*M-1
N. Wildwood, 4041....T-8
Northfield, 8624....Q-10
Northvale, 4640....D-13
Nutley, 27362....*E-7
Oak Ridge, 900....C-10
Oak Ridge Estates, 1600....T-1
Oakhurst, 3995....J-13
Oakland, 12754....D-11
Oaklyn, 4038....*F-6
Ocean Acres, 16142....N-11
Ocean Bch., 1800....L-13
Ocean City, 11701....Q-10
OCEAN CO., 576567....M-11
Ocean Gate, 2011....L-12
Ocean Grove, 3342....J-13
Oceanport, 5832....I-13
Ogdensburg, 2410....C-9
Old Bridge, 23753....H-11
Old Tappan, 5750....D-13
Oliver, 1408....E-9
Oradell, 7978....D-13
Orange, 32868....*G-5
Ortley Bch., 1209....L-13
Osbornsville, 850....K-12
Oxford, 1090....E-7
Palermo, 1200....R-9
Palisades Pk., 19622....*E-10
Palmyra, 7398....K-7
Paramus, 26342....D-13
Parkertown, 800....O-12
Parkway Pines, 1100....K-12
Parsippany, 7800....E-10
Passaic, 69781....E-12
PASSAIC CO., 501226....C-11
Paterson, 146199....D-12
Paulsboro, 6097....M-6
Peapack and Gladstone, 2582....F-9
Pebble Bch., 2000....I-13
Pemberton, 1409....L-9
Pemberton Hts., 2423....L-9
Pennington, 2585....J-9
Penns Grove, 5147....N-4
Pennsville, 11888....N-4
Pequannock, 15500....D-11
Perth Amboy, 50814....H-11
Petersburg, 900....R-9
Phillipsburg, 14950....F-6
Pine Bch., 2127....L-12
Pine Hill, 10233....M-7
Pine Lake Pk., 8707....L-12
Pinewald, 1700....M-12
Piscataway, 31000....G-10
Pitman, 9011....N-6
Plainfield, 49808....G-10
Plainsboro Ctr., 2712....I-9
Pleasantville, 20249....Q-10
Point Pleasant, 18392....K-13
Point Pleasant Bch., 4665....L-13
Pomona, 7124....P-10
Pompton Lakes, 11097....D-11
Port Monmouth, 3818....H-12
Port Norris, 1377....R-7
Port Reading, 3728....*L-5
Port Republic, 1115....O-10
Princeton, 28572....I-9
Princeton Jct., 2465....I-9
Prospect Pk., 5865....*B-6
Pumptown, 2000....L-2
Rahway, 27346....G-11
Ramblewood, 5907....F-3
Ramsey, 14473....C-12
Ramtown, 6242....K-12
Rancocas Hts., 750....*E-10
Rancocas Woods, 1400....*D-10
Raritan, 6881....G-9
Red Bank, 12206....I-13
Red Bank, 1100....*G-4
Richwood, 3459....N-6
Ridgefield, 11032....*E-10
Ridgefield Pk., 12729....*D-9
Ridgewood, 24958....*A-8
Ringwood, 12228....C-11
Rio Grande, 2670....S-8
River Edge, 11340....*B-9
River Vale, 9449....*A-10
Riverside, 8000....K-7
Riverton, 2779....K-7
Robbinsville, 3041....J-9
Robertsville, 11297....I-11
Rochelle Pk., 5528....C-8
Rockaway, 6438....E-10
Roebling, 3715....K-8
Roosevelt, 882....J-10
Roselle, 21085....*I-4
Roselle Pk., 13297....*E-1
Rosenhayn, 1098....F-6
Rumson, 7122....I-13
Runnemede, 8468....M-7
Rutherford, 18061....*E-7
Saddle Brook, 13155....*C-8
Salem, 5146....O-4
SALEM CO., 66083....O-5
Sayreville, 42704....H-11
Scotch Plains, 23500....G-11
Sea Bright, 1412....I-13
Sea Girt, 1828....K-13
Sea Isle City, 2114....S-8
Seabrook, 1484....P-6
Seabrook Farms, 1484....L-1
Seaside Hts., 2887....L-13
Seaside Pk., 1579....L-13
Secaucus, 15931....F-8
Sewaren, 2756....*M-4
Sewell, 2000....N-6
Shark River Hills, 3697....Q-2
Ship Bottom, 1156....O-12
Short Hills, 13165....F-11
Shrewsbury, 3809....Q-2
Sicklerville, 1800....N-7
Silver Ridge, 1133....L-12
Slackwood, 4300....J-9
Slackwoods, 4300....J-9
Smithville, 7242....P-11
Somerdale, 5151....M-7
Somers Pt., 10795....Q-9
Somerset, 22083....H-10
SOMERSET CO., 323444....H-9
Somerville, 12098....G-9
S. Amboy, 8631....H-11
S. Bound Brook, 4563....G-10
S. Hackensack, 2106....G-5
S. Orange, 16964....G-4
S. Plainfield, 23385....G-11
S. River, 16008....H-11
S. Toms River, 3684....L-12
Southard, 3400....K-12
Sparta, 1900....D-9
Spotswood, 8257....I-11
Spring Lake, 3567....K-13
Spring Lake Hts., 4713....J-13
Springfield, 15800....F-11
Springside, 1600....K-8
Stanhope, 3610....D-9
Stirling, 1800....F-10
Stone Hbr., 866....S-8
Stratford, 7258....M-7
Succasunna, 9152....E-9
Summit, 21457....F-11
Surf City, 1205....N-12
Sussex, 2130....B-9
SUSSEX CO., 149265....B-9
Swedesboro, 2584....N-5
Teaneck, 39260....*D-9
Tenafly, 14488....D-13
Thorofare, 1800....L-6
Tinton Falls, 17892....I-12
Titusville, 900....I-8
Toms River, 88791....L-12
Totowa, 10804....E-12
Town Bank, 1500....T-7
Trenton, 84913....J-8
Troy Hills, 5100....E-11
Tuckahoe, 800....Q-9
Tuckerton, 3347....O-11
Turnersville, 3742....N-7
Twin Rivers, 7443....J-10
Union, 56600....F-11
Union Bch., 6245....H-12
Union City, 66455....*G-9
UNION CO., 536499....G-11
Upper Saddle River, 8208....C-12
Ventnor City, 10650....Q-10
Verga, 800....*G-4
Vernon, 1713....B-10
Vernon Valley, 1626....B-10
Victory Gdns., 1520....E-10
Vienna, 981....E-8
Villas, 9483....S-7
Vincentown, 900....L-9
Vineland, 60724....P-7
Voorhees, 976....F-1
Waldwick, 9625....D-12
Wallington, 11335....*E-8
Wanamassa, 4532....J-13
Wanaque, 11116....D-11
Waretown, 1569....N-12
WARREN CO., 108692....E-8
Warrenville, 1000....G-10
Washington, 6461....F-7
Washington Hts., 2500....F-3
Watchung, 5801....G-10
Waterford Works, 1000....N-8
Wayne, 54700....D-11
Weehawken, 12554....*F-9
Wenonah, 2278....M-6
W. Atlantic City, 900....Q-10
W. Belmar, 2493....Q-3
W. Cape May, 1024....T-7
W. Creek, 800....O-11
W. Freehold, 13613....J-12
W. Long Branch, 8097....I-13
W. Milford, 4700....C-11
W. New York, 49708....E-13
W. Orange, 46200....F-11
Westfield, 30316....G-11
Westville, 4288....*G-5
Westville Grove, 1500....*G-5
Westwood, 10908....D-13
Wharton, 6522....E-10
White Horse, 9494....M-4
White House Sta., 2089....G-8
Whitesboro, 800....G-9
Whitesboro, 2300....S-8
Whiting, 950....L-11
Whitman Sq., 3500....N-7
Wildwood, 5325....T-8
Wildwood Crest, 3270....T-7
Williamstown, 15567....O-7
Willingboro, 31600....K-8
Winfield, 1470....*L-4
Winslow, 800....N-8
Wood-Lynne, 2978....*F-5
Wood-Ridge, 7626....*E-8
Woodbine, 2472....R-8
Woodbridge, 19265....G-11
Woodbury, 10174....M-6
Woodbury Hts., 3055....M-6
Woodland Pk., 10987....*D-6
Woodstown, 3505....N-5
Wrightstown, 802....K-9
Wyckoff, 16720....*A-7
Yardville, 7186....J-9

New Mexico
Map p. 68

Acomita, 800....E-3
Adobe Acres, 2500....E-8
Agua Fria, 2800....M-4
Alamogordo, 30403....K-6
Albuquerque, 545852....E-4
Algodones, 814....D-5
Alto, 800....K-6
Angel Fire, 1216....B-7
Anthony, 9360....L-5
Arenas Valley, 1522....K-2
Arroyo Seco, 1785....B-6
Artesia, 11301....J-8
Atoka, 1077....J-8
Aztec, 6763....B-3
Bayard, 2328....K-2
Belen, 7269....F-4
Bernalillo, 8320....D-4
BERNALILLO CO., 662564....E-4
Black Rock, 1323....E-1
Bloomfield, 8112....B-2
Bluewater, 628....E-3
Bosque Farms, 3904....E-4
Capitan, 1489....I-6
Carlsbad, 26138....K-8
Carrizozo, 996....I-5
CATRON CO., 3725....G-2
Cedar Crest, 958....E-5
Cedar Hill, 847....A-3
Chama, 1022....A-4
Chamberino, 919....L-4
Chaparral, 14631....L-5
CHAVES CO., 65645....G-9
Chimayo, 3177....C-6
Church Rock, 1128....D-2
CIBOLA CO., 27213....E-2
Cimarron, 1021....B-7
Claunch, 3025....G-5
Clayton, 2980....B-10
Cloudcroft, 674....L-6
Clovis, 37775....F-10
COLFAX CO., 13750....B-7
Columbus, 1664....M-3
Corrales, 8329....E-5
Crownpoint, 2278....D-2
Cuba, 731....C-4
CURRY CO., 48376....F-9
DE BACA CO., 2022....F-8
Deming, 14855....L-3
Dexter, 1266....I-8
Dixon, 926....C-6
Doña Ana, 1211....L-4
DOÑA ANA CO., 209233....K-4
Dulce, 2743....A-4
EDDY CO., 53829....J-8
Edgewood, 3735....E-5
El Rito, 808....C-5
Elephant Butte, 1431....I-4
Española, 10224....C-5
Estancia, 1655....E-5
Eunice, 2922....L-10
Fairacres, 824....L-4
Farmington, 45877....B-2
Five Points, 4200....E-4
Flora Vista, 2191....B-2
Ft. Sumner, 1031....F-8
Ft. Wingate, 950....E-1
Gallup, 21678....D-1
GRANT CO., 29514....L-1
Grants, 9182....E-3
GUADALUPE CO., 4687....E-7
Hagerman, 1257....I-8
HARDING CO., 695....C-9
Hatch, 1673....K-3
HIDALGO CO., 4894....K-1
High Rolls, 834....L-6
Hobbs, 34122....J-10
Hurley, 1297....K-2
Jal, 2047....J-10
Jarales, 2475....F-4
Jemez Pueblo, 1788....D-4
Kirtland, 7875....B-2
La Cienega, 3819....D-5
La Luz, 1697....K-6
La Mesa, 728....L-4
La Mesilla, 2196....L-4
La Plata, 612....A-2
La Puebla, 1186....C-5
La Union, 1106....K-4
Laguna, 1241....E-3
Las Cruces, 97618....L-4
Las Vegas, 13753....D-7
LEA CO., 64727....H-9
LINCOLN CO., 20497....G-6
Logan, 1042....D-9
Lordsburg, 2797....K-1
Los Alamos, 12019....C-5
LOS ALAMOS CO., 17950....C-5
Los Chavez, 5446....F-4
Los Lunas, 14835....E-4
Los Padillas, 2500....E-4
Los Ranchos de Albuquerque, 6024....E-8
Loving, 1413....K-9
Lovington, 11009....J-10
LUNA CO., 25095....J-2
Magdalena, 938....G-3
McINTOSH, 1484....E-5
McKINLEY CO., 71492....D-3
Melrose, 651....E-9
Mescalero, 1338....K-6
Mesilla, 2196....L-4
Mesquite, 1112....L-4
Midway, 971....I-8
Milan, 3245....E-3
MORA CO., 4881....C-7
Moriarty, 1910....E-5
Mosquero, 93....D-9
Mountainair, 928....F-5
Navajo, 1645....C-1
OTERO CO., 63797....L-6
Paradise Hills, 4256....K-7
Paraje, 777....E-3
Pecos, 1392....D-6
Pena Blanca, 709....D-5
Peralta, 3660....E-4
Placitas, 4977....D-5
Pojoaque Valley, 1907....C-5
Portales, 12280....F-10
QUAY CO., 9041....E-9
Questa, 1770....B-6
Ranchos de Taos, 2518....C-6
Raton, 6885....B-8
Reserve, 289....G-1
RIO ARRIBA CO., 40246....B-4
Rio Rancho, 87521....E-4
ROOSEVELT CO., 19846....G-9
Roswell, 48366....H-8
Ruidoso, 8029....H-6
Ruidoso Downs, 2815....H-6
Salem, 942....L-4
San Felipe Pueblo, 2404....D-5
SAN JUAN CO., 130044....B-2
San Juan Pueblo, 1143....C-5
SAN MIGUEL CO., 29393....D-7
San Rafael, 933....E-3
SANDOVAL CO., 131561....C-4
Santa Clara, 1686....K-2
Santa Fe, 67947....D-6
SANTA FE CO., 144170....D-5
Santa Rosa, 2848....E-8
Santa Teresa, 4258....K-4
Santo Domingo Pueblo, 2456....D-5
Shiprock, 8295....B-2
SIERRA CO., 11988....K-4
Silver City, 10315....J-2
Socorro, 9051....G-4
SOCORRO CO., 17866....G-5
Springer, 1047....C-8
Sunland Pk., 14106....K-5
Taos, 5716....B-6
TAOS CO., 32937....B-6
Taos Pueblo, 1135....B-6
Tatum, 798....H-10
Texico, 1130....F-10
Thoreau, 1865....D-2
Tierra Amarilla, 382....B-5
Tijeras, 541....E-5
Tome, 1867....E-4
TORRANCE CO., 16383....F-6
Truth or Consequences, 6475....J-3
Tucumcari, 5363....E-9
Tularosa, 2842....J-5
Twin Lakes, 1052....D-1
Tyrone, 637....L-1
UNION CO., 4549....B-9
University Pk., 4192....L-4
Vado, 3194....L-4
Valencia, 2192....E-4
VALENCIA CO., 76569....F-4
Waterflow, 1670....B-2
White Rock, 5725....D-5
White Sands, 1651....J-5
Zuni Pueblo, 6302....E-1

New York
Map pp. 69 – 71

Map keys — Atlas pages
NA – NN — 70 – 71
SA – SJ — 69

* City keyed to pp. 72 – 73

Adams, 1775....NF-12
Adams Ctr., 1568....NF-12
Addison, 1763....SH-8
Afton, 822....NM-14
Akron, 2868....NI-5
Albany, 97856....NK-19
ALBANY CO., 304204....NK-18
Albertson, 5182....*G-17
Albion, 6056....NE-6
Alden, 2605....NJ-5
Alexandria Bay, 1078....NC-12
Alfred, 4174....SH-7
Allegany, 1816....NM-5
ALLEGANY CO., 48946....NL-6
Altamont, 1720....NK-18
Altona, 730....NB-19
Amagansett, 1165....SE-13
Amawalk, 1390....SC-6
Amenia, 955....NM-20
Amherst, 45800....NJ-5
Amityville, 9523....SJ-7
Amsterdam, 18620....NJ-18
Andover, 1042....NM-7
Angelica, 869....NM-6
Angola, 2127....NK-3
Angola on the Lake, 1675....NK-3
Apalachin, 1131....NM-12
Arcade, 2071....NK-5
Arkport, 844....NL-7
Arlington, 4061....SA-6
Armonk, 4330....SD-7
Armor, 1550....NJ-4
Ashville, 800....NM-2
Athens, 1668....NL-19
Atlantic Bch., 1891....*J-16
Attica, 2547....NJ-6
Auburn, 27687....NI-10
Aurora, 724....NJ-10
Averill Park, 1693....NK-19
Avoca, 946....NL-8
Avon, 3394....NJ-7
Babylon, 12166....SJ-9
Bainbridge, 1355....NL-14
Baiting Hollow, 1642....SE-10
Baldwin, 24033....*J-18
Baldwin Hbr., 8102....*J-18
Baldwinsville, 7053....NI-11
Ballston Spa, 5409....NJ-19
Balmville, 3178....SB-5
Batavia, 15465....NI-6
Bath, 5786....NL-8
Baxter Estates, 999....*F-16
Bay Park, 2212....*J-17
Bay Shore, 26337....SF-9
Bayport, 8215....SF-9
Bayville, 7024....SE-6
Beacon, 15541....SB-6
Bedford, 1834....SD-7
Bedford Hills, 3001....SC-7
Belfast, 837....NL-6
Belle Terre, 792....SE-9
Bellerose, 1193....*H-16
Bellerose Ter., 2198....*H-16
Bellmore, 16218....*I-20
Bellport, 2084....SF-10
Belmont, 969....NM-6
Bergen, 1176....NI-6
Berlin, 800....NK-20
Bethpage, 16429....*H-20
Big Flats, 5277....NM-9
Binghamton, 47376....NM-12
Black River, 1348....NF-13
Blasdell, 2553....NJ-4
Blauvelt, 5689....SD-6
Bloomfield, 1361....NJ-8
Bloomingburg, 420....SB-4
Blue Pt., 4773....SJ-12
Boght Cors., 1150....NK-19
Bohemia, 10180....SF-9
Bolivar, 1047....NM-5
Boonville, 2072....NG-14
Brant Lake, 850....NG-19
Brentwood, 60664....SF-9
Brewster, 2390....SC-7
Briarcliff Manor, 7867....SD-7
Bridgehampton, 1756....SE-12
Brightwaters, 3103....SJ-10
Brighton, 36609....SI-9
Broadalbin, 1280....NJ-18
Brockport, 8366....NE-6
Brocton, 1547....NL-2
BRONX CO., 1385108....*D-11
Bronxville, 6323....*B-13
Brookhaven, 3451....SI-13
Brookville, 3465....*F-19
BROOME CO., 200600....NM-12
Brownville, 1119....NE-12
Brunswick, 800....NJ-19
Buchanan, 2230....SC-7
Buffalo, 261310....NJ-4
Bullville, 900....SB-4
Burnt Hills, 1620....NJ-19
Cadyville, 900....NB-19
Cairo, 1402....NL-18
Calcium, 3491....NE-13
Caledonia, 2201....NI-7
Calverton, 6510....SE-11
Cambridge, 1870....NI-20
Camden, 2231....NH-14
Camillus, 1213....NI-11
Campbell, 713....NM-9
Canajoharie, 2229....NJ-16
Canandaigua, 10545....NJ-8
Canastota, 4804....NI-13
Candor, 851....NM-11
Canisteo, 2270....NL-7
Canton, 6314....NC-14
Cape Vincent, 726....NE-11
Carle Place, 4981....*G-18
Carmel, 3600....SB-7
Carthage, 3747....NE-13
Castile, 1015....NK-6
Castleton-on-Hudson, 1473....NK-19
CATTARAUGUS CO., 80317....NL-4
CAYUGA CO., 80026....NI-10
Cayuga Hts., 3729....NL-11
Cazenovia, 2835....NJ-13
Cedarhurst, 6592....*K-15
Celoron, 1112....NM-2
Center Moriches, 7580....SF-11
Centereach, 31578....SE-9
Centerport, 5508....SE-8
Central Islip, 34450....SF-9
Central Sq., 1848....NH-12
Chadwicks, 1506....NI-14
Champlain, 1101....NA-19
Champlain Park, 1200....NB-20
Chappaqua, 1436....SD-7
Chateaugay, 833....NB-18
Chatham, 1770....NL-19
CHAUTAUQUA CO., 134905....NL-2
Cheektowaga, 75178....NE-10
CHEMUNG CO., 88830....NM-9
Chenango Bridge, 2883....NM-12
CHENANGO CO., 50477....NK-13
Chester, 3969....SC-4
Chili Ctr., 4350....SG-1
Chittenango, 5081....NI-13
Churchville, 1961....NI-7
Cicero, 1100....NI-12
Circleville, 1350....SB-4
Clarence, 2646....NI-4
Clarence Ctr., 2257....NI-4
Clark Mills, 1905....NI-14
Clarkson, 4358....NI-6
Clarksville, 800....NK-18
Claverack, 1000....NL-19
Clayton, 1978....NE-12
Cleveland, 750....NH-13
Clifton Park, 1200....NJ-19
Clifton Sprs., 2127....NJ-9
Clinton, 1942....NI-14
CLINTON CO., 82128....NB-19
Clinton Park, 800....NG-8
Clintondale, 1452....SA-5
Clyde, 2093....NI-10
Cobleskill, 4678....NK-17
Cohocton, 838....NK-8
Cohoes, 16168....NJ-19
Cold Spring, 2013....SC-6
Cold Spring Hbr., 5070....SH-8
Colonie, 7793....NK-19
COLUMBIA CO., 63096....NM-19
Commack, 36124....SE-8
Congers, 8363....SD-6
Conklin, 1800....NM-13
Constantia, 1182....NH-12
Cooperstown, 1852....NK-15
Copake, 1200....NM-20
Copiague, 21922....SJ-7
Coram, 39113....SE-10
Corfu, 709....NI-5
Corinth, 2559....NH-19
Corning, 11183....NM-9
Cornwall-on-Hudson, 3058....SC-5
Cortland, 19204....NK-12
CORTLAND CO., 49336....NK-12
Coxsackie, 2813....NL-19
Cross River, 980....SC-7
Croton Falls, 970....SC-7
Croton-on-Hudson, 8070....SC-6
Crown Pt., 1000....NE-20
Cuba, 1575....NM-5
Cuddebackville, 1100....SB-3
Cutchogue, 3349....SD-12
Dannemora, 3936....NB-19
Dansville, 4719....NK-7
Deer Park, 27745....SF-8
Deferiet, 293....NE-13
DELAWARE CO., 47980....NM-15
Delevan, 1089....NK-5
Delhi, 3087....NL-16
Delmar, 8300....NK-19
Depew, 15303....NJ-4
Deposit, 1663....NM-15
Derby, 1200....NK-3
Dexter, 1052....NE-12
Dix Hills, 26892....SE-8
Dobbs Ferry, 10875....SD-6
Dolgeville, 2206....NI-16
Dover Plains, 1323....SA-7
Dryden, 1890....NL-11
Dundee, 1690....NL-9
Dunkirk, 12563....NL-2
DUTCHESS CO., 297488....SA-7
Earlville, 872....NJ-14
E. Aurora, 6236....NJ-4
E. Farmingdale, 6484....SJ-8
E. Glenville, 6616....NJ-18
E. Greenbush, 4487....NK-19
E. Hampton, 1083....SE-13
E. Hills, 6955....SE-7
E. Islip, 14475....SJ-11
E. Marion, 926....SD-12
E. Massapequa, 19069....SJ-8
E. Meadow, 38132....*G-17
E. Northport, 20217....SE-8
E. Norwich, 2709....*E-19
E. Patchogue, 22469....SJ-13
E. Quogue, 4757....SE-11
E. Rochester, 6587....SG-4
E. Rockaway, 9818....*J-17
E. Setauket, 8000....SE-9
E. Shoreham, 6666....SG-14
E. Syracuse, 3084....SI-4
E. Williston, 2556....*G-17
Eastchester, 19554....*B-14
Eastport, 1831....SE-11
Eden, 3516....NK-3
Eggertsville, 15019....NJ-9
Elbridge, 1058....NI-11
Eldred, 750....SB-2
Elizabethtown, 754....ND-19
Ellenville, 4130....SA-4
Elma Ctr., 2571....NJ-4
Elmira, 29200....NM-10
Elmira Hts., 4097....NM-10
Elmont, 32657....*H-16
Elmsford, 4664....SD-6
Elsmere, 4200....NG-3
Elwood, 11177....SH-9
Endicott, 13392....NM-12
Endwell, 11446....SG-18
ERIE CO., 919040....NK-4
ESSEX CO., 39370....NE-18
Fair Haven, 745....NH-10
Fairmount, 10224....NI-11
Fairport, 5353....NI-8
Fairview, 3099....SA-5
Falconer, 2420....NM-3
Falconwood, 1500....ND-7
Fallsburg, 800....SA-3
Farmingdale, 8189....SJ-8
Farmingville, 15481....SE-10
Fayetteville, 4190....NI-12
Ferndale, 850....SA-3
Findley Lake, 800....NM-1
Fire Island Pines, 900....SF-9
Firthcliffe, 5000....SJ-12
Flanders, 4472....SE-11
Floral Park, 15863....*H-16
Florida, 2833....SC-4
Flower Hill, 4665....*F-16
Fluvanna, 900....NM-2
Fonda, 795....NJ-17
Forestport, 900....NG-14
Ft. Covington, 1200....NA-16
Ft. Edward, 3375....NH-19
Ft. Plain, 2322....NJ-16
Ft. Salonga, 10008....SI-15
Frankfort, 2564....NJ-15
FRANKLIN CO., 51599....NC-17
Franklin Park, 800....NK-13
Franklin Sq., 29320....*H-17
Franklinville, 1740....NL-5
Fredonia, 11230....NL-2
Freeport, 42860....SF-8
Frewsburg, 1965....NM-3
Friendship, 1218....NM-5
Fulton, 11896....NH-11
FULTON CO., 55531....NI-17
Fultonville, 784....NJ-17
Galeville, 4617....SI-4
Gang Mills, 4185....NM-8
Garden City, 22371....*H-18
Garden City Park, 7806....*H-17
Garden City South, 4024....*H-1
Gardiner, 950....SA-5
Gardnertown, 4373....SB-5
Garrison, 800....SC-6
Gasport, 1248....NI-4
Gates Ctr., 4910....NI-12
GENESEE CO., 60079....NJ-5
Geneseo, 8031....NK-7
Geneva, 13261....NJ-9
Germantown, 845....NM-19
Gerry, 800....NM-2
Getzville, 2300....NC-0
Glasco, 2099....NM-8
Glen Cove, 26964....SE-7
Glen Head, 4697....*F-18
Glenham, 2000....SB-6
Glenmont, 1200....NK-19
Glens Falls, 14700....NH-19
Glenwood Landing, 3779....*F-18
Gloversville, 15665....NI-17
Golden's Bridge, 1630....SC-7
Gordon Hts., 4042....SH-13
Goshen, 5454....SB-4
Gouverneur, 3949....NH-13
Gowanda, 2709....NL-3
Grand Gorge, 1000....NL-17
Grand Island, 800....NJ-3
Granville, 2644....NH-20
Great Bend, 843....NE-13
Great Neck, 9989....SF-7
Great Neck Estates, 2761....F-15
Great Neck Plaza, 6707....F-15
Great River, 1489....SJ-11
Greece, 14519....SE-2
Green Island, 2620....NE-5
Greene, 1701....NL-13
GREENE CO., 49221....NL-18
Greenlawn, 13742....SH-9
Greenport, 2197....SD-12
Greenport, 2169....NL-19
Greenville, 7116....SJ-5
Greenwich, 1777....NI-20
Groton, 2363....NL-11
Guilderland, 1900....NK-1
Guilderland Ctr., 860....NJ-18
Hadley, 1009....NH-19
Hagaman, 1292....NJ-18
Halesite, 2498....SH-8
Hamburg, 9409....NJ-4
Hamilton, 4239....NJ-14
HAMILTON CO., 4836....NF-16
Hamlin, 5521....NH-6
Hampton Bays, 13603....SE-12
Hampton Manor, 2417....NG-5
Hancock, 1031....NN-14
Hannawa Falls, 1042....NC-15
Harbor Isle, 1301....*K-17
Harriman, 2424....SC-5
Harris Hill, 5508....SE-1
Harrison, 27472....SE-7
Harrison, 13620....*A-16
Hartsdale, 5293....SJ-6
Hastings-on-Hudson, 7648....SD-6
Hauppauge, 20882....SE-9
Haverstraw, 11910....SD-6
Head of the Harbor, 1472....SG-11
Hempstead, 53891....SF-7
Henrietta, 1200....NG-3
Herkimer, 7743....NI-15
HERKIMER CO., 64519....NH-15
Herricks, 4295....*G-17
Heuvelton, 714....NC-14
Hewlett, 6819....*J-16
Hewlett Hbr., 1269....*J-16
Hicksville, 41547....SF-8
Highland, 5647....SA-6
Highland Falls, 3900....SC-6
Highland-on-the-Lake, 1800....NK-3
Hillcrest, 7558....SD-5
Hilton, 5886....NH-7
Hinsdale, 900....NM-5
Holbrook, 27135....SE-10
Holland, 1206....NK-5
Holley, 1802....NI-6
Holtsville, 19714....SE-10
Homer, 3291....NK-12
Homowack, 1450....SE-6
Honeoye Falls, 2674....NJ-7
Hoosick Falls, 3501....NJ-20
Horseheads, 6461....NM-10
Houghton, 1693....NL-5
Hudson, 6713....NL-19
Hudson Falls, 7281....NH-19
Hughsonville, 1400....SB-6
Huntington, 18403....SE-8
Huntington Bay, 1425....SH-8
Huntington Sta., 33029....SE-8
Hurley, 6314....SA-5
Hyde Park, 908....NN-18
Ilion, 8053....NI-15
Inwood, 9792....SJ-19
Irondequoit, 51692....NI-7
Island Park, 4655....SE-6
Islandia, 3135....SJ-11
Islip, 18689....SJ-11
Islip Ter., 5389....SJ-11
Ithaca, 29287....NL-11
Jamesport, 1710....SE-11
Jamestown, 31146....NM-2
JEFFERSON CO., 116229....NE-12
Jefferson Valley, 6700....SC-6
Jericho, 13567....SF-7
Johnson City, 15174....NM-12
Johnstown, 8743....NI-17
Jordan, 1368....NI-11
Kaser, 4724....SD-5
Katonah, 1679....SC-7
Keeseville, 1815....NC-19
Kenmore, 15423....NI-4
Kensington, 1161....*F-15
Kerhonkson, 1684....SA-4
Keuka Park, 1137....NK-9
Kinderhook, 1275....NL-19
Kings Park, 17282....SE-9
Kings Pt., 5005....*F-15
Kingston, 23456....SA-5
Kiryas Joel, 20175....SC-5
Lackawanna, 18141....NG-9
Lacona, 582....NG-12
Lake Carmel, 8282....SC-7
Lake Erie Bch., 3872....NK-3
Lake George, 906....NG-19
Lake Grove, 11163....SE-9
Lake Luzerne, 1227....NH-19
Lake Placid, 2521....ND-18
Lake Ronkonkoma, 20155....SE-9
Lake Success, 2934....*G-16
Lakeland, 2786....SJ-12
Lakeview, 5615....*I-17
Lakewood, 3002....NM-2
Lancaster, 10352....NJ-4
Lansing, 3529....NL-11
Larchmont, 6485....SE-4
Latham, 10131....NJ-19
Lattingtown, 1739....*E-18
Laurel, 1394....SD-11
Laurel Hollow, 1952....*F-20
Lawrence, 6483....*K-16
Le Roy, 4391....NJ-6
Levittown, 51881....SF-7
LEWIS CO., 27087....NG-13
Lewiston, 2701....NI-3
Liberty, 4392....SA-2
Lido Bch., 2897....SJ-17
Lima, 2459....NJ-7
Lime Lake, 867....NK-5
Lincoln Park, 2500....NH-11
Lindenhurst, 27253....SF-8
Little Falls, 4946....NI-16
Little Valley, 1143....NL-4
Liverpool, 2347....NI-12
Livingston Manor, 1221....SA-2
LIVINGSTON CO., 65393....NK-7
Livingston Manor, 1355....NN-16
Livonia, 1409....NJ-7
Lloyd Hbr., 3660....SE-8
Lockport, 21165....NI-4
Locust Grove, 9700....*F-20
Locust Valley, 3406....SE-7
Long Bch., 33275....SF-7
Lowville, 3470....NF-14
Lynbrook, 19427....*J-17
Lyndonville, 838....NH-5
Lyons, 3619....NI-9
Macedon, 1523....NI-8
MADISON CO., 73442....NJ-13
Madrid, 757....NB-15
Mahopac, 8369....SC-7
Malone, 5911....NB-18
Malverne, 8514....*I-17
Mamaroneck, 18929....SE-7
Manchester, 1709....NJ-8
Manhasset, 8080....*F-16
Manlius, 4704....NJ-12
Manorhaven, 6556....*E-16
Manorville, 14314....SE-10
Maplewood, 800....NE-5
Marathon, 919....NL-12
Marcellus, 1813....NI-11
Marion, 1511....NI-9
Marlboro, 3669....SB-6
Massapequa, 21685....SF-8
Massapequa Pk., 17008....SJ-8
Massena, 10936....NB-15
Mastic, 15481....SF-10
Mastic Bch., 12930....SF-10
Mattituck, 4219....SE-12
Mattydale, 6446....SI-3
Maybrook, 2958....SB-5
Mayfield, 832....NI-17
Mayville, 1711....NM-2
Maywood, 3400....NE-3
McGraw, 1053....NL-12
McKownville, 4850....NF-3
Mechanicstown, 6858....SB-4
Mechanicville, 5196....NJ-19
Medford, 24142....SF-10
Medina, 6065....NH-5
Melrose Park, 2294....NI-11
Melville, 18985....SE-8
Menands, 3990....NK-19
Mendon, 1000....NI-8
Merrick, 20097....*I-19
Mexico, 1624....NH-12
Middle Hope, 3000....SB-5
Middle Island, 10483....SH-13
Middleburgh, 1500....NK-17
Middleport, 1840....NH-5
Middletown, 28086....SB-4
Middleville, 1400....SG-10
Mill Neck, 997....*F-19
Millbrook, 1452....NN-19
Miller Place, 12339....SE-10
Millerton, 958....NM-20
Milton, 1403....SA-6
Mineola, 18799....SF-7
Minetto, 1069....NH-11
Mineville, 1269....ND-19
Minoa, 3449....NI-12
Modena, 900....SA-5
Mohawk, 2731....NJ-15
Mohegan Lake, 3600....SC-6
Mongaup Valley, 750....SA-2
Monroe, 8364....SC-5
MONROE CO., 744344....NH-7
Montauk, 3326....SD-14
Montgomery, 3814....SB-5
MONTGOMERY CO., 49708....NJ-16
Monticello, 6726....SA-3
Montour Falls, 17'1....NL-10
Montrose, 2731....SC-6
Moravia, 1282....NK-11
Morrisonville, 1545....NB-19
Morristville, 2199....NJ-13
Mt. Kisco, 9678....SD-5
Mt. Morris, 2986....NK-7
Mt. Sinai, 12118....SE-10
Mt. Vernon, 67292....*C-13
Mt. Vernon, 2800....SA-5
Mountain Lodge Park, 1588....SC-5
Mumford, 800....NI-7
Munsey Park, 2693....*F-16
Munsons Cors., 2728....NK-11
Muttontown, 3497....*E-19
Myers Cor., 6790....SA-6
Nanuet, 17882....SD-6
Napanoch, 1134....SA-4
Naples, 1041....NK-8
Nassau, 1133....NK-19
NASSAU CO., 1339532....SF-7
Nedrow, 2244....NJ-12
Nesconset, 13387....SH-11
New Baltimore, 960....NL-19
New Berlin, 1028....NK-14
New Cassel, 4059....SF-7
New City, 33559....SD-6
New Falconwood, 1200....ND-?
New Hampton, 1200....SC-4
New Hartford, 1847....NI-14
New Hyde Park, 9712....*H-16
New Lebanon, 950....NK-20
New Paltz, 6818....SA-5
New Rochelle, 77062....SE-7
New Windsor, 8922....SB-5
New York, 6175133....SF-6
NEW YORK CO., 1585873....*D-11
New York Mills, 3327....SA-12
Newark, 9*45....NI-9
Newark Valley, 997....NM-12
Newburgh, 28866....SB-5
Newfane, 3822....NH-4
Newfield, 759....NL-10
Newtonville, 2300....NE-4
NIAGARA CO., 216469....NH-4
Niagara Falls, 50193....NI-3
Nimmonsburg, 900....NM-12
Niskayuna, 4859....NJ-19
Nissequogue, 1749....SH-10
Niverville, 1662....NL-19
Norfolk, 1327....NB-15
N. Amityville, 17862....SJ-8
N. Babylon, 17509....SJ-9
N. Bay Shore, 14992....SJ-10
N. Bellmore, 19944....*I-19
N. Bellport, 11545....SJ-13
N. Bloomfield, 2260....NJ-8
N. Boston, 2521....NK-4
N. Chili 2300....NI-7
N. Collins, 1232....NK-3
N. Great River, 4001....SJ-11
N. Haven, 833....SD-13
N. Hills, 5075....*F-17
N. Hornell, 778....NL-7
N. Lindenhurst, 11652....SJ-9
N. Lynbrook, 793....*J-16
N. Massapequa, 17886....SJ-8
N. Merrick, 12272....*I-19
N. New Hyde Park, 14899....*G-16
N. Patchogue, 7246....SJ-13
N. Salem, 930....SC-7
N. Sea, 4458....SE-12
N. Syracuse, 6800....NI-12
N. Tonawanda, 31568....NI-4
N. Valley Stream, 16628....*I-16
Northport, 7401....SE-8
Northville, 1099....NI-17
Norwich, 7190....NL-14
Norwood, 1657....NB-15
Noyack, 3568....SE-12
Nunda, 1377....NK-6
Nyack, 6765....SD-6
Oakdale, 7974....SJ-12
Oakfield, 1813....NI-5
Oceanside, 32109....SJ-15
Ogdensburg, 11128....NC-14
Olcott, 1241....NH-4
Old Bethpage, 5523....SJ-8
Old Brookville, 2134....*F-18
Old Field, 918....SF-9
Old Forge, 756....NG-15
Old Westbury, 4671....*G-18
Olean, 14452....NM-5
Oneida, 11393....NI-13
ONEIDA CO., 234878....NH-13
Oneonta, 13901....NL-15
ONONDAGA CO., 467026....NJ-12
Onondaga Hill, 2000....SI-2
Ontario, 2160....NH-8
ONTARIO CO., 107931....NJ-8
ORANGE CO., 372813....SC-4
Orange Lake, 6982....SB-5
Orchard Park, 3246....NJ-4
Oriskany, 1400....NI-14
Oriskany Falls, 732....NJ-14
ORLEANS CO., 42883....NI-6
Ossining, 25060....SD-6
Oswego, 18142....NH-11
OSWEGO CO., 122109....NG-12
Otego, 1010....NL-15
Otisville, 1068....SC-4
OTSEGO CO., 62259....NK-15
Owego, 3896....NM-11
Oxford, 1450....NL-13
Oyster Bay, 6707....SE-7
Oyster Bay Cove, 2197....*D-20
Painted Post, 1809....NM-9
Palatine Bridge, 737....NJ-16
Palenville, 1037....NL-18
Palmyra, 3536....NI-8
Panama, 479....NM-2
Parc Lake, 1100....SE-4
Patterson, 1200....SB-7
Pawling, 2347....SB-7
Pearl River, 15876....SD-5
Peekskill, 23583....SC-6
Pelham, 6400....SE-6
Pelham Manor, 5486....*C-14
Penfield, 6300....NI-8
Penn Yan, 5159....NK-9
Perry, 3673....NK-6
Peru, 159'....NC-19
Phelps, 1989....NJ-9
Philadelphia, 1252....NE-13
Philmont, 1379....NL-19
Phoenix, 2382....NH-11
Pine Bush, 1780....SB-4
Pine Island, 1500....SC-4
Pine Plains, 1353....NM-19
Pine Valley, 813....NM-10
Pinehurst, 1850....NJ-3
Pittsford, 1355....NI-8
Plainedge, 8817....*H-20
Plainview, 26217....SF-8
Plandome, 1349....*F-16
Plandome Hts., 1005....*F-16
Plandome Manor, 872....*F-16
Plattekill, 1260....SB-5
Plattsburgh, 19989....NB-19
Pleasant Valley, 1145....SA-6
Pleasantdale, 1250....ND-5
Pleasantville, 7019....SD-6
Poestenkill, 1061....NK-19
Point Lookout, 1219....*K-19
Pomona, 3103....SD-5
Poquott, 953....SG-12
Port Byron, 1290....NI-10
Port Chester, 28967....SE-7
Port Dickinson, 1641....NM-12
Port Ewen, 3546....NM-18
Port Henry, 1194....NE-20
Port Jefferson, 7750....SE-9
Port Jefferson Station, 7838....SE-9
Port Jervis, 8828....SC-3
Port Leyden, 672....NG-14
Port Washington, 15846....SF-7
Port Washington North, 3154....*E-16
Portland, 950....NL-2
Portville, 1014....NM-5
Potsdam, 9428....NC-15
Poughkeepsie, 32736....SA-6
Prospect, 900....NH-15
Pulaski, 2365....NG-12
Purdys, 970....SC-7
PUTNAM CO., 99710....SB-7
Putnam Lake, 3844....SB-7
QUEENS CO., 2230722....SF-6
Queensbury, 830....NH-19
Queenston, 2701....NA-6
Quogue, 967....SF-11
Randolph, 1286....NM-3
Ransomville, 1419....NH-4
Rapids, 1636....NI-4
Ravena, 3268....NK-19
Red Hook, 1961....NM-19
Red Oaks Mill, 3613....SA-6
Remsen, 531....NH-14
Rensselaer, 9392....NK-19
RENSSELAER CO., 159429....NK-20
Rhinebeck, 2657....NM-18
Richfield Sprs., 1264....NJ-15
Richmond, 466730....SG-5
Richmondville, 918....NK-16
Ridge, 13336....SE-10
Rigney Bluff, 1090....NH-7
Riverhead, 13299....SE-11
Riverside, 3300....NK-17
Rochester, 210565....NI-7
Rock Hill, 1742....SA-3
Rockaway Point, 1400....SI-4
Rockdale, 1800....SA-6
ROCKLAND CO., 311687....SD-5
Rockville Centre, 24023....SF-7
Rocky Pt., 14014....SE-10
Rome, 33725....NI-14
Ronkonkoma, 19082....SF-1
Roosevelt, 16258....*I-18
Rosendale Vil., 1349....NM-18
Roslyn, 2770....SF-7
Roslyn Est., 1251....*F-17
Roslyn Hts., 6577....*F-17
Ross Cors., 800....NM-12
Rotterdam, 20652....NJ-18
Rotterdam Jct., 1000....NJ-18
Round Lake, 623....NJ-19
Rouses Pt., 2209....NA-20
Russell Gdns., 945....*F-16
Rye, 15720....SE-7
Rye Brook, 9347....SE-7
Sackets Hbr., 1450....NE-12
Sag Harbor, 2169....SE-12
Saint James, 13338....SE-9
St. Johnsville, 1732....NJ-16
ST. LAWRENCE CO., 111944....ND-15
Salamanca, 5815....NM-4
Salem, 964....NI-20
Sanborn, 1645....NI-4
Sands Pt., 2675....*E-17
Sandy Bch., 2731....NJ-4
Sandy Creek, 771....NG-12
Saranac Lake, 5406....NC-18
SARATOGA CO., 219607....NH-18
Saratoga Sprs., 26585....NI-19
Saugerties, 3971....NM-18
Sauquoit, 930....NJ-14
Savona, 827....NL-8
Sayville, 16853....SF-9
Scarsdale, 17166....SD-6
Schaghticoke, 592....NJ-19
Schenectady, 66135....NJ-18
SCHENECTADY CO., 154727....NJ-18
Schoharie, 922....NK-17
SCHOHARIE CO., 32749....NK-16
Schroon Lake, 833....NF-19
SCHUYLER CO., 18343....NL-10
Schuylerville, 1386....NI-19
Scotia, 7729....NJ-18
Scottsville, 2001....NJ-7
Sea Cliff, 4995....*E-18
Seaford, 15294....*I-20
Searingtown, 4915....*G-17
Selden, 19851....SE-10
SENECA CO., 35251....NJ-10
Seneca Falls, 6661....NJ-10
Seneca Knolls, 2011....SH-1
Setauket, 3300....SE-9
Shelter Island, 1333....SD-12
Shelter Island Hts., 1048....SD-12
Sherburne, 1367....NK-14
Sherrill, 3071....NJ-13
Sherrill, 730....NI-12
Shinnecock Hills, 2188....SE-12
Shirley, 27854....SF-10
Shokan, 1183....NM-17
Shortsville, 1439....NJ-8
Shrub Oak, 2011....SC-6
Sidney, 3900....NL-15
Sidney Ctr., 800....NL-15
Silver Creek, 2656....NK-2
Silver Sprs., 782....NK-6
Skaneateles, 2450....NJ-11
Skaneateles Falls, 800....NJ-11
Slate Hill, 800....SC-4
Sleepy Hollow, 9870....SD-6
Slingerlands, 2100....NK-19
Sloan, 3661....NJ-4
Sloatsburg, 3039....SD-5
Smithtown, 26470....SH-11
Sodus, 1819....NH-9
Sodus Pt., 900....NH-9
Solvay, 6584....NI-11
Sound Bch., 7612....SE-10
S. Corning, 1145....NM-9
S. Fallsburg, 2061....SA-3
S. Farmingdale, 14486....SJ-8
S. Floral Park, 1764....*H-16
S. Glens Falls, 3518....NH-19
S. Hempstead, 3243....*I-18
S. Hill, 6673....NL-11
S. Huntington, 9422....SH-9
S. Lockport, 8324....NI-4
S. Nyack, 3510....SD-6
S. Valley Stream, 5962....*J-16
Southampton, 3109....SE-12
Southold, 5748....SD-12
Southport, 7238....NM-10
Sparrow Bush, 1200....SC-3
Speigletown, 1200....NK-19
Spencer, 759....NM-11
Spencerport, 3601....NI-7
Spring Valley, 31347....SD-5
Springs, 6592....SD-13
Springville, 4296....NK-4
Staatsburg, 1000....NN-19
Stamford, 1119....NL-16
Stannards, 798....NM-6
Steamburg, 900....NM-3
Stephentown, 750....NK-20
Stewart Manor, 1896....*H-16
Stillwater, 1738....NJ-19
Stony Brook, 13740....SE-9
Stony Pt., 12147....SC-6
Stottville, 1375....NL-19
Suffern, 10723....SD-5
SUFFOLK CO., 1493350....SE-10
SULLIVAN CO., 77547....NN-15
Swan Lake, 1200....SA-2
Sycaway, 1950....NE-6
Sylvan Bch., 897....NI-13
Syosset, 18829....SF-8
Syracuse, 145170....NI-12
Tappan, 6613....SE-6
Terryville, 11770....SE-9
Theresa, 863....ND-13
Thiells, 5032....SC-6
Thornwood, 3759....SD-6
Ticonderoga, 3382....NF-20
Tillson, 1586....NN-18
TIOGA CO., 51125....NM-11
Tivoli, 1118....NM-18
Tomkins Cove, 850....SC-6
TOMPKINS CO., 101564....NL-10
Tonawanda, 15130....NC-8
Town Line, 2367....NJ-4
Tribes Hill, 1003....NJ-17
Troy, 50129....NJ-19
Trumansburg, 1797....NL-10
Tuckahoe, 6486....*B-13
Tuckahoe, 1373....SE-12
Tully, 873....NK-12
Tupper Lake, 3667....ND-17
Twin Orchards, 1600....SB-10
ULSTER CO., 182493....SA-4
Unadilla, 1128....NL-14
Union Ctr., 1500....NM-12
Union Sprs., 1197....NJ-10
Uniondale, 24759....*H-18
University Gardens, 4226....*G-16
Upper Brookville, 1698....*E-19
Utica, 62235....NI-14
Vails Gate, 3369....SB-5
Valatie, 1819....NL-19
Valhalla, 3162....SH-6
Valley Cottage, 9107....SD-6
Valley Stream, 37511....SF-7
Verdoy, 1000....NE-5
Vernon, 1172....NI-13
Verona, 852....NI-13
Vestal, 5000....NM-12
Vestal Ctr., 800....NM-12
Victor, 2696....NI-8
Village Green, 3891....SH-1
Village of the Branch, 1807....SH-11
Vista, 750....SD-8
Voorheesville, 2789....NK-18
Waddington, 972....NB-14
Wading River, 7719....SE-10
Walden, 6978....SB-5
Walker Valley, 853....SA-4
Wallkill, 2288....SB-5
Walton, 3088....NM-15
Wampsville, 543....NI-13
Wantagh, 18871....*I-20
Wappingers Falls, 5522....SB-6
Warnerville, 1000....NK-17
WARREN CO., 65707....NG-18
Warrensburg, 3103....NG-19
Warsaw, 3473....NJ-6
Warwick, 6731....SC-4
WASHINGTON CO., 63216....NH-20
Washingtonville, 5899....SB-5
Waterford, 1990....NJ-19
Waterloo, 5171....NJ-10
Watertown, 27023....NE-12
Waterville, 1583....NJ-14
Watervliet, 10254....NE-5
Watkins Glen, 1859....NL-10
Waverly, 4444....NM-11
Wawarsing, 800....SA-4
Wayland, 1865....NK-7
WAYNE CO., 93772....NI-9
Webster, 5399....NI-8
Weedsport, 1815....NI-10
Wellsville, 4679....NM-6
W. Babylon, 43213....SJ-8
W. Bay Shore, 4648....SJ-10
W. Carthage, 2012....NE-13
W. Corners, 1800....SB-9
W. Elmira, 4967....NN-10
W. Glens Falls, 7071....NH-19
W. Haverstraw, 10165....SD-6
W. Hempstead, 18862....*H-17
W. Hills, 5592....SH-8
W. Hurley, 1939....NM-18
W. Islip, 28335....SJ-10
West Nyack, 3661....SD-6
West Point, 6763....SC-6
W. Sand Lake, 2660....NK-19
W. Sayville, 5011....SJ-12
W. Seneca, 44711....NJ-4
W. Webster, 8700....NI-8
W. Winfield, 862....NJ-15
Westbury, 15199....SF-7
Westbury South, 9500....*G-19
WESTCHESTER CO., 949113....SD-7
Westfield, 3224....NM-1
Westhampton, 3079....SE-11
Westhampton Bch., 1721....SF-11
Westmere, 7284....NE-8
Westmoreland, 1000....NI-14
Westons Mills, 1472....NM-5
Westvale, 4963....SI-1
Wheatley Hts., 5130....SJ-9
White Plains, 56853....SD-7
Whitehall, 2614....NG-20
Whitesboro, 3772....SA-12
Whitney Pt., 964....NL-12
Williamson, 2495....NH-8
Williamsville, 5300....ND-10
Williston Park, 7287....*G-17
Willow Pt., 1700....SB-18
Willow Ridge Estates, 4800....SC-10
Wilmington, 937....NC-19
Wilson, 1264....NH-3
Windsor, 916....NM-13
Wolcott, 1701....NI-10
Woodbourne, 1200....SA-3
Woodbury, 10686....SG-20
Woodbury, 8907....SH-8
Woodmere, 17121....*J-16
Woodridge, 847....SA-3
Woodstock, 2088....NM-18
Worcester, 1113....NK-16
Wurtsboro, 1246....SB-3
Wyandanch, 10546....SJ-9
Wynantskill, 3276....NK-19
WYOMING CO., 42155....NK-5
Yaphank, 5945....SE-10
YATES CO., 25348....NK-9
Yonkers, 195976....SE-6
Yorkshire, 1180....NL-5
Yorktown Hts., 1781....SC-6
Yorkville, 2689....NI-14
Youngstown, 1935....NH-3
Youngsville, 850....SA-2
Yulan, 750....SA-2

North Carolina
Map pp. 74 – 75

* City keyed to p. 76

Aberdeen, 6350....G-9
Advance, 1138....D-7
Ahoskie, 5039....C-17
ALAMANCE CO., 151131....D-9
Albemarle, 15903....F-7
ALEXANDER CO., 37198....D-4
ALLEGHANY CO., 11155....B-4
Alliance, 776....G-17
Andrews, 1781....F-2
Angier, 4350....F-12
ANSON CO., 26948....H-7
Apex, 37476....E-11
Arapahoe, 556....G-17
Archdale, 11415....E-8
Arden, 800....E-1
Asheboro, 25012....E-8
Asheville, 83393....E-1
ASHE CO., 27281....B-3
Atlantic Bch., 1495....H-17
Aulander, 895....C-16
Ayden, 4932....F-18
Badin, 1974....F-9
Banner Elk, 1028....C-3
Bayboro, 1263....F-18
Bayleaf, 800....D-14
Beaufort, 4039....H-17
BEAUFORT CO., 47759....E-16
Belhaven, 1688....E-16
Belmont, 10076....G-5
Belwood, 950....F-4
Benson, 3311....F-12
Bent Creek, 1287....E-1
Bermuda Run, 1725....D-7
Bertie Co., 21282....D-16
Bessemer City, 5340....F-4
Bethel, 1577....D-15
Bethlehem, 4214....E-4
Beulaville, 1296....H-14
Biltmore Forest, 1343....N-8
Biscoe, 1700....F-9
Black Creek, 769....E-13
Black Mtn., 7848....E-1
BLADEN CO., 35190....I-12
Bladenboro, 1750....I-12
Blounts Creek, 1150....F-16
Blowing Rock, 1241....C-3
Bogue, 684....H-16
Boiling Sprs., 4647....F-3
Bolivia, 143....J-13
Boone, 17122....C-3
Boonville, 1222....C-6
Brevard, 7609....N-5
Broadway, 1229....F-10
Brogden, 2633....F-13
Brunswick, 1119....C-1
BRUNSWICK CO., 107431....J-12
Bryson City, 1424....L-3
Buies Creek, 2942....F-11
BUNCOMBE CO., 238318....E-1
Burgaw, 3872....I-14
BURKE CO., 90912....E-3
Burlington, 49963....D-9
Burnsville, 1693....D-1
Butner, 7591....C-11
Buxton, 1273....F-20
CABARRUS CO., 178011....F-6
Cajahs Mtn., 2823....D-3
Calabash, 1786....K-12
CALDWELL CO., 83029....D-3
Camden, 599....C-18
CAMDEN CO., 9980....B-18
Candor, 840....F-8
Canton, 4227....E-17
Cape Carteret, 1917....H-16
Carolina Bch., 5706....K-14
Carolina Shores, 3048....K-12
Carrboro, 19582....D-10
CARTERET CO., 66469....H-16
Carthage, 2205....F-9
Cary, 135234....E-11
Castle Hayne, 1202....I-14
CASWELL CO., 23719....C-9
CATAWBA CO., 154358....E-4
Cedar Pt., 1279....H-16
Chadbourn, 1856....J-11
Chapel Hill, 57233....D-10
Charlotte, 731424....F-5
CHATHAM CO., 63505....E-10
Cherokee, 2138....E-1
Cherryville, 5760....F-4
China Grv., 3563....E-6
Chocowinity, 820....E-6
CHOWAN CO., 14793....C-17
Claremont, 1352....E-5
Clarkton, 837....I-12
CLAY CO., 10587....G-2
Clayton, 16116....E-12
Clemmons, 18627....D-7
Cleveland, 871....E-6
CLEVELAND CO., 98078....F-3
Clinton, 8639....G-12
Clyde, 1223....L-4
Coats, 2112....F-11
Colfax, 1050....D-8
Columbia, 891....D-18
Columbus, 999....F-2
COLUMBUS CO., 58098....J-11
Concord, 79066....F-6
Connelly Sprs., 1669....E-4
Conover, 8165....E-4
Conway, 836....C-15
Cooleemee, 960....E-6
Cordova, 1775....H-8
Cornelius, 24866....F-5
Cramerton, 4165....G-5
CRAVEN CO., 103505....F-15
Creedmoor, 4124....C-11
Cricket, 1855....C-4
Crouse, 900....F-4
Cullowhee, 6228....F-2
CUMBERLAND CO., 319431....H-11
Currituck, 630....B-19
CURRITUCK CO., 23547....B-19
Dallas, 4488....F-5
Danbury, 189....C-7
DARE CO., 33920....E-19
Davidson, 10944....E-5
DAVIDSON CO., 162878....D-7
DAVIE CO., 41240....D-6
Denton, 1636....E-7
Denver, 2309....F-5
Dobbins Hts., 866....G-9
Dobson, 1586....C-6
Dortches, 935....D-13
Drexel, 1858....E-3
Dunn, 9263....F-12
DUPLIN CO., 58505....G-13
Durham, 228330....D-11
DURHAM CO., 267587....D-11
E. Flat Rock, 4995....F-1
E. Spencer, 1534....E-7
Eastover, 3628....G-11
Eden, 15527....B-8
Edenton, 5004....C-17
EDGECOMBE CO., 56552....D-14
Edneyville, 2367....F-1
Elizabeth City, 18683....C-18
Elizabethtown, 3583....I-12
Elkin, 4001....C-6
Ellenboro, 873....F-3
Ellerbe, 1054....G-9
Elm City, 1298....E-14
Elon, 9419....D-9
Emerald Isle, 3655....H-16
Emma, 1100....M-7
Enfield, 2532....C-14
Erwin, 4405....F-12
Etowah, 6944....F-1
Eureka Sprs., 2910....K-16
Fair Bluff, 951....J-11
Fairmont, 2663....I-10
Fairplains, 2120....C-5
Fairview, 3324....E-1
Faith, 807....E-6
Farmville, 4654....E-15
Fayetteville, 200564....H-11
Fearrington, 903....*B-8
Flat Rock, 3114....F-1
Flat Rock, 1556....B-6
Fletcher, 7187....F-1
Forest City, 7476....F-3
FORSYTH CO., 350670....C-7
Ft. Bragg, 29183....G-11
Foxfire, 902....G-9
Franklin, 3845....N-3
FRANKLIN CO., 60619....C-12
Franklinton, 2023....C-12
Franklinville, 1164....E-9
Fremont, 1255....E-13
Fuquay-Varina, 17937....E-11
Gamewell, 4051....D-3
Garner, 25745....E-12
Garysburg, 1057....B-14
Gaston, 1152....B-14
GASTON CO., 206086....G-4
Gastonia, 71741....G-5
GATES CO., 12197....B-17
Gatesville, 321....B-17
Gibsonville, 6410....D-9
Glen Alpine, 1517....E-3
Goldsboro, 36437....F-14
Graham, 14153....D-9
GRAHAM CO., 8861....L-2
Granite Falls, 4722....D-4
Granite Quarry, 2930....E-7
Grantsboro, 945....G-17
GRANVILLE CO., 59916....C-12
Green Level, 2100....D-10
GREENE CO., 21362....F-14
Greensboro, 269666....D-8
Greenville, 84554....E-15
Grifton, 2617....F-15
Grover, 708....G-4
GUILFORD CO., 488406....D-9
Half Moon, 8352....H-15
Halifax, 234....C-14
HALIFAX CO., 54691....C-14
Hamlet, 6495....H-9
Hampstead, 4083....I-14
Harkers Island, 1207....H-17
HARNETT CO., 114678....F-11
Harrisburg, 11526....F-6
Havelock, 20735....H-16
Haw River, 2298....D-10
Hays, 1851....C-5
HAYWOOD CO., 59036....K-4
Hemby Br., 1520....*J-7
Henderson, 15368....C-12
HENDERSON CO., 106740....N-7
Hendersonville, 13137....F-1
Hertford, 2143....C-18
HERTFORD CO., 24669....C-16
Hickory, 40010....E-4
Hickory, 860....*G-1
High Pt., 104371....D-8
High Shoals, 696....F-4
Highlands, 924....M-4
Hightsville, 739....I-13
Hillsborough, 6087....D-10
HOKE CO., 46952....G-10
Hollister, 674....C-13
Holly Ridge, 1268....I-15
Holly Sprs., 24661....E-11
Hope Mills, 15176....H-11
Hudson, 3776....D-4
Huntersville, 46773....F-5
HYDE CO., 5810....E-18
Indian Trail, 33518....F-7
IREDELL CO., 159437....D-5
Iron Sta., 755....E-5
Jacksonville, 70145....H-15
James City, 5899....G-16
Jamestown, 3382....D-8
Jefferson, 1611....B-4
JOHNSTON CO., 168878....E-12
JONES CO., 10153....G-15
Jonesville, 2285....C-5
Kannapolis, 42625....F-6
Kenansville, 855....G-13
Kenly, 1339....E-13
Kernersville, 23123....D-8
Kill Devil Hills, 6683....D-20
King, 6904....C-7
Kings Grant, 8113....L-20
Kings Mtn., 10296....G-4
Kingstown, 681....F-3
Kinston, 21677....F-15
Kitty Hawk, 3272....C-20
Knightdale, 11401....E-12
Lake Park, 3422....G-6
La Grange, 2873....F-14
L. Junaluska, 2734....L-4
L. Lure, 1192....F-2
Lake Pk., 3422....G-6
L. Waccamaw, 1480....J-12
Landis, 3109....E-6
Laurel Hill, 1254....H-9
Laurel Pk., 2180....F-1
Laurinburg, 15962....H-9
LEE CO., 57866....F-10
Leland, 13527....J-13
Lenoir, 18228....D-3
LENOIR CO., 59495....G-14
Lewisville, 12639....D-7
Lexington, 18931....E-7
Liberty, 2656....D-9
Lillington, 3194....F-11
LINCOLN CO., 78265....F-4
Lincolnton, 10486....F-4
Littleton, 674....B-13
Locust, 2930....F-7
Long View, 4871....E-4
Louisburg, 3359....C-12
Lowell, 3526....M-4
Lowesville, 2945....F-5
Lucama, 1108....E-13
Lumberton, 21542....I-11
MACON CO., 33922....M-3
MADISON CO., 20764....D-1
Maggie Valley, 1150....L-4
Magnolia, 939....G-13
Maiden, 3310....E-4
Manners, 826....C-1
Manteo, 1434....D-20
Marion, 7838....E-2
Marshall, 872....D-1
Marshallberg, 900....H-18
Marshville, 2402....G-7
Marvin, 5579....G-5
Matthews, 27198....G-6
Maury, 1685....F-14
Maxton, 2426....I-10
Mayodan, 2478....C-8
McAdenville, 651....*F-2
McDOWELL CO., 44996....E-2
Mebane, 11393....D-10
MECKLENBURG CO., 919628....G-5
Middlesex, 822....E-13
Midland, 3073....G-6
Midway, 4679....E-7
Millers Creek, 2112....C-4
Mint Hill, 22722....G-6
Mocksville, 5051....D-6
Monroe, 32797....G-6
MONTGOMERY CO., 27798....F-8
Montreat, 723....E-1
Mooresboro, 311....F-3
Mooresville, 32711....E-5
Moravian Falls, 1901....C-5
Morehead City, 8661....H-17
Morganton, 16918....E-3
Morrisville, 18576....E-11
Mt. Airy, 10388....B-6
Mt. Gilead, 1181....F-8
Mt. Holly, 13656....F-5
Mt. Olive, 4589....G-13
Mt. Pleasant, 1652....F-6
Murfreesboro, 2835....B-16
Murphy, 1627....M-1
Myrtle Grove, 8875....J-14
Nags Head, 2757....D-20
NASH CO., 95840....D-13
Nashville, 5352....D-13
Navassa, 1505....J-13
New Bern, 29524....G-16
NEW HANOVER CO., 202667....J-14
Newland, 698....C-2
Newport, 4150....H-17
Newton, 12968....E-4
N. Topsail Bch., 743....I-15
N. Wilkesboro, 4245....C-5
NORTHAMPTON CO., 22099....B-15
Northwest, 735....J-13
Norwood, 2379....G-7
Oak Island, 6783....K-13
Oak Ridge, 6185....C-8
Oakboro, 1859....G-7
Ogden, 6766....I-14
Old Fort, 908....E-2
ONSLOW CO., 177772....H-14
ORANGE CO., 133801....D-10
Oxford, 8461....C-12
PAMLICO CO., 13144....G-17
PASQUOTANK CO., 40661....C-18
Pembroke, 2973....I-10
PENDER CO., 52217....I-14
PERQUIMANS CO., 13453....C-17
PERSON CO., 39464....B-11
Pfafftown, 1750....C-7
Pikeville, 778....E-13
Pilot Mtn., 1477....C-6
Pine Knoll Shores, 1339....H-17
Pine Level, 1700....E-13
Pinebluff, 1337....G-9
Pinehurst, 13124....G-9
Pinetops, 1374....E-14
Pineville, 7479....J-14
Piney Green, 13293....H-15
Pink Hill, 552....G-14
Pisgah Forest, 2150....N-5
PITT CO., 168148....F-15
Pittsboro, 3743....E-10
Pleasant Gdn., 4489....D-8
Plymouth, 3878....D-17
POLK CO., 20510....F-1
Polkton, 3375....G-7
Princeton, 1194....F-13
Princeville, 2082....D-15
Pumpkin Ctr., 2222....H-15
Raeford, 4611....G-10
Raleigh, 403892....E-12
Ramseur, 1692....E-9
Randleman, 4113....E-8
RANDOLPH CO., 141752....E-8
Ranlo, 3434....M-14
Red Cross, 742....F-7
Red Oak, 3430....D-14
Red Sprs., 3428....H-10
Reidsville, 14520....C-9
Rich Sq., 958....C-15
Richlands, 1520....H-15
RICHMOND CO., 46639....G-8
River Bend, 3119....G-16
Roanoke Rapids, 15754....B-14
Robbins, 1097....F-9
Robbinsville, 620....L-2
Robersonville, 1488....D-15
ROBESON CO., 134168....H-10
Rockfish, 3298....G-11
Rockingham, 9558....H-8
ROCKINGHAM CO., 93643....C-8
Rockwell, 2108....E-7
Rocky Mount, 57477....D-14
Rocky Pt., 1602....I-14
Rolesville, 3786....D-12
Rose Hill, 1626....H-13
Rowland, 1037....I-10
Roxboro, 8362....C-11
Royal Pines, 4272....F-1
Rural Hall, 2937....C-7
RUTHERFORD CO., 67810....F-2
Rutherford College, 1341....E-4
Rutherfordton, 4213....F-2
St. James, 3165....K-13
St. Pauls, 2035....I-11
Salem, 2218....E-3
Salisbury, 33662....E-6
Saluda, 713....F-1
SAMPSON CO., 63431....G-12
Sanford, 28094....F-10
Sawmills, 5240....D-4
Saxapahaw, 1648....D-10
SCOTLAND CO., 36157....H-9
Scotland Neck, 2059....C-15
Seabreeze, 1969....I-14
Sedgefield, 1000....*C-6
Selma, 6073....E-13
Seven Lakes, 4888....F-9
Shallotte, 3675....K-12
Sharpsburg, 2024....D-14
Shelby, 20323....F-3
Siler City, 7887....E-9
Silver City, 882....H-10
Silver Lake, 5598....I-14
Skippers Cor., 2785....I-14
Smithfield, 10966....E-12
Sneads Ferry, 2646....I-15
Snow Hill, 1595....F-14
S. Gastonia, 5433....G-5
Southern Pines, 12334....G-9
Southern Shores, 2714....C-20
Southmont, 1470....E-7
Southport, 2833....K-13
Sparta, 1770....B-5
Spencer, 3267....E-7
Spindale, 4321....F-2
Spring Hope, 1320....D-13
Spring Lake, 11964....G-11
Spruce Pine, 2175....D-2
Stallings, 13831....G-6
Stanfield, 1486....G-7
Stanley, 3556....F-5
STANLY CO., 60585....F-7
Stantonsburg, 784....E-14
Star, 876....F-8
Statesville, 24532....E-5
Stedman, 1028....G-11
Stokesdale, 5047....C-8
STOKES CO., 47401....C-7
Stoneville, 1056....B-8
Stony Pt., 1317....D-5
Summerfield, 10232....C-8
Sunset Bch., 3572....K-12
Surf City, 1853....I-15
SURRY CO., 73673....C-6
SWAIN CO., 13981....L-2
Swannanoa, 4576....E-1
Swansboro, 2663....H-16
Sylva, 2588....L-4
Tabor City, 2511....J-11
Tarboro, 11415....D-15
Taylorsville, 2098....D-4
Thomasville, 26757....E-8
Toast, 1450....B-6
Tobaccoville, 2441....C-7
TRANSYLVANIA CO., 33090....M-5
Trent Woods, 4155....G-16
Trenton, 287....G-15
Trinity, 6614....E-8
Troutman, 2383....E-5
Troy, 3189....F-8
Tryon, 1646....F-1
Unionville, 5929....G-6
UNION CO., 201292....G-6
Valdese, 4490....E-3
Valley Hill, 2070....F-1
VANCE CO., 45422....C-12
Vanceboro, 1005....F-16
Vander, 1146....G-11
Vass, 720....G-10
Wadesboro, 5813....G-8
Wake Forest, 30117....D-12
WAKE CO., 900993....D-12
Walkertown, 4675....C-7
Wallace, 3880....H-13
Walnut Cove, 1425....C-7
Walnut Creek, 835....F-13
Warrenton, 862....B-13
WARREN CO., 20972....C-13
Warsaw, 3054....G-13
Washington, 9744....E-16
WASHINGTON CO., 13228....D-17
WATAUGA CO., 51079....C-3
Waxhaw, 9859....H-6
Waynesville, 9869....L-4
Weaverville, 3120....D-1
Welcome, 4162....D-7
Weldon, 1655....B-14
Wendell, 5845....E-12
Wentworth, 2807....C-8
Wesley Chapel, 7463....G-6
W. Jefferson, 1299....C-4
Westport, 4076....E-5
Whispering Pines, 2928....F-10
Whitakers, 744....C-14
White Lake, 802....I-12
White Plains, 1074....B-6
Whiteville, 5394....J-12
Wilkesboro, 3413....C-5
WILKES CO., 69340....C-5
Williamston, 5511....D-16
Wilmington, 106476....J-14
Wilson, 49167....E-14
WILSON CO., 81234....E-14
Wilsons Mill, 2277....E-12
Windsor, 3630....D-16
Wingate, 3491....G-7
Winston-Salem, 229617....D-7
Winterville, 9269....E-15
Winton, 769....B-16
Woodfin, 6123....D-1
Wrightsboro, 4496....K-19
Wrightsville Bch., 2477....J-14
Yadkinville, 2959....C-6
YADKIN CO., 38406....C-6
Yanceyville, 2039....C-10
Youngsville, 1157....D-12
YANCEY CO., 17818....D-1
Zebulon, 4433....D-13

North Dakota
Map p. 77

ADAMS CO., 2343....J-4
Amidon, 20....I-3
Ashley, 749....J-9
BARNES CO., 11066....H-11
Beach, 1019....H-2
Belcourt, 2078....B-8
Belfield, 800....H-3
BENSON CO., 6660....E-9
Beulah, 3121....G-5
BILLINGS CO., 783....G-2
Bismarck, 61272....H-7
Bottineau, 2211....D-7
BOTTINEAU CO., 6429....D-7
Bowbells, 336....D-5
Bowman, 1650....J-3
BOWMAN CO., 3151....J-2
BURKE CO., 1968....D-4
BURLEIGH CO., 81308....H-7
Burlington, 1060....E-6
Cando, 1115....D-9
Cannon Ball, 875....I-7
Carrington, 2065....G-9
Carson, 293....I-6
Casselton, 2329....H-11
Cavalier, 1302....D-12
CAVALIER CO., 3993....D-10
Center, 571....H-6
Cooperstown, 984....G-11
Crosby, 1070....C-3
Devils Lake, 7141....E-10
DICKEY CO., 5289....J-10
Dickinson, 17787....H-4
DIVIDE CO., 2071....D-3
Drayton, 824....D-12
DUNN CO., 3536....G-4
Dunseith, 773....D-8
EDDY CO., 2385....F-9
Elgin, 642....I-5
Ellendale, 1394....J-10
EMMONS CO., 3550....I-8
Enderlin, 886....I-11
Fargo, 105549....H-13
Fessenden, 479....F-9
Finley, 445....G-11
Forman, 504....J-12
Ft. Totten, 1243....E-10
Ft. Yates, 184....J-7
FOSTER CO., 3343....G-9
Garrison, 1453....F-6
Glen Ullin, 807....H-5
GOLDEN VALLEY CO., 1680....G-2
Grafton, 4284....E-12
Grand Forks, 52838....F-12
GRAND FORKS CO., 66861....F-12
GRANT CO., 2394....I-5
GRIGGS CO., 2420....G-11
Gwinner, 753....J-12
Hankinson, 919....J-13
Harvey, 1783....F-8
Harwood, 718....H-13
Hatton, 777....F-12
Hazen, 2411....G-5
Hebron, 747....H-5
HETTINGER CO., 2477....H-4
Hillsboro, 1603....G-13
Horace, 2430....H-13
Jamestown, 15427....H-10
Kenmare, 1096....D-5
KIDDER CO., 2435....G-8
Killdeer, 751....G-4
Kindred, 692....I-13
LA MOURE CO., 4139....I-10
Lakota, 672....E-10
Lamoure, 889....I-10
Langdon, 1878....D-10
Larimore, 1346....F-12
Lidgerwood, 652....J-12
Lincoln, 2406....H-7
Linton, 1097....I-8
Lisbon, 2154....I-12
LOGAN CO., 1990....I-9
Mandan, 18331....H-7
Manning, 74....G-4
Mapleton, 762....H-13
Mayville, 1858....G-12
McClusky, 380....G-7
McHENRY CO., 5395....E-7
McINTOSH CO., 2809....J-9
McKENZIE CO., 6360....F-2
McLEAN CO., 8962....F-6
Medora, 112....H-2
MERCER CO., 8424....G-5
Minot, 40888....E-6
Minnewaukan, 224....E-9
Mohall, 783....D-6
MORTON CO., 27471....I-5
Mott, 721....I-4
MOUNTRAIL CO., 7673....E-4
Napoleon, 792....I-8
NELSON CO., 3126....F-11
New England, 600....I-3
New Rockford, 1391....F-9
New Salem, 946....H-6
New Town, 1925....F-4
Northwood, 945....F-12
Oakes, 1856....J-11
OLIVER CO., 1846....G-5
Park River, 1403....E-12
Parshall, 903....F-5
PEMBINA CO., 7413....D-11
Pembina, 592....C-12
PIERCE CO., 4357....D-8
Portland, 606....G-12
RAMSEY CO., 11451....E-10
RANSOM CO., 5457....I-12
RENVILLE CO., 2470....C-5
RICHLAND CO., 16321....J-13
ROLETTE CO., 13937....D-8
Rolla, 1280....D-9
Rugby, 2876....E-8
SARGENT CO., 3829....J-12
SHERIDAN CO., 1321....F-7
SIOUX CO., 4153....K-6
SLOPE CO., 727....I-3
Stanley, 1458....E-4
Stanton, 366....G-5
STARK CO., 24199....H-4
Steele, 715....H-8
STEELE CO., 1975....F-11
STUTSMAN CO., 21100....H-9
Surrey, 934....E-6
Thompson, 986....F-13
Tioga, 1230....E-3
Towner, 533....E-7
TOWNER CO., 2246....D-9
TRAILL CO., 8121....F-12
Underwood, 778....G-6
Valley City, 6585....H-11
Velva, 1084....E-7
Wahpeton, 7766....J-13
Walhalla, 996....C-11
WALSH CO., 11119....E-11
WARD CO., 61675....E-5
Washburn, 1246....G-7
WELLS CO., 4207....G-8
W. Fargo, 25830....H-13
WILLIAMS CO., 22398....D-3
Williston, 14716....E-2
Wishek, 1002....J-9

Ohio
Map pp. 78 – 81

Map keys — Atlas pages
NA – NN — 78 – 79
SA – SN — 80 – 81

* City keyed to p. 112

Aberdeen, 1638....SK-6
Ada, 5952....NI-5
ADAMS CO., 28550....SH-7
Addyston, 938....SJ-1
Adena, 759....NM-15
Akron, 199110....NI-9
Albany, 826....SE-14
Alger, 860....NJ-5
ALLEN CO., 106331....NI-3
Alliance, 22322....NJ-15
Amberley, 3585....SK-4
Amelia, 4801....SK-8
Amherst, 12021....NF-10
Andersonville, 779....SE-8
Andover, 1145....NE-20
Anna, 1567....NK-3
Ansonia, 1174....NK-3
Antwerp, 1736....NF-1
Apple Creek, 1173....NI-15
Arcanum, 2129....SB-2
Archbold, 4346....NE-4
Arlington, 1455....NJ-5
Arlington Hts., 745....NH-20
Ashland, 20362....NI-12
ASHLAND CO., 53139....NI-12
Ashtabula, 19124....NC-19
ASHTABULA CO., 101497....NE-18
Ashville, 4097....SC-9
Athens, 23832....SE-13
ATHENS CO., 64757....SF-14
Attica, 899....NH-9
Atwater, 758....NH-15
AUGLAIZE CO., 45949....NK-4
Aurora, 15548....NG-16
Austintown, 29677....NH-19
Avon, 21193....NF-12
Avon Lake, 22581....NF-13
Avondale, 3500....NJ-13
Bainbridge, 3267....NF-16
Bainbridge, 860....SF-18
Baltic, 795....NL-15
Baltimore, 2966....SB-11
Barberton, 26550....NH-15
Barnesville, 4193....SA-17
Batavia, 1509....SK-7
Bay Vil., 15651....NF-14
Beach City, 1033....NK-15
Beachwood, 11953....SE-14
Beavercreek, 45193....SC-4
Bedford, 13074....NF-15
Bedford Hts., 10751....NF-16
Bellaire, 4278....SA-19
Bellbrook, 6943....SD-4
Belle Ctr., 813....NK-6
Bellefontaine, 13370....NK-5
Bellevue, 8202....NG-10
Bellville, 1918....NJ-11
BELMONT CO., 70400....NM-17
Beloit, 978....NI-18
Belpre, 6441....SF-16
Bentleyville, 864....NE-16
Berea, 19093....NF-14
Berlin, 898....NK-15
Berlin Hts., 714....NG-11
Bethel, 2711....SK-8
Bethesda, 1256....SA-18
Beverly, 1313....SD-15
Bevis, 1100....SJ-2
Bexley, 13057....SB-9
Blacklick Estates, 8682....SJ-20
Blanchester, 4243....SF-5
Bloomingburg, 938....SE-7
Bluffton, 4125....NI-5
Boardman, 35376....NH-19
Bolivar, 996....NK-15
Boston Hts., 1300....NG-15
Botkins, 1155....NL-4
Bowling Green, 30028....NF-6
Bradford, 1842....NN-2
Bradner, 985....NG-6
Bratenahl, 1197....SK-18
Brecksville, 13656....NG-15
Bremen, 1425....SD-11
Brewster, 2112....NK-15
Bridgeport, 1831....NN-19
Bridgetown North, 12569....SI-1
Brilliant, 1482....NM-20
Broadview Hts., 19400....NG-15
Brook Pk., 19212....NF-14
Brookfield Ctr., 1207....NE-14
Brooklyn, 11169....NF-15
Brooklyn Hts., 1543....SM-17
Brookville, 5884....SB-3
BROWN CO., 44846....SH-5
Brunswick, 34255....NG-14
Bryan, 8545....NF-2
Buckeye Lake, 2746....SB-12
Bucyrus, 12362....NJ-9
Burlington, 2676....SK-11
Burton, 1455....NF-17
Butler, 933....NK-11
BUTLER CO., 368130....SE-1
Byesville, 2438....SB-16
Cadiz, 3353....NM-18
Calcutta, 3742....NK-20
Caldwell, 1748....SC-16
Cambridge, 10635....SB-16
Camden, 2046....SD-2
Campbell, 8235....NH-20
Canal Fulton, 5479....NJ-15
Canal Winchester, 7101....SB-10
Canfield, 7515....NI-19
Canton, 73007....NK-16
Cardington, 2047....NL-9
Carey, 3674....NI-7
Carlisle, 4915....SD-3
CARROLL CO., 28836....NK-18
Carrollton, 3241....NK-18
Castalia, 852....NG-10
Cedarville, 4019....SC-6
Celina, 10400....NK-2
Centerburg, 1773....NM-10
Centerville, 23999....SD-4
Chagrin Falls, 4113....NF-16
CHAMPAIGN CO., 40097....NM-5
Champion Hts., 6498....NG-18
Chardon, 5148....NE-17
Chauncey, 1049....SE-14
Cherry Grv., 4378....SM-5
Chesapeake, 745....SK-12
Chesterland, 2521....NF-16
Cheviot, 8375....SJ-2
Chillicothe, 21901....SE-9
Chippewa Lake, 711....NH-13
Churchill, 2149....NH-19
Cincinnati, 296943....SJ-3
Circleville, 13314....SC-9
CLARK CO., 138333....SB-6
Clarktown, 958....SH-10
Clayton, 13209....SB-3
CLERMONT CO., 197363....SH-4
Cleveland, 396815....NF-15
Cleveland Hts., 46121....NF-15
Cleves, 3234....SI-1
Clinton, 1214....NH-15
CLINTON CO., 42040....SE-6
Clyde, 6325....NG-9
Coal Grv., 2165....SK-13
Coldwater, 4427....NL-2
Colerain Hts., 2600....SK-2
Columbiana, 6384....NH-13
COLUMBIANA CO., 107841....NJ-19
Columbus, 787033....SB-9
Columbus Grv., 2137....NI-4
Commercial Pt., 1582....SC-9
Conneaut, 12841....NC-20
Continental, 1153....NH-3
Convoy, 1085....NI-2
Cortland, 7104....NG-19
Coshocton, 11216....NM-14
COSHOCTON CO., 36901....NM-13
Covedale, 6447....SM-2
Covington, 2584....NM-3
Craig Bch., 1180....NH-18
CRAWFORD CO., 43784....NI-8
Crestline, 4630....NJ-10
Creston, 2171....NI-14
Cridersville, 1852....NJ-4
Crooksville, 2534....SC-13
Crystal Lakes, 1483....SC-5
Cuyahoga Falls, 49652....NH-15
CUYAHOGA CO., 1280122....NG-14
Dalton, 1830....NJ-15
Danville, 1044....NL-12
Darbydale, 793....SC-8
DARKE CO., 52959....NM-1
Dayton, 141527....SC-4
De Graff, 1285....NL-5
Deer Pk., 5736....SJ-3
Defiance, 16494....NF-3
DEFIANCE CO., 39037....NG-2
DeForest, 1100....NG-19
Delaware, 34753....NM-9
DELAWARE CO., 174214....NM-8
Delhi Hills, 20000....SJ-2
Delphos, 7101....NI-3
Delta, 3103....NE-5
Dennison, 2655....NL-16
Dent, 10497....SI-2
Deshler, 1799....NG-5
Devola, 2652....SE-16
Dillonvale, 3740....NM-19
Dover, 12826....NL-16
Doylestown, 3051....NI-14
Dresden, 1529....NN-13
Drexel, 2076....SM-5
Dry Run, 750....SE-5
Dublin, 41751....SJ-8
Dunkirk, 875....NI-6
Dunlap, 1719....SF-7
E. Alliance, 1175....NJ-17
E. Canton, 1591....NK-17
E. Cleveland, 17843....NF-15
E. Liverpool, 11195....NK-20
E. Palestine, 4721....NJ-20
E. Sparta, 819....NL-16
Eastlake, 18577....NE-16
Eaton, 8407....SD-1
Eaton Estates, 1222....NG-13
Edgerton, 2012....NF-1
Edgewater Pk., 700....SB-19
Edgewood, 4432....NC-19
Edon, 834....NE-1
Elida, 1905....NI-4
Elmore, 1410....NF-7
Elmwood Pl., 2188....SL-2
Elyria, 54533....NF-12
Englewood, 13465....SB-3
Enon, 2415....SB-5
ERIE CO., 77079....NF-11
Etna, 1215....SB-11
Euclid, 48920....NE-15
Evendale, 2767....SL-3
Fairborn, 32352....SB-5
Fairfax, 1699....SL-4
Fairfield, 42510....SE-2
FAIRFIELD CO., 146156....SB-11
Fairlawn, 7437....NH-15
Fairport Hbr., 3109....NE-17
Fairview Lakes, 1000....NF-10
Fairview Pk., 16826....NF-14
Farmersville, 1009....SC-3
Fayette, 1283....NE-4
FAYETTE CO., 29030....SD-8
Felicity, 818....SL-6
Findlay, 41202....NH-6
Finneytown, 12741....SK-3
Five Points, 1824....SA-10
Flushing, 879....NN-18
Forest, 1461....NI-7
Forest Pk., 18720....SF-2
Forestville, 10532....SG-3
Ft. Loramie, 1478....NL-3
Ft. McKinley, 3989....SC-3
Ft. Recovery, 1430....NL-1
Ft. Shawnee, 3726....NJ-4
Fostoria, 13441....NH-7
Frankfort, 1064....SE-8
Franklin, 11771....SD-3
FRANKLIN CO., 1163414....NN-10
Franklin Furnace, 1660....SL-12
Frazeysburg, 1326....NN-13
Fredericktown, 2493....NL-11
Fremont, 16734....NG-8
Fruit Hill, 3755....SK-5
FULTON CO., 42698....NE-5
Gahanna, 33248....SA-10
Galion, 10512....NJ-10
GALLIA CO., 30934....SH-12
Gallipolis, 3641....SH-13
Gambier, 2391....NL-12
Garfield Hts., 28849....NF-15
Garrettsville, 2325....NG-17
Gates Mills, 2270....NE-16
GEAUGA CO., 93389....NF-17
Geneva, 6215....ND-18
Geneva-on-the-Lake, 1288....ND-18
Genoa, 2336....NF-7
Georgetown, 4331....SH-5
Germantown, 5547....SD-3
Gibsonburg, 2581....NF-7
Girard, 9958....NH-19
Glandorf, 1001....NI-4
Glendale, 2155....SM-3
Gloucester, 1791....SD-13
Gnadenhutten, 1288....NL-16
Golf Manor, 3611....SK-4
Goshen, 720....SH-3
Grafton, 6636....NG-13
Grand Rapids, 965....NF-5
Grandview Hts., 6536....SB-9
Granville, 5646....NN-11
Gratis, 881....SD-2
Green, 25699....NI-16
Green Sprs., 1368....NG-9
GREENE CO., 161573....SC-6
Greenfield, 4639....SE-7
Greenford, 700....NI-19
Greenhills, 3615....SJ-3
Greentown, 3804....NI-16
Greenville, 13227....NM-2
Greenwich, 1476....NH-11
Groesbeck, 6788....SK-2
Grove City, 35575....SB-9
Groveport, 5363....SB-10
Grover Hill, 402....NH-2
GUERNSEY CO., 40087....NN-16
Hamersville, 547....SJ-5
Hamilton, 62477....SE-2
HAMILTON CO., 802374....SH-4
Hamilton Meadows, 2100....SE-2
HANCOCK CO., 74782....NI-5
Hanover, 921....NN-12
Hanoverton, 411....NI-19
HARDIN CO., 32058....NK-5
Harrison, 9897....SF-1
HARRISON CO., 15864....NM-17
Hartville, 2944....NI-16
Haskins, 1188....NF-6
Heath, 10310....SA-12
Hebron, 2336....SB-11
HENRY CO., 28215....NG-4
Hicksville, 3581....NG-1
HIGHLAND CO., 43589....SF-6
Highland Hts., 8345....SK-20
Highland Hills, 5573....SL-15
Highland Pk., 700....SG-2
Highpoint, 1503....SF-8
Hilliard, 28435....SA-8
Hillsboro, 6605....SF-7
Hiram, 1406....NG-17
HOCKING CO., 29380....SE-11
Holgate, 1109....NG-4
Holland, 1764....NB-1
HOLMES CO., 42366....NK-13
Hopewell, 1047....NB-13
Howland Ctr., 6351....NI-12
Hubbard, 7874....NH-20
Huber Hts., 38101....SB-4
Huber Ridge, 4604....SF-19
Hudson, 22262....NG-16
Hunter, 1500....SD-3
Huntington Valley, 1150....NF-16
Huron, 7149....NF-11
HURON CO., 59626....NH-11
Independence, 7133....NG-15
Ironton, 11129....SK-12
Jackson, 6397....SH-11
JACKSON CO., 33225....SH-11
Jamestown, 1993....SE-6
Jefferson, 3120....ND-19
JEFFERSON CO., 69709....NK-19
Jeffersonville, 1203....SD-7
Jerusalem Hts., 1700....NM-6
Johnstown, 4632....NN-10
Junction City, 819....SB-12
Kalida, 1542....NI-3
Kendall Hts., 850....NI-15
Kent, 28904....NH-16
Kenton, 8262....NK-6
Kenwood, 6981....SK-5
Kettering, 56163....SC-4
Kidron, 944....NJ-15
Killbuck, 817....NL-13
Kings Mills, 1319....SE-4
Kingston, 1032....SE-9
Kirtland, 6866....NE-16
KNOX CO., 60921....NM-11
La Croft, 1144....NK-20
Lagrange, 2103....NG-13
Lake Darby, 4662....SJ-8
LAKE CO., 230041....ND-17
L. Milton, 1100....NH-18
Lakemore, 3068....NI-16
Lakeview, 1072....NL-5
Lakewood, 52131....NF-15
Lancaster, 38780....SC-11
Laurel Ridge, 2350....NF-6
LAWRENCE CO., 62450....SI-11
Leavittsburg, 1973....NG-18
Lebanon, 20033....SE-3
Leesburg, 1314....SE-7
Leetonia, 1959....NJ-19
Leipsic, 2093....NH-5
Lewisburg, 1820....SD-2
Lexington, 4822....NJ-11
Liberty Ctr., 1180....NF-5
Lima, 38771....NJ-4
Lincoln Hts., 3286....SL-3
Lincoln Vil., 9032....SH-20
Lisbon, 2821....NJ-19
Lithopolis, 1106....SC-10
LICKING CO., 166492....NN-11
Lockland, 3449....SL-3
Lodi, 2746....NH-13
Logan, 7152....SD-12
LOGAN CO., 45858....NL-5
Logan Elm Vil., 1118....SD-9
London, 9904....SE-7
Lorain, 64097....NF-10
LORAIN CO., 301356....NG-12
Lordstown, 3417....NH-18
Loudonville, 2641....NK-12
Louisville, 9186....NJ-17
Loveland, 12081....SF-3
Loveland Pk., 1523....SF-3
Lowellville, 1155....NH-20
Lucas, 615....NJ-11
LUCAS CO., 441815....NE-5
Lucasville, 2757....SH-9
Luckey, 1012....NF-6
Lynchburg, 1499....SF-6
Lyndhurst, 14001....NE-16
Macedonia, 11188....NG-16
Mack, 11585....SL-1
Madeira, 8726....SK-5
Madison, 3184....ND-18
MADISON CO., 43435....NN-7
Madison-on-the-Lake, 950....ND-18
Magnolia, 978....NK-17
MAHONING CO., 238823....NI-18
Malvern, 1189....NK-17
Manchester, 2023....SK-7
Mansfield, 47821....NJ-11
Mantua, 1043....NG-17
Maple Hts., 23138....NG-15
Marblehead, 903....NF-9
Mariemont, 3403....SL-4
Marietta, 14085....SE-16
Marion, 36837....NK-8
MARION CO., 66501....NK-7
Marne, 783....NN-12
Marshallville, 756....NI-15
Martins Ferry, 6915....NN-19
Marysville, 22094....NM-7
Mason, 30712....SE-3
Massillon, 32149....NJ-15
Masury, 2064....NG-20
Maumee, 14286....NF-7
Mayfield, 3460....SK-20
Mayfield Hts., 19155....NE-16
McArthur, 1701....SF-12
McClure, 725....NG-4
McComb, 1648....NH-5
McConnelsville, 1784....SC-14
McDonald, 3263....NH-19
McKinley Hts., 1060....NI-19
Mechanicsburg, 1644....NN-6
Medina, 26678....NH-14
MEDINA CO., 172332....NH-13
Medway, 2000....SB-5
MEIGS CO., 23770....SG-13
Mentor, 47159....NE-16
Mentor-on-the-Lake, 7443....NE-16
MERCER CO., 40814....NK-1
MIAMI CO., 102506....NN-3
Miamisburg, 20181....SC-3
Middleburg Hts., 15946....NF-14
Middlefield, 2694....NF-17
Middleport, 2530....SG-14
Middletown, 48694....SD-3
Midvale, 754....NL-16
Milan, 1367....NG-11
Milford, 6709....SK-5
Millbury, 1200....NF-7
Millersburg, 3025....NL-14
Millersport, 1044....SB-11
Millville, 708....SE-1
Mineral City, 727....NL-16
Mineral Ridge, 3892....NH-19
Minerva, 3720....NK-18
Minerva Park, 1272....SJ-19
Mingo Jct., 3454....NN-20
Minster, 2805....NL-3
Mogadore, 3853....NI-16
Monfort Hts., 11948....SJ-2
Monroe, 12442....SE-3
MONROE CO., 14642....SC-18
Monroeville, 1400....NH-11
Montgomery, 10251....SK-5
MONTGOMERY CO., 535153....SC-3
Montpelier, 4072....NE-2
Moraine, 6307....SC-4
Moreland Hills, 3320....SM-20
MORGAN CO., 15054....SC-15
Morrow, 1188....SE-4
MORROW CO., 34827....NK-9
Mt. Carmel, 4741....SM-5
Mt. Gilead, 3660....NK-10
Mt. Healthy, 6098....SK-2
Mt. Orab, 3664....SG-5
Mt. Repose, 4672....SM-5
Mt. Sterling, 1782....SD-8
Mt. Vernon, 16990....NL-11
Mulberry, 3323....SM-5
Munroe Falls, 5012....NH-16
Napoleon, 8749....NF-4
Navarre, 1957....NK-15
Nelsonville, 5392....SE-13
Nevada, 760....NH-9
New Albany, 7724....SA-10
New Boston, 2272....SJ-10
New Bremen, 2978....NL-3
New Burlington, 5069....SJ-2
New California, 1411....NN-8
New Carlisle, 5785....SB-5
New Concord, 2491....SB-15
New Holland, 801....SD-8
New Knoxville, 879....NL-3
New Lebanon, 3995....SC-3
New Lexington, 4731....SC-13
New London, 2461....NH-11
New Madison, 892....SB-1
New Matamoras, 896....SE-18
New Miami, 2249....SE-2
New Middletown, 1621....NI-20
New Paris, 1629....SB-1
New Philadelphia, 17288....NL-16
New Richmond, 2582....SK-6
New Straitsville, 722....SD-13
New Vienna, 1224....SE-6
New Washington, 967....NI-10
New Waterford, 1238....NI-20
Newark, 47573....NN-12
Newburgh Hts., 2167....SM-18
Newcomerstown, 3822....NM-15
Newport, 1003....SE-17
Newton Falls, 4795....NG-18
Newtown, 2672....SK-5
Niles, 19266....NH-19
NOBLE CO., 14645....SC-16
N. Baltimore, 3432....NH-6
N. Bend, 857....SJ-1
N. Canton, 17488....NI-16
N. College Hill, 9397....SK-2
N. Fork Vil., 1700....SD-9
N. Kingsville, 2923....ND-20
N. Lewisburg, 1490....NN-6
N. Madison, 8547....ND-18
N. Olmsted, 32718....NF-14
N. Perry, 893....ND-17
N. Ridgeville, 29465....NF-13
N. Royalton, 30444....NG-15
N. Zanesville, 2816....NN-14
Northbrook, 10668....SK-2
Northfield, 3677....NG-16
Northridge, 8500....SB-4
Northridge, 7572....SA-6
Northwood, 5265....NF-6
Norton, 12085....NI-14
Norwalk, 17012....NG-11
Norwood, 19207....SK-4
Oak Harbor, 2759....NF-8
Oak Hill, 1551....SI-11
Oakwood, 9202....SC-4
Oakwood, 3667....SJ-17
Oberlin, 8286....NG-12
Obetz, 4532....SB-10
Olmsted Falls, 9024....NF-14
Ontario, 6225....NJ-11
Orange, 3323....SJ-20
Oregon, 20291....NE-7
Orrville, 8380....NI-14
Orwell, 1660....NE-18
Ottawa, 4460....NH-4
OTTAWA CO., 41428....NE-7
Ottawa Hills, 4517....NE-6
Ottoville, 976....NI-3
Owensville, 794....SH-4
Oxford, 21371....SE-1
Painesville, 19563....ND-17

Painesville on the Lake, 850 ND-17
Pandora, 1153 NI-5
Parma, 81601 NF-15
Parma Hts., 20718 NF-14
Pataskala, 14962 SA-11
Paulding, 3605 NH-2
PAULDING CO., 19614 NH-1
Payne, 1194 NH-1
Peebles, 1782 SH-7
Pemberville, 1371 NF-7
Pepper Pike, 5979 NF-16
Perry, 1663 ND-17
PERRY CO., 36058 SC-12
Perry Hts., 8441 NC-8
Perrysburg, 20623 NE-6
Perrysville, 735 NK-12
Petersburg, 950 NI-20
Philo, 733 SB-14
PICKAWAY CO., 55698 SD-9
Pickerington, 18291 SB-10
PIKE CO., 28709 SG-9
Piketon, 2181 SG-9
Pioneer, 1380 ND-2
Piqua, 20522 NN-3
Pisgah, 1000 SE-3
Plain City, 4225 NN-8
Pleasant Grv., 1742 SB-14
Pleasant Hill, 1200 NN-3
Pleasant Run, 4953 SJ-2
Pleasant Run Farm, 4654 SJ-2
Pleasantville, 960 SC-11
Plymouth, 1857 NI-10
Poland, 2555 NH-20
Pomeroy, 1852 SG-14
Port Clinton, 6056 NF-9
PORTAGE CO., 161419 NH-17
Portage Lakes, 6968 NI-15
Portsmouth, 20226 SI-9
Powell, 11500 NN-9
Powhatan Pt., 1592 SB-19
PREBLE CO., 42270 SC-1
Prospect, 1112 NL-8
PUTNAM CO., 34499 NI-4
Quincy, 706 NM-5
Randolph, 750 NH-17
Ravenna, 11724 NH-17
Reading, 10385 SF-3
Redbird, 2000 ND-17
Reedurban, 4400 NJ-16
Reminderville, 3404 NF-16
Reno, 1293 SE-17
Rensselaer Pk., 850 SK-3
Reynoldsburg, 35893 SB-10
Richfield, 3648 NG-15
RICHLAND CO., 124475 NI-11
Richmond Hts., 10546 NE-16
Richville, 3324 NJ-16
Richwood, 2229 NL-8
Rio Grande, 830 SH-12
Ripley, 1750 SI-5
Rittman, 6491 NI-14
Riverside, 25201 SC-4
Roaming Shores, 1508 NE-19
Rockford, 1120 NJ-2
Rocky River, 20213 NF-14
Rome, 1450 SK-12
Roseland, 2150 NJ-11
Rosemount, 2112 SI-9
Roseville, 1852 SC-13
Ross, 3417 SE-2
ROSS CO., 78064 SE-9
Rossford, 6293 NE-6
Russells Pt., 1391 NL-5
Sabina, 2564 SD-6
Sagamore Hills, 1930 NG-15
St. Bernard, 4368 SL-3
St. Clairsville, 5184 NN-18
St. Henry, 2427 NL-2
St. Marys, 8332 NK-3
St. Paris, 2089 NN-5
Salem, 12303 NI-18
Salineville, 1311 NK-19
Sandusky, 25793 NF-10
SANDUSKY CO., 60944 NF-8
Sardinia, 980 SG-5
Sawyerwood, 1540 NC-6
Schoenbrunn, 700 NL-16
Scio, 763 NL-18
SCIOTO CO., 79499 SH-9
Sciotodale, 1081 SI-10
Seaman, 944 SH-7
Sebring, 4420 NI-18
SENECA CO., 56745 NH-8
Seven Hills, 11804 NF-15
Seven Hills, 2000 SJ-2
Seven Mile, 751 SD-2
Seville, 2296 NH-14
Shadyside, 3785 SA-19
Shaker Hts., 28448 NF-15
Sharonville, 13560 SF-3
Shawnee Hills, 2171 SC-6
Sheffield, 3982 NF-13
Sheffield Lake, 9137 NF-13
Shelby, 9317 NI-10
SHELBY CO., 49423 NM-3
Sherwood, 827 NG-2
Shiloh, 11000 SB-4
Shreve, 1514 NJ-13
Sidney, 21229 NM-4
Silver Lake, 2519 NH-16
Silverton, 4788 SK-4
Skyline Acres, 1717 SK-2
Smithfield, 869 NM-19
Smithville, 1252 NI-14
Solon, 23348 NF-16
Somerset, 1481 SC-12
S. Amherst, 1688 NF-12
S. Bloomfield, 1744 SC-9
S. Charleston, 1693 SB-6
S. Euclid, 22295 NE-15
S. Hill Pk., 1040 NB-1
S. Lebanon, 4115 SE-4
South Point, 3958 *B-2
S. Russell, 3810 NF-16
S. Webster, 866 SH-10
S. Zanesville, 1989 SB-14
Spencer, 753 NH-13
Spencerville, 2223 NJ-3
Springboro, 17409 SD-4
Springdale, 11223 SJ-3
Springfield, 60608 SB-6
STARK CO., 375586 NJ-17
Steubenville, 18659 NL-20
Stow, 34837 NH-16
Strasburg, 2608 NK-16
Streetsboro, 16028 NG-16
Strongsville, 44750 NG-14
Struthers, 10713 NH-20
Stryker, 1335 NF-3
Sugarcreek, 2220 NK-15
Summerside, 5083 SG-3
Summerside Estates, 1700 SM-6
Summit, 700 NC-13
SUMMIT CO., 541781 NH-15
Sunbury, 4389 NM-10
Surrey Hill, 700 NB-12
Swanton, 3690 NE-5
Sycamore, 861 NI-8
Sylvania, 18965 ND-6
Syracuse, 826 SG-14
Tallmadge, 17537 NH-16
Terrace Pk., 2251 SL-5
The Plains, 3080 SE-13
The Vil. of Indian Hill, 5785 SK-5
Thornville, 991 SB-12
Tiffin, 17963 NH-8
Tiltonsville, 1372 NM-19
Tipp City, 9689 SB-4
Toledo, 287208 NE-7
Toronto, 5091 NL-20
Trenton, 11869 SD-3
Trotwood, 24431 SC-3
Troy, 25058 NN-3
TRUMBULL CO., 210312 NG-18
Turpin Hills, 5099 SM-4
Tuscarawas, 1056 NL-16
TUSCARAWAS CO., 92582 NM-16
Twinsburg, 18795 NG-16
Uhrichsville, 5413 NL-16
Union, 6419 SB-3
Union City, 1666 NM-1
UNION CO., 52300 NL-7
Uniontown, 3309 NI-16
University Hts., 13539 NF-15
Upper Arlington, 33771 SA-9
Upper Sandusky, 6596 NJ-8
Urbana, 11793 NN-5
Urbancrest, 960 SB-9
Utica, 2132 NM-11
Valley View, 2034 SN-18
Van Wert, 10846 NI-2
VAN WERT CO., 28744 NJ-2
Vandalia, 15246 SB-4
Venice Hts., 1300 NA-12
Vermilion, 10594 NF-12
Versailles, 2687 NM-2
Viking Vil., 1230 SM-5
Villa Nova, 800 NK-3
VINTON CO., 13435 SF-11
Wadsworth, 21567 NH-15
Wakeman, 1047 NG-12
Walbridge, 3019 NC-3
Walnut Creek, 878 NK-15
Walton Hills, 2281 SN-19
Wapakoneta, 9867 NK-4
Warren, 41557 NG-19
WARREN CO., 212693 SE-4
Warrensville Hts., 13542 NF-15
WASHINGTON CO., 61778 SD-16
Washington Court House, 14192 SD-7
Washingtonville, 801 NI-19
Waterville, 5523 NF-6
Wauseon, 7332 NE-4
Waverly, 4408 SG-9
Wayne, 887 NG-7
WAYNE CO., 114520 NI-14
Wayne Lakes Pk., 718 SA-2
Waynesburg, 923 NJ-17
Waynesfield, 847 NK-5
Waynesville, 2834 SD-4
Wellington, 4802 NH-12
Wellston, 5663 SG-11
Wellsville, 3541 NK-19
W. Alexandria, 1340 SC-2
W. Carrollton City, 13818 SC-3
W. Chester, 800 SE-3
W. Hill, 2273 NG-20
W. Jefferson, 4222 SB-8
W. Lafayette, 2321 NM-15
W. Liberty, 1805 NM-5
W. Milton, 4630 SB-3
W. Portsmouth, 3149 SI-9
W. Salem, 1464 NI-13
W. Union, 3241 SI-7
W. Unity, 1671 NE-3
Westerville, 36120 NN-9
Westfield Ctr., 1115 NH-14
Westlake, 32729 NF-14
Weston, 1590 NG-5
Wheelersburg, 6437 SI-10
White Oak, 19167 SF-2
Whitehall, 18062 SB-10
Whitehouse, 4149 NF-5
Wickliffe, 12750 NE-16
Wilberforce, 2271 SC-5
Wildbrook Acres, 1500 SK-3
Willard, 6236 NH-10
WILLIAMS CO., 37642 NE-2
Williamsburg, 2490 SG-4
Williamsport, 1023 SD-9
Willoughby, 22268 NE-16
Willoughby Hills, 9485 NE-16
Willowick, 14171 NE-16
Wilmington, 12520 SE-5
Winchester, 1051 SH-6
Windham, 2209 NG-18
Wintersville, 3924 NL-19
Withamsville, 7021 SG-3
WOOD CO., 125488 NG-6
Woodbourne, 6050 SN-8
Woodlawn, 3294 SK-3
Woodmere, 884 SL-20
Woodsfield, 2384 SC-18
Woodville, 2135 NF-7
Woodworth, 700 NI-19
Wooster, 26119 NJ-14
Wooster Hts., 850 NJ-11
Worthington, 13575 NN-9
WYANDOT CO., 22615 NJ-7
Wyoming, 8428 SK-3
Xenia, 25719 SC-5
Yellow Sprs., 3487 SC-5
Yorkville, 1079 NM-19
Youngstown, 66982 NH-19
Zanesville, 25487 SB-14

Oklahoma

Map pp. 82 – 83

Ada, 16810 H-15
Adair, 790 D-18
ADAIR CO., 22683 E-19
Afton, 1049 C-19
ALFALFA CO., 5642 C-11
Allen, 932 H-16
Altus, 19813 I-9
Alva, 4945 C-10
Anadarko, 6762 G-11
Antlers, 2453 J-17
Apache, 1444 H-11
Arapaho, 796 F-10
Ardmore, 24283 J-14
Arkoma, 1989 G-20
Arnett, 524 D-8
Atoka, 3107 I-16
ATOKA CO., 14182 J-16
Barnsdall, 1243 C-16
Bartlesville, 35750 C-16
Beaver, 1515 B-6
BEAVER CO., 5636 C-7
BECKHAM CO., 22119 G-8
Beggs, 1321 F-16
Bethany, 19051 F-13
Bethel Acres, 2895 G-14
Bixby, 20884 E-17
Blackwell, 7092 C-14
BLAINE CO., 11943 E-11
Blair, 818 H-9
Blanchard, 7670 G-13
Boise City, 1266 C-2
Boley, 1184 F-15
Bray, 1209 I-12
Bristow, 4222 E-16
Broken Arrow, 98850 E-17
Broken Bow, 4120 J-20
Brushy, 900 F-19
BRYAN CO., 42416 K-16
Buffalo, 1299 B-8
Burns Flat, 2057 G-9
Bushyhead, 1314 C-18
Byng, 1175 H-15
Cache, 2796 I-10
Caddo, 997 J-16
CADDO CO., 29600 H-11
Calera, 2164 K-16
CANADIAN CO., 115541 F-12
Carnegie, 1723 G-11
CARTER CO., 47557 J-13
Cashion, 802 E-13
Catoosa, 7151 D-17
Central High, 1199 I-12
Chandler, 3100 F-14
Checotah, 3335 F-18
Chelsea, 1964 C-18
Cherokee, 1498 C-11
CHEROKEE CO., 46987 E-19
Cherry Tree, 883 E-20
Cheyenne, 801 F-8
Chickasha, 16036 H-12
Choctaw, 11146 F-14
CHOCTAW CO., 15205 J-17
Chouteau, 2097 D-18
CIMARRON CO., 2475 B-2
Claremore, 18581 D-17
Clayton, 821 I-18
Cleora, 1463 C-19
Cleveland, 3251 D-15
CLEVELAND CO., 255755 G-13
Clinton, 9033 F-10
COAL CO., 5925 I-16
Coalgate, 1967 I-16
Colbert, 1140 K-15
Colcord, 815 D-19
Collinsville, 5606 D-17
Comanche, 1663 I-12
COMANCHE CO., 124098 I-11
Commerce, 2473 B-19
Cookson, 900 F-19
Copeland, 1629 C-19
Cordell, 2915 G-10
COTTON CO., 6193 J-11
Coweta, 9943 E-17
CRAIG CO., 15029 C-18
CREEK CO., 69967 E-15
Crescent, 1411 E-13
Cushing, 7826 E-15
CUSTER CO., 27469 F-9
Cyril, 1059 H-11
Davenport, 814 F-15
Davis, 2683 I-14
Del City, 21332 F-13
DELAWARE CO., 41487 C-19
Dewar, 888 F-17
Dewey, 3432 C-17
DEWEY CO., 4810 E-9
Dibble, 878 H-13
Dickson, 1207 J-14
Drumright, 2907 E-15
Duncan, 23431 I-12
Durant, 15856 J-16
Eastborough, 1000 F-6
Edmond, 81405 F-13
El Reno, 16749 F-12
Elgin, 2156 H-11
Elk City, 11693 F-9
ELLIS CO., 4151 D-8
Empire City, 955 I-12
Enid, 49379 D-12
Erick, 1052 G-8
Eufaula, 2813 G-18
Fairfax, 1380 C-15
Fairland, 1057 C-19
Fairview, 2579 D-11
Fletcher, 1177 H-11
Forest Pk., 998 K-5
Ft. Gibson, 4154 E-18
Frederick, 3940 I-10
Garber, 822 D-13
GARFIELD CO., 60580 C-12
GARVIN CO., 27576 I-13
Geary, 1280 F-11
Geronimo, 1268 I-11
Glenpool, 10808 E-16
Goldsby, 1801 G-13
Goodwell, 1293 C-4
Gore, 977 F-19
GRADY CO., 52431 H-12
Grandfield, 1038 J-10
Granite, 2065 H-9
GRANT CO., 4527 B-12
GREER CO., 6239 H-8
Grove, 6623 C-19
Guthrie, 10191 E-13
Guymon, 11442 C-4
Haileyville, 813 H-18
HARMON CO., 2922 H-7
HARPER CO., 3685 C-8
Harrah, 5095 F-14
Hartshorne, 2125 H-18
Haskell, 2007 E-17
HASKELL CO., 12769 G-18
Healdton, 2788 J-13
Heavener, 3414 H-20
Helena, 1403 C-11
Hennessey, 2131 E-12
Henryetta, 5927 F-17
Hinton, 3196 F-11
Hobart, 3756 H-9
Holdenville, 5771 G-16
Hollis, 2060 I-7
Hominy, 3565 D-16
Hooker, 1918 B-5
Howe, 802 H-20
HUGHES CO., 14003 G-16
Hugo, 5310 J-18
Hydro, 969 F-11
Idabel, 7010 K-19
Inola, 1788 D-18
JACKSON CO., 26446 I-8
Jay, 2448 D-19
JEFFERSON CO., 6472 J-12
Jenks, 16924 E-17
JOHNSTON CO., 10957 J-15
Jones, 2692 F-14
Kansas, 802 D-19
KAY CO., 46562 B-14
Kellyville, 1150 E-16
Kenwood, 1224 D-19
Kiefer, 1685 E-16
Kingfisher, 4633 E-12
KINGFISHER CO., 15034 E-12
Kingston, 1601 J-15
KIOWA CO., 9446 H-10
Konawa, 1298 H-15
Krebs, 2053 H-17
Langley, 819 C-19
Langston, 1724 E-14
LATIMER CO., 11154 H-18
Laverne, 1344 C-8
Lawton, 96867 I-11
LE FLORE CO., 50384 I-19
Lexington, 2152 H-13
LINCOLN CO., 34273 E-14
Lindsay, 2840 H-13
Locust Grv., 1423 D-18
LOGAN CO., 41848 E-13
Lone Grv., 5054 J-14
Longtown, 2739 G-18
LOVE CO., 9423 J-13
Luther, 1221 F-14
Madill, 3770 J-15
MAJOR CO., 7527 D-10
Mangum, 3010 H-8
Mannford, 3076 D-16
Mannsville, 863 J-15
Marietta, 2626 K-14
Marlow, 4662 I-12
MARSHALL CO., 15840 J-14
Maud, 1048 G-15
MAYES CO., 41259 D-18
Maysville, 1232 H-13
McAlester, 18383 H-17
MCCLAIN CO., 34506 H-13
MCCURTAIN CO., 33151 I-19
MCINTOSH CO., 20252 G-17
McLoud, 4044 F-14
Medford, 996 C-13
Meeker, 1144 F-14
Miami, 13570 B-19
Midwest City, 54371 F-13
Minco, 1632 G-12
Moore, 55081 G-13
Mooreland, 1190 D-9
Morris, 1479 F-17
Mounds, 1168 E-16
Mountain View, 795 G-10
Muldrow, 3466 F-20
MURRAY CO., 13488 I-14
Muskogee, 39223 E-18
MUSKOGEE CO., 70990 F-17
Mustang, 17395 G-13
Newcastle, 7685 G-13
Newkirk, 2317 B-14
Nichols Hills, 3710 J-4
Nicoma Pk., 2393 K-7
Ninnekah, 1002 H-12
Noble, 6481 G-13
NOBLE CO., 11561 C-14
Norman, 110925 G-13
N. Enid, 860 D-12
Nowata, 3731 C-17
NOWATA CO., 10536 B-17
Oakhurst, 2185 E-16
Oakland, 1057 J-15
Oilton, 1013 E-15
Okarche, 1215 F-12
Okeene, 1204 E-11
Okemah, 3223 F-16
OKFUSKEE CO., 12191 F-15
Oklahoma City, 579999 F-13
OKLAHOMA CO., 718633 F-13
Okmulgee, 12321 F-17
OKMULGEE CO., 40069 E-17
Oologah, 1146 D-17
OSAGE CO., 47472 C-15
OTTAWA CO., 31848 B-19
Owasso, 28915 D-17
Panama, 1413 G-20
Park Hill, 3909 E-19
Pauls Valley, 6187 H-14
Pawhuska, 3584 C-16
Pawnee, 2196 D-15
PAWNEE CO., 16577 D-14
PAYNE CO., 77350 E-14
Peggs, 813 E-19
Perkins, 2831 E-14
Perry, 5126 D-14
Piedmont, 5720 F-12
Pink, 2058 G-14
PITTSBURG CO., 45837 I-17
Pocola, 4056 G-20
Ponca City, 25387 C-14
Pond Creek, 856 C-12
PONTOTOC CO., 37492 I-15
Poteau, 8520 G-20
POTTAWATOMIE CO., 69442 G-14
Prague, 2386 F-15
Pryor, 9539 D-18
Purcell, 5884 H-13
PUSHMATAHA CO., 11572 I-18
Quapaw, 906 B-19
Quinton, 1051 G-18
Ringling, 1037 J-13
ROGER MILLS CO., 3647 F-8
ROGERS CO., 86905 D-17
Roland, 3169 F-20
Rush Sprs., 1231 H-12
Ryan, 816 J-12
Salina, 1396 D-18
Sallisaw, 8880 F-19
Sand Sprs., 18906 D-16
Sapulpa, 20544 E-16
Sayre, 4375 G-8
Seiling, 860 D-10
Seminole, 7488 G-15
SEMINOLE CO., 25482 H-15
Sentinel, 901 G-9
SEQUOYAH CO., 42391 F-20
Shady Pt., 1026 G-20
Shattuck, 1356 D-8
Shawnee, 29857 G-14
Skiatook, 7397 D-16
Slaughterville, 4137 G-13
Snyder, 1394 I-10
S. Coffeyville, 785 B-17
Spencer, 3912 J-6
Sperry, 1206 D-16
Spiro, 2164 G-20
STEPHENS CO., 45048 I-12
Sterling, 793 H-11
Stigler, 2685 G-19
Stillwater, 45688 E-14
Stilwell, 3949 E-20
Stratford, 1525 H-14
Stroud, 2690 F-15
Sulphur, 4929 I-14
Tahlequah, 15753 E-19
Talihina, 1114 H-19
Taloga, 299 E-10
Tecumseh, 6457 G-14
Temple, 1002 J-11
Texanna, 2261 G-18
TEXAS CO., 20640 B-4
Texhoma, 926 C-3
The Village, 8929 J-4
Thomas, 1181 F-10
TILLMAN CO., 7992 I-10
Timber Brook, 1000 E-17
Tipton, 847 I-9
Tishomingo, 3034 J-15
Tonkawa, 3216 C-13
Tulsa, 391906 D-17
TULSA CO., 603403 D-17
Turley, 2756 D-17
Tuttle, 6019 G-12
Tyrone, 762 B-5
Union City, 1645 G-12
Valley Brook, 765 L-5
Valliant, 754 J-19
Verdigris, 3993 D-17
Vian, 1466 F-19
Vinita, 5743 C-18
Wagoner, 8323 E-18
WAGONER CO., 73085 E-18
Walters, 2551 I-11
Warner, 1641 F-18
Warr Acres, 10043 J-3
WASHINGTON CO., 50976 C-17
WASHITA CO., 11629 G-9
Watonga, 5111 E-11
Waukomis, 1286 D-12
Waurika, 2064 J-12
Waynoka, 927 C-10
Weatherford, 10833 F-10
Weleetka, 998 G-16
Welling, 771 E-19
Wellston, 788 F-14
W. Siloam Sprs., 846 D-20
Westville, 1639 E-20
Wetumka, 1282 G-16
Wewoka, 3430 G-15
Wilburton, 2843 H-18
Wilson, 1724 J-13
Wister, 1102 H-19
WOODS CO., 8878 C-10
Woodward, 12051 D-9
WOODWARD CO., 20081 C-9
Wright City, 762 J-19
Wynnewood, 2212 I-14
Yale, 1227 D-15
Yukon, 22709 F-12

Oregon

Map pp. 84 – 85

Adair Vil., 840 F-4
Albany, 50158 F-4
Aloha, 49425 C-4
Amity, 1614 D-4
Ashland, 20078 M-4
Astoria, 9477 A-2
Athena, 1126 B-13
Aumsville, 3584 E-4
Aurora, 918 D-5
Baker City, 9828 E-15
BAKER CO., 16134 E-15
Bandon, 3066 J-1
Banks, 1777 C-4
Barview, 1844 J-1
Bay City, 1286 C-2
Beaverton, 89803 C-4
Bend, 76639 H-7
BENTON CO., 85579 G-3
Bly, 700 L-8
Boardman, 3220 B-11
Boring, 730 D-5
Brookings, 6336 M-1
Brownsville, 1668 G-4
Bunker Hill, 1444 J-1
Burns, 2806 I-12
Canby, 15829 D-5
Cannon Bch., 1690 B-2
Canyon City, 703 G-12
Canyonville, 1884 K-3
Carlton, 2007 D-4
Cascade Locks, 1144 C-6
Cave Jct., 1883 M-2
Cedar Hills, 8300 L-17
Cedar Mill, 14546 L-17
Central Pt., 17169 L-4
Charleston, 700 J-1
Chenoweth, 1855 C-8
Chiloquin, 734 L-6
Clackamas, 5177 M-19
CLACKAMAS CO., 375992 E-5
Clatskanie, 1737 B-4
CLATSOP CO., 37039 B-3
Coburg, 1035 G-4
Colton, 600 D-5
Columbia City, 1946 B-4
COLUMBIA CO., 49351 B-4
Condon, 682 D-10
Coos Bay, 15967 J-1
COOS CO., 63043 J-2
Coquille, 3866 J-1
Cornelius, 11869 C-4
Corvallis, 54462 F-3
Cottage Grv., 9686 H-4
Crescent, 770 I-7
Creswell, 5031 H-4
CROOK CO., 20978 H-10
Culver, 1357 F-8
CURRY CO., 22364 L-1
Dallas, 14583 E-3
Damascus, 10539 M-20
Dayton, 2534 D-4
Depoe Bay, 1398 E-2
DESCHUTES CO., 157733 H-8
Donald, 979 D-4
DOUGLAS CO., 107667 J-4
Drain, 1151 I-3
Dufur, 604 D-8
Dundee, 3162 D-4
Dunes City, 1303 H-2
Durham, 1351 M-18
Eagle Pt., 8469 L-4
Echo, 699 C-12
Elgin, 1711 C-14
Elmira, 600 H-3
Enterprise, 1940 C-16
Estacada, 2695 D-5
Eugene, 156185 H-4
Fairview, 8920 C-5
Falcon Hts., 800 M-7
Falls City, 947 E-3
Florence, 8466 H-2
Forest Grv., 21083 C-4
Fossil, 473 E-10
Four Cors., 15947 F-20
Fruitdale, 1177 L-3
Garibaldi, 779 C-2
Gaston, 637 C-4
Gearhart, 1462 B-2
Gervais, 2464 E-4
GILLIAM CO., 1871 D-10
Gladstone, 11497 M-19
Glasgow, 763 I-1
Glendale, 874 K-3
Gleneden Bch., 900 E-2
Glide, 1795 J-4
Gold Bch., 2253 L-1
Gold Hill, 1220 L-4
Grand Ronde, 1661 E-3
GRANT CO., 7445 E-13
Grants Pass, 34533 L-3
Green, 7515 J-3
Gresham, 105594 C-5
Halsey, 904 G-4
Happy Valley, 13903 M-20
Harbor, 2391 M-1
HARNEY CO., 7422 J-12
Harrisburg, 3567 G-4
Hauser, 700 I-1
Hayesville, 19936 E-20
Heppner, 1291 D-11
Hermiston, 16745 B-12
Hillsboro, 91611 C-4
Hines, 1563 I-12
Hood River, 7167 C-7
HOOD RIVER CO., 22346 C-7
Hubbard, 3173 D-4
Independence, 8590 E-4
Irrigon, 1826 B-11
Island City, 989 D-14
JACKSON CO., 203206 L-4
Jacksonville, 2785 M-4
Jefferson, 3098 F-4
JEFFERSON CO., 21720 F-8
John Day, 1744 G-12
Joseph, 1081 D-16
JOSEPHINE CO., 82713 L-3
Junction City, 5392 G-4
Keizer, 36478 E-4
Keno, 1100 M-6
King City, 3111 M-17
KLAMATH CO., 66380 L-7
Klamath Falls, 20840 M-6
La Grande, 13082 D-14
La Pine, 1653 I-7
Lafayette, 3742 D-4
LAKE CO., 7895 K-9
L. Oswego, 36619 D-5
Lakeside, 1699 I-1
Lakeview, 2294 M-10
LANE CO., 351715 H-4
Lebanon, 15518 F-4
Lincoln Bch., 2045 E-2
Lincoln City, 7930 E-2
LINCOLN CO., 46034 F-2
LINN CO., 116672 F-5
Lowell, 1045 H-4
Lyons, 1161 E-5
Madras, 6046 F-8
MALHEUR CO., 31313 J-15
Malin, 805 N-7
Mapleton, 900 H-2
MARION CO., 315335 E-6
Maywood Pk., 752 K-19
McMinnville, 32187 D-4
McNulty, 800 B-4
Medford, 74907 M-4
Melrose, 735 J-3
Merlin, 1615 L-3
Merrill, 844 N-7
Metolius, 710 F-8
Metzger, 3765 M-18
Mill City, 1855 F-5
Milton-Freewater, 7050 B-13
Milwaukie, 20291 M-19
Mission, 1037 C-13
Molalla, 8108 D-5
Monmouth, 9534 E-3
Monroe, 617 G-3
Moro, 324 C-9
MORROW CO., 11173 C-11
Mt. Angel, 3286 E-4
Mulino, 2103 D-5
MULTNOMAH CO., 735334 C-6
Myrtle Creek, 3439 K-3
Myrtle Pt., 2514 J-1
Netarts, 748 C-2
New Hope, 1515 L-3
Newberg, 22068 D-4
Newport, 9989 F-2
N. Bend, 9695 I-1
N. Plains, 1947 C-4
Nyssa, 3267 H-17
Oak Grv., 16629 M-19
Oakland, 927 I-3
Oakridge, 3205 H-5
Odell, 2255 C-7
Ontario, 11366 H-17
Oregon City, 31859 D-5
Pacific City, 1035 D-2
Pendleton, 16612 C-13
Philomath, 4584 F-3
Phoenix, 4538 M-4
Pilot Rock, 1502 C-13
POLK CO., 75403 E-3
Port Orford, 1133 K-1
Portland, 583776 C-5
Powell Butte, 770 G-8
Powers, 689 K-2
Prairie City, 909 F-13
Prineville, 9253 G-8
Rainier, 1895 B-4
Raleigh Hills, 5896 L-18
Redmond, 26215 G-8
Reedsport, 4154 I-2
Rhododendron, 800 D-6
Riddle, 1185 K-3
Rockaway Bch., 1312 C-2
Rogue River, 2131 L-3
Rose Lodge, 1894 E-2
Roseburg, 21181 J-3
Ruch, 840 M-4
St. Helens, 12883 B-4
Salem, 154637 E-4
Sandy, 9570 D-6
Scappoose, 6592 C-4
Scio, 838 F-4
Seal Rock, 600 F-2
Seaside, 6457 B-2
Selma, 695 M-2
Shady Cove, 2904 L-4
Sheridan, 6127 D-3
SHERMAN CO., 1765 D-9
Sherwood, 18194 D-4
Siletz, 1212 F-2
Silverton, 9222 E-4
Sisters, 2038 G-7
Springfield, 59403 H-4
Stanfield, 2043 C-12
Stayton, 7644 E-4
Sublimity, 2681 E-4
Sunnyside, 6791 M-20
Sunriver, 1393 H-7
Sutherlin, 7810 I-3
Sweet Home, 8925 G-5
Talent, 6066 M-4
Tangent, 1164 F-4
Terrebonne, 1257 G-8
The Dalles, 13620 C-8
Tigard, 48035 D-4
Tillamook, 4935 C-2
TILLAMOOK CO., 25250 C-3
Toledo, 3465 F-2
Trail, 702 L-4
Tri-City, 3931 K-3
Troutdale, 15962 C-5
Tualatin, 26054 D-4
Turner, 1854 E-4
Umatilla, 6906 B-12
UMATILLA CO., 75889 D-13
Union, 2121 D-15
UNION CO., 25748 D-14
Vale, 1874 H-16
Veneta, 4561 H-3
Vernonia, 2151 B-4
Waldport, 2033 F-2
Wallowa, 808 C-15
WALLOWA CO., 7008 C-16
Warm Sprs., 2945 F-8
Warren, 1787 B-4
Warrenton, 4989 A-2
WASCO CO., 25213 E-8
WASHINGTON CO., 529710 C-3
W. Linn, 25109 N-19
W. Slope, 6554 L-18
Weston, 667 B-13
WHEELER CO., 1441 F-10
White City, 7975 L-4
Willamina, 2025 E-3
Williams, 1072 M-3
Wilsonville, 19509 D-4
Winchester, 2700 J-3
Winston, 5379 J-3
Woodburn, 24080 D-4
Yachats, 690 G-2
Yamhill, 1024 D-4
YAMHILL CO., 99193 D-3
Yoncalla, 1047 I-3

Pennsylvania

Map pp. 86 – 89

Map keys	Atlas pages
EA – ET	88 – 89
WA – WT	86 – 87

* City keyed to p. 24
† City keyed to p. 66
‡ City keyed to p. 90

Abbottstown, 1011 EQ-4
Abington, 10000 ‡A-5
Acmetonia, 1500 ‡I-8
ADAMS CO., 101407 EP-2
Adamstown, 1789 EN-8
Akron, 3876 EO-7
Albion, 1516 WE-2
Alburtis, 2361 EM-10
Aldan, 4152 ‡F-2
Aliquippa, 9438 WL-3
Allandale, 1000 ET-3
ALLEGHENY CO., 1223348 WM-4
Allentown, 118032 EL-10
Allison Pk., 21552 WL-4
Almedia, 1078 EJ-6
Altoona, 46320 WM-11
Ambler, 6417 EO-12
Ambridge, 7050 WL-3
Ancient Oaks, 6661 EM-10
Andalusia, 3500 ‡B-8
Annville, 4767 EN-6
Apollo, 1647 WL-6
Archbald, 6984 EG-10
Ardmore, 12455 ‡D-2
Ardsley, 4500 ‡A-4
Arendtsville, 952 EP-2
ARMSTRONG CO., 68941 WL-6
Arnold, 5157 WL-5
Ashland, 2817 EK-7
Ashley, 2790 EI-9
Aspinwall, 2801 ‡J-7
Atglen, 1406 EP-8
Athens, 3367 EE-6
Atlas, 809 EK-6
Audubon, 8433 EO-11
Avalon, 4705 WM-3
Avella, 804 WN-2
Avis, 1484 EI-2
Avoca, 2661 EB-10
Avon, 1667 EN-6
Avondale, 1265 EQ-9
Avonia, 1205 WD-3
Avonmore, 1011 WM-6
Baden, 4135 WL-3
Bainbridge, 1355 EO-5
Bakerton, 900 WL-9
Bala-Cynwyd, 8000 ‡D-3
Baldwin, 19767 WN-4
Bally, 1090 EM-10
Bangor, 5273 EK-12
Bareville, 1250 EO-8
Bath, 2693 EL-11
Beaver, 4531 WL-2
BEAVER CO., 170539 WK-2
Beaver Falls, 8987 WK-2
Beaver Meadows, 869 EJ-9
Beaverdale, 1035 WN-9
Beavertown, 965 EL-3
Bechtelsville, 942 EN-10
Bedford, 2841 WP-10
BEDFORD CO., 49762 WO-10
Belair, 1310 ER-8
Belfast, 1257 EK-11
Bell Acres, 1388 WL-3
Belle Vernon, 1093 WO-4
Bellefonte, 6187 WK-14
Belleville, 1827 WL-14
Bellevue, 8370 WM-3
Bellwood, 1828 WL-11
Belmont, 2784 WT-2
Belmont Hills, 1500 ‡C-2
Ben Avon, 1781 ‡I-4
Bensalem, 3000 ‡A-8
Bentleyville, 2581 WO-4
Benton, 824 EI-6
BERKS CO., 411442 EM-8
Berlin, 2104 WP-8
Bernville, 955 EM-8
Berwick, 10477 EJ-7
Berwyn, 3631 EP-11
Bessemer, 1111 WJ-2
Bethel Pk., 32313 WN-4
Bethlehem, 74982 EL-11
Big Beaver, 1970 WK-2
Biglerville, 1200 EP-3
Birdsboro, 5163 EN-9
Bishop, 800 WN-3
Black Lick, 1462 WM-7
Blaine Hill, 1100 WN-4
BLAIR CO., 127089 WN-11
Blairsville, 3412 WM-7
Blakely, 6564 EG-10
Blandon, 7152 EM-9
Blawnox, 1432 ‡J-8
Bloomingdale, 2100 ES-9
Bloomsburg, 14855 EJ-6
Blossburg, 1538 EF-3
Blue Ball, 1031 EO-8
Blue Bell, 6067 EO-11
Blue Ridge Summit, 891 ER-2
Boalsburg, 3722 WK-13
Bobtown, 757 WQ-4
Boiling Sprs., 3225 EO-3
Bonneauville, 1800 EQ-3
Boothwyn, 4933 *A-10
Boswell, 1277 WO-8
Bowmanstown, 937 EK-10
Bowmansville, 2077 EO-8
Boyertown, 4055 EN-10
Brackenridge, 3260 WL-5
Braddock, 2159 ‡L-8
Braddock Hills, 1880 ‡K-8
Bradford, 8770 WD-10
BRADFORD CO., 62622 EE-5
Bradford Woods, 1171 WL-3
Breinigsville, 4138 EM-10
Brentwood, 9643 ‡L-6
Bressler, 1437 ET-4
Brickerville, 1309 EO-7
Bridgeport, 4554 ‡A-1
Bridgeville, 5148 WN-3
Bristol, 9726 EO-13
Brockway, 2072 WI-9
Brodheadsville, 1800 EJ-11
Brookhaven, 8006 EQ-11
Brookside, 2200 WC-4
Brookville, 3924 WI-8
Broomall, 10789 EP-11
Broughton, 3000 ‡M-6
Brownstown, 2816 EO-7
Brownsville, 2331 WP-4
Browntown, 1418 EB-9
Bryn Athyn, 1375 EO-12
Bryn Mawr, 3779 ‡C-1
Buck Hill Falls, 950 EI-11
Buckingham, 2000 EN-12
BUCKS CO., 625249 EM-11
Burgettstown, 1388 WM-2
Burnham, 2054 EL-1
Bushkill, 1200 EI-12
Butler, 13757 WK-4
BUTLER CO., 183862 WJ-4
Butztown, 1500 EA-5
California, 6795 WO-4
Caln, 1519 EP-9
CAMBRIA CO., 143679 WL-10
Cambridge Sprs., 2595 WE-4
CAMERON CO., 5085 WG-11
Camp Hill, 7888 EN-4
Campbelltown, 3616 EN-6
Canadensis, 1200 EI-11
Canonsburg, 8992 WN-3
Canton, 1976 EF-4
CARBON CO., 65249 EJ-9
Carbondale, 8891 EG-10
Carlisle, 18682 EO-3
Carnegie, 7972 ‡K-4
Carnot, 4500 ‡I-2
Carroll Valley, 3876 EQ-2
Carrolltown, 853 WL-9
Castanea, 1125 EI-2
Castle Shannon, 8316 ‡L-5
Catasauqua, 6436 EL-11
Catawissa, 1552 EJ-6
Cecil, 900 WN-3
Cedar Hts., 800 ‡B-2
Cedarbrook, 2800 ‡B-4
Cementon, 1538 EL-10
Center Valley, 900 EM-11
Centerville, 3263 WO-4
Centerville, 1700 ES-7
Central City, 1124 WO-9
CENTRE CO., 153990 EK-1
Centre Hall, 1265 WK-14
Chadds Ford, 1200 EQ-10
Chalfant, 800 ‡K-8
Chalfont, 4009 EN-12
Chambers Hill, 1500 ES-4
Chambersburg, 20268 EP-1
Charleroi, 4120 WO-4
Chase, 978 EA-7
Chatwood, 1000 EP-10
Cherryville, 1580 EK-10
Chester, 33972 EQ-11
CHESTER CO., 498886 EP-9
Chester Hts., 2531 EP-11
Chester Hill, 883 WK-12
Cheswick, 1746 ‡I-9
Chevy Chase Hts., 1502 WL-8
Chicora, 1043 WJ-5
Chinchilla, 2098 EA-13
Christiana, 1168 EP-8
Churchill, 3011 ‡K-8
Clairton, 6796 WN-4
Claridge, 1200 WN-5
Clarion, 5276 WI-6
CLARION CO., 39988 WJ-6
Clarks Green, 1476 EA-13
Clarks Summit, 5116 EG-9
Clay, 1559 EO-7
Claysburg, 1625 WN-10
Claysville, 829 WO-2
Clearfield, 6215 WJ-11
CLEARFIELD CO., 81642 WI-11
Clearview Estates, 2500 ET-2
Cleona, 2080 EN-6
Clifton Hts., 6652 ‡F-2
CLINTON CO., 39238 EI-1
Clymer, 1357 WL-8
Coaldale, 2281 EK-9
Coaltown, 1200 WJ-2
Coatesville, 13100 EP-9
Cochranton, 1136 WG-4
Collegeville, 5089 EO-11
Collingdale, 8786 ‡F-2
Colmar, 800 EN-12
Colonial Pk., 13229 EN-5
Colony Pk., 1076 ET-11
Columbia, 10400 EP-6
COLUMBIA CO., 67295 EI-6
Columbus, 824 WE-6
Colver, 959 WM-9
Colwyn, 2546 ‡F-3
Conestoga, 1258 EP-7
Conewago Hts., 900 EO-5
Confluence, 780 WQ-6
Conneautville, 774 WE-2
Connellsville, 7637 WP-5
Conshohocken, 7833 EO-11
Conway, 2176 WL-3
Conyngham, 1914 EJ-8
Coopersburg, 2386 EM-11
Coplay, 3192 EL-10
Coraopolis, 5677 WM-3
Coraopolis Hts., 1400 ‡J-2
Cornwall, 4112 EN-6
Cornwells Hts., 1391 ‡B-8
Corry, 6605 WE-5
Coudersport, 2546 WF-12
Countryside, 2500 ES-2
Crafton, 5951 WM-3
CRAWFORD CO., 88765 WF-4
Creighton, 1500 WL-5
Cresson, 1711 WM-10
Cressona, 1651 EL-7
Croydon, 9950 ‡B-9
CUMBERLAND CO., 235406 EO-3
Curtisville, 1064 WL-4
Curwensville, 2542 WJ-10
Dale, 1234 WN-8
Dallas, 2804 EH-8
Dallastown, 4049 EP-5
Dalton, 1234 EG-9
Danville, 4699 EJ-5
Darby, 10687 EP-12
Dauberville, 848 EM-8
Dauphin, 791 EN-4
DAUPHIN CO., 268100 EN-4
Davidsville, 1130 WO-8
Dawson Ridge, 1200 WL-2
DELAWARE CO., 558979 EP-11
Delmont, 2686 WM-6
Denver, 3861 EO-8
Derrick City, 1000 WD-10
Derry, 2688 WN-7
Devon, 1515 EP-11
Dewart, 1471 EI-4
Dickson City, 6070 EG-10
Dillsburg, 2563 EO-4
Dingmans Ferry, 1000 EI-13
Donora, 4781 WO-4
Dormont, 8593 WM-4
Dorneyville, 4406 EC-2
Dover, 2007 EP-4
Downingtown, 7891 EP-10
Doylestown, 8380 EN-12
Dravosburg, 1792 ‡M-7
Drexel Hill, 28043 EP-11
Drifton, 800 EJ-9
Dublin, 2158 EN-12
DuBois, 7794 WI-9
Duboistown, 1205 EI-4
Duke Ctr., 850 WE-11
Dunbar, 1042 WP-5
Duncannon, 1522 EN-4
Duncansville, 1233 WM-11
Dunmore, 14057 EH-10
Dunnstown, 1360 EI-2
Dupont, 2711 EC-10
Duquesne, 5565 ‡L-8
Duryea, 4917 EB-10
Earlston, 1122 WP-11
E. Bangor, 1172 EK-12
E. Berlin, 1521 EP-4
E. Berwick, 2007 EJ-7
E. Brady, 942 WJ-5
E. Conemaugh, 1220 WN-9
E. Earl, 1144 EO-8
E. Freedom, 972 WN-11
E. Greenville, 2951 EM-10
E. Lansdowne, 2668 ‡E-2
E. McKeesport, 2126 ‡L-9
E. Petersburg, 4506 EO-7
E. Pittsburgh, 1822 ‡L-8
E. Prospect, 905 EP-6
E. Stroudsburg, 9840 EJ-12
E. Washington, 2234 WO-3
E. York, 8777 WS-14
Easton, 26800 EL-12
Ebensburg, 3351 WM-9
Economy, 8970 WL-3
Eddington, 1906 ‡B-8
Eddington Gdns., 800 ‡A-8
Eddystone, 2410 ‡G-1
Edgemont, 900 ES-3
Edgewood, 3118 ‡K-7
Edgewood, 2384 EK-6
Edgeworth, 1680 WM-3
Edinboro, 6438 WE-3
Edwardsville, 4816 EA-7
Effort, 2269 EJ-11
Egypt, 2391 EA-2
Eldred, 825 WE-11
Elizabeth, 1493 WN-4
Elizabethtown, 11545 EO-6
Elizabethville, 1510 EM-5
ELK CO., 31946 WG-10
Elkins Pk., 4700 ‡B-5
Elkland, 1821 ED-2
Ellport, 1180 WK-3
Ellsworth, 1027 WO-4
Ellwood City, 7921 WK-2
Elmhurst, 830 EH-10
Elverson, 1225 EO-9
Elysburg, 2194 EK-6
Emigsville, 2672 EP-5
Emmaus, 11211 EM-10
Emporium, 2073 WG-12
Emsworth, 2449 WM-3
Enhaut, 1007 ET-4
Enlow, 1013 ‡K-2
Enola, 6111 EN-4
Ephrata, 13394 EO-7
Erie, 101786 WC-4
ERIE CO., 280566 WD-4
Erlen, 800 ‡B-4
Espy, 1642 EJ-6
Estherton, 1200 ER-3
Etna, 3451 ‡J-6
Evans City, 1833 WK-3
Evansburg, 2129 EO-11
Everett, 1834 WP-11
Everson, 793 WO-5
Exeter, 5652 EH-9
Export, 917 WM-5
Exton, 4842 EP-10
Factoryville, 1158 EG-9
Fairchance, 1975 WQ-5
Fairdale, 2059 WP-4
Fairfield, 1100 WC-4
Fairless Hills, 8466 EO-13
Fairoaks, 800 ‡H-2
Fairview, 2348 WD-3
Falls Creek, 1037 WI-9
Fallsington, 1300 †E-2
Fannettsburg, 950 WO-13
Farmersville, 991 EO-7
Farmington, 800 EB-4
Farmington, 767 WQ-6
Farrell, 5111 WI-2
FAYETTE CO., 136606 WP-5
Fayetteville, 3128 EP-1
Fellsburg, 1180 WO-4
Ferndale, 1636 WN-8
Fernway, 12414 WL-3
Fivepointville, 1156 EO-8
Fleetwood, 4085 EM-9
Flemington, 1330 EI-2
Flourtown, 4538 ‡A-3
Fogelsville, 950 EL-10
Folcroft, 6606 ‡F-2
Folsom, 8323 ‡F-1
Ford City, 2991 WK-6
Forest City, 1911 EF-10
FOREST CO., 7716 WG-7
Forest Grv., 2600 ‡J-4
Forest Hills, 6518 ‡K-8
Ft. Loudon, 886 WP-13
Ft. Washington, 5446 EO-12
Forty Fort, 4214 EH-9
Foster Brook, 1251 WD-10
Fountain Hill, 4597 EL-11
Fox Chapel, 5388 ‡I-7
Frackville, 3805 EK-7
Franklin, 6545 WH-5
FRANKLIN CO., 149618 WP-13
Franklin Pk., 13470 WL-3
Frazer, 2000 EP-10
Fredericksburg, 1357 EM-6
Freedom, 1569 WL-3
Freeland, 3531 EJ-9
Freemansburg, 2636 EB-5
Freeport, 1813 WL-5
Friedens, 1523 WP-8
Friedensburg, 858 EL-7
Friedensville, 800 EC-4
Frisco, 850 WK-3
Fullerton, 14925 EL-10
FULTON CO., 14845 WP-12
Gabby Hts., 1200 WO-2
Galeton, 1149 EF-1
Gallitzin, 1668 WM-10
Gap, 1931 EP-8
Garden View, 2503 EI-4
Gastonville, 2818 WN-4
Geistown, 2467 WN-9
Georgetown, 1640 EB-7
Georgetown, 1022 EP-8
Gettysburg, 7620 EQ-3
Ghennes Hts., 900 WO-4
Gibsonia, 2733 WL-4
Gilberton, 769 EK-7
Gilbertsville, 4832 EN-10
Girard, 3104 WD-3
Girardville, 1519 EK-7
Gladwyne, 4000 ‡C-2
Glassport, 4483 WN-4
Glen Lyon, 1873 EI-8
Glen Moore, 1000 ES-9
Glen Rock, 2025 EQ-5
Glenburn, 953 EG-9
Glenmoore, 900 EO-9
Glenolden, 7153 ‡F-2
Glenshaw, 8981 ‡I-6
Glenside, 8384 ‡A-4
Glenwillard, 1100 ‡H-2
Glenwood, 3000 ES-3
Goldsboro, 952 EO-5
Gordon, 763 EL-7
Gouldsboro, 890 EI-11
Grandview Hts., 2050 ES-9
Graterford, 900 EO-11
Gratz, 765 EL-5
Greeley, 1000 EH-12
Green Tree, 4432 ‡K-5
Greenawalds, 1200 EB-2
Greencastle, 3996 WQ-14
GREENE CO., 38686 WQ-3
Greenes, 894 EE-6
Greenfields, 1170 ES-12
Greenock, 2195 ‡M-9
Greensburg, 14892 WN-6
Greentown, 1000 EH-11
Greenville, 5919 WH-2
Greenwood, 2458 WM-11
Grill, 1468 ET-12
Grove City, 8322 WI-3
Halifax, 841 EM-4
Hallam, 2673 EP-6
Hallstead, 1303 ED-9
Hamburg, 4289 EM-8
Hamilton Pk., 3500 ES-8
Hamlin, 1100 EH-11
Hanover, 15289 EQ-4
Hanover, 800 EA-4
Harborcreek, 1500 WC-4
Harleigh, 1104 EJ-8
Harleysville, 9286 EN-11
Harmar Hts., 1050 ‡H-8
Harmarville, 1100 ‡I-8
Harmonville, 1500 ‡B-2
Harmony, 890 WK-3
Harrisburg, 49528 EN-4
Harrisville, 897 WI-4
Harveys Lake, 2791 EH-8
Harwick, 899 ‡H-9
Hastings, 1278 WL-9
Hatboro, 7360 EO-12
Hatfield, 3290 EN-11
Haverford, 6000 ‡D-2
Havertown, 30000 ‡D-1
Hawley, 1211 EG-12
Hayti, 950 EP-9
Hazleton, 25340 EJ-8
Hecktown, 1200 EL-11
Hegins, 812 EL-6
Heidelberg, 1244 WM-3
Hellertown, 5898 EL-11
Hereford, 930 EM-10
Herminie, 789 WN-5
Hermitage, 16220 WI-2
Hershey, 14257 EN-5
Highland Pk., 1900 ET-2
Highland Pk., 1380 EL-1
Highspire, 2399 EO-5
Hilldale, 1246 EB-9
Hiller, 1155 WP-4
Hilltown, 800 EN-12
Hokendauqua, 3378 EA-3
Holland, 5300 EO-13
Hollidaysburg, 5791 WM-11
Hollywood, 800 ‡B-5
Holmes, 2800 ‡F-2
Homer City, 1707 WM-7
Homestead, 3165 ‡K-7
Hometown, 1349 EK-8
Honesdale, 4480 EG-11
Honey Brook, 1713 EO-9
Hopwood, 2090 WP-5
Horsham, 14842 EO-12
Houserville, 1814 WK-13
Houston, 1296 WN-3
Houtzdale, 797 WK-11
Hudson, 1443 EB-8
Hughestown, 1392 EB-10
Hughesville, 2128 EI-5
Hummels Wharf, 1353 EK-4
Hummelstown, 4538 EN-5
Huntingdon, 7093 WM-12
HUNTINGDON CO., 45913 WN-12
Huntingdon Valley, 10000 ‡A-6
Hyde, 1399 WJ-11
Hyde Pk., 2528 ES-13
Hyndman, 910 WQ-9
Imperial, 2541 WM-3
Indiana, 13975 WL-7
INDIANA CO., 88880 WK-8
Indianola, 900 WL-4
Industry, 1835 WL-2
Ingram, 3330 ‡K-5
Inkerman, 1819 EB-9
Intercourse, 1274 EP-8
Iona, 800 EN-7
Irwin, 3973 WN-5
Ivyland, 1041 EO-12
Jacksonwald, 3393 ET-14
Jacobus, 1841 EQ-5
Jamison, 850 EN-12
Jeannette, 9654 WN-5
JEFFERSON CO., 45200 WH-8
Jefferson Hills, 10619 WN-4
Jenkintown, 4422 EO-12
Jermyn, 2169 EG-10
Jerome, 1017 WO-8
Jersey Shore, 4361 EI-3
Jessup, 4676 EG-10
Jim Thorpe, 4781 EK-9
Johnsonburg, 2483 WG-10
Johnstown, 20978 WN-8
Jonestown, 1905 EM-6
JUNIATA CO., 24636 EM-2
Juniata Gap, 1100 WA-12
Kane, 3730 WF-9
Kenhorst, 2877 ET-12
Kenilworth, 1907 EO-10
Kenmar, 4124 EI-4
Kennett Sq., 6072 EQ-10
Kersey, 937 WH-10
King of Prussia, 19936 EO-11
Kingston, 13182 EI-9
Kittanning, 4044 WK-6
Knox, 1146 WI-6
Koppel, 762 WK-2
Korn Krest, 850 EB-6
Kreamer, 822 EK-4
Kulpmont, 2924 EK-6
Kulpsville, 8194 EN-11
Kutztown, 5012 EM-9
Laboratory, 850 WO-3
LACKAWANNA CO., 214437 EH-10
Lafayette Hill, 6700 ‡B-3
Laflin, 1487 EB-9
L. Ariel, 1250 EG-11
Lake City, 3031 WD-2
L. Harmony, 850 EJ-10
L. Wynonah, 2640 EL-7
Lakemont, 1868 WM-11
Lamott, 800 ‡B-5
Lampeter, 1669 ET-10
Lancaster, 59322 EP-7
LANCASTER CO., 519445 EP-8
Landis Valley, 800 ER-9
Landisville, 1893 EO-6
Lansdale, 16269 EN-11
Lansdowne, 10620 ‡E-2
Lansford, 3941 EK-9
Laporte, 316 EH-6
Larksville, 4480 EI-8
Latrobe, 8338 WN-6
Laughlintown, 950 WO-7
Laureldale, 3911 EN-9
Laurys Sta., 1243 EL-10
Laverock, 1100 ‡B-4
Lawnton, 3813 ES-4
LAWRENCE CO., 91108 WI-2
Lawrence Pk., 3982 WC-4
Leaders Hts., 1200 WT-13
Lebanon, 25477 EN-6
LEBANON CO., 133568 EM-6
Lee Pk., 3600 EI-8
Leechburg, 2156 WL-5
Leesport, 1918 EM-8
Leetsdale, 1218 WL-3
LEHIGH CO., 349497 EL-10
Lehighton, 5500 EK-9
Leith, 900 WP-5
Lemont, 2270 WK-13
Lemont Furnace, 827 WP-5
Lemoyne, 4553 ET-3
Leola, 7214 EO-7
Level Green, 4020 WN-5
Levittown, 52983 EO-13
Lewisburg, 5792 EJ-4
Lewistown, 8338 EL-1
Liberty, 2551 ‡M-8
Library, 6000 ‡N-5
Lightner, 1400 WR-13
Lightstreet, 1093 EJ-6
Ligonier, 1573 WN-7
Lilly, 968 WM-10
Lima, 2735 EP-11
Lime Ridge, 890 EJ-7
Limerick, 800 EN-10
Lincoln, 1072 ‡M-8
Lincoln Pk., 1615 ET-11
Lincolnway, 1900 WS-12
Linconia, 950 ‡A-8
Linesville, 1040 WF-2
Linglestown, 6334 EN-5
Linntown, 1489 EJ-4
Linwood, 3281 *B-10
Lionville, 6189 EP-10
Lititz, 9369 EO-7
Littlestown, 4434 EQ-3
Liverpool, 955 EM-4
Llewellyn, 800 EL-7
Lock Haven, 9772 EI-2
Loganville, 1240 EQ-5
Long Pond, 900 EJ-10
Lorain, 759 WS-2
Lorane, 4236 EN-9
Loretto, 1302 WM-10
Lower Allen, 6694 ET-3
Lower Burrell, 11761 †H-10
Lucerne Mines, 937 WM-7
Luzerne, 2845 EH-9
LUZERNE CO., 320918 EH-8
LYCOMING CO., 116111 EH-3
Lykens, 1779 EM-5
Lyndora, 1300 WK-4
Lynnwood, 1300 EB-7
Macungie, 3074 EM-10
Madera, 1000 WK-11
Mahanoy City, 4162 EK-8
Mainland, 2000 EN-11
Malvern, 2998 EP-10
Manchester, 2763 EP-5
Manheim, 4858 EO-6
Manor, 3239 WN-5
Manor Ridge, 1000 ES-8
Mansfield, 3625 EE-3
Maplewood Pk., 1700 ‡F-1
Marcus Hook, 2397 EQ-11
Marienville, 3137 WG-8
Marietta, 2588 EP-6
Marion, 953 WQ-14
Mars, 1699 WL-4
Marshallton, 1441 EK-6
Martinsburg, 1958 WN-11
Marysville, 2534 EN-4
Masontown, 3450 WQ-4
Matamoras, 2469 EH-14
Mayfield, 1807 EG-10
Maytown, 3824 EO-6
McAdoo, 2300 EK-8
McAlisterville, 971 EL-3
McClure, 941 EL-2
McConnellsburg, 1220 WP-13
McConnellstown, 1194 WM-12
McDonald, 2149 WN-3
McGovern, 2742 WN-3
MCKEAN CO., 43450 WF-10
McKees Rocks, 6104 WM-3
McKeesport, 19731 WN-4
McMurray, 4647 WN-3
McSherrystown, 3038 EQ-4
Meadow Lands, 822 WN-3
Meadowbrook, 1000 ‡A-5
Meadville, 13388 WF-3
Mechanicsburg, 8981 EO-4
Mechanicsville, 3100 EJ-6
Media, 5327 EP-11
Melrose Pk., 6500 ‡B-5
Mercer, 2002 WI-3
MERCER CO., 116638 WH-2
Mercersburg, 1561 WQ-13
Meridian, 3881 WK-4
Meyersdale, 2184 WQ-8
Middleburg, 1309 EK-4
Middletown, 8901 EO-5
Middletown, 7378 EA-5
Midland, 2635 WL-2
Midway, 913 WN-2
MIFFLIN CO., 46682 EK-2
Mifflinburg, 3540 EK-4
Mifflintown, 936 EM-2
Mifflinville, 1253 EJ-7
Milesburg, 1123 WJ-13
Milford, 1021 EH-13
Milford Sq., 897 EM-11
Mill Hall, 1613 EI-2
Millbourne, 1159 ‡E-2
Millersburg, 2557 EM-4
Millersville, 8168 EP-7
Millheim, 904 EK-2
Millvale, 3744 ‡J-6
Millville, 948 EI-6
Milroy, 1498 EL-1
Milton, 7042 EJ-4
Minersville, 4397 EL-7
Mogeetown, 1400 ‡A-1
Mohnton, 3043 EN-8
Monaca, 5737 WL-3
Monessen, 7720 WO-4
Monongahela, 4300 WO-4
MONROE CO., 169842 EJ-11
Monroeville, 28386 WM-5
Mont Alto, 1705 EQ-1
Mont Clare, 1800 EO-10
Montandon, 903 EJ-4
Montgomery, 1579 EI-4
MONTGOMERY CO., 799874 EN-10
Montgomeryville, 12624 EN-12
MONTOUR CO., 18267 EJ-5
Montoursville, 4615 EI-4
Montrose, 1617 EE-9
Montrose Hill, 1600 ‡J-8
Moon, 1000 ‡I-2
Moon Crest, 2100 ‡I-3
Moosic, 5719 EH-9
Morgan, 800 WN-3
Morgantown, 826 EO-9
Morrisdale, 754 WJ-12
Morrisville, 8728 EO-14
Morrisville, 1265 WP-3
Morton, 2669 ‡F-1
Moscow, 2026 EH-10
Mt. Allen, 2000 EO-4
Mt. Carmel, 5893 EK-6
Mt. Cobb, 1799 EH-10
Mt. Holly Sprs., 2030 EO-3
Mt. Jewett, 919 WF-10
Mt. Joy, 7410 EO-6
Mt. Lebanon, 33100 ‡L-5
Mt. Nebo, 1500 ‡I-4
Mt. Oliver, 3403 ‡K-6
Mt. Penn, 3106 EN-9
Mt. Pleasant, 4454 WO-6
Mt. Pocono, 3170 EI-11
Mt. Union, 2447 WN-13
Mt. Vernon, 2200 ‡N-8
Mt. Wolf, 1393 EP-5
Mountain Top, 10982 EI-9
Mountainhome, 1182 EI-11
Mountville, 2802 EP-6
Muhlenberg Pk., 1420 ES-12
Muncy, 2477 EI-5
Mundys Cor., 1651 WM-9
Munhall, 11406 WM-4
Murrysville, 20079 WM-5
Muse, 2504 WN-3
Myerstown, 3062 EN-7
Nanticoke, 10465 EI-8
Nanty Glo, 2734 WM-9
Narberth, 4282 EP-12
Nassau Vil., 1500 ‡G-1
Natrona Hts., 2800 WL-5
Nazareth, 5746 EL-11
Neffsville, 1000 EO-7
Nemacolin, 937 WP-4
Nescopeck, 1583 EJ-7
Nesquehoning, 3349 EK-9
New Beaver, 1502 WK-2
New Bedford, 925 WI-2
New Berlin, 873 EK-4
New Berlinville, 1368 EN-10
New Bethlehem, 989 WJ-7
New Bloomfield, 1247 EM-3
New Brighton, 6025 WK-2
New Britain, 3152 EN-12
New Castle, 23273 WJ-2
New Columbia, 1013 EJ-4
New Cumberland, 7277 EO-4
New Derry, 800 WN-7
New Eagle, 2184 WO-4
New Freedom, 4464 EQ-5
New Holland, 5378 EO-8
New Hope, 2528 EN-13
New Kensington, 13116 WL-5
New Market, 816 ET-3
New Milford, 868 EE-9
New Oxford, 1783 EQ-3
New Philadelphia, 1085 EL-8
New Sheffield, 2000 WL-2
New Stanton, 2173 WN-5
New Tripoli, 898 EL-9
New Wilmington, 2466 WI-2
Newmanstown, 2478 EN-7
Newport, 1574 EM-3
Newtown, 2248 EN-13
Newtown, 1400 EB-7
Newtown Sq., 11300 EP-11
Newville, 1326 EO-2
Nicholson, 767 EF-9
Noll Acres, 1050 ET-1
Norristown, 34324 EO-11
N. Apollo, 1297 WL-6
N. Belle Vernon, 1971 WO-4
N. Bend, 800 WH-14
N. Braddock, 4857 ‡L-8
N. Catasauqua, 2849 EA-3
N. Charleroi, 1313 WO-4
North East, 4294 WC-5
N. Hills, 3000 ‡A-4
N. Irwin, 846 WN-5
N. Versailles, 10200 ‡L-8
N. Wales, 3229 EO-11
N. Warren, 1934 WE-8
N. York, 1914 EP-5
Northampton, 9926 EL-10
NORTHAMPTON CO., 297735 EK-11
Northern Cambria, 3835 WL-9
Northumberland, 3804 EK-5
NORTHUMBERLAND CO., 94528 EK-5
Norvelt, 948 WO-6
Norwood, 5890 ‡F-2
Nottingham, 3000 ‡A-8
Oakdale, 1459 WM-3
Oakland, 1600 WS-2
Oakland, 1569 WJ-2
Oakleigh, 1000 ES-4
Oakmont, 6303 WM-4
Oaks, 850 EO-11
Ohioville, 3533 WL-2
Oil City, 10557 WG-5
Oklahoma, 809 WL-6
Oklahoma, 782 WI-9
Old Forge, 8313 EH-9
Oley, 1282 EN-9
Oliver, 2535 WP-5
Olyphant, 5151 EG-10
Orchard Hills, 1952 WL-6
Oreland, 5678 ‡A-4
Orwigsburg, 3099 EL-8
Osceola Mills, 1141 WK-11
Overlook Hts., 1200 WS-5
Oxford, 5077 EQ-8
Paint, 1023 WN-9
Palmer Hts., 3762 EL-11
Palmerton, 5414 EK-10
Palmyra, 7320 EN-6
Palo Alto, 1032 EL-7
Paoli, 5575 EP-11
Paradise, 1129 EP-8
Park Forest Vil., 9660 WS-5
Park Hills, 2500 WT-5
Park View, 1300 ‡J-7
Park Way Mnr., 2000 EB-2
Parker, 840 WI-5
Parker Ford, 800 EO-10
Parkesburg, 3593 EP-9
Parkside, 2328 EQ-11
Parkville, 6706 EQ-4
Patton, 1769 WL-10
Paxtang, 1561 ES-4
Paxtonia, 5412 ER-4
Pen Argyl, 3595 EK-11
Pen Mar, 929 ER-2
Penbrook, 3008 ES-3
Penn Valley, 6000 ‡C-2
Penn Valley, 700 †E-2
Penn Wynne, 5697 ‡D-2
Penndel, 2328 EO-13
Penns Woods, 2600 ‡M-9
Pennsburg, 3843 EN-10
Pennside, 4215 ET-13
Pennwyn, 780 ET-12
Penryn, 1024 EO-7
Perkasie, 8511 EN-11
PERRY CO., 45969 EN-3
Perryopolis, 1784 WO-5
Philadelphia, 1526006 EP-12
PHILADELPHIA CO., 1526006 EO-12
Philipsburg, 2770 WK-12
Phoenixville, 16440 EO-10
PIKE CO., 57369 EH-12
Pilgrim Gdns., 1650 ‡E-1
Pine Grv., 2186 EM-6
Pine Grv. Mills, 1502 WL-13
Pineville, 950 EN-13
Pitcairn, 3294 ‡K-9
Pittsburgh, 305704 WM-4
Pittston, 7739 EH-9
Plains, 4335 EB-8
Pleasant Gap, 2879 WK-14
Pleasant Hills, 8268 ‡M-6
Pleasantville, 892 WG-6
Pleasureville, 1200 WR-13
Plum, 27126 WM-5
Plumsteadville, 2637 EN-12
Plymouth, 5951 EI-8
Plymouth Meeting, 6177 ‡A-2
Pocono Pines, 1409 EI-11
Pocono Summit, 1500 EI-11
Pt. Marion, 1159 WQ-4
Pt. Pleasant, 800 EM-12
Polk, 816 WH-5
Port Allegany, 2157 WE-11
Port Carbon, 1889 EL-7
Port Griffith, 1350 EB-9
Port Royal, 925 EM-2
Port Trevorton, 769 EL-4
Port Vue, 3798 ‡M-8
Portage, 2638 WN-10
POTTER CO., 17457 EE-1
Pottstown, 22377 EN-10
Pottsville, 14324 EL-7
Primos, 900 ‡F-2
Pringle, 979 EA-8
Progress, 9765 ES-3
Prospect, 1169 WJ-4
Prospect Pk., 6454 EP-11
Punxsutawney, 5962 WJ-8
Quakertown, 8979 EM-11
Quarryville, 2576 EP-7
Rankin, 2122 ‡K-7
Raubsville, 1088 EL-12
Reading, 88082 EN-9
Reamstown, 3361 EO-8
Red Hill, 2383 EN-10
Red Lion, 6373 EP-6
Reiffton, 4178 ET-13
Reinholds, 1803 EN-8
Renovo, 1228 WH-14
Republic, 1096 WP-4
Reynoldsville, 2759 WI-9
Rheems, 1598 EO-6
Richboro, 6563 EO-13
Richland, 1519 EN-7
Richlandtown, 1327 EM-11
Ridgeview, 800 ER-4
Ridgway, 4078 WH-9
Ridley Farms, 1500 ‡F-1
Ridley Pk., 7002 ‡G-1
Riegelsville, 868 EL-12
Rillton, 900 WN-5
Rimersburg, 951 WJ-6
Ringtown, 818 EK-7
River View Pk., 3380 ES-12
Riverside, 1932 EJ-5
Roaring Spr., 2585 WN-11
Robesonia, 2061 EN-8
Rochester, 3657 WL-2
Rochester Mills, 2802 WK-8
Rockledge, 2543 EO-12
Rockwood, 890 WP-7
Rohrerstown, 1200 ES-8
Roscoe, 812 WO-4
Rose Valley, 913 EP-11
Roseto, 1567 EK-12
Roslyn, 10000 ‡A-5
Rossmoyne, 1100 ET-2
Rothsville, 3044 EO-7
Roulette, 779 WF-12
Rouzerville, 917 EQ-1
Royalton, 907 EO-5
Royersford, 4752 EO-10
Ruffs Dale, 800 WO-5
Rural Ridge, 1000 WL-4
Rural Valley, 876 WK-7
Russell, 1408 WE-8
Russellton, 1440 WL-4
Rutherford, 4303 ES-4
Rutledge, 784 ‡F-1
Rydal, 1800 ‡A-5
Saddle Brook, 1160 EC-2
Saegertown, 997 WF-3
St. Clair, 3004 EL-7
St. Lawrence, 1809 EN-9
St. Marys, 13070 WH-10
St. Thomas, 900 WP-13
Salix, 1149 WN-9
Saltsburg, 873 WM-6
Salunga, 2695 EO-6
Sanatoga, 8378 EN-10
Sand Hill, 2496 EN-6
Sandy, 1429 WI-9
Saxonburg, 1525 WK-5
Saylorsburg, 1126 EK-11
Sayre, 5587 ED-6
Scalp Level, 778 WN-9
Schaefferstown, 941 EN-7
Schnecksville, 2935 EL-10
Schoeneck, 1056 EN-7
School Lane Hills, 1840 ES-8
SCHUYLKILL CO., 148289 EM-7
Schuylkill Haven, 5437 EL-7
Scotland, 1395 EP-1
Scottdale, 4384 WO-5
Scottsville, 2400 ‡H-2
Scranton, 76089 EH-10
Secane, 1700 ‡F-1
Selinsgrove, 5654 EK-4
Sellersville, 4249 EN-11
Seneca, 1065 WH-5
Seven Fields, 2887 WL-3
Sewickley, 3827 WM-3
Sewickley Hts., 810 ‡H-3
Shamokin, 7374 EK-6
Shamokin Dam, 1686 EK-5
Sharon, 14038 WI-2
Sharon Hill, 5697 ‡F-2
Sharpsburg, 3446 WM-4
Sharpsville, 4415 WH-2
Shavertown, 2019 EA-8
Sheffield, 1132 WF-8
Shenandoah, 5071 EK-7
Shenandoah Hts., 1233 EK-7
Shepherd Hills, 2030 EC-1
Shickshinny, 838 EI-7
Shillington, 5273 EN-8
Shiloh, 11218 EP-5
Shinglehouse, 1127 WD-12
Shippensburg, 5492 EP-1
Shiremanstown, 1569 EO-4
Shoemakersville, 1378 EM-8
Shrewsbury, 3823 EQ-5
Silkworth, 820 EH-8
Silverdale, 871 EN-11
Simpson, 1275 EG-10
Sinking Spr., 4008 EN-8
Skippack, 3758 EN-11
Slatington, 4232 EL-10
Slippery Rock, 3625 WJ-4
Smethport, 1655 WE-11
Smithfield, 4180 WM-12
Smithfield, 875 WQ-4
Snow Shoe, 765 WJ-13
SNYDER CO., 39702 EL-4
Somerset, 6277 WP-8
SOMERSET CO., 77742 WP-8
Souderton, 6618 EN-11
S. Coatesville, 1303 EP-9
S. Connellsville, 1970 WP-5
S. Fork, 928 WN-9
S. Greensburg, 2117 WN-6
S. Lakemont, 1100 WB-13
S. Pottstown, 2081 EN-10
S. Temple, 1424 ER-13
S. Uniontown, 1360 WP-5
S. Waverly, 1027 ED-6
S. Williamsport, 6379 EI-4
Southampton, 11500 EO-12
Southmont, 2284 WN-8
Southwest Greensburg, 2155 WN-6
Speers, 1154 WO-4
Spinnerstown, 1826 EM-11
Spring City, 3323 EO-10
Spring Grv., 2167 EQ-4
Spring Hill, 839 WN-10
Spring House, 3804 EO-12
Spring Mount, 2259 EN-11
Springdale, 3405 WM-5
Springfield, 23677 ‡E-1
Spry, 4891 WT-14
Stafore Estates, 1200 EA-4
State College, 42034 WK-13
State Line, 2709 WQ-14
Steelton, 5990 EO-4
Stewartstown, 2089 EQ-6
Stiles, 1113 EA-2
Stockertown, 927 EK-11
Stoneboro, 1051 WH-3
Stony Creek Mills, 1045 ET-13
Stonybrook, 2384 EP-5
Stormstown, 2366 WK-12
Stowe, 3695 EN-10
Strabane, 1100 WN-3
Strafford, 4500 EP-11
Strasburg, 2809 EP-7
Strodes Mills, 757 EM-1
Stroudsburg, 5567 EJ-12
Sturgeon, 1710 WM-3
Sugar Notch, 989 EI-8
Sugarcreek, 5294 WH-4
SULLIVAN CO., 6428 EH-6
Summerdale, 800 ER-2
Summit Hill, 3034 EK-9
Sunbury, 9905 EK-5
Sunnybrook, 1300 ‡A-4
Sunset Valley, 2700 ‡M-10
SUSQUEHANNA CO., 43356 EF-9
Susquehanna Depot, 1643 EE-10
Swarthmore, 6194 ‡F-1
Swissvale, 8983 ‡K-7
Swoyersville, 5062 EH-9
Sykesville, 1157 WJ-9
Sylvan Hills, 1000 WB-13
Tamaqua, 7107 EK-8
Tannersville, 1200 EJ-11
Tarentum, 4530 WL-5
Tatamy, 1203 EK-11
Taylor, 6263 EH-9
Telford, 4872 EN-11
Temple, 1877 EM-9
Terre Hill, 1295 EO-8
Thompsonville, 3520 ‡N-4
Thorndale, 3407 EP-9
Throop, 4088 EC-13
TIOGA CO., 41981 EF-3
Tionesta, 483 WG-6
Tipton, 1083 WL-11
Tire Hill, 900 WN-8
Titusville, 5601 WF-5
Tobyhanna, 1200 EI-11
Todd, 952 WN-12
Toftrees, 2053 WS-5
Topton, 2069 EM-9
Toughkenamon, 1492 EQ-9
Towanda, 2919 EF-6
Tower City, 1346 EL-6
Trafford, 3174 WN-5
Trainer, 1828 *B-10
Trappe, 3509 EO-11
Tremont, 1752 EL-6
Tresckow, 880 EK-8
Treveskyn, 1200 WN-3
Trevorton, 1834 EK-5
Trexlertown, 1988 EM-10
Trooper, 5744 EO-11
Troy, 1354 EF-5
Trucksville, 2152 EA-8
Trumbauersville, 974 EM-11
Tunkhannock, 1836 EG-8
Turtle Creek, 5349 WM-4
Tuscarora, 980 EK-8
Tyrone, 5477 WL-11
Union City, 3320 WE-5
UNION CO., 44947 EJ-3
Uniontown, 10372 WP-5
Unionville, 962 WJ-4
Unionville, 900 EP-9
Upland, 3239 EQ-11
Upper St. Clair, 19200 WN-3
Valley Forge, 1500 EO-11
Valley View, 1683 EL-6
Vandergrift, 5205 WL-6
Vandling, 751 EF-10
VENANGO CO., 54984 WG-5
Verona, 2474 WM-4
Versailles, 1515 WN-4
Vestaburg, 975 WP-4
Vinco, 1305 WM-9
Walmo, 900 WJ-2
Walnutport, 2070 EK-10
Warminster, 31400 EO-12
Warren, 9710 WE-8
WARREN CO., 41815 WE-7
Warrington, 7000 EN-12
Washington, 13663 WO-3
WASHINGTON CO., 207820 WN-2
Washington Crossing, 850 EN-13
Waterford, 1517 WD-4
Watsontown, 2351 EJ-4
Waymart, 1341 EG-11
WAYNE CO., 52822 EF-11
Wayne Hts., 2545 EQ-1
Waynesboro, 10568 EQ-1
Waynesburg, 4176 WP-3
Weatherly, 2525 EJ-9
Weigelstown, 12875 EP-5
Weldon, 4300 ‡A-4
Wellsboro, 3263 EF-2
Wendel, 1500 ‡N-10
Wernersville, 2494 EN-8
Wescosville, 5872 EC-2
Wesleyville, 3341 WC-4
W. Bristol, 5000 ‡B-9
W. Brownsville, 992 WP-4
W. Chester, 18461 EP-10
W. Conshohocken, 1320 ‡B-1
W. Enola, 800 ES-2
W. Fairview, 1282 ES-2
W. Grove, 2854 EQ-9
W. Hazleton, 4594 EJ-8
W. Homestead, 1929 ‡L-7
W. Kittanning, 1175 WK-6
W. Lancaster, 800 ES-8
W. Lawn, 1715 ET-11
W. Leechburg, 1294 WL-5
W. Mayfield, 1239 WK-2
W. Middlesex, 863 WI-2
W. Mifflin, 20313 WN-4
W. Milton, 900 EJ-4
W. Newton, 2633 WO-5
W. Pittsburg, 808 WJ-2
W. Pittston, 4868 EB-9
W. Reading, 4212 ET-12
W. View, 6771 WM-4
W. Wyoming, 2725 EA-9
W. Wyomissing, 3407 ET-12
W. York, 4617 EP-5
Westfield, 1064 EE-1
Westmont, 5181 WN-8
WESTMORELAND CO., 365169 WM-6
Westwood, 1000 WS-1
Wexford, 1100 WL-3
Whitaker, 1271 ‡L-7
White Haven, 1097 EJ-9
White Oak, 7862 WN-5
Whitehall, 13944 WN-4
Wiconisco, 921 EM-5
Wilkes-Barre, 41498 EI-9
Wilkinsburg, 15930 WM-4
Williamsburg, 1254 WM-12
Williamsport, 29381 EI-4
Williamstown, 1387 EM-5
Willow Grv., 15726 EO-12
Willow Street, 7578 EP-7
Wilmerding, 2190 ‡L-9
Wilson, 7896 EL-11
Wind Gap, 2720 EK-11
Windber, 4138 WO-9
Windsor, 1319 EP-6
Windsor Pk., 1100 ET-1
Winfield, 900 EK-4
Wolfdale, 2888 WO-2
Womelsdorf, 2810 EN-7
Woodland Hts., 1261 WH-5
Woodland Pk., 950 EH-3
Woodlawn, 1850 EL-10
Woodlyn, 9485 EQ-11
Woodside, 2425 †D-1
Woolrich, 800 EI-2
Wormleysburg, 3070 EN-4
Wrightsville, 2310 EP-6
Wyncote, 3044 ‡B-4
Wyndmoor, 5498 ‡B-4
Wynnewood, 7800 ‡D-2
Wyoming, 3073 EB-9
WYOMING CO., 28276 EG-7
Wyomissing, 10461 EN-8
Yardley, 2434 EN-13
Yeadon, 11762 ‡E-3
Yeagertown, 1050 EL-1
Yoe, 1018 EP-5
York, 43718 EP-5
YORK CO., 434972 EP-4
York Sprs., 833 EP-3
Yorkshire, 1700 WS-14
Youngsville, 1729 WE-7
Youngwood, 3050 WN-6
Zelienople, 3812 WK-3
Zieglersville, 900 EN-11
Zion, 2030 WK-14

Puerto Rico

Map p. 128

Arecibo, 44191 A-11
Bayamón, 185996 A-13
Caguas, 82243 B-13
Carolina, 157832 A-13
Cayey, 16680 B-13
Guaynabo, 75443 A-13
Humacao, 18629 B-13
Mayagüez, 70463 B-10
Ponce, 132502 C-11
San Germán, 10989 B-10
San Juan, 381931 A-13
Trujillo Alto, 48437 B-13

Rhode Island

Map p. 91

Abbott Run Valley, 1800 B-7
Adamsville, 600 G-9
Allenton, 650 G-6
Anthony, 3400 E-5
Arnold Mills, 640 B-7
Ashaway, 1485 I-3
Ashton, 910 B-6
Barrington, 16300 E-7
Berkeley, 910 B-6
Bonnet Shores, 1500 H-6
Bradford, 1406 I-3
Bridgetown, 2200 H-6
Bristol, 22400 F-8
BRISTOL CO., 49875 E-7
Burdickville, 500 I-3
Carolina, 970 H-4
Central Falls, 19376 C-7
Charlestown, 2000 I-4
Chepachet, 1675 C-4
Common Fence Pt., 900 F-8
Coventry, 8600 E-4
Cranston, 80387 D-6
Cumberland Hill, 7934 B-6
Davisville, 550 F-6
Diamond Hill, 910 B-6
E. Greenwich, 11800 F-6
E. Providence, 47037 D-7
Esmond, 5000 C-6
Forestdale, 550 B-5
Galilee, 560 I-5
Glendale, 860 B-4
Greene, 888 E-3
Greenville, 8658 C-5
Harmony, 985 C-5
Harris, 1250 E-5
Harrisville, 1605 B-4
Hope Valley, 1612 H-4
Hopkinton, 590 H-3
Island Pk., 1550 F-8
Jamestown, 5000 H-7
KENT CO., 166158 F-4
Kenyon, 550 H-4
Kingston, 6974 H-5
La Fayette, 760 G-6
Little Compton, 550 H-9
Lonsdale, 4200 C-6
Manville, 3200 B-6
Mapleville, 1600 B-4
Matunuck, 580 I-5
Melville, 1320 G-8
Middletown, 3800 G-7
Mt. View, 700 F-6
Narragansett Pier, 3409 I-6
New Shoreham, 830 L-5
Newport, 24672 H-7
NEWPORT CO., 82888 G-8
N. Kingstown, 3000 G-6
N. Providence, 32000 C-6
Oakland, 600 B-4
Pascoag, 4577 B-4
Pawtucket, 71148 C-7
Peace Dale, 3400 H-5
Pettaquamscutt Lake Shores, 750 H-6
Portsmouth, 4200 F-8
Primrose, 530 B-5
Providence, 178042 D-6
PROVIDENCE CO., 626667 C-4
Quidnessett, 2000 F-6
Quidnick, 2700 E-5
Saylesville, 3800 C-6
Shannock, 1100 H-4
Slatersville, 2400 A-5
Snug Hbr., 600 I-5
S. Hopkinton, 500 I-3
Tiverton, 7557 F-8
Union Vil., 2300 B-5
Usquepaug, 530 H-4
Valley Falls, 11547 C-7
Warren, 10600 E-8
Warwick, 82672 E-6
WASHINGTON CO., 126979 H-4
W. Kingston, 1400 H-5
W. Warwick, 29100 E-5
Westerly, 17936 I-2
Woonsocket, 41186 A-5

South Carolina

Map p. 92

* City keyed to p. 28

Abbeville, 5237 D-4
ABBEVILLE CO., 25417 D-4
Aiken, 29524 F-6
AIKEN CO., 160099 F-6
Allendale, 3482 G-7
ALLENDALE CO., 10419 H-6
Anderson, 26686 C-3
ANDERSON CO., 187126 C-3
Andrews, 2861 F-11
Arcadia, 2634 I-4
Arcadia Lakes, 861 F-3
Arial, 2543 B-3
Arthurtown, 1450 H-3
Awendaw, 1294 G-11
Bamberg, 3607 G-7
BAMBERG CO., 15987 G-7
Barnwell, 4750 G-7
BARNWELL CO., 22621 G-6
Batesburg-Leesville, 5362 E-6
Beaufort, 12361 I-8
BEAUFORT CO., 162233 I-8
Beech Island, 1500 F-5
Belle Meade, 1900 J-2
Belmont, 2400 F-5
Belton, 4134 C-4
Belvedere, 5792 *A-13
Ben Avon, 1700 J-6
Bennettsville, 9069 C-11
Berea, 14295 I-1
BERKELEY CO., 177843 G-10
Beverly Hills, 1500 D-9
Bishopville, 3471 D-9
Blacksburg, 1848 A-6
Blackville, 2406 F-7
Bluffton, 12530 J-8
Blythewood, 2034 D-8
Boiling Sprs., 8219 A-5
Bonneau Bch., 1929 F-10
Bowman, 968 F-8
Branchville, 1024 G-8
Bucksport, 876 E-12
Buffalo, 1266 B-6
Burnettown, 2673 F-5
Burton, 6976 I-8
CALHOUN CO., 15175 E-8
Calhoun Falls, 2004 D-4
Camden, 6838 D-8
Capitol View, 4000 E-8
Catawba, 1343 B-8
Cayce, 12528 G-2
Centerville, 6586 C-3
Centerville, 4400 H-10
Central, 5159 B-3
Chaparral Ranches, 5000 G-10
Chapin, 1445 D-7
Charleston, 120083 H-10
CHARLESTON CO., 350209 H-10
Cheraw, 5851 B-10
CHEROKEE CO., 55342 B-6
Cherokee Forest, 2100 I-3
Chesnee, 868 A-5
Chester, 5607 B-7
CHESTER CO., 33140 C-7
Chesterfield, 1472 B-10
CHESTERFIELD CO., 46734 C-9
Chestnut Hills, 1400 J-1
City View, 1345 I-1
CLARENDON CO., 34971 F-9
Clearwater, 4370 *B-14
Clemson, 13905 B-3
Clinton, 8490 C-5
Clover, 5094 A-7
COLLETON CO., 38892 H-8
Columbia, 129272 D-7
Conway, 17103 E-12
Cowpens, 2162 A-6
Dalzell, 3059 D-9
Darlington, 6289 D-10
DARLINGTON CO., 68681 C-10
Denmark, 3538 F-7
Denny Ter., 1750 F-2
Dentsville, 14062 F-3
Dillon, 6788 C-11
DILLON CO., 32062 C-12
DORCHESTER CO., 136555 G-9
Drayton, 1400 I-5
Due West, 1247 C-4
Duncan, 3181 B-5
Dunean, 3671 J-1
Easley, 19993 B-4
E. Gaffney, 3085 A-6
Eastover, 813 E-8
Edgefield, 4750 E-5
EDGEFIELD CO., 26985 E-5
Elgin, 2607 B-8
Elgin, 1311 D-8
Estill, 2040 H-7
Fairfax, 2025 H-7
FAIRFIELD CO., 23956 C-7
Fairforest, 1693 J-4
Florence, 37056 D-10
FLORENCE CO., 136885 D-10
Folly Bch., 2617 H-10
Forest Acres, 10361 G-3
Forestbrook, 4612 I-12
Ft. Lawn, 895 B-8
Ft. Mill, 10811 B-8
Fountain Inn, 7799 B-5
Gadsden, 1632 E-8
Gaffney, 12414 A-6
Gantt, 14229 J-1
Gaston, 1645 E-7
Georgetown, 9163 F-12
GEORGETOWN CO., 60158 F-11
Gloverville, 2831 F-5
Golden Grv., 2467 B-4
Goose Creek, 35938 G-10
Graniteville, 2614 F-5
Great Falls, 1979 C-8
Greenville, 58409 B-4
GREENVILLE CO., 451225 C-4
Greenwood, 23222 D-5
GREENWOOD CO., 69661 D-5
Greer, 25515 B-4
Hampton, 2808 H-7
HAMPTON CO., 21090 H-7
Hampton Hts., 1600 I-2
Hanahan, 17997 H-10
Hardeeville, 2952 J-7
Hartsville, 7764 C-10
Haskell Hts., 1000 E-2
Hazelwood Acres, 1000 G-4
Hilton Head Island, 37099 J-8
Holly Hill, 1277 F-9
Hollywood, 4714 H-9
Hollywood Hills, 950 F-2
Homeland Pk., 6296 C-3
Honea Path, 3597 C-4
Hopkins, 2882 E-8
HORRY CO., 269291 D-13
Inman, 2321 A-5
Inman Mills, 1050 A-5
Irmo, 11097 D-7
Isle of Palms, 4133 H-10
Iva, 1218 D-3
Jackson, 1700 F-6
JASPER CO., 24777 I-7
Joanna, 1539 C-5
Johnsonville, 1480 E-11
Johnston, 2362 E-5
Jonesville, 911 B-6
Judson, 2050 J-1
Kershaw, 1803 C-8
KERSHAW CO., 61697 C-8
Kiawah Island, 1626 I-10
Kingstree, 3328 E-10
Kingswood, 2100 F-1
La France, 900 C-3
Ladson, 13790 G-10
Lake City, 6675 E-11
L. Forest, 1000 I-3
L. View, 807 C-12
L. Wylie, 8841 A-7
Lamar, 989 D-10
Lancaster, 8526 B-8
LANCASTER CO., 76652 C-5
Landrum, 2376 A-5
Latta, 1379 C-11
Laurel Bay, 5891 I-8
Laurens, 9139 C-5
LAURENS CO., 66537 B-8
LEE CO., 19220 D-9
Lesslie, 3112 B-8
Lexington, 17870 E-7
LEXINGTON CO., 262391 E-7
Liberty, 3269 B-3
Lincoln Shire, 1400 E-2
Little River, 8960 E-13
Loris, 2396 D-13
Lugoff, 7434 D-8
Lyman, 3243 B-5
Manning, 4108 E-9
Marietta, 1200 A-4
Marion, 6939 D-11
MARION CO., 33062 D-11
MARLBORO CO., 28933 C-11
Mauldin, 22889 B-4
Mayo, 1592 A-5
McBee, 867 C-9
McColl, 2174 B-11
McCormick, 2783 E-4
MCCORMICK CO., 10233 E-4
Meadowlake, 2700 F-3
Meggett, 1226 H-9
Monarch Mill, 1811 B-6
Moncks Cor., 7885 G-10
Montmorenci, 900 F-6
Mt. Pleasant, 67843 C-13
Mullins, 4663 D-12
Murrells Inlet, 7547 F-12
Myrtle Bch., 27109 E-13
New Ellenton, 2052 F-6
Newberry, 10277 D-6
NEWBERRY CO., 37508 D-5
Newport, 4136 B-7
Ninety Six, 1998 D-5
Norris, 813 B-3
N. Augusta, 21348 *B-13
N. Charleston, 97471 A-12
N. Hartsville, 3251 C-10
N. Myrtle Bch., 13752 E-13
OCONEE CO., 74273 B-2
Olympia, 1200 G-2
Orangeburg, 13964 F-8
ORANGEBURG CO., 92501 F-8
Pacolet, 2235 B-6
Pageland, 2760 B-9
Pamplico, 1226 D-11
Paris, 1950 I-2
Park Pl., 1500 I-2
Pendleton, 2964 C-3
Pickens, 3126 B-3
PICKENS CO., 119224 B-3
Pierpont, 2700 A-11
Pine Valley, 1400 F-1
Pinopolis, 948 G-10
Pleasant Valley, 1200 J-2
Port Royal, 10678 I-8
Prosperity, 1180 D-6
Quinby, 932 D-11
Ravenel, 2465 H-9
Red Bank, 9617 E-7
RICHLAND CO., 384504 E-8
Ridgeland, 4036 I-7
Ridgeville, 1979 G-9
Ridgewood, 1600 F-2
Riverside, 2350 I-1
Rock Hill, 66154 B-7
Roebuck, 2200 B-5
St. George, 2084 G-9
St. Matthews, 2021 E-8
St. Stephen, 1697 F-10
Saluda, 3565 D-6
SALUDA CO., 19875 D-6
Sandwood, 2400 F-3
Sandy Sprs., 1200 C-3
Sans Souci, 7869 I-1
Santee, 961 F-9
Saxon, 3424 I-4
Scranton, 932 E-11
Seabrook Island, 1714 I-10
Seneca, 8102 B-3
Shannontown, 1500 E-9
Simpsonville, 18238 B-4
Socastee, 19952 E-12
S. Congaree, 2306 E-7
S. Forest Estates, 1000 J-2
Spartanburg, 37013 B-5
SPARTANBURG CO., 284307 B-5
Spring Mills, 1400 C-8
Springdale, 2636 E-7
Stateburg, 1380 E-9
Sullivans Island, 1791 H-10
Summerton, 1000 F-9
Summerville, 43392 G-10
Sumter, 40524 E-9
SUMTER CO., 107456 E-9
Surfside Bch., 3837 F-12
Swansea, 827 E-7
Taylors, 21617 B-4
Tega Cay, 7620 A-7
Tigerville, 1312 A-4
Timmonsville, 2320 D-10
Tirzah, 2150 B-7
Travelers Rest, 4576 B-4
Union, 8393 B-6
UNION CO., 28961 B-6
Utica, 1489 B-3
Valley Falls, 6299 H-4
Varnville, 2162 H-7
Wade Hampton, 20461 H-3
Walhalla, 4263 B-2
Wallace, 892 B-10
Walterboro, 5398 H-8
Ware Shoals, 2170 C-4
Warrenville, 1233 F-5
Watts Mills, 1635 C-5
Wedgefield, 1615 E-9
Wellford, 2378 B-5
W. Columbia, 14988 G-2
W. Gantt, 3050 J-2
W. Pelzer, 880 C-4
Westminster, 2418 B-2
Westview, 2000 J-4
Westville, 2200 I-1
Whitmire, 1441 C-6
Whitney, 1500 I-5
WILLIAMSBURG CO., 34423 F-11
Williamston, 3934 C-4
Williston, 3139 F-6
Windsor Estates, 2200 E-4
Winnsboro, 3550 C-7
Winnsboro Mills, 1898 C-7
Woodland Hills, 2700 F-1
Woodruff, 4090 B-5
Yemassee, 1027 H-8
York, 7736 B-7
YORK CO., 226073 B-7

South Dakota

Map p. 93

Aberdeen, 26091 B-10
Alcester, 807 G-13
Alexandria, 615 F-11
Antelope, 826 G-7
Arlington, 915 D-12
Armour, 699 F-10
Aurora, 532 D-13
AURORA CO., 2710 E-10
Avon, 590 G-11
Baltic, 1089 E-13
BEADLE CO., 17398 D-10
Belle Fourche, 5594 D-2
BENNETT CO., 3431 G-5
Beresford, 2005 G-13
Bison, 333 B-4
Blackhawk, 2892 E-3
BON HOMME CO., 7070 G-11
Bowdle, 502 B-8
Box Elder, 7800 E-3
Brandon, 8785 F-13
Britton, 1241 A-11
Brookings, 22056 D-12
BROOKINGS CO., 31965 D-12
BROWN CO., 36531 B-10
BRULE CO., 5255 F-9
Buffalo, 330 B-3
BUFFALO CO., 1912 E-9
Burke, 604 G-9
BUTTE CO., 10110 C-3
CAMPBELL CO., 1466 B-8
Canistota, 656 F-12
Canton, 3057 F-13
Castlewood, 627 C-12
Centerville, 882 G-12
Chamberlain, 2387 E-9
CHARLES MIX CO., 9129 G-10
Clark, 1139 C-11
CLARK CO., 3691 C-11
CLAY CO., 13864 G-12
Clear Lake, 1273 C-13
CODINGTON CO., 27227 C-12
Colman, 594 E-12
Colton, 687 E-12
Corsica, 592 F-10
CORSON CO., 4050 B-6
Crooks, 1269 F-12
Custer, 2067 E-2
CUSTER CO., 8216 F-2
DAVISON CO., 19504 F-10
DAY CO., 5710 C-11
De Smet, 1089 D-11
Deadwood, 1270 D-2
Dell Rapids, 3633 E-13
DEUEL CO., 4364 C-13
DEWEY CO., 5301 C-6
DOUGLAS CO., 3002 F-10
Dupree, 525 C-5
Eagle Butte, 1318 C-6
Edgemont, 774 F-2
EDMUNDS CO., 4071 B-8
Elk Pt., 1963 H-13
Elkton, 736 D-13
Estelline, 768 D-12
Eureka, 868 A-8
FALL RIVER CO., 7094 G-2
FAULK CO., 2364 C-9
Faulkton, 736 C-9
Flandreau, 2341 E-13
Ft. Pierre, 2078 D-7
Ft. Thompson, 1282 E-9
Freeman, 1306 F-12
Gann Valley, 14 E-9
Garretson, 1166 F-13
Gettysburg, 1162 C-8
GRANT CO., 7356 C-12
Gregory, 1295 G-9
GREGORY CO., 4271 G-9
Groton, 1458 B-10
HAAKON CO., 1937 D-5
HAMLIN CO., 5903 D-12
HAND CO., 3431 D-9
HANSON CO., 3331 F-11
HARDING CO., 1255 B-3
Harrisburg, 4089 F-13
Hartford, 2534 F-12
Hayti, 381 D-12
Highmore, 795 D-9
Hill City, 948 E-2
Hot Sprs., 3711 F-2
Howard, 858 E-11
HUGHES CO., 17022 D-8
Humboldt, 589 F-12
Huron, 12592 D-10
HUTCHINSON CO., 7343 F-11
HYDE CO., 1420 D-8
Ipswich, 954 B-9
JACKSON CO., 3031 F-5
Jefferson, 547 H-13
JERAULD CO., 2071 E-10
JONES CO., 1006 E-6
Kadoka, 654 E-5
Kennebec, 240 E-8
Kimball, 703 F-9
KINGSBURY CO., 5148 D-11
Kyle, 846 F-4
L. Andes, 879 G-10
LAKE CO., 11200 E-12
L. Preston, 599 D-12
LAWRENCE CO., 24097 E-2
Lead, 3124 D-2
Lemmon, 1227 A-5
Lennox, 2111 F-12
Leola, 457 A-9
LINCOLN CO., 44828 G-13
Lower Brule, 613 E-8
LYMAN CO., 3755 E-8
Madison, 6474 E-12
Marion, 784 F-12
MARSHALL CO., 4656 A-11
Martin, 1071 G-5
MCCOOK CO., 5618 E-12
McIntosh, 173 A-6
McLaughlin, 663 A-6
MCPHERSON CO., 2459 A-9
MEADE CO., 25434 D-3
MELLETTE CO., 2048 F-6
Menno, 608 G-11
Milbank, 3353 B-13
Miller, 1489 D-9
MINER CO., 2389 E-11
MINNEHAHA CO., 169468 E-12
Mission, 1182 G-7
Mitchell, 15254 F-11
Mobridge, 3465 B-7
MOODY CO., 6486 E-13
Mound City, 71 A-8
Murdo, 488 E-7
New Underwood, 660 E-3
Newell, 603 C-3
N. Sioux City, 2530 H-13
Oglala, 1290 G-4
OGLALA LAKOTA CO., 13586 F-4
Olivet, 74 G-11
Onida, 658 D-8
Parker, 1022 F-12
Parkston, 1508 F-11
Parmelee, 562 F-6
PENNINGTON CO., 100948 E-4
PERKINS CO., 2982 B-4
Philip, 779 E-5
Pierre, 13646 D-7
Pine Ridge, 3308 G-4
Plankinton, 707 F-10
Platte, 1230 F-9
Porcupine, 1062 G-4
POTTER CO., 2329 C-8
Rapid City, 67956 E-3
Redfield, 2333 C-10
ROBERTS CO., 10149 B-12
Rosebud, 1587 G-6
St. Francis, 709 G-6
Salem, 1347 F-12
SANBORN CO., 2355 E-10
Scotland, 841 G-11
Selby, 642 B-8
Sioux Falls, 153888 F-13
Sisseton, 2470 B-12
Spearfish, 10494 D-2
SPINK CO., 6415 C-10
Springfield, 1989 G-11
STANLEY CO., 2966 D-6
Sturgis, 6627 D-2
SULLY CO., 1373 D-7
Summerset, 1814 E-3
Tea, 3806 F-12
Timber Lake, 443 B-6
TODD CO., 9612 G-6
Tripp, 647 G-11
TRIPP CO., 5644 G-8
TURNER CO., 8347 F-12
Tyndall, 1067 G-11
UNION CO., 14399 G-13
Valley Sprs., 759 F-13
Veblen, 531 A-12
Vermillion, 10571 G-12
Viborg, 782 G-12
Volga, 1768 D-12
Wagner, 1566 G-10
Wall, 766 E-4
WALWORTH CO., 5438 B-8
Wanblee, 725 F-5
Watertown, 21482 C-12
Waubay, 576 B-12
Webster, 1886 B-11
Wessington Sprs., 956 E-10
White River, 581 F-7
Whitewood, 927 D-2
Winner, 2897 F-8
Woonsocket, 655 E-10
Worthing, 877 F-13
Yankton, 14454 G-12
YANKTON CO., 22438 G-12
ZIEBACH CO., 2801 C-5

Tennessee

Map pp. 94 – 95

† City keyed to p. 96

Adamsville, 2207 F-6
Alamo, 2461 D-4
Alcoa, 8449 D-19
Alexandria, 966 C-13
Algood, 3495 C-15
Altamont, 1045 F-14
ANDERSON CO., 75129 C-18
Apison, 2469 G-16
Ardmore, 1213 G-11
Arlington, 11517 F-3
Arrowhead, 950 *A-9
Ashland City, 4541 C-10
Athens, 13458 F-18
Atoka, 8387 F-2
Atwood, 938 D-6
Banner Hill, 1497 K-18
Bartlett, 54613 F-2
Baxter, 1365 C-15
Bean Sta., 2826 J-16
BEDFORD CO., 45058 E-12
Belle Meade, 2912 L-7
Bells, 2437 E-4
Benton, 1385 G-17
BENTON CO., 16489 C-7
Berrys Chapel, 3000 D-11
Bethel Sprs., 718 F-6
Biltmore, 1800 †M-5
Blaine, 1856 C-20
BLEDSOE CO., 12876 F-16
Bloomingdale, 9888 I-18
BLOUNT CO., 123010 E-20
Blountville, 3074 I-18
Bluff City, 1733 J-19
Bolivar, 5417 F-5
Bradford, 1048 C-5
BRADLEY CO., 98963 G-17
Brentwood, 37060 D-11
Briceville, 800 C-19
Bridwell Hts., 2700 †J-2
Brighton, 2735 E-2
Bristol, 26702 I-19
Brownsville, 10292 E-4
Bruceton, 1478 D-7
Bulls Gap, 738 K-16
Burns, 1468 D-10
Byrdstown, 803 B-16
Calderwood, 820 E-19
Camden, 3582 C-7
CAMPBELL CO., 40716 B-19
CANNON CO., 13801 D-13
CARROLL CO., 28522 D-6
Carson Spring, 700 L-16
CARTER CO., 57424 J-19
Carthage, 2306 C-14

Caryville, 2297 ... C-19
Celina, 1495 ... B-15
Centerville, 3644 ... D-9
Central, 2279 ... †M-4
Chapel Hill, 1445 ... E-11
Charlotte, 1235 ... C-10
Chattanooga, 167674 ... G-16
CHEATHAM CO., 39105 ... B-10
CHESTER CO., 17131 ... F-6
Church Hill, 6737 ... J-17
CLAIBORNE CO., 32213 ... B-20
Clarksville, 132929 ... B-10
CLAY CO., 7861 ... B-14
Cleveland, 41285 ... G-17
Clifton, 2694 ... F-8
Clinton, 9841 ... C-19
Coalfield, 2463 ... D-18
Coalmont, 841 ... F-14
COCKE CO., 35662 ... K-16
COFFEE CO., 52796 ... E-13
Collegedale, 8282 ... G-16
Collierville, 43965 ... G-3
Collinwood, 982 ... G-8
Colonial Hts., 6934 ... J-18
Columbia, 34681 ... E-10
Cookeville, 30435 ... C-15
Coopertown, 4278 ... B-11
Cornersville, 1194 ... F-11
Counce, 700 ... G-7
Covington, 9038 ... E-3
Cowan, 1737 ... G-13
Crab Orchard, 752 ... D-17
Crestwood Hills, 1600 ... K-11
CROCKETT CO., 14586 ... D-4
Cross Plains, 1714 ... B-11
Crossville, 10795 ... D-16
Crump, 1428 ... F-7
CUMBERLAND CO., 56053 ... D-17
Dandridge, 2812 ... K-15
DAVIDSON CO., 626681 ... C-11
Dayton, 7191 ... F-16
DE KALB CO., 18723 ... D-14
Decatur, 1598 ... E-17
DECATUR CO., 11757 ... E-7
Decaturville, 867 ... E-7
Decherd, 2361 ... G-13
Dickson, 14538 ... C-9
DICKSON CO., 49666 ... C-9
Dover, 1417 ... B-8
Dresden, 3005 ... C-6
Dunlap, 4815 ... F-15
Dyer, 2341 ... C-5
DYER CO., 38335 ... C-4
Dyersburg, 17145 ... C-4
Eagleton Vil., 5052 ... *B-9
E. Ridge, 20979 ... G-16
Eastview, 705 ... G-6
Elizabethton, 14176 ... J-19
Englewood, 1532 ... F-18
Erin, 1324 ... C-9
Erwin, 6097 ... K-18
Estill Sprs., 2055 ... F-13
Etowah, 3490 ... F-18
Fairfield Glade, 6989 ... D-17
Fairmount, 2825 ... G-15
Fairview, 7720 ... D-10
Fall Branch, 1291 ... J-17
Farragut, 20676 ... D-19
FAYETTE CO., 38413 ... F-3
Fayetteville, 6827 ... G-12
FENTRESS CO., 17959 ... B-17
Fincastle, 1618 ... B-19
Finley, 1000 ... C-3
Fordtown, 1900 ... †L-1
Forest Hills, 4812 ... C-11
Franklin, 62487 ... D-11
FRANKLIN CO., 41052 ... G-13
Friendsville, 913 ... E-19
Gainesboro, 962 ... B-14
Gallatin, 30278 ... B-12
Gallaway, 680 ... F-3
Gatlinburg, 3944 ... M-15
Germantown, 38844 ... G-2
GIBSON CO., 49683 ... D-5
GILES CO., 29485 ... F-10
Gleason, 1445 ... C-6
Goodlettsville, 15921 ... C-11
Gordonsville, 1213 ... C-14
GRAINGER CO., 22657 ... C-20
Gray, 1222 ... J-18
Graysville, 1502 ... F-16
Green Hill, 6618 ... C-12
Greenback, 1064 ... E-19
Greenbrier, 6433 ... B-11
GREENE CO., 68831 ... J-17
Greeneville, 15062 ... K-17
Greenfield, 2182 ... C-5
Grimsley, 1167 ... C-16
Gruetli-Laager, 1813 ... F-15
GRUNDY CO., 13703 ... F-14
Halls, 2255 ... D-4
Halls Crossroads, 1250 ... C-19
HAMBLEN CO., 62544 ... J-16
HAMILTON CO., 336463 ... F-16
Hampton, 2000 ... J-19
HANCOCK CO., 6819 ... J-15
HARDEMAN CO., 27253 ... G-4
HARDIN CO., 26026 ... G-7
Harriman, 6350 ... D-18
Harrison, 7769 ... L-14
Harrogate, 4389 ... B-20
Hartsville, 7870 ... B-13
HAWKINS CO., 56833 ... J-16
HAYWOOD CO., 18787 ... E-4
Helenwood, 865 ... B-18
Henderson, 6309 ... F-6
HENDERSON CO., 27769 ... E-6
Hendersonville, 51372 ... C-12
Henning, 945 ... E-3
HENRY CO., 32330 ... B-7
HICKMAN CO., 24690 ... E-9
Hickory Withe, 2600 ... F-3
Hohenwald, 3757 ... E-9
Hollow Rock, 718 ... D-7
Hopewell, 1874 ... F-17
HOUSTON CO., 8426 ... C-8
Humboldt, 8452 ... D-5
HUMPHREYS CO., 18538 ... C-8
Hunter, 1854 ... †M-5
Huntingdon, 3985 ... D-6
Huntland, 872 ... G-13
Huntsville, 1248 ... B-18
Indian Sprs., 2200 ... †J-2
Jacksboro, 2020 ... B-19
Jackson, 65211 ... E-5
JACKSON CO., 11638 ... C-14
Jamestown, 1959 ... B-17
Jasper, 3279 ... G-15
Jefferson City, 8047 ... K-15
JEFFERSON CO., 51407 ... C-20
Jellico, 2355 ... B-19
John Sevier, 800 ... I-14
Johnson City, 63152 ... J-18
JOHNSON CO., 18244 ... J-20
Jonesborough, 5051 ... J-18
Kenton, 1281 ... C-5
Kimball, 1395 ... G-14
Kimberlin Hts., 680 ... D-20
Kingsport, 48205 ... I-18
Kingston, 5934 ... D-18
Kingston Sprs., 2756 ... C-10
Kingston Woods, 840 ... K-11
KNOX CO., 432226 ... C-20
Knoxville, 178874 ... D-20
La Vergne, 32588 ... D-12
Lafayette, 4474 ... B-13
LaFollette, 7456 ... B-19
LAKE CO., 7832 ... C-3
Lake Tansi Vil., 3803 ... D-16
Lakeland, 12430 ... F-2
Lakesite, 1826 ... G-16
Lakewood, 2302 ... C-12
LAUDERDALE CO., 27815 ... D-3
LAWRENCE CO., 41869 ... F-9
Lawrenceburg, 10428 ... F-10
Lebanon, 26190 ... C-13
Lenoir City, 8642 ... D-19
LEWIS CO., 12161 ... E-9
Lewisburg, 11100 ... F-11
Lexington, 7652 ... E-6
LINCOLN CO., 33361 ... G-12
Linden, 908 ... E-8
Livingston, 4058 ... B-15
Lobelville, 897 ... D-8
Lookout Mtn., 1832 ... N-11
Loretto, 1714 ... G-9
Loudon, 5381 ... E-18
LOUDON CO., 48556 ... E-18
Louisville, 2439 ... D-19
Luttrell, 1074 ... C-20
Lyles, 734 ... D-10
Lynchburg, 6362 ... F-12
MACON CO., 22248 ... B-14
MADISON CO., 98294 ... E-5
Madisonville, 4577 ... E-18
Manchester, 10102 ... F-13
MARION CO., 28237 ... G-14
MARSHALL CO., 30617 ... F-11
Martin, 11473 ... B-5
Maryville, 27465 ... E-19
Mascot, 2411 ... C-20
Mason, 1609 ... F-3
Maury City, 674 ... D-4
MAURY CO., 80956 ... E-10
Maynardville, 2413 ... C-20
McEwen, 1750 ... C-9
McKenzie, 5310 ... C-6
MCMINN CO., 52266 ... F-17
McMinnville, 13605 ... E-14
MCNAIRY CO., 26075 ... F-6
Medina, 3479 ... D-5
MEIGS CO., 11753 ... F-17
Memphis, 646889 ... G-2
Middle Valley, 12684 ... G-16
Middleton, 706 ... G-5
Midtown, 1360 ... D-18
Midway, 2491 ... †N-2
Milan, 7851 ... D-5
Millersville, 6440 ... B-11
Millington, 10176 ... F-2
MONROE CO., 44519 ... F-19
Monteagle, 1192 ... F-14
Monterey, 2850 ... C-16
MONTGOMERY CO., 172331 ... B-9
MOORE CO., 6362 ... F-12
Mooresburg, 941 ... J-16
MORGAN CO., 21987 ... C-17
Morrison, 694 ... E-14
Morristown, 29137 ... K-16
Mosheim, 2362 ... K-17
Mt. Carmel, 5429 ... I-17
Mt. Juliet, 23671 ... C-12
Mt. Olive, 720 ... K-13
Mt. Pleasant, 4561 ... E-10
Mountain City, 2531 ... J-20
Munford, 5927 ... E-2
Murfreesboro, 108755 ... D-12
Nashville, 601222 ... C-11
New Hope, 1082 ... G-14
New Johnsonville, 1951 ... D-8
New Market, 1334 ... C-20
New Tazewell, 3037 ... B-20
New Union, 1431 ... E-13
Newbern, 3313 ... C-4
Newport, 6945 ... L-16
Niota, 719 ... E-18
Nolensville, 5861 ... D-12
Norris, 1491 ... C-19
Northcott, 800 ... †J-1
Oak Grove, 4425 ... J-18
Oak Hill, 4529 ... C-11
Oak Ridge, 29330 ... D-19
Oakland, 6623 ... F-3
Obion, 1119 ... C-4
OBION CO., 31807 ... B-4
Oliver Sprs., 3231 ... D-18
Olivet, 1350 ... F-7
Oneida, 3752 ... B-18
Ooltewah, 687 ... G-16
Orebank, 1300 ... †J-2
Orlinda, 859 ... B-11
OVERTON CO., 22083 ... C-15
Palmer, 672 ... F-15
Paris, 10156 ... C-7
Park City, 2442 ... G-12
Parsons, 2373 ... E-7
Pegram, 2093 ... C-10
PERRY CO., 7915 ... E-8
PICKETT CO., 5077 ... B-16
Pigeon Forge, 5875 ... D-20
Pikeville, 1608 ... E-16
Pine Crest, 2388 ... J-18
Piperton, 1445 ... G-3
Plainview, 2125 ... C-20
Pleasant View, 4149 ... B-10
POLK CO., 16825 ... G-18
Portland, 11480 ... B-12
Powells Crossroads, 1322 ... G-15
Pulaski, 7870 ... G-10
Puryear, 671 ... B-7
PUTNAM CO., 72321 ... C-15
Ramsey, 700 ... J-14
Red Bank, 11651 ... L-12
Red Boiling Sprs., 1112 ... B-14
RHEA CO., 31809 ... E-16
Riceville, 670 ... F-17
Rickman, 750 ... C-15
Ridgely, 1795 ... C-3
Ridgetop, 1874 ... B-11
Ripley, 8445 ... D-3
Roan Mtn., 1360 ... K-19
ROANE CO., 54181 ... E-18
ROBERTSON CO., 66283 ... B-11
Rockford, 856 ... D-19
Rockwood, 5562 ... D-17
Rocky Top, 1781 ... C-19
Rogersville, 4420 ... J-16
Russellville, 1200 ... K-16
Rutherford, 1151 ... C-5
RUTHERFORD CO., 262604 ... E-12
Ruthton, 900 ... I-19
Rutledge, 1122 ... J-15
St. Joseph, 782 ... G-9
Sale Creek, 2845 ... F-16
Savannah, 6982 ... F-7
SCOTT CO., 22228 ... B-18
Scotts Hill, 984 ... E-7
Selmer, 4396 ... G-6
SEQUATCHIE CO., 14112 ... F-15
SEVIER CO., 89889 ... D-20
Sevierville, 14807 ... D-20
Sewanee, 2311 ... G-14
Seymour, 10919 ... D-20
Sharon, 944 ... C-5
SHELBY CO., 927644 ... G-2
Shelbyville, 20335 ... F-12
Shooks Gap, 690 ... *A-9
Signal Mtn., 7554 ... G-15
SMITH CO., 19166 ... B-13
Smithville, 4530 ... D-14
Smyrna, 39974 ... D-12
Sneedville, 1387 ... J-16
Soddy-Daisy, 12714 ... F-16
Somerville, 3094 ... F-4
S. Carthage, 1322 ... C-14
S. Fulton, 2354 ... B-5
S. Pittsburg, 2992 ... G-14
Sparta, 4925 ... D-15
Spencer, 1601 ... E-15
Spring City, 1981 ... E-17
Spring Hill, 29036 ... E-11
Springfield, 16440 ... B-11
Spurgeon, 3957 ... J-18
STEWART CO., 13324 ... B-8
Strawberry Plains, 700 ... C-20
Suburban Hills, 1500 ... K-11
SULLIVAN CO., 156823 ... J-19
Summertown, 866 ... F-10
SUMNER CO., 160645 ... B-12
Surgoinsville, 1801 ... J-17
Sweetwater, 5764 ... E-18
Tazewell, 2218 ... B-20
Telford, 921 ... K-18
Tellico Plains, 880 ... F-18
Tennessee Ridge, 1368 ... C-8
Thompson's Sta., 2194 ... D-11
Three Way, 1709 ... D-5
TIPTON CO., 61081 ... E-2
Tiptonville, 4464 ... B-3
Tracy City, 1481 ... F-14
Trenton, 4264 ... D-5
Trezevant, 859 ... D-6
TROUSDALE CO., 7870 ... B-13
Troy, 1371 ... B-4
Tullahoma, 18655 ... F-13
Tusculum, 2663 ... K-17
Unicoi, 3632 ... K-18
UNICOI CO., 18313 ... K-18
Union City, 10895 ... B-5
UNION CO., 19109 ... B-20
Unionville, 1368 ... E-12
Valley Forge, 2200 ... †N-5
VAN BUREN CO., 5548 ... E-15
Vonore, 1474 ... E-19
Walden, 1898 ... G-15
Walnut Grove, 864 ... B-12
Walnut Hill, 2394 ... †J-4
WARREN CO., 39839 ... E-14
Wartburg, 918 ... C-18
WASHINGTON CO., 122979 ... K-18
Watertown, 1477 ... C-13
Waverly, 4105 ... C-8
WAYNE CO., 17021 ... F-8
Waynesboro, 2449 ... F-8
WEAKLEY CO., 35021 ... B-6
Westmoreland, 2206 ... B-13
White Bluff, 3206 ... C-10
WHITE CO., 25841 ... D-15
White House, 10255 ... B-12
White Pine, 2196 ... K-16
Whiteville, 4638 ... F-4
Whitwell, 1699 ... G-15
Wildwood, 1098 ... D-20
WILLIAMSON CO., 183182 ... D-10
WILSON CO., 113993 ... C-13
Winchester, 8530 ... G-13
Winfield, 967 ... B-18
Woodbury, 2680 ... D-13

Texas

Map pp. 98 – 101

Map keys	Atlas pages
EA – ET	100 – 101
WA – WT	98 – 99

* City keyed to p. 96
† City keyed to p. 97

Abernathy, 2805 ... WG-10
Abilene, 117063 ... WJ-14
Addison, 13056 ... †E-10
Agua Dulce, 812 ... EP-5
Alamo, 18353 ... WS-10
Alamo Hts., 7031 ... ER-10
Albany, 2034 ... EE-2
Aledo, 2716 ... EE-5
Algoa, 400 ... *I-7
Alice, 19104 ... EP-5
Allen, 84246 ... ED-7
Alpine, 5905 ... WN-7
Alto, 1225 ... EG-10
Alton, 12341 ... WR-9
Alvarado, 3785 ... EF-6
Alvin, 24236 ... EL-10
Alvord, 1334 ... ED-5
Amarillo, 190695 ... WD-10
Ames, 1003 ... EK-11
Anahuac, 2243 ... EK-11
Anderson, 222 ... EJ-9
ANDERSON CO., 58458 ... EG-9
Andrews, 11088 ... WJ-9
ANDREWS CO., 14786 ... WJ-8
ANGELINA CO., 86771 ... EI-11
Angleton, 18862 ... EM-10
Anna, 8249 ... ED-7
Anson, 2430 ... WI-14
Anthony, 5011 ... WK-1
Anton, 1126 ... WG-10
ARANSAS CO., 23158 ... EP-7
Aransas Pass, 8204 ... EP-7
Archer City, 1834 ... EC-3
ARCHER CO., 9054 ... EC-3
Arcola, 1642 ... EL-10
Argyle, 3282 ... ED-6
Arlington, 365438 ... EE-6
ARMSTRONG CO., 1901 ... WE-11
Arp, 970 ... EF-10
Asherton, 1084 ... WS-14
Aspermont, 919 ... WH-13
Atascocita, 65844 ... *A-7
ATASCOSA CO., 44911 ... EN-4
Athens, 12710 ... EF-9
Atlanta, 5675 ... ED-12
Aubrey, 2595 ... ED-6
Audobon Pk., 1200 ... *B-6
Austin, 790390 ... EK-5
AUSTIN CO., 28417 ... EK-8
Azle, 10947 ... EE-6
Bacliff, 8619 ... *H-9
BAILEY CO., 7165 ... WF-8
Baird, 1496 ... EF-2
Balch Sprs., 23728 ... †H-12
Balcones Hts., 2941 ... ER-9
Ballinger, 3767 ... WL-14
Bammel, 600 ... *A-4
Bandera, 857 ... EL-3
BANDERA CO., 20485 ... EL-2
Bangs, 1603 ... EG-2
Barker ... *D-1
Barrett, 3199 ... *C-8
Bartlett, 1623 ... EI-6
Bartonville, 1469 ... †C-6
Bastrop, 7218 ... EK-6
BASTROP CO., 74171 ... EK-6
Bay City, 17614 ... EM-9
BAYLOR CO., 3726 ... EC-2
Bayou Vista, 1537 ... EM-11
Baytown, 71802 ... EL-11
Beach City, 2198 ... EL-11
Beaumont, 118296 ... EK-12
Beaumont Pl., 8000 ... *C-7
Beckville, 847 ... EF-11
Bedford, 46979 ... †F-6
Bee Cave, 3925 ... EK-5
BEE CO., 31861 ... EO-6
Beeville, 12863 ... EO-5
BELL CO., 310235 ... EI-6
Bellaire, 16855 ... EL-10
Bellmead, 9901 ... EH-6
Bells, 1392 ... EC-8
Bellville, 4097 ... EK-8
Belton, 18216 ... EI-6
Benavides, 1362 ... EQ-4
Benbrook, 21234 ... EE-6
Benjamin, 258 ... WH-14
Berryville, 975 ... EF-9
Bertram, 1353 ... EJ-5
Beverly Hills, 1995 ... WT-7
Bevil Oaks, 1274 ... EK-12
BEXAR CO., 1714773 ... EM-4
Big Lake, 2936 ... WM-11
Big Sandy, 1343 ... EE-10
Big Spr., 27282 ... WJ-11
Bisbee ... †J-6
Bishop, 3134 ... EQ-5
Blanco, 1739 ... EK-4
BLANCO CO., 10497 ... EJ-4
Blooming Grv., 821 ... EG-7
Blossom, 1494 ... EC-9
Blue Ridge, 822 ... ED-8
Boerne, 10471 ... EL-3
Bogata, 1153 ... EC-10
Bonham, 10127 ... EC-8
Booker, 1516 ... WA-13
BORDEN CO., 641 ... WI-11
Borderland ... WQ-1
Borger, 13251 ... WC-11
BOSQUE CO., 18212 ... EG-5
Bosqueville ... WS-6
Bovina, 1868 ... WE-8
Bowie, 5218 ... EC-5
BOWIE CO., 92565 ... EC-11
Boyd, 1207 ... ED-5
Bracken, 80 ... EP-12
Brackettville, 1688 ... WQ-13
Brady, 5528 ... EI-2
Branch, 400 ... †B-14
Brazoria, 3019 ... EM-10
BRAZORIA CO., 313166 ... EM-10
BRAZOS CO., 194851 ... EI-8
Breckenridge, 5780 ... EE-3
Bremond, 929 ... EI-7
Brenham, 15716 ... EK-8
BREWSTER CO., 9232 ... WO-7
Briarcliff, 1438 ... EJ-5
Bridge City, 7840 ... EK-13
Bridgeport, 5976 ... ED-5
BRISCOE CO., 1637 ... WE-11
Bronte, 999 ... WK-13
BROOKS CO., 7223 ... ER-4
Brookshire, 4702 ... EL-9
Brookside Vil., 1523 ... *G-5
BROWN CO., 38106 ... EH-3
Brownfield, 9657 ... WH-9
Brownsboro, 1039 ... EF-9
Brownsville, 175023 ... ET-6
Brownwood, 19288 ... EG-3
Bruceville-Eddy, 1475 ... EH-6
Brushy Creek, 21764 ... WA-5
Bryan, 76201 ... EJ-8
Buda, 7295 ... EK-5
Buffalo, 1856 ... EH-8
Bullard, 2463 ... EF-10
Bulverde, 4630 ... EL-4
Bunker Hill Vil., 3633 ... *D-3
Burkburnett, 10811 ... EB-3
Burleson, 36690 ... EF-6
BURLESON CO., 17187 ... EJ-8
Burnet, 5987 ... EJ-4
BURNET CO., 42750 ... EI-4
Cactus, 3179 ... WB-10
Caddo Mills, 1338 ... ED-8
Caldwell, 4104 ... EJ-7
CALDWELL CO., 38066 ... EL-6
CALHOUN CO., 21381 ... EO-7
CALLAHAN CO., 13544 ... EF-2
Calvert, 1192 ... EI-7
Camelot, 4000 ... ER-12
Cameron, 5552 ... EI-7
CAMERON CO., 406220 ... ET-6
CAMP CO., 12401 ... EE-10
Campo Alto, 300 ... WS-10
Canadian, 2649 ... WB-13
Canton, 3581 ... EE-9
Canyon, 13303 ... WD-10
Carrizo Sprs., 5368 ... WS-14
Carrollton, 119097 ... EE-7
CARSON CO., 6182 ... WC-11
Carthage, 6779 ... EF-12
CASS CO., 30464 ... ED-11
Castle Hills, 4116 ... ER-10
CASTRO CO., 8062 ... WE-9
Castroville, 2680 ... EM-3
Cedar Hill, 45028 ... †J-8
Cedar Pk., 48937 ... EJ-5
Cedar Pt. ... *F-10
Celeste, 814 ... ED-8
Celina, 6028 ... ED-7
Center, 5193 ... EG-12
Centerville, 892 ... EH-9
Central Gdns., 4347 ... ER-13
Cesar Chavez, 1929 ... WR-11
CHAMBERS CO., 35096 ... EL-11
Chandler, 2734 ... EF-9
Channelview, 38289 ... *D-8
Channing, 363 ... WC-9
Charlotte, 1715 ... EN-3
CHEROKEE CO., 50845 ... EG-10
Chico, 1002 ... ED-5
Childress, 6105 ... WF-13
CHILDRESS CO., 7041 ... WE-13
China, 1160 ... EK-12
China Grv., 1179 ... ES-11
Cisco, 3899 ... EF-3
Clarendon, 2026 ... WE-12
Clarksville, 3285 ... EC-10
Claude, 1196 ... WD-11
CLAY CO., 10752 ... EC-4
Clear L. Shores, 1063 ... *G-9
Cleburne, 29337 ... EF-6
Cleveland, 7675 ... EJ-10
Cliffside ... WA-1
Clifton, 3442 ... EG-5
Clint, 926 ... WK-2
Cloverleaf, 22942 ... *D-7
Clute, 11211 ... EM-10
Clyde, 3713 ... EF-2
Coahoma, 817 ... WJ-11
COCHRAN CO., 3127 ... WG-8
Cockrell Hill, 4193 ... †H-9
COKE CO., 3320 ... WK-12
Coldspring, 853 ... EJ-10
Coleman, 4709 ... EG-2
COLEMAN CO., 8895 ... EH-2
College Sta., 93857 ... EJ-8
Colleyville, 22807 ... †F-6
COLLIN CO., 782341 ... ED-7
COLLINGSWORTH CO., 3057 ... WD-13
Collinsville, 1624 ... EC-7
Colorado City, 4146 ... WJ-12
COLORADO CO., 20874 ... EL-7
Columbus, 3655 ... EL-8
COMAL CO., 108472 ... EK-4
Comanche, 4335 ... EG-4
COMANCHE CO., 13974 ... EG-4
Combes, 2895 ... ET-5
Commerce, 8078 ... ED-8
CONCHO CO., 4087 ... WM-14
Concord Bridge, 1200 ... *C-2
Conroe, 56207 ... EJ-10
Converse, 18198 ... EL-4
COOKE CO., 38437 ... EC-6
Coolidge, 955 ... EG-7
Cooper, 1969 ... ED-9
Coppell, 38659 ... †E-8
Copper Canyon, 1334 ... †C-7
Copperas Cove, 32032 ... EI-5
Corinth, 19935 ... ED-6
Corpus Christi, 305215 ... EP-6
Corral City, 27 ... †C-5
Corrigan, 1595 ... EI-11
Corsicana, 23770 ... EG-8
CORYELL CO., 75388 ... EH-5
COTTLE CO., 1505 ... WF-13
Cotton Flat, 250 ... WH-6
Cotulla, 3603 ... EO-2
Crabb ... *G-1
Crandall, 2858 ... EE-8
Crane, 3353 ... WL-9
CRANE CO., 4375 ... WL-9
Crockett, 6950 ... EH-10
CROCKETT CO., 3719 ... WN-11
CROSBY CO., 6059 ... WH-11
Crosbyton, 1741 ... WG-11
Cross Mtn., 3124 ... EP-8
Cross Plains, 982 ... EG-2
Crowell, 948 ... WG-14
Crowley, 12838 ... EF-6
Crystal City, 7138 ... WR-14
Cuero, 6841 ... EM-6
CULBERSON CO., 2398 ... WL-5
Culleoka, 250 ... †B-14
Cumby, 777 ... ED-9
Cut and Shoot, 1070 ... EJ-10
Cypress ... *B-1
Cypress Meadow, 1500 ... *C-1
Daingerfield, 2560 ... ED-11
Daisetta, 966 ... EK-11
Dalhart, 7930 ... WB-9
DALLAM CO., 6703 ... WB-9
Dallas, 1197816 ... EE-7
DALLAS CO., 2368139 ... EF-7
Dalworthington Gdns., 2259 ... †H-6
Danbury, 1715 ... EM-10
Dawson, 807 ... EG-7
DAWSON CO., 13833 ... WI-10
Dayton, 7242 ... EK-11
De Kalb, 1699 ... EC-11
De Leon, 2246 ... EG-4
DE WITT CO., 20097 ... EM-6
DEAF SMITH CO., 19372 ... WD-9
Decatur, 6042 ... ED-5
DeCordova, 2683 ... EF-5
Deer Pk., 32010 ... EL-10
Del Rio, 35591 ... WQ-12
DELTA CO., 5231 ... ED-9
Denison, 22682 ... EC-7
Denton, 113383 ... ED-6
DENTON CO., 662614 ... ED-6
Denver City, 4479 ... WI-8
DeSoto, 49047 ... EE-7
Devine, 4350 ... EM-3
Diboll, 4776 ... EH-11
Dickens, 286 ... WG-12
DICKENS CO., 2444 ... WH-12
Dickinson, 18680 ... EL-11
Dilley, 3894 ... EN-3
DIMMIT CO., 9996 ... WS-14
Dimmitt, 4393 ... WE-9
Dish, 201 ... †B-4
DONLEY CO., 3677 ... WD-12
Donna, 15798 ... WS-11
Double Oak, 2867 ... †C-7
Dripping Sprs., 1788 ... EK-5
Dublin, 3654 ... EG-4
Dumas, 14691 ... WC-10
Duncanville, 38524 ... EE-7
DUVAL CO., 11782 ... EP-4
Eagle Lake, 3639 ... EL-8
Eagle Pass, 26248 ... WR-13
Early, 2762 ... EG-3
Earth, 1065 ... WF-9
E. Bernard, 2272 ... EL-9
E. Mountain, 797 ... EE-11
E. Tawakoni, 883 ... EE-8
Eastland, 3960 ... EF-3
EASTLAND CO., 18583 ... EF-3
ECTOR CO., 137130 ... WK-8
Eden, 2766 ... WM-14
Edgecliff Vil., 2776 ... †I-4
Edgewood, 1441 ... EE-9
Edinburg, 77100 ... ES-5
Edna, 5499 ... EM-7
EDWARDS CO., 2002 ... WP-13
El Campo, 11602 ... EM-8
El Cenizo, 3273 ... EQ-2
El Gato, 200 ... WT-11
El Lago, 2706 ... *G-8
El Paso, 649121 ... WK-1
EL PASO CO., 800647 ... WK-2
Eldorado, 1951 ... WM-12
Electra, 2791 ... EB-3
Elgin, 8135 ... EJ-6
Elkhart, 1371 ... EG-9
ELLIS CO., 149610 ... EF-7
Elmendorf, 1488 ... EM-4
Elsa, 5660 ... ET-5
Emory, 1239 ... EE-9
Ennis, 18513 ... EF-7
ERATH CO., 37890 ... EF-5
Escobares, 1188 ... ES-3
Euless, 51277 ... †F-7
Eustace, 991 ... EF-8
Everman, 6108 ... †I-4
Fair Oaks Ranch, 5986 ... EL-4
Fairfield, 2951 ... EG-8
Fairgreen, 2300 ... *C-5
Fairview, 7248 ... †B-12
Falfurrias, 4981 ... EQ-5
Fallbrook, 1500 ... *B-4
FALLS CO., 17866 ... EH-7
FANNIN CO., 33915 ... EC-8
Farmers Branch, 28616 ... †E-9
Farmersville, 3301 ... ED-8
Farwell, 1363 ... WF-8
FAYETTE CO., 24554 ... EL-7
Ferris, 2436 ... EF-7
Fifth Street, 2486 ... *G-3
FISHER CO., 3974 ... WI-13
Flatonia, 1383 ... EL-7
Florence, 1136 ... EI-5
Floresville, 6448 ... EM-5
Flower Mound, 64669 ... †D-7
FLOYD CO., 6446 ... WF-11
Floydada, 3038 ... WG-11
FOARD CO., 1336 ... WF-14
Forest Hill, 12355 ... †I-5
FT. BEND CO., 585375 ... EL-9
Ft. Davis, 1201 ... WN-6
Ft. Stockton, 8283 ... WM-8
Ft. Worth, 741206 ... EE-6
Four Cors., 12382 ... *F-1
Franklin, 1564 ... EI-8
FRANKLIN CO., 10605 ... ED-10
Frankston, 1229 ... EG-9
Fredericksburg, 10530 ... EK-3
Freeport, 12049 ... EM-10
Freer, 2818 ... EP-4
FREESTONE CO., 19816 ... EG-8
Fresno, 19069 ... *G-4
Friendswood, 35805 ... EL-10
FRIO CO., 17217 ... EN-2
Friona, 4123 ... WE-9
Frisco, 116989 ... ED-7
Fritch, 2117 ... WC-11
Fulshear, 1134 ... EL-9
Fulton, 1358 ... EP-7
Gail, 231 ... WI-11
GAINES CO., 17526 ... WI-9
Gainesville, 16002 ... EC-6
Galena Pk., 10887 ... *E-6
Galveston, 47743 ... EM-11
GALVESTON CO., 291309 ... EL-11
Ganado, 2003 ... EM-8
Garden City, 334 ... WK-11
Garden Ridge, 3259 ... EP-12
Garland, 226876 ... EE-7
Garrett, 806 ... EF-7
Garrison, 895 ... EG-11
GARZA CO., 6461 ... WH-11
Gatesville, 15751 ... EH-5
George West, 2445 ... EO-5
Georgetown, 47400 ... EJ-5
Gholson, 1061 ... EG-6
Giddings, 4881 ... EK-7
GILLESPIE CO., 24837 ... EJ-2
Gilmer, 4905 ... EE-10
Gladewater, 6441 ... EE-10
GLASSCOCK CO., 1226 ... WK-11
Glen Rose, 2444 ... EF-5
Glenn Hts., 11278 ... †J-10
Godley, 1009 ... EF-6
Goldthwaite, 1878 ... EH-4
Goliad, 1908 ... EN-6
GOLIAD CO., 7210 ... EO-6
Gonzales, 7237 ... EL-6
GONZALES CO., 19807 ... EM-6
Gorman, 1083 ... EF-3
Graham, 8903 ... ED-4
Granbury, 7978 ... EF-5
Grand Prairie, 175396 ... EE-7
Grand Saline, 3136 ... EE-9
Grandview, 1561 ... EF-6
Granger, 1419 ... EI-6
Granite Shoals, 4910 ... EI-4
Granjeno, 293 ... WT-9
Grapeland, 1489 ... EH-9
Grapevine, 46334 ... †E-6
GRAY CO., 22535 ... WD-12
GRAYSON CO., 120877 ... EC-7
Greatwood, 11538 ... *I-1
Greenville, 25557 ... ED-8
Greenwood Vil., 4000 ... *C-5
GREGG CO., 121730 ... EF-10
Gregory, 1907 ... EP-6
Grey Forest, 483 ... EP-8
GRIMES CO., 26604 ... EJ-8
Groesbeck, 4328 ... EH-7
Groves, 16144 ... EK-13
Groveton, 1057 ... EI-10
Gruver, 1194 ... WA-11
GUADALUPE CO., 131533 ... EL-5
Gun Barrel City, 5672 ... EF-8
Gunter, 1498 ... ED-7
Guthrie, 160 ... WG-13
Hackberry, 968 ... †B-9
Hale Ctr., 2252 ... WF-10
HALE CO., 36273 ... WG-10
HALL CO., 3353 ... WE-12
Hallettsville, 2550 ... EL-7
Hallsville, 3577 ... EE-11
Haltom City, 42409 ... †G-4
Hamilton, 3095 ... EG-4
HAMILTON CO., 8517 ... EH-4
Hamlin, 2124 ... WI-13
HANSFORD CO., 5613 ... WA-11
HARDEMAN CO., 4139 ... WF-14
Hardin, 819 ... EK-11
HARDIN CO., 54635 ... EJ-12
Harker Hts., 26700 ... EI-5
Harlingen, 64849 ... ET-6
HARRIS CO., 4092459 ... EK-9
HARRISON CO., 65631 ... EF-12
Hart, 1114 ... WF-10
HARTLEY CO., 6062 ... WC-9
Haskell, 3322 ... WH-14
HASKELL CO., 5899 ... WH-14
Hawkins, 1278 ... EE-10
HAYS CO., 157107 ... EK-4
Hearne, 4459 ... EI-7
Hebbronville, 4558 ... EQ-4
Hebron, 415 ... †D-9
Hedwig Vil., 2557 ... *D-3
Helotes, 7341 ... EL-3
Hemphill, 1198 ... EH-13
HEMPHILL CO., 3807 ... WC-13
Hempstead, 5770 ... EK-8
Henderson, 13712 ... EF-11
HENDERSON CO., 78532 ... EF-9
Henrietta, 3141 ... EC-4
Hereford, 15370 ... WE-9
Hewitt, 13549 ... EH-6
Hickory Creek, 3247 ... †B-7
Hico, 1379 ... EG-5
Hidalgo, 11198 ... ET-4
HIDALGO CO., 774769 ... ES-4
Hideaway, 3083 ... EF-9
Highland Pk., 8564 ... †F-10
Highland Vil., 15056 ... †C-7
HILL CO., 35089 ... EG-7
Hill Country Vil., 985 ... EQ-10
Hillcrest, 730 ... *I-6
Hillsboro, 8456 ... EG-6
Hilshire Vil., 746 ... *D-3
Hitchcock, 6961 ... EL-11
HOCKLEY CO., 22935 ... WH-9
Holland, 1121 ... EI-6
Holliday, 1758 ... EC-3
Hollywood Pk., 3062 ... EQ-10
Hondo, 8803 ... EM-3
Honey Grv., 1668 ... EC-8
HOOD CO., 51182 ... EF-5
Hooks, 2769 ... EC-11
HOPKINS CO., 35161 ... ED-9
Horizon City, 16735 ... WK-2
Houmont Pk., 2400 ... *C-7
Houston, 2099451 ... EL-10
HOUSTON CO., 23732 ... EH-9
HOWARD CO., 35012 ... WJ-11
Howe, 2600 ... EC-7
Hubbard, 1423 ... EG-7
Hudson, 4731 ... EH-11
HUDSPETH CO., 3476 ... WL-3
Hughes Sprs., 1760 ... ED-11
Humble, 15133 ... EK-10
HUNT CO., 86129 ... ED-8
Hunters Creek Vil., 4367 ... *D-3
Huntington, 2118 ... EH-11
Huntsville, 38548 ... EI-9
Hurst, 37337 ... †G-6
Hutchins, 5338 ... †I-11
HUTCHINSON CO., 22150 ... WB-11
Hutto, 14698 ... EJ-6
Idalou, 2250 ... WG-10
Impact, 35 ... EA-6
Ingleside, 9387 ... EP-6
Ingram, 1804 ... EK-2
Iowa Pk., 6355 ... EC-3
Iraan, 1229 ... WM-10
IRION CO., 1599 ... WL-12
Irving, 216290 ... EE-7
Italy, 1863 ... EF-7
Itasca, 1644 ... EF-6
Jacinto City, 10553 ... *D-6
JACK CO., 9044 ... ED-4
Jacksboro, 4511 ... ED-4
JACKSON CO., 14075 ... EN-8
Jacksonville, 14544 ... EG-10
Jamaica Bch., 983 ... EM-11
Jarrell, 984 ... EI-5
Jasper, 7590 ... EI-12
JASPER CO., 35710 ... EJ-12
Jayton, 534 ... WH-12
JEFF DAVIS CO., 2342 ... WM-6
Jefferson, 2106 ... EE-11
JEFFERSON CO., 252273 ... EL-12
Jersey Vil., 7620 ... EK-9
Jewett, 1167 ... EH-8
JIM HOGG CO., 5300 ... ER-3
JIM WELLS CO., 40838 ... EP-4
Joaquin, 824 ... EG-12
Johnson City, 1656 ... EK-4
JOHNSON CO., 150934 ... EF-6
Jollyville, 16151 ... WB-5
JONES CO., 20202 ... WI-14
Jones Creek, 2020 ... EM-10
Jonestown, 1834 ... EJ-5
Josephine, 812 ... ED-8
Joshua, 5910 ... EF-6
Jourdanton, 3871 ... EN-4
Junction, 2574 ... WN-14
Justin, 3246 ... ED-6
Karnes City, 3042 ... EN-5
KARNES CO., 14824 ... EN-5
Katy, 14102 ... EL-9
Kaufman, 6703 ... EE-8
KAUFMAN CO., 103350 ... EF-8
Keene, 6106 ... EF-6
Keller, 39627 ... †E-5
Kemah, 1773 ... *G-9
Kemp, 1154 ... EF-8
Kempner, 1089 ... EI-5
KENDALL CO., 33410 ... EK-3
Kenedy, 3296 ... EN-5
KENEDY CO., 416 ... ER-6
Kennedale, 6763 ... †I-5
KENT CO., 808 ... WI-12
Kerens, 1573 ... EF-8
Kermit, 5708 ... WK-8
KERR CO., 49625 ... EK-2
Kerrville, 22347 ... EK-3
Kilgore, 12975 ... EF-10
Killeen, 127921 ... EI-5
KIMBLE CO., 4607 ... WN-14
KING CO., 286 ... WG-13
Kingsville, 26213 ... EQ-5
KINNEY CO., 3598 ... WQ-13
Kirby, 8000 ... EL-4
Kirbyville, 2142 ... EI-13
KLEBERG CO., 32061 ... EQ-5
Knox City, 1130 ... WH-14
KNOX CO., 3719 ... WG-14
Kohrville, 400 ... *A-2
Kountze, 2123 ... EJ-12
Krum, 4157 ... ED-6
Kyle, 28016 ... EK-5
La Feria, 7302 ... ET-5
La Grange, 4641 ... EK-7
La Grulla, 1622 ... ET-4
La Homa, 11985 ... WR-8
La Joya, 3985 ... ET-4
La Marque, 14509 ... EL-11
La Porte, 33800 ... EL-11
LA SALLE CO., 6886 ... EO-2
La Vernia, 1034 ... EM-5
La Villa, 1957 ... ES-5
LaCoste, 1119 ... EM-3
Lacy-Lakeview, 6489 ... WR-7
Lago Vista, 6041 ... EJ-5
Laguna Vista, 3117 ... ET-6
L. Dallas, 7105 ... †B-8
L. Jackson, 26849 ... EM-10
L. Tanglewood, 796 ... WD-10
L. Worth, 4584 ... †G-3
Lakeport, 974 ... EF-11
Lakeside, 1307 ... †G-2
Lakeside City, 997 ... EC-4
Lakeway, 11391 ... EJ-5
Lakewood Vil., 545 ... †B-8
LAMAR CO., 49793 ... EC-9
LAMB CO., 13977 ... WG-9
Lamesa, 9422 ... WI-10
Lampasas, 6681 ... EI-4
LAMPASAS CO., 19677 ... EI-4
Lancaster, 36361 ... †J-10
Lantana, 6874 ... †C-6
Laredo, 236091 ... EQ-2
LAVACA CO., 19263 ... EM-7
League City, 83560 ... EL-10
Leakey, 425 ... WP-14
Leander, 26521 ... EJ-5
LEE CO., 16612 ... EJ-6
LEON CO., 16801 ... EI-8
Leon Valley, 10151 ... ER-8
Leonard, 1990 ... ED-8
Levelland, 13542 ... WG-9
Lewisville, 95290 ... †C-8
Lexington, 1177 ... EJ-7
Liberty, 8397 ... EK-11
LIBERTY CO., 75643 ... EJ-11
Liberty Grv., 50 ... †E-14
Liberty Hill, 967 ... EJ-5
LIMESTONE CO., 23384 ... EH-7
Lincoln Pk., 308 ... †A-8
Lindale, 4818 ... EF-9
Linden, 1988 ... ED-11
Lindsay, 1018 ... EC-6
Lipscomb, 37 ... WB-13
LIPSCOMB CO., 3302 ... WB-13
Little River-Academy, 1961 ... EI-6
Littlefield, 6372 ... WG-9
Live Oak, 13131 ... EL-4
LIVE OAK CO., 11531 ... EO-4
Livingston, 5335 ... EI-11
Llano, 3232 ... EJ-3
LLANO CO., 19301 ... EI-3
Lockhart, 12698 ... EL-5
Lockney, 1842 ... WF-11
Lometa, 856 ... EI-4
Lone Star, 1581 ... EE-11
Longview, 80455 ... EE-11
Lorena, 1691 ... EH-6
Lorenzo, 1147 ... WG-11
Los Fresnos, 5542 ... ET-6
Los Indios, 1083 ... ET-5
Lott, 759 ... EI-7
LOVING CO., 82 ... WK-7
Lowry Crossing, 1711 ... †A-13
Lubbock, 229573 ... WH-10
LUBBOCK CO., 278831 ... WG-10
Lucas, 5166 ... †C-13
Lufkin, 35067 ... EH-11
Luling, 5411 ... EL-5
Lumberton, 11943 ... EJ-12
Lyford, 2611 ... ES-5
LYNN CO., 5915 ... WH-10
Lytle, 2492 ... EM-3
Mabank, 3035 ... EF-8
MADISON CO., 13664 ... EI-8
Madisonville, 4396 ... EI-9
Magnolia, 1393 ... EK-9
Magnolia Gdns. ... *C-8
Malakoff, 2324 ... EF-8
Manor, 5037 ... EJ-6
Mansfield, 56368 ... EF-6
Manvel, 5179 ... EL-10
Marble Falls, 6077 ... EJ-4
Marfa, 1981 ... WN-6
Marion, 1066 ... EL-5
MARION CO., 10546 ... EE-11
Marlin, 5967 ... EH-7
Marshall, 23523 ... EE-11
Marshall Creek, 431 ... †D-5
Mart, 2209 ... EH-7
MARTIN CO., 4799 ... WJ-10
Martindale, 1116 ... EL-5
Martinez ... ES-12
Mason, 2114 ... EJ-2
MASON CO., 4012 ... EJ-2
Matador, 607 ... WG-12
MATAGORDA CO., 36702 ... EN-9
Mathis, 4942 ... EO-5
Maud, 1056 ... ED-11
MAVERICK CO., 54258 ... WR-13
Maypearl, 934 ... EF-6
McAllen, 129877 ... ET-4
McCamey, 1887 ... WM-9
MCCULLOCH CO., 8283 ... EH-2
McGregor, 4987 ... EH-6
McKinney, 131117 ... ED-7
McLean, 778 ... WD-12
MCLENNAN CO., 234906 ... EH-6
MCMULLEN CO., 707 ... EO-4
McNair, 1400 ... *D-9
McNeil, 30 ... WB-6
Meadows Pl., 4660 ... *F-2
MEDINA CO., 46006 ... EM-2
Melissa, 4695 ... ED-7
Memphis, 2290 ... WE-13
Menard, 1471 ... WM-14
MENARD CO., 2242 ... WN-14
Mentone, 19 ... WK-7
Mercedes, 15570 ... ET-5
Meridian, 1493 ... EG-5
Merkel, 2590 ... WJ-13
Mertzon, 781 ... WM-12
Mesquite, 139824 ... EE-7
Mexia, 7459 ... EG-8
Miami, 597 ... WC-12
Midland, 111147 ... WK-10
MIDLAND CO., 136872 ... WK-10
Midlothian, 18037 ... EF-7
Mila Doce, 6222 ... WS-12
MILAM CO., 24757 ... EI-7
Miles, 829 ... WL-13
MILLS CO., 4936 ... EH-4
Mineola, 4515 ... EE-9
Mineral Wells, 16788 ... EE-4
Mission, 77058 ... ET-4
Mission Bend, 36501 ... *E-1
Missouri City, 67358 ... EL-10
MITCHELL CO., 9403 ... WK-12
Monahans, 6953 ... WL-8
Mont Belvieu, 3835 ... EK-11
Montague, 304 ... EC-5
MONTAGUE CO., 19719 ... EC-5
MONTGOMERY CO., 455746 ... EJ-9
Moody, 1371 ... EH-6
MOORE CO., 21904 ... WC-10
Morgan's Pt., 339 ... *F-9
Morgan's Pt. Resort, 4170 ... EI-6
MORRIS CO., 12934 ... ED-11
Morton, 2006 ... WG-9
MOTLEY CO., 1210 ... WF-12
Moulton, 886 ... EL-6
Mt. Pleasant, 15564 ... ED-10
Mt. Vernon, 2662 ... ED-10
Muenster, 1544 ... EC-6
Muleshoe, 5158 ... WF-9
Munday, 1300 ... WH-14
Muniz, 1370 ... WR-11
Murphy, 17708 ... †D-13
Mustang Ridge, 861 ... EK-5
Nacogdoches, 32996 ... EG-11
NACOGDOCHES CO., 64524 ... EH-11
Naples, 1378 ... ED-11
Nash, 2960 ... EC-12
Nassau Bay, 4002 ... *G-8
Natalia, 1431 ... EM-3
NAVARRO CO., 47735 ... EG-7
Navasota, 7049 ... EJ-8
Nederland, 17547 ... EK-12
Needville, 2823 ... EL-9
Nevada, 822 ... ED-8
New Boston, 4550 ... EC-11
New Braunfels, 57740 ... EL-5
New Deal, 794 ... WG-10
New Fairview, 1258 ... ED-6
New Hope, 614 ... †A-13
New London, 998 ... EF-10
New Summerfield, 1111 ... EG-10
New Territory, 15186 ... *G-1
New Waverly, 1032 ... EJ-10
Newark, 1005 ... EE-6
Newton, 2478 ... EI-13
NEWTON CO., 14445 ... EI-13
Nixon, 2385 ... EM-5
Nocona, 3033 ... EC-5
NOLAN CO., 15216 ... WJ-13
Nolanville, 4259 ... EI-5
Noonday, 777 ... EF-10
N. Alamo, 3235 ... WS-10
N. Houston, 2000 ... *B-3
N. Richland Hills, 63343 ... EE-6
N. San Antonio Hills, 100 ... ER-7
Northlake, 1724 ... †C-5
Northline Ter., 2700 ... *C-4
NUECES CO., 340223 ... EP-5
Nurillo, 7344 ... WR-10
Oak L. Estates, 2000 ... *F-1
Oak Pt., 2786 ... †A-8
Oak Ridge N., 3049 ... EK-10
OCHILTREE CO., 10223 ... WB-12
Odem, 2389 ... EP-6
Odessa, 99940 ... WK-9
O'Donnell, 831 ... WI-10
Old River-Winfree, 1245 ... EK-11
OLDHAM CO., 2052 ... WC-9
Olivarez, 3827 ... WS-12
Olmos Pk., 2237 ... ER-10
Olney, 3285 ... ED-3
Olton, 2215 ... WF-10
Omaha, 1021 ... ED-11
Onalaska, 1764 ... EI-10
Orange, 18595 ... EK-13
ORANGE CO., 81837 ... EK-12
Orange Grv., 1318 ... EP-5
Ore City, 1144 ... EE-11
Overton, 2554 ... EF-10
Ovilla, 3492 ... †J-9
Oyster Creek, 1111 ... EM-10
Ozona, 3225 ... WN-11
Paducah, 1186 ... WG-13
Paint Rock, 273 ... WL-14
Palacios, 4718 ... EN-8
Palestine, 18712 ... EG-9
Palmer, 2000 ... EF-7
Palmhurst, 2607 ... WS-9
Palmview, 5460 ... WS-10
Palo Pinto, 333 ... EE-4
PALO PINTO CO., 28111 ... EE-4
Pampa, 17994 ... WC-12
Panhandle, 2452 ... WD-11
PANOLA CO., 23796 ... EF-12
Pantego, 2394 ... †H-6
Paris, 25171 ... EC-9
Parker, 3811 ... †C-13
PARKER CO., 116927 ... EE-5
PARMER CO., 10269 ... WE-8
Pasadena, 149043 ... EL-10
Payne Sprs., 767 ... EF-8
Pearland, 91252 ... EL-10
Pearsall, 9146 ... EN-3
Pecan Grv., 15963 ... *F-1
Pecos, 8780 ... WL-7
PECOS CO., 15507 ... WN-8
Penitas, 4403 ... ET-4
Perryton, 8802 ... WA-12
Petersburg, 1202 ... WG-11
Pflugerville, 46936 ... EJ-5
Pharr, 70400 ... ET-5
Pilot Pt., 3856 ... ED-7
Pine Island, 988 ... EK-9
Pinehurst, 2097 ... EK-13
Pineland, 850 ... EH-12
Piney Pt. Vil., 3125 ... *D-3
Pittsburg, 4497 ... ED-10
Plains, 1481 ... WH-8
Plainview, 22194 ... WF-10
Plano, 259841 ... EE-7
Pleak, 1044 ... EL-9
Pleasanton, 8934 ... EN-4
Point, 820 ... EE-9
POLK CO., 45413 ... EI-11
Ponder, 1395 ... ED-6
Port Aransas, 3480 ... EP-7
Port Arthur, 53818 ... EK-13
Port Isabel, 5006 ... ET-7
Port Lavaca, 12248 ... EN-8
Port Neches, 13040 ... EK-13
Portland, 15099 ... EP-6
Post, 5376 ... WH-11
Poteet, 3260 ... EM-4
Poth, 1908 ... EM-5
POTTER CO., 121073 ... WD-10
Pottsboro, 2160 ... EC-7
Prairie View, 5576 ... EK-9
Premont, 2653 ... EQ-5
Presidio, 4426 ... WP-5
PRESIDIO CO., 7818 ... WO-5
Princeton, 6807 ... ED-7
Progreso, 5507 ... ET-5
Prosper, 9423 ... ED-7
Providence Vil., 4786 ... †A-8
Quanah, 2641 ... WF-14
Queen City, 1476 ... ED-12
Quinlan, 1394 ... EE-8
Quitman, 1809 ... EE-9
RAINS CO., 10914 ... EE-9
Ralls, 1944 ... WG-11
Rancho Viejo, 2437 ... ET-6
RANDALL CO., 120725 ... WE-10
Ranger, 2468 ... EF-3
Rankin, 778 ... WM-10
Ransom Canyon, 1096 ... WH-10
Raymondville, 11284 ... ES-5
REAGAN CO., 3367 ... WL-11
REAL CO., 3309 ... WP-14
Red Lick, 1008 ... EC-12
Red Oak, 10769 ... EF-7
RED RIVER CO., 12860 ... EC-10
Redwater, 1057 ... ED-12
REEVES CO., 13783 ... WL-6
Refugio, 2890 ... EO-6
REFUGIO CO., 7383 ... EO-7
Rendon, 12552 ... †J-5
Reno, 3166 ... EC-9
Reno, 2494 ... EE-5
Rhome, 1522 ... ED-6
Rice, 923 ... EF-7
Richardson, 99223 ... †E-11
Richland Hills, 7801 ... †G-5
Richmond, 11679 ... EL-9
Richwood, 3510 ... EM-10
Ridgeheights, 200 ... WH-10
Riesel, 1007 ... EH-7
Rio Bravo, 4794 ... EQ-2
Rio Grande City, 13834 ... ES-3
Rio Hondo, 2356 ... ET-6
Rio Vista, 873 ... EF-6
Rising Star, 835 ... EG-3
River Oaks, 7427 ... †G-3
Roanoke, 5962 ... EE-6
Robert Lee, 1049 ... WK-13
ROBERTS CO., 929 ... WC-12
ROBERTSON CO., 16622 ... EI-7
Robinson, 10509 ... EH-6
Robstown, 11487 ... EP-6
Roby, 643 ... WI-13
Rockdale, 5595 ... EJ-7
Rockport, 8766 ... EP-7
Rocksprings, 1182 ... WO-13
Rockwall, 37490 ... EE-7
ROCKWALL CO., 78337 ... EE-8
Rogers, 1218 ... EI-6
Rolling Hills, 500 ... WA-2
Rollingwood, 1412 ... WE-5
Roma, 9765 ... ES-3
Roscoe, 1322 ... WJ-13
Rose City, 502 ... EQ-14
Rosebud, 1412 ... EI-7
Rosenberg, 30618 ... EL-9
Rotan, 1508 ... WI-13
Round Rock, 99887 ... EJ-5
Rowlett, 56199 ... †E-13
Royse City, 9349 ... EE-8
Runaway Bay, 1286 ... ED-5
Runge, 1031 ... EN-5
RUNNELS CO., 10501 ... WK-13
Rushwood, 3600 ... *B-4
Rusk, 5551 ... EG-10
RUSK CO., 53330 ... EG-11
Sabinal, 1695 ... EM-2
SABINE CO., 10834 ... EG-12
Sachse, 20329 ... †D-13
St. Francis Vil., 500 ... †J-2
St. Hedwig, 2094 ... EM-4
St. Jo, 1043 ... EC-5
St. Paul, 1066 ... †C-13
Salado, 2126 ... EI-6
San Angelo, 93200 ... WL-13
San Antonio, 1327407 ... EM-4
San Augustine, 2108 ... EH-12
SAN AUGUSTINE CO., 8865 ... EH-12
San Benito, 24250 ... ET-6
San Diego, 4488 ... EP-4
SAN JACINTO CO., 26384 ... EJ-10
San Juan, 33856 ... WS-10
San Leon, 4970 ... *H-10
San Marcos, 44894 ... EL-5
SAN PATRICIO CO., 64804 ... EP-6
San Saba, 3099 ... EI-3
SAN SABA CO., 6131 ... EI-3
Sanderson, 837 ... WO-9
Sanger, 6916 ... ED-6
Sansom Pk., 4686 ... †G-3
Santa Anna, 1099 ... EG-2
Santa Fe, 12222 ... EL-10
Santa Rosa, 2873 ... ET-5
Sarita, 238 ... EQ-5
Savoy, 831 ... EC-8
Sayers, 30 ... ET-12
Schertz, 31465 ... EL-4
SCHLEICHER CO., 3461 ... WM-13
Schulenburg, 2852 ... EL-7
Scissors, 3186 ... WT-11
SCURRY CO., 16921 ... WI-12
Seabrook, 11952 ... EL-11
Seadrift, 1364 ... EO-7
Seagoville, 14835 ... EE-7
Seagraves, 2417 ... WI-9
Sealy, 6019 ... EL-8
Seguin, 25175 ... EL-5
Selma, 5540 ... EQ-12
Seminole, 6430 ... WI-9
Seven Pts., 1455 ... EF-8
Seymour, 2740 ... EC-2
SHACKELFORD CO., 3378 ... EE-2
Shady Shores, 2612 ... †B-7
Shallowater, 2484 ... WG-10
Shamrock, 1910 ... WD-13
Shavano Pk., 3035 ... EQ-9
SHELBY CO., 25448 ... EG-12
Shenandoah, 2134 ... EK-10
Shepherd, 2319 ... EJ-11
Sherman, 38521 ... EC-7
SHERMAN CO., 3034 ... WB-10
Shiner, 2069 ... EL-6
Shoreacres, 1493 ... *F-9
Sienna Plantation, 13721 ... *H-3
Sierra Blanca, 553 ... WL-4
Silsbee, 6611 ... EJ-12
Silverton, 731 ... WF-11
Sinton, 5665 ... EP-6
Slaton, 6121 ... WH-11
SMITH CO., 209714 ... EF-9
Smithville, 3817 ... EK-6
Snyder, 11202 ... WI-12
Socorro, 32013 ... WK-2
Somerset, 1631 ... EM-4
SOMERVELL CO., 8490 ... EF-5
Somerville, 1376 ... EJ-8
Sonora, 3027 ... WN-12
Sour Lake, 1813 ... EK-12
S. Alamo, 3361 ... WT-11
S. Houston, 16983 ... *F-6
S. Padre Island, 2816 ... ET-7
Southlake, 26575 ... †E-6
Southmayd, 992 ... EC-7
Southside Pl., 1715 ... *E-4
Southton, 100 ... ET-11
Spearman, 3368 ... WB-11
Splendora, 1615 ... EK-10
Spring Valley, 3611 ... *D-3
Springtown, 2658 ... EE-5
Spur, 1318 ... WH-12
Stafford, 17693 ... *F-3
Stamford, 3124 ... WI-14
Stanton, 2492 ... WK-10
STARR CO., 60968 ... ES-3
STEPHENS CO., 9630 ... EE-3
Stephenville, 17123 ... EF-4
Sterling City, 888 ... WK-12
STERLING CO., 1143 ... WL-11
Stinnett, 1881 ... WC-11
Stockdale, 1442 ... EM-5
STONEWALL CO., 1490 ... WH-13
Stony, 50 ... †J-1
Stratford, 2017 ... WA-10
Sudan, 958 ... WF-9
Sugar Land, 78817 ... EL-9
Sullivan City, 4002 ... ET-4
Sulphur Sprs., 15449 ... ED-9
Sundown, 1397 ... WH-9
Sunnyvale, 5130 ... †G-13
Sunray, 1926 ... WB-10
Sunset Valley, 749 ... WF-4
SUTTON CO., 4128 ... WN-13
Sweeny, 3684 ... EM-9
Sweetwater, 10906 ... WJ-13
SWISHER CO., 7854 ... WE-10
Taft, 3048 ... EP-6
Tahoka, 2673 ... WH-10
Tara, 1100 ... *G-1
TARRANT CO., 1809034 ... EE-6
Tatum, 1385 ... EF-11
Taylor, 15191 ... EJ-6
TAYLOR CO., 131506 ... WK-14
Taylor Lake Vil., 3544 ... *G-8
Teague, 3560 ... EH-8
Temple, 66102 ... EI-6
Tenaha, 1160 ... EG-12
Terrell, 15816 ... EE-8
TERRELL CO., 984 ... WO-9
Terrell Hills, 4878 ... ER-10
TERRY CO., 12651 ... WH-9
Texarkana, 36411 ... EC-12
Texas City, 45099 ... EL-11
The Colony, 36328 ... ED-7
The Hills, 2472 ... EK-5
Thorndale, 1336 ... EJ-5
Thrall, 839 ... EJ-6
Three Rivers, 1848 ... EO-4
Throckmorton, 828 ... ED-2
THROCKMORTON CO., 1641 ... ED-2
Tilden, 261 ... EO-4
Timpson, 1155 ... EG-11
Tioga, 803 ... ED-7
TITUS CO., 32334 ... ED-10
Tom Bean, 1045 ... EC-7
TOM GREEN CO., 110224 ... WM-13
Tomball, 10753 ... EK-9
Tool, 2240 ... EF-8
Town West ... *F-2
TRAVIS CO., 1024266 ... EJ-5
Trinidad, 886 ... EF-8
Trinity, 2697 ... EI-10
TRINITY CO., 14585 ... EI-10
Trophy Club, 8024 ... †D-5
Troup, 1869 ... EF-10
Troy, 1645 ... EI-6
Tulia, 4967 ... WE-10
Tye, 1242 ... WJ-14
Tyler, 96900 ... EF-10
TYLER CO., 21766 ... EI-11
Uhland, 1014 ... EK-5
Universal City, 18530 ... EQ-12
University Pk., 23068 ... †F-10
UPSHUR CO., 39309 ... EE-10
UPTON CO., 3355 ... WL-10
Uvalde, 15751 ... WQ-14
UVALDE CO., 26405 ... WQ-14
VAL VERDE CO., 48879 ... WO-11
Valley Mills, 1203 ... EH-6
Valley View, 757 ... ED-6
Van, 2632 ... EF-9
Van Alstyne, 3046 ... ED-7
Van Horn, 2063 ... WM-4
VAN ZANDT CO., 52579 ... EE-9
Vega, 884 ... WD-9
Venus, 2960 ... EF-6
Vernon, 11002 ... EB-2
Victoria, 62592 ... EN-7
VICTORIA CO., 86793 ... EN-7
Vidor, 10579 ... EK-12
Village of Tiki Island, 968 ... *B-8
Vinton, 1971 ... WK-1
Von Ormy, 1085 ... EM-4
Waco, 124805 ... EH-6
Waelder, 1065 ... EL-6
Wake Vil., 5492 ... EC-12
WALKER CO., 67861 ... EI-9
Waller, 2326 ... EK-9
WALLER CO., 43205 ... EK-9
Wallis, 1252 ... EL-9
Walnut Sprs., 827 ... EG-5
WARD CO., 10658 ... WL-7
WASHINGTON CO., 33718 ... EK-7
Waskom, 2160 ... EE-12
Watauga, 23497 ... †F-5
Waxahachie, 29621 ... EF-7
Weatherford, 25250 ... EE-5
WEBB CO., 250304 ... WT-14
Webster, 10400 ... *G-8
Weimar, 2151 ... EL-7
Wellington, 2189 ... WE-13
Wells, 790 ... EH-10
Wells Branch, 12120 ... WB-6
Weslaco, 35570 ... ET-5
West, 2807 ... EG-6
W. Columbia, 3905 ... EM-9
W. Lake Hills, 3063 ... WE-4
W. Orange, 3443 ... EK-13
W. Sharyland, 2309 ... WR-9
W. Tawakoni, 1576 ... EE-8
W. University Place, 14787 ... *E-4
Westfield, 800 ... *A-4
Westlake, 992 ... †D-6
Weston Lakes, 2482 ... EL-9
Westover Hills, 682 ... †H-3
Westworth Vil., 2472 ... †H-3
Wharton, 8832 ... EM-8
WHARTON CO., 41280 ... EM-8
Wheeler, 1592 ... WC-13
WHEELER CO., 5410 ... WD-13
White Deer, 1000 ... WC-11
White Oak, 6469 ... EE-10
White Settlement, 16116 ... †G-2
Whitehouse, 7660 ... EF-10
Whitesboro, 3793 ... EC-7
Whitewright, 1604 ... EC-8
Whitney, 2087 ... EG-6
WICHITA CO., 131500 ... EB-3
Wichita Falls, 104553 ... EC-4
WILBARGER CO., 13535 ... EC-2
WILLACY CO., 22134 ... ES-6
WILLIAMSON CO., 422679 ... EJ-6
Willis, 5662 ... EJ-10
Wills Pt., 3524 ... EE-8
Wilmer, 3682 ... †J-12
WILSON CO., 42918 ... EN-4
Winchester Country, 2000 ... *B-2
Windcrest, 5364 ... ER-11
Windemere, 1037 ... WB-7
Wink, 940 ... WK-8
WINKLER CO., 7110 ... WK-8
Winnsboro, 3434 ... EE-10
Winters, 2562 ... WK-14
WISE CO., 59127 ... ED-5
Wolfe City, 1412 ... ED-8
Wolfforth, 3670 ... WH-10
WOOD CO., 41964 ... EE-9
Woodcreek, 1457 ... EK-5
Woodlake, 800 ... ER-11
Woodsboro, 1512 ... EO-6
Woodville, 2586 ... EI-12
Woodway, 8452 ... EH-6
Wortham, 1073 ... EG-8
Wylie, 41427 ... EE-7
Yoakum, 5815 ... EM-6
YOAKUM CO., 7879 ... WH-8
Yorktown, 2092 ... EM-6
YOUNG CO., 18550 ... ED-3
Zapata, 5089 ... ER-2
ZAPATA CO., 14018 ... ER-2
ZAVALA CO., 11677 ... EM-2

Utah

Map pp. 102 – 103

American Fork, 26263 ... E-9
Annabella, 795 ... J-8
Apple Valley, 701 ... N-6
Aurora, 1016 ... I-8
Ballard, 801 ... E-12
Bear River City, 853 ... B-8
Beaver, 3112 ... K-7
BEAVER CO., 6629 ... J-6
Blanding, 3375 ... L-13
Bluffdale, 7598 ... E-8
Bountiful, 42552 ... D-8
BOX ELDER CO., 49975 ... B-5
Brigham City, 17899 ... B-8
CACHE CO., 112656 ... B-9
CARBON CO., 21403 ... G-11
Carbonville, 1567 ... G-10
Castle Dale, 1630 ... H-10
Cedar City, 28857 ... L-6
Centerfield, 1367 ... H-8
Centerville, 15335 ... D-8
Central, 613 ... M-5
Clarkston, 666 ... A-8
Clearfield, 30112 ... C-8
Clinton, 20426 ... C-8
Coalville, 1363 ... D-9
Copperton, 826 ... E-8
Corinne, 685 ... B-8
Cottonwood Hts., 33433 ... I-19
DAGGETT CO., 1059 ... D-12
Daniel, 938 ... E-9
DAVIS CO., 306479 ... D-7
Delta, 3436 ... H-7
Draper, 42274 ... E-8
Duchesne, 1690 ... F-11
DUCHESNE CO., 18607 ... E-11
Dugway, 795 ... F-7
Eagle Mtn., 21415 ... E-8
E. Carbon City, 1301 ... G-11
Eden, 600 ... C-9
Elk Ridge, 2436 ... F-9
Elsinore, 847 ... J-8
Elwood, 1034 ... B-8
EMERY CO., 10976 ... H-11
Enoch, 5803 ... L-6
Enterprise, 1711 ... L-5
Ephraim, 6135 ... H-9
Erda, 4642 ... E-8
Escalante, 797 ... L-9
Eureka, 669 ... F-8
Fairview, 1247 ... G-9
Farmington, 18275 ... D-8
Farr West, 5928 ... A-2
Ferron, 1626 ... I-10
Fillmore, 2435 ... I-7
Ft. Duchesne, 714 ... E-12
Fountain Green, 1071 ... G-9
Francis, 1077 ... E-10
Fruit Hts., 4987 ... F-3
GARFIELD CO., 5172 ... L-10
Garland, 2400 ... B-8
Genola, 1370 ... F-8
Goshen, 921 ... F-8
GRAND CO., 9225 ... I-13
Granite, 1932 ... J-20
Grantsville, 8893 ... E-7
Green River, 952 ... I-12
Gunnison, 3285 ... H-8
Harrisville, 5567 ... A-2
Heber City, 11362 ... E-9
Helper, 2201 ... G-10
Henefer, 766 ... D-9
Herriman, 21785 ... K-17
Hideout, 656 ... E-9
Hildale, 2726 ... N-6
Hinckley, 696 ... H-7
Holladay, 26472 ... E-8
Honeyville, 1441 ... B-8
Hooper, 7218 ... C-8
Huntington, 2129 ... H-10
Huntsville, 608 ... C-9
Hurricane, 13748 ... N-5
Hyde Pk., 3833 ... L-20
Hyrum, 7609 ... B-8
IRON CO., 46163 ... L-5
Ivins, 6753 ... M-5
JUAB CO., 10246 ... G-6
Junction, 191 ... K-8
Kamas, 1811 ... E-10
Kanab, 4312 ... N-7
KANE CO., 7125 ... M-9
Kaysville, 27300 ... D-8
Kearns, 35731 ... H-17
La Verkin, 4060 ... M-5
Layton, 67311 ... C-8
Leeds, 820 ... M-5
Lehi, 47407 ... E-8
Levan, 841 ... G-8
Lewiston, 1766 ... A-8
Lindon, 10070 ... F-1
Loa, 572 ... J-9
Logan, 48174 ... B-8
Maeser, 3601 ... E-13
Magna, 26505 ... G-16
Manila, 310 ... D-13
Manti, 3276 ... H-9
Mantua, 687 ... B-8
Mapleton, 7979 ... F-9
Marriott-Slaterville, 1701 ... B-2
Mendon, 1282 ... B-8
Midvale, 27964 ... I-19
Midway, 3845 ... E-9
Milford, 1409 ... J-6
MILLARD CO., 12503 ... H-6
Millcreek, 62139 ... H-19
Minersville, 907 ... K-6
Moab, 5046 ... J-13
Mona, 1547 ... G-8
Monroe, 2256 ... J-8
Monticello, 1972 ... L-14
Morgan, 3687 ... D-9
MORGAN CO., 9469 ... C-9
Moroni, 1423 ... G-9
Mt. Pleasant, 3260 ... G-9
Murray, 46746 ... H-19
Naples, 1755 ... E-13
Nephi, 5389 ... G-8
Newton, 789 ... A-8
N. Logan, 8269 ... M-20
N. Ogden, 17357 ... C-8
N. Salt Lake, 16322 ... E-18
Oakley, 1470 ... D-10
Ogden, 82825 ... C-8
Orangeville, 1470 ... H-10
Orem, 88328 ... E-9
Panguitch, 1520 ... L-7
Paradise, 904 ... B-8
Park City, 7558 ... E-9
Parowan, 2790 ... L-6
Payson, 18294 ... F-9
Perry, 4512 ... B-8
PIUTE CO., 1556 ... J-8
Plain City, 5476 ... C-8
Pleasant Grv., 33509 ... E-9
Price, 8715 ... G-11
Providence, 7075 ... B-9
Provo, 112488 ... F-9
Randolph, 464 ... B-10
Redmond, 730 ... I-8
RICH CO., 2264 ... B-9
Richfield, 7551 ... I-8
Richmond, 2470 ... A-9
River Hts., 1734 ... N-20
Riverdale, 8426 ... C-2
Riverside, 760 ... B-8
Riverton, 38753 ... E-8
Roosevelt, 6046 ... E-12
Roy, 36884 ... C-8
St. George, 72897 ... N-5
Salem, 6423 ... F-9
Salina, 2489 ... I-8
Salt Lake City, 186440 ... D-8
SALT LAKE CO., 1029655 ... E-19
SAN JUAN CO., 14746 ... K-13
Sandy, 87461 ... E-8
SANPETE CO., 27822 ... H-9
Santa Clara, 6003 ... N-5
Santaquin, 9128 ... F-9
Saratoga Sprs., 17781 ... E-8
SEVIER CO., 20802 ... I-9
Smithfield, 9495 ... B-8
S. Jordan, 50418 ... I-17
S. Ogden, 16532 ... C-2
S. Salt Lake, 23617 ... G-19
S. Weber, 6051 ... D-3
Spanish Fork, 34691 ... F-9
Spring City, 988 ... H-9
Spring Glen, 1126 ... G-10
Springville, 29466 ... F-9
Stansbury Pk., 5145 ... E-8
Stockton, 616 ... E-7
SUMMIT CO., 36324 ... D-10
Sunset, 5122 ... D-2
Syracuse, 24331 ... E-1
Taylorsville, 58652 ... H-17
Tooele, 31605 ... E-8
TOOELE CO., 58218 ... D-6
Toquerville, 1370 ... M-5
Tremonton, 7647 ... B-8
Uintah, 1322 ... C-8
UINTAH CO., 32588 ... G-13
UTAH CO., 516564 ... F-8
Vernal, 9089 ... E-13
WASATCH CO., 23530 ... F-10
Washington, 18761 ... N-5
WASHINGTON CO., 138115 ... M-5
Washington Ter., 9067 ... C-2
WAYNE CO., 2778 ... J-10
WEBER CO., 231236 ... C-9
Wellington, 1676 ... G-11
Wellsville, 3432 ... B-8
Wendover, 1400 ... D-4
W. Bountiful, 5265 ... D-18
W. Haven, 10272 ... B-2
W. Jordan, 103712 ... E-8
West Point, 9511 ... D-1
W. Valley City, 129480 ... D-8
Willard, 1772 ... C-8
Woods Cross, 9761 ... D-8

Vermont

Map p. 104

ADDISON CO., 36821 ... F-3
Arlington, 1213 ... L-2
Barre, 9052 ... F-5
Barton, 737 ... C-6
Bellows Falls, 3148 ... K-5
Bennington, 9074 ... M-2
BENNINGTON CO., 37125 ... L-2
Bethel, 569 ... H-4
Bradford, 788 ... G-6
Brandon, 1648 ... H-3
Brattleboro, 7414 ... M-5
Bristol, 2030 ... F-3
Burlington, 42417 ... D-2
CALEDONIA CO., 31227 ... D-6
Castleton, 1485 ... I-2
Chelsea, 500 ... G-5
Chester, 1005 ... K-5
CHITTENDEN CO., 156545 ... E-3
Derby Ctr., 597 ... B-6
Derby Line, 673 ... A-7
E. Arlington, 620 ... L-3
E. Barre, 826 ... F-5
Enosburg Falls, 1329 ... E-4
Essex Ctr., 850 ... D-3
ESSEX CO., 6306 ... C-8
Essex Jct., 9271 ... D-3
Fair Haven, 2269 ... I-2
FRANKLIN CO., 47746 ... C-3
GRAND ISLE CO., 6970 ... B-2
Graniteville, 784 ... F-5
Guildhall, 100 ... D-9
Hardwick, 1345 ... D-6
Hinesburg, 658 ... E-3
Hyde Park, 462 ... C-5
Island Pond, 821 ... B-7
Jeffersonville, 729 ... C-4
Jericho, 1329 ... D-3
Johnson, 1443 ... C-4
LAMOILLE CO., 24475 ... D-4
Ludlow, 811 ... J-4
Lyndonville, 1207 ... D-7
Manchester, 749 ... K-3
Manchester Ctr., 2120 ... K-3
Middlebury, 6588 ... G-2
Milton, 1861 ... C-3
Montpelier, 7855 ... E-5
Morrisville, 1958 ... D-5
Newfane, 118 ... L-4
Newport, 4589 ... B-6
N. Bennington, 1643 ... L-2
N. Clarendon, 550 ... I-3
N. Hero, 190 ... B-2
N. Springfield, 573 ... J-5
N. Troy, 620 ... A-5
Northfield, 2101 ... F-4
Norwich, 878 ... H-6
ORANGE CO., 28936 ... F-5
Orleans, 818 ... B-6
ORLEANS CO., 27231 ... B-5
Pittsford, 740 ... H-3
Poultney, 1612 ... I-2
Proctor, 1740 ... H-3
Quechee, 656 ... I-5
Randolph, 1974 ... G-4
Richford, 1361 ... A-4
Richmond, 723 ... D-3
Rutland, 16495 ... I-3
RUTLAND CO., 61642 ... I-2
St. Albans, 6918 ... B-3
St. Johnsbury, 6193 ... D-7
Saxtons River, 565 ... K-5
Shelburne, 592 ... E-2
S. Barre, 1219 ... F-5
S. Burlington, 17904 ... D-2
S. Royalton, 694 ... H-5
S. Shaftsbury, 683 ... L-2
Springfield, 3979 ... J-5
Swanton, 2386 ... B-3
Vergennes, 2588 ... F-2
Wallingford, 830 ... I-3
WASHINGTON CO., 59534 ... D-5
Waterbury, 1763 ... E-4
Websterville, 550 ... F-5
W. Brattleboro, 2740 ... M-5
W. Rutland, 2024 ... I-3
White River Jct., 2286 ... H-6
Wilder, 1690 ... H-6
Williamstown, 1162 ... F-5
WINDHAM CO., 44513 ... L-5
Windsor, 2066 ... I-5
WINDSOR CO., 56670 ... I-5
Winooski, 7267 ... D-2
Woodstock, 900 ... I-5

Virginia

Map pp. 106 – 107

† City keyed to p. 105
‡ City keyed to p. 111

Abingdon, 8191 ... D-6
Accomac, 519 ... I-19
ACCOMACK CO., 33164 ... I-20
Adwolf, 1530 ... M-1
ALBEMARLE CO., 98970 ... H-10
Alexandria, 139966 ... E-15
ALLEGHANY CO., 16250 ... I-5
Allison Gap, 700 ... D-7
Altavista, 3450 ... K-8
AMELIA CO., 12690 ... J-12
Amelia Court House, 1099 ... K-12
Amherst, 2231 ... J-9
AMHERST CO., 32353 ... I-8
Annalee Hts., 1800 ... ‡G-4
Annandale, 41008 ... E-14
Appalachia, 1754 ... C-4
Appomattox, 1733 ... K-9
APPOMATTOX CO., 14973 ... J-9
Aquia Hbr., 6727 ... F-14
Arlington, 207627 ... D-15
Arrington, 708 ... I-9
Arvonia, 750 ... I-11
Ashburn, 43511 ... D-14
Ashland, 7225 ... I-14
Atkins, 1143 ... L-1
Atlantic, 862 ... H-20
AUGUSTA CO., 73750 ... G-9
Austinville, 850 ... L-3
Bailey's Crossroads, 23643 ... ‡H-5
Bassett, 1100 ... M-6
Basye, 1253 ... E-9
BATH CO., 4731 ... H-7
Bealeton, 4435 ... F-13
Bedford, 6222 ... K-7
BEDFORD CO., 68676 ... K-7
Bel Air, 1500 ... ‡G-4
Bellair, 1400 ... †B-1
Belle Haven, 6518 ... ‡I-6
Belleview, 2300 ... ‡E-3
Bellwood, 6352 ... †E-8
Belvedere, 2200 ... ‡H-4
Benns Church, 872 ... L-17
Bensley, 5819 ... †E-8
Berryville, 4185 ... C-12
Big Stone Gap, 5614 ... D-4
Blacksburg, 42620 ... K-4
Blackstone, 3621 ... L-12
Blairs, 916 ... M-8
Bland, 409 ... K-2
BLAND CO., 6824 ... K-2
Blevinstown, 800 ... ‡H-1
Blue Ridge, 3084 ... J-6
Bluefield, 5444 ... K-2
Boissevain, 900 ... K-1
Bon Air, 16366 ... J-13
BOTETOURT CO., 33148 ... I-6
Bowling Green, 1111 ... H-14
Boydton, 431 ... M-11
Bracey, 1554 ... M-12
Brambleton, 9845 ... D-13
Brandermill, 13173 ... †E-5
Bridgewater, 5644 ... F-9
Brightwood, 1001 ... F-11
Bristol, 17835 ... E-5
Broadway, 3691 ... E-9
Brookneal, 1112 ... L-9
Broyhill Pk., 3700 ... ‡G-3
BRUNSWICK CO., 17434 ... L-12
Buchanan, 1178 ... J-7
BUCHANAN CO., 24098 ... B-6
Buckingham, 350 ... J-10
Buckingham Cir., 900 ... †C-1
BUCKINGHAM CO., 17146 ... I-10
Bucknell Manor, 2350 ... ‡I-6
Buena Vista, 6650 ... I-8
Burke, 41055 ... ‡I-2
CAMPBELL CO., 54842 ... K-9
Cana, 1254 ... M-4
Cape Charles, 1009 ... K-18
Captains Cove, 1042 ... H-20
CAROLINE CO., 28545 ... H-14
CARROLL CO., 30042 ... M-4
Carrollton, 4574 ... †K-3
Carrsbrook, 950 ... H-11
Castlewood, 2045 ... D-5
Cave Spr., 24922 ... K-6
Cedar Bluff, 1137 ... C-7
Centreville, 71135 ... E-14
Chamberlayne, 5456 ... †B-8
Chantilly, 23039 ... D-14
Chapel Acres, 1200 ... ‡J-3
Charles City, 133 ... J-15
CHARLES CITY CO., 7256 ... J-15
CHARLOTTE CO., 12586 ... L-10
Charlotte Court House, 543 ... L-10
Charlottesville, 43475 ... H-10
Chase City, 2351 ... M-11
Chatham, 1269 ... M-8
Chatmoss, 1698 ... M-6
Chesapeake, 222209 ... L-18
Chester, 20987 ... J-14
Chester Gap, 839 ... E-12
Chesterbrook, 1600 ... ‡F-4
Chesterfield, 3560 ... J-14
CHESTERFIELD CO., 316236 ... K-13
Chilhowie, 1781 ... M-1
Chincoteague, 2941 ... H-20
Christiansburg, 21041 ... K-4
CLARKE CO., 14034 ... D-12
Clarksville, 1139 ... M-10
Claypool Hill, 1776 ... C-7
Clifton Forge, 3884 ... I-6
Clintwood, 1414 ... C-5
Cloverdale, 3119 ... J-6
Cluster Sprs., 811 ... M-9
Coeburn, 2139 ... C-5
Collinsville, 7335 ... M-6
Colonial Bch., 3542 ... G-15
Colonial Hts., 17411 ... K-14
Concord, 1458 ... K-9
Courtland, 1284 ... M-15
Covington, 5961 ... I-6
CRAIG CO., 5190 ... J-5
Craigsville, 923 ... H-8
Crewe, 2326 ... K-12
Crimora, 2209 ... G-9
Crozet, 5565 ... H-10
Culmore, 5200 ... ‡G-4
Culpeper, 16379 ... F-12
CULPEPER CO., 46689 ... F-12
Cumberland, 393 ... J-11
CUMBERLAND CO., 10052 ... J-11
Dahlgren, 2653 ... F-15
Dale City, 65969 ... E-14
Daleville, 2557 ... J-6
Damascus, 814 ... E-7
Danville, 43055 ... N-8
Dare, 1500 ... †H-4
Dayton, 1530 ... F-9
Deltaville, 1119 ... J-17
DICKENSON CO., 15903 ... C-5
Dinwiddie, 200 ... L-13
DINWIDDIE CO., 28001 ... L-13
Dooms, 1327 ... G-9
Dranesville, 11921 ... ‡D-1
Dryden, 1208 ... D-3
Dublin, 2534 ... K-4
Dumbarton, 7879 ... †B-7
Dumfries, 4961 ... F-14
Dunn Loring, 8803 ... ‡F-3
E. Highland Pk., 14796 ... †B-8
E. Lexington, 1463 ... I-8
Eastville, 305 ... J-19
Edinburg, 1041 ... E-10
Ednam Forest, 700 ... †B-1
Elkton, 2726 ... F-10
Elliston, 902 ... K-5
Emory, 1251 ... D-7
Emporia, 5927 ... M-14
Enon, 3466 ... K-14
ESSEX CO., 11151 ... H-15
Ettrick, 6682 ... K-14
Exmore, 1460 ... J-19
Fairfax, 22565 ... D-14
FAIRFAX CO., 1081726 ... D-14
Fairfax Sta., 12030 ... ‡I-1
Fairlawn, 2367 ... K-4
Falls Church, 12332 ... D-14
Falmouth, 4274 ... G-14
Farmville, 8216 ... K-11
FAUQUIER CO., 65203 ... E-12
Ferrum, 2043 ... L-6
Ferry Farms, 4000 ... G-14
Fieldale, 879 ... M-6
Fincastle, 353 ... J-6
First Colony, 900 ... †F-1
Fishersville, 7462 ... H-9
Five Mile Fork, 700 ... G-13
Floyd, 425 ... L-5
FLOYD CO., 15279 ... L-5
FLUVANNA CO., 25691 ... I-11
Forest, 9106 ... J-8
Forksville, 1000 ... M-12
Ft. Hunt, 16045 ... ‡J-6
Franconia, 18245 ... ‡I-4
Franklin, 8582 ... M-15
FRANKLIN CO., 56159 ... L-6
Franklin Pk., 1800 ... ‡F-4
FREDERICK CO., 78305 ... C-11
Fredericksburg, 24286 ... G-14
Front Royal, 14440 ... D-11
Gainesville, 11481 ... E-13
Galax, 7042 ... M-3
Gate City, 2034 ... E-4
GILES CO., 17286 ... K-3
Glade Spr., 1456 ... D-7
Glasgow, 1133 ... I-7
Glen Allen, 14774 ... †A-7
Glenvar, 976 ... K-5
Gloucester, 2951 ... J-17
GLOUCESTER CO., 36858 ... J-16
Gloucester Pt., 9402 ... K-17
Goochland, 861 ... I-12
GOOCHLAND CO., 21717 ... I-12
Gordonsville, 1496 ... G-11
Grafton, 1050 ... †H-4
Gratton, 937 ... K-1
GRAYSON CO., 15533 ... M-2
Great Falls, 15427 ... ‡D-2
GREENE CO., 18403 ... G-11
GREENSVILLE CO., 12243 ... M-13
Greenville, 832 ... H-8
Gretna, 1267 ... L-8
Grottoes, 2668 ... G-9
Groveton, 14598 ... ‡I-5
Grundy, 1021 ... B-6
Halifax, 1309 ... M-9
HALIFAX CO., 36241 ... M-9
Hampden Sydney, 1450 ... K-11
Hampton, 137436 ... L-17
Hanover, 252 ... I-14
HANOVER CO., 99863 ... I-13
Harrisonburg, 48914 ... F-9
Harriston, 909 ... G-9
Hayes, 1000 ... †F-4
Haymarket, 1782 ... E-13
Heathsville, 142 ... H-17
HENRICO CO., 306935 ... J-14
HENRY CO., 54151 ... N-6
Henry Fork, 1234 ... L-6
Herndon, 23292 ... D-14
HIGHLAND CO., 2321 ... G-7
Highland Sprs., 15711 ... J-14
Hillsville, 2681 ... M-3
Hillwood, 1650 ... ‡G-4
Hollins, 14673 ... K-6
Hollymead, 7690 ... G-11
Holmes Run Acres, 1400 ... ‡G-3
Honaker, 1449 ... C-6
Hopewell, 22591 ... K-14
Horse Pasture, 2227 ... M-6
Hot Sprs., 738 ... H-6
Huntington, 11267 ... ‡I-6
Hurt, 1304 ... L-8
Hybla Valley, 15801 ... ‡J-5
Idylwood, 17288 ... ‡G-3
Independence, 947 ... M-2
Independent Hill, 7419 ... E-14
Isle of Wight, 70 ... L-16
ISLE OF WIGHT CO., 35270 ... L-16
JAMES CITY CO., 67009 ... K-16
Jefferson Vil., 2500 ... ‡G-4
Jolivue, 1129 ... G-9
Jonesville, 1034 ... D-2
Kenbridge, 1257 ... L-12
Keysville, 832 ... L-11
Kilmarnock, 1487 ... I-17
KING & QUEEN CO., 6945 ... I-15
King & Queen Court House, 85 ... I-16
King George, 4457 ... G-15
KING GEORGE CO., 23584 ... G-15
King William, 252 ... I-15
KING WILLIAM CO., 15935 ... I-15
Kings Pk., 4333 ... ‡H-3
L. Monticello, 9920 ... H-11
Lakeside, 11849 ... †B-7
Lancaster, 80 ... I-17
LANCASTER CO., 11391 ... I-17
Langley, 1450 ... ‡E-4
Laurel, 16713 ... I-14
Lawrenceville, 1438 ... M-13
Lebanon, 3424 ... D-6
LEE CO., 25587 ... D-2
Leesburg, 42616 ... C-13
Lexington, 7042 ... I-7
Lincolnia, 22855 ... ‡H-4
Lincolnia Hts., 1800 ... ‡H-4
Linton Hall, 35725 ... E-13
Lorton, 18610 ... E-14
LOUDOUN CO., 312311 ... D-13
Louisa, 1555 ... H-12
LOUISA CO., 33153 ... H-12
Lovettsville, 1613 ... C-13
Lovingston, 520 ... I-9
Lunenburg, 165 ... L-11
LUNENBURG CO., 12914 ... L-11
Luray, 4895 ... E-11
Lynchburg, 75568 ... J-8
Lyndhurst, 1490 ... H-9
Madison, 229 ... F-11
MADISON CO., 13308 ... F-11
Madison Hts., 11285 ... J-8
Manassas, 37821 ... E-14
Manassas Pk., 14273 ... E-14
Mantua, 7135 ... ‡G-3
Marion, 5968 ... L-1
Marshall, 1480 ... D-12
Martinsville, 13821 ... M-6
Marumsco, 35036 ... E-14
Mathews, 555 ... J-17
MATHEWS CO., 8978 ... J-17
Matoaca, 2403 ... †H-7
Maurertown, 770 ... D-11
McLean, 48115 ... ‡F-4
Meadowview, 967 ... D-6
Mechanicsville, 36348 ... I-14
MECKLENBURG CO., 32727 ... M-11
Merrifield, 15212 ... ‡G-3
MIDDLESEX CO., 10959 ... J-17
Middletown, 1265 ... D-11
Montclair, 19570 ... E-14
Monterey, 147 ... F-7
MONTGOMERY CO., 94392 ... K-4
Montrose, 7993 ... †D-9
Montross, 384 ... G-16
Motley, 1015 ... L-8
Mt. Hermon, 3966 ... M-8
Mt. Jackson, 1994 ... E-10
Mt. Vernon, 12416 ... E-15
Mountain Road, 1100 ... M-9
Narrows, 2029 ... K-3
Natural Br., 1500 ... I-7
Nellysford, 1076 ... H-9
NELSON CO., 15020 ... I-9
New Alexandria, 950 ... ‡I-6
New Baltimore, 8119 ... E-13
New Castle, 153 ... J-5
New Hope, 797 ... G-9
New Kent, 239 ... J-15
NEW KENT CO., 18429 ... J-15
New Market, 2146 ... E-10
Newington, 12943 ... ‡J-4
Newport News, 180719 ... L-17
Nokesville, 1354 ... E-13
Norfolk, 242803 ... L-18
Norge, 1000 ... J-16
N. Garden, 900 ... H-10
N. Shore, 3094 ... L-7
N. Springfield, 7274 ... ‡H-3
NORTHAMPTON CO., 12389 ... J-19
Northfields, 1400 ... †A-3
NORTHUMBERLAND CO., 12330 ... H-17
Norton, 3958 ... C-4
Nottoway, 84 ... K-12
NOTTOWAY CO., 15853 ... K-12
Oak Level, 857 ... M-6
Oakton, 34166 ... ‡G-2
Occoquan, 934 ... E-14
Onancock, 1263 ... I-19
Orange, 4721 ... G-12
ORANGE CO., 33481 ... G-12
Ordinary, 1000 ... †E-4
PAGE CO., 24042 ... F-10
Palmyra, 104 ... H-11
Parklawn, 2400 ... ‡H-4
Parksley, 842 ... I-19
PATRICK CO., 18490 ... M-4
Patrick Sprs., 1845 ... M-5
Pearisburg, 2786 ... K-3
Pembroke, 1128 ... K-4
Penhook, 801 ... L-7
Pennington Gap, 1781 ... D-3
Petersburg, 32420 ... K-14
Pimmit Hills, 6094 ... ‡F-3
PITTSYLVANIA CO., 63506 ... L-8
Poquoson, 12150 ... K-17
Portsmouth, 95535 ... L-17
Pound, 1037 ... C-4
Powhatan, 700 ... J-12
POWHATAN CO., 28046 ... J-12
Prices Fork, 1066 ... K-4
PRINCE EDWARD CO., 23368 ... K-10
Prince George, 2066 ... K-14
PRINCE GEORGE CO., 35725 ... K-14
PRINCE WILLIAM CO., 402002 ... E-13
Pulaski, 9086 ... L-3
PULASKI CO., 34872 ... K-3
Purcellville, 7727 ... C-13
Quail Oaks, 1400 ... †F-8
Queens Lake, 1400 ... †E-2
Radford, 16408 ... K-4
RAPPAHANNOCK CO., 7373 ... E-11
Raven, 2270 ... C-7
Ravensworth, 2466 ... ‡H-3
Ravenwood, 2550 ... ‡G-4
Reston, 58404 ... D-14
Rich Creek, 774 ... J-3
Richlands, 5823 ... C-7
Richmond, 204214 ... J-14
RICHMOND CO., 9254 ... H-16
Ridgeway, 742 ... N-6
Riner, 859 ... L-4
Roanoke, 97032 ... K-6
ROANOKE CO., 92376 ... J-5
ROCKBRIDGE CO., 22307 ... H-8
ROCKINGHAM CO., 76314 ... F-9
Rocky Mount, 4799 ... L-6
Rose Hill, 799 ... D-2
Ruckersville, 1141 ... G-11
Rural Retreat, 1483 ... L-2
Rushmere, 1018 ... K-16
RUSSELL CO., 28897 ... C-6
Rustburg, 1431 ... K-9
St. Paul, 970 ... C-5
Salem, 24802 ... K-6
Saltville, 2077 ... D-7
Saluda, 769 ... I-16
Sandston, 7571 ... †C-10
SCOTT CO., 23177 ... D-4
Seaford, 2700 ... K-17
Seven Cors., 9255 ... ‡G-4
Seven Mile Ford, 783 ... M-1
Shawnee Land, 1873 ... C-11
Shawsville, 1310 ... K-5
Shenandoah, 2373 ... F-10
SHENANDOAH CO., 41993 ... E-10
Short Pump, 24729 ... †A-5
Smithfield, 8089 ... L-16
SMYTH CO., 32208 ... M-1
S. Boston, 8142 ... M-9
S. Hill, 4650 ... M-12
SOUTHAMPTON CO., 18570 ... L-15
Spotsylvania, 4239 ... G-13
SPOTSYLVANIA CO., 122397 ... H-13
Springfield, 30484 ... ‡I-4
Stafford, 1600 ... F-14
STAFFORD CO., 128961 ... F-13
Stanardsville, 367 ... G-11
Stanley, 1689 ... F-10
Stanleytown, 1422 ... M-6
Staunton, 23746 ... G-9
Stephens City, 1829 ... D-11
Sterling, 27822 ... D-14
Strasburg, 6398 ... D-11
Stuart, 1408 ... M-5
Stuarts Draft, 9235 ... H-9
Suffolk, 84585 ... M-17
Sugar Grv., 758 ... M-1
Sugar Loaf, 2500 ... H-1
Sugarland Run, 11799 ... ‡C-1
Surry, 244 ... K-16
SURRY CO., 7058 ... K-15
Sussex, 256 ... L-14
SUSSEX CO., 12087 ... L-14
Tabb, 950 ... K-17
Tangier, 727 ... H-18
Tappahannock, 2375 ... H-16
Tazewell, 4627 ... K-1
TAZEWELL CO., 45078 ... L-1
Timberlake, 12183 ... K-8
Timberville, 2522 ... E-10
Toano, 1200 ... J-16
Triangle, 8188 ... F-14
Tuckahoe, 44990 ... I-13
Tyler Pk., 1250 ... ‡G-4
Tysons Corner, 19627 ... ‡F-3
Varina, 3000 ... †E-9
Verona, 4239 ... G-9
Victoria, 1725 ... L-11
Vienna, 15687 ... D-14
Vinton, 8098 ... K-6
Virginia Beach, 437994 ... L-18
Virginia Hills, 2840 ... ‡I-5
Wakefield, 927 ... L-15
Warm Sprs., 123 ... H-6
WARREN CO., 37575 ... D-12
Warrenton, 9611 ... E-13
Warsaw, 1512 ... H-16
Washington, 135 ... E-11
WASHINGTON CO., 54876 ... D-7
Waverly, 2149 ... L-15
Waynesboro, 21006 ... H-9
Waynewood, 3450 ... ‡J-6
Weber City, 1327 ... E-4
Wellington, 1750 ... ‡J-6
West Point, 3306 ... J-16
W. Springfield, 22460 ... ‡I-3
Westmoreland, 900 ... †A-3
WESTMORELAND CO., 17454 ... G-15
Weyanoke, 1500 ... ‡H-4
Weyers Cave, 2473 ... G-9
Wicomico, 1350 ... K-17
Williamsburg, 14068 ... K-16
Wilton Woods, 1400 ... ‡I-5
Winchester, 26203 ... C-11
Windsor, 2626 ... M-16
Wise, 3286 ... C-4
WISE CO., 41452 ... C-4
Woodlake, 7319 ... J-13
Woodlawn, 2343 ... M-3
Woodstock, 5097 ... D-10
WYTHE CO., 29235 ... L-2
Wytheville, 8211 ... L-2
YORK CO., 65464 ... J-16
York Ter., 800 ... †F-2
Yorktown, 195 ... K-17

Washington

Map pp. 108 – 109

* City keyed to p. 110

Aberdeen, 16896 ... H-3
ADAMS CO., 18728 ... I-16
Ahtanum, 3601 ... J-11
Airway Hts., 6114 ... F-18
Alderton, 2893 ... *N-9
Alderwood, 1760 ... B-7
Algona, 3014 ... *K-9
Allyn, 1963 ... G-6
Amboy, 1608 ... L-7
Anacortes, 15778 ... C-6
Arlington, 17926 ... D-8
Asotin, 1251 ... J-20
ASOTIN CO., 21623 ... K-19
Auburn, 70180 ... G-7
Basin City, 1092 ... J-15
Battle Ground, 17571 ... M-6
Bayview, 696 ... C-7
Belfair, 3931 ... G-6
Bellevue, 122363 ... *E-9
Bellingham, 80885 ... B-7
Benton City, 3038 ... K-14
BENTON CO., 175177 ... J-13
Big Lake, 1835 ... C-7
Bingen, 712 ... M-9
Birch Bay, 8413 ... A-6
Black Diamond, 4151 ... G-8
Blaine, 4684 ... A-6
Bonney Lake, 17374 ... H-7
Bothell, 33505 ... *A-9
Bremerton, 37729 ... F-6
Brewster, 2370 ... D-13
Bridgeport, 2409 ... E-13
Brier, 6087 ... *A-8
Brinnon, 797 ... F-6
Browns Pt., 1950 ... *K-6
Bryant, 1870 ... D-7
Bryn Mawr, 1500 ... *G-9
Buckley, 4354 ... H-8
Buena, 990 ... J-12
Burbank, 3291 ... K-15
Burien, 33313 ... G-7
Burlington, 8388 ... C-7
Camano, 13347 ... D-7
Camas, 19355 ... M-7
Carbonado, 610 ... H-8
Carlsborg, 995 ... D-5
Carnation, 1786 ... F-8
Carson, 2279 ... M-8
Cascade Valley, 2246 ... H-14
Cascade Vista, 7800 ... *H-10
Cashmere, 3063 ... F-11
Castle Rock, 1982 ... K-5
Cathlamet, 532 ... K-4
Central Pk., 2685 ... H-4
Centralia, 16336 ... I-5
Chehalis, 7259 ... I-5
Chelan, 3890 ... E-13
CHELAN CO., 72453 ... E-11
Cheney, 10590 ... F-19
Chewelah, 2607 ... D-18
Chimacum, 800 ... E-6
CLALLAM CO., 71404 ... E-4
CLARK CO., 425363 ... M-7
Clarkston, 7229 ... J-20
Cle Elum, 1872 ... G-10
Clear Lake, 1419 ... H-7
Clear Lake, 1002 ... C-7
Clearview, 3324 ... E-8
Clinton, 928 ... E-7
Clyde Hill, 2984 ... *D-9
Colfax, 2805 ... I-19
College Pl., 8765 ... L-17
COLUMBIA CO., 4078 ... K-18
Colville, 4673 ... C-18
Concrete, 705 ... C-8
Connell, 4209 ... I-15
Cosmopolis, 1649 ... H-3
Coulee Dam, 1098 ... E-15
Country Homes, 5841 ... *A-2
Coupeville, 1831 ... D-6
Covington, 17575 ... G-8
COWLITZ CO., 102410 ... K-6
Dallesport, 1202 ... M-10
Darrington, 1347 ... D-9
Davenport, 1734 ... F-17
Dayton, 2526 ... K-18
Deer Pk., 3652 ... E-19
Des Moines, 29673 ... G-7
Desert Aire, 1626 ... I-13
DOUGLAS CO., 38431 ... F-13
DuPont, 8199 ... H-6
Duvall, 6695 ... F-8
E. Wenatchee, 13190 ... G-12
Eastgate, 4958 ... *E-10
Eastsound, 1100 ... B-6
Eatonville, 2758 ... I-7
Edgewood, 9387 ... *L-8
Edmonds, 39709 ... *A-7
Electric City, 968 ... E-15
Elk Plain, 14205 ... H-7
Ellensburg, 18174 ... H-11
Elma, 3107 ... H-4
Entiat, 1112 ... F-12
Enumclaw, 10669 ... G-8
Ephrata, 7664 ... G-14
Everett, 103019 ... E-7
Everson, 2481 ... A-7
Fairfield, 612 ... G-19
Fairwood, 19102 ... *H-10
Federal Way, 89306 ... G-7
Ferndale, 11415 ... B-6
FERRY CO., 7551 ... C-16
Fife, 9173 ... *L-7
Finley, 6012 ... K-15
Fircrest, 6497 ... *L-5
Fords Prairie, 1959 ... I-5
Forks, 3532 ... E-2
FRANKLIN CO., 78163 ... J-15
Freeland, 2045 ... E-7
Friday Hbr., 2162 ... C-5
GARFIELD CO., 2266 ... J-18
Garrett, 1419 ... K-17
Geneva, 2321 ... *F-3
Gig Hbr., 7126 ... G-6
Gleed, 2906 ... I-11
Gold Bar, 2075 ... E-9
Goldendale, 3407 ... L-11
Graham, 23491 ... H-7
Grand Coulee, 988 ... E-15
Grand Mound, 2981 ... I-5
Grandview, 10862 ... K-13
Granger, 3246 ... K-12
Granite Falls, 3364 ... D-8
GRANT CO., 89120 ... G-15
Grapeview, 954 ... G-6
Grayland, 953 ... I-3
GRAYS HARBOR CO., 72797 ... G-3
Hansville, 3091 ... E-7
Harrah, 625 ... J-11
Hobart, 6221 ... G-8
Hollywood, 800 ... *B-10
Hoquiam, 8726 ... H-3
Ilwaco, 936 ... K-3
ISLAND CO., 78506 ... D-6
Issaquah, 30434 ... F-8
JEFFERSON CO., 29872 ... F-4
Kalama, 2344 ... L-6
Kelso, 11925 ... K-5
Kenmore, 20460 ... *A-8
Kennewick, 73917 ... K-15
Kent, 92411 ... G-7
Kettle Falls, 1595 ... B-17
KING CO., 1931249 ... F-9
Kingsgate, 13065 ... *B-10
Kingston, 2099 ... E-7
Kirkland, 48787 ... *C-9
KITSAP CO., 251133 ... F-6
Kittitas, 1381 ... H-12
KITTITAS CO., 40915 ... H-11
KLICKITAT CO., 20318 ... L-12
La Center, 2800 ... L-6
La Conner, 891 ... C-7
Lacey, 42393 ... H-6
L. Forest Pk., 12598 ... *A-8
L. Stevens, 28069 ... E-8
Lakeland, 12000 ... *K-8
Lakeview Pk., 915 ... G-14
Lakewood, 58163 ... H-7
Leavenworth, 1965 ... F-11
LEWIS CO., 75455 ... I-6
Lexington, 800 ... K-6
LINCOLN CO., 10570 ... F-16
Lofall, 2289 ... E-6
Long Bch., 1392 ... J-3
Longbranch, 3784 ... G-6
Longview, 36648 ... K-5
Longview Hts., 3851 ... K-5
Loon Lake, 783 ... D-18
Lynden, 11951 ... A-7
Lynnwood, 35836 ... E-7
Mabton, 2286 ... K-13
Manchester, 5413 ... *F-5
Manson, 1468 ... E-12
Maple Valley, 22684 ... G-8
Maplewood Hts., 3300 ... *H-10
Marysville, 60020 ... D-7
MASON CO., 60699 ... H-5
Mattawa, 4437 ... I-13
McCleary, 1653 ... H-5
McKenna, 716 ... H-6
McMillin, 1547 ... H-7
Mead, 7275 ... E-19
Medical Lake, 5060 ... F-18
Medina, 2969 ... *D-9
Mercer Island, 22699 ... *E-9
Midland, 8962 ... *N-6
Mill Creek, 18244 ... E-7
Millwood, 1786 ... *B-4
Milton, 6968 ... *L-8
Monroe, 17304 ... E-8
Montesano, 3976 ... H-4
Morgan Acres, 1500 ... *B-3
Morton, 1126 ... J-7
Moses Lake, 20366 ... H-14
Mossyrock, 759 ... J-7
Mt. Pleasant, 1200 ... D-5
Mt. Vernon, 31743 ... C-7
Mountlake Ter., 19909 ... *A-8
Moxee City, 3308 ... J-12
Mukilteo, 20254 ... E-7
Naches, 795 ... I-11
Napavine, 1766 ... J-6
Neah Bay, 865 ... C-2
Newcastle, 10380 ... *F-10
Newport, 2126 ... D-20
Nooksack, 1338 ... A-7
Normandy Pk., 6335 ... *H-7
N. Bend, 5731 ... F-8
N. Bonneville, 956 ... M-8
N. Puyallup, 1743 ... *M-8
Oak Hbr., 22075 ... D-6
Oakville, 684 ... I-5
Ocean Pk., 1573 ... J-3
Ocean Shores, 5569 ... H-3
Odessa, 910 ... G-16
Okanogan, 2552 ... C-14
OKANOGAN CO., 41120 ... B-13
Olympia, 46478 ... H-6
Omak, 4845 ... C-14
Onalaska, 621 ... J-6
Orchards, 19556 ... M-6
Oroville, 1686 ... A-14
Orting, 6746 ... H-7
Othello, 7364 ... I-15
Pacific, 6606 ... *L-9
PACIFIC CO., 20920 ... J-4
Palouse, 998 ... H-20
Parkland, 35803 ... H-7
Parkwood, 7126 ... *F-4
Pasadena Pk., 1700 ... *B-4
Pasco, 59781 ... K-15
Pateros, 667 ... D-13
Pe Ell, 632 ... J-5
PEND OREILLE CO., 13001 ... B-19
Peshastin, 900 ... F-11
PIERCE CO., 795225 ... I-7
Pt. Roberts, 1314 ... A-5
Pomeroy, 1425 ... J-19
Port Angeles, 19038 ... D-4
Port Orchard, 11144 ... F-6
Port Townsend, 9113 ... D-6
Poulsbo, 9200 ... F-6
Prosser, 5714 ... K-13
Pullman, 29799 ... I-20
Purdy, 1544 ... G-6
Puyallup, 37022 ... H-7
Quincy, 6750 ... G-13
Rainier, 1794 ... I-6
Randle, 850 ... J-8
Ravensdale, 1101 ... G-8
Raymond, 2882 ... I-4
Redmond, 54144 ... *C-10
Renton, 90927 ... G-7
Republic, 1073 ... B-16
Richland, 48058 ... K-14
Ridgefield, 4763 ... L-6
Ritzville, 1673 ... H-17
Rochester, 2388 ... I-5
Rock Island, 788 ... G-12
Roslyn, 893 ... G-10
Roy, 793 ... H-6
Royal City, 2140 ... I-13
Ruston, 749 ... *K-5
Salmon Creek, 19686 ... M-6
Sammamish, 45780 ... F-8
SAN JUAN CO., 15769 ... C-5
Satsop, 675 ... H-4
Satus, 750 ... K-12
SeaTac, 26909 ... G-7
Seattle, 608660 ... F-7
Seaview, 650 ... J-3
Sedro-Woolley, 10540 ... C-7
Selah, 7147 ... I-11
Sequim, 6606 ... D-5
Shelton, 9834 ... G-5
Shoreline, 53007 ... *B-7
Silverdale, 19204 ... F-6
SKAGIT CO., 116901 ... C-8
SKAMANIA CO., 11066 ... L-8
Skokomish, 617 ... G-5
Skyway, 8500 ... *G-9
Smokey Pt., 1556 ... D-7
Snohomish, 9098 ... E-8
SNOHOMISH CO., 713335 ... E-9
Snoqualmie, 10670 ... F-8
Soap Lake, 1514 ... G-14
S. Bend, 1637 ... I-3
S. Hill, 52431 ... *N-8
S. Wenatchee, 1553 ... G-12
Southworth, 2185 ... *G-5
Spanaway, 27227 ... H-7
Spokane, 208916 ... F-19
SPOKANE CO., 471221 ... F-19
Spokane Valley, 89755 ... F-19
Stanwood, 6231 ... D-7
Steilacoom, 5985 ... H-6
STEVENS CO., 43531 ... D-18
Stevenson, 1465 ... M-8
Sudden Valley, 6441 ... B-7
Sultan, 4651 ... E-8
Sumas, 1307 ... A-7
Summit, 7985 ... *N-7
Sumner, 9451 ... G-7
Suncrest, 1500 ... E-18
Sunnyside, 15858 ... K-13
Sunnyslope, 3252 ... G-12
Tacoma, 198397 ... G-7
Taholah, 840 ... G-2
Tanglewilde, 5892 ... L-4
Tanner, 1018 ... G-8
Tekoa, 778 ... G-20
Tenino, 1695 ... I-6
Terrace Hts., 6937 ... M-16
THURSTON CO., 252264 ... I-6
Tieton, 1191 ... I-11
Toledo, 725 ... J-6
Tonasket, 1032 ... B-14
Toppenish, 8949 ... J-12
Town & Country, 4857 ... *A-2
Tukwila, 19107 ... *G-8
Tumwater, 17371 ... H-6
Twisp, 919 ... C-12
Union, 631 ... G-5
Union Gap, 6047 ... J-11
University Pl., 31144 ... G-7
Vader, 621 ... J-5
Vancouver, 161791 ... M-6
Vashon, 10624 ... G-7
Vashon Hts., 700 ... *G-6
WAHKIAKUM CO., 3978 ... J-4
Waitsburg, 1217 ... K-17
Walla Walla, 31731 ... K-17
WALLA WALLA CO., 58781 ... J-16
Wapato, 4997 ... J-12
Warden, 2692 ... H-15
Warm Bch., 2437 ... D-7
Washougal, 14095 ... M-7
Waterville, 1138 ... F-12
Wenatchee, 31925 ... G-12
W. Richland, 11811 ... K-14
Westport, 2099 ... H-3
WHATCOM CO., 201140 ... B-8
White Ctr., 13495 ... *F-7
White Salmon, 2224 ... M-9
White Swan, 793 ... J-11
WHITMAN CO., 44776 ... H-18
Wilbur, 884 ... E-16
Winlock, 1339 ... J-5
Wollochet, 6651 ... *L-4
Woodinville, 10938 ... *B-10
Woodland, 5509 ... L-6
Woodway, 1307 ... *A-7
Yacolt, 1566 ... L-7
Yakima, 91067 ... J-11
YAKIMA CO., 243231 ... J-12
Yarrow Pt., 1001 ... *D-9
Yelm, 6848 ... H-6
Zillah, 2964 ... J-12

West Virginia

Map p. 112

* City keyed to p. 46

Alderson, 1184 ... L-6
Alum Creek, 1749 ... J-3
Anmoore, 770 ... G-7
Ansted, 1404 ... J-5
Arthurdale, 1500 ... F-8
Athens, 1048 ... M-5
BARBOUR CO., 16589 ... G-8
Barboursville, 3964 ... I-2
Barrackville, 1302 ... F-7
Beaver, 1308 ... L-5
Beckley, 17614 ... L-4
Belington, 1921 ... G-8

Canada Cities and Towns

Populations are from latest available census or are Rand McNally estimates

Mexico Cities and Towns (map p. 128)

Populations are from 2010 Mexican Census or are Rand McNally estimates

*, †, ‡, § See explanation under state title in this index. County and parish names are listed in capital letters and in boldface type. Independent cities (not in any county) are shown in italics.